P9-DNJ-954

Chicago Public Library
C
P
L
REFERENCE
Form 178 rev. 11-00

ENCYCLOPEDIA OF AMERICAN HISTORY

The Development of the Industrial United States 1870 to 1899

VOLUME VI

ENCYCLOPEDIA OF AMERICAN HISTORY

Volume I
THREE WORLDS MEET
Beginnings to 1607

Volume II
COLONIZATION AND SETTLEMENT
1608 to 1760

Volume III
REVOLUTION AND NEW NATION
1761 to 1812

Volume IV
EXPANSION AND REFORM
1813 to 1855

Volume V
CIVIL WAR AND RECONSTRUCTION
1856 to 1869

Volume VI
THE DEVELOPMENT OF THE INDUSTRIAL UNITED STATES
1870 to 1899

Volume VII
THE EMERGENCE OF MODERN AMERICA
1900 to 1928

Volume VIII
THE GREAT DEPRESSION AND WORLD WAR II
1929 to 1945

Volume IX
POSTWAR UNITED STATES
1946 to 1968

Volume X
CONTEMPORARY UNITED STATES
1969 to the Present

Volume XI
COMPREHENSIVE INDEX

ENCYCLOPEDIA OF AMERICAN HISTORY

The Development of the Industrial United States 1870 to 1899

VOLUME VI

Ari Hoogenboom, Editor
Gary B. Nash, General Editor

Facts On File, Inc.

Encyclopedia of American History:
The Development of the Industrial United States (1870 to 1899)

Editorial Director: Laurie E. Likoff
Editor in Chief: Owen Lancer
Chief Copy Editor: Michael G. Laraque
Associate Editor: Dorothy Cummings
Production Director: Olivia McKean
Production Manager: Rachel L. Berlin
Production Associate: Theresa Montoya
Art Director: Cathy Rincon
Interior Designer: Joan M. Toro
Desktop Designers: Erika K. Arroyo and David C. Strelecky
Maps and Illustrations: Dale E. Williams and Jeremy Eagle

Facts On File, Inc.
132 West 31st Street
New York NY 10001

Library of Congress Cataloging-in-Publication Data

Encyclopedia of American history / Gary B. Nash, general editor.
p. cm.
Includes bibliographical references and indexes.
Contents: v. 1. Three worlds meet — v. 2. Colonization and settlement — v. 3. Revolution and new nation — v. 4. Expansion and reform — v. 5. Civil War and Reconstruction — v. 6. The development of the industrial United States — v. 7. The emergence of modern America — v. 8. The Great Depression and World War II — v. 9. Postwar United States — v. 10. Contemporary United States. — v. 11 Comprehensive index
ISBN 0-8160-4371-X (set) ISBN 0-8160-4366-3 (v. 6)
1. United States—History—Encyclopedias. I. Nash, Gary B.
E174 .E53 2002
973′.03—dc21 2001051278

Printed in the United States of America

VB Hermitage 10 9 8 7 6 5 4 3 2 1

This book is printed on acid-free paper.

Contents

List of Entries

About the Editors

General Editor: Gary B. Nash received a Ph.D from Princeton University. He is currently director of the National Center for History in the Schools at the University of California, Los Angeles, where he teaches American history of the colonial and Revolutionary era. He is a published author of college and precollegiate history texts. Among his best-selling works is *The American People: Creating a Nation and Society* (Addison Wesley, Longman), now in its fifth edition.

Nash is an elected member of the Society of American Historians, American Academy of Arts and Sciences, and the American Philosophical Society. He has served as past president of the Organization of American Historians, 1994–95, and was a founding member of the National Council for History Education, 1990.

Volume Editor: Ari Hoogenboom, professor emeritus, Brooklyn College, City University of New York, received a Ph.D. from Columbia University. He is the author of *The Gilded Age* (Prentice Hall, 1967) and *Rutherford B. Hayes: Warrior and President* (University Press of Kansas, 1995), among other books and articles.

Foreword

The Encyclopedia of American History series is designed as a handy reference to the most important individuals, events, and topics in U.S. history. In 10 volumes, the encyclopedia covers the period from the 15th century, when European explorers first made their way across the Atlantic Ocean to the Americas, to the present day. The encyclopedia is written for precollegiate as well as college students, for parents of young learners in the schools, and for the general public. The volume editors are distinguished historians of American history. In writing individual entries, each editor has drawn upon the expertise of scores of specialists. This ensures the scholarly quality of the entire series. Articles contributed by the various volume editors are uncredited.

This 10-volume encyclopedia of "American history" is broadly conceived to include the historical experience of the various peoples of North America. Thus, in the first volume, many essays treat the history of a great range of indigenous people before contact with Europeans. In the same vein, readers will find essays in the first several volumes that sketch Spanish, Dutch, and French explorers and colonizers who opened up territories for European settlement that later would become part of the United States. The venues and cast of characters in the American historical drama are thus widened beyond traditional encyclopedias.

In creating the eras of American history that define the chronological limits of each volume, and in addressing major topics in each era, the encyclopedia follows the architecture of *The National Standards for United States History, Revised Edition* (Los Angeles: National Center for History in the Schools, 1996). Mandated by the U.S. Congress, the national standards for U.S. history have been widely used by states and school districts in organizing curricular frameworks and have been followed by many other curriculum-building efforts.

Entries are cross-referenced, when appropriate, with *See also* citations at the end of articles. At the end of most entries, a listing of articles and books allows readers to turn to specialized sources and historical accounts. In each volume, an array of maps provide geographical context, while numerous illustrations help vivify the material covered in the text. A time line is included to provide students with a chronological reference to major events occurring in the given era. The selection of historical documents in the back of each volume gives students experience with the raw documents that historians use when researching history. A comprehensive index to each volume also facilitates the reader's access to particular information.

In each volume, long entries are provided for major categories of American historical experience. These categories may include: African Americans, agriculture, art and architecture, business, economy, education, family life, foreign policy, immigration, labor, Native Americans, politics, population, religion, urbanization, and women. By following these essays from volume to volume, the reader can access what might be called a mini-history of each broad topic, for example, family life, immigration, or religion.

— Gary B. Nash
University of California, Los Angeles

Introduction

The period from 1870 to 1899 has earned more nicknames than any other period in American history. Having so many aliases is in keeping with its dubious—yet undeserved—reputation, which several of its a.k.a.'s have helped perpetuate. The era's most enduring name, the "Gilded Age," was bestowed by Mark Twain and Charles Dudley Warner in a novel of that name. Some of its other names have a positive ring. Historians have noted that the period witnessed the "Emergence of Modern America" or "America in Transition," or that Americans were involved in a "Search for Order" in the "Age of Energy" or the "Age of Industrialism." Other names have stressed negative aspects of the time—already implied in the term *Gilded Age*—and have referred to it as the "Age of Excess" or the "Era of Good Stealings." Edith Wharton, however, in her most enduring novel, called it the "Age of Innocence."

The late 19th-century United States was not the unique possessor of these characteristics. Society is always in transition, seeking a semblance of order, becoming more modern, and losing the innocence of its past. People have been making technological advances since before the dawn of history and always have expended energy profligately. Every era has its examples of excess and corruption. Indeed, as these words are being written in late January 2002, newspapers are running stories about the monumental irresponsibility of a major corporation to its employees and investors (with the connivance of a respected auditing firm) and of its ties to the highest political circles.

Nevertheless, the characterizations of novelists and historians contain a germ of truth, if not the whole kernel. The late 19th-century United States experienced the most astonishing expansion of industry in human history. It built the world's largest network of railroads, and its production of steel outstripped that of Great Britain and Germany, its nearest competitors. There were heavy social costs. Laborers in the United States worked longer and harder on any given day than their European counterparts, but they earned more money and were less inclined toward radicalism. Additionally, the United States was the most democratic nation in the world, and workers participated in the political process. Cities grew rapidly and housing was often inadequate, but over the years most workers improved their lot, and in these small increments the promise of America was kept for immigrants who flocked to the United States. Despite the spectacular and ruthless settlement of the West and the revolutionary changes in agriculture, industrialization and urbanization dominated late 19th-century America.

The rapid development of factories and the monumental growth of cities made 1870 to 1899 watershed years, a period dividing an earlier America from a later America, an age that really was one of "transition" and "emergence." Agricultural and rural America became industrial and urban America. Local and regional economies gave way to a national economy. An unorganized society of individuals became institutionalized as professionals established national organizations of lawyers, economists, historians, and other groups. A nation that gloried in its isolation in 1870 gloried in its imperialism by 1899. A people whose vast majority had believed literally in the Bible were by 1899 often figuratively interpreting Scriptures to accommodate the Darwinian hypothesis of evolution.

There was enough gilt in an upwardly mobile society, boasting of many self-made people who exhibited nouveau riche characteristics, to be called a "Gilded Age." But there was gold under the gilt. Any age that could boast writers like Mark Twain and Henry James, painters like Thomas Eakins and Mary Cassatt, architects like Henry H. Richardson and Louis Sullivan, engineers like James B. Eads and Washington A. Roebling, inventors like Thomas A. Edison and Alexander Graham Bell, scientists like George Washington Carver and Othneil Charles Marsh, thinkers like Charles S. Peirce and William James, historians like Henry Adams and Frederick Jackson Turner, sociologists like William Graham Sumner and Lester Frank Ward, and reformers like Susan B. Anthony and Ida Bell Wells-Barnett had considerably more value than mere gilt.

— Ari Hoogenboom
Brooklyn, New York

ENTRIES
A TO Z

Adams, Henry (1838–1918)

Born in Boston on February 16, 1838, the historian Henry Adams was both privileged and challenged as the great-grandson and grandson of Presidents John Adams and John Quincy Adams and the son of Charles Francis Adams, who would become Abraham Lincoln's minister to Great Britain. After graduating from Harvard in 1858, Adams spent two years abroad studying and touring. Returning home, he studied law briefly and then accompanied his father as his private secretary to Britain, where he hobnobbed with literary, political, and reform leaders.

Back in the United States in 1868, Adams, inspired by his heritage and by English liberal intellectuals, moved to Washington and wrote political articles that promoted the liberal agenda—CIVIL SERVICE REFORM, free trade, the gold standard, and anti-imperialism—for journals of opinion like *THE NATION*. Adams was disappointed that President Ulysses S. Grant not only failed to adopt this agenda but also distanced himself from its intellectually elite supporters and, worse, cottoned to spoils-minded Republican party leaders like ROSCOE CONKLING. Adams bitterly attacked Grant and supported the establishment of the LIBERAL REPUBLICAN PARTY, which he hoped would nominate his father for president in 1872, but he was further disappointed when it nominated Horace Greeley. His optimistic dream of leading and guiding (with intellectuals like himself) the American democracy into the paths of liberal reform was destroyed.

In 1870 Adams returned to Boston to accept an assistant professorship in medieval history at Harvard and the editorship of the *North American Review*. He also taught courses in early American history. Reflecting trends abroad, he introduced seminars and encouraged his students to use scientific methods in studying the past. In 1872 he married Marian "Clover" Hooper. Despite his success at Harvard, Adams preferred to be close to the center of power in Washington, and after resigning his editorship in 1876, he gave up his professorship in 1877 and returned to the capital.

Adams had left teaching, but he remained fascinated by history both for its own sake and as a medium for expressing and illustrating his increasing pessimism about the United States. In Washington he began extensive archival research on the early years of the 19th century—the time when his great-grandfather left office and, in Adams's opinion, the time when the seeds of American decline were sewn. The Adamses also travelled abroad, where he examined archives in the major European capitals. In Washington they associated with political leaders—President RUTHERFORD B. HAYES enjoyed their conversation, even with Adams declaring, "Our system of Gov't has failed utterly in many respects"—and were at the core of the scintillating "Five of Hearts," which also included Clara and author/diplomat JOHN HAY and geologist CLARENCE KING. Adams published biographies of Albert Gallatin (1879) and John Randolph (1882) and the novels *Democracy* (1880) and *Esther* (1884), but in 1885 he was devastated when his wife Clover committed suicide, and his outlook became more bleak. His nine-volume *History of the United States during the Administrations of Thomas Jefferson and James Madison* (1889–91) is beautifully written, carefully researched, and provocative with its suggestion that the material progress of the United States undermined the republican virtues of the Founding Fathers.

His *History* completed, Adams circled the globe from 1890 to 1892 with the artist John La Farge, especially enjoying his long stay in Paris. Henceforth Adams spent part of each year there, took up medieval history anew, and used it—as he did American history—to express his pessimistic view of the future. He designed his historical work *Mont-Saint-Michel and Chartres* (1904) to demonstrate the unity he found in medieval culture as symbolized by the Virgin Mary, and he wrote his classic autobiography *The Education of Henry Adams* (privately printed in 1904) to illustrate the multiplicity of the 20th century, symbolized by the dehumanizing powerful dynamo. In his closing years Adams continued to counteract SOCIAL DARWINISM, with its notions of progress derived from biology, by applying physicist JOSIAH WILLARD GIBBS's "Rule of Phase" (stressing the dissipation of energy) to a disintegrating society. Adams died in Washington on March 27, 1918, while World War I raged, and confirmed his dire prophesies.

Further reading: David R. Contosta, *Henry Adams and the American Experiment* (Boston: Little, Brown, 1980); Ernest Samuels, *Henry Adams,* 3 vols. (Cambridge: Harvard University Press, 1948–64).

advertising

Advertising can be traced back to the earliest days of recorded history, but modern advertising has its roots in the post–Civil War era. The major elements dominating advertising during this period include the rise of popular MAGAZINES; the ascendancy of large, cheap, metropolitan NEWSPAPERS using new technologies to improve their appearance; the growth of consumer-orientated industries; and the creation of advertising agencies, whose profits rested on reaching large audiences for their clients. The most important factor in the evolution of advertising was the existence of a large urban middle class with financial resources allowing them to buy a wide variety of consumer goods. Especially crucial for the rise of advertising was the large number of middle-class women who had time and money to shop.

Of course, newspapers and magazines go back to the 18th century in the United States, and both organs carried advertising. But before the Civil War these ads were uninteresting because the papers were limited by current technologies. New methods of printing led to the multiplication of urban journals known as the Penny Press. By the late 19th century, both newspapers and magazines carried photographs

Advertisement for children's shoes, ca. 1874 *(Library of Congress)*

Advertisement for the Climax mowing machine, ca. 1871 *(Library of Congress)*

and were visually appealing to readers. Newspapers, which before the war consisted of four sheets, were much larger, running 20 or more pages filled for the most part with advertising. Ads by DEPARTMENT STORES, the latest retailing innovation, were the major source of revenue for these papers.

The number of magazines introduced in the late 19th century doubled between 1880 and 1890, with virtually all of them featuring fancy advertisements aimed particularly at women. Cyrus Curtis founded the *Ladies' Home Journal,* which became the base of a publishing empire aimed largely at affluent middle-class buyers. The *Journal* and its many imitators became the vehicle for the sale of a wide variety of food items, cosmetics, and ready-made clothing. Without the advertising in these journals, it is unlikely that new products such as Campbell's Soup would have reached the tables of millions of American homes or that Fels-Naptha would have become the preferred soap of American consumers. The success of Lydia E. Pinkham's Vegetable Compound for "female complaints" was entirely due to its magazine advertisements.

A group of entrepreneurs—including George P. Rowell, F. Wayland Ayer, and J. Walter Thompson—used the revolution in newspapers and magazines to found advertising agencies that established them as middlemen between industrialists, retailers, and publishers. These agencies negotiated rates for advertisers, designed the ads, and did market research to determine the best place to advertise and the efficiency of these ads. Thompson specialized in magazines and in the 1890s placed almost 90 percent of all advertisements in these journals. Larger industries and retailers developed departments devoted exclusively to advertising that worked closely with these agencies.

Advertising in the late 19th century was intimately linked with the development of consumerism and with the creation of a vast array of new products. The purchase of luxury goods was changed by advertising from something that was regarded as un-Christian and immoral to an act that promoted personal and national well-being. It is unlikely that the vast increase in industrialism would have succeeded without advertising. Few would have bought canned soup without the "um um good" advertisements of Campbell's Soup.

Further reading: Pamela Walker Laird, *Advertising Progress* (Baltimore: Johns Hopkins Press, 1998); James D. Norris, *Advertising and the Transformation of American Society, 1865–1920* (New York: Greenwood, 1990); Daniel Pope, *The Making of Modern Advertising* (New York: Basic Books, 1983).

— Herbert Ershkowitz

Aesthetic movement

The Aesthetic movement describes the philosophy and products of designers who created, as they termed it, "art for art's sake." Costly materials, complex craftsmanship, elaborate patterning, and learned references in motifs were emphasized in the fine and decorative arts of the Aesthetic movement, even at the expense of narrative and functionality.

The underpinnings of the movement can be found with design reformers and art critics such as William Morris and Clarence Cook, who were disturbed by the shoddy products of industry. The movement began in Britain and was swiftly disseminated through the burgeoning illustrated media, through international expositions, and through societies and clubs. While the Aesthetic movement was being formulated by artists and luxury craftsmen, its basic stylistic formulas were adopted by manufacturers of goods at all price levels. The Aesthetic movement was fueled by the era's concern with creating beautiful domestic environments that would foster high levels of aesthetic and moral sensibility. Women, as creators and consumers, were central to the movement.

Multiplicity and synchronicity within single objects and assemblages characterized the Aesthetic movement. Furniture incorporated ceramic tiles, patinated hardware, and painted surfaces within carved woodwork. The Herter Brothers and other interior designers flourished by harmonizing furniture and textiles of their own design with objects commercially produced. Some painters branched out to work in other media: JAMES ABBOTT MCNEILL WHISTLER created the Peacock Room (1876–77, Freer Gallery of Art), and John La Farge was an innovator in stained glass. Retailers like Daniel Cottier with shops in New York City, London, and Sydney promoted aesthetic taste by selling antiques as well as contemporary goods. Industrialists became collectors and sought fine objects from all eras; designers not only incorporated collections into interiors but drew inspiration from them. Classical antiquity, colonial America, Japan, and the natural world were particularly rich design sources; motifs from all places and times were combined elegantly.

Aesthetic-movement objects were made by individual artisans and by large factories. Some influential figures, such as ceramist and metalworker M. Louise McLaughlin, worked largely alone. Others, such as LOUIS COMFORT TIFFANY, designer of interiors, jewelry, and stained glass, were the heads of large firms. Upper-class women with leisure time were actively hand-painting china, carving wood, and creating every sort of textile. At SETTLEMENT HOUSES and through other philanthropic endeavors, leisured women encouraged old-world crafts in the name of the new aestheticism. New technologies in the printing industry led to a bloom of wallpapers with saturated hues and complex patterning. The commercial potteries of Staffordshire in England provided dinner services to the American market, while numerous small art potteries, such as Rookwood in Cincinnati and the Chelsea Keramic Art Works in Chelsea, Massachusetts, made vases, tiles, and more. Tiffany and Company in New York City sold jewelry and silver in the aesthetic style alongside more traditional models; countless manufacturers and retailers did the same. The Aesthetic movement embraced no single style; it was a philosophy that encouraged manufacturers and consumers to live artfully.

Further reading: Dorren Bolger Burke et al., *In Pursuit of Beauty: Americans and the Aesthetic Movement* (New York: Metropolitan Museum of Art and Rizzoli, 1986).

— Karen Zukowski

African-American churches, growth of

Baptists

African slaves, who arrived in America as Muslims or followers of traditional African religions, slowly accepted Christianity. The Baptists converted many enslaved persons during a period of great Baptist growth from 1750 to 1850. Slaves usually attended white churches, where they were segregated in separate pews or excluded in a hidden balcony commonly known as "nigger heaven." The first black Baptist church was organized in 1775 by David George at Silver Bluff, South Carolina, near Savannah, Georgia, but most black Americans were unable to have their own churches in the early years of the 19th century as whites sought to use religion to control them. Many enslaved persons, however, wanted their religious experience to reflect their African and, later, their African-American cultures and traditions. They stole off to canebrakes or woods to worship early in the morning away from the watchful eyes of owners, overseers, or night patrols. Blacks organized

Baptist churches in the North, notably the Jay Street Baptist Church (originally known as African Meeting House) in Boston in 1805 and the Abyssinian Baptist Church in lower Manhattan in 1808.

Black Baptist churches flourished after the Civil War as former slaves left the white churches to organize their own. Their growth was enhanced by the establishment of colleges with the assistance of white religious bodies. Many of these historically black colleges were seminaries for the training of ministers and teachers. Among the earlier black seminaries were Wayland Seminary (Virginia Union University) and Raleigh Institute (Shaw University), both founded in 1865. They were followed by the establishment of Augusta Institute (Morehouse College), 1867; Benedict College, 1870; Natchez Seminary (Jackson State University), 1877; Florida Baptist Institute (Florida Memorial College), 1879; and Atlanta Baptist Female Seminary (Spelman College), 1881.

Each Baptist congregation is independent and selects pastors and other church officials. This autonomy helped the Baptist church to spread in the South and elsewhere as AFRICAN AMERICANS migrated to points North and West. In 1895 the American National Baptist Convention and the Tripartite Union merged to form the National Baptist Convention, U.S.A. (NBC). Two years later the Lott Carey Baptist Foreign Mission Convention was organized by dissatisfied parties within the NBC who eschewed white support for mission work. Both became active participants in the African mission field. Among mainstream denominations, the Baptists were more apt to be encouraged by the church's leadership to express themselves emotionally in worship. The vast majority of African-American Protestants are members of the Baptist Church.

African Methodist Episcopalians (AME)

Next to the black Baptists, the AME Church is the largest African-American denomination in the United States. Richard Allen was the founder of this denomination. Allen was born a slave in Philadelphia in 1760. He preached to black worshipers in St. George Methodist Episcopal Church until a desire for a church of their own and a racial altercation led to his ejection from a "white" pew, which caused him and his followers to build Bethel AME Church in 1794. The AME Church was incorporated in 1816 with Allen as its first bishop. African Methodism spread to New York, New England, Maryland, the District of Columbia, and the Ohio Valley. Prior to the Civil War, congregations were established in Kentucky, Missouri, and Louisiana. Many churches were founded in the Midwest by missionary Paul Quinn. Other missionaries brought the church to California. During the 1820s a mission was established in Haiti.

At the end of the Civil War, James Lynch and James D. S. Hall were the first two missionaries commissioned to convert the newly freed slaves. In May 1865 Bishop Daniel A. Payne—assisted by Theophilus G. Steward, James A. Handy, and James H. A. Johnson—reestablished the church in South Carolina. (It had been banned in 1822 when African Methodists were implicated in the Denmark Vesey insurrection.) From April 1865 to May 1866 about two-thirds of black members of the Methodist Episcopal Church, South, set up their own churches outside of that denomination. Like the Baptists, many African Methodists took control of church buildings that they had built as slaves for white Christians. To their credit, many whites cooperated and allowed the former slaves to take charge of the buildings. African Methodism spread rapidly to North Carolina, Georgia, Alabama, Florida, and into the Southwest due to the missionary spirit of African Methodist Civil War chaplains HENRY M. TURNER, David Stevens, Garland H. White, and William H. Hunter as well as AME soldiers.

Like the Baptists, the AME Church established seminaries and colleges to train ministers. Among them were Wilberforce University (1856), Allen University (1880), Morris Brown College (1881), Paul Quinn College (1881), and Kittrell College (1886). The British Methodist Episcopal Church, which was organized after splitting from the AME Church in 1856, reunited with the mother church in 1884, adding congregations in Canada, Bermuda, and British Guiana. Bishop Henry M. Turner organized churches into conferences in Liberia and Sierra Leone in 1891 and five years later in South Africa. Between 1890 and 1916 the AME Church grew from 494,777 members to 548,355, and the number of churches increased from 2,481 to 6,636.

African Methodist Episcopal Zion (AMEZ)

There were few independent black churches in the late 18th century, when black members of the John Street Methodist Church in New York City felt the sting of racial discrimination. In 1796 Peter Williams and William Miller started a separate congregation. From 1816 to 1824 black Methodists moved to establish a separate denomination. In 1816 a separate circuit was established for African Methodists with a petition from Zion Church and Asbury Church to the Methodist Episcopal Conference of New York. In 1820 they formed a separate conference within the Methodist Episcopal body, but in 1821 they rejected an affiliation with the AME Church. In 1824 the AMEZ conference declared its independence from the Methodist Episcopal Church.

Like other black denominations, the AMEZ Church gained members during the Civil War as its missionaries followed black soldiers. Bishop Joseph J. Clinton commissioned James Hood and others to conduct mission work in the South during and after the Civil War. In the 1870s and following decades, the AMEZ extended mission work to the Midwest, the Far West, Canada, the Caribbean, and Africa. While smaller in numbers and congregations than either the black Baptists or the AME Church, the AMEZ Church made remarkable strides from 1821, when it counted 1,400 members and 22 ministers. By 1871 membership had increased to nearly 400,000. Like other black denominations, the AMEZ used its seminary, Livingstone College, in North Carolina, to train ministers for mission work in Africa. Throughout the late 19th century until the present, Africans have attended Livingstone College, where they further their education to assist in the African mission field.

Further reading: Paul E. Johnson, ed., *African-American Christianity: Essays in History* (Berkeley: University of California Press, 1994); C. Eric Lincoln and Lawrence H. Mamiya, *The Black Church in the African-American Experience* (Durham, N.C.: Duke University Press, 1990).

— William Seraile

African Americans

Between 1870 and 1900, the African-American population jumped from about 460,000 to 910,000 in the North and West and from 4.4 million to 7.9 million in the South. In the years following the Civil War, major adjustment problems gripped the South, where both races faced new situations. For African Americans, freedom was an experience to be tasted and tested; for Southern whites, black freedom was a challenge to be circumscribed and, where possible, checked.

By 1870 congressional Reconstruction was in full swing. The former Confederate states were required to write new constitutions, some of which funded public schools, railroad construction, and other public improvements. Abrogating previous restrictive laws, most of these basic documents set a democratic tone for the former Confederacy. The Fifteenth Amendment (1870) to the U.S. Constitution permitted black men to vote, and by 1875 Congress passed the CIVIL RIGHTS ACT prohibiting racial discrimination in public accommodations. Schools for black children and adults were opened across the South, and several colleges, like Howard University in the District of Columbia and Fisk University in Nashville, Tennessee, began somewhat tentatively to offer higher education to black Americans. Supported by federal troops, the offices of the Freedmen's Bureau across the South provided legal and protective assistance to former slaves. Black men not only voted, they were elected to federal and state offices. Two black U.S. senators, Hiram Revels and Blanche K. Bruce, represented Mississippi, while four African Americans were elected to the Congress from South Carolina and Mississippi. At the state level, P. B. S. Pinchback served as acting governor of Louisiana for a short time. Three states elected black secretaries of state, and four elected black state superintendents of education. James Lynch, secretary of state for Mississippi (1869–72), a perceptive and ambitious minister-editor, exemplified the effectiveness of African Americans who served in public office during Reconstruction. In addition to handling routine duties, Lynch began the process of straightening out the confusion over public lands to enable the state to locate taxable lands for schools and internal improvements. Pressured by divisions within and outside the race and by discrimination, Lynch and other black public officials were not always able to realize their full potential.

As the 1870s wore on, the gloss of full citizenship for southern blacks wore off. The number of federal troops was reduced to the point of ineffectiveness. States were slowly "redeemed" (that is, returned to local white control), and whites found ways to undo some of the progress that blacks had achieved. Black schools were underfunded compared with white schools; black officeholders were slowly squeezed out; and black farmers were pinched by mounting debt. Agriculture was the major employer for blacks, plantations the major unit, and cotton the major crop. Few African Americans could overcome the obstacles to be landowners, so the vast majority were tenants who faced three options. They could work on a cash system and pay rent; they could borrow on credit to buy seeds and other needs, repaying the planter when the crop was harvested; or they could sharecrop, splitting the harvest's income into shares for planter and tenant. The almost inevitable result of these systems was an unbearable debt burden. A black man summed it up for a visitor: "White man sit down the whole year; Nigger work day and night and make crop; Nigger hardly gits bread and meat; white man sittin' down gits all. *It's wrong.*"

The North slowly tired of supporting southern Reconstruction, and by 1876 Republicans were looking for a way out. RUTHERFORD B. HAYES, as their presidential candidate, sought to calm the waters by appealing to Southern leaders to treat their racial work force equitably. Historians have characterized Hayes's victory in the disputed election of 1876 as the result of an agreement between him and Southern Democrats to withdraw the remaining troops from the South. The evidence for such a deal is circumstantial at best, but it is true that Hayes was anxious to restore peace within the South and between the North and South. Soon after his inauguration in March 1877, Hayes withdrew federal troops from the two remaining Republican states (South Carolina and Louisiana), formally ending Reconstruction. White Southerners rejoiced and slowly began the process of exercising total control over the black minority, initially by fraud and intimidation and eventually by restrictive JIM CROW LAWS in the 1890s and the early 20th century.

Freedom for many African Americans came to mean scratching for subsistence, and some sought new surroundings, moving from plantation to plantation, from rural areas to cities, from state to state. The Louisiana sugar plantations and the Virginia and North Carolina tobacco farms hired workers for wages, but the pay was low and the work seasonal. A few found employment building railroads, mining coal or phosphate, making turpentine, or lumbering. A handful eyed a different kind of freedom available in the North and West and began the slow drift out of the South. In 1879 about 6,000 men, women, and children headed for Kansas, an exodus impelled by poverty and widening white terrorism. Most of the migrants put down roots there, overcoming white resistance and poor soil. Northern and western black Americans had full citizenship rights, limited civil rights, and greater mobility than their Southern brethren, but they faced stiff discrimination in employment, housing, and social affairs. In 1883 the U.S. SUPREME COURT invalidated the Civil Rights Act of 1875, and Northern states—following an earlier lead of Massachusetts, New York, and Kansas—began to enact mild statutes to protect the rights of African Americans to be served in restaurants, seated in theaters, and housed in inns and hotels.

The black response to southern oppression and northern indifference was to concentrate on their own well-being. AFRICAN-AMERICAN CHURCHES multiplied, led by black Baptists and Methodists and three black denominations: the African Methodist Episcopal (AME), the AME Zion, and the Colored [later Christian] ME. Colleges for blacks proliferated, offering industrial education and little more than a high-school curriculum. African Americans realized that education was essential to achieve even a limited financial stability. Tuskegee Institute in Alabama, emphasizing industrial education, was established by the state in 1881 with a young Hampton Institute graduate as principal. BOOKER T. WASHINGTON carefully used this position as a springboard to national leadership. He spoke persuasively to the National Education Association in Madison, Wisconsin, in 1884, and 11 years later he delivered his famous ATLANTA COMPROMISE speech in Georgia, in which he counseled separation of the races coupled with mutual understanding. "In all things purely social," he asserted, "we can be as separate as the fingers, yet one as the hand in all things essential to mutual progress." The white South happily accepted his separation premise and doggedly rejected mutuality.

Other African-American men and women rose to leadership in the last two decades of the century. IDA WELLS-BARNETT crusaded against lynching here and in England, using her capability as a speaker and her competence as a writer to rally support. Mary Church Terrell and Josephine St. Pierre Ruffin activated the National Association of Colored Women (1896) to give women a voice in black affairs. Editors T. Thomas Fortune in New York and Harry Smith in Cleveland stood out among an often argumentative group of able editors of weekly black newspapers. Frederick Douglass used his position as an elder statesman to agitate for and mediate within the race. His death in 1895 created a vacuum that was soon filled by Booker T. Washington, whose leadership after the turn of the century was contested by W. E. B. Du Bois. The Massachusetts-born Du Bois was the first black Harvard Ph.D., and before 1900 he was the author of two substantial books and the editor of a precedent-breaking series of race studies at Atlanta University. Du Bois used his considerable skills to oppose Washington's emphasis on industrial education to the exclusion of the liberal arts, his accommodating posture with whites, and his expanding control over black organizations, newspapers, and fund-raising.

By the 1890s white domination over southern blacks was secure. Jim Crow laws maintained total segregation, and the U.S. Supreme Court decision in *PLESSY V. FERGUSON* (1896) confirmed their constitutionality. The right to vote was closed down. Terrorism in the form of LYNCHING reached its horrible heights between 1880 and 1900, with an average of 100 reported lynching murders a year and an unknown number unreported. The victims usually were accused, without substantiation, of rape and then killed without a court trial. In the North and West, blacks steeled themselves against an ever-present prejudice and sought refuge among themselves.

During these difficult decades a distinct black culture evolved, derived partly from African origins, partly from the long stretch of slavery, and partly from the race's own creativity. New patterns of religious practice emerged, featuring greater emotional participation. There was also new music in the form of spirituals, gospel, and different vocal and instrumental interpretations. The music was popularized by the Fisk University Jubilee Singers, a student group that entertained throughout the country and abroad beginning in 1876. African-American artists like HENRY O. TANNER, poets like PAUL LAURENCE DUNBAR, and authors like Charles W. Chesnutt achieved national or international reputations. Chesnutt's novels and short stories unflinchingly probed racial subjects, while Tanner's artistic interest was more general. Tanner was a resident of France for most of his productive life, and his success was a model for younger black artists. Dunbar had a short life, but his works often captured the down-home character of southern blacks while occasionally and subtly underlining the race's discriminatory difficulties. One of his best-known poems expresses African-American bitterness and the techniques used to hide it: "We wear the mask that grins and lies. / It hides our cheeks and shades our eyes / . . . With torn and bleeding hearts we smile. . . ." Early in the next century, two national organizations—the National Urban League (NUL) and the National Association for the Advancement of Colored People (NAACP)—were established in part to encourage African Americans to drop the mask. Both organizations began a sustained campaign to capture citizens' rights for all black people.

The final three decades of the 19th century were discouraging years for African Americans. In differing degrees and with differing methods, whites in the North and South attempted to restrict black livelihood, destroy black personhood, and erode black identity. Despite these efforts, African Americans created strong family and social ties, a vibrant subculture, and the beginnings of an organizational structure to sustain them through the next century.

Further reading: Robin D. G. Kelley and Earl Lewis, eds., *To Make Our World Anew: A History of African Americans* (New York: Oxford University Press, 2000); Philip A. Klinkner and Rogers M. Smith, *The Unsteady March: The Rise and Decline of Racial Equality in America* (Chicago: University of Chicago Press, 1999); Leon F. Litwack, *Trouble in Mind: Black Southerners in the Age of Jim Crow* (New York: Random House, 1998).

— Leslie H. Fishel jr.

agriculture

American agriculture in the late 19th century underwent a profound revolution. Vast areas were put into cultivation; machines and techniques were improved and used more widely; and farmers increased their indebtedness, specialized more and more on money crops, became increasingly dependent on changeable markets, and had less and less control over their profits. With less diversification and greater dependence on a money crop, profits were determined by the elements (more than ever), interest rates, freight rates, and world supply and demand.

Expansion

From 1870 to 1900 farm acreage jumped from 408 million to 839 million, largely because RAILROADS crisscrossed the nation and connected arable land with markets. Although

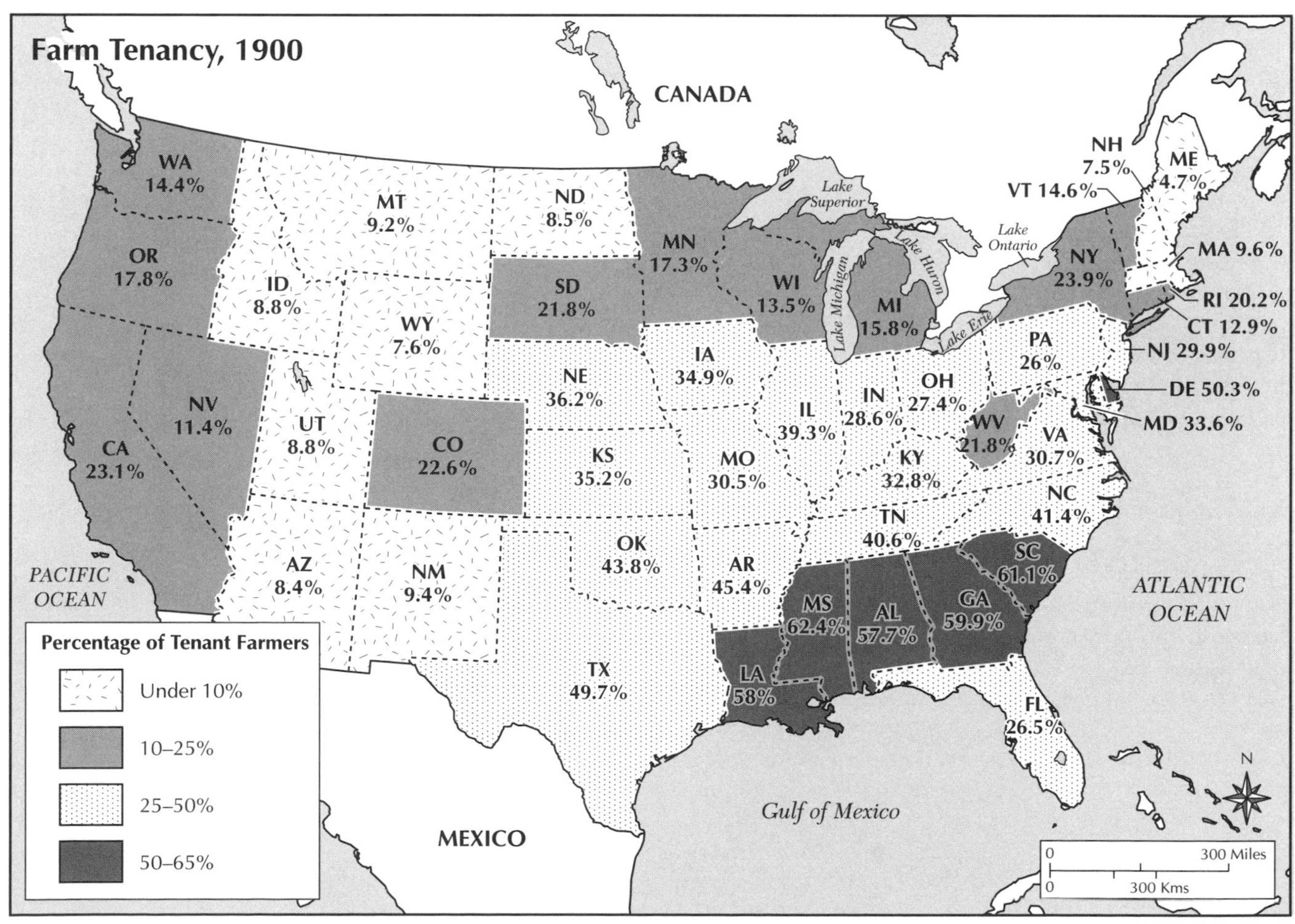

the Homestead Act (1862) enabled settlers to acquire 160 acres of public land as long as they remained on it for five years, most of the farms created from 1870 to 1900 were on land purchased from railroads and land speculators. The railroads had received land grants from the federal government to encourage them to build in sparsely settled territories. Their acreage was usually more fertile and accessible to their tracks than land available under the Homestead Act, and since the railroads were anxious to attract settlers to increase the volume of their freight, they sold the land for a reasonable price. Since the cost of converting virgin land into a productive farm with its buildings and machinery was high in comparison with the cost of good land, it was sound economics for farmers to purchase the most productive land available.

Machines

The basic principles of most of the machines used in the Gilded Age—steel plows, disk harrows, grain drills and corn planters, harvesters, binders, threshers—were patented by 1870. All, however, were significantly improved over the next three decades. For example, from 1868 to 1877 James Oliver developed the modern plow. Sulky plows and steam plows were improved, but steam plows were used only on giant wheat farms in the Far West. Binders were improved in 1878 with a twine knotter that eliminated the need for wire; threshers grew in capacity and utilized steam power; and by 1880 combines were used in California, but not east of the Rockies before 1910. Apart from steam plows and threshers, horses and mules powered farm machinery. Neither the cultivation of cotton nor tobacco was significantly affected by the introduction of machinery in the Gilded Age. An effective mechanical cotton picker was not developed until the 20th century. The dairy industry, however, was revolutionized after 1879 with the introduction of the centrifugal cream separator and the later development of the cream tester.

Techniques

Manly Miles of the University of Illinois built a silo in 1875, and by 1900 silos were in use throughout the corn belt. Farmers in arid areas relied on irrigation and experimented with methods of dry farming. Federal and state governments established schools and agencies to improve farming techniques. The federal government established the Department of Agriculture in 1862 and elevated it to cabinet status in 1889. The department disseminated information through hundreds of publications, studied plant and animal diseases and their cures, explored how to preserve soil fertility, and collected statistics, among other duties. In 1862 the Morrill Land Grant Act provided for the establishment of agricultural and mechanical (A&M) colleges in each state, and by 1898, 64 had been established with departments of general agriculture as well as specialized departments in animal industry, dairy husbandry, agricultural chemistry, and other areas. These schools also had model demonstration farms. Connecticut set up an agricultural experiment station in 1875, and several states followed suit until in 1887 the federal Hatch Act subsidized these stations in all states and territories. These stations coordinated their work with the A&M colleges and the Department of Agriculture in educating farmers.

Specialization

Mechanization led to specialization in cash crops for two reasons. Farmers wished to utilize the full productive capacity of their expensive machinery, and they needed cash to pay debts incurred in acquiring those machines. In addition, railroads and refrigerator cars enabled each section of the country to become more specialized. The centers of wheat and corn belts moved west as did hog, cattle, and sheep raising. New England and the middle states were switching from corn and wheat to dairy farming and truck gardening. The South continued to specialize in tobacco and cotton, not because of mechanization but because of the perpetual indebtedness of tenant farmers.

Markets

Planting more cash crops made farmers more dependent on markets than when their production was more diversified. With rapid urban growth in the Gilded Age, domestic markets grew rapidly, but farm production grew even more rapidly. While the population less than doubled from 40 million in 1870 to 76 million in 1900, corn production more than doubled from 1.1 billion bushels to 2.7 billion bushels, and wheat also more than doubled from 254 million bushels to 599 million bushels. While cotton and tobacco exports grew at a relatively steady rate, wheat exports fluctuated wildly. In 1870, 37 million bushels were exported and in 1900 102 million bushels, but wheat exports fell as low as 46 million bushels in 1889, only to rise three years later to 157 million bushels.

Agricultural Depression

From 1870 to 1900 American agriculture was depressed mainly because of overproduction. In the late 1860s wheat sold for over two dollars a bushel and corn for 78 cents a bushel, but in 1870 wheat was barely over one dollar and corn was at 52 cents. By 1895 wheat had fallen to half a dollar while corn in 1896 hit 21 cents.

In 1900 prices had rebounded to 62 cents for wheat and 35 cents for corn. With deflation prices declined, interest rates rose, and debtors had to produce more to pay their debts. Overproduction, however, drove prices lower, and the thousands of individual farmers had no way to control production. Wheat prices, furthermore, were set by worldwide conditions, and American farmers were competing with Canadians, Argentineans, Hungarians, and Ukrainians. Farmers sold their wheat in a world market but purchased manufactured goods in a protected national market. Middlemen profited in buying crops from farmers and in selling goods to farmers. Finally, although railroad rates were declining, farmers felt they were not declining as fast as the prices they received for their crops, and they knew they paid higher discriminatory rates for short hauls than urban shippers, with access to competing lines, paid for long hauls. This agricultural malaise led to the populist revolt of the 1890s.

Further reading: Fred A. Shannon, *The Farmers Last Frontier: Agriculture, 1860–1897* (New York: Holt, Rinehart and Winston, 1945).

Alabama claims

See Washington, Treaty of

Alcott, Louisa May (1832–1888)

The author of some of the most popular and enduring juvenile fiction ever, Louisa May Alcott was born in Germantown, Pennsylvania, on November 29, 1832, and grew up in Boston and Concord, Massachusetts. Her father was Bronson Alcott, the educational innovator and transcendentalist. Although he was part of a distinguished intellectual circle—close family friends included Ralph Waldo Emerson and Henry David Thoreau—he was incapable of earning a sustained income, and his family frequently lived in poverty.

As a teenager, to help support her family, Alcott began working as a seamstress, a governess, and a domestic worker, among other jobs. She also began to write for publication. Her first published piece was a poem in *Peterson's Magazine* in 1851, and she followed it up with a variety of thrillers and potboilers that were published anonymously or under pseudonyms in publications like the *Saturday Evening Gazette* and the *Atlantic Monthly*.

In 1862 she briefly became an army nurse and served in a hospital in Washington, D.C., before contracting typhoid fever. She was treated with mercury, which permanently damaged her health, but she used that experience to write *Hospital Sketches,* which appeared in *Commonwealth* (May–June 1863) and was reprinted that same year in book form. In 1864 she published *Moods,* a novel about a young woman who feels forced by circumstance to marry a man she merely likes. Meanwhile, she continued to crank out sensational stories for magazines.

In 1868 she tried her hand at a book for adolescent girls. The result was *Little Women,* which was published in two separate volumes, the first in 1868 and the second in 1869. It was based on Alcott's own family, and Jo, the tomboy heroine who chaffs under pressure to be ladylike, was based on Alcott herself. Within four years, *Little Women* had sold 82,000 copies, unprecedented numbers for juvenile fiction. Its success enabled Alcott to provide for her parents, but it also led to relentless pressure to produce more books, which added to her difficulties in her final years (she died on March 6, 1888) as her health broke down.

Alcott followed up *Little Women* with *An Old-Fashioned Girl* (1870), a novel about a small-town girl trying to hold on to her values during an extended visit to a wealthy family in worldly Boston; *Little Men* (1871), a sequel to *Little Women,* in which Jo and her husband run a boy's school, based in large part on the educational theories of Bronson Alcott; *Eight Cousins* (1875), about a sickly orphan girl whose health improves after she begins to spend time with her boisterous male cousins; *Rose in Bloom* (1876), a sequel to *Eight Cousins; Under the Lilacs* (1878), about a circus runaway; *Jack and Jill* (1880), about a boy and a girl convalescing after a sledding accident; and *Jo's Boys* (1886), a sequel to *Little Men.* All were successful, but none matched the sales figures of *Little Women.*

Alcott also published scores of short stories for children and adolescents and two more adult novels: *Work* (1873) and *A Modern Mephistopheles* (1877), about a young poet who sells himself for literary fame. But it was her adolescent books that brought her the bulk of her success and her enduring fame. She did not always enjoy writing them, referring to them at one point as "moral pap for the young," but their success was no accident—Alcott remembered what it was like to be 14 or 15, and many of the problems her heroines struggled with were universal. In addition, her books hit the market at a time when an entirely new consumer group was emerging: middle-class girls, 12 to 16 years old, who were anxious to read about girls like themselves and had enough money to purchase moderately priced books.

Further reading: Sarah Elbert, *A Hunger for Home: Louisa May Alcott's Place in American Culture* (New Brunswick: Rutgers University Press, 1987); Madeleine B. Stern, *Louisa May Alcott* (Norman: University of Oklahoma Press, 1950).

— Lynn Hoogenboom

Alger, Horatio (1834–1899)

Born in Revere, Massachusetts, on January 13, 1834, Horatio Alger, the author of moral, melodramatic books for boys, graduated from Harvard in 1852, sewed wild oats on a trip to Europe, and then for three years worked for local newspapers before attending Harvard Divinity School. After earning his divinity degree, Alger again traveled abroad and in 1864 became minister of the Brewster, Massachusetts, Unitarian church. Two years later, accused of being a pederast, he was dismissed.

Having already published sentimental poems and stories as well as sensational—but moral—novels, Alger moved to New York City to make his way as a writer. He did some tutoring for the wealthy and some social work at the Newsboys' Lodging House, where he lived most of the time and drew on his observations in his books for boys. His most successful book, *Ragged Dick: Or Street Life in New York,* appeared in 1867, and Alger produced over a hundred more like it.

In a typical Alger tale, a poor boy of sterling character leaves the farm (perhaps to earn money to help his widowed mother); goes to the city; gets a job in a department store; is honest, diligent, and frugal; and by an extraordinary stroke of good luck comes to the attention of the merchant prince who owns the store.

By the end of the book the boy is on his way to a managerial position. Alger's books have come to symbolize the "rags to riches" American dream. They were enormously popular among boys, not so much for the moralistic lessons and traditional values dispensed, but more for their adventurous and melodramatic character and the assurance that ultimately the hero (who eschewed gambling) would nevertheless hit the jackpot in the world of business.

In 1896 Alger moved to Natick, Massachusetts, to live with his sister and to write a great adult novel, but he failed to begin it before he died on July 18, 1899.

Further reading: Carol Nackenoff, *The Fictional Republic: Horatio Alger and American Political Discourse* (New York: Oxford University Press; 1994); Gary Scharnhorst and Jack Bales, *The Lost Life of Horatio Alger, Jr.* (Bloomington: Indiana University Press, 1985).

Altgeld, John Peter (1847–1902)

Democratic politician John Peter Altgeld was born to John Peter and Mary Altgeld on December 30, 1847, at Nieder Selters in Nassau, Germany. His parents brought him to the United States and settled in Richland County, Ohio, when he was only three months old. In 1864 he served in the Ohio Home Guards briefly, taught school for two years, and in 1869 at the age of 21 moved west to Missouri. He read law, was admitted to the bar in 1871, and in 1874 he was elected state's attorney for Andrew County with Democratic-Granger support. Despite this apparent success, he resigned and moved to Chicago one year later.

At first Altgeld did not do well in Chicago. He slept in his office for two years before he could afford living quarters.

By 1879, however, he was secure enough to begin speculating in real estate. Over the next 11 years he parlayed a $500 initial investment into a $500,000 fortune. During this time he continued to practice law and to write. In 1884 he published *Our Penal Machinery and Its Victims,* suggesting that the poor had a less than equal chance in America. Another publication, *The Immigrant's Answer* (1890), responded to nativist attacks against aliens. He was also an effective politician, elected as a judge for the Superior Court of Cook County in 1886 and, six years later, became the Democratic Party's successful candidate for governor.

Shortly after his inauguration, Altgeld, pressed by Clarence Darrow and other liberals, considered pardoning those convicted of the bombing during the HAYMARKET RIOT. After careful study he pardoned the three who were still alive, in June 1893. Altgeld suggested that the bomb was most likely thrown as an act of individual revenge, because the Chicago police often clubbed strikers who gave no offense. He also dismissed much of the evidence as "pure fabrication," objected to the method of jury selection, and noted the obvious prejudice of Judge Joseph Gary. The press denounced Altgeld as an anarchist, a demagogue, a fomenter of lawlessness, and an apologist for murder.

The outcry did not deter Altgeld from supporting those he considered disenfranchised. He appointed Alzina P. Stevens assistant factory inspector for Illinois and supported her assault upon the sweatshop system. He protested the use of federal troops during the PULLMAN STRIKE of 1894, stating that President GROVER CLEVELAND's action was "unnecessary, unjustifiable, and unconstitutional."

Altgeld played a major role in the Democratic Party's repudiation of Cleveland. At its 1896 convention he helped write its platform, calling for the free coinage of silver (FREE-SILVER MOVEMENT), and his influence was so great that he would have been a serious contender for the nomination had he not been born abroad and thus ineligible for the U.S. presidency. The Illinois Democratic Party nominated him in 1896 for a second gubernatorial term, but although he ran well ahead of the Democratic Party's national ticket in Illinois, he lost. Altgeld also suffered financial as well as political reverses, but he remained active as a lawyer and in politics. He was an outspoken advocate of municipal ownership of streetcar lines and an opponent of IMPERIALISM; indeed, he died in Joliet, Illinois, on March 12, 1902, just after delivering a speech attacking imperialism. The poet Vachel Lindsay celebrated Altgeld in his poem "The Eagle That Is Forgotten."

Further reading: Harry Barnard, *Eagle Forgotten: The Life of John Peter Altgeld* (Secaucus, N.J.: L. Stuart, 1968);

Ray Ginger, *Altgeld's America: The Lincoln Ideal* versus *Changing Realities* (Chicago: Quadrangle Books, 1965).

— Harold W. Aurand

American Federation of Labor (AFL)

The American Federation of Labor (AFL) grew out of a conflict between trade unions and the KNIGHTS OF LABOR (Knights). In 1885 the Knights raided the territory of Local 144 of the Cigarmakers International in New York. Outraged, the president of Local 144, SAMUEL GOMPERS, called a conference with other trade unionists to discuss options. The conference demanded, among other things, that the Knights cease recruiting members from established trade unions and stop issuing their own union labels. Knowing that the Knights would not accede to these demands, the group called for another, larger conference. Responding to the call, delegates from 25 labor unions met in Columbus, Ohio, in December 1886 and created the AFL.

An executive council, elected by an annual convention controlled by the national trade unions (each national received one vote for every 100 members), was the AFL's primary policy-enforcing body. The council was responsible for adjudicating jurisdictional disputes among member unions, helping form new national trade unions, and judging the merits of proposed boycotts. It also established state federations and, in some cases, local central bodies to coordinate union activities at those levels. A per capita tax levied on its affiliates provided most of the organization's income.

Since each affiliate retained its autonomy, the AFL had little real power. It tended to determine jurisdictional disputes, for example, in favor of the stronger contender rather than upon the merits of the case. But the best illustration of its weakness was its inability to enforce its constitutional prohibition against discrimination. Although it denied affiliation to the boilermakers union because its constitution contained a "white only" clause, it was powerless against members practicing de facto exclusion. At the turn of the century only one, of its more than 50 affiliates, the United Mine Workers of America, had a sizable African-American membership.

The exclusionary policy of AFL member unions extended to women and the unskilled. By 1895 less than 6 percent of all union members were women. Formed to protect their skilled members from the encroachment of machines, craft unions spurned industrial workers. Moreover, they feared that if industrial workers were permitted membership, the more numerous unskilled laborers would force their skilled brethren into hopeless strikes.

AFL unions believed that collective bargaining, supported by strikes and boycotts, was the best means to improve economic conditions for their members. A series of disastrous strikes such as the HOMESTEAD STRIKE generated questions about the effectiveness of wage-conscious unionism. Led by socialists, those favoring a more political tack attempted to have the 1892 convention convert itself into an independent political party. Gompers, however, defeated the movement. The following year the political actionists defeated Gompers's bid for reelection, but their victory was fleeting, as Gompers was elected president again in 1895. Under his leadership the AFL remained committed to pursuing economic goals while rewarding its friends and punishing its enemies in elections, regardless of party affiliation. Over the years the policy proved effective. The exclusionary practices of most AFL unions, however, limited the beneficiaries of these gains to skilled white males, creating, in a sense, an aristocracy of labor.

Further reading: Stuart B. Kaufman, *Samuel Gompers and the Origins of the American Federation of Labor, 1848–1896* (Westport, Conn.: Greenwood, 1973).

— Harold W. Aurand

American Protective Association (APA)

Nativists flocked to the American Protective Association in the Gilded Age. American NATIVISM was often linked to anti-Catholicism, which had deep roots in the Anglo-American Protestant culture of the United States. Nativist groups used anti-Catholic rhetoric to arouse the long-standing fears and misgivings that Americans had of Catholics. Several developments in the 1870s and 1880s exacerbated anti-Catholic suspicions: the rise to political power of Irish and German Catholics in some of the nation's major cities; the rapid expansion of parish and parochial schools and the controversy over public aid to those schools; and the perceived Catholic influence over organized labor.

On March 13, 1887, Henry F. Bowers, a self-taught Iowa lawyer, founded the American Protective Association (APA), which became the largest American nativist organization of the late 19th century. The APA was an oath-bound organization open to anyone committed to bringing a halt to immigration and resisting the so-called Catholic menace. It absorbed many of the smaller nativist societies that had sprung up in the years immediately following the Civil War. By 1894 membership in the APA had reached a reported 500,000 people, with councils (local chapters) in cities throughout the Middle West, Northeast, and Far West.

The growth of the APA was partially the result of new leadership. In 1893 William J. Traynor replaced Bowers as the organization's supreme president. Traynor had been the president of the Michigan council and was a vocal, committed nativist who not only had experience in promoting several anti-Catholic groups but also possessed a keen sense of politics. His vigorous leadership, however, was not the sole cause of the increase in membership. The economic depression of 1893 had stimulated anti-Catholic and anti-immigrant feelings in America and served as a powerful recruiting tool. The members of the APA portrayed immigrants as "job stealers" and accused Catholics of plotting to disrupt the nation's economic system and paving the way for the pope to seize power.

By the late 1890s, the APA began to weaken. Not only was the organization beset by internal dissension, but nativism was also being gradually eclipsed by more pressing issues. Like its Know-Nothing predecessor in the 1850s, the APA created much nativist excitement and anti-Catholic anxiety, but unlike the Know-Nothings, it had little political success.

See also IMMIGRATION; IMMIGRATION RESTRICTIONS.

Further reading: David H. Bennett, *The Party of Fear: From Nativist Movements to the New Right* (Chapel Hill: University of North Carolina Press, 1988); Donald L. Kinzer, *An Episode in Anti-Catholicism: The American Protective Association* (Seattle: University of Washington Press, 1964).

— Phillip Papas

American Woman Suffrage Association (AWSA)
See women's rights

anarchists
See labor, radical

Anthony, Susan B. (1820–1906)

The most visible force behind the battle for woman suffrage, Susan Brownell Anthony was the daughter of a well-to-do Quaker mill owner. Born in Adams, Massachusetts, on February 15, 1820, she grew up in Battenville, New York. She worked as a teacher from 1839 until 1849, when she left teaching to manage her family's farm and became absorbed in reform movements.

In 1850 she met Elizabeth Cady Stanton, a leader of the first women's rights convention in Seneca Falls, New York, in 1848. Their mutual interests in abolition and women's issues led to a professional partnership that lasted until Stanton's death in 1902. Stanton, who had strong writing and oratorical skills, honed the message while Anthony provided the organizational skills.

In the years leading up to the Civil War, Anthony was a primary organizer of a series of women's rights conventions, and from 1854 on she organized yearly petition drives in New York demanding woman suffrage and property rights for married women. From 1856 until the beginning of the Civil War, Anthony was also the principal New York agent (or lobbyist) for the American Anti-Slavery Society. In 1863 Anthony and Stanton organized the Women's Loyal National League, which collected 400,000 signatures on a petition calling for the abolition of slavery. After the war, as the corresponding secretary for the American Equal Rights Association (AERA), Anthony oversaw petitions to Congress advocating universal suffrage and coordinated several campaigns to amend state constitutions.

Susan B. Anthony *(Library of Congress)*

In 1867 she campaigned in Kansas for proposals for African-American and woman suffrage. Both were defeated, and that campaign opened a rift within the equal-rights movement when, midway through the campaign, the Republican Party withdrew support for the woman suffrage amendment. In order to complete her campaign, Anthony accepted the help of George Francis Train, a Democrat and blatant racist. She and Stanton also accepted his financing of their newspaper, *The Revolution,* which made its debut in January 1868 and lasted only until 1870, when it was turned over to a new owner. It opposed the Fourteenth and Fifteenth Amendments on the grounds that both excluded women, and it departed from the AERA position in favor of universal suffrage by running articles favorable to educated suffrage. With Anthony and Stanton's positions diverging from those of the AERA, they set up their own organization, the National Woman Suffrage Association (NWSA) in 1869. LUCY STONE, disturbed by Anthony and Stanton's hostility to the Fourteenth and Fifteenth Amendments, formed a rival organization, the American Woman Suffrage Association (AWSA), that same year.

Anthony's opposition to the Fourteenth and Fifteenth Amendments did not keep her from testing the theory that those amendments, which linked voting rights with citizenship, actually had granted women the right to vote. In 1872, after Anthony and a group of followers voted in Rochester, New York, she was arrested for violating federal law. At her trial, a hostile judge pronounced her guilty without polling the jury and fined her $100. She refused to pay the fine, but since she was not jailed she was unable to appeal her case to the SUPREME COURT. In *Minor v. Happersett* (1875), the case that eventually decided the issue, in which the Supreme Court ruled that the Fourteenth and Fifteenth Amendments did not give women the right to vote.

At the Fourth of July ceremonies at the PHILADELPHIA CENTENNIAL EXPOSITION of 1876, Anthony and two colleagues received a flurry of publicity when they interrupted the official celebration and presented the keynote speaker with a "Women's Declaration of 1876," which asked for women's rights in fulfillment of the ideals of 1776.

From 1870 to 1900 Anthony lectured everywhere, gave hundreds of interviews to local newspapers, and forged links with various women's organizations, which had burgeoned in the latter half of the 19th century. While few of these organizations endorsed suffrage, they proved willing to work with Anthony on other women's issues and eventually welcomed her as a speaker at their conventions. By the 1890s Anthony had access to the platforms of every significant women's group in the country. She campaigned for a woman suffrage amendment everywhere, taking the skills she had developed in her early campaigns in New York State and reapplying them on a national level. Although she never came close to getting the amendment passed, she did manage to move the issue from the political fringes to the mainstream. And while she had taken the brunt of the ridicule and vitriol that was heaped on suffragists in the early days, by the 1890s she was widely respected, even revered, for her unflinching devotion to her cause.

In 1890 the NWSA and AWSA merged into the National American Woman Suffrage Association (NAWSA). Anthony insisted that Stanton, longtime president of the NWSA, be president of the merged association. When Stanton retired as NAWSA president in 1892, Anthony replaced her and remained president of the organization until 1900, when she was 80. Although she slowed down a bit, she continued to campaign for woman suffrage up until a month before her death on March 13, 1906.

See also WOMEN'S RIGHTS.

Further reading: Kathleen Barry, *Susan B. Anthony: A Biography of a Singular Feminist* (New York: New York University Press, 1988).

— Lynn Hoogenboom

Anti-Imperialist League

The Anti-Imperialist League grew out of the opposition to the war with Spain and its consequences. Prominent Americans spoke out against military intervention to free CUBA from Spain before war was declared in April 1898. Once U.S. forces seized Spain's insular possessions, these spokespeople began to organize to prevent colonialism.

On June 15, 1898, a rally at Boston's historic Faneuil Hall formed a committee of correspondence, which resulted in an Anti-Imperialist League five months later. At first its efforts focused on a petition campaign to block permanent acquisition of the newly conquered territory. The outbreak in February 1899 of the Philippine Rebellion against American rule inspired others to form anti-imperialist leagues. Outside of New England, the Single Tax followers of Henry George were responsible for forming branch offices. Finally, in October 1899 activists established the American Anti-Imperialist League with its national office in Chicago and George S. Boutwell, a former member of Ulysses S. Grant's cabinet, as its president.

The anti-imperialists shared high status and advanced years but lacked a clear-cut alternative foreign policy program. Most were economic conservatives and were uneasy when WILLIAM JENNINGS BRYAN took up the fight against IMPERIALISM as the Democratic presidential candidate in 1900. While Bryan claimed FOREIGN POLICY issues were the center of his candidacy, he continued to advocate FREE-SILVER monetization. This stand alienated such anti-imperialists as ANDREW CARNEGIE and Senator GEORGE F. HOAR. Some defectors in the New York office withdrew to form a nonpartisan organization, while others established Liberty Leagues to advocate Philippine independence.

After 1901 the seven remaining league offices continued to criticize the Philippine-American War, but they were again disappointed when the DEMOCRATIC PARTY chose a lackluster candidate to oppose Theodore Roosevelt in the 1904 election. The national office moved to Boston and the league survived until 1921.

See also FILIPINO INSURRECTION; SPANISH-AMERICAN WAR.

Further reading: Robert L. Beisner, *Twelve against Empire: The Anti-Imperialists, 1898–1900* (New York: McGraw-Hill, 1968); E. Berkeley Tompkins, *Anti-Imperialism in the United States: The Great Debate, 1890–1920* (Philadelphia: University of Pennsylvania Press, 1970).

— Bruce Abrams

Anti-Saloon League

See Prohibition Party

Apache War

The Apache War was marked by frequent skirmishes and battles from the early 1870s into the 1880s. Apache Indians first clashed with Spaniards during the colonial era, then with Mexico after Mexican independence, and finally with the United States after it won control of the Southwest from Mexico in 1848. After settlers began to mine copper ore, especially in Arizona, where many Apache lived, the situation deteriorated. To control it the federal government aimed to consolidate the disparate Apache bands at the San Carlos Reservation in eastern Arizona.

In 1871 citizens of Tucson, Arizona, reacted to repeated Chiricahua Apache raids by attacking Camp Grant, a federal government-sponsored settlement, and killing up to 150 Apache, including many women and children. President Ulysses S. Grant, appalled by the vigilantism, ordered General George Crook to stabilize the region. After Apache raids continued, Crook led western forces against the Apache, successfully using Native American "scouts" to fight other Indians. Crook led several bloody campaigns against the Apache until a tenuous peace was negotiated with the Chiricahua band in 1874. That same year President Grant put their copper-producing reservation lands in the public domain, opening them up to mining interests. This move led to the resettlement of Chiricahua Apache to the reservation at San Carlos in 1876. Roughly half the Chiricahua complied with the removal order while the remainder fled to Mexico.

Among the recalcitrant Chiricahua Apache, a warrior named GERONIMO emerged as a war leader. Geronimo had fled to Mexico in 1876 and began to use the Ojo Caliente Reservation in New Mexico, where the Warm Springs Apache were located, as a base to organize raids. As a result, the Warm Springs Reservation was shut down by authorities in 1877, and officials began planning to remove 400 Warm Springs Apache and Geronimo's band of Chiricahua Apache to the San Carlos Reservation. Fearing resistance, officials arrested Geronimo and several other leaders. Conditions at San Carlos were abysmal, and the displaced Warm Springs Apache, led by their war chief Victorio, broke away from the reservation in September 1877, eventually crossing the border into Mexico and beginning a three-year period during which the band raided settlements along the border in Mexico and the United States. The raids ended in 1880, when Victorio and his band were killed by Mexican soldiers.

The Warm Springs Apache who had been sent back to San Carlos joined with Geronimo, who had returned there in the interim. During this time officials became increasingly concerned about an Apache rebellion after tribal members began practicing the Ghost Dance religion, which involved communing with ancestors via a trancelike dance. Tension between the Apache and the U.S. Army led to an Apache attack on August 30, 1881. Geronimo again fled to Mexico with other Apache, engaging American troops at the border. Apache warriors reentered the United States in April 1882, attacking reservation policemen at San Carlos on April 19, during which time Geronimo freed a group of Apache, fleeing to Mexico with the fugitives. Determined to bring peace to the territory, General Crook entered Mexico in 1883 with 200 scouts, and in February 1884 Geronimo surrendered, returning to San Carlos. In May 1885 Geronimo again left San Carlos, this time with 130 fugitives, which set off skirmishes along the border of the United States and Mexico as the two countries joined forces to fight the Apache. In September 1886 Geronimo again surrendered, accepting a deal to relocate the Apache to Florida for a period of two years before being allowed to return to the West. However, Geronimo was not allowed to return, and he died at Fort Sill, Oklahoma, in 1909.

Further reading: Dee Brown, *Bury My Heart at Wounded Knee: An Indian History of the American West* (New York: Henry Holt, 1970).

— Scott Sendrow

art and architecture

The growth and diversification typical of America's political, economic, and social life in the late 19th century were also reflected in its art and architecture. As America industrialized and its economic power grew, it became a political power on the world stage, finally becoming an empire with the acquisition of the Philippines. Architecture reflected this growing commercial and political power. The first of the skeleton-frame SKYSCRAPERS was designed by William Le Baron Jenny and constructed in Chicago in 1883. That same year, what was then the longest suspension bridge ever built, the Brooklyn Bridge, opened in New York City. The City Beautiful movement promulgated design reform along the lines of models provided by the Roman Empire and France's Louis XIV (the Sun King). Increasing IMMIGRATION and increasing specialization of the work force fueled America's economic engine. Class distinctions became more finely drawn, and the arts reflected these hierarchies. Domestic architectural form embodied them, as developers built suburbs of tidy Queen Anne houses along trolley lines and as industrialists erected monumental chateaux and palazzi along Manhattan's Fifth Avenue. Women and men moved in separate spheres, and home life, where children were raised and culture fostered, belonged to women. The cult of domesticity justified art in the home, and civic philanthropy demanded art in museums. Thus were the arts popularized and democratized in the late 19th century.

America's painters, sculptors, and architects, its designers of decorative arts, and its landscape designers—all developed a new professionalism in response to these changing social conditions. Training abroad, especially in the École des Beaux-Arts in Paris, became imperative. Artists joined established organizations, such as the art academies of the nation's major cities, and formed new ones. Organizations representing specialized constituencies, such as the American Institute of Architects, the National Sculpture Society, and the Women's Exchange, sprang up or consolidated power. These organizations not only defined working practices and standards but through their exhibition facilities also offered opportunities for patronage. American artists vigorously participated in world's fairs, where their work could be measured against that of their European peers. To rid themselves of any association with manual laborers, artists became scholars and connoisseurs. They collected art and displayed it in their studios, they wrote for magazines, and they joined private clubs.

A cosmopolitanism that sprang from academic and aesthetic idealism became the stylistic marker of late 19th-century American art. Earlier, a Ruskinian literalism espousing truth to nature, a confident nationalism, and the prevailing Protestantism had produced an emphatically didactic art. In contrast, late 19th-century art as a body depicted a broader array of subjects, with each work of art being more narrowly focused. Erudite mixing of sources, exquisite technique, and poetic mood were typical of late 19th-century art. Psychological insight replaced mid-century sentimentality, finely tuned understatement replaced drama, and evocation replaced specificity.

Cosmopolitan artists expressed the new tone through historicism and exoticism. These themes were especially apparent in PAINTING and SCULPTURE, though they were present in all the arts. Certain cultures and times were rich mines: the American colonial era, 17th- and 18-century England, and the peasant life of Holland and northern France. Artists examined non-Christian cultures and perceived a colorful barbarity and sensuality in the Islamic world and a refined simplicity in still-feudal Japan. Representation of the human form, at the core of the curricula of the academies of Paris, Munich, London, and Rome, was paramount in the arts of painting and sculpture.

Through ethnographic exactitude, history painters sought to make a small moment of the historical past or the geographically remote vividly alive. Charles Sprague Pearce, in his *A Village Funeral, Brittany* (1891, Danforth Museum of Art, Framingham, Mass.), shows French peasants gathered to say goodbye to the departed and gives equal attention to the particularity of the women's caps and the universality of their grieving faces. The same sort of exactitude governed Tiffany and Company as it crafted the Viking punch bowl (1892, Metropolitan Museum of Art, New York), a work that incorporates motifs from medieval manuscripts and Viking ships. Not all historicist art was so exact, however: Daniel Pabst's tall case clock (1884, Wurts House Foundation, Philadelphia) grafted gothic and neo-Greco ornamentation upon Chippendale form. The aim of art with historical and exotic themes was to draw the viewer into another culture and time in order to marvel at its finer moments, finding in it affinities with the modern age.

The classical world—ancient Greece and Rome as well as Renaissance Italy—became the wellspring from which artists fashioned a movement scholars have termed the American Renaissance. Parallels were drawn between America and these cultures, where democracy, empire-building, and commerce were understood to have flourished. Cultural critics like Harvard professor Charles Eliot Norton advocated the importance of the classical world. In all the arts, classical models and motifs were investigated, internalized, and reconfigured in a respectful spirit of scientific eclecticism. Abbott Handerson Thayer painted his daughter as Nike, thus making a Greek goddess corporeal. Charles Adams Platt and others adapted the Italian villa garden for the new American country house. The American Renaissance reached its apogee at the WORLD'S COLUMBIAN EXPOSITION in Chicago in 1893. Architect Daniel Burnham supervised the development of a 686-acre site where architecture, sculpture, and urban design were unified by Renaissance ideals and motifs.

Aestheticism, the credo of "art for art's sake," underlay most efforts in the visual arts in the late 19th century. This aestheticism, especially when it found expression in the decorative arts, has been termed the AESTHETIC MOVEMENT. The idea that style, technique, and materials were of more consequence than content or function was promulgated for an American audience by writers such as Matthew Arnold and Oscar Wilde. In his art and his life, JAMES ABBOTT MCNEILL WHISTLER also set an early and influential example as an aesthete. Aestheticism was not expressed in a particular style, but sumptuousness, elegance, and bravura craftsmanship were its hallmarks. Historical models displaying virtuosity in all media were revered. Painters went to Holland and Spain to study the brushwork of Frans Hals and Diego Velázquez, while the intricate rococo marquetry of Jean-Henri Riesener was imitated with great success by cabinetmakers. The lily, the sunflower, and the iris became symbols of the aesthetic ideal, serving, too, as motifs for the decorative arts and for gardens. As the emphasis on form and materials progressed, greater abstraction was the result. The muscular "modern gothic" of Frank Furness's architecture and Isaac E. Scott's furniture were only two expressions among many in which nature was schematized by a profound understanding of organic form. The sensuous curves of the female body, sometimes unrecognizable as such, became the leitmotif for Art Nouveau, a style that appeared at the end of the century. Art Nouveau sought to create a new nature-based yet nonreferential art that distilled beauty to its essentials. It was the logical outcome of aestheticism and pointed the way to modernism.

Further reading: The Brooklyn Museum, *The American Renaissance 1876–1917* (New York: The Brooklyn Museum, 1979); Dorren Bolger Burke et al., *In Pursuit of Beauty: Americans and the Aesthetic Movement* (New York: Metropolitan Museum of Art and Rizzoli, 1986); Detroit Institute of Arts, *The Quest for Unity: American Art between World's Fairs 1876–1893* (Detroit: Detroit Institute of Arts, 1983); H. Barbara Weinberg, *The Lure of Paris: Nineteenth-Century American Painters and Their French Teachers* (New York: Abbeville, 1991).

— Karen Zukowski

Arthur, Chester Alan (1829–1886)

Chester Alan Arthur, the 21st president of the United States, was the son of an aggressive abolitionist Baptist minister. He was born October 5, 1829, in Vermont and grew up in upstate New York. After graduating from Union College in 1848, Arthur taught school and studied law in his spare time before moving to New York City, where he clerked and studied in a law office. Admitted to the New York bar in 1854, Arthur participated in the Lemmon Slave case (1852–60), which freed slaves temporarily housed in New York while in transit from one slave state to another. He successfully represented Elizabeth Jennings, an African-American teacher who sued after she was brutally evicted from a segregated streetcar in 1855. The victory of Arthur and Jennings led shortly thereafter to the integration of New York's street railways.

Arthur helped found the New York Republican Party and became a favorite of Governor Edwin D. Morgan, who appointed him quartermaster general of New York during the Civil War. Arthur—with the vast responsibility of feeding, housing, clothing, and equipping thousands of volunteers—was vigorous yet diplomatic, effective yet efficient, and proved to be a superb administrator. When Arthur lost his commission following Republican defeat in 1862, he had already acquired a love of politics; a taste for fine clothes, food, and wine; and shared with his wife, Ellen Herndon, whom he married in 1859, the desire for an elegant residence.

Arthur was lucky in his pursuit of both money and politics. He was a successful lobbyist, served on the Republican state committee, and collected political assessments from civil servants with his friend Thomas Murphy, whom he succeeded as collector of the Port of New York in 1871. As collector he headed the New York customhouse, the largest federal office in the land, which—with its politically active personnel and the campaign assessments they paid—made it the key to the political control of New York. Initially Arthur's princely compensation, mostly in fees and moieties, was approximately $50,000 annually, but the CIVIL SERVICE REFORM movement in 1874 eliminated the fees and moieties and reduced his salary to a still very comfortable $12,000 annually. Administering the customhouse with the twin interests of his patron, Senator ROSCOE CONKLING, and the U.S. Treasury in mind, Arthur—an honest spoilsman—was as efficient as possible in collecting tariffs while maintaining Conkling's machine.

President RUTHERFORD B. HAYES, hating Conkling and anxious to remove the New York customhouse from politics and make it a showcase for civil service reform, replaced Arthur in 1878 after a long struggle. Conkling, arguing that senators should control appointments in their states (senatorial courtesy), initially prevented Arthur's removal, but ultimately Hayes prevailed. Ironically, however, when the deadlocked 1880 Republican convention frustrated Conkling and his fellow STALWARTS by rejecting Ulysses S. Grant and nominating JAMES A. GARFIELD, Garfield's friends offered the vice presidential nomination to the New York delegation, and it named Chester A. Arthur. The Garfield-Arthur ticket was elected, and as vice

Chester Alan Arthur *(Library of Congress)*

president, Arthur presided over the Senate when Conkling again challenged a president over naming the New York collector and again lost. Garfield, however, could not enjoy his victory. On July 2, 1881, he was assassinated by a deranged office seeker who claimed to be a Stalwart and proclaimed that Arthur was president. Garfield lingered until September 19, when Arthur, to the dismay of reformers, did become president.

Arthur was a spoilsman and a machine politician, but he was also a good administrator and proved to be an able president. He had the good sense to recognize that Garfield's tragic death circumscribed his actions. His refusal to appoint Conkling to his cabinet alienated his friend, but it reassured all except the Stalwarts and preserved Arthur's independence. He did not call off the investigation and prosecution of those involved in the STAR ROUTE FRAUDS (in the Post Office Department), even though he had worked with them in the 1880 campaign. And while he did not think that appointments to office on the basis of open competitive examinations secured the best people, when Congress passed the Pendleton Civil Service Reform Bill (1883) he signed it and conscientiously enforced it. Arthur's reaction to the huge Treasury surplus resulting from increased foreign trade after the 1879 return to the gold standard was statesmanlike. To reduce revenue he preferred a simplified tariff schedule with more items on the duty-free list. An 1882 commission appointed by Arthur recommended significant tariff reductions in a comprehensive package, but congressmen in a piecemeal fashion revised these proposed rates upward until overall reductions were slight and the rationale for them was lost in the act known as the Mongrel Tariff (1883). Congressmen preferred to dispose of the surplus with a pork-barrel River and Harbor Act (1882), an $18-million Treasury raid for questionable projects in their districts, which Arthur vetoed to no avail, since Congress overrode his veto. Arthur also vetoed a bill that restricted Chinese immigration for 20 years as an unreasonable length of time, but he did sign into law the Chinese Exclusion Act (1882), which restricted Chinese immigration for 10 years. Less controversial were the appropriations approved by Arthur for the buildup of a modern American navy in place of the few rotting and rusting vessels left over from the Civil War.

Arthur, a large majestic man who looked every inch a president, was actually in poor health. He suffered from Bright's disease, a kidney ailment, and was not a serious candidate for the presidential nomination in 1884. He died on November 18, 1886, a year and a half after leaving the office he had filled far better than virtually everyone expected.

Further reading: Thomas C. Reeves, *Gentleman Boss: The Life of Chester Alan Arthur* (New York: Knopf, 1975).

Atlanta Compromise

See Washington, Booker T.

Australian ballot

See elections, conduct of

B

banking, investment

Financing the enormous industrial expansion of the late 19th century required the marketing of securities—stocks and bonds—which in turn led to the growth of investment banking. Earlier, state governments had financed canals and corporations and built railroads by selling bonds directly to wealthy individuals or to private bankers who would either keep them or resell them to investors. During the Civil War the federal government went $2.6 billion into debt. Most of it was in bonds, and more than half of those were sold far and wide for a commission by its aggressive agent, the private banking house of JAY COOKE & Company. After the war Cooke organized a syndicate that underwrote (took entire issues of) Pennsylvania Railroad (PRR) bonds, marketed them, and bought those it could not sell. Cooke later agreed to market $100 million in Northern Pacific Railroad (NP) bonds, and when sales slowed he put Cooke & Company money into the enterprise, only to have his company fail in 1873 and precipitate a financial panic.

Other investment bankers more than took the place of Jay Cooke. Kuhn, Loeb & Company dated from 1867 but came into its own after 1875, when Jacob Schiff, who had extensive contacts with bankers and investors in Germany and elsewhere on the continent of Europe, married Therese Loeb and became a partner in the firm. The most famous of the private banking firms was J. P. MORGAN & Company. Morgan's father was an American private banker in London, which gave the son valuable contacts in Great Britain. Although most investment banking was handled by private banks, the First National Bank and the National City Bank, both of New York City, also marketed securities.

Immediately after the Civil War investment bankers were primarily concerned with marketing U.S. securities that managed the public debt, but they were soon heavily involved with railroads. Initially the bankers were detached from the management of the railroads whose bonds they underwrote and sold to clients. But when railroad leaders mismanaged, or plunged their roads into bankruptcy, or forced reorganizations (by investment bankers) that scaled down the value of bonds, the reputation of investment bankers suffered, which made the sale of future bonds most difficult.

To protect their interests and the interests of their clients, Morgan, Schiff, and other bankers shared in management by serving on boards of directors. Morgan, for example, arranged a syndicate in the early 1880s to underwrite the sale of some of W. H. Vanderbilt's stock in the New York Central Railroad (NYC) and also became a member of its board of directors. Morgan promoted order and harmony and deplored cutthroat competition and instability. In the early 1880s, when the PRR and NYC began a costly war by building lines paralleling each other's main lines, Morgan in 1885 (on his yacht in the Hudson River) convinced managers of both roads to make peace, with the NYC abandoning the South Pennsylvania Railroad and Vanderbilt buying the West Shore line up the Hudson. Although not as spectacular as Morgan, Schiff financed, reorganized, and was on the board of directors of several leading railroads, including the Union Pacific (UP), which he reorganized in 1896. Schiff's support of Edward H. Harriman, who controlled the UP and the Southern Pacific, led to a spectacular battle with Morgan and his favorite railroad man JAMES J. HILL, who controlled the Great Northern (GN) and NP, over control of the Chicago Burlington & Quincy (CB&Q). The result was the compromise Northern Securities Company (a holding company), which gave the Harriman-Schiff forces a share in the management of the GN, NP, and CB&Q. The SUPREME COURT, however, declared the Northern Securities Company a monopoly and broke it up in 1904. The ties between Morgan and Hill and between Schiff and Harriman illustrate that railroads and industrial corporations were generally bound to one private banking house and did not move from one investment banker to another.

Investment bankers in the 1870s and 1880s generally dealt with government or railroad bonds, but in time they began to finance industrial development and combinations by underwriting stock issues. In the late 1870s the House of Morgan became interested in financing THOMAS A. EDISON's electric light, and in 1892 Morgan helped establish the General Electric Company. The most spectacular combinations occurred in the steel industry and were financed by Morgan. In 1898 the Federal Steel Company was capitalized at $200 million, and in 1901 Morgan financed the creation of the first billion-dollar corporation, United States Steel.

Further reading: Vincent P. Carosso, *Investment Banking in America: A History* (Cambridge: Harvard University Press, 1970); Ron Chernow, *The House of Morgan* (New York: Simon & Schuster, 1990).

barbed wire

Although the Homestead Act (1862) encouraged rapid westward settlement in the latter half of the 19th century, a major obstacle for farmers and ranchers was the high cost of fencing. In some cases, fencing costs equaled that of raising the livestock. A major technological advancement was the invention of barbed wire, which kept costs down for fledgling farmers and ranchers and helped to further populate the West.

Eastern farmers used timber and stones, which were readily available in forested areas, to construct fences. Prairie lands lacked these resources, however, which accounted for the high initial costs of establishing a farm. Although early western farmers used natural borders like streams to protect land from grazing cattle, increased settlement limited these options. Ranchers faced similar problems in preventing their stock from wandering astray. Indeed, ranchers and farmers feuded as to who should pay for fencing. The farmer needed to keep cattle from grazing on his land, while the rancher had to keep cattle from straying. Hedges were used, especially the osage orange plant, but these proved costly as well.

Michael Keely took out a patent for "thorny fence" in 1868, a precursor of barbed wire, but it was Joseph F. Glidden of De Kalb, Illinois, who understood its wider potential. After first seeing the invention at an Illinois country fair, Glidden patented a version in 1874 that featured two small pieces of sharpened wire twisted together in opposite directions around a main strand of wire that was made to be stretched between two fence posts. That same year Glidden patented a second version that became the most successful and popular form of barbed wire. This version featured one small piece of sharpened wire twisted around a main strand, which was then twisted around a second main strand so that the barb did not slip or twist. Glidden and his partners started manufacturing this barbed wire in 1874, and in 1876 Glidden sold his share to the Washburn & Moen Manufacturing Company of Worcester, Massachusetts. Production of barbed wire grew exponentially during the 1870s, from 2.8 million pounds in 1876 to 80.5 million pounds by 1880. In time Washburn & Moen's virtual monopoly based on Glidden patents passed on to the American Steel and Wire Company, which in the 20th century was a part of the United States Steel Corporation.

The "steel thorn hedge" was cheaper than hedges or wooden fences, preserved valuable soil space by not shading crops, took up little space, stayed secure under high winds, did not cause snow drifts, and was dog and wolf proof. Barbed wire was "just what the people of the treeless states have needed for years," as a contemporary advertisement noted.

The introduction of barbed wire also allowed for better control of cattle breeding and, in part, contributed to the boom in the agricultural sector in the late 19th century. It also led to the decline of open-range grazing and the long drives of cattle by cowboys to railheads. Another advantage of barbed wire was that it discouraged trespassing. However, overzealous farmers and ranchers sometimes blocked even post roads and water sources with barbed-wire fences, which led to fence-cutting threats, acts of violence by those shut out. To deal with this problem, Congress passed the Illegal Fencing Act of February 25, 1885, the enforcement of which President GROVER CLEVELAND especially urged.

Further reading: Fred A. Shannon, *The Farmer's Last Frontier: Agriculture, 1860–1897* (New York: Holt, Rinehart and Winston, 1945).

— Scott Sendrow

Barnum, Phineas T. (1810–1891)

The son of Philo F. Barnum, a farmer and shopkeeper, and Irena Taylor, Phineas Taylor Barnum, showman and circus manager, was born on July 5, 1810, in Bethel, Connecticut, where he attended public schools until his early teens. Barnum became familiar with the art of salesmanship from an early age by acting as an independent candy peddler. Upon the death of his father when Barnum was 15 years of age, he took a job clerking in a general store and gave early evidence of initiative and imagination by creating and promoting a lottery that offered as prizes discarded bottles he had purchased for almost nothing. He clerked briefly in Brooklyn, New York, and in 1828 he returned to Bethel to open his own fruit and candy store. The next year he married Charity Hallett, with whom he had four children.

Barnum started an anticlerical and abolitionist weekly newspaper, *The Herald of Freedom and Gospel Witness,* in 1831 and kept it going until 1834. The following year he moved to New York City where, after a stint as a grocer and boardinghouse keeper, he made his entry into show business by purchasing the rights to exhibit Joice Heth, an elderly African American who claimed to be 161 years old and to have been the nurse of George Washington. Her stories of the infancy of the father of the country brought in a good sum, but she died a year later at the age of about 80, according to an autopsy. Subsequent exhibits and enterprises yielded Barnum little until 1841 when for a shoestring he bought Scudder's American Museum. There he showed everything from jugglers and tightrope walkers to bearded ladies and albinos to modern machinery and dioramas. His exhibits included the "Feejee Mermaid," which was obviously a monkey's head stitched to a fish's tail, and the "Great Model of Niagara Falls," which was only 18 inches tall, but the public flocked to his shows. No one complained, even when charged 25 cents to see a strange horse whose head was where its tail should be, but which turned out to be merely a horse backed into its stall. His most popular attractions were a 25-inch-tall midget he called General Tom Thumb, who captivated Europe in 1844, and the Swedish concert singer Jenny Lind, whom he took on a profitable tour through America in 1850.

In 1871 Barnum opened a circus in Brooklyn, which he billed with characteristic swagger as The Greatest Show on Earth. Ten years later he joined English showman James Anthony Bailey, with whom he developed the first three-ring circus. Featuring aerialists, acrobats, clowns, and sideshows, as well as Jumbo, the largest elephant in captivity, the spectacular ensemble toured the nation successfully by rail. Barnum also served two terms in the Connecticut state legislature, from 1865 to 1869, and was mayor of Bridgeport, Connecticut, in 1875–76.

Barnum has been described as "pure brass without any gilding, yet in picturesque and capable effrontery the very embodiment of the age," and indeed he rejoiced in the self-bestowed title "Prince of Humbugs." He wrote several books, including an autobiography (1855), a history of American swindlers, and a book entitled *The Art of Money-Getting; or Hints and Helps on How to Make a Fortune* (1882), which accurately reflected the brash, cynical, and grandiose spirit of the period. It is estimated that his humbuggery brought him more than $4 million, and when he died on April 7, 1891, his obituaries received more space than any except for a president of the United States.

Further reading: Neil Harris, *Humbug: The Art of P. T. Barnum* (Chicago: University of Chicago Press, 1981); A. H. Saxon, *P. T. Barnum: The Legend and the Man* (New York: Knopf, 1989).

— Dennis Wepman

baseball

By 1870 baseball was considered America's "national game." Baseball had spread from the Northeast to the Midwest, and the National Association of Base Ball Clubs (NAB) had grown to 300 amateur teams. In 1869 the Cincinnati Reds fielded an all-salaried team under player-manager Harry Wright. While the Reds did not return a profit, their undefeated record that season boosted professional baseball and ignited a smoldering dispute between amateurs and professionals, with the amateurs walking out of the 1870 NAB annual meeting. The professionals retaliated in March 1871 by forming the National Association of Professional Base Ball Players (NA), thus destroying the amateur association and starting major-league baseball.

The player-controlled NA, the first professional major league, suffered serious problems and lasted only from 1871 through 1875. Most clubs lost money, as attendance averaged under 3,000 a game. Players jumped contracts, showed poor discipline, and dealt with gamblers. The NA also lacked a fixed playing schedule. Teams played each rival five times, with dates arranged by correspondence. However, with each team paying an entry fee of only $10, the outclassed teams frequently dropped out, thus disrupting the schedule. Conflicts arose over playing dates, ticket pricing, the division of gate receipts, and poor officiating by volunteer umpires. The NA lacked competitive balance, too, as evidenced by the Boston Red Stockings, who won four pennants in five years. Nevertheless, the NA popularized professional baseball. The Boston Red Stockings drew large crowds, with their attendance figures peaking at 70,000 in 1875. Boston manager Harry Wright's innovations in equipment procurement, training of players, and park administration set standards for future promoters. Expanded newspaper coverage and annual guides, edited by Henry Chadwick, enhanced fan interest.

In 1876 Chicago promoter William Hulbert organized a new league controlled by club owners. The National League of Professional Base Ball Clubs (NL), limited to eight well-financed teams from cities with populations of at least 75,000, was organized along east-west lines. Hulbert barred liquor sales, gamblers, and Sunday games. Teams were ordered to play each rival 10 times or face expulsion, and a fixed playing schedule was introduced in 1877. Players faced strict disciplinary codes and were bound to teams by rigid contracts. Albert Spalding supplied the league's balls and published its guidebook.

The NL struggled initially with low attendance and low player salaries. Philadelphia and New York were expelled after 1876 for failing to play their quota of games. In 1877 gamblers bribed four Louisville players to throw the NL pennant. The offending players were barred from the NL for life, and Milwaukee replaced the Louisville club. The NL also faced stiff competition from the rival International Association in 1877 and 1878, but the latter folded in 1879. To bind star players to a team, NL owners in 1879 inserted reserve clauses (the right to rehire players for the following

A print showing the game of baseball, ca. 1890 *(Library of Congress)*

season) in their playing contracts, and in 1883 the NL owners solidified their control by extending the reserve clause to the contracts for all players.

Professional baseball prospered in the 1880s with improved NL attendance and profits. The rival American Association (AA), formed in 1882, featured 25-cent admission prices, optional liquor sales, and Sunday games. The upstart AA also raided the NL roster. The National Agreement of 1883 recognized the AA as a major league, but the AA had to agree to stop roster raids and accept the reserve clause. In 1884 the two major-league organizations crushed a new rival, the Union Association. Attendance at major-league games peaked at 2 million in 1889. Some clubs grossed $100,000, and playing schedules increased to 140 games. The NL competed in postseason championships with the AA and dominated them after 1886, with the St. Louis Browns, operated by promoter Chris Von der Ahe, winning four consecutive pennants. Von der Ahe increased attendance with sideshows, liquor sales, and Sunday games.

During the 1880s, baseball evolved further by extending the pitching distance to 50 feet, permitting overhand pitching, adopting a single strike zone, and establishing the four-ball/three-strike rule. *The Sporting News* and *Sporting Life* spread the popularity of baseball by reporting the diamond exploits of stars King Kelly, Cap Anson, and Dan Brouthers. In 1887 Chicago sold Kelly to Boston for a record $10,000.

Baseball, however, was troubled. Salaries averaged $2,000, with stars earning at least $5,000. Major- and minor-league clubs excluded black players by 1890. White major leaguers protested the reserve clause, harsh disciplinary rules, and a threatened salary cap. Disgruntled NL players in 1885 joined the Brotherhood of Professional Base Ball Players (BP), led by John M. Ward, a star player and lawyer. The BP in 1887 sought recognition as a collective-bargaining agency, but the owners continued the reserve clause and salary cap. Ward persuaded the BP to field a rival Players League (PL) in 1890 and promised players fair shares of power and profits. But the bitter, costly PL war of 1890 ended major-league baseball's brief golden age. The PL lured most star players and fielded eight well-stocked teams in seven NL cities. The PL outdrew the NL and AA, but financial losses savaged all three leagues. The NL forced the PL to sue for peace at the end of the season, allowing PL players to return to their former clubs without penalties. The AA battled with the NL over reassignment of players in 1891 and collapsed after the 1891 season. The NL emerged victorious, annexing four AA teams and buying out the others for $130,000.

From 1892 to 1899, the single, 12-team NL dominated major league baseball. Owners became business magnates, but they could not match the old dual leagues in attendance and profits. The Boston, Baltimore, and Brooklyn teams outclassed the others. The NL sought unsuccessfully to boost attendance by staging postseason Temple Cup matches, increasing playing schedules to 154 games, and trying split-season formats. In 1899 the owners dropped the four weakest teams and restored an eight-team format in 1900. Owners limited player salaries to $2,400 and adopted stricter disciplinary standards. The Baltimore Orioles and Cleveland Spiders boosted fan interest by using aggressive tactics like brawling, umpire-baiting, and bench-jockeying (taunting opponents from the bench). Defense improved with bigger gloves and better catcher's equipment. In 1893 the pitching distance was increased to 60 feet, six inches. Hitters broke batting and home-run marks until pitchers adjusted. By 1900 scientific baseball prevailed, featuring bunting, stealing, hit and run, and sacrificing. Concession stands and Sunday games were standard. The eight-team NL reigned as the only major league, but it was soon challenged by the formation of the American League.

Further reading: David Nemec, *The Great Encyclopedia of 19th Century Major League Baseball* (New York: Donald I. Fine Books, 1997); Benjamin G. Rader, *Baseball: A History of America's Game* (Urbana: University of Illinois Press, 1992); Harold Seymour, *Baseball: The Golden Age* (New York: Oxford University Press, 1971); David Quentin Voigt, *American Baseball: From Gentleman's Sport to the Commissioners System* (Norman: University of Oklahoma Press, 1966).

— David L. Porter

Beach, Amy Marcy Cheney (Mrs. H. H. A. Beach) (1867–1944)

Amy Marcy Beach was the first important American woman composer and was considered by some to be the finest composer of her generation. Amy Marcy Cheney was born into a prominent New England family in Henniker, New Hampshire, on September 5, 1867. She was the only child of Charles Abbott Cheney, a paper manufacturer and importer, and Clara Imogene Marcy, a singer and pianist. Amy showed exceptional musical ability as a child. She gave her first public piano recital at age seven, which included works of Handel, Beethoven, and Chopin, as well as her own compositions. The family moved to Chelsea, Massachusetts, in 1871 and settled in Boston in 1875, where Amy studied piano with Ernst Perabo and Karl Baermann, two of that city's leading piano teachers. Her subsequent musical training was somewhat unorthodox. She studied harmony for one year with Junius Hill, but following the advice of Wilhelm Gericke, director of the Boston Symphony Orchestra, she designed her own course of independent study, employing the treatises and compositions of the great masters as models. Beach made her professional debut at age 16 in Boston on October 24, 1883, playing Chopin's Rondo in E-flat and Moscheles's Concerto in G Minor with an orchestra led by Adolf Neuendorff. In 1885 she performed Chopin's F Minor Concerto with the Boston Symphony Orchestra under the direction of Gericke and Mendelssohn's Concerto no. 2 with the Theodore Thomas Orchestra. Her first published composition, a setting of Longfellow's *The Rainy Day,* was issued in 1883.

In December 1885 she married Henry Harris Aubrey Beach, a prominent Boston physician on the faculty of Harvard Medical School and an amateur musician. He was a widower 24 years her senior. After her marriage, in accordance with her husband's wishes, she concentrated on composition rather than performance, perhaps giving one or two recitals per year.

Her first large-scale composition, the Mass in E-flat, op. 5, was published in 1890 and was premiered by the Boston Handel and Haydn Society in 1892 with soloists, chorus, and orchestra under the direction of Carl Zerrahn. Other important works soon followed. *Eilende Wolken,* a concert aria, was premiered by the New York Symphony Society under Walter Damrosche later that year. The Boston Symphony Orchestra premiered the *Gaelic* Symphony in E minor, op. 32, in 1896 and the Piano Concerto in C-sharp Minor, op. 45, in 1900 with the composer at the piano. These were the first works by a woman composer performed by these organizations. Beach received a number of important commissions, including the *Festival Jublilate,* op. 17, commissioned for the May 1, 1893, dedication of the Women's Building of the WORLD'S COLUMBIAN EXPOSITION in Chicago. She was a prolific composer of songs, and some achieved great popularity, including *Ecstasy,* op. 19, no. 2, and *The Year's at the Spring,* op. 44, no. 1.

Dr. H. H. A. Beach died in 1910 and Amy's mother died the following year. In 1911 Amy sailed for Europe, where she gradually resumed her performing career. From 1912 to 1914 she toured Europe, performing her piano concerto and other works to great acclaim. In 1914 she returned to the United States in triumph, committed to 30 concerts for the 1914–15 season. She lived briefly in New York and San Francisco before settling in Hillsborough, New Hampshire, in 1916. After 1916 she toured extensively during the winter and spent the summers in Hillsborough, at her home on Cape Cod, and after 1921 as a fellow at the MacDowell colony, where most of her later works were completed. In 1942 a two-day festival of her works was organized in Washington, D.C., in honor of her 75th birthday. She died in New York on December 27, 1944, of a heart ailment.

Beach's early works are in the late Romantic style, exhibiting the influence of Brahms, Wagner, and her Boston contemporaries. Her first (and perhaps most lasting) success was as a composer of art songs, and these demonstrate her gift for text setting and a fluency of melody that is characteristic of all her work. Yet it was her early large-scale works, such as the Mass and the *Gaelic* Symphony, that established her reputation, both in Europe and the United States, as a composer of the first order. She made frequent use of folk melodies, including American, Inuit, Scottish, Irish, and other European melodies, in her works. Her later compositions reflect the influence of Debussy and impressionism and are characterized by chromaticism, unresolved dissonance, and a leaner harmonic style.

Beach was a highly intelligent, disciplined woman. She spoke fluent French and German; was interested in philosophy, science, and religion; and made an important contribution to the field of ornithology by transcribing bird calls into musical notation. She served as a leader of the Music Teachers National Association and the Music Educators National conference and, in 1925, cofounded and served as first president of the Society of American Women Composers.

Further reading: Adrienne Fried Block, *Amy Beach, Passionate Victorian: The Life and Work of an American Composer, 1867–1944* (New York: Oxford University Press, 1998); Walter S. Jenkins, *The Remarkable Mrs. Beach: American Composer: A Biographical Account Based on Her Diaries, Letters, Newspaper Clippings, and Personal Reminiscences* (Warren, Mich.: Harmonie Park Press, 1994).

— William Peek

Beecher, Henry Ward (1813–1887)

In the late 19th century, Henry Ward Beecher was the most famous clergyman in the United States. Born in Litchfield, Connecticut, on June 24, 1813, Beecher was the eighth son of Lyman Beecher (also a clergyman) and the brother of the author Harriet Beecher Stowe. He graduated from Amherst College in 1834, studied at Lane Theological Seminary (Cincinnati, Ohio), where his father was president, entered the ministry in 1837, and that same year married Eunice Bullard White. After serving two churches in Indiana, he was called in 1847 to the new Plymouth Church of Brooklyn, New York, where he served until his death 40 years later.

Beecher's reputation was based on his melodramatic preaching, which he perfected early in his career. He later wrote that a "sermon succeeds by focusing on the single objective of effecting moral change in the hearer." In his emphasis on moral character over doctrine, Beecher was an early advocate of the liberal theology that would come to dominate the Protestant scene during the last quarter of the century. He also was an early practitioner of social preaching, early on insisting on his right to preach on secular issues such as abolition, suffrage, and labor.

In the first half of his ministry he was so popular that he preached to 2,500 on a regular basis. His dramatic, personal, intimate, spontaneous style helped, but it was his abolitionism that was key to his early popularity, leading some to call Plymouth Church the Grand Central Station of the Underground Railroad. He is perhaps most famous for "auctioning" a slave from his dais, to demonstrate the evils of the "peculiar institution," and it is reported that men threw money and women threw jewelry on stage to redeem the young black woman he presented.

Henry Ward Beecher *(Library of Congress)*

After the Civil War his embrace of liberal theology made him a precursor of the SOCIAL GOSPEL. He advocated evolution as God's plan and accepted the new scholarship of the Bible. He opposed restrictions on IMMIGRATION, supported the right of labor to organize unions, favored CIVIL SERVICE REFORM, and joined the 1884 MUGWUMP defection from the Republican Party to support Democrat GROVER CLEVELAND for president.

In addition to his preaching, he published a weekly column in the *Independent;* edited the *Christian Union;* lectured widely, including the *Yale Lectures on Preaching* (3 vols., 1872–74); wrote a novel (*Norwood,* 1867); and was the biographer of Jesus Christ.

Because he had courted celebrity successfully, the charge in 1872 by VICTORIA WOODHULL in *Woodhull and Claflin's Weekly* that Beecher had seduced the wife of his journalistic protégé Theodore Tilton resulted in the spectacular BEECHER-TILTON SCANDAL. Tilton brought charges against Beecher first in a church trial (1874) and then for alienation of affection in a civil suit (1875). Though Beecher was not convicted, the taint of doubt never entirely left him. After his death on March 8, 1887, a monument celebrating his abolitionist work was erected in downtown Brooklyn.

Further reading: Milton Rugoff, *The Beechers: An American Family in the Nineteenth Century* (New York: Harper & Row, 1981).

— W. Frederick Wooden

Beecher-Tilton scandal (1872–1878)

Lacking only the frankness of modern times, the Beecher-Tilton scandal was in every other sense as lurid and fascinating as any modern sex scandal. And it might have been covered up had not a flamboyant, radical, feminist journalist been in need of a sensational story to recoup her own fortunes. In November 1872 VICTORIA WOODHULL described in *Woodhull and Claflin's Weekly* an adulterous affair between the celebrated preacher HENRY WARD BEECHER and his Plymouth Church parishioner Elizabeth Tilton, the wife of his protégé, the editor of the *Independent,* Theodore Tilton. The affair began in 1866; Elizabeth confessed it to her husband Tilton in July 1870; in December he wrote of it to Beecher and demanded he resign his pulpit; a mutual friend, Frank Moulton, urged both Tilton and Beecher to be silent; and to keep Tilton quiet, Moulton and Beecher bankrolled a publishing venture, *The Golden Age,* for him in 1871. But Tilton—who wrote a campaign biography of Woodhull (published in 1871) for her disastrous 1872 presidential campaign—told her, and Woodhull told the world.

When the affair became public a Plymouth Church committee, appointed by Beecher, investigated, found Beecher innocent, and in 1873 withdrew Tilton's membership for his comments in the press. Moreover, the connection between Tilton and Woodhull, who was notorious as an advocate of free love, enabled Beecher's supporters to attack Tilton's character. Thus goaded, Tilton filed a civil suit against Beecher for alienation of affection. The six-month trial in 1875 was a national sensation and ended on the equivocal note of a hung jury. A virtual acquittal, as far as Beecher was concerned, there was, nonetheless, another church trial in 1876, which also exonerated Beecher. But in 1878 Elizabeth Tilton confessed publicly that she had committed adultery, and Plymouth Church removed her membership. Her estranged husband, unable to make a living because of the scandal, moved to Paris in 1883. Beecher remained minister of Plymouth Church until his death in 1887, diminished but not destroyed.

Further reading: Richard Wightman Fox, *Trials of Intimacy: Love and Loss in the Beecher Tilton Scandal* (Chicago: University of Chicago Press, 1999); Altina L. Waller, *Reverend Beecher and Mrs. Tilton: Sex and Class in Victorian America* (Amherst: University of Massachusetts Press, 1982).

— W. Frederick Wooden

Bell, Alexander Graham (1847–1922)

Born in Edinburgh on March 3, 1847, the son of a noted teacher of speech, Alexander Graham Bell, inventor of the telephone, accompanied his parents when they immigrated to Ontario, Canada, in 1870. Ambitious to achieve and surpass his father's distinction, young Bell set up for himself as a teacher of speech to the deaf in Boston, the leading center of American science and technology. That environment reawakened Bell's earlier tentative notion of a system to send several telegraph messages at once over a single wire by means of intermittent currents of different frequencies. Experimenting by night while teaching by day, he circumvented certain snags by using continuous induced "undulatory" currents, which would reproduce both frequency and amplitude instead of frequency alone, as in intermittent currents. Frequency and amplitude are the essential elements of intelligible speech. In the summer of 1874, Bell recognized the theoretical possibility of thereby transmitting speech electrically, but he assumed it would be too weak to hear. On June 2, 1875, while working on his multiple telegraph, he plainly heard such a sound. After further thought and experiments, he designed and, on March 7, 1876, patented the telephone. The first intelligible sentence heard on it—"Mr. Watson, come here, I want to see you"—was transmitted on March 10, 1876. In June 1876 he successfully demonstrated it to the judges at the PHILADELPHIA CENTENNIAL EXPOSITION. Bell then worked to improve his telephone's performance and range, publicizing it in lecture tours.

In 1877 Bell's father-in-law Gardiner Hubbard organized the Bell Telephone Company and ran it with great success. Bell served as its technical adviser until the early '80s, then turned to other interests. However, he continued on occasion to do the Bell Telephone Company and its successors a vital service by testifying in convincing detail against a number of claimants to priority in conceiving the telephone. The best-known of these was an electrical inventor named Elisha Gray, who captured public attention by virtue of having filed a caveat (stating an untested idea) a few hours after Bell filed a patent application. Since Bell could document his conception as early as October 1874, and Gray only claimed it for his as of November 1875, the verdict for Bell was inevitable.

Bell had received stock in lieu of royalties and sold most of it at an early date. He therefore did not become immensely wealthy, although he was rich enough to remain active as an educator and advocate for the deaf. In later years he also devised the audiometer and studied the genetics of deafness. He invented a device for transmitting telephonic communication by means of a light beam, though it was not then commercially practical. He led a team that greatly improved the usefulness of Edison's phonograph and spent a score of years after 1891 working on heavier-than-air flight, although the Wright brothers succeeded first. Bell strove unsuccessfully for years to breed a strain of twin-bearing sheep. He was more successful in improving hydrofoil boats and produced one that held the world's speed record for 10 years. He and his father supported the struggling journal *Science* for nearly a decade in the 1880s and 1890s, and he lived to see it develop, in other hands, into the official organ of the American Association for the Advancement of Science and become one of the world's leading general-science journals. Bell also conceived, demonstrated, and patented a system of constructing large bridges and buildings quickly and cheaply from mass-produced tetrahedral frames. Thus he anticipated the space-frame architecture of Buckminster Fuller, but his system's immense usefulness was not grasped at the time. Bell was still conceiving new ideas at the time of his death from diabetes on August 2, 1922.

Further reading: Robert V. Bruce, *Bell: Alexander Graham Bell and the Conquest of Solitude* (Ithaca, N.Y.: Cornell University Press, 1989).

— Robert V. Bruce

Bellamy, Edward (1850–1898)

Edward Bellamy, utopian socialist, was born on March 28, 1850, in Chicopee Falls, Massachusetts. The son of a minister known for his charitable works, Bellamy developed compassion for the plight of the poor as he grew up in an industrial community. The intense religious training he received at home would be reflected by frequent quotes from the Bible in his later writing. His well-educated mother (she read Greek and Latin) insisted that her children read nonfiction, especially history. Inspired by such heroic military characters as Alexander the Great, Bellamy aspired to a career in the army, but he failed the physical examination for West Point at age 17.

Disappointed, he spent a year with an older brother, Frederick, at Union College pursuing an independent course of study. A two-year (1868–69) sojourn in Dresden, Germany, exposed him to German socialism. Upon his return to America he read law, passed the bar examination in 1871, and opened an office in Chicopee Falls. But his first case, the eviction of a widow, caused him to leave the legal profession. He then became a journalist and a writer, successfully submitting short stories to such magazines as *Scribner's*. The best known of his earlier novels, *The Duke of Stockbridge* (serialized in 1879), accurately described the socioeconomic inequities that sparked Shays's Rebellion.

Bellamy put forth his vision of an ideal society in two books, *Looking Backward* (1888), the best known, and *Equality* (1897). His just society achieved equality and abundance by nationalizing the economy to derive the efficiency of large-scale operations. Everyone, except the lazy, received an equal annual income, determined by dividing the gross national product by the population, issued as a credit in the only surviving bank. Differentiated prices for various items, however, permitted individual lifestyles. Universal public service was required. Everyone was organized into four armies—the industrial, the invalid, the women's (dropped in *Equality*), and the professional—which guaranteed the production of goods and services by those who were able. Nonconformists and the lazy were consigned to solitary confinement until they agreed to work.

Education by example rather than revolution secured this ideal world. The process began with community ownership of public service facilities. The federal government assumed ownership and operation of railroads, coal mines, and other key industries. Impressed with the resulting efficiencies and lower prices, the people demanded continued nationalization until all forms of private property disappeared. The resulting economic equality eradicated greed, corruption, and social inequities caused by competition for private property.

Bellamy's ideas received wide attention in a society dislocated in the 1890s by an economic depression. Soon Nationalist clubs sprang up across the country. At first they emphasized persuasive education through journals and lectures, but later they actively supported the POPULIST PARTY. The idea of a cooperative society also influenced Eugene Debs, a labor leader and perennial presidential candidate for the SOCIALIST PARTY.

Further reading: Sylvia E. Bowman, *Edward Bellamy* (Boston: Twayne, 1986); John L. Thomas, *Alternative America: Henry George, Edward Bellamy, Henry Demarest Lloyd and the Adversary Tradition* (Cambridge, Mass.: Harvard University Press, 1983).

— Harold W. Aurand

Bering Sea dispute (1892)

This diplomatic conflict between the United States and Great Britain originated in the 1880s when Canadian hunters began harvesting seals in the North Pacific, depleting the herds that nested on Pribilof Islands, a U.S. territory. Those islands, in the Bering Sea north of Alaska's Aleutian Islands, are the breeding grounds of 80 percent of the world's fur-bearing seals. In 1870 the U.S. government gave a monopoly on seal hunting to the Alaska Commercial Company. The agreement stipulated that the company would pay a rental fee and royalties for the harvested skins and was allowed to hunt only 100,000 male seals per year. The killing of females was strictly forbidden. For the next 10 years the company's profits soared and so did the seal population. As the price of sealskins increased, Canadian hunters began to engage in pelagic sealing (killing seals in the open sea) and to kill females. As a result the seal herd declined rapidly. In 1886 the United States, traditionally the defender of freedom of the seas, arrested several Canadian hunters in international waters.

Negotiations aimed at resolving the crisis stalled between Britain and the United States. The Canadians denied they were depleting the seal population and refused to accept any restrictions, while Britain maintained that the Bering Sea was not a "closed" American sea like Chesapeake Bay. To relieve tensions and revive negotiations, Secretary of State Thomas F. Bayard convinced President GROVER CLEVELAND to stop all arrests on the high seas. As a result, on November 22, 1887, a joint commission met in Washington to resolve the issue. Its work resulted in the Bayard-Chamberlain Treaty, signed on February 15, 1888, which the Senate then refused to ratify. Attempting to salvage something from the talks, both nations informally agreed to let American fisherman fish the coastal waters of Canada while Canadians could still engage in pelagic sealing.

This agreement, however, did not last. On March 2, 1889, Congress authorized—and BENJAMIN HARRISON, Cleveland's successor, soon resumed—the arrest of Canadian sealers in the Bering Sea. The British protested, dispatched four warships to the Bering Sea, and called for a joint commission to investigate the problem for two years, during which time pelagic sealing was to be prohibited. American seizures subsequently stopped. Despite war talk, diplomacy resulted in the Anglo-American arbitration treaty of February 29, 1892, which created an international (French, Swedish, and Italian) panel to resolve the sealing dispute.

In 1893 the panel denied that the Bering Sea was a closed sea and ruled that the United States owed Canada damages for the sealing vessels it had seized. Pelagic sealing was forbidden within 60 miles of the Pribilof Islands, and sealing on the high seas was prohibited from May 1 to July 31. Damages to Canadian shipping were assessed at $425,000. When Congress refused to appropriate the money, a joint commission met and increased the damages to $473,151.26. In June 1898, amid much grousing, Congress paid the amount.

Further reading: Charles C. Tansill, *The Foreign Policy of Thomas F. Bayard: 1885–1897* (New York: Fordham University Press, 1940); Alice F. Tyler, *The Foreign Policy of James G. Blaine* (Hamden, Conn.: Archon Books, 1945).

— Timothy E. Vislocky

Bessemer process

For centuries STEEL had been laboriously made from pig iron by beating the hot iron on an anvil until the flying sparks had reduced its carbon content to 2 percent. In 1847 an American, William Kelly, and in 1855 an Englishman, Henry Bessemer—neither one experienced enough in the iron trade to have a closed mind—independently discovered that a blast of air forced through molten iron would burn off its carbon rapidly, and doing so generated enough heat to keep the iron molten. American manufacturers had little faith in the neophyte Kelly or his counterintuitive idea, but Bessemer had already made a fortune and a reputation from other inventions. Bessemer was able to design, construct, and demonstrate a converter in the form of a large, pear-shaped vessel into which a blast of air could be forced and which could then be tilted to pour out a dazzling, white-hot gusher of molten steel. The old process had required a worker to labor 15 days to produce 50 pounds of steel. The Bessemer process turned out five tons of steel in 30 minutes.

The Bessemer process ran into trouble when it was found to work only on low-phosphorus pig iron, the supply of which was limited in England. Swedish ore, however, was low in phosphorus, as were the rich ore deposits in the Marquette region of Michigan, made accessible by the Sault Ste. Marie Canal in 1855. Alexander Holley, an energetic and eloquent American journalist sent to England by the Union government to report on British technology during the Civil War, saw the Bessemer converter in action and was converted himself. Upon his return he became its foremost prophet and promoter in the United States. He led in forming a pool of the Kelly and Bessemer patents in 1866. Holley also devised major improvements in the design of the converters. He designed six of the 11 Bessemer plants operating in the United States in 1880 and was consulted on three others. The remaining two were copied from one of the first six.

At Chicago in 1885 the world's first true SKYSCRAPER—that is, one supported not by its walls but by a steel skeleton—used steel from ANDREW CARNEGIE's works for the last half of its framework. By then the age of steel had arrived: Steel was recognized as by far the most available and reliable metal for all kinds of structures and machines.

By the end of the century the Siemens-Martin open-hearth process was outstripping Bessemer's converters. The new process, developed in England and France, was more flexible in the kinds of scrap and ore that could be fed into it and was easier to control. By 1950, 90 percent of the steel produced in Great Britain and the United States was open hearth. After 1960 the newer all-oxygen process replaced both the Bessemer and open-hearth processes. Nevertheless the Bessemer process had secured its place in history by physically transmuting the instruments of industry, transportation, and construction.

Further reading: John N. Ingham, *Making Iron and Steel: Independent Mills in Pittsburgh, 1820–1920* (Columbus: Ohio State University Press, 1991); Joseph Wall, *Andrew Carnegie* (New York: Oxford University Press, 1970).

— Robert V. Bruce

bicycling, 1870–1900

A bicycle craze gripped Gilded Age America. The earliest bicycles were far from safe. Americans originally rode the vélocipède, a crude French bicycle. The high two-wheel bike consisted of a wooden frame and tires covered by iron. The bike, called "the bone shaker," could not be used on streets and caused frequent injuries. Young people saw the Harlan brothers use the bike in acrobatic acts and practiced secretly in barns and abandoned lofts. During the 1870s, the English marketed a more popular bicycle in the United States. This bicycle was an iron frame with a huge wheel in front and a small one in back, both with solid rubber tires. Riders, perched about seven feet above the ground, risked permanent injuries from falls.

Bicycling became a popular pastime. Boston lawyer Charles Pratt, the father of American cycling, founded the Boston Bicycling Club and a periodical, *Bicycling World.*

A lithograph for the Springfield Bicycle Club, Springfield, Massachusetts, 1883 *(Library of Congress)*

On May 30, 1880, he summoned American bicyclists to Newport, Rhode Island, where they formed the League of American Wheelmen, which soon boasted 10,000 members. The number of cyclists grew from 20,000 in 1882 to over 100,000 by 1890, and clubs formed in most American towns. Bicycle parades, competitive drills, hill climbs, and races became popular. On July 4, 1884, so many riders jammed the Boston Common that the planned race was canceled. Thomas Stevens excited the nation with his bicycle trip around the world, leaving his San Francisco home in April 1883 and arriving in Boston that August. He went on to bike across Europe through the Middle East, India, and the Orient, returning to San Francisco in 1887 amid a wild municipal celebration.

Initially women found bicycle riding difficult because of the high front tire. Manufacturers in the 1880s offered a cheaper, light-frame "safety bicycle" with moderate-sized wheels of equal proportion. The frame was indented in the middle to accommodate fashionable long skirts. Women loved the safety bicycle, which was simple to operate. Their Michaux Club of Manhattan performed intricate bicycle drills to popular music.

The invention of the safety bicycle and a substantial drop in bicycle prices led to a cycling craze in the 1890s. Ten million bicycles were on the road, and countless enthusiasts joined bicycle clubs, read cycling magazines, and attended races. The classic 1890s tune, "Daisy Bell," popularized the bicycle, too, ending with "But you'll look sweet upon the seat, / Of a bicycle built for two."

Velodromes for racing sprang up in several eastern cities. Large crowds watched the racers careen around the board tracks at full tilt. Manufacturers paid the racers to promote the Imperial, Monarch, Columbia, and other bikes. Albert Shock excelled at endurance racing, pedaling 1,009 miles in 72 hours. The six-day race also flourished, with contestants completing as many laps as possible in six days. However, the New York State legislature declared these bike races inhumane after it learned that contestants circled the tracks without relief for 144 hours. Charles Murphy in June 1899 pedaled a paced mile in just 57.8 seconds on a wooden track between rails over a level stretch at Hempstead, New York.

Major Taylor, a black racer from Indianapolis, broke the racial barrier in professional bicycling. Taylor, the world's fastest bicyclist, won the national sprint championships in 1898, 1899, and 1900 and broke many world records. Taylor attracted large crowds but frequently faced racial slurs. White riders colluded in throwing him from his bicycle, and he was physically attacked by a white bicyclist after a race. Promoters prohibited him from racing in all southern and several northern tracks. The League of American Wheelmen originally allowed African Americans into membership, but when southern white affiliates began withdrawing in the early 1890s, the league restricted memberships to whites in 1894.

The bicycle craze was short lived. In the 20th century, the automobile provided a more convenient mode of getting out into the countryside, and it gradually replaced the bicycle in popularity.

Further reading: Peter Nye, *Hearts of Lions: The History of American Bicycle Racing* (New York: Norton, 1988); Andrew Ritchie, *Major Taylor: The Extraordinary Career of a Champion Bicycle Racer* (Mill Valley, Calif.: Bicycle Books, 1988); Robert A. Smith, *A Social History of the Bicycle* (New York: McGraw-Hill, 1972).

— David L. Porter

Bierstadt, Albert See painting

bimetallism

For most of its existence, the United States recognized gold and silver as the basis for the dollar, adhering to what is known as bimetallism. Beginning in the 1870s, the government's monetary policy changed. The Coinage Act of 1873 demonetized silver by removing the silver dollar from circulation. This law made gold the only monetary standard for the nation. Increased silver production soon caused the price of silver to drop, and if it were coined as in the past, the money supply would be increased and have an inflationary effect. Western silver mining interests and debtor groups referred to the Coinage Act as the CRIME OF '73 and demanded the unlimited remonetization of silver (FREE-SILVER MOVEMENT).

By the mid 1870s the demand for a return to bimetallism was gaining momentum, but CONGRESS made only a token response with passage of the BLAND-ALLISON ACT over President RUTHERFORD B. HAYES's veto in 1878. This law required the Treasury to purchase and coin not less than $2 million or more than $4 million of silver monthly. As a result silver dollars were again minted, but not in sufficient numbers to drive the United States from the monetary gold standard or to cause inflation. Bimetallists wanted more action from the government.

Congress followed up the Bland-Allison Act with the Sherman Silver Purchase Act of 1890. This law increased the amount of silver coinage in circulation by obligating the government to purchase 4.5 million ounces of silver per month. Supporters of sound-money principles (the gold standard) feared that the Sherman Silver Purchase Act threatened the stability of the nation's money supply. In 1893 an economic depression set in, and President GROVER CLEVELAND, an advocate of sound-money principles, blamed the financial crisis on the Sherman Silver Purchase Act. Cleveland's view prevailed, and Congress repealed the Sherman Silver Purchase Act on November 1, 1893.

The repeal of the Sherman Silver Purchase Act set the stage for one of the most bitter and emotionally charged political contests in American history. Bimetallists such as William H. Harvey, the author of *Coin's Financial School* (1894), and Ignatius Donnelly led protests against the law's repeal. The PEOPLE'S PARTY (Populist Party) also joined the bimetallist movement. In 1896 the Democrats and the Populists nominated WILLIAM J. BRYAN for president on a platform calling for the "free" (unlimited) coinage of silver. Bryan, however, was overwhelmingly defeated by the Republican candidate, WILLIAM MCKINLEY, who supported the gold standard. Bryan's defeat was a major setback for bimetallism. In 1900 Congress enacted the Gold Standard Act, which recognized the gold dollar as the standard of value in the United States. Bimetallists were silenced until the Great Depression of the 1930s.

See also CURRENCY ISSUE.

Further reading: Milton Friedman and Anna J. Schwartz, *Monetary History of the United States, 1867–1960* (Princeton: Princeton University Press, 1971); Walter T. K. Nugent, *Money and American Society, 1865–1880* (New York: The Free Press, 1968).

— Phillip Papas

Black Hills gold rush

The first of three SIOUX WARS (the War of the Bozeman Road [which by connecting the Oregon Trial with mining camps encroached on hunting grounds] from 1866 to 1868) ended with the U.S. Army pulling back from its posts along that road and with the Treaty of Fort Laramie (1868) creating the Great Sioux Reservation of western South Dakota, including the Black Hills. Several Sioux leaders, however, did not agree to that treaty. Prospectors suspected that there was gold in the Black Hills, and in 1874 a cavalry expedition under General George A. Custer—supposedly exploring a road route between Forts Abraham Lincoln (Bismarck) and Laramie—happened to have prospectors along who confirmed that there indeed was gold in those hills.

The news that summer that Custer's expedition had discovered gold brought white prospectors flooding into the Black Hills, trespassing on Sioux (Lakota) land in search of the valuable metal despite Indian hostility. In the winter of 1875–76, there were 15,000 miners at the town of Custer in the heart of the Black Hills. The federal government tried to purchase or lease the Black Hills, but the land was sacred to the Sioux, and the effort failed. Unable to control the swarms of miners descending on the Black Hills, federal officials in December 1875 ordered the uncooperative Lakota to relocate to distant reservations in six weeks (an impossibility in winter) or come under attack. When they failed to comply with the order, the army in March 1876 attacked the Oglala Sioux and their allies the Northern Cheyenne. But in June the Lakota, led by CRAZY HORSE and SITTING BULL, struck back and defeated General George Crook on June 17, 1876, at the Battle of the Rosebud. Eight days later, on June 25, they annihilated Custer's command at the Battle of the Little Bighorn, often referred to as Custer's Last Stand. Despite this initial success, the Sioux resistance was soon broken. Crazy Horse surrendered and Sitting Bull fled to Canada.

The gold rush followed a classic pattern. Thousands rushed from Custer to new diggings at Deadwood Gulch in the summer of 1876. Both towns were plagued by violence, vice, and inflation. Initially, individual miners could do well, since the gold was located in "placer" gravel and easily extracted, but it was not long before large-scale mines appeared, and these required a considerable infusion of capital from financial centers. Nevertheless, many of the miners, attracted by their surroundings, remained in the area.

Further reading: Donald Jackson, *Custer's Gold: The United States Cavalry Expedition of 1874* (New Haven: Yale University Press, 1966).

— Scott Sendrow

Blackwell, Antoinette Brown (1825–1921)

Antoinette Brown Blackwell was the first woman ordained a minister of a congregation in a regular Protestant denomination; she was also a prominent advocate for WOMEN'S RIGHTS. Antoinette Brown was born on May 20, 1825, in Henrietta, New York, where her father was a farmer and justice of the peace. She became a teacher at age 16 and entered Oberlin College at age 21. After graduating from the literary course (which did not award a bachelor's degree) in 1847, she applied to study theology. The faculty refused to allow her regular enrollment, so she became a resident graduate and was not given a degree. After completing her studies in 1850, she decided to hold off on her ordainment until it could take place in a church in which she held pastoral responsibilities.

For the next three years she worked as a lecturer, speaking on women's rights, antislavery, and temperance. In 1850 she attended and spoke at the first National Women's Rights Convention in Worcester, Massachusetts, of which LUCY STONE, a friend from Oberlin, was a primary organizer. In the summer of 1853 she gained national prominence at the World's Temperance Convention in New York when she strove for three hours to be heard over the shouts of angry male delegates. That same year she was ordained as a minister at the Congregational Church in South Butler, New York, but growing doubts about some Congregational tenets led her to resign a year later. She eventually became a Unitarian.

In 1855 she worked as a volunteer in the slums and prisons of New York and wrote about her experiences in a series of articles in the *New York Tribune.* These were collected in a book, *Shadows of Our Social System* (1856). In 1856 she married Samuel Blackwell, whose sister Elizabeth was the first female doctor and whose brother Henry married Lucy Stone. They lived primarily in northern New Jersey and had seven children, five of whom survived to adulthood.

Blackwell was more socially conservative than many of her suffragist colleagues. She was opposed to divorce, and when Elizabeth Cady Stanton and SUSAN B. ANTHONY advocated liberalized divorce laws at the National Women's Rights Convention in 1860, Blackwell led the opposition. In the late 1860s, when Anthony and Stanton's opposition to the Fourteenth and Fifteenth Amendments (on the grounds that women should have been given the vote along with African-American men) caused a split between them and Stone, Blackwell sided with Stone, becoming active in Stone's American Woman Suffrage Association. Unlike Stone, though, Blackwell remained on friendly terms with both Anthony and Stanton.

Blackwell had wide-ranging intellectual interests. She helped found the Association for the Advancement of Women in 1873. In 1878 she requested and received recognition from the American Unitarian Association as a minister. An effective orator, she spoke frequently at suffrage meetings on both the state and national levels, usually on specific resolutions. Between 1869 and 1915, Blackwell wrote six books on theological and scientific issues. These books, including *The Sexes throughout Nature* (1875) and *The Philosophy of Individuality* (1893), were devoted primarily to reconciling her views on theology and feminism with the theories of Darwin and Spencer. She also published a novel and a book of poems.

Blackwell was the only pioneer suffragist to live to see the ratification of the Nineteenth Amendment. In 1920, at age 95, she cast her first vote and died a year later on November 5.

Further reading: Elizabeth Cazden, *Antoinette Brown Blackwell: A Biography* (Old Westbury, N.Y.: Feminist Press, 1983).

— Lynn Hoogenboom

Blackwell, Elizabeth (1821–1910)

The first woman in modern times to earn a medical degree, Elizabeth Blackwell was born on February 3, 1821, near Bristol, England, and moved with her family to the United States in 1832. The Blackwells settled initially in New York, where her father, who had owned a sugar refinery in England, tried to develop the use of beet sugar. His efforts failed, and in 1838 they moved to Cincinnati, where her father died a few months later.

For the next four years Blackwell helped her mother and two sisters run a private school that supported the family. She then taught for a year in Henderson, Kentucky, where she developed a strong interest in pursuing a career in medicine. She continued to teach for two more years while pursuing private medical studies with doctors in Asheville, North Carolina, and Charleston, South Carolina.

In 1847 she began applying to medical schools. After she was turned down by every medical school in New York City and Philadelphia, she began applying to rural schools. She was finally accepted by Geneva College in central New York. The acceptance, she later learned, had been a fluke: The faculty referred her application to the students, confident that they would oppose her admission, and the students, thinking they were dealing with a hoax, voted to accept her.

Her early days in medical school were exceedingly rough. She was ostracized by the townspeople and was initially barred from classroom demonstrations. But her quiet persistence eventually won her a degree of acceptance. She graduated from Geneva on January 23, 1849, and continued her studies in Europe at La Maternité in Paris and St. Bartholomew's Hospital in London. In Paris, she lost sight in one eye after catching purulent ophthalmia from an infant she had treated. That ended her hopes of becoming a surgeon.

She returned to New York in 1851 and found herself barred from practicing in city hospitals and dispensaries. She had few patients, so she began a series of lectures on hygiene. (She had a particular interest in preventative medicine and public health.) Her message appealed to Quaker women, who attended her lectures, became patients, and eventually brought her to the attention of prominent Quaker men whose financial support helped her launch her more ambitious projects.

In 1853 she opened a dispensary in the tenement district. By the end of the first year, she had treated 200 women there. In 1856 her sister Dr. Emily Blackwell joined her practice, and in 1857 she expanded her dispensary into a hospital, the New York Infirmary for Women and Children. During the Civil War, both she and her sister contributed to the Union effort by selecting and training nurses.

In 1868 Blackwell opened the Women's Medical College of the New York Infirmary. It was not the first medical school for women; by this point there were women's medical colleges in Boston and Philadelphia. But Blackwell, knowing that women doctors would be under greater scrutiny, set unusually high standards, including entrance examinations, longer-than-usual terms, plenty of clinical experience, and an examining board that was independent of the faculty.

Once the college was operating successfully, Blackwell left it in the hands of her sister, and in 1869 she returned to England for good. She set up a successful practice in London, accepting the chair of gynecology at the New Hospital and London School of Medicine for Women in 1875. A year later she began to suffer health problems and reluctantly retired. She remained active in her retirement, however, writing a number of books and articles on medical and behavioral issues and involving herself in reform and in the antivivisection movement. She died on May 31, 1910.

Further reading: Elinor Rice Hays, *Those Extraordinary Blackwells: The Story of a Journey to a Better World* (New York: Harcourt Brace, 1967).

— Lynn Hoogenboom

Blaine, James Gillespie (1830–1893)

James G. Blaine, perhaps the most outstanding Republican politician of the Gilded Age, was born on January 31, 1830, in West Brownsville, Pennsylvania, the son of Ephraim Lyon Blaine and Louise Gillespie. Blaine graduated from Washington and Jefferson College (1847) and taught school while studying law. In 1850 he married Harriet Stanwood, with whom he had six children. Blaine settled in Augusta, Maine, in 1854 and became the editor of the *Kennebec Journal.* In 1859 he became chairman of the Republican State Committee and began his first of three terms in the Maine legislature (1859–62), where he served as speaker (1861–62). In 1860 Blaine supported Abraham Lincoln for the Republican presidential nomination even though several members of Maine's REPUBLICAN PARTY favored William Seward.

In 1862 Blaine was elected to the U.S. House of Representatives and began a long and illustrious career in CONGRESS. He served in the House until 1876 (as its Speaker from 1869 to 1875) and as a senator from 1876 to 1881. Blaine also held the office of secretary of state under Presidents JAMES A. GARFIELD (1881) and BENJAMIN HARRISON (1889–92).

Rank-and-file Republicans, especially from the West, adored Blaine. He was a staunch party man but not an extremist. Although Blaine could "wave the bloody shirt" to attract voters, he was a moderate on Reconstruction. He advocated protective tariffs but also supported reciprocity agreements as a means of increasing American trade abroad. Blaine favored sound-money principles but did not lose the support of inflationary minded Republicans.

In 1876 Blaine emerged as a contender for the Republican presidential nomination. However, accusations that he had received $64,000 from the Union Pacific Railroad (which as Speaker of the House he was in a position to help) for some nearly worthless Little Rock and Fort Smith Railroad bonds tarnished his reputation and cost him the nomination. Shortly thereafter he was elected by the Maine legislature to the U.S. Senate. At the deadlocked 1880 Republican National Convention, Blaine threw his support to James A. Garfield, who was nominated on the 36th ballot. After his election to the presidency, Garfield appointed Blaine secretary of state. In this office, Blaine pursued an aggressive FOREIGN POLICY designed to expand American foreign trade and influence abroad. He was particularly interested in U.S. relations with Latin America and sought to block European influence in that part of the world. Among his foreign policy initiatives, Blaine promoted Pan-Americanism and attempted to gain exclusive control for the United States over any proposed isthmian canal. He resigned as secretary of state following the assassination of President Garfield in 1881.

Despite questions about his character, Blaine remained the most popular Republican in the United States. At the 1884 Republican National Convention in Chicago, Blaine was nominated on the fourth ballot. He faced a difficult battle, since the DEMOCRATIC PARTY nominated reform-minded governor of New York GROVER CLEVELAND for the presidency. Blaine's questionable reputation and opposition to CIVIL SERVICE REFORM led a small but influential group of reform-minded Republicans known as the MUGWUMPS to bolt from the party and support Cleveland. The ensuing campaign focused more on personal attacks than on the issues. The Republicans charged that Cleveland had fathered an illegitimate child, which he courageously acknowledged. The Democrats answered by accusing Blaine of aiding the railroads at public expense, a charge he unconvincingly denied. Although he was popular in New York, Blaine lost the state by 1,149 votes along with its 36 electoral votes, giving Cleveland a victory of 219 to 182 in the electoral college.

Following the election, Blaine semiretired from public life. In 1888 he refused the Republican Party's presidential nomination. Instead, Blaine decided to support the nomination of Benjamin Harrison of Indiana. When Harrison defeated the incumbent Cleveland, he rewarded Blaine by returning him to the State Department. Blaine served under Harrison in that capacity from 1889 to 1892 and focused his attention on protecting American commercial interests overseas. Again he was particularly concerned with U.S. commercial relations in the Western Hemisphere. He organized the first Pan-American Conference (1889–90); tried to obtain a naval base in Haiti; favored the annexation of HAWAII; attempted to negotiate a treaty with Nicaragua for an isthmian canal; favored the Berlin Conference whereby the United States, Great Britain, and Germany agreed to a three-power protectorate over SAMOA; tried to settle a dispute with Great Britain over seal hunting in the Bering Sea; secured a commercial reciprocity amendment to the MCKINLEY TARIFF of 1890; and was instrumental in negotiating reciprocity treaties with several Latin American nations. Thus, Blaine-Harrison policies initiated U.S. expansionism in Latin America, the Caribbean, and the Pacific.

Blaine, however, fell ill after March 1891 and finally resigned from the cabinet in June 1892. He received mild support for the Republican presidential nomination that year, which President Harrison easily won. Blaine died on January 27, 1893, in Washington, D.C.

See also CURRENCY ISSUE; TARIFF ISSUE.

Further reading: Edward P. Crapol, *James G. Blaine: Architect of Empire* (Wilmington, Del.: Scholarly Resources, 2000); H. Wayne Morgan, *From Hayes to McKinley: National Party Politics, 1877–1896* (Syracuse, N.Y.: Syracuse University Press, 1969); David S. Muzzey, *James G. Blaine: A Political Idol of Other Days* (New York: Dodd, Mead, 1934).

— Phillip Papas

Bland-Allison Act (1878)

During the economic depression of the mid-1870s, several groups of farmers and western silver mine operators joined together in urging the government to adopt a monetary policy of BIMETALLISM. The Coinage Act of 1873 had taken the silver dollar out of circulation just before the market value of silver dropped dramatically, when its coinage would have been inflationary. Silver advocates called that act the CRIME OF '73 and demanded that CONGRESS remonetize silver. The silver issue dominated the American political scene throughout the late 19th century.

The silver movement rapidly gained momentum after 1873. In the fall of 1877, the U.S. House of Representatives passed a bill calling for the "free" (unlimited) coinage of silver at the ratio of 16 parts of silver to one part of gold. Known as the Bland Bill, it was introduced by Representative Richard P. ("Silver Dick") Bland of Missouri and, had it become law, it would have driven gold (one part of which was worth more than 16 parts of silver) out of circulation. The bill, however, was amended and weakened in the Senate by William B. Allison of Iowa. In February 1878 the amended Bland-Allison Act was passed over President RUTHERFORD B. HAYES's veto.

The Bland-Allison Act required that the government purchase at market price no less than $2 million or no more than $4 million worth of silver monthly and mint it into silver dollars. No administration from 1878 to 1890 ever purchased more than the minimum $2 million of silver and gold was not driven out of circulation. Despite protests from silver advocates, the Bland-Allison Act remained unchanged until it was superseded by the Sherman Silver Purchase Act of 1890.

See also CURRENCY ISSUE; FREE SILVER MOVEMENT.

Further reading: Walter T. K. Nugent, *Money and American Society, 1865–1880* (New York: The Free Press, 1968).

— Phillip Papas

blues See music: art, folk, popular

Boomers See Sooners

Boston fire (1872) See cities and urban life

Boxer Rebellion See Volume VII

boxing

Prior to innovations in the Gilded Age, boxing was an unregulated working-class sport dominated by Irish Americans and outlawed in most places. Participants fought with bare knuckles, relying on wrestling skills and brute strength. Rounds ended only when a boxer was struck down by an opponent's fists or thrown to the turf with a wrestling hold. Once down, a boxer had 30 seconds to recover before reaching the scratch line in the center of the ring. Bouts ended when a fighter was unable to reach the scratch line or conceded defeat.

The 1865 marquis of Queensberry rules brought more structure to the sport. The rules required the use of gloves, limited rounds to three minutes, provided for 10-second knockouts, and prohibited wrestling holds. The use of gloves appeared to curb brutality, thus making the sport more acceptable. The rules, however, did not win acceptance for nearly three decades in the United States, where New York City served as the boxing center. Charges of corruption hurt the sport's credibility, and even championship fights were farces.

Boxing entered a new era in the 1880s. Richard Kyle Fox, publisher and editor of the notoriously sensational *The National Police Gazette,* pleaded for the legalization of boxing. Fox offered belts and other prizes for winners of boxing championships. He also campaigned to unseat heavyweight champion John L. Sullivan and to name champions in six different weight divisions. Key metropolitan saloons, especially Harry Hill's saloon on Bleecker Street in New York City, also promoted boxing. Boxing matches were held at Hill's saloon, where large bets were made and contracts were signed for larger matches elsewhere. Hill was the nation's best-known and most esteemed boxing stakeholder and referee.

Members of athletic clubs in New York, New Orleans, and San Francisco promoted boxing and tried to get politicians to modify state laws or city ordinances that banned prizefighting. As the sport became more fashionable, wealthier young men took sparring lessons. Middleweight champion Mike Donovan taught boxing at the New York Athletic Club, which scheduled the first national amateur boxing championships. The athletic clubs instituted reforms to improve the sport, encouraging a round limit for bouts and using Fox's weight-division system. They also began arranging indoor matches, charging admission, offering purses to the winners, and promoting the growing acceptance of the 1865 marquis of Queensberry rules, which made boxing faster-paced and more commercially appealing.

John L. Sullivan, nicknamed "the Boston strong boy," popularized boxing with his love of fighting and flamboyant lifestyle. Sullivan, born to Irish immigrants in Boston, Massachusetts, became the first truly national sports hero. He gave boxing exhibition matches in Boston theaters and music halls in the 1870s and knocked out Irishman Paddy Ryan in the ninth round for the heavyweight championship at Mississippi City, Mississippi, in February 1882. He launched nationwide tours, offering $1,000 to anyone who lasted four rounds against him. Only one challenger performed the feat. From January 1884 to December 1886, Sullivan won 14 official fights. In March 1888, Sullivan—who suffered from alcoholism, overweight, and poor health—fought English champion Charley Mitchell to an

John L. Sullivan, in a lithograph by Currier & Ives, ca. 1883 *(Library of Congress)*

embarrassing 39-round draw at Chantilly, France. In July 1889 he fought Jake Kilrain in the last bare-knuckle bout. Wrestler-trainer William Muldoon conditioned him for the fight. Sullivan battled Kilrain under the intense Richburg, Mississippi, sun for 75 rounds before Kilrain's seconds conceded. Public interest intensified in September 1892, when Sullivan defended his heavyweight title against James J. Corbett in New Orleans, Louisiana. Sullivan, who had returned to binge drinking and excessive eating and had passed his prime, fared poorly. Corbett knocked him out in the 21st round with a right across the jaw.

The Sullivan-Corbett fight marked a pivotal turning point in boxing history. Major newspapers, locked in circulation wars, began openly supporting boxing. The bout was arranged in the offices of JOSEPH PULITZER's *New York World* rather than in a saloon or Fox's offices. The heavyweight championship fight was the first to be held indoors under electric lights, to use gloves, to employ the marquis of Queensberry rules, and to be sponsored by an athletic club. Corbett brought greater respectability to boxing, having attended college, worked as a bank clerk, and learned boxing at an elite athletic club. Sullivan remained a celebrity after losing to Corbett, performing in vaudeville acts and giving temperance lectures.

Nevertheless, the fight game remained a working-class, ethnic sport shrouded by shady characters and illegal almost everywhere. Boxing continued as a chaotic, disorderly sport, lacking a national regulatory body or a rational system for determining champions. Fraudulent tactics, such as "carrying" an opponent, "taking a dive," and "fixing records," prevailed into the 20th century.

Further reading: Nat Fleischer and Sam Andre, *A Pictorial History of Boxing* (New York: The Citadel Press, 1959); Elliott J. Gorn, *The Manly Art: Bare-Knuckle Prize Fighting in America* (Ithaca, N.Y.: Cornell University Press, 1986); Michael T. Isenberg, *John L. Sullivan and His World* (Urbana: University of Illinois Press, 1988).

— David L. Porter

Bradwell, Myra Colby (1831–1894)

Editor and publisher of the most influential legal journal west of the Alleghenies, Myra Colby Bradwell was born on February 12, 1831, in Manchester, Vermont, grew up in Western New York, then moved with her family to Illinois. In 1852 she married James Bolesworth Bradwell; they had four children, two of whom survived to adulthood. At the time of their marriage, her husband was reading for the law, and Bradwell began to study the subject as well. They first lived in Memphis, Tennessee, where they both taught school before moving to Chicago in 1854. Her husband was admitted to the Illinois bar and became a successful lawyer; she worked for his firm, helping with research and writing. In 1861 her husband was elected county judge of Cook County.

In 1868 Bradwell founded the Chicago *Legal News*, the first weekly law journal published in the Midwest. Through her husband's influence, she received a special charter exempting her from the Illinois law that prevented married women from entering contracts, so she was able to run both the business and the editorial sides of her publication. At the same time the Bradwells set up a printing, binding, and publishing firm, Chicago Legal News Company, that printed stationery, legal forms, and briefs as well as publications.

Legal News was a resounding success, printing legal news of the entire country and covering local legal matters in depth. In her editorial columns, Bradwell attacked lawyers and judges for incompetence, evaluated legislation and court opinions, and kept a steady watch on the standards of the legal profession. These editorial columns were highly influential among lawyers in the Midwest. She pushed hard for legal and political equality for women and was instrumental in getting Illinois laws passed giving married women the right to their own earnings (1869), making women eligible to hold school offices (1873), giving women equal guardianship of children (1873), and making women eligible to become notaries public (1875).

In the CHICAGO FIRE of 1871, the Bradwells lost all their possessions—except for the subscription book of the *Legal News*, which their 13-year-old daughter alertly grabbed. Three days later, Bradwell managed to publish the *Legal News* on schedule. Back issues saved by downstate lawyers were used to establish legal facts for which all other evidence had disappeared, and the Bradwells successfully rebuilt their businesses.

In the meantime, Bradwell was conducting an ongoing battle to be admitted to the Illinois bar. In 1869 she passed the examination but was denied admission solely on the basis of her sex. She appealed the case, lost in the state supreme court, and took it to the U.S. SUPREME COURT. In 1873, in *Bradwell v. Illinois*, the Supreme Court upheld the Illinois decision. In 1872, however, before that decision was handed down, the Illinois legislature, prodded by Bradwell's case, passed a bill prohibiting the state from enforcing occupational exclusion on the basis of sex.

Bradwell was also active in the woman suffrage movement. She and her husband were involved in the founding of the American Woman Suffrage Association, and for many years she was on the executive committee of the Illinois Woman Suffrage Association. She continued to manage the *Legal News*—and through it to exercise a strong influence over the legal profession—until her death on February 14, 1894.

Further reading: Eve Cary and Kathleen Willert Peratis, *Women and the Law* (Skokie, Ill.: National Textbook Company, 1977).

— Lynn Hoogenboom

Bradwell v. Illinois (1873)

See Bradwell, Myra Colby

bridges

The construction of ever bolder bridges in the late 19th century demonstrated American engineering ingenuity and industrial capability while facilitating the commerce that sustained industrial expansion. A few large masonry bridges were built during this era, including the 23-arch-span "Great Stone Bridge" crossing the Mississippi at Minneapolis in 1883. Wooden covered bridges continued to be built in rural areas, but by and large the era demonstrates the triumph of the iron-and-steel bridge.

The Civil War era marked a change in bridge-building technology from the carpenter-craftsman to engineering mass prefabrication. The Fink through-truss bridge in 1858 was one of the first all-metal truss bridges in the United States, and by the 1870s a number of bridge companies were offering competing truss designs: The Wrought Iron Bridge Company of Canton, Ohio; the King Iron Bridge & Manufacturing Company of Cleveland; the Keystone Bridge Company of Pittsburgh (owned by ANDREW CARNEGIE) and the Phoenixville Bridge Works and Union Bridge Company, both of Pennsylvania; and the Berlin Iron Bridge Company of Connecticut were among the larger companies building railroad and highway bridges. They were joined by a number of smaller firms offering their wares to local road commissioners. The companies would provide a bridge in "kit" form, with girders and components delivered in a package. The prevalence of the pin-connected "American Standard" bridge design, with tension and compression members joined by swivel pins, facilitated bridge erection by unskilled local labor. Unfortunately, they did not always get it right. In the 1870s and 1880s more than 200 iron bridges failed.

Early truss bridges used wrought iron for tension members and less expensive cast iron for compression beams. With production costs for wrought iron decreasing substantially in the 1870s, wrought iron could be used both for tension and compression members, and cast iron was gradually eliminated as a material in bridge construction. The BESSEMER PROCESS, first used practically in the United States in 1865, dramatically reduced the cost of steel production, and by the 1890s steel was generally replacing wrought iron. Because steel has superior strength compared with wrought iron, it was possible to design longer spans capable of carrying greater loads.

Steel gained an early advantage in the great river crossings, where its strength outweighed its greater cost. John Roebling (1806–69) had used wrought-iron wire in his early designs, including the surviving 1849 suspension-bridge canal aqueduct at Lackawaxen, Pennsylvania, and the 1,000-foot long Covington-Cincinnati suspension bridge in 1866. For his greatest design, the Brooklyn Bridge, he made a controversial recommendation of steel wire, but he died in 1869 from a bridge-related accident before the final decision was reached. His son, Washington Roebling (1837–1926), took over construction and made the decision in 1876 to use Bessemer steel wire for the great cables. Although suffering severely from caisson sickness (or the bends, a painful—even fatal—condition caused by gas bubbles in tissues after too rapid decompression from watertight chambers—caissons—used to dig the bridge's foundation in the East River), Roebling supervised construction from a distance until the bridge was finally opened in 1883.

Prior to the Brooklyn Bridge, steel had first been used extensively in the huge Eads Bridge spanning the Mississippi at St. Louis. JAMES BUCHANAN EADS designed it with three arch spans of 502, 520, and 502 feet, with the main arch members constructed of steel. Other great bridges, including the Poughkeepsie Bridge across the Hudson, were also of steel. The Poughkeepsie Bridge, with a series of truss spans carrying the track 212 feet above the water, was the longest steel bridge at 6,767 feet.

River navigation often requires a movable bridge. The standard design through much of this era was the swing truss. This design requires a central pivot, which narrows the available channel. In the 1890s, the swing truss was replaced by the rolling bascule design, first appearing in 1893 with the Van Buren Street bascule in Chicago.

By the end of the era, steel had replaced iron, and national corporations had replaced the proliferation of bridge companies that flourished after 1870. In 1900 Andrew Carnegie's Keystone Bridge Company and 25 others were consolidated into the American Bridge Company, soon to become part of the United States Steel Corporation.

Further reading: Eric DeLony, *Landmark American Bridges* (Boston: Little, Brown, 1993); David Plowden, *Bridges: The Spans of North America* (New York: Viking Press, 1974).

— Francis H. Parker

Brown, Olympia (1835–1926)

Olympia Brown, a minister and a suffragist, was born in Prairie Ronde, Michigan, on January 5, 1835, and grew up on a farm. Her parents were Universalists and valued education sufficiently to send Brown to Mt. Holyoke Female Seminary in Massachusetts in 1854, but she felt stifled by its religious orthodoxy and left after one year. In 1856 she went to Antioch College in Ohio and graduated in 1860. While there, she heard ANTOINETTE BROWN BLACKWELL, a Congregational minister, preach and resolved to become a minister, but it was difficult to gain admission into a divinity school. After several rejections Brown was admitted in 1861 into the Canton School of Theology at St. Lawrence University in New York. Despite encountering prejudice, she graduated in June 1863, and later that month—after some controversy—was ordained by the Northern Universalist Association. While Blackwell had the distinction of being the first American woman minister ordained by a congregation (1853), Olympia Brown was the first to be ordained by a denomination. Small in stature but large in voice, she was an excellent speaker and preached in several Vermont churches before she was installed in 1864 as the minister of the Weymouth, Massachusetts, Universalist Church.

Brown had been an advocate of WOMEN'S RIGHTS since she was a child, and her parents received—and she read—the weekly edition of Horace Greeley's *New York Tribune.* In 1866, at the invitation of SUSAN B. ANTHONY, Brown attended a woman suffrage meeting in New York City; met Anthony, Elizabeth Cady Stanton, and LUCY STONE, and joined them as charter members of the American Equal Rights Association. The following year Brown spoke in New York State for woman suffrage and, at the behest of Stone and her husband Henry Blackwell, journeyed to Kansas, where from July to October she gave over 200 speeches in support of a suffrage amendment to its constitution. In 1868 Brown organized the meeting in Boston that established the New England Woman Suffrage Association. Differing in tactics, suffragists in 1869 split into two organizations: Anthony's more confrontational National Woman Suffrage Association (NWSA), which was incensed by the exclusion of women from the Fifteenth Amendment (extending the vote to black males, whom, she believed, in some cases, to be less qualified) and advocated immediate redress; and Stone's more patient American Woman Suffrage Association (AWSA), which was unwilling to destroy the prewar abolitionist-women's rights alliance and concentrated its efforts on state and local levels. Brown, although friendly with the AWSA, leaned toward the militant NWSA.

In 1870 Brown accepted a call to be minister of the Bridgeport, Connecticut, Universalist Church. There she met and married in 1873 John Henry Willis, a businessman, and following the example of Lucy Stone, she retained her maiden name. They had two children. Her family, which had been most supportive in her ministerial and reform endeavors, was concerned that marriage might harm her career, but Willis proved to be a helpful mate. In 1878 the family moved to Racine, Wisconsin. In 1887 she gave up her pastoral work and devoted her energies to the cause of woman suffrage.

In 1884 Brown became a vice president of the NWSA and, the same year, was elected president of the Wisconsin Woman Suffrage Association (WWSA), serving until 1912. Broadly interpreting the Wisconsin law as allowing women to vote in elections "pertaining to school matters," Brown in 1887—in the aggressive spirit of the NWSA—tried to vote in a Racine election but was refused, took her case to court, lost, and ran up a considerable debt for the WWSA. After the NWSA and the AWSA united to form the National American Woman Suffrage Association (NAWSA) in 1890, Brown objected to its emphasis on state campaigns and in 1892 formed the Federal Suffrage Association, but its influence was minimal. In 1912 younger suffragists in Wisconsin, having formed the Political Equality League, eclipsed and then merged with the WWSA. Brown disapproved and resigned her presidency of the WWSA. The following year, however, she was elected to the advisory board of Alice Paul and Lucy Burns's Congressional Union, which later became the National Women's Party. In 1920, thanks to the Nineteenth Amendment for which she had fought so long, Brown finally voted in her first election. She died in Baltimore on October 23, 1926.

Further reading: Dana Greene, ed., *Suffrage and Religious Principle: Speeches and Writings of Olympia Brown* (Metuchen, N.J.: Scarecrow Press, 1983); Catherine F. Hitchings, *Universalist and Unitarian Women Ministers*, 2d ed. (Boston: Unitarian Universalist Historical Society, 1985).

Bryan, William Jennings (1860–1925)

William Jennings Bryan, Democratic presidential candidate and secretary of state, was born on March 19, 1860, in Salem, Illinois, the son of Silas Bryan and Mariah Elizabeth Jennings. An 1881 graduate of Illinois College in Jacksonville, Illinois, Bryan also spent two years at Union College of Law in Chicago, graduating in 1883. From 1883 to 1887 he practiced law in Jacksonville. Bryan married Mary Baird in 1884, with whom he had three children.

In 1887 Bryan moved to Nebraska in search of new career opportunities. He rose rapidly in the local DEMO-

William Jennings Bryan *(Library of Congress)*

CRATIC PARTY ranks and in 1890 was nominated for the U.S. House of Representatives in a normally Republican district that included Lincoln and Omaha. Although Bryan's main focus throughout the campaign was the TARIFF ISSUE, he also took advantage of Nebraska's newly created PEOPLE'S PARTY (Populist Party) by endorsing some of its proposals, such as the direct election of U.S. senators and BIMETALLISM, and won the election by 6,713 votes.

In Congress, Bryan gained national attention by advocating a federal income tax and strongly opposing repeal of the 1890 Sherman Silver Purchase Act. His relentless criticism of President GROVER CLEVELAND over his demand for its repeal pushed Bryan to the forefront of the FREE-SILVER MOVEMENT. Free-Silver advocates sought to achieve an inflated currency through the unlimited coinage of silver. It was a hotly contested issue in late-19th-century America, and Bryan rode it to political stardom.

When the 1896 Democratic National Convention met in Chicago, Free-Silver advocates were firmly in control. Bryan attended the convention as a member of the Nebraska delegation. He served on the platform committee and was chosen by its members to address the convention on the Free-Silver issue. Bryan captivated his audience by stating: "Having behind us the producing masses of this nation and the world, supported by the commercial interests, the laboring interests, and the toilers everywhere, we will answer their demand for a gold standard by saying to them: You shall not press down upon the brow of labor this crown of thorns, you shall not crucify mankind upon a cross of gold." The "cross of gold" speech won Bryan the Democratic presidential nomination on the fifth ballot. In the 1896 presidential election, Bryan faced the Republican candidate WILLIAM MCKINLEY of Ohio. McKinley ran on a platform that endorsed the gold standard and a high protective tariff. Bryan's nomination and the Democratic Party's adoption of Free Silver created a dilemma for the Populists. If they supported Bryan, they could possibly lose their identity as a party, but if they nominated their own candidate, they would split the protest vote and elect McKinley. The Populists decided to support Bryan but nominated one of their own, Thomas E. Watson, for vice president. McKinley defeated Bryan by 7,104,779 to 6,502,925 popular votes and collected 271 electoral votes to Bryan's 176. Nearly 80 percent of the eligible electorate voted in one of highest turnouts in American history.

During the SPANISH-AMERICAN WAR (1898), the governor of Nebraska named Bryan colonel of the Third Nebraska Volunteer Regiment. However, the regiment did not serve outside the United States. In December 1898 the Treaty of Paris, which formally ended the war, required Spain to cede the Philippine Islands to the United States in return for $20 million. Although a staunch anti-imperialist, Bryan surprisingly urged the Senate to ratify the treaty. Bryan had opposed annexation but defended his position by arguing that to reject the treaty would leave the United States technically still at war with Spain and the fate of the Philippines undetermined. He argued that it was better to accept the islands and then grant them independence. His opponents charged that Bryan supported ratification only because he hoped to make the issue the subject of a national referendum in the presidential election of 1900, when he expected to be the Democratic candidate once again. The Senate ratified the Treaty of Paris on February 6, 1899, and Bryan was renominated in 1900.

The Republicans also renominated President McKinley in 1900. The Republicans focused on the nation's prosperity, arguing that it had resulted from the gold standard and the protectionist Dingley Tariff of 1897. Bryan campaigned on a platform that condemned IMPERIALISM and again called for Free Silver. President McKinley won 7.2 million votes to Bryan's 6.4 million and captured 292 electoral votes to Bryan's 155. The election demonstrated that Bryan was less popular in 1900 than he was in 1896, and it failed to revive the silver issue or to condemn imperialism.

Nevertheless, Bryan remained a progressive force in the Democratic Party. He favored a strong national government to regulate big business, advocated woman suffrage, and supported prohibition. Although strongly supported by organized labor, Bryan in 1908 was again defeated for the presidency, but in 1913 he became Woodrow Wilson's secretary of state. After trying to pursue an even-handed policy of neutrality during World War I, he resigned in 1915, since Wilson tilted in favor of the Allies. Bryan did, however, favor American entry into the League of Nations. He was also a fundamentalist Christian opponent of evolution and, just prior to his death on July 26, 1925, helped convict John Scopes, who had defied Tennessee law by teaching evolution.

Further reading: Robert W. Cherny, *A Righteous Cause: The Life of William Jennings Bryan* (Boston: Little, Brown, 1985); Paolo E. Coletta, *William Jennings Bryan,* 3 vols. (Lincoln: University of Nebraska Press, 1964–69).

— Phillip Papas

Bryce, James, first viscount Bryce (1838–1922)

James Bryce, a keen observer of American democracy in the Gilded Age, was born in Belfast, Ireland, on May 10, 1838, the eldest of five children of James Bryce, a Scots Presbyterian schoolmaster, and Margaret Young. He was educated at the University of Glasgow and at Oxford, where in 1863 he won the Arnold Historical Essay Prize for "The Holy Roman Empire," which he enlarged and published in book form the following year. Bryce was admitted to the bar in 1867 and served as Regis professor of civil law at Oxford from 1870 to 1893, as a Liberal member of the House of Commons from 1880 to 1907, and as the British ambassador to the United States from 1907 to 1913. Before taking that post he had made four trips to America between 1870 and 1890. On his visits, Bryce discussed several topics with many of the leading political, educational, and literary figures of America. Perhaps the most influential of these sources was EDWIN L. GODKIN, editor of *THE NATION*. Informed by travels and conversations, Bryce wrote *The American Commonwealth* (1888), which ranks with Alexis de Tocqueville's *Democracy in America* (1835) for its perceptive analysis of American political institutions.

In *The American Commonwealth,* Bryce gave his readers a keen yet sympathetic insight into American life, expressing his admiration for the American people and their government. He believed America's uniqueness stemmed from the soundness of its founding principles. Bryce was especially intrigued by the American ideal of equality in economic and educational opportunities and by the formation of political decisions that respected both majority rule and minority rights. He discussed the roles played by political parties and public opinion in American politics. Although he found much to admire in America, Bryce criticized the rapid growth of cities and their lack of individuality. He was also critical of the American political system's inability to formulate new approaches to solve the nation's growing social problems; the lack of a legal basis for American political parties; the role of urban political machines; the American drive toward material success; the concentration of power in the central government; the American penchant for exploiting the nation's natural resources; and the relative weakness of state and local governments.

Bryce retired as ambassador to the United States in April 1913. Elevated to the British peerage as a viscount in 1914, Bryce later that year was appointed to the International Court of Justice at The Hague. During the First World War, Bryce presided over a British commission investigating alleged German atrocities in Belgium and France. After the war, Bryce advocated the creation of the League of Nations. He died in Sidmouth, Devon, England, on January 22, 1922.

Further reading: Edmund Ions, *James Bryce and American Democracy, 1870–1922* (New York: Humanities Press, 1970).

— Phillip Papas

buffalo, extermination of

Although the buffalo stocks are safe now, the species was once considered all but extinct. The extermination of the buffalo occurred throughout the course of the 19 century, culminating in 10 to 15 years of intense slaughter when the animal was nearly hunted to extinction.

Buffalo, or, properly, the American bison (*buffalo* is the accurate name of African and Asian varieties of the species), were plentiful in North America due to several centuries of climatic change that increased the buffalo's numbers and expanded the area that it inhabited. Historians estimate that there were once 25 million of the animals in North America. For the Plains Indians, especially the Sioux, who utilized all parts of the animal, the buffalo was sacred. Native Americans eventually traded the animal's robe, which consisted of a buffalo's hair attached to its hide, with early European settlers.

By the 1840s drought, overgrazing, and complications from the introduction of horses and cattle (including imported diseases) to the region began threatening native buffalo herds. A particularly devastating drought in 1867 killed many buffalo. Horses not only made hunting the animal easier but also competed with buffalo for grazing lands. The removal to the West during the 1840s of Indians who hunted the animal in the western fringes of its habitat also contributed slightly to diminished numbers there.

By 1870 there were still several million buffalo in North America. The animal became particularly threatened after new railroad service in the plains facilitated moving the meat to far-off markets and built demand for the animal. Further encroachment by white settlers continued to transform western lands into cattle farms, which diminished grazing areas for the buffalo. White settlers also hunted the animal for its meat, tongue, and robe, but since the robe was the main prize, hunters were forced to wait until winter when the robes were especially thick, which helped to replenish stocks. In 1870, however, tanners discovered that buffalo hides were useful, and hunters began shooting the animal for its hide all year, which also contributed to the animal's quick disappearance. By 1872 more than 500,000 had been killed for only their hides.

By 1880 all the wild buffalo in the southern plains had been killed. The SIOUX WARS (1876–77) delayed extinction in the northern plains, but by 1879 the species was extinct in Wyoming and eastern Nebraska. The last buffalo were killed in Montana and the Dakotas in 1883.

The extermination of the buffalo destroyed the culture and economy of the Plains Indians, forcing them to settle and to turn to agriculture. Recognizing this fact, the U.S. Army encouraged the slaughter of buffalo, whose near extinction was a significant factor in subduing the Plains Indians.

Further reading: William T. Hornaday, *The Extermination of the American Bison* (Washington, D.C.: Government Printing Office, 1889); Mari Sandoz, *The Buffalo Hunters.* (New York: Hastings House, 1954).

— Scott Sendrow

Buffalo Soldiers

After Union soldiers defeated the Confederate army in the Civil War (1861–65), troops were moved to the West to subdue hostile Native American tribes and clear the way for further western settlement. Most of the more than 2 million Union soldiers during the Civil War were volunteers, and of these, 178,000 were African-American. Faced with a severely understaffed regular army of just 16,000 soldiers and nearly 200,000 Native Americans spread out over an area of 1 million square miles, the U.S. Army continued to enlist African Americans who became known as Buffalo Soldiers. They formed the all-black Ninth and 10th Cavalries and the 38th, 39th, 40th, and 41st Infantries. They were called Buffalo Soldiers by Native American warriors who encountered the Ninth and 10th Cavalries in Texas in 1867. In 1869 the infantry units were combined into the 24th and 25th Infantry Regiments and assigned to the Texas frontier. There they escorted trains and stagecoaches, built roads and telegraph lines, and guarded water sources and supply lines.

The African-American soldiers earned praise for their discipline and high morale. At the same time, they were hampered by racism within the military and larger society. High-ranking politicians and officers, among them General William T. Sherman, retained prejudices regarding African Americans that ensured that their work would be difficult and underappreciated. Black soldiers also faced discrimination in the communities in which they served, despite the fact that they were protecting civilians. Nevertheless, the use of black soldiers during this period was an important first step on the long road to normalizing race relations in the United States. Throughout their service, desertion rates and numbers of court-martials remained lower than those for white regiments. While in military service, many former slaves were educated by army chaplains, a vital component in their transition to civilian life.

In 1880, after Texas was deemed relatively safe, the 24th Infantry was transferred to Indian Territory (present-day Oklahoma) and the 25th was moved to the Department of Dakota, serving there and in Montana until the end of the Indian Wars in 1891. A group of African-American soldiers guarded the famous Sioux war chief SITTING BULL when he was imprisoned after surrendering to the army in 1881. In 1888 the 24th was moved to Arizona, where it served until it secured the region. The history of the Buffalo Soldiers was largely forgotten until the 20th century, when historians and African Americans rediscovered the troops, who now are remembered with admiration and pride.

Further reading: Arlen L. Fowler, *The Black Infantry in the West, 1869–1891* (Norman: University of Oklahoma Press, 1971).

— Scott Sendrow

business and government

Laissez-faire—nonintervention by government in economic affairs—is an untried panacea. The late 19th century, the Gilded Age, in the United States, is widely regarded as a period of laissez-faire; indeed much lip service was paid to that concept, but government was far from quiescent at that time. Initially, much of the intervention in economic matters benefited substantial business interests, but by the late 1880s the demand for government regulation of RAILROADS and TRUSTS became irresistible.

The post–Civil War industrial expansion was accelerated by government aid to business. The most conspicuous form of governmental intervention in the economy was in protective TARIFF legislation. Prior to the Civil War the United States was on the road to free trade, with rates of approximately 20 percent, but the 1860 Republican Party platform called for a protective tariff, and the secession of southern states enabled Congress to pass the Morrill Tariff in 1861 and subsequent revisions from 1862 to 1869 that raised rates to 47 percent. In the 1870s and 1880s the tariff was reduced slightly, but the protective feature was retained. The McKinley Tariff of 1890 raised rates to 49.5 percent and provided the flexibility of reciprocity to either raise or lower rates to secure favorable trading agreements with other nations. The Wilson-Gorman Tariff of 1894 was a hodgepodge that lowered rates, but in 1897 the Dingley Tariff jacked rates up to 57 percent, where they remained until lowered to 38 percent in 1909 by the Payne-Aldrich Tariff. The protective tariff was a substantial subsidy levied by the federal government on American consumers for the benefit of American business. The tariff effectively excluded foreign manufacturers from the enormous and rapidly expanding American market.

The federal government in the post–Civil War era also disposed of much of the vast national domain in order to develop the West rapidly. This largesse primarily benefited business interests. Mineral and timberlands were sold at ridiculously low prices. In 1873 Congress approved the sale of land rich in iron ore deposits for $1.25 an acre, and its Timber and Stone Act of 1878 allowed for the sale of timberland at $2.50 an acre. Transcontinental railroads were by far the greatest beneficiaries of federal largesse. Although railroads forfeited some acreage by failing to fulfill requirements, they were given approximately 130 million acres of the national domain. In addition, states gave railroads about 49 million acres of state lands. These land grants were justified because the roads were to be built through territory sparsely populated by Native Americans and not likely to produce any freight until settled by whites. As a result, the land-grant railroads became agents of colonization. Although Congress called a halt to land grants in 1871, railroads benefited from them into the 20th century. Just how necessary the grants were has been questioned because, without a land grant, JAMES J. HILL built the Great Northern Railway to the Pacific by 1893 on the profits of settlements he developed along his right of way. Yet if the building of the Union Pacific and the Central Pacific had been delayed until the regions through which they ran matured, the first continental railroad may not have been completed until the 1890s.

The federal government did not as a rule give outright cash subsidies to industries from its treasury. The tariffs subsidized industry out of the pockets of consumers, and the federal government gave railroads land, not cash. It did advance money to the Union Pacific and Central Pacific, but those loans were paid back in the 1890s. The federal government did, however, subsidize the ailing American merchant marine with generous mail contracts for steamship lines connecting the United States with South America, Japan, and China via Hawaii. In addition, the Merchant Marine Act of 1891 gave a small per-mile bounty (66 $^2/_3$ cents to $4.00, depending on the size of the vessel) on outward bound voyages. These subsidies did little to arrest the decline of the once proud American merchant marine.

The federal government also regulated—albeit not harshly—as well as subsidized industry. A NATIONAL BANKING SYSTEM had been created during the Civil War that gave the federal government some control over the banking system and did provide more financial stability. Banks could issue banknotes secured by government bonds deposited with the comptroller of the currency, and a death tax of 10 percent on state banknotes eliminated them from circulation. National banks, however, served the monetary needs of the Northeast better than those of the South and West, where there were not enough banknotes available. The reserve requirements of the national banks also enabled a few great New York banks to centralize the system. Decentralization and greater federal control would come with the Federal Reserve System in 1913.

Since railroads were monopolies in most rural areas and competitive where they converged in urban areas, they charged less where they encountered competition and more where shippers had no alternative transportation. Railroads also would offer large-volume shippers rebates while requiring shippers of small amounts to pay the published rate. Freight-rate discrimination angered farmers, small business owners, and communities because it diminished their profits and even threatened their survival. In the late 1860s and the 1870s the GRANGERS advocated RAILROAD REGULATION and secured legislation creating tough commissions to set nondiscriminatory rates. The SUPREME COURT in *Munn v. Illinois* (1877) upheld state regulation of railroads even if they were engaged in interstate commerce. In 1886 the Court reversed itself in *Wabash v. Illinois,* declaring that the regulation of interstate commerce is the responsibility of Congress. In 1887 Congress responded with the Interstate Commerce Act (ICA), which prohibited rebates, the long-and-short-haul abuse; called for "reasonable and just" rates; outlawed pools of freight and earnings; and established the Interstate Commerce Commission (ICC) to investigate, recommend and, if ignored, go to the courts to compel obedience. The passage of the ICA marked the shift of the federal government from promoting railroads to restraining railroads. The ICC was reasonably successful in administering the ICA until 1897 when the Supreme Court, in the *Maximum Freight Rates* case, denied that the ICC could set rates and, in the *Alabama Midland* decision, undermined the effectiveness of the long-and-short-haul clause. Effective railroad regulation was postponed until the 20th century.

The development in the Gilded Age of huge industrial combinations called TRUSTS gave rise to a significant antimonopoly movement that the federal government could not ignore. Yet while virtually everyone—farmers and laborers, reformers and most businesspeople—was hostile to trusts, virtually everyone favored individualism, suspected strong government, and opposed economic equality. They wanted equality of economic opportunity and for the government to regulate business to restore the competition that existed in an earlier era. Although by the 1890s 15 states had constitutional provisions against monopolies and 27 states had laws against them, these prohibitions were ineffectual. By 1890 it was obvious to Congress that federal action was necessary, and with virtual unanimity it passed the SHERMAN ANTITRUST ACT, which reiterated the common-law prohibition of monopolies, combinations, or conspiracies in restraint of trade. The wording of the act was vague, but it put Congress on record as opposed to monopoly the same year it increased significantly the protective tariff. The Sherman Act was to be enforced by the attorney general, and violators were to be prosecuted in the courts. Prior to the administration of Theodore Roosevelt (1901–9) the act was ineffectual. Given the merger mania that swept the United States in the 1890s, neither attorney generals nor the Supreme Court seriously challenged monopolies. The Sherman Act was invoked only 18 times from 1890 to 1901, and four of those times it was used against organized labor. The Supreme Court, in *U.S. v. E. C. Knight Company* (1895), denied that the American Sugar Refining Company, which controlled 98 percent of the nation's sugar refining capacity, was restraining trade. Taking a narrow view, the Court regarded manufacturing—even of commodities shipped across state lines—as separate from commerce and trade. The Sherman Act, nevertheless, was law and would be available in the Progressive Era.

Further reading: Morton Keller, *Affairs of State: Public Life in Late Nineteenth Century America* (Cambridge, Mass.: Harvard University Press, 1977); Edward C. Kirkland, *Industry Comes of Age: Business, Labor, and Public Policy, 1860–1897* (New York: Holt, Rinehart and Winston, 1961).

business cycles

In the decades between 1870 and 1900 the United States experienced remarkable economic growth—averaging about 4 percent a year—a process that helped to raise the standard of living per capita by about 2 percent a year. The population also grew from 40 million in 1870 to 76 million in 1900, while the labor force increased at an even greater rate, expanding from 13 million to 29 million. During these years industry hurtled past AGRICULTURE as the major engine of economic development. In 1870 the agricultural sector supplied 47 percent of the value added to the economy while industry took a 43 percent share. By the end of the century the figures were entirely reversed, with industry garnering 65 percent of value added while agriculture was reduced to 35 percent.

This rapid growth, and industry's rise to dominance, did not take place smoothly or without sharp ups and downs but proceeded within a context of what economists would later call "business cycles," pronounced periodic swings in output, employment, and prices. Laypeople would term these swings "boom-and-bust" cycles, and the Gilded Age economy seemed to be pockmarked with them, especially the busts that ranged in duration from many months to several years and in severity from mild to deep. Notable among them were the depression following the Panic of 1873, the Panic of 1884, and the depression after the Panic of 1893. To some contemporary critics of the new industrial society, these periodic spasms of mass unemployment, bankruptcies, and social insecurity were evils endemic to industrial capitalism. EDWARD BELLAMY made this point in his utopian novel *Looking Backward* (1888). "Your system," he wrote, "was liable to periodic convulsions, overwhelming alike the wise and the unwise, the successful cutthroat as well as its victim. I refer to the business crises at intervals of five to ten years, which wrecked the industries of the nation."

Contrary to what Bellamy implied, such economic crises were not unique to the Gilded Age. In the early decades of the 19th century, when agriculture was preeminent, boom and bust fluctuations were frequent and extensive. In the years between 1816 and 1847, two economic downturns of great severity, the Panics of 1819 and 1837, followed periods of prosperity and roiled the American economy with widespread bankruptcies, deflation, severe unemployment, and general social distress. And although the nation enjoyed a long period of prosperity after 1843, the two decades preceeding the Civil War also witnessed a sharp crisis in 1854 and a brief, nasty depression from 1857 to 1858.

Yet, the business cycles of the Gilded Age were different in some ways from their predecessors. As industrial capitalism transformed the country, what had formerly been an economy dependent on agriculture and exports of cotton and wheat for its prosperity now became a self-sufficient economy of complex characteristics. Because of this fundamental shift, the business cycles of this period took another shape and displayed unique attributes. In the preindustrial era, cyclical fluctuations arose largely because of excessive speculation in new agricultural lands and an unstable money supply, currency, and banking system. In the Gilded Age, however, business cycles were mainly due to changes in the rate of investments in factories, railroads, and mines and to alterations in the supply of money brought about by structural changes in the banking and financial systems. Also, as a result of dramatic improvements in COMMUNICATIONS and transportation—the invention of the TELEPHONE, widespread usage of the telegraph, the expansion and integration of the RAILROADS—and the economic and geographical interdependency arising therefrom, changes in business activity more easily and forcefully rippled through the economy. As a consequence, the two major depressions of the Gilded Age, beginning in 1873 and 1893 (the Panic of 1884 was not as severe), were two of the worst downturns the nation had ever experienced. And although they were different in detail, each, including that of 1884, followed the same general pattern of development and were linked to investment swings in the new, dynamic sectors of the economy, particularly the railroads.

The depression of 1873 began with the collapse of the country's leading brokerage house, Jay Cooke & Company, an event that reverberated throughout the nation. Jay Cooke, known as the "financer of the Civil War," had expanded his activities following the conflict beyond that of handling government securities. He became a major broker and financer of ventures in coal, iron, and especially railroads. These and other investments stimulated rapid growth in transportation, mining, and large-scale cattle raising. But as was often the case in periods of prosperity and profit-making, there were excessive investments in speculative enterprises. Too many railroad lines were built; too many cattle ranches put too many cattle out to pasture; and too much silver was mined. And as billions of dollars in foreign capital flowed into the country, there was a constant drain of gold to service the burgeoning debt. With the unexpected failure of Jay Cooke, panic ensued. Commodity prices and prices for manufactured goods plunged. The stock exchange closed for 10 days; credit dried up; and stunned depositors initiated runs at hundreds of banks. Between 1873 and 1878, there were almost 50,000 bankruptcies, with losses estimated in the billions. The panic soon turned into a severe retrenchment, then a depression, and unemployment skyrocketed to levels never seen before. All segments of the increasingly integrated economy appeared to grind to a halt. For the first time in history, the majority of Americans appeared to be caught in the coils of an economic crisis not of their making and over which they had no control.

Many analysts regard this depression as the worst of all the economic downturns of the 19th century and, with the possible exception of the Great Depression of 1929, the most severe in the nation's history. But hard statistical data that accurately measures the severity of the depression of 1873 is lacking. It was not until the 1880s and 1890s that many state and local governments, especially in the East, began to establish agencies to collect data on such things as employment, housing, and immigration. As a result, the depression beginning in 1893 offers a better window into the economic crises of the period.

While perhaps not as serious at the 1873 contraction, the depression of the 1890s appeared to be, by almost any measure, a bad one. Perhaps 20 percent if not more of the workforce experienced unemployment at one time or another. Almost 50 percent of all businesses failed. More than 156 railroads, controlling 30,000 miles of track and with a capitalization in excess of 2.5 billion dollars went under. At its worst, the economy is estimated to have contracted about 25 percent below its pre-depression level.

The factors responsible for this downturn were similar to those of 1873, although this time it was the collapse of the great British banking house, Baring Brothers, which helped trigger the crisis. Having overextended itself in Argentina, Baring was forced to liquidate its holdings in American securities, particularly railroads. This precipitated a heavy outflow of gold, which put a strain on American banks. The banks might have been able to withstand the drain on their gold reserves but for the fact that, for political reasons, the Treasury Department was then engaged in trying to support the price of silver by buying 4.5 million ounces of that metal per month under the terms of the recently enacted Sherman Silver Purchase Act (1890) and issuing Treasury notes, redeemable in gold, for those purchases. This required a large supply of gold to maintain redemption. Bankers, concerned about their falling gold reserves, petitioned the Treasury for conversion of greenbacks and other paper into gold. But the government's gold reserves were clearly inadequate to the task, and the possibility that the government might have to suspend payments in gold sent shivers through Wall Street and set off a panic in the spring of 1893. Again the financial panic spread disruption to other areas of the economy. Railroads went under. Investors found that many of their holdings were worthless. As prices for their goods fell, manufacturers of all sorts retrenched or closed their doors, banks failed, and credit became scarce. Once more the economic system seemed to be in disarray after another boom-and-bust cycle.

But was the underlying economy truly in such bad shape or were all of these crises just a lot of sound and fury signifying nothing? One recent historian has advanced the argument that the panics and depressions of the era were largely mirages of little economic significance. When viewed from the perspective of long-term growth trends during the period, he claims, the depressions were not "of any great seriousness or duration." To be sure, the pace and rate of economic activity fluctuated and was erratic. And, yes, factories might close for short periods of time, unemployment might increase, and public confidence might fall. "But it was," he concludes, "in the main, a time of rapid expansion," and it was that expansion of production that had a much greater impact on American history and development than the downturns that accompanied it.

Still, whatever their long-term significance, those periodically recurring business cycles and breakdowns were real, and economists in the 20th century have analyzed them extensively and developed numerous theories seeking to explain their causes. One of the pioneers in the understanding of business-cycle behavior was Wesley C. Mitchell, who presented a theory of self-generating cycles. Basically, his theory held that when prospects for profits improved, business activity increased, and when prospects became less certain, business declined. After a period of depression, the stage was set anew for a revival and a combination of forces then converted incipient prosperity into another boom, which once again eventuated into a bust. Other scholars have built on Mitchell's analysis, some looking for the key initiating forces or starters of the process, others constructing theories to explain the cycles on the grounds of monetary or investment factors. But however much economists might differ in their analysis of the whys and wherefores of the business cycle, all students of the phenomena agree that it is deeply embedded within the capitalist system and must be taken into consideration by policy makers if its worst tendencies are to be avoided.

Further reading: Rendigs Fells, *American Business Cycles, 1865–1897* (Chapel Hill: University of North Carolina Press, 1959).

— Jerome L. Sternstein

C

cable cars See transportation, urban

Canada and the United States

Unresolved issues stemming from America's Civil War and the persistence of dreams of annexation framed the diplomatic agenda involving Canada and the United States in the postwar years. Briefly, the Americans wanted compensation from the British for building Confederate commerce raiders that disrupted Union shipping. The U.S. government also resented the Canadians for harboring Confederate guerrillas, and the Canadians resented raids by Irish nationalists (called Fenians). Fearful of their economic future, Canadians sought to consolidate their separate provinces, while British policy makers wanted to discourage American expansionist ambitions. As a result, the British North American Act created the Dominion of Canada out of four colonies in 1867 as a semiautonomous federation, with foreign policy remaining in the hands of Great Britain. From 1870 to 1900 and beyond, Canadians believed—with some justification—that Britain sacrificed their interests in controversies with the United States to promote Anglo-American accord.

Annexationists in CONGRESS, such as Senate Foreign Relations Committee chairman Charles Sumner, unrealistically urged that the British surrender Canada to settle American claims for merchant ships destroyed by Confederate raiders built in Britain and to recoup the enormous cost of prolonging the war. But President Ulysses S. Grant and his secretary of state, Hamilton Fish, unwilling to antagonize Britain, did not press for annexation and settled instead for the arbitration of outstanding disputes with Britain and Canada in the TREATY OF WASHINGTON of 1871. The treaty gave the United States fishing rights in Canadian waters and navigation rights on the St. Lawrence River, while Canadians could fish in less-productive waters as far south as Delaware Bay. Arbitrators awarded the United States $15.5 million to settle the *Alabama* claims for lost shipping; Britain received $5.5 million to make up for the unequal fishing rights the Canadians received; and the United States got the disputed San Juan Islands between the present state of Washington and Canada's Vancouver Island in the Pacific Northwest.

Congress, however, was unhappy with the 1871 fisheries settlement and withdrew from the agreement as of July 1, 1885. Canadians fell back on an 1818 treaty and began arresting American fishing boats; Congress retaliated with threats against Canadian imports. Canada, amid economic difficulties, wanted to resolve the fisheries dispute and to secure a reciprocity treaty that would allow agricultural products to enter the United States duty-free, which would help to restore prosperity and stave off sentiment in Canada for annexation. A further complication arose with the BERING SEA DISPUTE over American seizures of Canadian schooners caught killing seals in international waters. That dispute was resolved by an 1892 arbitration treaty (the United States had to pay damages for illegal seizures), but attempts to negotiate a solution to the ongoing fisheries dispute failed until 1909, and reciprocity—because it was tangled up in the question of annexation—was delayed well into the 20th century.

Further reading: Donald Creighton, *Canada's First Century: 1867–1967* (New York: St. Martin's Press, 1970); Donald F. Warner, *The Idea of Continental Union: Agitation for the Annexation of Canada to the United States, 1849–1893* (Lexington: University of Kentucky Press, 1960).

— Bruce Abrams

Carnegie, Andrew (1835–1919)

Born in Dunfermline, Scotland, on November 25, 1835, industrialist and philanthropist Andrew Carnegie was the son of a handloom weaver who had married into a prominent radical family active in the Chartist movement, which

Andrew Carnegie *(Library of Congress)*

advocated sweeping parliamentary reform, and harbored antimonarchial republican views. Steam-powered looms soon impoverished the family, and upon the insistence of Margaret, Carnegie's strong-minded mother, they migrated to Allegheny City (now Pittsburgh's North Side), Pennsylvania, where Carnegie, at 12 years of age, got his first job as a $1.20-a-week bobbin boy in a cotton textile factory. Despite living in a slum, Carnegie reveled in the political equality and economic opportunity of his adopted country. With only four years of schooling, Carnegie took advantage of the practice of Colonel James Anderson, founder of the James Anderson Library Institute of Allegheny City, of allowing working boys to use his large personal library free of charge. On the lookout for better jobs, Carnegie tended a steam engine; delivered telegrams; became a telegraph operator; and, as one of the first to take messages by ear, had the good luck to be discovered by THOMAS A. SCOTT, head of the western division of the Pennsylvania Railroad, who hired him as his telegrapher and secretary at $35 a month. Scott made Carnegie his protégé, tutoring him on investments. When Scott became the railroad's general superintendent in 1859, Carnegie became superintendent of the western division. By 1865 Carnegie had so expanded his investments that he left the railroad to manage them.

His most interesting venture was the Keystone Bridge Company, which specialized in building railroad BRIDGES, the most famous of which is the JAMES B. EADS Bridge over the Mississippi at St. Louis. To secure iron beams for Keystone, Carnegie in 1864 created the Cyclops Iron Company, and the following year he forced a competitor to merge and form Union Mills. The insistence by Eads that Keystone supply steel rather than iron for his bridge and the preference of railroads for British steel rails made by the BESSEMER PROCESS to American iron rails led Carnegie in 1872 to commence building the largest Bessemer plant in the United States. Within a decade, Carnegie headed the incredibly efficient Carnegie Steel Company and dominated the steel industry. The company was a partnership, not a corporation, with Carnegie owning more than half of it and exercising complete control, while his partners owned a small percentage and worked extremely hard to cut production costs. Carnegie rewarded efficiency, eliminating inefficient managers, destroying labor unions, installing the latest machines, and adopting new technology to maintain a competitive edge. He also cut costs by expanding vertically, acquiring iron mines, coal fields (for coke), and steamships and a railroad to transport iron ore from the Great Lakes to the Pittsburgh district.

Carnegie's mixed heritage of his father's radical idealism and his mother's aggressive, acquisitive realism (honed by the family's struggle to survive) account for his complex, contradictory nature. His mother's spirit dominated his business career, but his father's generous, humane spirit was not eradicated. It surfaced in 1886 when, in a magazine article, Carnegie recognized labor's right to organize; but in 1892 he was his mother's boy when he ordered his partner HENRY CLAY FRICK to break the Amalgamated Association of Iron and Steel Workers, thus provoking the bloody HOMESTEAD STRIKE. While engaged in his relentless pursuit of profits, Carnegie feared that the accumulation of wealth was a form of idolatry, but in 1889 he rationalized his wealth by espousing the idea of stewardship in his article "The Gospel of Wealth." He argued that those who had the talent to acquire a fortune were best equipped to distribute it most beneficially for society. In 1901 Carnegie sold his company to U.S. Steel for $480 million (his own share was $225 million), which allowed him to engage full time in philanthropy.

An avid reader from childhood, he donated 2,811 buildings for public libraries upon the condition that community taxes would maintain the buildings and purchase books. He provided pensions for Carnegie Steel workers and also for college teachers. Carnegie was an ANTI-IMPERIALIST and an advocate of peace, and he created the Carnegie Endowment for International Peace. He also built the Pan-American Union Building in Washington, D.C., the Central American Court of Justice in Costa Rica (to arbitrate disputes), and the Hague Peace Palace in the Netherlands to house the World Court. Since so much of his fortune was made in Pittsburgh, he focused many of his philanthropic efforts there, forming the Carnegie Institute, which supported a concert hall, art museum, and library. He also supported Pittsburgh's Carnegie Institute of Technology. Finally, he established the Carnegie Corporation of New York to administer what was left of his fortune. Carnegie's optimistic hopes for the arbitration of disputes and peace were dashed in 1914 by the outbreak of World War I, which left him badly shaken. He died on August 11, 1919, at his vacation home in Lenox, Massachusetts.

Further reading: Joseph Frazier Wall, *Andrew Carnegie* (New York: Oxford University Press, 1970).

Carver, George Washington (ca. 1864–1943)

George Washington Carver, an African-American scientist and educator, devoted his life to improving southern agriculture. Born of enslaved parents in Diamond Grove, Missouri, Carver's father apparently died before he was born, and his mother was abducted by slave raiders. Consequently, Carver was raised and tutored by his mother's former owners on their small farm. When Carver went off to school at nearby Neosho in the mid-1870s he knew as much as his teacher, so he moved to Kansas and then Iowa, working, homesteading, and trying to secure an education. He was a multitalented young man who was an able pianist and especially interested in both growing and painting plants. He enrolled in 1890 as an art major at Simpson College in Indianola, Iowa, but although an able artist (one of his paintings would be exhibited at the WORLD'S COLUMBIAN EXPOSITION), he realized that opportunities for a black artist were severely limited. In 1891—at approximately 27 years of age—he entered Iowa State University of Science and Technology at Ames and found his life's work.

Carver was an excellent student, earning his bachelor of science degree in 1894 and his master of science in 1896. He impressed and was impressed by outstanding agriculturalists associated with that institution, including three future U.S. secretaries of agriculture: James Wilson, Henry C. Wallace, and Henry A. Wallace, who was six years old when Carver introduced him to plant fertilization. At the time, Carver was in charge of the college greenhouse and conducting experiments on plant propagation.

Carver was not patronized because of his race; he deserved the recognition he received and could have joined the Iowa State faculty. Instead, he accepted the invitation and challenge of BOOKER T. WASHINGTON to head the agricultural work at Tuskegee Institute in 1896. He soon also became director of Tuskegee's agricultural experiment station. For almost 50 years he taught and experimented and became a legend in his own lifetime. He was intensely interested in educating African-American farmers in methods of cultivation and the necessity of a balanced diet. A movable school of agriculture and home economics in a well-equipped wagon set forth from Tuskegee to carry these messages to impoverished rural black farm families.

Carver soon realized that the southern farmers were plagued by overspecialization in cotton, which produced soil exhaustion. To counter this problem, he advocated crop diversification, specifically the planting of peanuts and sweet potatoes in place of cotton. To popularize their growth, he conducted experiments in his laboratory at Tuskegee to counter the diseases peanuts were prone to and to identify new uses for peanuts and sweet potatoes. Both became major commercial crops in Carver's lifetime.

Carver was selfless. He never took out any patents on the uses of the peanut or sweet potato he discovered because he wanted them to be widely and freely used. He could have left Tuskegee for well-paying jobs elsewhere. Indeed, despite his low salary at Tuskegee, he sometimes refused to accept raises in pay. A devout Presbyterian, Carver was one of the rare individuals who in every way lived up to the Christian ideal. He died on January 5, 1943.

Further reading: Linda O. McMurry, *George Washington Carver: Scientist and Symbol* (New York: Oxford University Press, 1981).

Cassatt, Mary (1844–1926)

Mary Cassatt applied the stylistic tenets of avant-garde French art to the themes of motherhood and childhood. Born in Allegheny City (now Pittsburgh's North Side) on May 22, 1844, into an affluent Pennsylvania family, Cassatt matriculated at the Pennsylvania Academy of the Fine Arts in 1860. After the Civil War, she went to Paris with her family for further study. As a woman, she was barred from the École des Beaux-Arts, but she studied privately with one of its most important teachers, Jean-Léon Gérôme. She received additional training from other French painters and worked in several French art colonies. After 1875 she divided her time between Paris and the French countryside, returning to America for only a few short visits. She never married, and for most of her life lived with family members. After exhibiting in the Paris Salon six times, she became disillusioned with its politics and aesthetics, and in 1879 she showed with the impressionists. She exhibited three more times with them and then with a similarly dissident group, the Société Français des Peintres-Graveurs. She was influenced by her friends Edgar Degas, Auguste Renoir, and Berthe Morisot and by Japanese art. A retrospective exhibition in 1893 at the gallery of Paul Durand-Ruel in Paris established Cassatt as a major figure in modern painting and launched her acceptance in the United States. She was forced to stop making art in 1914 when her eyesight became clouded by cataracts, and she died in Mesnil-Theribus, France, on June 13, 1926.

Throughout her career Cassatt painted portraits mainly of family members (including her brother Alexander, president of the Pennsylvania Railroad). These, like *Lady at a Tea Table* (1883, Metropolitan Museum of Art, New York), are quiet, straightforward, even unflattering portrayals of the sitter. Around 1880 she began to focus on women and children in neutral domestic settings, developing the theme in both oils and pastels. She displayed a genius for capturing prosaic but telling postures and facial expressions in images of mothers holding or washing children, and women reading, crocheting, and taking tea. After seeing a large exhibition of Japanese prints in 1890, she began working in drypoint and aquatint, inking the plates herself. The resulting series of 10 prints inaugurated her continued work in the medium and influenced other printmakers. She produced a mural for the Women's Building at the WORLD'S COLUMBIAN EXPOSITION of 1893 in Chicago. Titled *Modern Woman,* it showed women and girls picking apples, their bright, contemporary dresses brilliantly lit.

Like the other Impressionists, Cassatt wanted to forge a style for the depiction of modern life. In simple compositions using flat planes of color pushed close to the picture plane, she made icons of timeless themes. Her prints combine color and line, ignoring Western conventions for depicting space. Both paintings and prints became increasingly abstract. In *The Boating Party* (1893–94, National Gallery of Art, Washington, D.C.) a family, oars, and a sail are arrayed in a set of diagonals, and *Under the Horse Chestnut* (1896–97, Museum of Fine Arts, Boston), a print showing a half-reclining woman holding a nude child, is composed of little more than flat planes of blue, green, yellow, and beige tones.

Further reading: Nancy Mowll Mathews, *Cassatt: A Retrospective* (New York: Hugh Lauter Levin Associates, 1996); Nancy Mowll Mathews, *Mary Cassatt: A Life* (New York: Villard Books, 1994).

— Karen Zukowski

cattle kingdom

Cattle raising became an important industry in the Gilded Age. The Spanish brought the first cattle to the New World in the 16th century and later raised them in the Rio Grande Valley and along the California coast. These original stocks were the ancestors of the Texas longhorn. After the United States annexed Texas in 1848, the growth of the cattle industry was interrupted only by the Civil War (1861–65). After 1865 the "cattle kingdom" in the West expanded greatly, aided by the suppression of western Indian tribes and the extermination of the buffalo. Although it tended to be lean and its meat tough, the Texas longhorn was the favorite breed in the cattle kingdom. It proved to be a resilient animal that could withstand cold temperatures and travel great distances with little water to shipping points.

RAILROADS that had expanded west following the Civil War facilitated moving the meat to markets as Europeans and easterners invested in cattle during the late 1870s. By the early 1880s the cattle industry had become a lucrative trade. Texas cattle were driven north by cowboys (rough-hewn ranch hands) on cattle trails to open-range pastures in the Great Plains, where the animals could graze on abundant and free grasslands. Abilene, Kansas, the terminus of the Chisholm Trail, was served by the Kansas Pacific Railroad and became one of the first big transfer points for Texas cattle. The cattle kingdom contributed to the decline of the buffalo, since both cattle and buffalo competed for grassland. The Texas longhorn also brought Texas fever, a disease carried by ticks, which harmed buffalo and other local cattle.

By 1880 there were over 4 million cattle in a swath of land stretching from Texas to Montana and the Dakotas. During the Gilded Age the MEATPACKING industry in midwestern cities perfected a process whereby cattle were slaughtered and the carcasses prepared for shipment to eastern markets via refrigerated railroad cars. By the mid-1880s the number of cattle had almost doubled to 7.5 million, and overgrazing became a significant problem, only to be compounded by a series of mild winters, which led to further overgrazing. The wide distribution of BARBED WIRE beginning in 1884 helped to shut out grazing cattle from farmlands, further limiting available grassland. Fence cutting became a problem, leading to federal legislation regulating fencing. Meager grazing areas meant that cattle needed more and more acreage to survive, which contributed to the degradation of grasslands in the plains. The winters of 1885–86 and 1886–87 were particularly brutal, and many cattle froze to death, which led to further problems in an already flagging nationwide economy with ranchers unable to pay their creditors. By the 1890s cattle drives were becoming a thing of the past as railroads expanded and ranchers began to grow hay to feed cattlestocks, starting a dependency on irrigation and a new set of problems over water allocation.

Further reading: Maurice Frink, W. Turrentine Jackson, and Agnes Spring, *When Grass Was King: Contributions to the Western Range Cattle Industry* (Boulder: University of Colorado Press, 1956); Robert V. Hine and John Mack

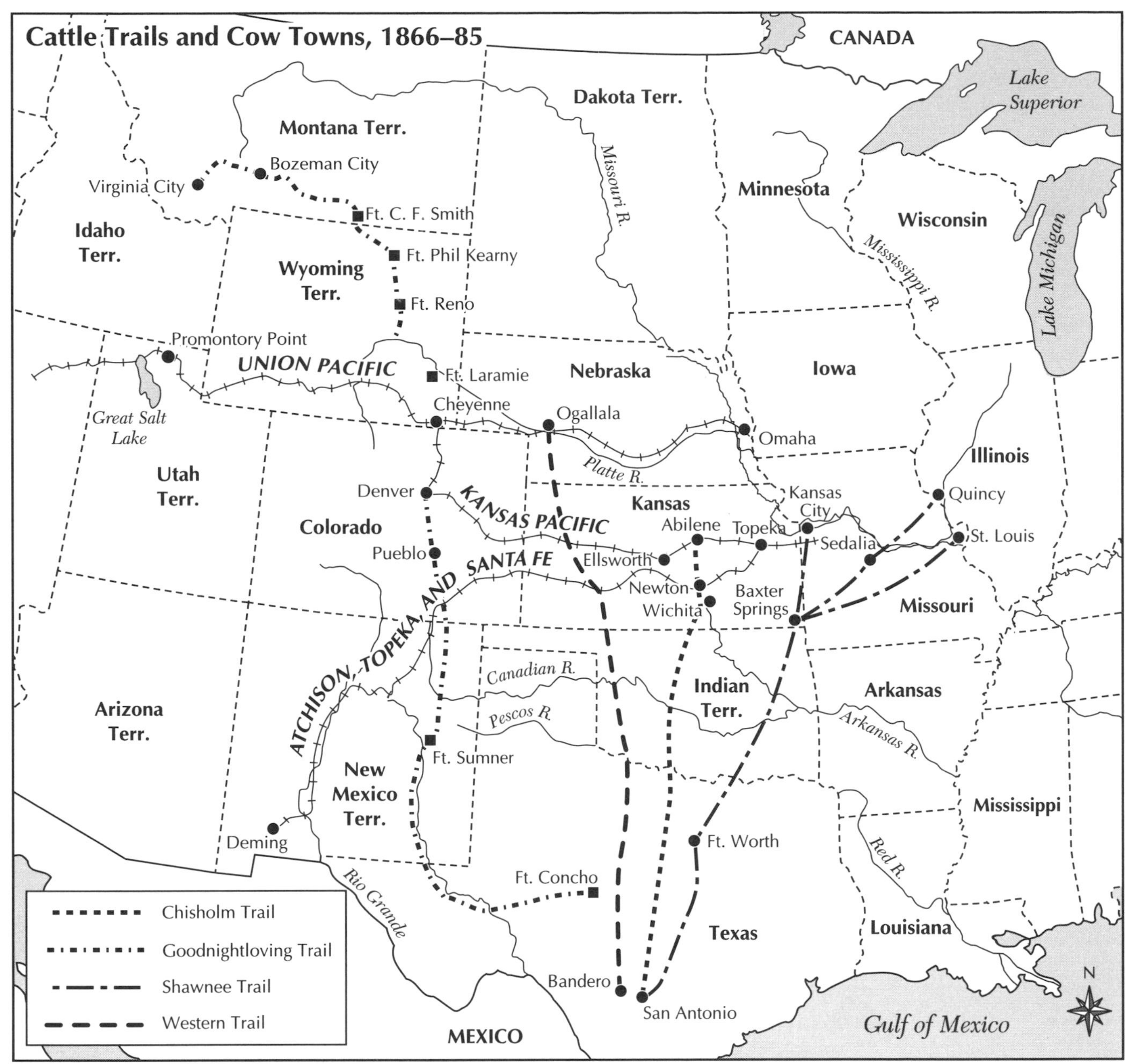

Faragher, *The American West: A New Interpretive History* (New Haven: Yale University Press, 2000).

— Scott Sendrow

chain stores

By the late 19th century a national transportation system had developed, communications were more rapid, more and more commodities were produced, and the purchasing power of the masses had improved. Markets had become national rather than local or regional, and most shoppers were no longer members of a wealthy elite but, rather, represented a broader spectrum of society. These changing conditions enabled chain stores to flourish. Direct purchases of large orders at low prices from manufacturers, which were then sold with small markups at several similar (chain) stores, achieved efficiency by eliminating middlemen and, because of enormous volume, yielded substantial profits. Although chain stores existed prior to the Gilded Age, two of the most spectacular examples expanded enormously in that period: the Great Atlantic and Pacific Tea Company (A&P) and the five-and-ten-cent stores of Frank W. Woolworth.

In 1863 George F. Gilman and George Huntington Hartford started the Great American Tea Company with a flamboyantly decorated store in New York City. They imported tea directly from China in ships owned by Gilman's father, and by eliminating intermediaries they could sell tea at one-third the price of their competitors. They soon opened more stores, added coffee, spices, and other commodities to their wares, and had 25 stores in operation by 1865. Hartford developed "Thea Nectar" from damaged tea; cheap to produce and sold at a low price, it became a very popular and profitable product. In 1869 Gilman and Hartford formed the A&P on the basis of a handshake. Their friendship and respect for each other was such that they felt no need for a legal partnership. They expanded their stores to other cities throughout the Northeast and as far west as St. Louis and St. Paul, growing to 100 stores by 1880 and almost 200 stores by 1900. When Gilman died in 1901 the A&P was grossing $5.5 million annually. In 1902 Hartford reorganized the A&P as a corporation, but in his and his son's hands it remained a family-owned business. In the 20th century the A&P continued to expand (16,000 stores in 1930), established economy stores in 1912, and in 1913 began selling foods under its own lables.

In 1879 Woolworth opened his "Great 5-Cent Store" in Utica, New York, but it failed because of its poor location. Later that year a second venture, in Lancaster, Pennsylvania, proved successful, but of three further ventures over the next three years, one was a moderate success and the other two failures. Woolworth, however, persisted and established more stores, utilizing partners to minimize his risk. He pioneered mass retailing and made his stores attractive by displaying merchandise on counters for customers to inspect. In 1886 he moved his headquarters to New York to facilitate large purchases of goods for cash directly from manufacturers, thus securing a bargain price and eliminating intermediaries. Dealing directly with a manufacturer, for example, enabled him to retail a quarter of a pound of candy for five cents. Always on the lookout for cheap sources of merchandise, Woolworth, on his first trip to Europe, discovered that German toys and Christmas decorations and Bohemian crockery could be imported and sold at bargain prices. By 1900 Woolworth had 59 uniformly decorated (in red) five-and-ten-cent stores in the United States and Canada. By 1912 Woolworth's stores had multiplied 10-fold to 596, and in 1913 the Woolworth Building—then the tallest and still one of the most beautiful SKYSCRAPERS in the world—was dedicated by President Woodrow Wilson. It cost $13 million, and Woolworth paid for it from the profits of his five-and-tens.

Further reading: Godrey M. Lebhar, *Chain Stores in America, 1859–1962,* 3d ed. (New York: Chain Store Pub. Corp, 1963); John P. Nichols, *The Chain Store Tells Its Story* (New York: Institute of Distribution, 1940); Andrew Seth and Geoffrey Randall, *The Grocers: The Rise and Rise of the Supermarket Chains* (London: Kogane Page, 1999).

Chase, William Merritt (1849–1916)

Well known for his portraits, landscapes, and still lifes, William Merritt Chase was one of the Gilded Age's most versatile painters. He was also one of the most prominent figures in the bustling art world of New York City, active as a collector and a teacher, and an outstanding artist. Born on November 1, 1849, and raised in Indiana, Chase was in New York City by 1869, studying painting at the National Academy of Design. In the autumn of 1872 Chase enrolled in the Royal Academy of Munich, where Karl von Piloty became his mentor. Over the next six years, Chase and a contingent of American classmates painted and traveled together to study the great paintings.

One of the first of his generation to establish himself in the United States after European training, Chase returned to New York City in 1878 as an instructor for the newly formed Art Students League. He opened a studio filled with an intriguing assortment of furniture, fabrics, artworks, and pets, including a Russian wolfhound, and he frequently depleted his bank account to purchase these furnishings. He became a kingpin in artists' organizations, especially the Society of American Artists. Chase married Alice Gerson in 1886 and eventually became the father of eight children, all of whom lived to adulthood. The elements of Chase's orbit—studio, students, colleagues, family, and home—appeared frequently on his canvases.

Even while maintaining a prodigious output of his own paintings, Chase became one of the country's most important teachers. In 1896 he founded his own school of art in New York City, where he taught until 1907. Supported by a group of wealthy amateur painters, from 1891 to 1902 he conducted a summer school of painting in Shinnecock on Long Island in New York. He also maintained long affiliations with the Art Students League and the Pennsylvania Academy of the Fine Arts. Work with Chase included not only classroom instruction but trips to museums, his own studio, and, in the summer, to Europe to look at old-master paintings. Chase had hundreds of pupils, including many women and future modernists, such as Charles Sheeler and Georgia O'Keefe.

When he was a young man, Chase was asked by potential backers if he would like to travel to Europe for further study. Chase replied: "My God . . . I'd rather go to Europe than to heaven." Indeed, a bravura style assimilated from a variety of European artists of various eras became Chase's hallmark. Chase admired Velázquez's brushwork, Frans Hals's chiaroscuro, and the modern conflation of space practiced by Edouard Manet and Alfred Stevens. To these techniques Chase added his own powers of observation, demonstrating an unerring ability to convey texture and light and an unfaltering ability to craft exquisite compositions. Among the best-known of Chase's works are his landscapes depicting the sandy dunes near Shinnecock, such as *Idle Hours* (1894, Amon Carter Museum, Fort Worth, Texas), portraits such as *JAMES ABBOTT MCNEILL WHISTLER* (1885, Metropolitan Museum of Art, New York), and numerous fish still lifes, such as *An English Cod* (1904, Corcoran Gallery of Art, Washington, D.C.). Chase died on October 25, 1916, in New York City.

Further reading: Keith L. Bryant Jr., *William Merritt Chase: A Genteel Bohemian* (Columbia: University of Missouri Press, 1991); Barbara Dayer Gallati, *William Merritt Chase* (New York: Harry N. Abrams and the National Museum of American Art, 1995).

— Karen Zukowski

Chautauqua Institute

The Chautauqua Institute began as an adult summer-education program located at a campsite on Lake Chautauqua in western New York State. It was started in 1869 by Methodist Episcopal bishop John H. Vincent (1832–1920) and Lewis Miller, a businessman from Akron, Ohio. The Institute's founders initially designed it for Sunday-school superintendents and teachers who wanted to improve their programs, but they soon broadened its goals.

The Chautauqua Institute reflected the American faith in popular education and the belief that a democratic republic needed citizens who could join in private organizations for mutual improvement. The origins of the Chautauqua Institute can be found in the early 19th-century lyceums, which sponsored lectures, debates, and concerts and which bridged the gap between a community's tiny number of college graduates and the vast majority of literate adults with a common-school education.

As the lyceum movement waned after the Civil War, the Chautauqua leaders adopted its approach and began to offer secular programs in art, music, literature, science, and social issues to summer vacationers who wanted to combine physical relaxation with mental stimulation. Speakers at Protestant churches encouraged attendance by families as well as single persons at the institute, where the joys of healthy, clean, rural living would be combined with the virtues of listening to great speakers address the issues of the day. Between lectures concerning such topics as the tariff, women's voting rights, or the implications of Darwinian thought on American society, participants enjoyed bountiful meals, boating, swimming, and church services. Easily accessible by rail, Chautauqua was visited by comfortably wealthy, intellectually active Americans.

In 1878, under the leadership of William R. Harper, a Yale University Hebrew scholar who later became president of the University of Chicago, Chautauqua developed a year-round home-reading program that also promoted its summer program. Between 1880 and 1900 Chautauqua participants (both home study and summer) increased as the number of well-to-do educated Americans with leisure time increased. During the first quarter of the 20th century, traveling Chautauqua programs (including drama and popular music) appeared throughout the country and appealed to educated Americans of all ethnic and religious backgrounds. By 1930, however, with the coming of radio and the movies and the spread of high schools throughout the country, summer attendance and home-reading enrollment in Chautauqua programs drastically declined.

Further reading: Ann Boylan, *Sunday School: The Formation of an American Institution, 1790–1880* (New Haven: Yale University Press, 1988); Lawrence Cremin, *A History of Education in American Culture* (New York: Holt, Rinehart, and Winston, 1953); Joseph Edward Sould, *The Chautaugua Movement: An Episode in the Contemping American Location* (New York: State University of New York, 1961).

— Harry Stein

Chicago Fire (1871)

See cities and urban life

Chicago World's Fair (1893)

See World's Columbian Exposition

Chilean-American relations

Located far down the Pacific coast of South America, Chile had a stormy relationship with the United States in the last quarter of the 19th century. The ill will stemmed from the tensions surrounding the War of the Pacific (1879–84), during which Chile fought Peru and Bolivia for control of the nitrate-rich regions of Arica and Tacna. The war started when Bolivia, in violation of a treaty, raised taxes on Chilean nitrate companies operating in the Antofagasta region of Bolivia. Chile responded by invading the region. Bolivia declared war and was joined by Peru, with whom Bolivia had a secret defense treaty. Chile's highly trained army quickly knocked Bolivia out of the war, captured Arica and Tacna, and went on to occupy Peru's capital, Lima.

Great Britain had a great amount of money invested in Chile and attempted to negotiate a peace settlement. The United States saw those overtures as a threat to its plans for increased economic and political influence in the Americas and sought to solve the situation itself. It did not want Chile to acquire land by force of arms, fearing that the precedent would launch South America into a chaos of land grabbing. In 1881 JAMES G. BLAINE, secretary of state under President JAMES A. GARFIELD, attempted to rally the other Latin American nations to force Chile to relinquish the captured regions, but his efforts only further antagonized Chile.

Blaine's levelheaded and methodical successor, Frederick Frelinghuysen, adopted a more conciliatory approach when he took office in December 1881. Knowing full well that the United States—given the state of its army and navy—could not intervene, the new secretary did not try to prevent Chile from keeping the nitrate fields as part of the 1883 Treaty of Ancon with Peru and the 1884 Treaty of Valparaiso with Bolivia. Although Chile achieved its goals, it would resent American diplomatic efforts to prevent its expansion for years to come.

Problems with Chile arose again in 1891. At the time Chile was embroiled in a civil war, with congressional forces revolting against those of President José Manuel Balmaceda. The rebels purchased weapons in the United States and were shipping them out of San Diego on a freighter named the *Itata.* The United States sought to detain the ship and, although it slipped away, eventually recovered it only to have American courts free it as improperly detained. Back in Chile the Congressionalists forced Balmaceda to flee and seek the protection of the American embassy. The Congressionalists became furious when the American minister Patrick Egan refused to surrender the Chilean president and other refugees to the mob outside the legation.

Although Balmaceda committed suicide on September 19, 1891, the situation deteriorated even further when on October 16 a fight broke out in Valparaiso at the True Blue Saloon. Two American sailors from the USS *Baltimore* were killed and several were injured by a mob of Chilean sailors and civilians who apparently were assisted by the Chilean police in the attack. President BENJAMIN HARRISON considered the incident an affront to national honor and demanded that Chile express regret for the incident and offer reparations. The Chilean minister to the United States, Manuel Antonio Matta, refused to oblige, and the newly installed president of Chile, Pedro Montt, denied that Chile was at fault and countered that the United States was guilty of provocations and indiscretions. On January 25, 1892, Harrison requested CONGRESS to authorize the use of force against Chile if Matta did not admit to wrongdoing. The U.S. Navy (significantly stronger since 1881) had been preparing for an attack for months and had a fleet of 17 warships ready for action in the event Montt refused to apologize. But when Harrison sent his bellicose message to Congress, Chile's apology rescinding its accusations had been received and was being decoded. The apology ended the crisis. Just before Christmas of 1892 the refugees were allowed to leave the legation and board an American warship, and although a Chilean court ultimately exonerated the police of any wrongdoing in the *Baltimore* incident, Chile paid a $75,000 indemnity that effectively put the entire matter to rest. The Chilean imbroglio of 1891–92 was the first use of naval power by the United States to enhance the effectiveness of its diplomacy.

Further reading: Henry C. Evans Jr., *Chile and Its Relations with the United States* (Durham, N.C.: Duke University Press, 1927); David M. Pletcher, *The Awkward Years: American Foreign Relations under Garfield and Arthur* (Columbia: University of Missouri Press, 1962); Alice F. Tyler, *Foreign Policy of James G. Blaine* (Hamden, Conn.: Archon Books, 1945).

— Timothy E. Vislocky

Chinese Exclusion Act (1882)

Congress designed the Chinese Exclusion Act to halt the flood of Chinese immigration into the country and to deport Chinese who were allegedly living in the United States illegally. The presence of Chinese immigrants had been an issue for some time in western states, where Chinese settled in large numbers during the gold rush of the 1850s. As heavy competition and the dwindling number of gold fields winnowed out all but the most resourceful of miners, the Chinese began to move into the vast railroad construction projects that sought to unite the two coasts of the nation. The completion of the transcontinental railway decreased the cost of eastern-manufactured goods and forced western manufacturers to look for a source of low-cost labor. They found it in the thousands of now-unemployed Chinese railroad workers.

Agitation for limiting Chinese immigration began during the depression of 1873. Jobs were scarce and competition for them was fierce. White laborers saw the hiring of Chinese workers at low wages by cost-conscious manufacturers as acts of job thievery. Anti-Chinese riots erupted in several western cities. Mob violence, especially in California, was accompanied by political action as western politicians sought to end Chinese immigration. Congress produced such a bill in 1879, but it was vetoed by President RUTHERFORD B. HAYES on the grounds that the bill would force the United States to abrogate a provision of the Burlingame Treaty, which allowed unrestricted Chinese immigration. Hayes subsequently negotiated a new treaty with China that regulated immigration.

The issue came up again in 1882 when Republican senator John Miller of California proposed a bill that would have restricted Chinese immigration for 20 years and made the Chinese residing in the United States ineligible for citizenship. President CHESTER A. ARTHUR vetoed the bill as undemocratic, but a revised bill passed by wide margins in

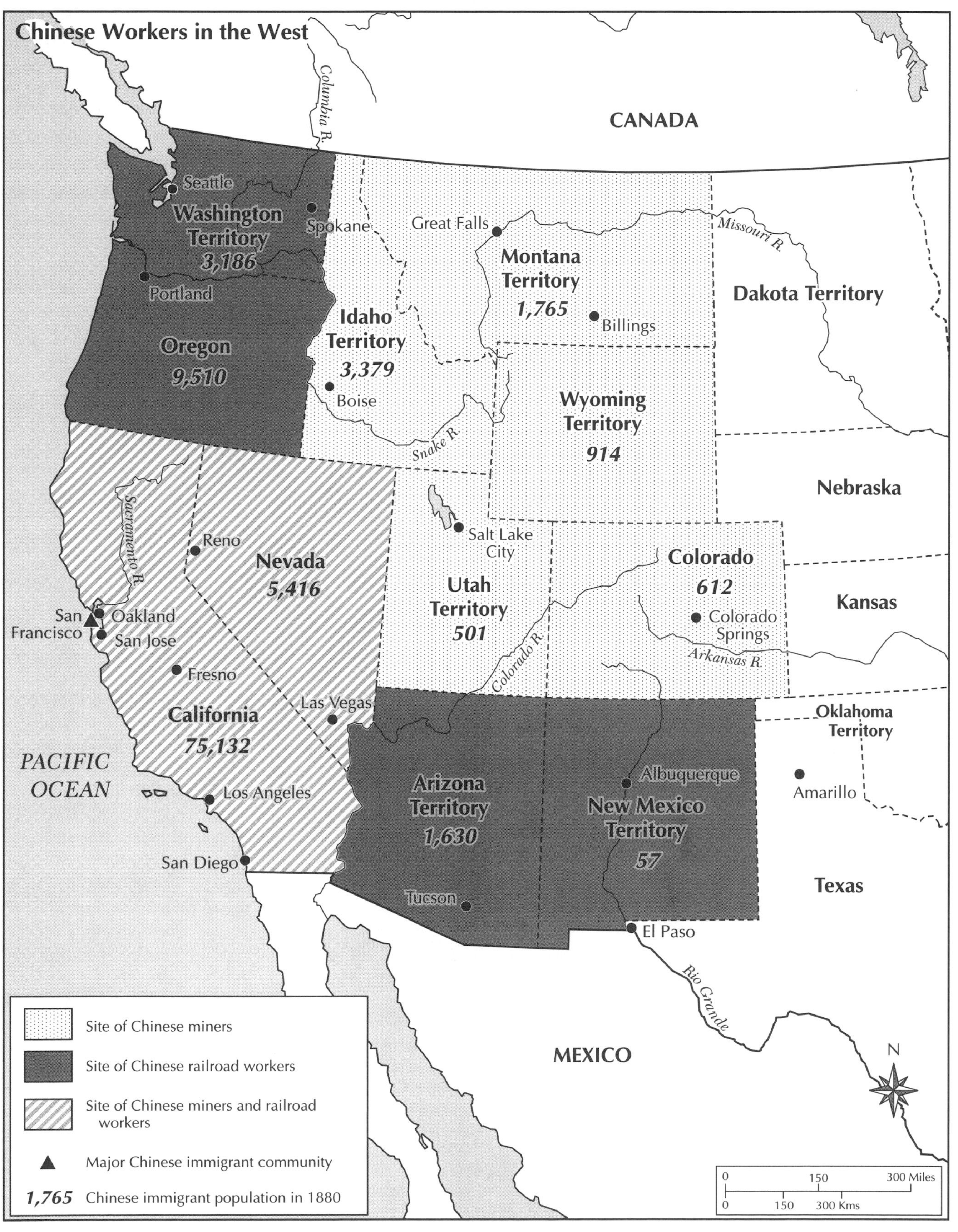
Chinese Workers in the West
CANADA
Columbia R.
Seattle
Washington Territory 3,186
Spokane
Portland
Oregon 9,510
Idaho Territory 3,379
Boise
Snake R.
Great Falls
Montana Territory 1,765
Billings
Missouri R.
Dakota Territory
Wyoming Territory 914
Nebraska
Salt Lake City
Utah Territory 501
Colorado 612
Colorado Springs
Arkansas R.
Kansas
Colorado R.
Sacramento R.
Reno
Nevada 5,416
San Francisco
Oakland
San Jose
Fresno
California 75,132
Las Vegas
Los Angeles
San Diego
PACIFIC OCEAN
Arizona Territory 1,630
Tucson
Albuquerque
New Mexico Territory 57
El Paso
Oklahoma Territory
Amarillo
Texas
Rio Grande
MEXICO
N
Site of Chinese miners
Site of Chinese railroad workers
Site of Chinese miners and railroad workers
Major Chinese immigrant community
1,765 Chinese immigrant population in 1880
0 150 300 Miles
0 150 300 Kms

This cartoon by Thomas Nast shows a Democratic tiger and a Republican elephant joining forces to remove a Chinese immigrant who hangs on desperately to a tree labeled "Freedom to all." *(Library of Congress)*

the House and Senate and was reluctantly signed by Arthur. The moratorium was reduced to 10 years, but the Chinese were still barred from becoming citizens. In order to maintain good trade relations, Arthur's secretary of state, Frederick Frelinghuysen, tried to curb California racists and lobbied for a ban on American exports of opium to China. The Chinese minister was mollified, and relations between the United States and China remained cordial.

Further reading: Justus Donecke, *The Presidencies of James A. Garfield & Chester A. Arthur* (Lawrence: University Press of Kansas, 1981); Ari Hoogenboom, *The Presidency of Rutherford B. Hayes* (Lawrence: University Press of Kansas, 1988); Alexander Saxton, *The Indispensable Enemy: Labar and the Anti-Chinese Movement in California* (Berkeley: University of California Press, 1971).

— Timothy E. Vislocky

Christian Science

Along with Mormonism, Adventism, and Pentecostalism, Christian Science is one of a few large, successful American religious groups and was the creation of one person, MARY BAKER EDDY (1821–1910). *Christian Science* is the term used by Eddy, but the germs of her ideas originated with Phineas Quimby. Following years of ill health and emotional precariousness, she was treated by Quimby, who promoted a mystical Christianity that could effect physical healing. He used the phrases "science of health" and "Christian science" to describe his theories. Eddy found herself healed and became a disciple of his ideas, but his sudden death in January 1866 and a personal accident turned her from disciple into apostle.

Eddy dated the religion of Christian Science from her fall on ice in February 1866, which injured her back. She had a revelation "on the third day" after reading Matthew 9:2 (associating a young man's palsy with his sins), and she arose, like him, from her bed. The next decade was spent in poverty as she elaborated on what she had learned from Quimby, developed her own ideas, and began to envision a Christian Science Church. Its first worship service was held in June 1875, and that fall she published the first edition of *Science and Health,* her principle work. The Church of Christ (Scientist) was chartered in 1879. Eddy, however, was a difficult person, and the new church was plagued with crises, splits, and lawsuits. The faithful few who remained loyal made her, at the age of 60, their pastor.

Eddy was a gifted teacher, and through the Massachusetts Metaphysical College, which she chartered in 1881, she attracted several hundred students eager to learn her insights, namely that matter—including sickness and death—is an illusion, and to be trained as "practitioners" to deal with the illusion of illness. These students became de facto missionaries who could and would organize Christian Science societies. In 1882 there were only 50 members of the original congregation, but by 1890 there were 110 churches and societies, 250 practitioners, and *The Journal of Christian Science.* Concerned by defections, Eddy reorganized the church, terminated the Metaphysical College in 1889, and dissolved the Christian Science Association in 1892, centralizing denominational affairs in the new "Mother Church" in Boston (dedicated in 1895). All other Christian Science churches were branches of it. Twelve "charter" and 20 "first" members controlled membership, and the church was run by a board of directors appointed by Eddy. An agency of the board also assumed the functions the college had performed.

Christian Science continued to grow rapidly and by 1910 exceeded 100,000 members. Ironically as the church grew, Eddy became more secluded and frail, lending her an air of mystery and encouraging a reverence that held her followers' loyalty across the country. She died in 1910, but Eddy noted that the world of the sense is mere "belief. . . . Matter and death are mortal illusions."

Although Eddy was a commanding personality, circumstances in New England and the United States contributed to the success of Christian Science. One was its appeal to and empowerment of women, who had begun to demand new roles in the 19th century. Another was its understanding of prosperity as a sign of spiritual health, which appealed to the new middle class. A third was its focus on health which, while metaphysical, had a rational and empirical emphasis and contrasted with emotional faith healing. And finally, thanks to Eddy, Christian Science was well organized.

Further reading: Stephen Gottschalk, *The Emergence of Christian Science in American Religious Life* (Berkeley: University of California Press, 1973); Robert Peel, *Mary Baker Eddy,* 3 vols. (Boston: Christian Science Publishing Society, 1966–77).

— W. Frederick Wooden

cities and urban life

The three decades from 1870 to 1900 constituted a period of astounding urban growth, reflected in the increased number of larger cities and the growing portion of the population that lived in larger cities. The U.S. population increased from 40 to 76 million, an increase of 91 percent. The rural population grew by 17 million, from 28.7 to 45.8 million, and the urban population increased by 20.3 million, from 9.9 to 30.2 million. Thus, while the rural population increased by 60 percent, the urban population more than tripled.

In 1870, 14 cities exceeded the 100,000 mark; by 1900, there were 35. Combined, these larger cities grew by 238 percent and accounted for 27 percent of the nation's total population growth from 1870 to 1900. Residents in these 35 cities comprised more than 18 percent of the entire population of the United States, or one of every five and one-half people. These larger cities were heavily concentrated in the Northeast, Middle-Atlantic, and upper Midwest. Indeed, in 1900 there were more cities larger than 100,000 in New Jersey (three) than in either the Old South or the Far West.

This growth was even more concentrated, because the 10 largest cities in the country accounted for 16 percent of the total national population growth; by 1900 one in eight Americans resided in these 10 largest cities. Moreover, the five largest cities accounted for 13 percent of the nation's total population growth, with the result that in 1900 one in every 10 persons in the United States lived in one of these five cities. Finally, the three largest cities from 1880 to 1900 were New York, Chicago, and Philadelphia, with populations of 3.4, 1.7, and 1.3 million, respectively, in 1900. Together these three were responsible for one-ninth of the nation's total population growth, and one in 12 of all U.S. residents lived in them.

IMMIGRATION fueled much of this urban population growth, especially in eastern and midwestern cities. Between 1880 and 1900 nearly 9 million immigrants came to the United States. While the immigrant stream had first flowed from the northern European countries, by 1900 the larger portion was arriving from eastern and southern Europe. This immigrant stream dramatically affected larger cities: One-third of the residents in the five largest cities in 1900 were foreign-born, and two-fifths of the residents reported that at least one parent was foreign-born. But the combination of foreign-born and those with at least one foreign-born parent comprised over three-fourths the population in many industrial cities, including Milwaukee (where it constituted more than four of every five residents), Detroit, Chicago, New York, and San Francisco.

Why were all these people moving to cities? The answer was simple: jobs and perceived opportunity. Trade and manufacturing expanded dramatically, creating strong demand for labor. Manufacturers set up shop either close to the materials needed to produce their goods or close to their markets. Transportation access was crucial, so virtually all the burgeoning cities were on the sea coasts, rivers, or the Great Lakes. Those not located on navigable bodies of water were amply served by railroads, which had also become crucial even for the continued growth of cities with excellent water transportation. As cities grew, they became their own generators of economic and employment opportunity. The construction of factories, housing, offices, and infrastructure were major activities as cities doubled in size during a single decade. At the turn of the century, construction trades often accounted for one-third of the jobs in a city.

This rapid growth strained existing urban systems and created the need for new services and the delivery of services on an unprecedented scale. The needs were so compelling they demanded resources: human, material, and financial. Solutions involved application of new technologies, attracting and then placing restrictions on the resources of private investors, developing the political will to raise the necessary public funds, and creating the organizational mechanisms for supplying and maintaining these services. Ultimately, such efforts called for the conception of the city as a system of systems, a view that was not always realized. Town planning still consisted largely of street layouts created by private developers, usually in a grid form—the easiest way to subdivide and market land—without any particular sense of their relationship to the entire city.

Rapid, large-scale urban growth could not have occurred without new and improved transport systems. Only main streets were paved at the outset of this period, and as development spread outward most new streets were not paved. Few cities could keep up with the pace of growth outward, so street conditions remained problematic, especially in the rapidly growing cities in the West and Midwest. Moreover, many streets and roads were in a perpetual state of chaos due to the continuing additions to and maintenance of gas lines, electric lines, water and sewer mains, and streetcar tracks. Horsecar lines and, by the late 1880s and 1890s, electric streetcar lines extended the distances residents could travel, especially for work. These conveyances both followed and stimulated the extension of residences beyond previously imposed travel limits.

Provision of sanitary sewers and a dependable, safe water supply were other imperatives for this new scale of urban living. Most new urban housing was still single-family dwellings on small plots of land, though in the larger cities substantial portions of the population lived in varying forms of multifamily structures. One general characteristic of the various forms of housing for the huge new additions of workers was crowding, as many people were forced by financial constraints to live in small spaces. This crowding together created additional strains on sewer and water resources. At the outset of this era, private wells were

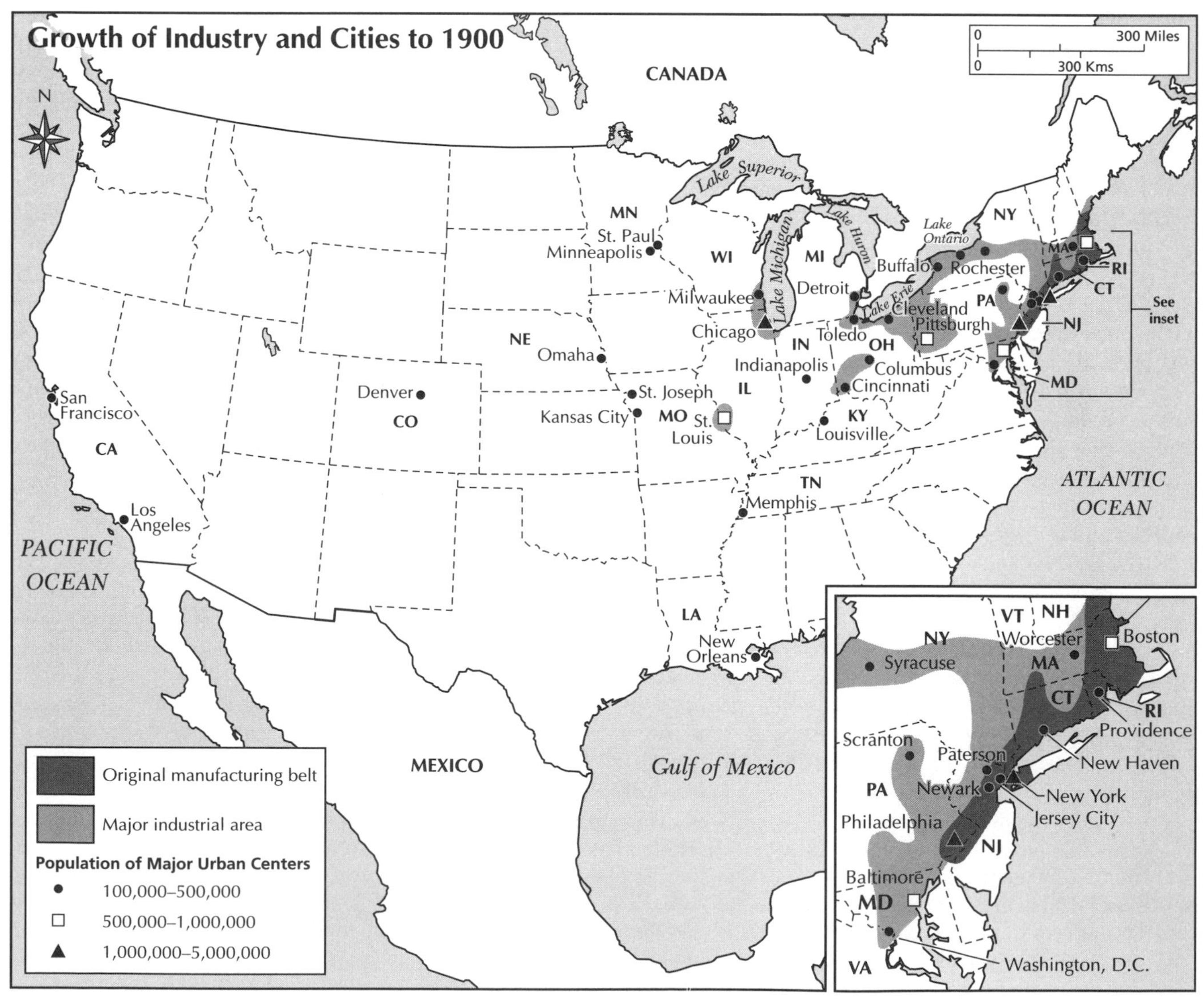

the main source of water and septic systems the main means of sewage disposal, both usually on the same small plot. By the 1870s an increasing number of places accepted the concept of the city as a self-flushing mechanism powered by water. Thus, if water were continuously delivered to households, water closets could replace backyard privies, and the flow of water would create self-cleansing sewers that could supplant septic tanks and cesspools. These concerns were part of the larger issues of public health and the perceived connection between open filth and the spread of diseases. Periodic urban outbreaks, most notably the 1878 yellow fever epidemic in Memphis in which one of every nine residents died, gave a strong sense of immediacy to the issue of sanitary reform throughout this era.

This era also saw the gradual transition from volunteer firemen to the establishment of professional municipal fire departments. Cites were ever-increasing masses of combustible materials, with buildings largely made of wood, masonry structures with wooden roofs, and even sidewalks and streets of wood. Inadequacies of the water supply meant few and scattered fire hydrants. The quantity, maintenance, and technical adequacy of fire-fighting equipment were generally problematic. A number of conflagrations called attention to these shortcomings. Boston suffered a fire on November 9–10, 1872, that destroyed 766 buildings in a 60-acre swath, including seven wharves and several ships tied there. The fire department was virtually helpless to combat the flames. The most famous fire was in Chicago on October 8–9, 1871. A long drought and strong winds exacerbated the inadequate condition of fire-fighting equipment and shortage of manpower; the fire finally ended because it was blown to the shores of Lake Michigan, and a steady rain fell through the second day. The burnt district encompassed a 2,000-acre area four miles long and three-quarters of a mile wide. Some 18,000 buildings were gone; the estimated death toll was 300; and 90,000 people were rendered homeless.

Ironically, the dynamism and growth pressures present in Chicago turned the horrible event into a development opportunity. The previous two decades of development that had seen the city grow from 30,000 to 300,000 had paradoxically made the land more valuable without structures than with them. So, trade continued to increase, and real estate values quickly attained and surpassed those before the fire. Major urban fires provided powerful impetus to enact and/or tighten building codes, boost investment in fire-fighting equipment, increase the number and training of full-time firefighters, and improve the system of water distribution.

In the 1890s the slogan that "municipal government is business, not politics" was promoted by business leaders and other civic reformers and made its way into the political-governmental vocabulary. The growth of cities required increasing technical preparation and competence to address the delivery of necessary public services. There was a need for foresight and vision and for leaders who would look at the "big picture" beyond narrow parochial interests. By century's end there was a growing sense that cities ought to become more beautiful, more efficient, and healthier places in which to live and do business. Yet because cities had become such diverse, multifaceted collections of people, activities, and interests, the allocation of resources and provision of services required more political sensitivity than mere technical preparation could deliver.

Further reading: Raymond A. Mohl, *The New City: Urban America in the Industrial Age, 1860–1920* (Arlington Heights, Ill.: Harlan Davidson, 1985); Eric H. Monkkonen, *America Becomes Urban: The Development of U.S. Cities and Towns, 1780–1980* (Berkeley: University of California Press, 1988); Jon C. Teaford, *The Unheralded Triumph: City Government in America, 1870–1900* (Baltimore: Johns Hopkins University Press, 1984).

— J. Paul Mitchell

Civil Rights Act of 1875 See Volume V

civil rights cases (1883)

Congress passed the Civil Rights Act of 1875, which prohibited discrimination on account of color, race, or previous condition of servitude on railroads or other forms of public conveyances, or in theaters, restaurants, inns, or other forms of public accommodation. Convicted persons were subjected to fines of not less than $500 and possible imprisonment. In 1883 five cases of violation were examined by the U.S. SUPREME COURT. AFRICAN AMERICANS were denied: service in a Kansas City restaurant, a seat in the dress circle of a San Francisco theater, admission to a New York City opera house, accommodations in a Missouri hotel, and a seat in the ladies car of a railroad train in Tennessee.

The Supreme Court ruled 8-1 that the 1875 Civil Rights Act was unconstitutional. Justice Joseph Bradley declared for the majority that the Thirteenth Amendment, which abolished slavery, was not applicable to the law and that the Fourteenth Amendment "interdicted discriminatory action only by the states and not by private persons." He added that the act of denying accommodation by an owner of an inn, a public carrier, or place of amusement is not tantamount to "imposing any badge of slavery or servitude upon the applicant." Bradley noted that slavery could not be cited as the cause of every act of discrimination because blacks were no longer slaves nor were they any longer "the special favorite of the laws."

In his lone dissent Justice JOHN MARSHALL HARLAN—a former slaveholder from Kentucky—said Bradley's opinion was "narrow and artificial" and that the Thirteenth Amendment not only abolished slavery but in conferring freedom gave Congress the power to destroy the "badges of slavery." He noted that railroad corporations, inns, theaters, and other public facilities were "agents or instruments of the state" and thereby liable.

Black activists and their supporters, aware that the court's decision would encourage segregation, were dismayed. Timothy Thomas Fortune, editor of the New York *Globe,* wrote that "the colored people of the United States feel today as if they had been baptized in ice water," and the Detroit *Plain Dealer* noted that the court's ruling "comes like an avalanche carrying our fondest hopes down the hill of despair."

Indeed, the decision of the Supreme Court emboldened southerners who opposed racial integration. In less than two decades the Court's decision in *PLESSY V. FERGUSON* and the enactment of JIM CROW LAWS would effectively create a rigid segregated system in the southern states that would not be seriously challenged until the Civil Rights movement of the 1950s and 1960s.

Further reading: Henry J. Abraham and Barbara A. Perry, *Freedom and the Court: Civil Rights and Liberties in the United States,* 7th ed. (New York: Oxford University Press, 1998); Loren Miller, *The Petitioners: The Story of the Supreme Court of the United States* (Cleveland: Meridian Books, 1967).

— William Seraile

civil service reform

With the rise of mass-based parties in the era of Andrew Jackson, politicians used civil servants to organize and finance their political campaigns. Public employees were assessed a percentage of their salaries for party purposes and—especially those in the field service outside Washington—performed the tasks of running conventions, campaigning, conveying supporters to the polls, and manning those polls. The appointment of civil servants was a vital concern for senators and congressmen because their political lives depended on patronage, and since the "spoils" of office belonged to the victors, civil servants had to reelect their patrons to keep their jobs. With each change of party, civil servants were rotated out of office and replaced by political appointees who, except for their inexperience, were like the previous appointees. The "spoils system" made the public service inefficient at best and corrupt at worst. Still, the major political parties—especially the party in power—argued that the American democracy, the one with the widest suffrage and most complex elections in the world, could not function without it.

The Civil War caused an extremely high turnover of civil servants (many of whom were suspected of treason) at the same time that the service was being subjected to unprecedented demands. Shortly after the war ended, Representative Thomas A. Jenckes, a Rhode Island Republican, inaugurated a movement to reform the civil service by introducing a bill requiring that nonpolicy-making civil servants be appointed on the basis of competitive examinations open to all. The idea of a nonpartisan civil service appealed to intellectuals sickened by the hurly burly of political campaigns and to merchants angered by incompetent and corrupt customhouse employees. Although the Jenckes bill never passed, CONGRESS in 1871, recognizing the strength of the reform movement, enabled President Ulysses S. Grant to appoint a commission to devise rules for examining applicants for positions in the civil service. Prior to the 1872 election Grant favored the idea, and his commission, headed by George William Curtis, drew up rules. After the election Congress starved the commission, and Grant departed from the rules to appoint ROSCOE CONKLING's candidate as surveyor of the New York customhouse rather than promote the deputy surveyor. Curtis resigned, Grant abandoned the rules completely, and "spoilsmen" rejoiced.

Civil service reform was set back, but not for long. Shortly after President RUTHERFORD B. HAYES took office in 1877, he forbade assessments of civil servants and their management of caucuses, conventions, and campaigns. Following a long struggle, he removed Conkling's lieutenant CHESTER A. ARTHUR as head of the New York customhouse and then insisted that it be made a showcase for reform. Although Hayes's successor, JAMES A. GARFIELD, moved to restore the spoils system in the New York customhouse, he was assassinated by a deranged office seeker before that was accomplished. The civil service reform movement, headed by George William Curtis, capitalized on Garfield's tragic death by blaming the spoils system for his murder and calling for passage of a reform bill as a memorial for the slain president. Congressmen and senators, reluctant to give up their patronage (which provided the political soldiers in their electoral campaigns), would not pass the Pendleton Civil Service Reform Act until Republicans suffered a severe defeat in the 1882 congressional election. The "lame duck" Congress in 1883 passed the reform bill, which prohibited political assessments of all civil servants and "classified" 10 percent of the service under the "merit system" of open competitive examinations for appointments to office. Subsequent presidents enlarged the classified service to freeze their political appointments under existing civil service rules until, in 1900, roughly 45 percent of all civil servants were classified.

By 1900 the Pendleton Act had a significant effect. A previously unprofessional civil service was becoming a professionalized bureaucracy. Civil servants were better educated, and loyalty to a patron in Congress and concerns over local politics were giving way to concerns of a federal office whose interests were national. Since civil servants were no longer forced to contribute time and money to political campaigns, political parties turned increasingly to corporations for political contributions, with a corresponding increase in corporate influence over public policy.

The civil service mirrored the development—in late-19th-century American society—of professionalism, nationalism, and the power of businesspeople. On the other hand, the reformed bureaucracy had acquired the capacity to accomplish the wide range of regulatory tasks assigned to it during the 20th century. Civil service reform was the fundamental reform for the Progressive Era.

Further reading: Ari Hoogenboom, *Outlawing the Spoils: A History of the Civil Service Reform Movement, 1865–1883* (Urbana: University of Illinois Press, 1961); Stephen Skowronek, *Building a New American State: The Expansion of National Administrative Capacities, 1877–1920* (Cambridge, U.K.: Cambridge University Press, 1982).

class consciousness

In comparison to Europe, the United States has been relatively free of class consciousness, but Americans have been acutely aware of race and ethnicity, with racial and ethnic prejudices often reinforced by differences in status. This tendency was strong in the Gilded Age in large part because of the huge influx of immigrants from eastern and southern Europe and China and by the migration of American blacks from the country into the city. The newcomers for the most part secured "foreign jobs"—the least desirable tasks at the lowest pay—and lived in poor housing in ethnic enclaves in city slums. Their poverty added to the contempt in which they were regarded (because of their Catholicism, Judaism, skin color, or strange tongues) by the children of earlier immigrants. Irish Americans were caricatured unmercifully in *Harper's Weekly* by THOMAS NAST (an immigrant from Germany), while eastern Europeans were disparaged as "Hunkies," southern Europeans as "Dagos," and Jews as "Sheenies."

Ironically, while racial and ethnic prejudices were strengthened by status in the society at large, the same prejudices were echoed even within the working class, which was also divided by ethnic and religious differences. Employers like Captain William Jones, who managed ANDREW CARNEGIE's J. Edgar Thompson Steel Works, preferred to hire "young American boys judicially mixed" in ethnic backgrounds. However, this was not easily accomplished in the 1880s in Pennsylvania's anthracite regions. The KNIGHTS OF LABOR was predominantly Irish, and the Amalgamated Association of Miners was English, Welsh, and German. Both unions tried, unsuccessfully, to attract either Slavs (who were mostly Poles) or Italians. By 1897, following the Lattimer massacre of immigrant strikers, the United Mine Workers had managed to unite the various ethnic groups. Even then, their leader John Mitchell still had to remind them that the coal they dug was not Irish coal or Slavic coal, but simply coal.

Industrial conditions were sufficiently harsh during the Gilded Age for workers to join labor unions, but workers were not class conscious enough to create a significant radical labor movement to overthrow, either peacefully or violently, the capitalist system. Apart from divisive ethnic and religious diversity, working-class consciousness was also hampered by the widespread belief in and hope for upward social mobility, a dream shared by virtually all Americans. Although very few individuals rose from rags to riches—Carnegie was a spectacular exception—modest gains were registered. The children of immigrants were often more skilled and enjoyed better housing than their parents, and their children were apt to be better educated, to own property, and to climb a rung up the social ladder. The American dream was realized, not spectacularly, but in small increments over generations, and these gains were sufficient to keep the hopes of all alive. Americans were also extremely mobile, and their frequent moves were made in anticipation of a better life.

The American political system also served to mute working-class consciousness. With universal male suffrage (blacks voted in large numbers in the South from the 1860s to the 1890s), most workers had the vote and thus were courted by the major parties. Although both the Republicans and Democrats had elitist leaders, they paid sufficient attention to labor to discourage the growth of labor or socialist parties. For example, both parties stressed that their opposite views of the TARIFF ISSUE would benefit workers and their families. The labor vote divided between the two major parties and was further subdivided into ethnic and religious groups with little love for each other. Moreover, there was no solidarity between rural and urban laborers. Attempts to build a farmer-laborer political alliance failed most spectacularly in the 1896 presidential campaign of WILLIAM JENNINGS BRYAN. Workers felt more comfortable with WILLIAM MCKINLEY's promises of industrial prosperity with sound money and protection than Bryan's promise of farm relief through inflation.

Further reading: Stephan Thernstrom, *Poverty and Progress: Social Mobility in a Nineteenth Century City* (Cambridge: Harvard University Press, 1964); Stephan

Thernstrom, *The Other Bostonians: Poverty and Progress in the American Metropolis, 1880–1970* (Cambridge, Mass.: Harvard University Press, 1973).

Clemens, Samuel Langhorne

See Twain, Mark

Cleveland, Grover (1837–1908)

Grover Cleveland, a two-term president of the United States, was born in Caldwell, New Jersey, on March 18, 1837. He was the fifth of nine children born to Richard Falley Cleveland, a Presbyterian minister, and Ann Neal. Cleveland had only a rudimentary formal education. The death of his father in 1853 removed any hope Cleveland may have had of attending college. In 1855 he settled in Buffalo, New York, where he studied law and joined the DEMOCRATIC PARTY. He was admitted to the New York bar in 1859. Cleveland remained a bachelor until June 1886, when he married Frances Folsom in the Blue Room of the White House. They had five children.

In public life Cleveland was noted for his honesty and frugality. In 1863 he became the assistant district attorney for Erie County, New York, and in 1871 was elected sheriff. Between terms in public office, Cleveland became one of the most successful private attorneys in Buffalo. His meteoric rise to the presidency began in 1881 when he was elected mayor of Buffalo with the support of a coalition of Democrats, reform-minded Republicans, and independents. As mayor, Cleveland stopped an attempt to defraud the city of $200,000 on a street-cleaning contract and vetoed several bills passed by Buffalo's aldermen that he felt perpetuated political graft. Rising above partisan politics as mayor earned Cleveland both the nomination and election in 1882 as governor of New York.

Grover Cleveland *(Library of Congress)*

Cleveland brought to the governor's mansion the same dedication to "good government" and independence that he had shown as mayor of Buffalo. Most state governments at this time operated on the spoils system, whereby politicians in office gave government jobs to those members of their party who had assisted them in getting elected. However, Cleveland appointed people to office based not on their party affiliation but on their skills. As governor, Cleveland signed the first state CIVIL SERVICE REFORM law in America. He also liberally used his veto power on appropriations bills and often challenged TAMMANY HALL, New York City's Democratic machine.

In 1884 the Republicans nominated JAMES G. BLAINE of Maine for president. Political pundits of the day realized that the candidate who carried New York would win the election. At their 1884 national convention, the Democrats nominated Cleveland for president. In a bitterly fought campaign, Cleveland narrowly won New York, defeated Blaine by a count of 219 electoral votes to 182, and became the first Democratic president since the Civil War. As president, Cleveland extended the merit system (civil service reform) for federal employees, promoted a policy of tariff reduction, was an advocate of "sound money" principles, and used the presidential veto power to reject bills that he believed would drain the national treasury. By scrutinizing veterans pensions bills closely, he offended the powerful GRAND ARMY OF THE REPUBLIC (GAR) veterans organization.

Cleveland was renominated by the Democrats in 1888 but lost the election to BENJAMIN HARRISON. Although Cleveland led Harrison in the popular vote 5,540,050 to 5,444,337, Harrison carried the electoral college by a vote of 233 to 168. Clever exploitation of the TARIFF ISSUE, however, enabled Cleveland to defeat Harrison in the 1892 election and become the only president in American history to serve two nonconsecutive terms in office (1885–89, 1893–97).

Within four months of Cleveland's second inauguration a panic gripped Wall Street that plunged the nation into a severe depression. The nation's gold reserve, which had been dwindling as a result of the Sherman Silver Purchase Act of 1890, dropped below the $100-million mark just prior to the panic, and after the onset of the panic it fell rapidly to $80 million by the end of 1893, threatening to drive the United States from the gold standard. Cleveland believed that the cause of this financial crisis was fear of inflation caused by agitation over Free Silver. He was firmly opposed to any schemes of currency inflation and called for the repeal of the Sherman Act, which obligated the government to purchase 4.5 million ounces of silver monthly that could be redeemed in gold. In 1893 the law was repealed as several Republicans and northeastern Democrats sided with the president. Cleveland's campaign against that act alienated southern and western Democrats. They were further alienated by bond sales in 1894 and 1895 to bankers at exorbitant rates to shore up the gold reserve, which fell as low as $41 million in early 1895. Cleveland saved the gold standard but at an enormous political cost.

Conflicts between business and labor also marked Cleveland's second administration. During the PULLMAN STRIKE (1894) the American Railway Union, led by Eugene V. Debs, protested a cut in wages at the Pullman Palace Car Company, called for a boycott of Pullman cars, and paralyzed the major midwestern rail lines. In response to the crisis, Cleveland broke the strike by deploying federal troops on the pretext that the strikers had impeded the delivery of the U.S. mail.

In foreign affairs, Cleveland steadfastly refused to aid rebel movements in HAWAII and CUBA. In 1895 he invoked the Monroe Doctrine to force an arbitrated settlement of a boundary dispute between British Guiana and Venezuela. The dispute was settled a year later by an arbitration commission.

Cleveland's stubborn independence led to his repudiation by the Democratic Party. In 1896 it embraced inflation, nominated WILLIAM J. BRYAN for president, and went down in defeat. Cleveland retired from public office to Princeton, New Jersey, where he died on June 24, 1908.

See also CURRENCY ISSUE; FREE-SILVER MOVEMENT.

Further reading: J. Rogers Hollingsworth, *The Whirligig of Politics: The Democracy of Cleveland and Bryan* (Chicago: University of Chicago Press, 1963); Horace Samuel Merrill, *Bourbon Leader: Grover Cleveland and the Democratic Party* (Boston: Little, Brown, 1957); Allan Nevins, *Grover Cleveland: A Study in Courage* (New York: Dodd, Mead, 1932); Richard Welch, *The Presidencies of Grover Cleveland* (Lawrence: University of Kansas Press, 1988).

— Phillip Papas

Cody, William Frederick (Buffalo Bill) (1846–1917)

William Cody, scout and showman, was born in Scott County, Iowa, on February 26, 1846, but in 1854 his family moved to the vicinity of Fort Leavenworth, Kansas. His schooling was sporadic at best, and after his father died in 1857 he worked as a messenger and as a teamster, joined the Pikes Peak gold rush to Colorado in 1859, turned to trapping, returned to Kansas broke in 1860, and then rode for the Pony Express. When the Civil War began he joined the antislavery guerrillas called Jayhawkers, and in 1863 the Ninth Kansas Cavalry employed him as a scout in its campaigns against the Kiowa and Comanche. Cody then volunteered for the Seventh Kansas Cavalry in early 1864 and soldiered in Tennessee, Missouri, Arkansas, and Kansas. After the Civil War Cody married Louisa Frederici in St. Louis in 1866 and then returned to Kansas. From 1867 to 1868 he earned the nickname of Buffalo Bill by supplying the construction gang of the Kansas & Pacific Railroad with the meat of 12 buffalo a day. He then returned to scouting, again as a civilian employee, for the Fifth Cavalry of the U.S. Army in campaigns against the Plains Indians.

Cody's life took a melodramatic twist in 1869 after an interview with Ned Buntline, the pseudonym of dime novelist Edward Z. C. Judson. Buntline, who never let the facts get in the way of an adventurous tale, wrote *Buffalo Bill: King of the Border Men,* which bore no resemblance to Cody's experiences but made him a celebrity. Exploiting the popularity of the Buffalo Bill he created, Buntline wrote the play *Scouts of the Prairies,* which opened in Chicago in December 1872 with Cody playing himself. Over the next decade until the 1882–83 season, Cody was on the stage playing himself in dramas that mingled facts and fiction. Cody continued to scout and risked his life on the frontier in mild weather and then acted heroic on urban stages in winters. For bravery in an April 1872 battle with Indians, Congress awarded him the Medal of Honor (rescinded in 1916, since Cody was a civilian employee and that medal is intended for military personnel), and in July 1876 he killed Yellow Hand, the son of a Cheyenne chief, in a celebrated duel that he subsequently reenacted countless times as he toured the country. His theatrical career enabled Cody to acquire a substantial ranch in Nebraska, but his career as a scout led him to move to Wyoming. In 1894 he served as a guide for a fossil-gathering expedition of Professor OTHNIEL C. MARSH in the Big Horn Basin. Cody was attracted to that area and received a substantial grant of land from Wyoming on which he developed an even more celebrated ranch.

In 1883 Cody began touring with the "Buffalo Bill Wild West Show" and continued to do so until 1912. The show re-created exciting scenes like an Indian raid on a stagecoach, celebrated the daring of Pony Express riders, and exhibited skillful riders, ropers, and marksmen. Cody himself was an expert horseman and a great shot, but the most famous marksman in the show was a woman named Annie Oakley. And Cody's most famous celebrity

W. F. (Buffalo Bill) Cody shown standing sixth man from the left *(Library of Congress)*

was SITTING BULL, who toured with the show in 1886, just 10 years after he and the Sioux wiped out GEORGE ARMSTRONG CUSTER and his command at Little Big Horn. The Wild West Show toured Europe with great success, and it was a hit at the Chicago WORLD'S COLUMBIAN EXPOSITION in 1893. The show created and perpetuated myths about the West in general and about Buffalo Bill in particular, and it had an incalculable influence on how Americans have perceived cowboys and Indians and the settlement of the West. Cody died in Denver, Colorado, on January 10, 1917.

Further reading: Sarah J. Blackstone, *Buckskins, Bullets, and Business: A History of Buffalo Bill's Wild West* (Westport, Conn.: Brenchwood Press, 1986); Don Russell, *The Lives and Legends of Buffalo Bill* (Norman: University of Oklahoma Press, 1960).

Coeur d'Alene miners' strike (1892)

The primary cause of the Coeur d'Alene miners' strike was technological change. Silver and lead mine operators in the Coeur d'Alene district of northern Idaho began installing steam-powered drilling machines in their mines. The new machines increased the number of low-skilled jobs such as shovelers while eliminating the jobs of highly skilled hand-drill miners. In contrast with other American labor unions that insisted on a wage differential based upon skill, the strong labor movement in the area reacted to technological displacement by winning a standard wage, the rate paid skilled miners, for all underground employees.

The uniform wage removed the cost efficiencies the operators hoped to gain by replacing their skilled men, and in an industry suffering from falling prices, labor costs were an important issue. Not surprisingly, the operators decided to destroy the union and its uniform wage scale. In 1891 they organized the Mine Owners Protective Association to ensure a united front against labor. The Protective Association hired the Pinkerton Detective Agency to infiltrate the union.

As the PINKERTONS gathered inside information, the operators ceased all mining in the region in January 1892. Although it was a ploy to force lower railroad rates, the shutdown had the additional effect of depriving the mine workers of an income, thus weakening their ability to resist employer aggression. On March 18 the mine owners announced that since the railroads had granted them rate relief, they would reopen the mines on the first of April. But they also announced a new wage scale that would be based upon skill. The union rejected the new wage scale and management responded by stating that the mines would remain closed until June.

But within a few days of this announcement, the operators began importing strikebreakers. Confrontation between union members and the strikebreakers and their heavily armed guards escalated on July 11 with a five-hour firefight at the Frisco mine that ended with the strikers dynamiting the processing mill. In another gunfight at a nearby mine five men were killed. Later that day a small army of armed strikers gained control of a third mine and threatened to destroy it if the strikebreakers were not fired.

The violence prompted Governor Norman Willey to order the National Guard into the region and to request and receive additional help from the federal government. Martial law was declared in the region, and the military force pursued a decidedly promanagement course. It removed local officials who were sympathetic to the strikers, arrested more than 300 union men and placed them in unsanitary "bull pens," closed down the union commissary, and protected the imported strikebreakers. The governor finally lifted martial law on November 19 when the strike was broken.

The strike's failure, however, inspired the union movement among the hard-rock miners. In May 1893 representatives from the broken union attended a meeting with delegates from other unions in the Rocky Mountain region to form the Western Federation of Miners, which would recruit more than 200,000 members by the turn of the century.

Further reading: Robert W. Smith, *The Coeur d'Alene Mining War of 1892* (Corvallis: Oregon State University, 1963).

— Harold W. Aurand

colleges See education, higher

communications

By 1870 most American communities were in instant touch with each other by telegraph, and as RAILROADS expanded during the Gilded Age people and products could move from one corner of the nation to another in days. A generation earlier—prior to the revolution in communications—months were required to send messages, goods, or travel across the nation. The economic effects of cheap and fast communication were profound. Local and regional markets gave way to a national market (indeed, a world market for growers of wheat). Manufacturers secured their raw materials from far and wide and, if anything, distributed their less bulky and more valuable products even further. Orders could be placed instantly, delivered speedily, and paid for promptly, thus providing a quicker return on capital invested than in times past. The social effects of the communications revolution echoed the economic effects. It made possible the two great population shifts in the Gilded Age: the settlement of the West and the growth of huge cities. It also helped reduce provincialism in America by binding its regions closer together with wire and rails.

The growth of a nationwide rail network was the key factor in the rapid movement of goods and people. In 1870 there were 53,000 miles of railroad track (the transcontinental railroad had been completed the year before), and by 1900 trackage had almost multiplied four times to 193,000 miles. Railroads also made possible the vast improvement in mail service in two ways. They not only moved the mail much more quickly than in the past, but also gave rise in the 1860s to the railway post office: mail cars on passenger trains, where the mail was sorted while moving down the track. Montgomery Blair, Lincoln's postmaster general, not only authorized the first railway post office but also home delivery in cities and a money-order system. In addition, in 1879 Congress aided rural Americans and mail-order houses when it provided that packages of up to four pounds could be mailed throughout the country at the flat rate of one cent an ounce. These innovations all had their greatest impact in the Gilded Age. The 468 million postage stamps sold in 1870 increased to almost 4 billion in 1900, indicating a dramatic increase in personal and business letters, which exerted a powerful cultural, social, and economic centripetal force.

The first practical telegraph line (from Washington to Baltimore) that went into operation in 1844 was owned by the federal government, but by 1847 the government had decided not to provide telegraph service as it did mail service and sold the line to private interests. Initially the telegraph industry was chaotic with numerous companies, but by 1870 the Western Union Telegraph Company consolidated over 90 percent of the business into one system that it continued to expand. In 1870 it had 3,972 offices and 112,000 miles of wire; by 1900 these had grown to 22,000 offices and 933,000 miles of wire. The telegraph was of importance to business in general, especially after the invention of the stock ticker in 1866, and of great value to newspapers. It led to the establishment of the New York Associated Press, which transmitted news items to subscribers throughout the country over the Western Union wires. At times during the Gilded Age, Western Union's position as the sole transmitter of business and general news caused alarm and led to calls for a postal telegraph system as an alternative to the Western Union monopoly. Postmaster Generals John A. J. Creswell in the 1870s and John Wanamaker in the 1890s advocated the postal telegraph, but nothing came of their efforts.

ALEXANDER GRAHAM BELL's telephone made a great impression when demonstrated at the PHILADELPHIA CENTENNIAL EXPOSITION in 1876, but its significant impact awaited the widespread distribution of telephones in operation. Although in 1878 President RUTHERFORD B. HAYES had a telephone in the White House that connected with one in the Treasury Department, the White House's nerve center was not a switchboard but its telegraph office, and it would remain so until the 20th century. Telephones, however, did proliferate until there were 1.4 million in 1900 (one for every 54 Americans), making 7.7 million local calls but only 193,000 toll calls daily. Long-distance calls were limited in the Gilded Age. Service between New York and Chicago was instituted in 1892, but transcontinental service between New York and San Francisco was not available until 1915. Among businesses, newspapers were quick to utilize the telephone. The telephone was on its way to becoming the "nervous system" of the 20th-century metropolis—the conqueror of time, space, and solitude, and an instrument used to bring the human family into closer touch.

Further reading: Robert V. Bruce, *Bell: Alexander Graham Bell and the Conquest of Solitude* (Boston: Little, Brown, 1973); Wayne E. Fuller, *The American Mail: Enlarger of the Common Life* (Chicago: University of Chicago Press, 1972); Paul Israel, *From Machine Shop to Industrial Laboratory: Telegraphy and the Changing Context of American Invention, 1830–1920* (Baltimore: Johns Hopkins University Press, 1992).

Compromise of 1877

See presidential campaigns

Comstock, Anthony (1844–1915)

Anthony Constock, the zealous guardian of public morals, was born on March 7, 1844, in New Canaan, Connecticut, the son of Polly Lockwood Comstock, who died when he was 10 years old, and Thomas Anthony Comstock, a farmer and sawmill owner. Anthony Comstock was raised in a strict household of limited financial means, attended Wykoff's Academy in New Canaan, and spent one year in high school in New Britain, Connecticut, before lack of funds forced him to leave in 1861. He worked as a grocer's clerk for the next two years, and when an older brother died in the Battle of Gettysburg, he volunteered to take his place in the 17th Connecticut Volunteer Infantry, where he served until 1865. After his discharge, he returned to his grocery-store job, traveled briefly in New England and the South, and around 1871 moved to New York City, where he took a job as a porter in a commission house.

Always concerned about public morals, Comstock was deeply distressed by the dissolute life he found in the city and by the government's failure to control it. In 1873 he initiated a personal crusade against pornography and, with the support of such prominent New York citizens as J. PIERPONT MORGAN, created a committee of the Young Men's Christian Association (YMCA), of which he was an active member, to combat it. So fierce were his efforts that some members of the YMCA accused him of entrapment, and he called on his supporters to help organize an independent New York branch of the London Society for the Suppression of Vice. As the secretary and main agent of the society, unpaid until about 1907, he devoted himself full time to social reform. That year he was made a special agent of the U.S. Post Office Department, which authorized him to cull the mail for improper material, and his organization lobbied CONGRESS successfully to pass a law against sending obscene material through the mails. By the end of his life, he boasted that the New York Society for the Suppression of Vice had been responsible for the arrest of 3,670 criminals and the destruction of 160 tons of obscene literature and pictures.

Although he was chiefly known for his campaign against what he considered obscene literature and art, Comstock also opposed abortion, birth control, gambling, fraudulent banking schemes, and medical quackery, and he inveighed against popular romances and adventure books, which he called "vampire literature" and believed led young readers into sin. He wrote *Frauds Exposed* (1880), reporting on his crusade against the use of the mail to promote swindles and immoral social practices, and *Gambling Outrages* (1887), about the pernicious influence of horse racing.

In both he defended his ruthless and often devious methods of trapping and persecuting the evildoers he perceived as corrupting society. His efforts at suppressing George Bernard Shaw's 1905 play *Mrs. Warren's Profession,* a sympathetic presentation of prostitution, led that playwright to coin the term "comstockery," which entered the language as a synonym for narrow-minded prudery and moralistic censorship. Comstock died on September 21, 1915.

Further reading: Nicola Beisel, *Imperiled Innocents: Anthony Comstock and Family Reproduction in Victorian America* (Princeton: Princeton University Press, 1997);

Heywood Broun and Margaret Leech, *Anthony Comstock: Roundsman of the Lord* (New York: A. C. Boni, 1927); Paul S. Boyer, *Purity in Print: The Vice-Society Movement and Book Censorships in America* (New York: Scribner 1968); ———. *Urban Masses and Moral Order in America, 1820–1920* (Cambridge, Mass.: Harvard University Press, 1978).

— Dennis Wepman

Congress

In the division of power among Congress, the president, and the SUPREME COURT, Congress had the largest share throughout the late 19th century. The ebb and flow of power within the federal government is the product of the times, personalities, and traditions. The Civil War (1861–65) required President Abraham Lincoln to enhance the power of the executive, but the policies and behavior of his inept successor Andrew Johnson (1865–69) eroded presidential prestige and enabled Congress to dominate the Reconstruction process. By 1870, although President Ulysses S. Grant was very popular, Congress had reoccupied its traditional position as the maker of laws and the president was, once again, primarily the administrator of those laws. Presidents did address problems and call for legislation in their annual messages to Congress, but Congress responded to those pleas in its own way or not at all.

Congressional power, in large part, depended on congressional dominance of the political process. Presidents, presidential nominees, and national committees were only nominally at the head of their political parties. The national parties were loose alliances of highly organized state and local parties that were, for the most part, firmly in control of senators and congressmen. In playing their dual roles as legislators and party leaders, they tended to emphasize organization rather than issues. To staff their political machines they relied on civil servants (postmasters, customhouse officers, internal revenue collectors, and so on) in their states and districts. Civil service appointments, nominally in the hands of the president and heads of departments, were actually made—especially outside Washington—on the recommendation of senators and representatives. CIVIL SERVICE REFORM was anathema to virtually all of them, since appointments on the basis of competitive examinations open to all would result in a politically neutral civil service and destroy their machines.

The outstanding political leaders of the late 19th century were often found in Congress but were rarely identified with a cause or a principle. The most prominent Republican of that era was not a president, but was JAMES G. BLAINE, who spent 20 years in Congress, was nominated for the presidency (and lost), and was a two-time secretary of state. Blaine actually did embrace some issues (protective tariff, Pan-Americanism, IMPERIALISM), but he was idolized by Republican regulars as a party organization man. Most members of the House of Representatives served only a few two-year terms before moving on to the Senate, like ROSCOE CONKLING, or to a governorship, like RUTHERFORD B. HAYES. Senators, in contrast, served for much longer periods because they were elected for six-year terms by state legislatures, which as heads of state parties they dominated. Conkling, a Republican senator from New York (1867–81), was perhaps the most prominent member of the Senate in the 1870s, but he is identified with no issue, bill, or act of Congress and is remembered for resigning the Senate in a petulant rage after being denied the patronage of the New York customhouse. Conkling is an extreme example, but virtually all senators and representatives paid close attention to patronage matters.

Organization remained important, but the trend in the 1880s and especially in the 1890s was toward the embracing of issues. Rapid industrial and urban growth and economic depressions spawned problems and pressures that could not be ignored. In addition, civil service reform legislation (1883) reduced the patronage and dried up the flow of cash from civil servants into party coffers. At the same time, industrialists increased their contributions and, as a consequence, their influence in politics. Senator Nelson Aldrich, a Rhode Island Republican who served from 1881 to 1911, championed the interests of big business in general and the protective tariff in particular while a loan from the American Sugar Refining Company enabled him to build his personal fortune. Along with Aldrich, Representative WILLIAM MCKINLEY was a major influence on the 1890 MCKINLEY TARIFF, and although the latter's identification with that measure led to an initial defeat, it also led to his ultimate nomination and election as president in 1896. On the other hand, the plight of America's farmers led WILLIAM JENNINGS BRYAN, who in the 1890s served briefly in the House, to advocate FREE SILVER, which in 1896 secured for him the Democratic nomination for the presidency.

Congress, while moving to embrace issues in the 1880s and 1890s, was not particularly influenced by the presidency. Congress legislated but did so under pressure from constituents. Presidents played little or no role in formulating, and at times opposed, major legislation. Responding to demands for currency expansion, Congress in 1874 passed a mildly inflationary bill, which President Grant vetoed. In 1878 Congress passed the BLAND-ALLISON ACT—providing for the coinage of 2 million to 4 million silver dollars monthly—over Hayes's veto. Under the lash of public opinion, Congress adopted the 1883 PENDLETON ACT, which was written by Dorman B. Eaton of the New York Civil Service Reform Association. Although he did not like it, President CHESTER A. ARTHUR felt compelled to sign it into law. President GROVER CLEVELAND approved the Interstate Commerce Act (1887) but had nothing to do with either its form or its passage. After the Supreme Court declared state regulation of interstate commerce unconstitutional, public opinion again forced Congress to act.

Congress, reflecting local business interests, all but ignored presidential pleas when constructing tariff legislation. Arthur's call for a 20 percent reduction resulted in minor reductions in the Mongrel Tariff (1883), and Cleveland's calls for reductions were either ignored (Mills Bill, 1888) or decimated (Wilson-Gorman Tariff, 1894). The reciprocity feature of the 1890 McKinley Tariff reflected Secretary of State Blaine's views, but its high rates and the even greater protectionism of the 1897 Dingley Tariff were the creations of Congress.

By 1900 Congress remained the paramount branch of the federal government, but it was more disciplined than in 1870, and an economic crisis and a war in the 1890s had by 1900 enhanced the power of the presidency. Speaker of the House THOMAS B. REED (1889–91, 1895–99) forced the adoption of rules that expedited legislation, and the Senate by the late 1890s was led by Aldrich and a few other long-term Republican cohorts. But while Congress became more focused, the modern presidency, exploiting issues and rallying public opinion, began to emerge with William McKinley and would flower with Theodore Roosevelt and other 20th-century presidents who would dominate Congress.

Further reading: George B. Galloway, *History of the House of Representatives,* 2d. rev. ed. (New York: Crowell, 1976); Ronald M. Peters Jr., *The American Speakership: The Office in Historical Perspective* (Baltimore: Johns Hopkins Press, 1990); David J. Rothman, *Politics and Power: The United States Senate, 1869–1901* (Cambridge: Harvard University Press, 1966).

Conkling, Roscoe (1829–1888)

Although he served in both houses of Congress, Roscoe Conkling's renown is not as a legislator but as the quintessential spoilsman of the Gilded Age, the political boss of New York. Born in Albany, New York, on October 30, 1829, Conkling was the son of Alfred Conkling, a federal district judge (1825–52) and minister to Mexico (1852–53). Roscoe Conkling studied law in Utica, New York, passed the bar examination in 1850, entered politics as a Whig, joined the Republicans with the demise of the Whig Party, and became mayor of Utica. In 1858 Conkling was elected to CONGRESS, serving in the House (1859–63, 1865–67) and the Senate (1867–81).

Although regarded as a leader of the Senate during the 1870s, Conkling is not associated with any acts of Congress or even bills before it. Handsome, vain, and arrogant, he was a skilled debater and an eloquent orator, but he was more inspired by politics than by issues. His speech opposing the Legal Tender Act of 1862 (Conkling consistently opposed currency inflation) was exceptional; the speeches his auditors remembered to their dying day, and which are still quoted, were made at political conventions. At the 1877 New York State Republican Convention, for example, Conkling vehemently attacked the editor and civil service reformer George William Curtis, lecturing him "that parties are not built up by deportment, or by ladies' magazines, or gush" and sneering that "when Dr. Johnson defined patriotism as the last refuge of a scoundrel, he was unconscious of the then undeveloped capabilities and uses of the word reform."

Conkling was infuriated with Curtis, reformers, and especially President RUTHERFORD B. HAYES because they threatened his control of the New York Republican Party, which was based on his control of the New York customhouse, post office, and other federal patronage plums awarded him by President Ulysses S. Grant, with whom Conkling was closely allied. In 1877 Hayes had not only banned political assessments of civil servants and ordered them to cease their management of political conventions and campaigns, but he had also moved to fire Conkling's lieutenant, CHESTER A. ARTHUR, as head of the New York customhouse. Conkling fought back, arguing "senatorial courtesy" (the established practice of allowing senators to designate appointees to field offices in their states), and for a time he prevented Senate confirmation of a successor to Arthur, but Hayes ultimately prevailed and, to Conkling's chagrin, made the customhouse a showcase for CIVIL SERVICE REFORM.

Conkling, however, hoped to regain control of the customhouse with the next administration. He and fellow STALWARTS worked mightily to secure Grant's nomination for a third term in 1880 (Conkling's nominating speech was perhaps the greatest of his career) but failed. Although disappointed with the Republican nominee, JAMES A. GARFIELD (and not at all happy that Arthur accepted the second place on the ticket), Conkling and his followers, after initially sitting on their hands, campaigned and Garfield triumphed. The Stalwarts were activated by what they took to be the promise of patronage—specifically the New York customhouse—but President Garfield awarded the customhouse to a lieutenant of Conkling's arch enemy, JAMES G. BLAINE. Conkling once again appealed to senatorial courtesy and once again went down to defeat. He resigned his seat, expecting the New York state legislature to reelect and vindicate him, but it failed to do so.

Out of politics and practicing law in New York City, Conkling ironically had a greater influence on policy (as distinct from politics) than he had had as a senator. In 1882 he argued before the SUPREME COURT that the DUE PRO-

CESS CLAUSE should apply to corporations as well as to individuals, an interpretation the Court subsequently adopted. Conkling died in New York City on April 18, 1888.

Further reading: David M. Jordan, *Roscoe Conkling of New York: Voice in the Senate* (Ithaca, N.Y.: Cornell University Press, 1971).

conservation

The American conservation movement from 1870 to 1900 is marked by several significant federally sponsored acts, including the congressional establishment of the first national park, Yellowstone National Park, in 1872; the founding of the National Forest Reserve program in 1891; and the creation of government offices to oversee natural resources. For the first time in American history, federal legislation protected wildlife by establishing refuges and encouraged the careful management of natural resources.

Two sometimes conflicting goals defined conservation efforts at the end of the 19th century: preservation and conservation. Economic growth following the Civil War and the continuing westward expansion stripped the land of forests and wildlife. The rapid depletion of natural resources, as well as a belief in the sanctity of nature, inspired preservationists like JOHN MUIR to call on policy makers to preserve wilderness for its own sake. Conservationists, influenced by utilitarian ideas, recognized the economic incentives in successfully managing the environment, specifically timber resources, as they moved to maximize yield and profit. During this time, scenic tourism, outdoor activities such as hiking and bird watching, and landscape architecture grew in popularity as Americans embraced nature and both the conservation and preservation movements.

CONGRESS established initial federal stewardship positions under either the Department of Agriculture or the Department of the Interior. The Interior Department oversaw the U.S. GEOLOGICAL SURVEY, which was established in 1879. At the state level, in 1885 New York created the Adirondack Forest Preserve and the New York State Reservation at Niagara Falls. Capitalizing on tourism at Niagara Falls, New York retained the services of noted landscape architects Frederick Law Olmsted (1822–1903) and Calvert Vaux (1824–95) to beautify the surrounding area to draw more visitors. In 1892 New York created Adirondack Park, amending its constitution in 1894 to ban logging activities there, which was a victory for preservationists.

The federal push to manage logging and protect forests started in earnest in the late 1880s. In 1886 Congress established the Division of Forestry in the Department of Agriculture, the forerunner of the U.S. Forest Service.

Congress then passed the Forest Reserve Act in 1891, which allowed the president to create forest reserves, a precursor of the national forest system. President BENJAMIN HARRISON immediately took advantage of this legislation, setting aside land in Wyoming for reserves. In 1896 the American Academy of Sciences established a committee on forests, calling for a scientific forest management policy to manage timber resources, a shift from preservation goals. In response, Congress passed a forest management act in 1897, also known as the Organic Act, that designated forest reserves as resources for timber, mining, and grazing. In 1898 Gifford Pinchot (1865–1946), who headed the Academy of Sciences committee on forests, was appointed chief of the Division of Forestry in the Department of Agriculture. Pinchot had studied forestry in Europe, where the stress was on management principles rather than preservation, and he focused on bringing together public-interest and forest-industry groups as he built support for the academy's ideas about scientific forest management. Pinchot would eventually clash with John Muir over the issue of grazing rights and conservation policy.

Strong initiatives to promote economic wildlife management also date to the late 1880s. Congress established the Division of Economic Ornithology and Mammalogy under the auspices of the Department of Agriculture in 1886; the office would later become the Bureau of Biological Survey. In 1889 Congress moved to protect Alaskan salmon fisheries, and in 1891 President Harrison created the first national wildlife refuge in Alaska: the Afognak Forest and Fish-Culture Reserve. In 1894 Congress banned hunting in Yellowstone National Park, thus setting a precedent for species preservation in national parks.

Other large national parks conceived during this era include California's Sequoia and Yosemite National Parks, which were established by Congress within days of each other in 1890. Mount Rainier National Park in the state of Washington was established in 1899. Several still-extant private organizations dedicated to preservation began in the 1890s, an indication of public support for an early form of environmentalism. In 1892 John Muir founded the Sierra Club and in 1896 the first Audubon Society was established in Massachusetts. At the close of the 19th century, the National Park movement had become a global phenomenon, with national parks established across the British Commonwealth, Mexico, and Russia.

Further reading: Stephen Fox, *John Muir and His Legacy: The American Conservation Movement* (Madison: University of Wisconsin Press, 1981); Roderick Frazier Nash, *American Environmentalism: Readings in Conservation History* (New York: McGraw-Hill, 1990); Dyan Zaslowsky and T. H. Watkins, *These American Lands:*

Parks, Wilderness, and the Public Lands (Washington, D.C.: Island Press, 1994).

— Scott Sendrow

contract labor

The term *contract labor* generally refers to alien workers imported under the Contract Labor Act of 1864. Designed to address the labor shortage accompanying the Civil War, the law permitted employers to recruit workers in Europe and advance them the cost of their transportation to America. The loan was secured by a lien, for not more than 12 months, against the immigrants' wages and all property that they might acquire in the United States. As a further inducement, the law exempted immigrants from the military draft.

Organizations such as the American Emigrant Company, capitalized at $1 million, quickly formed to recruit workers and supply them to manufacturers. Established immigrants also took advantage of the law, using their knowledge of English and American customs to exploit their compatriots after they arrived. Some of the most unscrupulous brought over entire families, placing the men in jobs, forcing the women into prostitution, and driving the children into the streets to shine shoes, beg, or steal for them.

Although contract laborers were relatively few in number, American workers blamed them for lowering wages and denounced them as strikebreakers. Both the National Labor Union and the KNIGHTS OF LABOR agitated for the repeal of the 1864 law, and their efforts finally resulted in the passage of the Foran Act in 1885. That act, however, contained a major loophole in that it forbade only prevoyage contracts. But even without this loophole, the act was difficult to enforce. The exact number of immigrant contract laborers is unknown, but the practice most likely continues to this day.

Convicts were another form of contract labored as governments sought to recoup the cost of keeping prisoners. In some instances prisons became factories manufacturing products for general consumption. Some states even leased their inmates to employers on a per diem basis. Organized labor protested that consumer goods produced by convicts represented unfair wage competition and demanded that it be stopped. Northern states began abolishing their convict labor systems in the 1880s, and the federal government stopped contracting its prisoners in 1887. By 1900 the system prevailed only in the South.

Further reading: H. S. Neli, "The Italian Padrone System in the United States," *Labor History* (1964): 153–167.

— Harold W. Aurand

Cooke, Jay See Volume V

corruption, political

In the popular imagination as well as in scholarly works, the Gilded Age is perceived as an especially debased period of American history. It was corrupt and its corrupters were often blatant, but it also abounded in active and vociferous reformers who publicized and at times exaggerated the shortcomings of the day. The Gilded Age, however, was not the only era in which politicians rigged elections, policymaking officials accepted bribes, administrators awarded padded contracts for public works and services, and civil servants extorted or stole money.

Prior to the adoption of the secret ballot in the 1890s, voters were frequently purchased in swing states like Indiana or marched to the polls on company time in Pennsylvania, where they voted as directed by their coal mine or steel mill boss. Lax registration procedures in cities enabled the Republican machine in Philadelphia, for example, or the Democratic machine in New York, to use "repeaters" who cast votes for fictitious names and for those long since dead. Voters were also "colonized" across state lines. Ballot boxes were "stuffed" with votes no one had cast legitimately. While some northern industrialists intimidated employees, southern white supremacists intimidated blacks. In the most violent and disgraceful election in American history they gained control of Mississippi in 1875 by threatening, beating, and murdering blacks to keep them from voting. By 1900 the secret ballot had reduced cheating at the polls, but southern blacks were totally disfranchised.

Throughout the country, however, most potential voters could vote and most votes were cast legitimately, but a close election could be determined by fraud or violence, and the four elections from 1876 to 1888 were close. Republican fraud prevailed over Democratic violence in the disputed presidential election of 1876, but it is impossible to determine who would have won if all enfranchised voters had been allowed to vote and their votes accurately counted. It is impossible to say whether or not zealous Republicans threw out too many Democratic votes to make up for intimidated black Republicans. In 1888 the successful Republican nominee BENJAMIN HARRISON thanked God for his victory, but his cynical campaign manager Matthew Quay observed that God had nothing to do with it, quipping that a number of men risked the penitentiary to put Harrison in the White House.

With the spectacular rise of industry in the late 19th century, businesspeople were anxious to curry favor with powerful politicians who were in a position to make or break a venture. Railroads, some of which were dependent on land grants and all of which were subject to some governmental regulation as public carriers, were especially active in influencing politicians, but so too were large-scale importers and distillers. These supplicants attempted to seduce power brokers using a variety of methods, ranging from flattery in mansions and on boats to investment opportunities, generous loans, exorbitant fees, and outright bribery. JAY GOULD and James Fisk of the Erie Railroad in 1868 bribed the New York state legislature with $1 million to legitimize the issuance of watered stock. The following year—after entertaining and temporarily duping President Ulysses S. Grant—they briefly cornered the gold market, sold short, made $11 million, and ruined many. During the Gilded Age, the Pennsylvania Railroad dominated the government of Pennsylvania, and the real capital of California reputedly was not Sacramento but the offices of the Southern Pacific Railroad.

Congressmen were also corrupted. Several accepted stock in the Credit Mobilier, the construction company controlled by insiders that made exorbitant profits in building the Union Pacific Railroad with federal funds. Speaker of the House JAMES G. BLAINE received $64,000 from the Union Pacific (which he was in a position to help) for some nearly worthless Little Rock & Fort Smith Railroad bonds, a payment that cost him the presidency. JAMES A. GARFIELD, however, gained the presidency despite having received a $329 Credit Mobilier dividend (he said it was a $300 loan) and a $5,000 fee from a paving firm that he helped secure a contract for Washington streets. That fee was chicken feed compared with Boss William M. Tweed's $1 million from the Erie Railroad for his legal services or the $5 million loan to Senator Nelson Aldrich—the major architect of Gilded Age tariff rates—from the American Sugar Refining Company, the major importer of the nation's most valuable import.

Garfield was not alone in making money from a government contract. The New York County Courthouse built by the TWEED RING for $12 million (three times what it should have cost) enriched insiders by padding contracts. Construction projects were especially lucrative for local politicians, and some like George W. Plunkitt of Tammany Hall differentiated between honest and dishonest graft. Plunkitt would have no part in outright stealing, but he saw no harm in profiting personally from the inside information politicians were often privy to. Urban bosses regularly awarded transportation franchises in exchange for hefty political contributions. The most spectacular example of padded contracts on the federal level were the STAR ROUTE FRAUDS. In the late 1870s contracts for mail service in remote corners of the West were fraudulently increased by approximately $2 million, and this money helped finance the 1880 Republican presidential campaign. Postal officials who perpetrated the star route frauds—and urban bosses who padded contracts and sold franchises—funneled most of the money they realized into political party organizations in an effort to perpetuate their power.

Civil servants involved in collecting taxes often took bribes. The New York customhouse was notorious in the

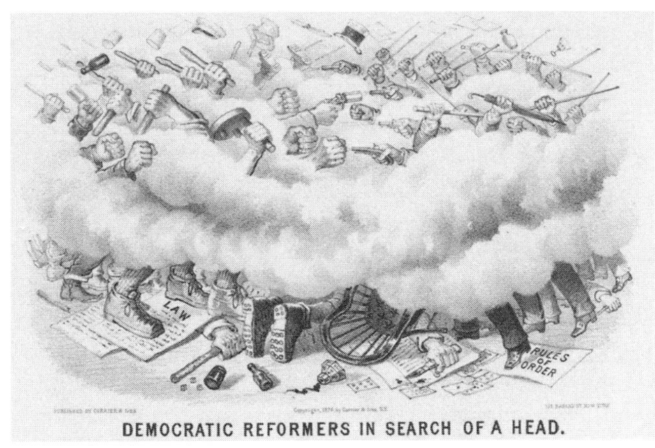

This cartoon is a parody on the strife and corruption within the New York Democratic Party *(Harper's Weekly)*

1870s among New Yorkers for taking advantage of importers, but non-New Yorkers claimed it allowed New York firms to skirt regulations and achieve an advantage over competing merchants in other cities with honest customs officials. In St. Louis a group of distillers and internal revenue agents with ties to Grant's personal secretary defrauded the government of large sums of money in a conspiracy known as the Whiskey Ring.

With the passage of the 1883 Pendleton Act, CIVIL SERVICE REFORM decreased blatant political corruption. As public officers became less partisan and more professional, and with the outlawing of political assessments, politicians depended less and less on civil servants (and what by hook or by crook they could realize from their positions) for funding campaigns. And as the public service became politically neutral, politicians turned instead to businessmen for contributions and became increasingly amenable to their demands, further blurring the line between a contribution and a bribe.

Further reading: Mark Wahlgren Summers, *The Era of Good Stealings* (New York: Oxford University Press, 1993).

Coxey's Army (1894)

In 1893 the United States experienced one of the greatest financial collapses in its history, and one of its results was Coxey's Army. The Panic of 1893 brought about the most severe economic depression the nation had yet experienced. All across the United States, businesses filed for bankruptcy, banks failed, factories and mines shut down, agricultural prices declined, and a large number of Americans were laid off from their jobs. The economic depression undermined the public's confidence in the economy and caused social unrest among the nation's unemployed. Several small groups or "armies" of the unemployed began to organize demonstrations and called on the government to take measures to relieve unemployment.

In 1894 Jacob S. Coxey, an Ohio businessman, social reformer, and Populist concerned about the families of unemployed Americans, began to advocate a vast program of public works financed by inflated currency to provide jobs for the unemployed. He demanded that CONGRESS authorize the federal government to print and distribute $500 million in paper money to state and local governments to hire unemployed workers for road construction projects. Individuals hired to work on government-sponsored construction projects would receive at least $1.50 a day in wages. In spring 1894, Coxey planned to gather a large group of unemployed workers and "send a petition to Washington with boots on." He envisioned an enormous grassroots march to the capital to promote his ideas.

On Easter Sunday, Coxey left Massillon, Ohio, with several hundred followers. The group became known as "Coxey's Army" and drew nationwide attention. Other "armies" sprang up about the country and headed for Washington hoping to persuade Congress to authorize federal programs that would provide work. Conservatives feared that the demonstrators would swell to more than 100,000 people and foment a revolution, but their fears were exaggerated. Of all the armies that set out for Washington, Coxey's Army was the only group to actually reach the nation's capital.

When Coxey's Army arrived in Washington on May Day, it numbered only 500 instead of the threatened 100,000. The marchers found armed police lining the streets and blocking the approaches to the Capitol. When Coxey and two others tried to reach the Capitol, the police clubbed and then arrested them for trespassing. Coxey's followers were dispersed by club-wielding police and detained in makeshift camps. Coxey was sentenced to 20 days in jail. The callous treatment of Coxey and his supporters convinced many unemployed Americans that the government had little interest in their plight. Although Coxey's Army and others like it were disbanded, public discontent over the government's response to the economic crisis remained. Ironically, the essence of Coxey's major idea was later implemented during the Great Depression of the 1930s.

See also CURRENCY ISSUE; PEOPLE'S PARTY.

Further reading: Carlos A. Schwantes, *Coxey's Army: An American Odyssey* (Lincoln: University of Nebraska Press, 1985).

— Phillip Papas

Crane, Stephen (1871–1900)

Realistic novelist Stephen Crane was born on November 1, 1871, in Newark, New Jersey, the 14th and last child of Jonathan Townley Crane, a Methodist minister and writer of religious books who died when the boy was eight years old, and Mary Helen Peck, a correspondent for religious newspapers. In 1882 his family settled in Asbury Park, New Jersey, where he attended Pennington Academy; he later went to the Hudson River Institute in Claverack, New York, a military academy, and spent a term each at Lafayette College in Pennsylvania and Syracuse University in New York. While in college he helped finance his education by selling articles to the Detroit *Free Press* and the *New York Tribune*, and in 1891 he left school for New York to make his living as a writer.

Crane spent the next few years struggling to support himself as a freelance reporter, placing occasional stories with the *Herald* and the *Tribune*, but his imaginative accounts of news events were seldom acceptable to editors. Living in the poorest neighborhoods, he became acquainted with city life at the bottom of the social and economic scale, and during this period he rewrote a novel he had sketched out while in college. Set in the New York slums, *Maggie: A Girl of the Streets* was too harshly realistic to find a publisher, and in 1893 Crane borrowed $700 to have it printed privately under the pseudonym Johnston Smith. It sold only 100 copies, but its powerful picture of the degradation of city life won the respect of several important writers, including WILLIAM DEAN HOWELLS, then the dean of American letters, and HAMLIN GARLAND.

Crane's novel *The Red Badge of Courage*, an account of a terrified young recruit's first experience of battle, was published with Howells's help in 1895. It established Crane's reputation as a writer of extraordinary psychological insight but earned him only $90. It did, however, win him many newspaper assignments. He traveled in the West and Mexico for a newspaper syndicate and, in addition to travel articles, wrote several distinguished short stories. In 1897 he was hired to report on the rebellion in CUBA and was sent to Greece to write about that country's war with Turkey. The next year he reported the SPANISH-AMERICAN WAR. In 1898, while battling an illness contracted in his strenuous travels as a correspondent, he married Cora Taylor, the madam of a brothel in Jacksonville, Florida.

Strongly influenced in his prose by the French naturalist writers, he was also affected by the poetry of EMILY DICKINSON, whom he was one of the first to appreciate. In 1895 he published *The Black Riders*, a volume of highly personal free verse viewed by many critics as a forerunner of imagism in American poetry. His collection *War is Kind* (1899) provided further inspiration for modernism in American verse. In 1899 Crane, now seriously ill, moved with his wife to England, where he came to know such literary figures as HENRY JAMES and Joseph Conrad. Deeply in debt, he frantically wrote potboilers during his last year but also produced some of his best work, including *The*

Monster and Other Stories (1899), an exploration of racism. His reputation as America's first major realist writer has continued to grow since his death at age 28 on June 5, 1900.

Further reading: John Berryman, *Stephen Crane,* rev. ed. (New York: Cooper Square Press, 2001); David Halliburton, *The Color of Sky: A Study of Stephen Grace* (Cambridge: Cambridge University Press, 1989).

— Dennis Wepman

Crazy Horse (Tashunca-uitco) (ca. 1840–1877)

A renowned Oglala Sioux warrior, Crazy Horse is best known for defeating General GEORGE ARMSTRONG CUSTER at the Battle of the Little Bighorn in 1876. Crazy Horse was born to an Oglala father and a Miniconjou mother near what is modern-day Rapid City, South Dakota. The warrior spent time with both the Oglala and Brulé Sioux Indian tribes, and he received his name, translated as His Horse is Crazy, from his father, who believed his son would grow into a great warrior.

Crazy Horse became a hunter and warrior at a young age and soon led raids against rival tribes and white settlers. In 1868 Crazy Horse, while still in his early 20s, earned his status of a "shirt-wearer," or head warrior, among the Oglala. (He would later lose this honor in 1870 after being shot by the jealous husband of a woman with whom he was romantically linked.) Crazy Horse rose to prominence during the War for the Bozeman Trail (1866–68), fighting alongside Oglala warrior RED CLOUD against the U.S. Army over the establishment of Fort Phil Kearny at the base of the Bighorn Mountains. The Sioux were successful in earning a stalemate against the army, which led to the 1868 Treaty of Fort Laramie that recognized the Black Hills and the Yellowstone River Basin as Oglala Lakota territory and established a Sioux reservation in South Dakota. Red Cloud accepted the treaty and peace, but Crazy Horse accepted neither and became the leader of the nontreaty Sioux, hostile both to rival tribes and white incursions.

Following the economic crisis stemming from the Panic of 1873, white settlers, who suspected that the Black Hills region of the Oglala's land was a potential source of gold, called on the federal government to purchase the area from the tribe. At the same time, the army wanted to establish a strategic base in the Black Hills to guard against Indian attacks, which led to General Custer's expedition into the Black Hills region in July 1874. When the expedition discovered gold, white prospectors rushed into the Black Hills. The U.S. government subsequently attempted to lease the Black Hills from the Oglala, but when the tribe declined, the government tried in the dead of winter to force all Oglala to a reservation out of the region. In 1876 troops attacked the Oglala who had not complied, beginning the SIOUX WAR of the Black Hills (1876–77). During the early stages of the war, the army did badly. Through his personal links, Crazy Horse brought together other Lakota as well as the Northern Cheyenne Nation and successfully defended the upper Rosebud portion of the Black Hills in the Battle of Rosebud Creek on June 17, 1876. Crazy Horse's subsequent charges on June 25, 1876, annihilated General Custer's command at the Battle of the Little Bighorn (Custer's Last Stand).

Although successful in ensuing battles, Crazy Horse and his forces surrendered on May 5, 1877, at Camp Robinson, Nebraska, brokering an agreement to establish a reservation for the Oglala Sioux. This arrangement failed to materialize, and General Crook, worried that Crazy Horse might escape to lead another uprising, ordered his imprisonment. In carrying out that order a soldier bayonetted and killed Crazy Horse on September 5, 1877, at Camp Robinson.

Further reading: Stephen E. Ambrose, *Crazy Horse and Custer: The Parallel Lives of Two American Warriors* (Garden City, N.Y.: Doubleday, 1975); Larry McMurtry, *Crazy Horse* (New York: Viking, 1999); Mari Sandoz, *Crazy Horse: The Strange Man of the Oglalas* (New York: Knopf, 1942).

— Scott Sendrow

Crime of '73 (1873)

Up to 1873, the United States had followed a monetary policy of BIMETALLISM, which recognized both gold and silver as the basis for the dollar. The government had coined silver at the ratio of 16 to one: there was 16 times as much silver in a silver dollar as there was gold in a gold dollar. The 16-to-one ratio, however, had undervalued silver ever since the 1849 California gold rush lowered the price of gold. Subsequently, silver-mine owners sold their product commercially rather than to the government for coins, virtually taking silver dollars out of circulation. Since the silver dollar had almost disappeared, several monetary experts urged Congress to stop the coinage of silver and place the United States on the gold standard.

The Coinage Act of 1873 demonetized silver and made the gold dollar the monetary standard for the nation. Ironically, just as the Coinage Act passed, the discovery of new silver mines in Nevada and other parts of the Far West increased the production of silver, thus leading to a decline in its price. In 1873 the United States also entered a period of economic depression. The American farmer was struck hardest as agricultural prices plummeted. Because of declining agricultural prices and the desire of western silver producers to see the demand for silver increase, farming and western silver interests joined together in demanding the "free" (unlimited) coinage of silver at the 16-to-one ratio. Farmers supported the FREE-SILVER MOVEMENT to increase the nation's money supply, which they believed would bring about the recovery of agricultural prices. Western silver-mine operators simply wanted the government to purchase their surpluses.

Free-silver advocates described the Coinage Act of 1873 as the Crime of '73. They insisted that the law was at the center of a conspiracy orchestrated by eastern creditors (bankers and financiers) to control the money supply and prevent price recovery. This conspiracy, it was said, intended to replace silver, which represented the "people's money," with gold, the currency of bankers and big business. Defenders of the Coinage Act argued that it was enacted in anticipation of a decline in silver prices because of the new discoveries made in the Far West. These discoveries had increased the silver supply by 20 percent. It was argued that if silver had not been demonetized, then bimetallism at the 16-to-one ratio would have caused a run on the nation's gold reserve and driven gold out of circulation.

Advocates of Free Silver urged the restoration of the "free and unlimited coinage" of silver at the 16-to-one ratio, but they had only limited success. The Coinage Act was partially repealed by the BLAND-ALLISON ACT (1878), which authorized the government to purchase, at market prices, not less than $2 million and not more than $4 million worth of silver monthly and mint it into silver dollars. It in turn was superseded by the Sherman Silver Purchase Act (1890, repealed 1893), which required the government to purchase 4.5 million ounces of silver monthly. Neither act drove the United States from the gold standard.

See also CURRENCY ISSUE.

Further reading: Walter T. K. Nugent, *Money and American Society, 1865–1880* (New York: The Free Press, 1968); Allen Weinstein, *Prelude to Populism: Origins of the Silver Issue, 1867–1878* (New Haven, Conn.: Yale University Press, 1970).

— Phillip Papas

Crummell, Alexander (1819–1898)

Alexander Crummell, missionary, educator, and Pan-African advocate, was the son of Boston Crummell, who had been kidnapped in West Africa and enslaved in New York. Boston declared himself free to his owner without any reprisals. After marrying Charity Hicks, a free woman, Boston established an oyster house at 6 Varick Street in Manhattan. It was at this location that *Freedom's Journal,* the nation's first black newspaper, was published in 1827. Alexander Crummell, who was born on March 3, 1819, attended the African Free School in Manhattan and then Noyes Academy in Canaan, New Hampshire, where a mob forced the integrated school to close. He transferred to Oneida Institute in Whitesboro, New York. Encouraged by Reverend Peter Williams, a cofounder of *Freedom's Journal,* Crummell applied for admission to the General Theological Seminary of the Protestant Episcopal Church but was rejected because he was black. Crummell, nevertheless, studied privately for the ministry and in 1844 was ordained a priest. He experienced poverty while shepherding small groups in Providence, Philadelphia, and New York and working in the antislavery movement. In 1847 he went to England to raise a building fund for the New York Church of the Messiah. Supported by British philanthropists, Crummell studied at Queens College, Cambridge University, graduating in 1853.

Unwilling to return to the United States and endure racism within the church, Crummell—who was influenced by Peter Williams's black nationalist ideology—emigrated to Liberia, where for nearly 20 years he worked as a missionary, educator, and a public moralist. A victim of Liberia's colorphobia politics (light-complexioned mulattoes dominated society), the dark-complexioned Crummell returned to the United States in 1872 and remained in Washington, D.C., until his death on September 10, 1898.

Crummell, stern and unyielding in his beliefs, was most passionate about uplifting the black race. Crummell noted in 1875, in "The Social Principle Among a People; and Its Bearing on Their Progress and Development," that black men needed to engage in a cooperative spirit to establish farms, businesses, and mechanical enterprises. He told them never to forget that they were colored men or to "give up all distinctive effort, as colored men, in schools, churches, associations and friendly societies." He eschewed agitation, which he viewed as mainly "wind and vanity." Instead, Crummell proposed that blacks needed to gain superiority to end racial prejudice. He argued that as their character rose, whites would forget that they were people of color. While he recognized that African Americans needed power, he believed that it came from character and that "character is the product of religion, intelligence, virtue, family order, superiority, wealth and the show of industrial forces. THESE ARE FORCES WHICH WE DO NOT POSSESS," he proclaimed.

Crummell was an early supporter of colonization programs, but he later became disdainful of African values and traditions, preferring the value system of upper-class New Englanders. Despite his own emigration to Liberia, Crummell in later years was critical of emigration schemes proposed by HENRY M. TURNER and others. Crummell believed that individuals had a responsibility to uplift the masses from ignorance and that salvation would come from their own resources rather than from either white philanthropists or an appeal to white guilt. He was proud of being a Negro and considered "colored," then popular among the elite (and which he had used earlier) as a "milk bastard term." Crummell organized the American Negro Academy in 1897 as an organization to advance the race through the leadership and contributions of "a talented tenth." While he did not wish to neglect industrial education, he argued that the race needed scholars and thinkers who were willing to use their intelligence "to transform and stimulate the souls of a race of a people." He noted that intelligent scholars must be inspired with "the notion of leadership and duty . . . for all true and lofty scholarship is weighted with the burdens and responsibilities of life and humanity." Crummell, an inspirational advocate of black self-reliance and a pioneer of Pan-Africanism, believed that the key to African-American leadership lay in a thorough grounding in the classics, social sciences, and liberal arts. After his death on September 10, 1898, the Academy attracted a who's who of black America throughout the first two decades of the 20th century.

Further reading: Wilson J. Moses, *Alexander Crummell: A Study of Civilization and Discontent* (New York: Oxford University Press, 1989); Gregory U. Rigsby, *Alexander Crummell: Pioneer in Nineteenth-Century Pan-African Thought* (New York: Greenwood Press, 1987).

— William Seraile

Cuba

Located 90 miles off the coast of Florida, Cuba was a colony of Spain that became the principal battlefield of the SPANISH-AMERICAN WAR. In the late 19th century Cuba twice attempted to throw off the yoke of Spanish domination. In 1868 a band of free whites and mulattoes touched off an insurrection, subsequently called the Ten Years' War, that would involve upwards of 12,000 combatants and eventually capture several large towns. The United States refused to intervene, considering the whole affair an internal problem of Spain.

But the insurrectionist cause had great sympathy among the American public that was translated into action. The rebels were aided by arms and by American soldiers of fortune known as filibusters, much to the annoyance of the Spanish authorities. In 1873 a former Confederate blockade runner, the *Virginius,* loaded with arms and filibusters, was captured by the Spanish. The governor of Santiago, Captain-General Juan Burriel, convened a court-martial that convicted the crew and passengers of piracy and sentenced them to death. When the United States learned that 53 people had been executed, the Grant administration demanded that Spain return the ship and its survivors to the United States, pay an indemnity, and punish Burriel. If such action were not taken within 12 days, the U.S. minister to Spain was instructed to close the legation and return home. One day after the deadline Spain agreed to the demands and paid an $80,000 indemnity. Spain delayed punishing Burriel for four years, by which time the general had passed away. The *VIRGINIUS* AFFAIR served to increase anti-Spanish feeling among Americans but did not lead to intervention.

The Ten Years' War ended in 1878, but another insurrection began in 1895. Spain responded by sending General Valeriano Weyler y Nicholau, a ruthless soldier of mixed Prussian and Spanish ancestry, who adopted a policy called *reconcentrado.* The plan involved herding the populace into fortified towns in order to prevent them from supplying aid to the rebels. Villagers were burned out of their homes and farms. The plan caused widespread starvation and disease as people lost their means of feeding themselves. The plan did little to abate the insurrection, but American sympathy for the rebels was progressively increased by the Cuban junta, a propaganda machine operated by revolutionary exiles that lobbied the American press and CONGRESS for Cuban independence. When the rebel leader General Máximo Gómez responded in kind and began burning the plantations of the rich Creoles, Cuba quickly descended into a hopeless cycle of violence. The chaos also threatened the nearly $50 million worth of American investments in the island, most of it in sugar plantations and railways. Although Congress passed resolutions in support of the rebels, President GROVER CLEVELAND maintained a strict noninterventionist policy regarding Cuba.

Matters boiled over in 1898 when a series of events triggered the Spanish-American War. On February 9, 1898, the *New York Journal* published the DE LÔME LETTER. The Spanish minister to the United States, Enrique Dupuy de Lôme, wrote the letter to an acquaintance in Havana. In the letter he described Cleveland's successor WILLIAM McKINLEY as "weak and a bidder for the admiration of the crowd." The furor over the letter forced de Lôme to resign. Two weeks later the battleship USS *Maine* was destroyed in Havana Harbor. When a naval court of inquiry determined that it had been sunk by a mine but failed to identify who perpetrated the deed, the press and public insisted on attributing the sinking to Spanish treachery. On April 19, 1898, Congress declared war on Spain but added the Teller Amendment, which pledged that the United States would not annex Cuba. Despite logistical mistakes, American troops landed in Cuba on June 22 and within four months had captured Santiago and forced the Spanish to surrender. The Americans suffered a minimal amount of battle casualties during the Cuban campaign, but nearly 5,000 died from tropical diseases.

As a result of the Teller Amendment and the 1898 Treaty of Paris with Spain, Cuba became independent. But the unsettled condition of the island and fears that a European power (especially Germany) might get a foothold there gave rise to second thoughts about annexation. Although the Teller Amendment prevented annexation, the Platt Amendment to the 1901 Army Appropriation Act (which the United States insisted Cuba incorporate into its constitution) gave the United States the right to intervene in Cuban affairs to preserve its "independence." Cuba remained a quasi protectorate of the United States until 1934, when it abandoned the Platt Amendment.

See also *MAINE*, REMEMBER THE; ROUGH RIDERS.

Further reading: Ivan Musicant, *Empire by Default: The Spanish-American War and the Dawn of the American Century* (New York: Henry Holt and Co., 1998); G. J. A. O'Toole, *The Spanish War: An American Epic, 1898* (New York: Norton, 1984).

— Timothy E. Vislocky

currency issue

The composition of the nation's currency was a major political issue of the late 19th century. BIMETALLISM (currency based on gold and silver) was federal monetary policy until 1873. The government coined silver at the ratio of 16-to-one; the silver dollar contained 16 times more silver than there was gold in a gold dollar. During the Civil War, however, the government printed $450 million in paper currency called "greenbacks," a fiat currency that was not backed by any specie. Greenbacks could not be redeemed in gold, and as their value declined they drove gold and silver out of circulation. In addition, national banks were allowed by the National Banking Act of 1863 to issue $300 million in notes redeemable in greenbacks, thus making these notes, in effect, equal to greenbacks.

The suspension of specie payments did not sit well with bankers and other creditors. Following the war, they called for the retirement of greenbacks and a resumption of specie payments. Such a policy would lead to deflation by keeping the value of the dollar—and thus interest rates and the value of debts owed to creditors—high. Debtor groups, especially in the cash-strapped South and West, pressured the government to further inflate the currency supply by placing more greenbacks into circulation. They believed the ensuing inflation (rise in prices and lowered interest rates) would make it easier to pay off their debts.

A major issue tied to the currency question was the constitutionality of the Legal Tender Act of 1862, which authorized the Treasury to issue the greenbacks. At the time it was argued that this measure was necessary to finance the Union war effort. Following the war, proponents of sound, or hard, money—a currency based on the gold standard—called for the resumption of specie payments. In 1866 Congress passed the Contraction Act, which initiated a policy of gradual reduction of the greenbacks in circulation. Debtors immediately attacked the law because it made their debts harder to pay off. Others blamed it for the worsening economic conditions of 1867. The constitutionality of the Legal Tender Act was finally taken up by the SUPREME COURT in a set of cases known collectively as the LEGAL TENDER CASES (1870–71). In *Hepburn v. Griswold* (1870), the Court decided that the greenbacks issued during the Civil War were not legal tender for debts incurred prior to the act's passage in 1862, but the Court quickly reversed the Hepburn decision in *Knox v. Lee* (1871), holding that greenbacks were valid legal tender for pre-as well as post-1862 debts. Although the Knox decision dealt hard-money advocates a serious setback, they would not allow themselves to be defeated.

In 1873 Congress enacted the Coinage Act, which effectively demonetized silver, making the gold dollar the monetary standard for the nation. The 16-to-one ratio had undervalued silver ever since the 1849 California gold rush lowered the price of gold. As a result, silver-mine operators sold their product commercially rather than to the government at a loss, virtually taking the silver dollar out of circulation. Since silver was being used for purposes other than coinage and the silver dollar had almost disappeared from circulation anyway, experts urged Congress to demonetize it. Two years after Congress demonetized silver, it enacted the Specie Resumption Act, authorizing the Treasury to resume, by January 1, 1879, the redemption of greenbacks in gold. As of that date the United States was back on the gold standard.

Reacting to the Specie Resumption Act, the advocates of "soft money" (greenbacks) conferred in Cleveland and Cincinnati, Ohio; held a convention in May 1876 in Indianapolis, Indiana; and organized a National Independent (Greenback) Party. These Greenbackers—farmers, labor reformers, and businessmen—called for the repeal of the Specie Resumption Act and nominated the 85-year-old philanthropist Peter Cooper for president. Cooper received only 80,000 votes, but the GREENBACK-LABOR PARTY was far more successful in the congressional elections of 1878, polling more than 1 million votes. In 1880 the party's presidential candidate General James B. Weaver of Iowa polled 300,000 votes. However, by the mid-1880s the Greenback Party began to disintegrate. As a consequence, Greenbackers joined with another group of currency inflationists, the advocates of Free Silver, to create a powerful political movement in late-19th-century America.

Shortly after Congress enacted the Coinage Act, new mines in Nevada and other parts of the Far West increased the production of silver and thus lowered its value. If the government had kept silver in circulation, the subsequent deflationary price spiral might not have occurred. Instead,

This cartoon depicts Senator John Sherman delivering silver "eggs" to Secretary of the Treasury John G. Carlisle, who will turn them into gold. *(New York Public Library)*

the nation entered a period of economic depression, with American farmers struck the hardest as agricultural prices declined. Because of falling farm prices and the desire of western silver producers to see demand for their product increase, debtor farmers and western silver-mining interests began to call for the remonetization of silver at the old ratio of 16-to-one. The removal of the silver dollar from circulation and the redemption of greenbacks were viewed as part of a larger scheme orchestrated by bankers and other financiers (chief supporters of the hard-money philosophy) to control the money supply and prevent price recovery.

In 1878 silverites won a partial victory when Congress passed the BLAND-ALLISON ACT authorizing a limited, but not free, coinage of silver. The law required the government to buy no less than $2 million or more than $4 million worth of silver monthly and then to mint it into silver dollars. The Sherman Silver Purchase Act of 1890 increased the amount of silver coinage in circulation by obligating the government to purchase 4.5 million ounces of silver monthly. The silver was to be paid for in Treasury notes of full legal-tender value that could be redeemed in "coin" at the discretion of the government. Treasury officials interpreted this provision as meaning redemption in gold, placing a great strain on the nation's gold reserve.

When the economic depression following the Panic of 1893 set in, hard-money advocates blamed the downturn on the Sherman Silver Purchase Act. President GROVER CLEVELAND, a hard-money advocate, called for and secured its repeal in 1893 with the support of several congressional Republicans and Democrats (mostly from the Northeast), thereby alienating the southern and western factions of both parties.

The calls for the free coinage of silver became more strident following the repeal of the Sherman Silver Purchase Act and set the stage for one of the most bitter and emotionally charged political contests in American history. Between 1894 and 1900 pro-silver literature flooded the nation. From William H. Harvey's *Coin's Financial School* (1894) and Ignatius Donnelly's *The American People's Money* (1895) to L. Frank Baum's classic *The Wonderful Wizard of Oz* (1900), authors argued the virtues and merits of silver. In 1896 both the Democratic Party and the PEOPLE'S PARTY (Populists) adopted Free Silver as their main campaign theme and nominated WILLIAM JENNINGS BRYAN for president. However, Bryan was defeated that year by the Republican presidential candidate WILLIAM MCKINLEY, who ran on a platform supporting the gold standard. Bryan's defeat was a major setback for the FREE-SILVER MOVEMENT from which it never recovered. In 1900 Congress passed the GOLD STANDARD ACT, which declared gold the nation's monetary standard of value and ended the silver controversy.

See also CRIME OF '73; FARMERS' ALLIANCES; OMAHA PLATFORM; POLITICAL PARTIES, THIRD; SIMPSON, JERRY.

Further reading: Walter T. K. Nugent, *Money and American Society, 1865–1880* (New York: The Free Press, 1968); Robert P. Sharkey, *Money, Class, and Party: An Economic Study of the Civil War and Reconstruction* (Baltimore: Johns Hopkins University Press, 1959); Irwin Unger, *The Greenback Era: A Social and Political History of American Finance, 1865–1879* (Princeton, N.J.: Princeton University Press, 1964).

— Phillip Papas

Currier and Ives See illustration, photography, and the graphic arts

Curtis, George William See civil service reform

Custer, George Armstrong See Sioux wars

D

dairy industry See agriculture

Darwinism See Darwinism and religion; science; Social Darwinism

Darwinism and religion

The intellectual challenge of 19th-century science appeared to erode the basis of Judeo-Christian RELIGIONS. Scientific methods, discoveries, and theories in geology, biology, and history questioned the literal text of the Bible, but the challenge of biology provoked a major religious controversy. When Charles Darwin in his *Origin of Species* (1859) theorized (on the basis of evidence) that plants and animals evolved over eons through natural selection and were not created by God in a few days, the effect was unsettling. As the implications of Darwinism became apparent, Christians divided into liberal and orthodox groups. The liberals accommodated their theology to the new scholarship, while the orthodox adhered to their faith that the Bible was literally the word of God. For liberals, John Fiske's *Outlines of Cosmic Philosophy* (1874) reconciled theism and evolution by arguing that there was no conflict between science and religion. He relegated religion to what the leading apostle of evolution, Herbert Spencer, called "the Unknowable." Indeed, liberals came to view evolution as God's plan. HENRY WARD BEECHER associated evolution and progress with Christianity and civilization. By 1900 preachers were citing evolution as a proof of Christianity rather than a challenge to it.

The extent of liberal acceptance of the implications of Darwinism varied. Some saw religion as a natural phenomenon, with Christianity subject to the same tests of integrity as any other faith or secular idea, but most liberals still believed that Christianity was special and not just one among many valid religions. By 1900 the seminaries and urban ministers of the major Protestant denominations were comfortable with an evolutionary philosophy that apparently confirmed the superiority of Christianity because it seemed to be the "most" evolved of the world's religions. Ironically, Darwinism was initially perceived as a threat by Protestants and then used a generation later by JOSIAH STRONG and others to sustain a belief in American Protestant Anglo-Saxon superiority and to inspire missionary activity.

Orthodox Protestants, who tended to be rural and working class, also varied their responses as they rejected evolution. The entire South was orthodox, while in the North mainstream Protestant denominations had orthodox and liberal wings or factions. The acceptance of Darwinism in scholarly seminaries and in fashionable churches led to a resurgence of millennialism within mainstream churches and in the growth of new denominations like the Seventh-Day Adventists and Jehovah's Witnesses. The emphasis on prophesies of the imminent second coming (advent) of Christ and the end of the world led to an emphasis on the literal, not the metaphorical, truth of the Bible.

Adventism was also embraced by those in mainstream churches who reacted against modernity. Orthodox scholars organized two Prophecy Conferences (in 1878 and 1886) and an annual Niagara Bible Conference to share in recognizing signs of the end and to uphold a literal belief in the Bible. Through their Bible study they decided that God had ordained a system of "dispensations" or eras following upon each other and ending with the last days. A close associate of DWIGHT L. MOODY, Cyrus Ingerson Scofield (1843–1921), was its chief advocate. Scofield, a Congregational minister, consolidated the dispensational scheme into seven ages concluding with the Great Sabbath or the Millennium of Christ ushered in by the Second Coming and the end of days. His work endures today in the popular *Scofield Reference Bible* (1909). Vital to the dispensational analysis of history and the Bible is the need to assert the literal and infallible authority of the Bible, and from that need, the 20th-century Fundamentalist movement developed.

Further reading: Paul A. Carter, *The Spiritual Crisis of the Gilded Age* (DeKalb: Northern Illinois University Press, 1971); Jon H. Roberts, *Darwinism and the Divine in America: Protestant Intellectuals and Organic Evolution, 1859–1900* (Madison: University of Wisconsin Press, 1988).

— W. Frederick Wooden

Dawes Severalty Act (1887)

Public sentiment toward the plight of Native Americans combined with the desire of western interests to obtain more land led to the Dawes Act of 1887. It dissolved tribes as legal entities, opened up Indian lands to individual ownership, and broke the Native American tradition of collective landholding. The act, which at the time was considered a humanitarian reform, formed the basis of U.S. policy toward Native Americans until the 1930s.

The Dawes Act of 1887 allowed reservation land to be distributed among individual members of Native American tribes. The author of the act was Massachusetts senator Henry L. Dawes (1816–1903), who was long interested in ameliorating conditions for poverty-stricken Native Americans. For several years, advocacy groups such as the Indian Rights Association pushed for the passage of the law, which until the 1880s never had sufficient political support. By the end of 1886, however, both the secretary of the Interior and commissioner of Indian Affairs supported enacting a lands-in-severalty law, and it was narrowly approved by the House. President GROVER CLEVELAND signed the bill into law on February 8, 1887.

Under the act every head of a family in the tribe would receive 160 acres of land and 40 acres for each minor child. Adults without a family (and orphans) would receive 80 acres. If the land was suitable only for grazing the acreage was to be doubled. Native Americans were allowed to choose which land to take title to, and land was put in a trust title whereby the federal government retained full title for a period of 25 years, during which the land could not be sold or taxed. At the expiration of that period Native Americans received full title to their land and full U.S. citizenship (which would also assimilate Indians into the larger American society). Oklahoma's so-called Five Civilized Tribes (the Cherokee, Choctaw, Chickasaw, Creek, and Seminole) and the Osage tribe were exempt from the act until 1898, when western land was at a premium. The Burke Act of 1906 allowed the secretary of the Interior to waive the 25-year trustee period and sped up the process of achieving full ownership and citizenship. Although most Indians had achieved full citizenship before 1924, in that year Congress conferred citizenship on all Native Americans.

Reformers believed that passage of the Dawes Act would help Native Americans realize the benefits of individual land ownership and help them participate fully in the life of the United States. Its goal was assimilation rather than self-determination. Western cattle interests, which had leased portions of the land for grazing, tended to oppose the legislation, but governments in the West widely supported the act, since the surplus land was opened up to white settlers.

The act undermined the collective, communal tradition within tribal structures and imposed an individualistic concept of land ownership. Even Dawes remarked that if the act was abused or administered incorrectly it would lead to minimal or even negative effects for Indian tribes. Indeed, over time, the long wait for full title to land was considered an impediment, and reservation land decreased dramatically; reservation land just before the passage of the law amounted to 137 million acres, but by the 1930s only 50 million acres were still owned by Native Americans.

The Dawes Act did not realize the hopes of its humanitarian authors. Its lack of success was due in part to a dearth of government support, especially for western tribes without a strong farming tradition. Native Americans often quickly lost their land once full title was taken. The land was sometimes bought by speculators, who in turn sold it to settlers. Indians also faced problems paying the taxes that were levied after full title to the land was granted. Because of the act, by the 1930s two-thirds of Native Americans were without property, and a large proportion of them were reduced to receiving government support to live. Defenders of the Dawes Act, however, stress that had it not been passed, the vast reservation lands would have been seized by white settlers (as in the past), and Native Americans would have ended up with even less land than the Dawes Act salvaged for them.

Further reading: Francis Paul Prucha, *The Great Father: The United States Government and the American Indians* (Lincoln: University of Nebraska Press, 1986).

— Scott Sendrow

Debs, Eugene Victor See Volume VII

de Lôme letter (1898)

The Spanish minister to the United States, Don Enrique Dupuy de Lôme, wrote a letter to an acquaintance in CUBA that contained insulting references to President WILLIAM MCKINLEY. Written in December 1897 after McKinley's annual address to Congress, the letter accused the president of being "weak and a bidder for the admiration of the crowd, . . . a would-be politician who tries to leave a door open behind himself while keeping on good terms with the jingoes of his party." The letter, stolen in the Havana post office and published by William Randolph Hearst's *New*

York Journal on February 9, 1898, under the screaming headline "WORST INSULT TO THE UNITED STATES IN ITS HISTORY," could not have come at a worse time. Tensions had been growing between the United States and Spain. The conduct of Spain's seemingly endless and brutal campaign to squash Cuba's independence movement offended American sensibilities and threatened its economic interests in the island. At the same time Spain fumed at the inability of the United States to prevent arms from flowing from American shores to the Cuban rebels.

McKinley quite properly ignored the letter, realizing that to respond to insults was beneath the dignity of the office of chief executive. Actually, de Lôme was mistaken about McKinley; he was a clever, effective politician who had survived four years of bloody Civil War battles and would not lightly go to war. De Lôme realized he had blundered and resigned the day after the letter was published, sparing himself the indignity of being recalled. But the effects of the letter did not die down with the Spanish minister's departure. Talk of resolutions to award belligerency status to the Cuban rebels and declarations of war were bandied about in the halls of CONGRESS until Spain officially apologized on February 14. The apology, however, did little to curb the growth of anti-Spanish feeling among the American people.

Further reading: Ivan Musicant, *Empire by Default: The Spanish-American War and the Dawn of the American Century* (New York: Henry Holt & Co., 1998); Joseph E. Wisan, *The Cuban Crisis as Reflected in the New York Press, 1895–1898* (New York: Columbia University Press, 1934.)

— Timothy E. Vislocky

Democratic Party

The immediate post–Civil War years were crucial to the development of America's major political parties. The Republicans emerged from the war as the victorious defenders of freedom and the Union. Their firm grip on CONGRESS assured them of control over the direction of southern Reconstruction as well as the federal government for at least a decade. Conversely, the Civil War weakened and discredited the Democratic Party. Slavery, secession, and war had split the party, but emancipation, union, and peace settled those issues, and Democrats in the North and South reunited in opposition to Radical Reconstruction policies. As white supremacists gained control of the South and with negrophobia alive in the North, the Democratic Party had become a formidable force by 1876.

As with all major parties, there was much diversity among the Democrats. For the most part, they were Americans who were growing tired with the course of Reconstruction and were troubled by the changes to society brought on by rapid industrialization. Although Republicans were far from centralized, the Democratic Party was an especially loose collection of state and local parties. Lacking cohesion, it was difficult to impose unity on the party's membership. Among the Democratic partisans were small farmers, industrial laborers, small businessmen, and Irish and German Catholic immigrants, but the party also included some bankers, railroad operators, and industrialists. Each of these constituencies brought their own agenda to the party, but the party's most consistent base of political support was the SOLID SOUTH and urban political machines such as TAMMANY HALL in New York City. Ultimately, the Democratic Party's diversity made it unstable.

The Democrats developed neither leaders nor an agenda that could unite the disparate elements of the party. They failed because the party returned to the traditional doctrines of states rights, decentralization, fiscal conservatism, and limited government. Following such a political strategy, Democrats developed remedies to the country's complex problems—business regulation, political reform, and labor legislation—based on local circumstances and individual initiatives. This approach succeeded on the state level, but these were limited victories. The emphasis on local and state government weakened the Democratic Party's ability to develop national leaders. Instead, the party depended on a group of powerful regional political leaders who were unwilling to subordinate local interests to make the national party cohesive and competitive.

Because they lacked national leaders, the Democrats found themselves under the political control of one or more competing factions. By the 1880s, the views of its conservative wing, the so-called Bourbons, began to take precedence. The Bourbons were centered mainly in the Northeast and had ties to the nation's financial and corporate communities. They called for a reduction in tariff rates, a currency system based on the gold standard, and "administrative economy." Simply put, the Bourbons wanted to restrict government activity to a minimum. The Bourbons were joined by several southern Democrats who advocated a NEW SOUTH based on industrial development and laissez-faire economic principles.

The reliance on Bourbon ideology led to intraparty strife. Democrats who were concerned with the social inequities caused by the nation's rapid industrialization believed that the Bourbons were aiding the destruction of the small family farm and the exploitation of American workers. This liberal faction led movements calling for federal regulation of large corporations and the RAILROADS. Intraparty strife also arose over the CURRENCY ISSUE, with Democrats in the economically depressed rural regions of the South and West advocating a policy of currency inflation by increasing the supply of paper money (greenbacks) in circulation or through the unlimited coinage of silver

(FREE-SILVER MOVEMENT). Another persistent issue with Democrats in these regions, as well as in the cities of the Northeast, was the availability of federal appropriations and subsidies that the Bourbons, as advocates of administrative economy, opposed. The TARIFF ISSUE also sparked division among the Democratic faithful.

Despite the intraparty differences, the Democrats slowly began to close the political gap between themselves and the Republicans. They won the House of Representatives in 1874 and the Senate in 1878. SAMUEL J. TILDEN won the popular vote for the presidency in 1876 (but lost the vote in the electoral college), and the election of 1884 brought GROVER CLEVELAND to the White House. Cleveland was the first Democrat elected president since James Buchanan in 1856, and he has the further distinction of being the only president in American history to serve two nonconsecutive terms in office (1885–89, 1893–97). For the Democratic Party, Cleveland's election meant an end to 24 years of political impotence on the national level. Unfortunately for Cleveland and the Democrats, they controlled the presidency and Congress when the Panic of 1893 inaugurated a devastating economic depression.

The erosion of Democratic power during the depression was confirmed in 1896 when the rural, southern-western faction recaptured the party under the leadership of WILLIAM JENNINGS BRYAN. Bryan and his supporters attacked both the Republicans and the Bourbons for manipulating government power for the benefit of the wealthy, industrial elite. They shared with the PEOPLE'S PARTY (Populists) the belief that increased federal regulation of railroads and public utilities, currency inflation based on the Free-Silver ideal, and the abolition of the NATIONAL BANKING SYSTEM could restore balance within America's economic system. Such policies could especially help small farmers living under the pressure of declining agricultural prices and high shipping costs. Furthermore, Bryan espoused an antiurbanism that alienated the Democratic political machines in the nation's major cities. These machine organizations had provided the party with a major core of constituents among immigrants and Catholics, and their lack of support for Bryan and his ideals contributed to his defeat in the 1896 presidential election. After Bryan's defeat, the Democrats remained the minority party until the 1930s.

See also GEORGE WASHINGTON PLUNKITT.

Further reading: J. Rogers Hollingsworth, *The Whirligig of Politics: The Democracy of Cleveland and Bryan* (Chicago: University of Chicago Press, 1963); Horace Merrill, *Bourbon Leader: Grover Cleveland and the Democratic Party* (Boston: Little, Brown, 1957); H. Wayne Morgan, *From Hayes to the McKinley: National Party Politics, 1877–1896* (Syracuse, N.Y.: Syracuse University Press, 1969).

— Phillip Papas

department stores

In the late 19th and early 20th centuries, large stores selling every imaginable type of product, both domestically produced and imported, dominated retailing in the United States. Department stores were found in every major city in the country, and many of these metropolises had four or more of these giant outlets. By 1900 department stores gave the downtown areas much of their romantic look, attracting shoppers (particularly women) from rural and suburban areas and even acting as a magnet for tourists. In the pre–World War I period, these department stores also helped pioneer the gothic architectural appearance that came to dominate urban centers until the 1940s.

Before the Civil War, peddlers, general country stores, and small, specialized urban shops dominated retailing in the United States. A few stores displayed greater stability and developed local and even national reputations, such as Tiffany's and Brooks Brothers in New York City. Alexander H. Stewart was the most famous merchant, selling a large array of women's dry goods out of his Marble Palace on Broadway. Although Stewart's three-story building introduced a number of innovations such as a nonnegotiable price for all items and the customer's ability to return unwanted goods, his merchandise was quite limited in scope. While Stewart was a model for many merchants, the major influence on American retailing was Paris's Bon Marché, a true department store that sold all kinds of goods for women, children, men, and the home.

American entrepreneurs such as John Wanamaker of Philadelphia; Adam Gimbel of Milwaukee, Philadelphia, and New York; Edward Filene of Boston; and Marshall Field of Chicago imitated the French model. They created stores with multidepartments, each headed by a buyer who had autonomy in picking merchandise and hiring and firing employees within their own specialty. John Wanamaker served on the board of the PHILADELPHIA CENTENNIAL EXPOSITION in 1876 and was so impressed by the wide array of merchandise sold there that he opened a department store to capitalize upon that event in 1877. An innovative merchandiser, Wanamaker soon had departments selling everything from artwork to pianos, from Paris women's clothing to ready-made menswear. Because of his use of technology—escalators, indoor electric lighting, and pneumatic tubes for sending cash—the Philadelphian became a model for other retailers.

Nathan Straus, who bought Macy's, and Marshall Field became the other major promoters of department stores. Each of these merchants and many of the approximately

500 retailers who opened emporiums in virtually every state in the Union turned their stores into entertainment centers, fashion galleries, and theaters. Wanamaker, for example, brought Leopold Stokowski to conduct in the store and had an exhibit of hundreds of photographs taken of Native Americans in the West. Straus brought models from France to exhibit the latest Paris fashions. Something was going on almost every day in Marshall Field's. Prices in these stores were quite competitive, driving many small-store owners out of business.

Department stores underwent major changes in the 20th century. The Great Depression of the 1930s forced many of these stores either into bankruptcy or to become a part of an emerging department store conglomerate like Federated Stores. After World War II, suburbanization made the central business district increasingly irrelevant for the retail shopper. To cope with this problem, major department stores cannibalized their business by building small suburban stores, which were pale reflections of their former-palaces. By 2000 most of the older chains such as Macy's, Wanamaker's, and Filene's were part of a larger organization and had lost their identity, and the retailing boom of discount shopping threatened even these stores.

Further reading: Stephen Elias, *Alexander T. Stewart: The Forgotten Merchant Prince* (Westport, Conn.: Praeger, 1992); Herbert B. Ershkowitz, *John Wanamaker, Philadelphia Merchant* (Conshohocken, Pa.: Combined Publishing, 1999); Robert Hendrickson, *The Grand Emporiums: The Illustrated History of the Great Department Stores* (New York: Stein and Day, 1979).

— Herbert Ershkowitz

Dependents Pension Act (1890) See Grand Army of the Republic

depressions, economic See business cycles

Dewey, George (1837–1917)

Admiral George Dewey is renowned for having defeated a Spanish fleet at the Battle of Manila Bay in 1898 during the SPANISH-AMERICAN WAR. Born in Vermont on December 26, 1837, Dewey entered the United States Naval Academy in 1854 and graduated in 1858. With the outbreak of the Civil War he was promoted to lieutenant and was the executive officer on the sidewheel steamer *Mississippi* in Admiral David Farragut's fleet that captured New Orleans.

The post–Civil War period was a dark time for Dewey, since CONGRESS allowed the navy's ships to either rot or rust. Promotion was slow and opportunities for distinction were nonexistent. Dewey commanded steam sloops (a naval "sloop" was a vessel with guns on one deck) and served on shore in the Lighthouse Service and in 1895 as president of the Board of Inspection and Survey. In that capacity he supervised inspections of the navy's new battleships. Dewey pined after greatness and feared that he would only be known as "George Dewey who entered the Navy at a certain date and retired as Rear Admiral at the age limit."

But Dewey was saved from obscurity on October 21, 1897, by Assistant Secretary of the Navy Theodore Roosevelt, who selected him as the commander of the navy's Asiatic Squadron. The strong possibility of war with Spain soon became a reality on April 20, 1898. Dewey had already been ordered to be ready for battle and was cabled a few days later to "use his utmost endeavor" to capture or destroy the Spanish fleet in the Philippine Islands. On May 1 at 5:22 A.M. Dewey spotted the Spanish fleet off Cavite in Manila Bay. When the American fleet was within 5,400 yards he coolly told the captain of his flagship *Olympia* "you may fire when you are ready, Gridley." After shelling the hopelessly outgunned Spanish squadron for two hours, all 10 of its ships were sunk or disabled and 381 of her seamen were either dead or wounded. At 12:30 P.M. the battle ended when the Spanish hoisted white flags above the shore batteries at Cavite. For his success Dewey was promoted to rear admiral.

After the war Dewey was promoted to admiral and Congress passed special legislation that allowed him to serve past the navy's mandatory retirement age. From 1900 until his death on January 16, 1917, Dewey served on the General Board of the Navy.

Further reading: Ivan Musicant, *Empire by Default: The Spanish-American War and the Dawn of the American Century* (New York: Henry Holt & Co. 1998); Ronald Spector, *Admiral of the New Navy: The Life and Career of George Dewey* (Baton Rouge: Louisiana State University Press, 1974).

— Timothy E. Vislocky

Dickinson, Emily (1830–1886)

The poet Emily Elizabeth Dickinson was a daughter of Edward Dickinson, a prominent attorney and scion of one of the most distinguished families in his community, and Emily Norcross, and was born on December 10, 1830, to a family of culture and privilege in Amherst, Massachusetts. Her formal education was limited to attendance at the Amherst Academy and a single year at Mount Holyoke Female Seminary when she was 17. From the time she left school in 1848, she rarely left Amherst except for an occasional trip to Philadelphia or Boston between 1851 and

1855 and one to Washington when her father was elected to the U.S. House of Representatives in 1854. From the age of 25 until her death she almost never went farther from the family home than her garden gate.

Finding the religious atmosphere of her community oppressive, Dickinson became increasingly reclusive as she grew older, rejecting at once the smug sanctimoniousness of the New England puritanism around her and the cultural pretensions of the academic life in her college town. She was recognized by family and friends as an original and talented woman, but she never attempted to win public esteem for the brief, seemingly fragmentary poems she began to write around 1858, preferring to copy them out on pages she stitched together by hand and kept hidden in her bureau drawers.

The intensity of the lyrical expression in her elliptical and often gnomic verse has given rise to speculation about a star-crossed love that never came to light, but no evidence exists of any frustrated romance apart from some unexpressed schoolgirl crushes. Her social life dwindled to nothing, and her personal relationships were apparently limited to family, a few close friendships, and correspondence with literary celebrities of the time. Thomas Wentworth Higginson, the literary editor of the *Atlantic Monthly,* generously praised her work and gave her advice, which she usually ignored, to help "clarify" her deliberately ambiguous verse. Of the seven poems by Dickinson published in her lifetime, all appeared anonymously and apparently against her will. Her personal isolation increased during her 30s, and she earned a local reputation for eccentricity as she refused to meet visitors, wore nothing but white, and sent gifts of food to neighbors accompanied by cryptic messages.

After her death on May 15, 1886, nearly 1,800 of her brief, enigmatic lyrics were discovered in her bedroom, and her sister Lavinia induced a family friend to publish a selection of them in 1890. Critical response was mixed, but the work was generally dismissed as crude and obscure. Derided in the press for its "hit or miss grammar and appalling rhymes," her lyrics on pain and death, love and loss, nature, and the quest for God nevertheless met with considerable popular success, and 11 editions sold out in the year of its publication. Two more collections and a selection of her letters appeared in 1894 and 1896 and were praised by WILLIAM DEAN HOWELLS and other arbiters of literary taste. Admired by later poets of the modernist school for her innovative prosody, rebellious spirit, and emotional depth, Dickinson has had few imitators but has taken her place as one of the most influential poets in American literature.

Further reading: Richard B. Sewell, *The Life of Emily Dickinson* (New York: Farrar, Straus and Giroux, 1974).

— Dennis Wepman

dime novels

Between 1870 and 1900 dime novels were the principal, though not exclusive, form of mass-produced popular fiction in the United States. Demand for inexpensive, unsophisticated novels was a by-product of 19th-century school laws, which had increased literacy among the working classes. Improvements in printing technology and shipping made it possible for enterprising publishers to profit by supplying fiction for the masses. "Story papers," which emerged during the 1840s and 1850s, initiated the mass distribution of popular fiction. Robert Bonner's *New York Ledger* and Street and Smith's *New York Weekly* were the industry leaders, but as many as 50 weekly story papers had national circulations that exceeded 100,000. The papers provided serialized fiction, usually sentimental romances and melodramatic tales of Native Americans, at five cents per issue. To get a complete novel, readers would have to acquire four or five issues. By comparison, dime novels supplied the entire novel right away and at half the price.

Dime novels first came to prominence during the 1860s, though the new format did not entirely displace story papers until the 1880s. Publisher Erastus Beadle struck gold when he launched a series of 10-cent novels in a new format, initially 4-inch-by-6-1/2-inch pamphlets of about 100 pages. The covers were burnt-orange or salmon colored, and the paper was cheap. The books sold well, especially among Union soldiers, who found them to be entertaining, accessible, and convenient.

The earliest Beadle dime novel was *Malaeska, The Indian Wife of the White Hunter* (1860), by Ann Sophia Stephens, a popular novelist and prominent editor of women's magazines. The success of Beadle's first series soon inspired competitors to launch their own lines of dime novels. Other leading publishers of the new cheap fiction were George Munro, Robert DeWitt, Norman Munro, Frank Tousey, and Street and Smith. Beadle and the others assembled stables of hack writers, many of them recruited from the story papers. The more prolific of these authors could turn out 1,000 words an hour for 12 hours at a time. They produced standardized assembly-line literature for mass consumption.

Though best known as a format for Westerns and urban detective stories, many dime novels were set during the American Revolution, the War of 1812, and the Mexican War. The stories were typically tales of adventure, whether on the high seas, the Great Plains, or the forests. They took their heroic ideal from James Fenimore Cooper's early 19th-century Leather-Stocking Tales. Eventually, the dime novel generated its own stock heroes, most notably frontiersmen Deadwood Dick and Buffalo Bill and detective Nick Carter.

Although his books frequently depicted violence and bloodshed, Erastus Beadle insisted that his authors adhere to Victorian standards of virtue and taste. But dime novels promulgated a new class of heroine that departed from the genteel notions of womanhood associated with VICTORIANISM. Popular fiction broke new ground by occasionally presenting assertive, even Amazonian women. Frequently dressed as men, these heroines sailed on pirate ships, tamed wild animals, confronted death, and overcame difficult physical challenges. Like their male counterparts, they were self-reliant, resourceful, and virtuous.

Dime novels may have created a new heroine, but they also exploited negative stereotypes of Native Americans. Mass fiction displayed a fascination with Indians, but typically depicted them as menacing, deceptive, untrustworthy, vengeful, and backward but cunning. The effect was to establish the moral and physical superiority of the books' white protagonists.

Altogether, dime novels conveyed a distorted image of the American past. As literary historian Jack Salzman has observed, "the dime novel provided the new working class with tales of adventure and excitement that were . . . implicitly political in their nationalism and patriotic fervor—as well as their racism and sexism."

Just as dime novels misrepresented the past, so too did they misconstrue the present, most notably in HORATIO ALGER's popular tales of newsboys and bootblacks who rose from rags to respectability through a combination of luck and pluck. Alger simply ignored the social ills and inexorable economic forces identified by contemporary journalists and novelists, such as STEPHEN CRANE and Frank Norris. But if sales were any indication, Alger's view of America eclipsed the harsh visions of Crane, Norris, and other realists. Scholars attribute to Alger no fewer than 119 titles, with combined sales of approximately 20 million.

To meet the tremendous demand for cheap fiction, the publishers of Alger's books and other dime novels devised efficient production and distribution strategies. They typically printed a first run of 40,000 to 60,000 copies of a single title, though it was not unusual for demand to require additional printings of between 400,000 and 1 million copies. Publishers sold their books at newsstands using circulation systems already in place for the marketing of newspapers and magazines. The American News Company, for instance, was for many years the principal distributor of dime novels, especially the Beadle line. During the peak years of the dime novel, the larger publishers issued thousands of titles that collectively sold in the millions. Given their impact on the publishing business and on American culture, Beadle and his fellow publishers were, as historian Henry Nash Smith has pointed out, the cultural equivalent of industrial magnates like ANDREW CARNEGIE, and John D. Rockefeller.

See also CODY, WILLIAM FREDERICK; LITERATURE.

The cover of a dime novel entitled *The Lost Trail,* 1864 *(Denver Public Library)*

Further reading: Michael Denning, *Mechanic Accents: Dime Novels and Working-Class Culture in America* (London: Verso, 1987); Russel Nye, *The Unembarrassed Muse: The Popular Arts in America* (New York: Dial Press, 1970); Jack Salzman, "Literature for the Populace," in *Columbia Literary History of the United States,* eds. Emory Elliott et al. (New York: Columbia University Press, 1987); Henry Nash Smith, *Virgin Land: The American West as Symbol and Myth* (Cambridge, Mass.: Harvard University Press, 1950).

— William Hughes

due process clause (1868)

After the Civil War, the United States SUPREME COURT interpreted the due process clause of the Fourteenth Amendment, passed initially to protect the rights of AFRICAN AMERICANS, to shield private property from state government regulation. The Fourteenth Amendment provides that no state shall "deprive any person of life, liberty, or property, without due process of law." The Court narrowed the protection of the due process clause for individuals in the 1883 CIVIL RIGHTS CASES (denial of equal access to public accommodations was a private, not a state, matter) and in the 1896 *PLESSY V. FERGUSON* decision (state-mandated segregation did not violate due process). While the Court reduced the protection of human rights by the due process clause, some justices—initially a minority—found in that clause, beginning in the 1870s, the means of protecting property rights from state regulation.

In the slaughterhouse cases of 1873, the Court limited the application of the Fourteenth Amendment. The state of Louisiana law gave the Crescent City Live Stock Landing and Slaughterhouse Company a monopoly over the butchering trade in New Orleans. A rival group of independent butchers sued, claiming that the law deprived them of their "privileges and immunities" as citizens without due process of law. By the slim margin of 5 to 4, the Court rejected the claims of the independent butchers. The majority held that the protections guaranteed by the Fourteenth Amendment, in particular that of due process, were intended to apply to former slaves and not to questions of economic regulation. But among the dissenters was Justice Stephen J. Field, who argued for a broader definition of due process that would narrow state "police power" and would protect property rights from state regulation. In the most famous of the Granger cases, *Munn v. Illinois* (1877), the Court upheld an Illinois Warehouse Act on the grounds that states had the authority to regulate private property when it was used in the public interest. Again, in a stinging dissent, Field argued that the due process clause protected private business from state regulation. His dissent in this case anticipated the future direction of the Court in its definition of the Fourteenth Amendment.

By the 1880s, the Court adopted Field's broad interpretation of the due process clause. In the case of *Santa Clara v. Southern Pacific Railroad Company* (1886), the Court accepted the argument that the word "persons" in the Fourteenth Amendment applied equally to corporations and individuals; therefore, corporations could enjoy the same benefits of due process and equal protection as did individuals. The due process clause thus insulated corporations from unreasonable state regulation and also protected freedom of contract to the extent that the Court, in time, overturned maximum hour and minimum wage legislation. From the end of the 19th century to well into the 20th century, the Court was a bastion of judicial conservatism and a champion of laissez-faire capitalism.

Further reading: William E. Nelson, *The Fourteenth Amendment: From Political Principle to Judicial Doctrine* (Cambridge, Mass.: Harvard University Press, 1988).

— Phillip Papas

Dunbar, Paul Laurence (1872–1906)

Born on June 27, 1872, in Dayton, Ohio, the son of former slaves, Paul Dunbar edited the high school newspaper, wrote his class's song, and graduated with honors. Unable to find a job in journalism, he became an elevator operator in his home town and spent his spare time writing poetry. He came to the attention of and was encouraged by several white men, including the Indiana poet James Whitcomb Riley. Before his 21st birthday he had published his first book of poetry, *Oak and Ivy*. His second book, *Majors and Minors*, received a favorable review from WILLIAM DEAN HOWELLS, editor of the prestigious *Harper's Monthly*, who then gladly wrote an introduction to Dunbar's third volume of poetry, *Lyrics of Lowly Life* (1896). He praised Dunbar's dialect poems as artistically "literary interpretation[s]" but dismissed Dunbar's poetic English offerings as "very good" or better, but not really a "contribution" to American poetry.

Dunbar's short life was scarred by financial pressures, tuberculosis, alcoholism, and a failed marriage. Two intense compulsions added complications to these wounds: The first was reflected in the Howells introduction; Dunbar wanted to be honored for his straight, not his dialect, poetry, but such recognition never came. His despair echoes in two stanzas of "The Poet," which begin "He sang of life, serenely sweet / With, now and then, a deeper note" and closed with the lament "But, ah, the world, it turned to praise / A jingle in a broken tongue." Dunbar wrote dialect poetry to earn a living, to satisfy a publishing market. Recent scholars now acknowledge his supreme artistry in reproducing southern black speech. No other author or poet has matched his accuracy.

Dunbar's dialect poetry resonates when read aloud. The rhythm of "When Malindy Sings" suggests the beauty of Malindy's voice, "But fu' real melojous music / Dat jes' strikes yo' hea't and clings / Jes yo' stan' an' listen wif me / When Malindy sings." The poem flows like music. Critics have complained that Dunbar's dialect paints AFRICAN AMERICANS as ignorant and servile. The dialect in Dunbar's poetry mirrored the speech of some southern blacks in his time. It was not demeaning. Every once in a while Dunbar slipped in a race-pride allusion. In "When Malindy Sings," for example, the narrator tells Miss Lucy to "Put dat music book away," because no matter how hard she tries, she'll never be able to sing like Malindy.

Race pride, or what one scholar has called "racial fire," was a second compulsion in Dunbar's life. He felt the oppressive prejudice of the day, as evidenced by his many letters to newspapers. A few of his poems reflect his heated resentment at the way blacks were treated. "Rights Security" demonstrates this feeling with subtle intensity: Whatever blows might fall, we praise "that man who will not compromise with wrong / . . . Minorities, since time began / have shown the better side of man."

Paul Laurence Dunbar *(Library of Congress)*

In a more revealing mood, Dunbar wrote his well-known "We Wear the Mask," which "grins and lies" while "With torn and bleeding hearts, we smile." Dunbar was neither cheerleader nor apologist for his race. His poetry probed a variety of human thoughts and emotions, including pride of race and repugnance of prejudice.

A friend wrote that though Dunbar was courtly in manner, polished in speech, and modest in behavior, he carried "a sac of bitterness" born of his reception as an artist, his ill-fated marriage to the talented Alice Moore (later Alice Dunbar-Nelson), his painful illness, and the pinch of finances. Animated in personality, he was an appealing performer who read his poems with expressive passion. He was also a prolific writer, producing more than 400 poems, four novels, four volumes of short stories, and collaborating on several musical revues. His last and best novel, *The Sport of the Gods* (1902), one of the first to tackle the theme of northern migration, followed a southern black family to Harlem, where the gilt and glamour almost destroy them.

Largely forgotten for most of the 20th century, Dunbar's poetry is now slowly gaining acknowledgment for its lyrical quality, its careful but courageous racial fire, and the beauty of what the contemporary poet Nikki Giovanni, calls "plantation speech." Dunbar was, Giovanni concludes in a telling phrase, "a natural resource for our people." Dunbar died on February 9, 1906.

Further reading: Henry Louis Gates and Nellie Y. McKay, eds., *The Norton Anthology of African American Literature* (New York, Norton, 1997), 884–86; Jay Martin, ed., *A Singer in the Dawn* (New York, Dodd, Mead, 1975); Lida Keck Wiggins, *The Life and Works of Paul Laurence Dunbar* (New York: Dodd, Mead, 1907).

— Leslie H. Fishel, jr.

E

Eads, James Buchanan (1820–1887)

Perhaps the most distinguished American engineer in the Gilded Age, James Eads was born beside the Ohio River in Lawrenceburg, Indiana, on May 23, 1820. He became a steamboat clerk on the Mississippi in 1839; when his boat sank, he perceived business opportunities in cargo salvage. He designed a diving bell in 1842 and started a salvage business. He later expanded into clearing river snags, made a fortune, and retired in 1857. During the Civil War, Eads designed and built ironclad gunboats for the Union, and these played a key role in gaining control of the Mississippi and its tributaries.

In 1866 Eads's proposal for a bridge across the Mississippi at St. Louis was adopted, and he became its engineer-in-chief in 1867. A major problem was constructing piers from bedrock up through the sandy bottom of the river. Eads used a pressurized caisson, floated into position and sunk to the bottom, within which excavators could work with compressed air to keep out the water. The first caisson reached bedrock 100 feet below the river surface in 1870. Records show that 119 men suffered from "the bends," and 14 died before it was learned that slow decompression was necessary after working under compressed air. In 1873 laborers began erecting the steel arches of the bridge. With three spans, each more than 500 feet long, the bridge marked the first extensive use of steel in bridge construction.

The great bridge officially opened on July 4, 1874, after Eads demonstrated its strength by driving 14 locomotives back and forth across it. An estimated 300,000 people attended the celebration, a municipal triumph for St. Louis. The bridge would carry increasingly heavy trains for 100 years. Closed to rail traffic in 1974, it reopened in 1993 to carry light-rail Metrolink trains across the Mississippi. The bridge is not only a vital transportation link; its functional beauty also inspired the architectural work of LOUIS SULLIVAN.

In 1873 Eads began investigating another problem: how to maintain navigation for ocean ships at the shallow mouth of the Mississippi. He argued against proposals for a canal to bypass the shallow sandbars and suggested building jetties to direct the river flow and scour a channel. Despite opposition, Eads's proposal was accepted in 1875. Construction of the jetties began the same year, and by 1879 the channel was 30 feet deep and routinely used by oceangoing steamers.

Eads's final great project, never accomplished, was to have been a multitrack ship railway to carry ocean liners from the Gulf of Mexico across the Isthmus of Tehuantepec to the Pacific. Eads began investigating the possibility in 1879 as an alternative to an ill-conceived proposal by the French promoter Ferdinand de Lesseps to construct a sea-level isthmian canal across Panama. Eads would lobby for his project until his death in 1887. Not until 1914 would the Panama Canal (with locks) be opened to traffic.

In 1920 Eads was elected to the Hall of Fame for Great Americans, and in the 1932 the deans of the American colleges of engineering named Eads one of the five greatest engineers of all time, ranking him alongside Leonardo da Vinci and Thomas Edison.

See also BRIDGES.

Further reading: Quinta Scott and Howard Miller, *The Eads Bridge* (Columbia: University of Missouri Press, (1979).

— Francis H. Parker

Eakins, Thomas (1844–1916)

Best known as a painter, Thomas Eakins also used the mediums of photography, sculpture, and watercolor to conduct uncompromising explorations of the human form. Eakins's life and art are linked with Philadelphia, where he was born on July 25, 1844. The son of a master calligrapher, Eakins excelled at mathematics and mechanical drawing in high school. He studied art at the Pennsylvania Academy of the Fine Arts and anatomy at Jefferson Medical College.

In 1866 he began four years of studying painting and sculpture in Paris, his only significant time away from Philadelphia. Along with Eadweard Muybridge, Eakins did pioneering work in motion photography in the late 1870s. As a teacher at the academy, Eakins championed the study of anatomy for both men and women, and by the early 1880s the school was one of the most progressive institutions worldwide. In 1886, however, Eakins removed a male model's loincloth in a women's or mixed life-drawing class, and he was fired. The incident, often cited as an archetype of Victorian prudery, was only one among Eakins's unconventional tactics, which also included a domineering manner, vulgar speech, and nude photography sessions involving himself and his students. Upon Eakins's dismissal, loyal pupils founded the Art Students' League of Philadelphia, and Eakins taught there until 1893. He also taught anatomy at other institutions in Philadelphia, New York, and Washington. Most of Eakins's art was uncommissioned and he sold few works; crucial financial support came from his father. Eakins's reputation as the consummate American realist was only established after his death on June 25, 1916, in Philadelphia.

Hallmarks of Eakins's style, which varied little over the course of his career, include a limited tonal palette, dark shadows cut by shafts of light, and a great wealth of specific detail. In oils, watercolors, and sculpture Eakins executed portraits and genre topics, such as American colonial themes, an Arcadian series, and the sports of sculling, hunting, sailing, and boxing. His realism was built upon a laborious armature of preparation that included perspective drawings and wax mannequins for the study of light. Figure studies, some with frankly erotic themes, were conducted with photography; these were private, study works. All these methods were investigations into the underpinnings of appearances.

Eakins's first masterwork was *The Gross Clinic* (1875, Jefferson Medical College, Philadelphia). In a crowded surgical amphitheater, Dr. Samuel Gross removes diseased

Thomas Eakins's *Max Schmitt in a Single Scull,* 1871 *(Metropolitan Museum of Art)*

bone tissue from the thigh of a prone patient, the incision and his bloody hands making shocking red points amid Rembrandtesque shadows. Most critics could not commend the painting; one noted, "power it has, but very little art." In *The Swimming Hole* (ca. 1883–84, Amon Carter Museum, Fort Worth, Texas) Eakins constructed a pyramidal composition of five nude youths diving, swimming, and lounging, moving the prosaic scene back to an idyllic age. In the searing *The Artist's Wife and His Setter Dog* (1884–ca. 89), Metropolitan Museum of Art, New York), a thin Susan Macdowell Eakins sits slumped in a chair, red-rimmed eyes and an empty, upturned palm almost beseeching the viewer. It takes its place among Eakins's brutally frank, meditative, melancholy portraits, which remain his most memorable works.

Further reading: William Innes Homer, *Thomas Eakins: His Life and Art* (New York: Abbeville Press, 1992); John Wilmerding, *Thomas Eakins (1844–1916) and the Heart of American Life* (London: National Portrait Gallery, 1993).

— Karen Zukowski

Eastman, George (1854–1932)

George Eastman, inventor, entrepreneur, and philanthropist, was born on July 12, 1854, in Waterville, New York, the son of a nurseryman and educator who moved with his family to Rochester, New York, when George was five, and died two years later, leaving the family poor. George quit school at age 13 to help support his mother and sisters. Methodical, efficient, and bent on self-improvement, he worked up from office boy to bank clerk. When, in 1877, he happened to take up photography, he added to his qualities a passionate single-mindedness verging on obsession. Photography still required the preparation and development of a wet-plate negative on the spot and at the time of an exposure, a process involving a bulky camera, tripod, plates, paper, storage box, a tent used as darkroom, and a wide array of chemicals and chemical apparatus. To carry and cope with all this demanded unusual patience, skill, and muscle. Eastman had all those, but he was also determined to find a better way. In 1878 he found it in the dry-plate process just developed in England, whereby plates could be prepared in advance and taken at leisure to a fixed laboratory for development.

Eastman experimented tirelessly with the process and began selling plates to others. In 1880 he patented an improved apparatus and in 1881 opened a factory in Rochester. He faced stiff competition, but he also saw the potential in exploiting a vast market of unhandy amateurs by continually making the process simpler and cheaper. He invented roll film, a roll holder attached to the camera, and bromide printing paper suitable for darkroom development. He also demonstrated a brilliant grasp of marketing, coining the catchy brand name "Kodak" (based on a feeling that "K" was a "strong" letter), reaching out to a world market (beginning with a London branch in 1885), and spending lavishly on advertisements for which he wrote most of the copy. In 1888 he introduced a portable box camera, which held a roll for 100 photos, and urged buyers to send their rolls and cameras to Rochester for development. He wrote a slogan that became a worldwide catch phrase: "You press the button, we do the rest." Constant improvement led to the "Brownie" camera of 1900, which sold for a dollar and came in a bright yellow package, a triumph of product identification.

In a series of acquisitions and reincorporations, Eastman's personal fortune reached the million-dollar mark by the end of the century. He gave a third of it to Eastman employees worldwide, and he subsequently pioneered in employee benefits: medical insurance, pensions, and profit sharing. In 1901 he organized his enterprises as a holding company. This drive toward monopoly ran up against federal antitrust laws, but he preserved his dominance in photography by strategic concessions. After 1901 he diverted more of his energies to philanthropy, which he had engaged in since his teens. Eventually, being a lifelong bachelor, he distributed the bulk of his $100 million fortune for the benefit of the public, avoiding personal publicity. He gave the Massachusetts Institute of Technology $20 million as a gift from "Mr. Smith." He also helped support African-American education through Tuskegee and Hampton Institutes, classical music (in which he delighted), medical research, dental clinics, parks, local political reform, and improvements in the city of Rochester. As a debilitating spinal affliction came upon him in his 70s, he put his affairs in order, bequeathing his estate to worthy causes. On March 14, 1932, leaving a terse note—"My work is done. Why wait?"—he shot himself through the heart.

Further reading: Elizabeth Brayer, *George Eastman: A Biography* (Baltimore: Johns Hopkins University Press, 1996).

— Robert V. Bruce

Eddy, Mary Baker (1821–1910)

Mary Baker Eddy, the founder of CHRISTIAN SCIENCE, was born on July 16, 1821, near Concord, New Hampshire. Although she was an emotional, sickly child who attended school irregularly, she had a aura of excitement about her and after age 12 occasionally published poetry. In 1843 she married George Washington Glover, who died six months later, leaving her pregnant and penniless. After returning to her parents' home in poor health, she gave birth to a son,

Mary Baker Eddy *(Library of Congress)*

who grew up abandoned by her and illiterate. Despite her ill health, in 1853 she married Daniel Patterson, an itinerant dentist. They were divorced in 1873.

Eddy's search for health brought her in 1862 to Phineas Parkhurst Quimby of Portland, Maine, whose direct mental healing hinted at modern psychological theories. Without denying illness, he maintained that its cause was often in the mind of the sufferer. Blooming under his guidance, Eddy became physically strong and a convert to his beliefs, copying out his manuscripts (one of which he called "Christ or Science"). When Quimby died four years later, Eddy reluctantly prepared to proclaim his healing message.

Working alone, without financial backing and estranged from her family and husband, Eddy wrote and in 1875 published *Science and Health,* the handbook of the Christian Science movement. Insisting that the mind could triumph over illness, her book made a religion of Quimby's theories, which she called her own and in many instances plagiarized. In her book's 381 revisions, Eddy gradually altered Quimby's teachings, linking them to the Bible. Unlike him, she denied the reality of illness and death, claiming they were not of the "Father Mother God" who created everything. When her followers appeared ill, they were to seek help from Christian Science practitioners, not medical doctors. Possessing bad teeth and needing glasses, Eddy allowed Christian Scientists to see dentists and optometrists. A believer in demonology, she blamed problems and deaths (including that of Asa Gilbert Eddy, whom she married in 1877 and who died in 1882) on the "malicious animal magnetism" of disgruntled former followers.

Eddy was both an energetic teacher and a pragmatic organizer. She formed the Christian Science Association in 1876 and chartered the Church of Christ (Scientist) in 1879 and, in 1881, the Massachusetts Metaphysical College, which granted degrees for nearly a decade. For $300 tuition (making Eddy the highest paid teacher of her day), adherents could attend her lectures and become teachers and healing practitioners. The trainees (mostly women, including numerous widows) acquired a lucrative profession and brought new believers to the movement, particularly after 1883 when the monthly *Journal of Christian Science* publicized their triumphs. Valuing good publicity, Eddy established in 1898 the weekly *Christian Science Sentinel* and in 1908 the daily *Christian Science Monitor.*

Eddy shrewdly shaped her denomination to increase her power, and during the last 20 years of her life she was the most famous woman in America. Annoyed by deteriorating health and her church's everyday problems, she began secluding herself in 1887, but nevertheless tightened control of her denomination by creating in 1892 "The Mother Church" with a self-perpetuating board of directors. In semiretirement, her emotional outbursts, her consulting with doctors and taking morphine to relieve her painful kidney stones, and her increasing paranoia were less noticed. She died on December 3, 1910, and left most of her $2.5 million estate to her church, which, despite numerous lawsuits and unfavorable publicity, had grown to nearly 100,000 members.

Further reading: Stephen Mottschalk, *The Emergence of Christian Science in American Religious Life* (Berkeley: University of California Press, 1973); Robert Peel, *Mary Baker Eddy,* 3 vols. (Boston: Christian Science Publishing Society, 1966–77).

— Olive Hoogenboom

Edison, Thomas Alva (1847–1931)

Thomas Edison, the most renowned inventor of the Gilded Age, was born on February 11, 1847, in the small town of Milan, Ohio. He did not have an easy start in life: Edison lost part of his hearing as a boy, his family fell on hard times, and his formal schooling was meager. He peddled candy and newspapers on railroad trains and set up a small electrical lab in a baggage car. Able to overhear the clicking of a railroad telegraph, he became a skilled operator and, in the tradition of the craft, moved from job to job. In 1868 he arrived in Boston, the center of American science and technology, where he resolved to be a full-time inventor. His first invention, an electric legislative vote recorder, was not wanted by politicians, who needed time to dicker during a vote. Edison thus learned to study the market before inventing for it. He also devised an improved stock ticker. When his Boston credit ran out in 1869 he moved to New York City. There he sold his stock ticker rights for enough to finance his own business in Newark.

From 1870 to 1876 Edison concentrated on improving telegraphy, in 1874 producing his most complex and notable invention in that field, the quadruplex telegraph, which could send two messages each way over a single wire. In 1876 he set out to establish an "invention factory" that would turn out "a minor invention every ten days and a big thing every six months or so." The plain two-story wooden building in the hamlet of Menlo Park, New Jersey, foreshadowed the modern industrial research laboratory. Edison put together and brilliantly led a dedicated team of skilled workers and scientific specialists. There and elsewhere in New Jersey over the next 15 years he changed the world and called whole new industries into being with a succession of inventions unequaled by any one person before or since, including his carbon-button telephone transmitter, phonograph, electric light, and integrated system of electrical generation and transmission. The public mythologized him as "the wizard of Menlo Park." Ultimately more than 1,000 patents bore his name, though not all were primarily his creation.

After the 1880s Edison changed his style. He came up with no more strikingly original and fundamental inventions, although his team did much to develop motion pictures. Instead, perhaps sensing that the day of the great independent inventors was passing or perhaps because his own incandescent genius was fading as he aged, he turned to massive projects such as ore separation and cement manufacture, both processes that required giant machinery and heavy infusions of capital. He struggled to join the American pantheon of great industrialists, but the new role was not natural to him and he failed, losing much of his fortune. Nevertheless, his triumphs in basic invention have made him a figure of undying fame and legend in American history. The technology he created is, and is likely to remain, an indispensable and inextricable part of human life. When Edison died on October 18, 1931, it was suggested that in observance of his death all dynamos be stopped momentarily, but the cost and disruption of even so fleeting an event was recognized as unthinkable.

Further reading: Paul Israel, *Edison: A Life of Invention* (New York: Wiley, 1998).

— Robert V. Bruce

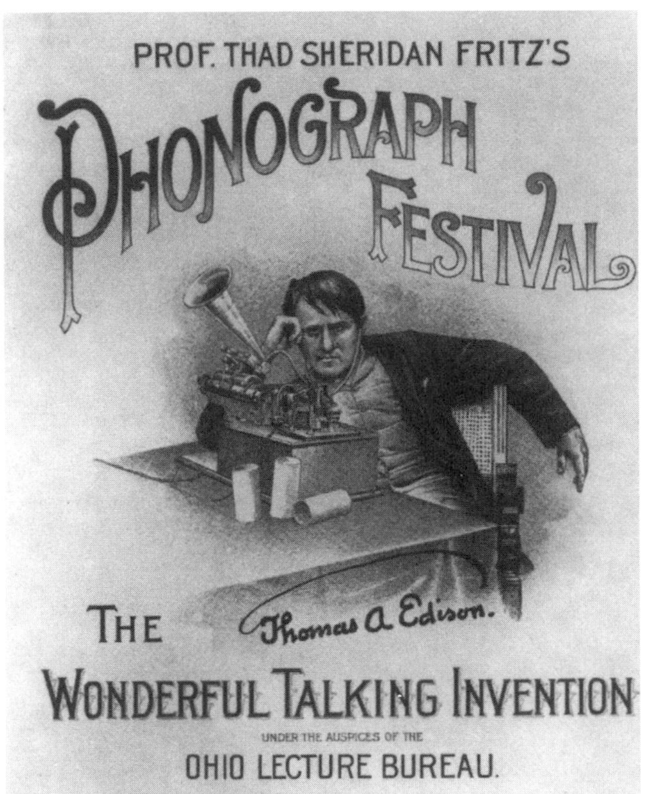

Thomas Alva Edison, with phonograph *(Library of Congress)*

education

Two themes dominated American education from 1870 to 1900. One was the great expansion in the number of schools and people in both teaching and learning. Education became increasingly important as the nation's population grew from natural expansion and IMMIGRATION, and millions of people entered school. The other theme was that the local village, town, or city shaped the educational experience of young Americans. They were not educated by a centralized school system as in Germany, Japan, France, or Great Britain. The minimal federal aid given to education helped establish land-grant agricultural and technical universities under state control. Many Republican congressmen wanted federal funds to be spent on local community schools in impoverished districts, to subsidize the education of black children in particular, but their efforts never became law. Furthermore, in most states, governors, legislators, and judges had little direct influence

One-room schoolhouse and its attendees, Hecla, Montana, 1893 *(Library of Congress)*

on students and teachers. Public education was locally controlled.

Schools aimed to prepare students for a place in a rapidly changing society while building personal and civic character. Between 1870 and 1900 the United States continued the rapid industrialization and urbanization that had begun a generation earlier. By 1880, for example, 50 percent of New Jersey's population lived in communities of more than 2,500 people, and the revolutions in transportation, marketing, and communications were creating a national integrated economy that affected even small rural villages. Local farm producers and their markets were facing competition from rail-transported meat and flour from Chicago and Minneapolis. Fruit shipped from Washington and Oregon to eastern urban centers was sold cheaper than products grown 20 miles away.

Despite the national economy, American children did not have a common educational experience. With the federal Constitution silent about education, that function fell to the states and, in practice, to the thousands of dissimilar communities that formed local school systems. Moreover, schools for AFRICAN AMERICANS and NATIVE AMERICANS were different from those of other children. In 1900, 90 percent of the nation's black children lived in the South and attended segregated schools deemed constitutional by the SUPREME COURT's 1896 *PLESSY V. FERGUSON* "separate but equal" decision. Outside the South, African Americans often attended integrated schools, especially in rural areas and small towns. Native Americans, whose schools were a federal responsibility, were the most poorly educated segment of the population. Schools on reservations were inadequate, and those children who attended the few Indian boarding schools, like the one at Carlisle, Pennsylvania, were intentionally far removed from their community to promote their assimilation into white society. Women of all races had fewer opportunities for education beyond the eighth grade, although only 5 percent of all graduates—regardless of race or gender—went on for more education. Nevertheless, growing numbers of women were going on to teacher education (normal schools), commercial, and nursing schools. Less than 1 percent of the 18-to-22-year-old female population went to the recently created women's colleges, such as Vassar, Smith, Radcliffe, Bryn Mawr, or Mills.

Why did parents send their children to school? Why did states foster schools and permit local communities to raise taxes for their operation? What influence did the rapidly changing economy have on these decisions? Historians have widely differing answers to these questions. Some believe that community schools were created to preserve and protect traditional American beliefs during a time when many Americans were leaving their farms and small towns for new homes in cities or for new farms and small towns on the frontier. With mobility undermining the ties of family, church, and community, education would provide some social glue, an element of stability. Schools could help young citizens adjust to changes and provide them with a common experience. Children could become individuals caring for their own interests as well as patriotic citizens preserving common national goals.

Other scholars believe that schools, especially in cities, were designed to control those who were poor and those who were recent arrivals. The rich desired to use education to "tame the poor" by getting them to accept inequality as an economic reality. Other "school controllers" were motivated by fears of moral decline. They saw Christian society threatened by drinking, prostitution, crime, political corruption, and—a more immediate temptation for youngsters—undesirable children's books. Through discipline and the teaching of high ideals, schools could counteract these influences and set children on the right path.

These theories, however, are not relevant for the majority of Gilded Age children who went to school in rural communities rather than in growing cities. From 1870 to 1900, 25 to 40 percent of all Americans lived in towns of more than 2,500. Rural schools were not created to cope with immigration, to respond to rapid economic change and population shifts, to shield the innocent minds of children from sin, or to teach poor children to accept inequality and not be influenced by foreign ideas to overthrow the government and reconstitute society.

Rural schools had three basic objectives. First, they wanted to train students to become self-reliant citizens who were thrifty, sober, orderly, serious, and competitive. Local taxpayers, loosely controlled by state governments, gave almost every child (the exceptions were among African-American and Indian children) an opportunity for a common-school, eight-year eduction so that they could become free citizens in charge of their own futures. Second, although the schools were secular, American republican and democratic ideals were taught to the point that they had religious overtones. America was the redeemer-savior-nation (one that could rescue a world of decadent monarchies), and children could carry out both their personal ambitions and responsibilities as citizens within God's plan. Finally, as either farmers or small business owners, young Americans needed education so that they could compete with producers at home and abroad. The careful education of children would enable a well-regulated society to balance its need for stability with the individual's desire for success.

Educational goals were carried out primarily in state-regulated community schools. Between 1865 and 1900 every state established requirements for minimal annual attendance, teaching certificates, basic curricula, and graduating tests. Local communities could tax and receive state aid if they carried out these minimal requirements. Very few other state regulations affected students and teachers. Many states also sponsored two- or three-day meetings where teachers could convene and learn new skills. Every small rural location had an elementary school teaching children through the eighth grade. Only 5 percent of the nation's children attended high schools, which were located in larger towns. Talented high school students from rural communities often had to board in larger towns and either pay tuition or establish residency.

The most salient change in Gilded Age primary schools was that more women than men taught school. In New Jersey, for example, male teachers outnumbered female teachers before the Civil War, but at its close in 1865 almost twice as many women were teaching as men, and by 1895 women outnumbered men by six to one. Teaching was a rapidly growing field for ambitious and qualified women who preferred it (especially with opportunities in rural areas or small towns) to urban employment as nurses or in business. However, few teachers remained in their jobs for more than a few years. In many counties the teaching force changed by 90 percent or more within a five-year period. Low wages for the largely female teaching force—and their individual desires to marry and raise a family—account for this shift.

Parochial schools were the most important trend in private education. A Roman Catholic educational system emerged in many urban areas following the call of the 1883

Council of Bishops in Baltimore for the expansion of Catholic schools in as many dioceses as possible. Catholics were unable to convince state legislatures that their schools merited state aid, even when bishops were willing to admit non-Catholic students (who would not participate in religious education) and to place their schools under state regulations. The expansion of private Catholic education paralleled the less significant growth of Protestant-based private schools.

Formal public and parochial school systems were not the only alternatives; there were also informal arrangements. An occasional bright teenager could be prepared for college entrance examinations by a tutor. Educational opportunities for adults existed. Farmers could learn the newest techniques by attending county fairs or by contact with agents of state departments of agriculture. In cities, businesspeople could pick up information at trade expositions, while any citizen could take courses sponsored by the CHAUTAUQUA MOVEMENT or at Young Mens Christian Associations (YMCA) and SETTLEMENT HOUSES. Courses were also available for immigrants who needed basic reading skills and knowledge to pass citizenship tests (which contained questions like What is a ballot?).

Between 1870 and 1900 publicly funded schools and informal educational opportunities could be found in every state and territory in communities of all sizes and wealth. A basic, locally administered common-school education was a national experience for nearly all children. The amount of money spent on public education varied greatly from state to state and from community to community within a state, and no state helped poor school districts by equalizing expenditures statewide. Virtually all Americans received a common-school education, but its quality varied considerably.

Further reading: Lawrence Cremin, *The American Common School: A Historical Conception* (New York: Teachers College Press, 1951); Wayne Fuller, *The Old Country School: The Story of Rural Education in the Midwest* (Chicago: University of Chicago Press, 1982); Joel Spring, *Education and the Rise of the American Corporate State* (Boston: Beacon Press, 1972); David B. Tyack, *The One Best System: A History of American Urban Education* (Cambridge, Mass.: Harvard University Press, 1974).

— Harry Stein

education, federal aid to

Through its land policy, the federal government from its inception supported common schools, but education was regarded as a state responsibility, exercised by local communities subject to state oversight. Using the sale of public lands to support education had its origins in the colonial period and was adopted by the Congress of the Articles of Confederation. Its Land Ordinance of 1785 created a system for surveying western lands into six-mile-square townships. In each township, one of its 36 sections was designated to support common schools. In the late 19th century, two sections (and in the early 20th century, four sections) in each state as it entered the Union were set aside for education.

In the late 19th century reformers tried to secure substantial federal aid for impoverished school districts, primarily in the South and West. Republican senator Henry W. Blair introduced a bill in 1881 to distribute among states, on the basis of illiteracy, $120 million over a 10-year period. The chief beneficiaries would be African-American children. Although the Senate passed the bill three times, it was killed in the House of Representatives by racist southerners and parsimonious northerners and never passed.

The federal government also supported higher education and research. Prior to the Civil War, public land granted to states as they entered the Union resulted in the establishment of state universities in Michigan, Indiana, and Wisconsin. In the 1840s and 1850s numerous advocates of an increased federal role in improving agricultural methods studied European models and petitioned CONGRESS for the funding of research and teacher training. In 1857 Republican senator Justin Morrill of Vermont introduced a bill encouraging the growth of higher education through the sale of public lands, and by 1859 it passed Congress only to be vetoed by President James Buchanan, who believed it would unconstitutionally encroach on states' rights by expanding federal power over education. Southern Democrats prevented an override of the veto.

In May and July 1862, with the nation at war and southern Democrats absent, the Republican Congress, with President Abraham Lincoln's approval, created the Department of Agriculture (which immediately began research on seed development and plant diseases) and signed Morrill's Land-Grant College Bill into law. The Morrill Act gave each state 30,000 acres of land for each senator and representative in Congress, and the states were free to sell these lands and use the proceeds to establish agricultural and mechanical colleges. As a result, land-grant institutions were created in every state, but the Morrill Act never provided enough money for the total support of a school. The federal government also provided special land grants for normal schools, schools of mines, military institutes, and segregated schools. An additional Morrill Act (1890) gave $25,000 annually to each land-grant college for studies related to the "industries of life." This term was used to prevent diverting the money to the liberal arts departments that existed in those institutions.

The 1887 Hatch Act, which gave states money for agricultural research stations, grew out of the work of land-grant universities and the Department of Agriculture. Department officials and college professors had for years been meeting in efforts to disseminate the results of agricultural experimentation to farmers. The research stations were designed to meet that need. By 1899, 56 research stations based in farming areas produced 445 reports and bulletins reaching more than a half-million farmers.

During the Gilded Age—a period of unparalleled agricultural and industrial expansion—the federal government recognized the value of technical training and scientific experimentation and, in limited but precise and important ways, encouraged higher education and the distribution of useful information.

Further reading: Fred A. Shannon, *The Farmer's Last Frontier: Agriculture, 1860–1897* (New York: Holt, Rinehart and Winston, 1945).

— Harry Stein

education, higher

From 1870 to 1900 the number of American institutions of higher learning jumped from 563 to 977, and the percentage of 18-to-21-year-old students increased from 1.7 to 4.1. These colleges and universities fall into three categories: privately endowed universities offering graduate as well as undergraduate programs; a large number of small, usually church-sponsored, liberal arts colleges; and public-supported state universities and land-grant colleges (encouraged by the Morrill Act of 1862), as well as the unusual City College of New York, established in 1847. Public-supported institutions offered technical and liberal arts training.

Graduate training expanded from 1870 to 1900. Before 1870, Harvard's Lawrence Scientific School and Yale's Sheffield Scientific School, as well as their schools of law and medicine, offered postgraduate training but few doctor of philosophy (Ph.D.) degrees. Aspiring American scholars went to Europe, especially Germany, for the Ph.D. until Johns Hopkins University, from its inception in 1876, emphasized graduate studies. Its president, Daniel Coit Gilman, made research the "soul" of the university and strived to combine the strengths of a traditional liberal arts college with a graduate program designed not only to preserve knowledge but also to discover and apply scientific knowledge. The Hopkins medical school, established in 1893, applied Gilman's concepts. Its outstanding faculty, high admission standards (open to women), affiliation with a teaching hospital, and sound financial footing made it the preeminent medical school in America in 1900.

During the last three decades of the 19th century, many American colleges and universities began offering their students a wide variety of majors and courses they could elect to meet degree requirements. This elective system was controversial. Charles William Eliot, Harvard's president, argued that the changing American economy and society needed college graduates who had been free to choose their course of study. Yale's president, Noah Porter, countered that while the elective system might benefit some earnest students, the vast majority were neither mature nor informed enough to make such crucial choices. He believed that a uniform college program should concentrate the attention of students on history, literature, and science before they began the pursuit of money through technical training. Porter also believed that the elective system would be costly, difficult to manage, and—by reducing common experiences—blur the identity of, and the camaraderie within, a college class. In 1885 James McCosh, the president of Princeton, took a moderate position combining Eliot's flexibility and Porter's rigidity. McCosh said the student should elect the college and major of his choice, but the faculty should determine the appropriate sequence of courses leading to a degree. All students at Princeton, whatever their major, had to study the trinity of language and literature, science, and philosophy.

Trends in higher education reflected the phenomenal growth of American agriculture and industry. The establishment of graduate programs, agricultural and mechanical colleges, and more flexible, practical curricula served the needs of a society organizing and reshaping itself. Despite the greater availability of higher learning in the late 19th century, only one out of 25 American youths attended college in 1900.

Further reading: Laurence R. Veysey, *The Emergence of the American University* (Chicago: University of Chicago Press, 1965).

— Harry Stein

education, philanthropy and

Following the Civil War, money from wealthy American philanthropists, especially businessmen, began to influence both private and public education in the United States. These funds were directed toward primary education in the impoverished and war-devastated Southern states and higher education elsewhere. Antebellum Southern states had invested little in common schools. After the war, if they were to teach theretofore neglected white and black children, they would have to rebuild, expand, and rethink their educational systems. This was a tall order in the postwar Reconstruction period, and Northerners recognized the need to raise private funds from churches and individuals to supplement the educational efforts of the federally financed Freedmen's Bureau.

Private and federal funding for Southern education focused on the secondary and college level to train teachers (black and white) for common, agricultural, and trade schools. Between 1865 and 1869 the American Missionary Association cooperated with the Freedmen's Bureau to establish Howard University in Washington, D.C., and seven other Negro institutions, including Fisk University in Nashville, Tennessee, and Atlanta University in Georgia. Individual philanthropists joined in this federal-religious effort to rebuild Southern education. Beginning in 1867 George Peabody, a London, England, merchant and financier by way of Massachusetts and Baltimore, set aside $3.5 million to establish the Peabody Education Fund. Peabody's aim was to "benefit the destitute areas of the South" and especially to aid the "children of the common people" by rebuilding its school system. He hoped that educational opportunity could bind the republic's wounds and improve the Southern economy. The Peabody Fund was administered by a board of trustees that included Presidents Ulysses S. Grant and RUTHERFORD B. HAYES. It was ultimately used to establish the George Peabody College for Teachers in Nashville (now part of Vanderbilt University).

In 1882, inspired by Peabody's example and the successful work of the fund's managers, John Slater, a Connecticut textile industrialist, donated $1 million to create the Slater Fund for "the uplifting of the lately emancipated population of the Southern States." Rutherford B. Hayes chaired the Slater Fund trustees, and under his leadership the fund invested in secondary and industrial training schools across the South, including Hampton Institute in Virginia, to produce prosperous black artisans, farmers, and businessmen. The Slater Fund also supported the efforts of individual scholars such as W. E. B. Du Bois, who went to Germany to further his graduate training in Berlin.

With few exceptions white southerners welcomed the support of these funds because their industrial education focus was nonthreatening. The funds carefully followed local social customs and did not attempt to integrate schools or, as was the case of the Peabody Fund, support the mixed-race common schools that existed in New Orleans until the mid-1870s. Although the Slater Fund aided Du Bois, the funds ignored his elitist notion that educational investment should concentrate on the "black talented tenth" who would attend universities and lead the black race. Between 1870 and 1900 northern philanthropy was a conservative but constructive force in southern society. In 1870, 80 percent of the African-American population 10 years or older was illiterate; by 1900 illiteracy had been reduced to 45 percent.

Philanthropists also established innovative universities in the post–Civil War years. Ezra Cornell founded Cornell University in 1868 by combining his $500,000 endowment with New York State's Morrill Act land grant. The new institution was unusual in that instruction was offered in agriculture and engineering, as the Morrill Act intended, as well as in the liberal arts; the classics were taught, but students could substitute German and French for Greek; it was open to the poor as well as to the rich and, starting in 1872, to women as well as to men; and there were no religious requirements for either faculty or students. Cornell was noted for its "liberal, progressive, and practical spirit."

Among other philanthropists, Johns Hopkins endowed both Johns Hopkins University and Johns Hopkins Hospital, which he intended to be a teaching hospital for the university's medical school. Hopkins died before the university opened in 1876, but unlike other American universities, it emphasized a graduate program designed to advance rather than to preserve knowledge. Leland Stanford endowed Stanford University, opened in 1891, with the largest American philanthropic gift up to that time. Stanford was coeducational and nonsectarian from its beginning, and Leland Stanford wished it to offer a broad curriculum in the arts and sciences as well as manual training. In the 1880s industrial training was in vogue not only for former slaves but also for the children of the affluent. John D. Rockefeller began contributing heavily to the University of Chicago in 1889 ($35 million by 1910), but unlike most philanthropists, he made no effort to influence its trustees, president, faculty, or curriculum.

Although virtually all American children were educated in public schools, philanthropic aid helped reduce illiteracy by training more teachers. And while states, complying with the Morrill Act, established universities with broad-based practical curricula, philanthropists established private universities that differed from traditional institutions like Harvard, Yale, and Princeton.

Further reading: B. Edward McClelland, *The Social History of American Education* (Champaign: University of Illinois Press, 1988).

— Harry Stein

elections, conduct of

With the exception of largely ineffectual federal Enforcement Acts, late-19th-century elections—federal, state, and local—were controlled by the states. In 1870 there was no secret balloting in the United States, although oral voting survived in only a few places in the South. Printed ballots, which with many elective offices tended to be lengthy, were prepared by political parties with only their candidates and none of their opponents listed. Voting a split ticket required the erasing ("scratching") of a candidate and writing in his opponent's name while party regulars at the polls, at the very least, glared their disapproval. Understandably, straight party voting was the rule and scratchers were rare. Voters were not only subjected to peer pressure but also economic pressure. Employers, making certain they hired the votes as well as the labor of their workers, supplied them with ballots and marched them to the polls. In large cities, political machines falsified registration lists with names from tombstones and often sought to discourage respectable voters by siting the polls at disreputable locations. Civil servants whose jobs depended on the outcome of the election, or those who wanted to replace them, effectively got out the vote.

By 1900 some significant changes had occurred. Purchasing and influencing voters through economic or peer pressure was greatly reduced and split-ticket voting greatly increased by the use of the Australian or secret ballot, which had been adopted by all states. Government-printed ballots listed all candidates, and voters marked the ballots in the privacy of a booth. Stringent voter registration requirements reduced fraud, but this also discouraged lower socioeconomic groups from voting. In addition, black southerners, who had exercised universal male suffrage in 1870, were by 1900, despite the Fifteenth Amendment, completely disfranchised by intimidation, literacy tests, poll taxes (in every southern state by 1904), or by the GRANDFATHER CLAUSE in their constitutions, which denied the vote to the descendants of those who could not vote in 1867 (in South Carolina [1895] and Louisiana [1898]). Thanks to CIVIL SERVICE REFORM, government employees were no longer active in getting out the vote, and that factor—along with registration laws, the "solid" Democratic South, and huge Republican majorities in the rest of the country—led to lower voter turnout. But as a harbinger of a more democratic era for them, women had won the vote by state action in the western states of Wyoming, Colorado, Utah, and Idaho in 1900.

Further reading: Paul Klepner, *Who Voted? The Dynamics of Electoral Turnout, 1870–1980* (New York: Praeger, 1982).

elective system See education, higher

elevated railroads (els) See transportation, urban

Ellis Island See immigration

entertainment, popular

The second half of the 19th century was an age of mass entertainment in the United States. Urban audiences had ready access to THEATER, minstrelsy, vaudeville, and other popular amusements, while showboats, touring troupes, tent shows, repertory companies, circuses, and Wild West shows took comedy, drama, MUSIC, and action to the hinterlands. In addition to this wide array of live entertainments, there were technical marvels such as dioramas, panoramas, cycloramas, and—by the end of the century—motion pictures, not to mention the wonders and oddities on display at museums and expositions.

Minstrelsy was the principal form of popular entertainment in America during the middle third of the 19th century. Unlike most musical or theatrical performances of the period, minstrelsy was largely, though not exclusively, indigenous entertainment. It was, as Eric Lott has written, "the national art of the moment." Minstrel shows typically included songs, dances, instrumental specialties, comic dialogues, novelty acts, parodies of "stump speeches," and burlesques. The performers were white entertainers who mimicked AFRICAN AMERICANS by wearing burnt-cork makeup (blackface), speaking in exaggerated dialect, exploiting well-established stereotypes, and performing music that ostensibly originated in the slave communities of antebellum plantations. Some black troupes (who also performed in blackface) toured the eastern states during the antebellum period and the Civil War, often appearing before abolitionist groups, but minstrelsy was essentially a white enterprise. Even the black companies came under white management by the 1870s. Managers, actors, and songwriters were typically northerners who had little or no knowledge of African Americans or of the plantation life that they romanticized.

This ignorance hardly mattered to either the performers or the audiences, for minstrelsy did not strive for authenticity; its function was to entertain and lampoon. In so doing, minstrels depicted plantation blacks as shiftless, ignorant (but cunning), and contented. Northern blacks were dandies, con men, gamblers, and womanizers. Black women, on the other hand, were not subjected to such derision. The comedy was not limited to African-American stereotypes. The stump speech, for instance, mocked pomposity, verbosity, and bogus intellectualism while satirizing abolitionism, temperance, women's rights, and other current issues. The burlesque numbers enabled minstrels to lampoon high culture—Shakespeare, opera, and classical music.

Minstrelsy reached its peak about 1860, when there were about 100 companies nationwide, 10 in New York City. By 1880 the number of companies had declined to about 30. The content and format had begun to change during the 1870s. One company, Primrose and West, kept the basic structure but dispensed with blackface altogether, dressing its performers as 18th-century French courtiers. Another promoter, J. H. Haverly, combined four companies into one and promoted his United Mastodon Minstrels as a spectacle, comparable to the circus. He included tightrope walkers, acrobats, clowns, bareback riders, and a brass band. Over time the comedy routines made less use of African-American stereotypes; the new objects of ridicule were immigrants, especially the Irish. Cultural historians attribute the decline of minstrelsy to many factors, including the PANIC OF 1873, the rise of variety, burlesque, and vaudeville shows, as well as postbellum concerns about African Americans. Race was no longer a laughing matter; the theatrical depiction of slave life had become the preserve of reformist melodramas such as *Uncle Tom's Cabin*.

Race, understandably, remains an important issue in critiques and cultural histories of minstrelsy. During the antebellum period, Frederick Douglass, the great African-American abolitionist, described minstrels as "filthy scum of white society, who have stolen from us a complexion denied them by nature, in which to make money, and pander to the corrupt taste of their white fellow-citizens." Russel B. Nye, writing in 1970, maintained that minstrelsy's obvious artificiality minimized the social effects of its negative African-American stereotypes. Robert C. Toll in 1976 stressed the popular appeal and entertainment value of the shows while acknowledging the harmful lingering effects of minstrel stereotypes. More recently, William L. Mahar (1999) and Eric Lott (1993) depicted minstrelsy as a two-way medium of cultural diffusion between blacks and whites.

Vaudeville superseded minstrelsy in popularity during the last 20 years of the 19th century. Vaudeville was principally an outgrowth of variety and burlesque, though it also perpetuated elements of minstrelsy. (Prominent vaudevillians such as Al Jolson and Eddie Cantor were performing in blackface even as late as the 1920s.) Variety, which had the greatest influence on vaudeville, was a hodgepodge of low comedy, songs, specialty acts (jugglers, hypnotists, acrobats), and dancing girls. The venue for variety was the concert saloon, with the audience consisting of men who wanted to be entertained while they imbibed. The blend of booze and sexuality in the disreputable atmosphere of the saloon caused respectable women to stay away from the shows and led moralists and reformers to charge that concert saloons were dens of vice. Variety shows that featured scantily clad women were called leg shows. The more risqué of these evolved into burlesque, although the traditional burlesque theater specialized in comedy skits and parodies of well-known plays and novels. By the 1890s these separate strands had merged. The typical burlesque show of the late 19th century included song-and-dance routines, double-entendre jokes, and slapstick, but partially dressed women were the principal attraction. The more daring shows presented "exotic" dancers, who did a variation of the belly dance. (Striptease was a much later innovation.) The performer who called herself Little Egypt became a celebrity by doing such a dance in Chicago at the WORLD'S COLUMBIAN EXPOSITION in 1893.

A key figure in the emergence of vaudeville was Tony Pastor, a singer and songwriter who operated variety theaters in New Jersey and New York City after 1865. A devout Catholic who had once sung at temperance rallies, Pastor revamped variety by prohibiting alcohol and forbidding vulgar comedy and suggestive dances in his shows. His goal was to attract middle-class families to his theaters by providing popular entertainment in a respectable venue. Pastor's formula, which he continued to call variety, was adopted by the emerging vaudeville theaters of the 1880s and 1890s. In Boston, B. F. Keith and Edward F. Albee employed a similar strategy, but enhanced by continuous performances in opulent new theaters designed to appeal to a broader and more affluent audience than those who went to concert saloons and burlesque houses. The policy of continuous performances enabled patrons to arrive at their convenience anytime between 9:30 A.M. and 10:00 P.M. and see a complete performance. By acquiring a circuit of theaters and creating their own booking agency, Keith and Albee dominated the vaudeville business in the eastern United States. Martin Beck's Orpheum Circuit was equally influential west of the Mississippi. Black performers worked the so-called Chitlin Circuit, a network of segregated theaters scattered between New York and New Orleans, controlled by the Theatre Owners Booking Association.

Between 1880 and 1920, when vaudeville was the reigning form of popular entertainment in the United States, every city had at least one vaudeville house. New York City had 10, including the Palace Theater, vaudeville's premier venue. Small towns and rural areas had to make do with occasional touring companies and tent shows. Vaudeville succeeded by virtue of its "cheerful frivolity," as one writer put it, as well as its peculiar blend of wholesomeness and urban sophistication, and the tempo and precision of its staging.

Successful vaudeville performers were those who timed, tested, and refined their material to achieve maximum impact during their brief turn in the spotlight. Shows typically opened with a "dumb act" (acrobats, jugglers, mimes, or trained animals). Then came comedians, ventriloquists, magicians, song-and-dance acts, skits, virtuoso instrumentalists, knife throwers, bird whistlers, and so on. The first half of the show always closed with a dynamic showstopper that made audiences eager for more. A similar lineup followed the intermission, except that the headliner came on next to closing. Among the leading vaudeville stars of the 1890s were comedians Weber and Fields, Sandow the Strong Man, dancer Eva Tanguay, and singer Lillian Russell. The final presentation was the "chaser," designed to hasten the crowd to the exits so a new audience could take its place. During the late 1890s motion pictures, then a mere novelty, served this function.

During its vogue, vaudeville, particularly the comedians, reflected the changing ethnic character of its audiences. With its broad appeal to pluralistic urban spectators, vaudeville provided unique opportunities for performers of varied ethnic backgrounds. African Americans were an exception to this trend. Even the great Bert Williams, one of the few African-American entertainers not restricted to the "Chitlin Circuit," did his act in blackface. Vaudeville also stereotyped Germans, Irish, and Jews, though the performers often shared the ethnic identities of their comic personas. Thus, white ethnic stereotypes provided employment opportunities for Irish and Jewish comics and singers. Vaudeville also offered prospects for women, who could find respectable employment, opportunities for self-expression, even wealth and fame in a business that welcomed their talents and allure.

The period after the Civil War also saw the beginning of a golden age for circus in America, thanks in large part to P. T. BARNUM, the nation's leading showman. Barnum launched his circus on a grand scale in 1871, then in 1880 teamed with James A. Bailey to create a unique spectacle: simultaneous acts in three rings surrounded by a hippodrome track for parades and races. Barnum promoted this "greatest show on earth" with parades and well-calculated publicity stunts. Jumbo, billed as the world's largest elephant, was the show's star attraction until the great beast was killed in a railroad accident in 1885. After Jumbo's demise the circus headlined the trapeze acts and tightrope walkers, supported by the usual clowns, equestrians, and wild animal routines. Barnum and Bailey were the first to make effective use of the nation's burgeoning railroad system, moving their circus from town to town and thus maximizing the number of performances by minimizing the time between show dates. Barnum & Bailey's main competition came from the Ringling Bros. Circus, formed in 1884. (The Ringlings acquired Barnum & Bailey in 1906 but operated it separately until 1918, when they merged their troupes to create the gigantic Ringling Bros. and Barnum & Bailey Circus.)

Wild West shows combined elements of the circus with the frontier myth to form a uniquely American spectacle. P. T. Barnum staged a Wild West show in 1874, but it was

Poster for Buffalo Bill's Wild West Show *(Library of Congress)*

Colonel WILLIAM F. CODY ("Buffalo Bill") who made the most of the "equestrian drama," as he called the genre. Cody, the renowned buffalo hunter and U.S. Army scout, was the hero of DIME NOVELS by Ned Buntline (Edward E. C. Judson) and in 1872–73 had appeared on stage in a play by Buntline. He returned to the West to fight under General GEORGE ARMSTRONG CUSTER and Philip H. Sheridan in the Indian wars of the 1870s, but in 1882 at North Platte, Nebraska, he mounted an outdoor show featuring exhibitions of roping, riding, sharpshooting, and a dramatic reenactment of a stagecoach robbery. The initial public response convinced Cody that a grander version of the show would be a great attraction across the country. He enlarged his cast, added buffaloes and NATIVE AMERICANS for greater authenticity, and staged an exciting Pony Express ride. Cody's first national tour culminated with a successful engagement at New York's Madison Square Garden. In 1885 Cody hired the great Sioux warrior and holy man SITTING BULL and sharpshooter Annie Oakley. His 1887 European tour caused a sensation in the Old World. Circus magnate James Bailey gained control of the company in 1894, though Cody remained with the show. The logistical expertise Bailey had gained in the circus business enabled the troupe to barnstorm the country with maximum efficiency. Cody's success inspired competing shows such as the Miller Brothers 101 Ranch and Pawnee Bill's Show. Reformed bandits Cole Younger and Frank James had a show that reenacted famous bank robberies.

Wild West shows survived until the 1930s. By then movies were the principal interpreters and purveyors of America's frontier legends. The shows, however, had a lasting impact on American popular culture. They romanticized the frontier experience and immortalized the plainsmen who opened up the West. They glorified courage, resourcefulness, and personal freedom in a boundless land, but they also justified frontier violence by promoting negative stereotypes of Native Americans. Some modern critics contend that the spectacles simultaneously defamed and exploited their Show Indians; others note that the Show Indians welcomed opportunities to get away from oppressive reservations, travel the world, and enjoy a degree of economic independence. And, they add, by performing native dances, replicating their traditional village encampments, and reenacting heroic battles, Show Indians sustained for a time their cultural identities in the face of powerful pressures for assimilation.

If so, Show Indians would have been an exception, for popular entertainment in the latter years of the 19th century was, on the whole, an agency of assimilation. Vaudeville, for instance, provided an element of shared culture for people of diverse ethnicity, both on stage and in the audience. Show business during this period also operated on the principle that bigger is better, with shows and venues growing larger and more opulent. And, like other contemporary enterprises, the entertainment industry adopted a strategy of consolidation, often to the disadvantage of the performers. Finally, the rise of mass amusements marked the continuing decline of VICTORIANISM and the notion that leisure activities should not merely amuse but also build character.

Further reading: Gunther Barth, *City People: The Rise of Modern City Culture in Nineteenth-Century America* (New York: Oxford University Press, 1980); Eric Lott, *Love and Theft: Blackface Minstrelsy and the American Working Class* (New York: Oxford University Press, 1993); William J. Mahar, *Behind the Burnt Cork Mask: Early Blackface Minstrelsy and Antebellum American Popular Culture* (Urbana: University of Illinois Press, 1999); L. G. Moses, *Wild West Shows and the Images of American Indians, 1883–1933* (Albuquerque: University of New Mexico Press, 1996); Russel B. Nye, *The Unembarrassed Muse: The Popular Arts in America* (New York: Dial Press, 1970); Robert W. Synder, *The Voice of the City: Vaudeville and Popular Culture in New York City* (New York: Oxford University Press, 1989); Robert C. Toll, *On With the Show: The First Century of Show Business in America* (New York: Oxford University Press, 1976).

— William Hughes

F

farmers' alliances

The term *farmers' alliances* was used to refer to the two powerful organizations that succeeded the PATRONS OF HUSBANDRY (the Granger movement) as the leading vehicles of agrarian protest in the post–Civil War period: the Northwestern Alliance and the Southern Alliance. Like the Grangers, the alliances were principally concerned with: declining agricultural prices, escalating railroad rates (shipping costs), problems with credit, land speculators, and the exploitation of farmers by the "money power" (banks and big business). Applying self-help solutions to their problems, they formed cooperatives and other marketing mechanisms such as stores, processing plants, and banks. These facilities were designed to break farmers' dependence on the "finishing merchants" who acted as the middlemen in an economic cycle that kept farmers in perpetual debt. They favored an inflation of the money supply either through an increase in the amount of greenbacks (paper currency) in circulation or the free and unlimited coinage of silver (FREE SILVER). Alliance members also attacked the NATIONAL BANKING SYSTEM as a tool used by corrupt financiers and politicians to make an easy profit. In some ways, then, the alliances sought to create a new American society where economic competition would be replaced by cooperation.

As early as 1875, a group of Texas farmers had united to form an alliance against local cattle ranchers, railroad operators, and land speculators, but it was short-lived. A new farmers' organization, the Southern Farmers' Alliance, emerged in the 1880s to take its place. After 1886 Charles W. Macune and William Lamb led the Southern Farmers' Alliance. It quickly expanded from Texas into neighboring southern states, and by 1890 the Southern Farmers' Alliance had evolved into the National Farmers' Alliance and Industrial Union. It became affiliated with an organization of African-American farmers known as the Colored Farmers' Alliance and with the KNIGHTS OF LABOR.

Milton George, the editor of the *Western Rural*, a Chicago-based agricultural journal, founded the Northwestern Alliance in 1880. George wanted the new organization to combat what he believed were the unfair practices of RAILROADS against the nation's farmers. Under George's leadership, the Northwestern Alliance established several local alliances in the Dakotas, Kansas, Minnesota, and Nebraska. Yet, the Northwestern Alliance never formulated a cohesive program and had great difficulty in attracting and keeping members.

Although the Alliance movement would eventually become far more widespread than the Granger movement, it suffered setbacks. Alliance cooperatives did not always work well, in part because the market forces were too strong to overcome but also because of mismanagement. These economic frustrations led several Alliance members to seek other avenues to remedy their situation. By the late 1880s, they helped steer the Alliance movement into electoral politics through the creation of a national political party.

Meeting in Ocala, Florida, in 1890, representatives of the farmers' alliances made demands that Macune helped formulate. The Ocala demands called for the direct election of U.S. senators; a graduated federal income tax; an end to protective tariffs and the National Banking System; 2-percent federal loans to farmers; the establishment of federal "subtreasuries" for the storage of surplus crops on which the 2-percent loans to farmers could be based; prohibition of land ownership by aliens; the free and unlimited coinage of silver at a ratio of 16-to-one; and effective government regulation and, if necessary, control of railroads and public utilities.

Of these demands, the establishment of a subtreasury system was most important. Farmers could hold their crops in government warehouses and claim Treasury notes for up to 80 percent of the local market value of the crops. The loan was to be repaid when the crops were sold. The idea was that the subtreasury system would help farmers pay their annual debts because they could hold on to their crops until market prices were more favorable.

Subsequently, leaders of the farmers' alliance discussed plans for the organization of a national political party at meetings held in Cincinnati (1891) and St. Louis (1892). They would follow the lead of Alliance members in Kansas who had already launched the PEOPLE'S PARTY in that state during the summer of 1890. In July 1892 several Alliance members were among the delegates and spectators who met at Omaha, Nebraska, in what was the first national convention of the PEOPLE'S (Populist) PARTY. The OMAHA PLATFORM in many ways mirrored the Ocala demands.

The creation of the People's Party effectively brought an end to the Alliance movement. The leaders of the Northwestern Alliance in their enthusiasm for the new party forgot the original purpose of their protest movement, while the members of the Southern Farmers' Alliance steadfastly identified with the DEMOCRATIC PARTY and were reluctant to join the Populists. By the middle 1890s, the Alliance movement had lost its vitality on the national stage as the Democrats and the emerging People's Party co-opted its ideas.

See also POLITICAL PARTIES, THIRD; SIMPSON, JERRY.

Further reading: Lawrence Goodwyn, *Democratic Promise: The Populist Movement in America* (New York: Oxford University Press, 1976); John D. Hicks, *The Populist Revolt: A History of the Farmers Alliance and the People's Party* (Lincoln: University of Nebraska Press, 1961); Theodore Saloutos, *Farmer Movements in the South, 1865–1933* (Lincoln: University of Nebraska Press, 1964); Michael Schwartz, *Radical Protest and Social Structure: The Southern Farmers Alliance and Cotton Tenancy, 1880–1890* (New York: Academic Press, 1976).

— Phillip Papas

Filipino insurrection (1899–1902)

The Filipino insurrection was a three-year conflict that began in 1899 after the SPANISH-AMERICAN WAR, and the United States declared itself sovereign over the entire archipelago of the Philippines. The struggle against the Americans had its beginnings in the Filipino revolt against the Spanish. Its first phase ended in 1896 when Primo de Rivera, then prime minister of Spain, negotiated a settlement whereby Spain promised economic and political reforms and the rebel leader Emilio Aguinaldo would receive 800,000 pesos and leave the country. The rebels, exiled in Hong Kong, were well organized and anxious for another try at winning their independence.

They did not have a long wait. The American invasion of the Philippines at the start of the Spanish-American War in 1898 was seen by the rebels as a new opportunity to rid the islands of Spanish domination. Admiral GEORGE DEWEY, who was in Hong Kong preparing his fleet for the battle that would make him famous, offered veiled assurances to Aguinaldo that the United States would win independence for the Philippines in exchange for their support against the Spanish. When Aguinaldo arrived in Luzon after the Battle of Manila Bay, many Filipinos flocked to the cause. Within a short time Aguinaldo had enough troops to effectively block Manila from being supplied by land. Trouble, however, began in August 1898 after the United States tricked the rebels into yielding a portion of their entrenchments and then (with the connivance of the Spanish authorities) captured Manila without the Filipino army. Aguinaldo was further angered by continued American evasiveness as to their intentions in the archipelago.

By February 1899 Filipino troops faced American lines in a tense standoff that flashed into a conflagration when Private Walter Grayson, a Nebraska volunteer, shot and killed several Filipino soldiers while he was on patrol. United States troops then stormed the Filipino lines, killing many soldiers; a bloody war had begun. While troops under General Marcus Mills seized the Visayan Islands to the west, General Arthur MacArthur, father of the more famous General Douglas MacArthur, headed north of Manila on Luzon to Malalos. Badly defeated in pitched battles that followed, the Filipinos switched to guerrilla tactics that the Americans, with only 24,000 troops, could not counter effectively, thus necessitating reinforcement by 46,000 more men. Aguinaldo hoped that guerrilla warfare would protract the war and wear down the already tepid public support for it in the United States.

The Americans won the hearts and minds of some Filipinos by setting up schools and local government and by constructing hospitals, roads, and sewers, but guerrilla activity and terrorism continued unabated. The inability to distinguish between friend and foe created frustration and fear among American troops, who increasingly tried to bring peace through brutality.

Internal dissent within the independence movement and the capture and defection of many of its leaders did more to slow the rebels' momentum than American military might. The insurrection could be said to have finally ended in March 1902, when Aguinaldo was captured in a daring raid perpetrated by American and loyal Filipino troops, but resistance in the southern Philippines continued for years after Aguinaldo's capture.

The costs of this war was appalling. Between 100,000 and 200,000 Filipino civilians died of starvation or were killed during the war. Military casualties for the rebels amounted to about 20,000, while American losses were 4,234 killed and 2,818 wounded. In addition, many surviving veterans would die back home from the tropical diseases they contracted during the war.

Further reading: Stanley Karnow, *In Our Image: America's Empire in the Philippines* (New York: Random House, 1989).

— Timothy E. Vislocky

flour milling

The expansion of grain-growing regions, the development of a rail network, and the building of storage facilities in the Gilded Age made possible the development of large-scale, year-round flour milling, but a process was needed to mill the hard spring wheat grown on the northern prairies. Cadwallader Colden Washburn, a Minneapolis flour miller, solved that problem in 1879 by utilizing technologies developed in Hungary (where rollers rather than millstones were used to break the hard wheat) and France (where purifiers with air blowers separated unwanted particles from the flour). Washburn also designed a mill that derived maximum efficiency from this machinery to produce flour rapidly and cheaply.

The "new process" mill was adopted by the Pillsbury brothers and other Minneapolis millers, and that city soon dominated the industry. By 1882 Minneapolis produced 3 million bushels of flour annually, or one–twenty-third of the nation's entire output. By 1890 it milled more than 7 million bushels or one-twelfth of all the flour milled in the United States. The huge volume of flour shipments out of Minneapolis and competing RAILROADS enabled millers there to secure rebates and gain a larger share of the market. Indeed, discriminatory freight rates favoring Minneapolis flour ruined New York millers and led to demands in that state for railroad regulation.

Further reading: John Storck and Walter Dorwin Teague, *Flour for Man's Bread: A History of Milling* (Minneapolis: University of Minnesota Press, 1952).

football

College football originated in informal matches. Students played both the soccer and rugby versions in pickup games and interclass rivalries. In November 1869 Rutgers University defeated Princeton University, 6-4, in the first intercollegiate football game at New Brunswick, New Jersey. The contest combined rugby and soccer. Princeton won a rematch, 8-0, at home a week later. Harvard University and McGill University in the spring of 1874 played a rugby style of football. Harvard defeated Yale University, 4-0, in their inaugural game in 1875. In November 1876 Columbia University, Harvard, Princeton, and Yale formed the Intercollegiate Football Association to standardize rules. Harvard's rugby style prevailed over Yale's soccer style, with play continuing until the ball went out of bounds. Opponents stopped the ball carrier by nearly any means. Football did not have a line of scrimmage, a series of downs, or forward passing. New rules added blocking, alternating ball possessions, and a fixed numbers of downs. Students operated college football teams, selecting, coaching, training, organizing, and financing the squads. Student captains trained and disciplined their teams, while other undergraduates held fund drives and raised subscriptions. Faculty and administration gradually intervened in the organization and oversight of the sport, but students continued to direct on-field activities.

Walter Camp transformed rugby-style football into American football. An all-around athlete at Yale from 1876 to 1882, the six-foot 200 pounder starred at halfback for six years as an undergraduate and medical student. He captained his final three years, picking the starters and deciding plays. Camp abandoned medicine to join the New Haven Clock Company (ultimately becoming its president), but he also directed the Yale football team and built it into a powerful winning program. Camp analyzed the team's work with student coaches each evening, institutionalized regular practice and training, and stressed team work, strategy, tactics, and character building.

Camp represented Yale for 48 years at football's annual rules conventions. In 1878 he pushed through a rule restricting starters to 11 players, and in 1880 he secured a rule establishing the scrimmage line. Organized plays further transformed English rugby into American football. To speed football, Camp in 1882 proposed a series of downs (three) to gain a set number of yards (initially five), new styles of blocking, and tackling below the waist. The committee established a scoring system, awarding one point for a safety, two for touchdowns, four for conversions after touchdowns, and five for field goals. Camp tried to outlaw the flying wedge, a play conceived by Princeton in 1884. The flying wedge placed the ball carrier in the crook of a V-shaped mass of offensive linemen who stampeded into the defense on each play. Camp proposed penalizing teams five yards for crossing the scrimmage line before the ball was snapped. In 1893 Camp became secretary of the intercollegiate football rules committee, securing the sport's future. The group eliminated the flying wedge and other dangerous plays.

Besides being an innovator, organizer, and tactician, Camp was football's most prominent national spokesman, promoter, and defender. He headed a blue-ribbon commission to investigate football brutality and concluded that football had markedly benefited players both physically and mentally. Camp also promoted football by selecting an all-America team beginning in 1889. Yale, Harvard, Princeton, and Pennsylvania dominated college football, often trouncing smaller schools and boasting all but two all-America players between 1889 and 1898.

By the 1890s college football had gained a degree of popularity among the middle and upper classes and became a national sport. The Ivy League and Western Conference were formed, rivalries were established, and teams traveled longer distances for intersectional games. As football's popularity increased, the alumni gained virtually

Football game between Yale and Princeton *(Library of Congress)*

complete control over college sports. Universities began to see football as a means of making money. Yale football receipts grew to $100,000 yearly, one-eighth of the institution's total income. The annual Thanksgiving Day championship game between the two best college teams eventually drew more than 40,000 spectators in New York City and started the winter social season.

Football provoked considerable controversy. It was a brutal sport, causing frequent injuries: In a 19-year period, 50 players died from injuries. Football also developed a win-at-any-cost mentality. Players and alumni emphasized victory so much that many colleges engaged in shady, dishonest recruiting practices. Tramp athletes made a career of playing college football. Martin Thayer performed for 13 years at nine schools, while James Hogan played football at three other schools after being expelled from Yale. As college football truly became a spectacle, university officials began denouncing the sport. Dean Shailer Mathews of the University of Chicago protested, "Football is a boy-killing, education-prostituting gladiatorial sport," while President Nicholas Murray Butler of Columbia University called football "madness and slaughter." By 1900 college football needed to reform or face extinction.

Further reading: Ivan N. Kaye, *Good Clean Violence: A History of College Football* (Philadelphia: J. B. Lippincott Co., 1973); Michael Oriard, *Reading Football: How the Popular Press Created an American Sporting Spectacle* (Chapel Hill: University of North Carolina Press, 1993); Ronald A. Smith, *Sports and Freedom: The Rise of Big Time Time College Athletics* (New York: Oxford University Press, 1988).

— David L. Porter

foreign policy

Through its territorial acquisitions in 1898 at the close of the SPANISH-AMERICAN WAR, the United States achieved world-power status. Historians have stressed that expansion before 1900 resulted either from Manifest Destiny, an American variant of a worldwide ultranationalistic urge for foreign conquest and colonies (IMPERIALISM), or from American industrialism and its need for markets for its products.

Undoubtedly, the move by the United States onto the world stage had both internal and external causes as it experienced unprecedented economic growth in an age of increasing nationalistic rivalries. Changing global patterns required presidents to be increasingly engaged in the conduct of international relations. This growth of presidential direction and power is the most significant development in American foreign policy in the late 19th century. The period began with the Senate humiliating Ulysses S. Grant by rejecting the SANTO DOMINGO ANNEXATION Treaty in February 1870 and it ended in 1900 with WILLIAM MCKINLEY sending an expeditionary force of 5,000 troops to help put down the Boxer Rebellion in China without consulting CONGRESS. The transformation of America's role in the world helped transform the American PRESIDENCY.

In 1870 Americans concentrated on the Western Hemisphere and were concerned by the presence of European powers: France had only recently withdrawn an army from Mexico, where it had supported a government headed by an Austrian-born emperor. The Dominion of Canada, although it had local autonomy, was a part of the British Empire. In the Caribbean, all the islands except Haiti were under the suzerainty of a European state. More importantly, Britain—not the United States—dominated the foreign trade of Latin America. Any assertion of U.S. interests had to take into consideration the commanding position of Europe in the Caribbean and in Latin America.

The United States, however, had enormous potential power. By 1885 it was the world's most productive manufacturer. Steel production exceeded that of Britain the following year, while energy consumption surpassed all other nations by 1890. Agricultural production did not lag behind: In the years from 1865 to 1890, wheat and corn production grew by 256 and 222 percent, respectively. The arrival of 11.5 million European immigrants in the last three decades of the century provided labor in fields and factories. Over the period from 1873 to 1913, the U.S. economy grew at an average annual rate of 5 percent compared with Britain's 1.6 percent over the same period.

American policymakers, however, were aware that American power was latent. America's small army was deployed against NATIVE AMERICANS on the frontier while its deteriorating navy (prior to its strengthening in the 1880s) was supposed to protect the coasts and in no way could enforce foreign policy. The State Department in 1869 employed only 31 clerks, and its staff by 1881 had grown to only 50. While prominent politicians and intellectuals might find representing the nation abroad rewarding, few Americans aspired to a diplomatic career, which still had the taint of Europe's aristocracy. Exams for consular service originated in the early 1890s in the wake of CIVIL SERVICE REFORM, but few Americans were experienced in conducting international affairs.

In a world dominated by European political and military power, American diplomats had few opportunities to assert themselves. European powers subjugated Africa and Asia. Where formal colonies did not exist, the European powers exercised control through protectorates and spheres of influence. However, this redounded to the benefit of American businessmen and missionaries, who enjoyed the entitlements of white men. Most-favored-nation clauses in treaties with the states of East Asia enabled Americans to obtain the same advantages as British subjects.

Until the late 1890s U.S. foreign affairs were overshadowed by domestic matters. Despite minor territorial disputes with Britain, America's borders were secure, and its attention was focused on Reconstruction, financial panics and ensuing depressions, violent strikes, and differences over the printing of greenbacks and the minting of silver. Foreign crises occurred only intermittently, but in the final decade of the century, with increasing rapidity, problems arose involving Chile, HAWAII, Venezuela, CUBA, and China.

This quickening diplomatic pace reflected the accelerating pace of life in the late 19th century. The revolution in industrial production was accompanied by a revolution in the communication and retrieval of information. Telegraph lines and submarine cables provided instant communication around the globe, and information could be stored in a legible, accessible form thanks to the introduction of the typewriter, tabs, index cards, and file folders in modern offices. The U.S. State Department, however, with its archaic filing and indexing practices, remained haphazard in its record keeping (relying heavily on the memories of old hands) until the 20th century.

International rivalry increased for markets in both farm produce and industrial goods. By the 1870s American farmers found themselves competing in a global marketplace. More significantly, American businessmen and farmers became convinced that growth depended on finding foreign markets. This belief became commonplace even before the disastrous economic depression that began in 1893. Commentators of the time took satisfaction in the rising proportion of manufactured goods among exports, which reached one-third of the total exports by the end of the century.

Rivalry among the great powers also played a part in the rising American concern with foreign policy. The newly industrialized powers of Germany, Russia, and Japan joined the competition for colonies in Africa and Asia, and American traders and investors had to contend with Germans as well as the British in Latin America and the Japanese in Hawaii. Americans had confidence that their products compared favorably with foreign rivals unless handicapped by barriers to trade, and to ensure favorable terms of trade the United States negotiated reciprocal tariff reductions with Hawaii and Latin America. Congress, representing particular interests that were frequently threatened by imports, viewed with unease the presidential power contained in the reciprocal treaties and frequently undermined these agreements.

The foreign crises of the 1890s increased the power of presidents. Civil service reform and the incipient regulation of business favored the executive over the legislative branch, but these were minor contributions to the modern presidency when compared with the demands of an effective foreign policy. America's status in world affairs was enhanced by the naval buildup begun in the 1880s and the investiture of larger and better-paid staffs of embassies abroad, including the appointment of military and naval attachés that began in 1889. The reach of the presidents of the 1890s was therefore longer than their predecessors.

In 1870 Grant's hope of annexing Santo Domingo was frustrated by the Senate, but the wartime emergency in 1898 conferred almost unrestricted power on William McKinley as commander in chief. Traditional restraints on expansion and other foreign policy goals weakened at this time of heightened nationalism. McKinley was a masterful political manager, but he could not have enhanced the powers of the president without the opportunity to intervene in Cuba against Spain. The triumph of the expansionists with the declaration of war against Spain was not total, since Congress asserted that Cuban independence was the goal of intervention. But when American military forces occupied Spanish possessions, the economic and strategic arguments of expansionists prevailed, and the United States opted to control Cuba as a protectorate and Puerto Rico and the Philippines as colonies. McKinley, who made the key decision, embraced imperialism to thwart other imperialist powers. American presidents were no longer merely interested in upholding the Monroe Doctrine in the Western Hemisphere, where the United States was paramount; rather, as the century came to a close, they were prepared to assume new responsibilities across the wide Pacific Ocean.

Further reading: Charles S. Campbell *The Transformation of American Foreign Relations, 1865–1900* (New York: Harper & Row, 1976); Walter LaFeber, *The New Empire: An Interpretation of American Expansion, 1860–1898* (Ithaca, N.Y.: Cornell University Press, 1963); Ernest R. May, *Imperial Democracy: The Emergency of America as a Great Power* (New York: Harper & Row, 1961); Fareed Zakaria, *From Wealth to Power: The Unusual Origins of America's World Role* (Princeton, N.J.: Princeton University Press, 1998).

— Bruce Abrams

Forest Reserve Act (1891)

The federal push to manage logging and protect forests started in earnest in the late 1880s. CONGRESS responded by passing the Forest Reserve Act in 1891, which allowed the president to create forest reserves, a precursor of the national forest system.

In the colonial period, the British Crown—and early in the history of the United States, the federal government—reserved the right to preserve timber on lands in the public domain (for shipbuilding in particular), although early laws were not enforced, and a laissez-faire tradition built up around logging. Secretary of the Interior CARL SCHURZ was the first to attempt to enforce these early laws. Having been raised in Germany, where economic forest management techniques had been long established, Schurz took seriously the dangers of depleted forest lands. Schurz removed corrupt land agents, punished those who logged federally held lands, and developed a system of selling timber rights while retaining federal title of forest lands. Congress, however, pardoned violators if they paid a paltry $1.25 an acre for land that they had cleared.

Not consistently hostile to the environment, Congress established a permanent Division of Forestry in the Department of Agriculture in 1886, the forerunner of the United States Forest Service, and subsequent studies confirmed that overharvesting would lead to a dire situation within a matter of years. Forest fires, exacerbated by logging, had already burned millions of acres, provoked intense flooding in watershed areas, and also compelled the federal government to protect forests.

The original Forest Reserve bill was narrow in its scope, but the Division of Forestry and Department of the Interior influenced legislators to attach a rider that allowed the president to set apart and reserve public lands covered in timber as public reservations. President BENJAMIN HARRISON immediately took advantage of this legislation, setting aside forests next to Yellowstone National Park in Wyoming as reserves. He added 13 million more acres of protected forest in four additional reserves. President GROVER CLEVELAND added 20 million more acres but also asked Congress to define the goal of the reserves. In response, Congress passed the Forest Management Act in 1897, which designated Forest Reserves as resources for timber, mining, and grazing, leading to the current forest management policy.

Further reading: Dyan Zaslowsky and T. H. Watkins, *These American Lands: Parks, Wilderness, and the Public Lands* (Washington, D.C.: Island Press, 1994).

— Scott Sendrow

Free-Silver movement

The term *Free Silver* refers to the demand made by agrarian and silver-mining interests in the late 19th century for the free and unlimited coinage of silver at a ratio of 16-to-1 (i.e., 16 ounces of silver for every one ounce of gold). The

Free-Silver movement emerged from the debate over what should give the dollar its value. Americans who adhered to the "sound money" philosophy believed that it was the government's duty to maintain a stable value of currency and that the best way for it to accomplish this was by the redemption of currency in gold. The gold standard was supported by bankers, some business interests, and many industrial workers whose real wages were thereby protected from inflation. On the other hand, many Americans, business owners as well as farmers, in the cash-strapped agricultural sections of the South and West argued that the government should manage the money supply to relieve any economic suffering caused by declining agricultural prices in the late 19th century.

In 1873 the government demonetized silver just prior to a fall in its market value, and shortly thereafter the nation's agrarian and silver-mining interests denounced this as the "CRIME OF '73"

American farmers believed that prices were determined by the amount of currency in circulation and that the free and unlimited coinage of silver would bring about a general price inflation, thus increasing the amount of money they would receive for their crops and easing their burden of debt. Silver-mine operators joined the call for Free Silver after 1873 simply because they wanted the government to purchase more of their product.

CONGRESS enacted the BLAND-ALLISON ACT in 1878, but this law did not meet the demands for the free and unlimited coinage of silver. Instead, the law limited the amount of silver the government could purchase and mint into silver dollars to not less than $2 million and not more than $4 million worth of silver per month. The Sherman Silver Purchase Act of 1890 required the government to purchase and coin 4.5 million ounces of silver monthly. These silver dollars could be redeemed in gold dollars but had to be put back into circulation, which placed a great strain on the nation's gold reserve. President GROVER CLEVELAND, an opponent of inflationary currency schemes, blamed the Sherman Silver Purchase Act for the financial panic that ensued in 1893 and called on Congress to repeal the law. Congress heeded the president's demand and repealed the Sherman Silver Purchase Act.

Between 1893 and 1896, the Free-Silver movement picked up much support. In 1896 both the DEMOCRATIC PARTY and the PEOPLE'S PARTY (Populist Party) adopted Free Silver as their main campaign theme and nominated WILLIAM J. BRYAN for president. Bryan and Free Silver, however, were overwhelmingly defeated by the Republican candidate, WILLIAM MCKINLEY of Ohio, who ran on a platform supporting the gold standard. As a result the GOLD STANDARD ACT OF 1900 declared the gold dollar to be the official American standard of value.

See also BIMETALLISM; CURRENCY ISSUE; FARMERS' ALLIANCES; MINING; OMAHA PLATFORM; SIMPSON, JERRY.

Further reading: Walter T. K. Nugent, *Money and American Society, 1865–1880* (New York: Free Press, 1968); Allen Weinstein, *Prelude to Populism: Origins of the Silver Issue, 1867–1878* (New Haven, Conn.: Yale University Press, 1970).

— Phillip Papas

Frick, Henry Clay (1849–1919)

Henry Clay Frick, the industrialist, was born on December 19, 1849, to John W. and Elizabeth Overholt Frick at West Overton, Pennsylvania. He attended school until age 14, when he accepted a position in his uncle Christopher Overholt's store in Mount Pleasant, Pennsylvania. While living with his uncle he attended the Mount Pleasant Institute. He also studied for a brief time at Otterbein College in Westerville, Ohio. After spending two years with his uncle, he moved to Pittsburgh where he sold ribbons and bows during the day and attended a business school during the evening. In 1868 he accepted his grandfather's offer to become bookkeeper for his Old Overholt Distillery in Broadford, Pennsylvania.

Frick quickly recognized the potential of the rich coking coal fields in the Broadford region. He formed a partnership, H. C. Frick and Company, to purchase coal land and build coking ovens. The firm survived the depression of 1873 by selling below cost and paying its workers in script good only at its company store. Frick used whatever cash he could scrape together to buy out his bankrupt competitors. When the depression ended, H. C. Frick and Company owned almost 10,000 coke ovens and was the major supplier of coke to Pittsburgh's rapidly expanding iron and steel industry.

ANDREW CARNEGIE, who was Frick's biggest customer, bought into the reorganized H. C. Frick Coke Company and soon secured the majority of its stock, retaining Frick as president. An 1887 miners' strike, however, illustrated a discordant note between the two capitalists. Frick, the coal man, wanted to break the union. But Carnegie, the steel man, was concerned over the supply of coke at his furnaces and ordered Frick to settle the strike. Frick resigned as president of the coke company. Although Carnegie did not care for Frick personally he recognized his ability, and six months later he reinstated Frick and made him a partner in Carnegie Brothers and Company and, two years later, its chairman of the board.

Running both businesses, Frick set out in 1891 to destroy the miners' union. After building up a large reserve of coke at the furnaces, Frick offered his miners a contract he knew they could not accept. When they struck he replaced them with strikebreakers protected by sheriff's deputies. On April 20, 1891, deputized guards killed nine strikers at Frick's Morewood Mines. The violence effectively destroyed the union. A year later Frick, with Carnegie's consent, employed the same tactics to destroy the iron workers' union during the HOMESTEAD STRIKE, but Carnegie, concerned about his image, tried to duck his responsibility by blaming Frick for the violence. Carnegie's claim that he could have averted the violence damaged their relationship and failed to convince the public, which sympathized with Frick after he survived an assassination attempt by anarchist Alexander Berkman.

While most noted for his ruthless antiunion stance, Frick was a capable manager. He directed the reorganization of Carnegie's steel interest, keeping the coke company a separate entity; bought large tracks of land in the Mesabi iron ore range in Minnesota; and purchased the Duquesne Iron Works, Carnegie's major competitor in the steel rail business. In 1889 when Frick took over the chairmanship, Carnegie Steel's profits were $3.5 million, but in 1899 they were $21 million. Despite this service, Carnegie forced Frick out of the steel company that year when they disagreed over the price of Frick's coke used by Carnegie Steel. The two became bitter enemies when Frick sued Carnegie for attempting to cheat him out of the full value of his share in the steel business. In their out-of-court settlement Frick received 11 percent of Carnegie Steel, which ultimately was worth about 12 times the $5 million Carnegie offered him.

Although Carnegie and other business associates of Frick thought him provincial and uncultivated, interested only in coke and steel, Frick acquired one of the finest collections of European art in the world and housed it in a magnificent mansion in New York City.

Further reading: Samuel A. Schreiner Jr., *Henry Clay Frick: The Gospel of Greed* (New York: St. Martin's Press, 1995).

— Harold W. Aurand

G

Gage, Matilda Joslyn (1826–1898)

Born on March 25, 1826, in Cicero, New York, Matilda Gage, a radical feminist, was tutored in Greek, mathematics, and physiology and taught to think for herself by her father, who was a physician, an abolitionist, a WOMEN'S RIGHTS advocate, and a free thinker. She married a prosperous merchant at 18, had five children, and suffered from poor health. Nevertheless in 1852, "trembling in every limb," she began her participation in the women's rights movement by addressing its convention at Syracuse, New York, but in a voice so weak her stirring words were scarcely heard. She improved somewhat as a speaker, but her major contribution to the women's rights movement was as an organizer, thinker, and writer.

In 1869 she was a charter member of the National Woman Suffrage Association (NWSA) and the New York State Woman Suffrage Association. She tried unsuccessfully to vote in 1872 and served as president of the NWSA from 1875 to 1876, giving way to her friend Elizabeth Cady Stanton. Gage, Stanton, and SUSAN B. ANTHONY wrote the Declaration of Rights, which Anthony read to a startled Fourth of July audience at the 1876 PHILADELPHIA CENTENNIAL EXPOSITION. Gage contributed to NWSA's paper *The Revolution,* and from 1878 to 1881 she edited the NWSA monthly *National Citizen and the Ballot Box.* She also coauthored with Stanton and Anthony the first three volumes of the six-volume *History of Woman Suffrage* (1881–1922). Trying to make up for the neglect of women, Gage was not above exaggerating the accomplishments of her sex in *Woman as Inventor* (1870) and in *Who Planned the Tennessee Campaign of 1862? or Anna Ella Carroll v. Ulysses S. Grant* (1880).

By the late 1870s Gage had become discouraged by the slow progress of the suffrage movement. She was convinced that Christian doctrines fostered in men a "belief in women's inferiority" and that church and state were obstacles to equality and freedom. Her attempts to convert the NWSA to the view that Christianity was the enemy, however, aroused intense opposition among the devout, conservative elements in that organization. By 1890 Gage was sufficiently alienated from the NWSA to establish the Woman's National Liberal Union, which proclaimed the role of religion in subjugating women and struggled for constitutional amendments guaranteeing woman suffrage and the separation of church and state. Her *Woman, Church, and State* (1893), which she regarded as her most important book, elaborated on these views. Gage spent her last years in Chicago with her daughter Maud—the wife of L. Frank Baum, the author of *THE WIZARD OF OZ.* Just prior to her death on March 18, 1898, she wrote a speech for the National American Woman Suffrage Association celebrating the 50th anniversary of the Seneca Falls Convention, which had marked the beginning of the women's rights movement.

Further reading: William Leach, *True Love and Perfect Union: The Feminist Reform of Sex and Society* (Middletown, Conn.: Wesleyan University Press, 1980).

Galveston flood (September 8, 1900)

The most devastating hurricane in U.S. history struck Galveston, Texas, on September 8, 1900, killing 6,000 people (more than one-sixth of that city's population). At the time of the storm, Galveston was the major American port west of New Orleans on the Gulf of Mexico. Situated on a low-lying island (basically an outer bank, a sandbar) between Galveston Bay and the Gulf, it was vulnerable to hurricanes because of its location and lack of altitude. The storm that hit Galveston was one of the most powerful ever recorded and did not dissipate until after it had headed east, crossed the Atlantic Ocean, and passed over Europe into Siberia. The barometric reading when its center was at Galveston was the lowest recorded in the United States up to that date. The storm surge (the extreme tide that accompanies a hurricane) flooded the entire city, caused most of the deaths, damaged virtually every structure, and cost about $20 million.

The flood had two long-range effects: One was on the city of Galveston itself, and the other was on the form of government adopted by many other cities. Although Galveston regained its status as a major port, it was no longer the preeminent commercial center of Texas. Faced with a crisis of monumental proportions, Galveston needed a city government far more efficient than the typical model featuring a weak mayor and an unwieldy council, with no clear-cut delineation of responsibilities. The citizens responded by simply dissolving the existing government and appointing five powerful commissioners to head the various departments (fire, police, etc.) that functioned as a council. This commission form of government eliminated unwieldiness and pinpointed responsibility. In 1901 a new charter made the commission form of government permanent for Galveston, with one of the commissioners serving as mayor for ceremonial purposes. The commissioners conducted city business—legislation, appointments, and contracts—in open meetings.

The Galveston commission rebuilt the city, restored its credit, and constructed a 17-foot-high seawall to protect the city in the future. This commission form of government appealed to progressive municipal reformers and was widely copied, especially in the South, in the early 20th century.

Further reading: Kai T. Erikson, *A New Species of Trouble: Explorations in Disaster, Trauma and Community* (New York: Norton, 1994); Bradley R. Rice, *Progressive Cities: The Commission Government Movement in America 1901–1920* (Austin: University of Texas Press, 1977); C. Vann Woodward, *Origins of the New South, 1877–1913* (Baton Rouge: Louisiana State University Press, 1951).

Garfield, James Abram (1831–1881)

James A. Garfield was an American president who actually did begin life in a log cabin. Born on November 19, 1831, near Cleveland, Ohio, Garfield was left destitute when his father died two years later. Despite their poverty, his mother convinced him to get an education, and he discovered his lifelong love of learning at Geauga Academy. He was also attracted to religion, joining the Disciples of Christ and, in time, becoming a lay preacher. Working as a carpenter and then as a teacher, Garfield financed his studies and graduated from Williams College in Massachusetts in 1856. He returned to Ohio to teach at the Western Reserve Eclectic Institute at Hiram, where he was named president in 1858. That same year he married Lucretia Rudolph after a long courtship. Troubled at first, their marriage endured and then flourished with children and love. Awakened to the evils of slavery, Garfield studied law, entered politics, and won a seat in the Ohio senate, but he was irresolute about his future. The outbreak of the Civil War ended his vacillation. As a prominent politician he was commissioned a lieutenant colonel, and by luck, merit (serving gallantly at Chicamauga), and well-placed friends was promoted to major general by late 1863.

As a war hero Garfield was elected to the U.S. House of Representatives in 1862, where he served from 1863 to 1880. Initially the youngest man in CONGRESS, his intelligence, grasp of details, and eloquence quickly made him a leader in the House. At the same time Garfield had a streak of self-doubt in his makeup. Anxious to please, he was not an extreme partisan and when faced with complex issues, he was prone to waver. Garfield's colleagues thought him inconsistent and even weak, yet his capacity—especially in the area of government finance—was such that he became the undoubted leader of House Republicans after JAMES G. BLAINE left for the Senate in 1876. On the two issues he regarded as moral—emancipation and sound currency based on gold—Garfield was unwavering; on two other issues he favored—CIVIL SERVICE REFORM and free trade—he was less steadfast. Garfield did not wish to depoliticize the civil service, and he wanted to protect the products of his district. As a powerful politician with five children and a low income, Garfield on occasion sold his influence. Having invested nothing, he received from Credit Mobilier a $329 dividend or, as he claimed, a $300 loan that he repaid. His $5,000 fee from the DeGolyer McClelland Company for his help in securing a paving contract in Washington, D.C., was most questionable (Garfield was chair of the crucial Appropriations Committee), and yet it did not prevent his nomination for the presidency.

When the 1880 Republican Convention deadlocked over the candidacies of Ulysses S. Grant, Blaine, and JOHN SHERMAN, the Blaine and Sherman delegates turned to Garfield and nominated him. To be elected he had to carry New York and needed the support of its Republican machine headed by Senator ROSCOE CONKLING, who happened to have been the chief STALWART supporter of Grant at the recent convention. Ambiguously agreeable, Garfield activated Conkling's lieutenants, as well as other spoilsmen, with vague promises of patronage. He also encouraged the collection of political assessments from civil servants. Reformers worried that Garfield's "fiber" was not "steel," but the Democrats were even less apt to reform the civil service.

Garfield's strategy of opposing nobody won the election, but it paralyzed his administration and led to his demise. His superb understanding of the workings of the federal government and the issues before it were irrelevant because he had raised expectations he could not or would not fulfill. Conkling got some patronage, but the biggest

James A. Garfield (*Library of Congress*)

plum, collector of the Port of New York, went to his arch-enemy Secretary of State Blaine. Conkling was outraged and urged his colleagues not to confirm the nomination on the grounds that it violated senatorial courtesy (the practice that enabled senators to dictate to the president who should be nominated in their states). The struggle lasted two months, and when Conkling realized he would lose, he resigned, expecting that the New York legislature would show its support by returning him to the Senate. It did not, and Conkling had committed political suicide.

Garfield had triumphed, but he never had an opportunity to get his administration on track. On July 2 a deranged office seeker, shouting that he was a Stalwart, assassinated Garfield. He lingered for more than two months, but blood poisoning set in and he died on September 19, 1881. Reformers, claiming that Garfield had been murdered by the spoils system, pushed through the PENDLETON CIVIL SERVICE REFORM ACT (1883) as a memorial to Garfield. Ironically he had little sympathy for its prohibition of political assessments and for its reliance on open competitive examinations to secure qualified nonpartisan appointees to office.

Further reading: Allan Peskin, *Garfield: A Biography* (Kent, Ohio: Kent State University Press, 1978).

Garland, Hamlin (1860–1940)

Hannibal Hamlin Garland, a realistic novelist, was born on the frontier near West Salem, Wisconsin, on September 14, 1860, to farmers Richard Hayes and Isabelle Charlotte McClintock. Garland spent his early youth traveling westward with his family through Wisconsin, Minnesota, and Iowa, where he participated in the strenuous labor of running his father's homestead. He attended the Cedar Valley Seminary in Iowa, from which he graduated in 1881, and taught school in Illinois for a season. In 1883 he rejoined his family, who had moved to South Dakota after losing their farm to a plague of insects. For two painful years he worked his own claim near his father's, but the toil proved so arduous and unrewarding that he sold his farm for $200 and moved to Boston.

Nourishing his literary appetites and ambitions at the Boston Public Library—where he spent entire days reading poetry, fiction, philosophy, and social theory—Garland was soon as well informed as any college graduate. After attending a few lectures at the Boston School of Oratory, he was appointed an instructor in English and American literature there. Around 1886 he began contributing brief sketches to local newspapers, and the next year *Harper's Weekly* published a story about the rural life he remembered. By 1890 he was making a modest living as a free-lance writer and had come to know the literary community in Boston, where he received encouragement from WILLIAM DEAN HOWELLS, the leading novelist and critic of the period. In 1891 he published his first book, *Main-Travelled Roads,* a collection of starkly realistic stories set in the Midwest, an area he called the Middle Border; in each of whose farm houses, as he was later to write, he saw an "individual message of sordid struggle and half-hidden despair."

During the next decade Garland produced a stream of books, including several novels and collections of short stories and a volume each of poetry and literary criticism. In all his early work he demonstrated and argued for his belief in a harsh realism that he termed "veritism." His 1892 novel *A Spoil of Office* was an exposé of political corruption on the western frontier and a tract for the POPULIST PARTY. That same year he published *A Member of the Third House,* dramatizing the cruel power of the railroad lobbies, and his later novels protested the fraudulent land practices of bankers, the condition of women on the frontier, and the exploitation of the Plains Indians. In 1899 he settled in Chicago, where he married Zulime Taft, the sister of the noted sculptor Lorado Taft; the couple had two daughters.

Following a series of commercially successful romantic novels in which he seemed to have forsworn his bleak vision of rural life, Garland returned to New York in 1916, and the next year published *A Son of the Middle Border*, the first of four volumes of autobiography that resumed his theme of the hardships and frustrations of pioneer life. This book and its Pulitzer Prize-winning 1921 sequel *A Daughter of the Middle Border* were to become his lasting legacy to American letters. A pioneer realist and an eloquent advocate for the rural poor, he provided a vivid picture of agrarian poverty in an age of industrialization, and his honest, often grim depiction of pioneer life did much to dispel the romantic myth of the midwestern farmer. Garland died in California on March 4, 1940.

Further reading: Jean Halloway, *Hamlin Garland: A Biography* (Austin: University of Texas Press, 1960).

— Dennis Wepman

General Allotment Act (1887)

See Dawes Severalty Act

Geological Survey, U.S.

On March 3, 1879, CONGRESS and President RUTHERFORD B. HAYES established the U.S. Geological Survey (USGS) as an Interior Department agency for "the classification of the public lands and examination of the Geological Structure, mineral resources and products of the national domain." The politicians and scientists who shaped the USGS legislation intended the new agency to aid the nation's struggling economy by supporting the mining industry's efforts to supply minerals for construction and currency. They also hoped to improve the civil service by increasing economy, efficiency, harmony, and utility in federal mapping and science surveys. The new law discontinued the three competing federal geological and geographical surveys of the public domain in the West led by Ferdinand Vandeveer Hayden (Interior), JOHN WESLEY POWELL (Interior), and First Lieutenant George Montague Wheeler (Army Crops of Engineers). The USGS absorbed some of the functions of these organizations, whose combined appropriations for 1878–79 totaled more than the new agency's funds for 1879–80. To protect the impartiality and integrity of USGS data and analyses, the founding statue prohibited its employees from speculating in the lands and resources under study or conducting outside consulting.

The USGS "organic act" also named the Smithsonian Institution's National Museum as the repository for USGS scientific collections, detailed the nature of USGS publications and exchanges, and established a Public Lands Commission (PLC) to codify laws and recommend improvements in management. CLARENCE (RIVERS) KING and Powell served on the PLC; Powell, under Smithsonian overview, also led the new Bureau of Ethnology (BE). Some of the disestablished survey's functions in botany and zoology passed to the commissioner of agriculture. The reformers did not succeed in establishing within either the Interior or War Departments a separate mapping agency for all geodetic, land-parceling, and topographic surveys, nor did they improve the Interior's administration of the public lands by its General Land Office (GLO).

President Hayes nominated King as director of the USGS. King, in helping to shape the USGS (1878–79) and then direct its operations (1879–81), drew on his experience while serving in the state-sponsored Geological Survey of California (1863–66) and leading the U.S. Geological Exploration of the 40th parallel (1867–79) for the Army Engineers. Continuing his policies, King intended USGS-mandated studies of mineral resources principally to yield immediate results of practical value to industry and a scientific classification of the national domain, which the attorney general's office determined to be those public lands (mostly in the West) still federally owned. King also expected the results in economic geology to increase an understanding of the classification and origin of ore deposits and, with the subordinate investigations in general geology, also to advance knowledge of the earth and its history.

In 1881 King resigned and advised President JAMES A. GARFIELD to appoint Powell as his successor. A year later King's and Director Powell's friends in the 47th Congress convinced their colleagues and President CHESTER ARTHUR to authorize USGS activities nationwide to support the completion of the reliable national geologic map sought by King. Under this rubric, Powell remade the USGS as an agency for topographic mapping (by design and default the needed national program) and basic research in general geology, but at the expense of economic geology. He continued to lead the BE and often merged with it USGS personnel and operations. Congress increased USGS appropriations through most of the 1880s. The 50th Congress and President GROVER CLEVELAND also gave Powell an opportunity in 1888 to pursue his long-standing goal of reforming land and water use in the West by authorizing and funding the Irrigation Survey (IS) within the USGS. But from 1890 to 1894, three Congresses and Presidents BENJAMIN HARRISON and Cleveland, seeking more economic geology, repudiated Powell's programs, principally because they did not yield the requested practical assessments of mineral and water resources. Powell's views and policies, unchanged by King's advice, contributed to the attorney general's decision to close the public domain to entry until the IS fixed the dam and reservoir sites. That decision also denied to six new states the federal-dowry lands due them at statehood. Powell's policies also left the USGS unable to respond effectively to a renewed currency crisis by facilitating new discoveries of precious metals. Congress first terminated the IS, then selectively slashed USGS statutory staff and operating expenses, and finally encouraged Powell to resign by reducing his salary.

Charles Doolittle Walcott, hired by King in 1879, replaced Powell as director. In 1893 Interior Secretary Hoke Smith had advanced Walcott from chief paleontologist to geologist-in-charge of geology and paleontology to reform the USGS geologic unit decimated by Powell's agencywide reduction-in-force in 1892 in response to the congressional cuts. For the public good and to reward Walcott's success, King and Smith urged the 53rd Congress and President Cleveland to make Walcott the third director in 1894. To renew USGS usefulness to the nation, Director Walcott expanded the agency's mission to include any economic, educational, or other practical objective that could be advanced by a greater knowledge of the earth and its resources. Walcott's balanced program of applied and basic research restored congressional confidence, and the legislators increased USGS appropriations beyond those granted Powell. Walcott restored the USGS program in economic geology, reorganized the agency's other geological work, professionalized its topographic-mapping program, and began successful and continuously funded studies of water resources and arid-land reclamation, native peoples' lands, forest reserves, as well as tests of fuels and structural materials. By 1900 Walcott completed definitions of the USGS geologic, hydrologic, and topographic units, which remained the agency's principal scientific and mapping components until the Interior Department's research biologists joined the USGS. Most of the other units Walcott managed, and those later transferred to the USGS that did not develop or retain scientific or mapping programs, subsequently became other Interior Department bureaus: Reclamation (1907), Mines (1910), Grazing (1935, then combined with GLO in 1946 as Land Management), and Minerals Management (1982). Additional functions went to existing agencies in other federal departments: Forest Service (1905) and the Bureau of Standards (1910). Walcott resigned as USGS Director in 1907 to become the Smithsonian's fourth secretary.

Further reading: T. G. Manning, *Government in Science: The U.S. Geological Survey, 1867* [sic]*–1894* (Lexington: University of Kentucky Press, 1967); M. C. Rabbitt, *Minerals, Lands, and Geology for the Common Defence and General Welfare,* 3 vols. [to 1939] (Washington, D.C.: Government Printing Office, 1979–86); E. L. Yochelson, *Charles Doolittle Walcott, Paleontologist* (Kent, Ohio: Kent State University Press, 1998).

— Clifford M. Nelson

George, Henry (1839–1897)

Henry George, economist, journalist, and reformer, was born on September 2, 1839, in Philadelphia, Pennsylvania, the son of Richard Samuel Henry George and Catherine Pratt Vallance. Following a brief rudimentary education, George clerked in a store and then shipped out to Australia and India. He returned to Philadelphia and learned to set type. In 1858 George decided to seek his fortune in San Francisco, where he worked as a printer and writer for various newspapers in the city. He also joined five other printers in the publication of the *Evening Journal* and worked for four years, hoping to make it competitive with San Francisco's other newspapers. George married Annie Corsina Fox in 1861 and together they had four children. The *Evening Journal,* however, did not work out. George lost everything he had invested in the project, and he endured poverty to the point that by 1865 he actually begged in the streets.

His luck changed in 1866 when he landed a job at the San Francisco *Times* as a printer. He also served on the paper's editorial staff before becoming its managing editor. In October 1868 George traveled to New York City on newspaper business and was struck by the great disparity between wealth and poverty in America and began his search for its root cause.

Within a few years George believed he had found the answer. The monopolization of land and natural resources caused the great divide between the rich and the poor. In 1871 he published *Our Land and Land Policy,* which advanced the idea that land formed the basis of wealth in American society and that economic inequality stemmed from the ability of a few to profit from rising land values. Eight years later George published *Progress and Poverty,* in which he argued that rising land values made owners rich simply because of an increased demand for living and working space. This demand was especially acute in the nation's cities. Since the rise in property values was caused by the increased market demand rather than by owners' improvements, it represented an "unearned increment" that George argued should be taxed. His solution—calling for replacing all taxes with a "single tax" on the increment—attracted many supporters, and single-tax clubs were organized throughout the United States.

In August 1880 George moved to New York, where he lectured and contributed to various magazines. The following year, George published *The Irish Land Question* and became a correspondent for the *Irish World and American Industrial Liberator.* He made two trips to the British Isles, lecturing, writing, and meeting with leaders of the Irish Land League and British Radical Liberals. His reports on Ireland made him enormously popular in New York among the Irish and with the supporters of the Central Labor Union.

With the support of organized labor, George ran for mayor of New York City in 1886. Although the Democrat Abram S. Hewitt was elected with 90,552 votes, George finished a surprising second ahead of the Republican candidate Theodore Roosevelt. George received 60,110 votes. In 1887 he unsuccessfully ran for the office of secretary of state under the banner of the Union Labor Party. Following several years of intense lecturing in the United States and overseas, George ran again for mayor of New York City in 1897. However, he died of a stroke on October 29, 1897, four days before the election was held.

Further reading: Charles A. Barker, *Henry George* (New York: Oxford University Press, 1955); Steven B. Cord, *Henry George: Dreamer or Realist?* (Philadelphia: University of Pennsylvania Press, 1965); Rhoda Hellman, *Henry George Reconsidered* (New York: Carlton Press, 1987).

— Phillip Papas

Geronimo (Goyahkla) (ca. 1823–1909)

A renowned Chiricahua Apache warrior, Goyahkla (One Who Yawns) was most likely born along the upper stretches of the Gila River in what is modern-day Arizona. Over time he became known by the Spanish name of Geronimo, which was given to him following a successful charge he led against Mexican infantry. During his youth Geronimo experienced a period of relative peace with both the Mexican and American governments. He began traveling with the Nednhi band of Chiricahua Apache, who came from the Sierra Madre of Mexico, joining them on raids and earning a place on the Apache council of warriors while still a teenager. He further linked himself with the Nednhi Apache by marrying a Nednhi woman in the late 1830s. Geronimo had many wives (perhaps up to nine) and often traveled with his current wife's band, which some have speculated may have been a reason he was never made a chief.

The Apache tribe, nestled along the border between Mexico and the United States, frequently encountered soldiers from both countries on their raids. In 1850 Mexican troops killed Geronimo's mother, wife, and three children while he and other male members of the tribe were on a trading expedition, prompting him to begin a personal crusade against Mexican troops in particular. Geronimo and his Apache brethren continued to raid Mexican and American settlements on both sides of the border, and they were forced to contend with hostile mining interests over the course of the 1850s and 1860s. Geronimo and other Apache leaders used the Ojo Caliente Reservation in New Mexico as a base to organize raids, causing federal authorities to shut it down in 1877 and transfer the 400 Warm Springs and Chiricahua Apache to the San Carlos Reservation in Arizona. Fearing resistance, officials arrested Geronimo and several other leaders. Geronimo spent a year at San Carlos, escaping to Mexico where he participated in raids, only to return to San Carlos and surrender in 1879 after Mexican authorities began hunting for him.

Geronimo *(New York Public Library)*

Officials became increasingly concerned about an Apache uprising after the Apache began practicing the Ghost Dance religion, which involved communing with ancestors via a trancelike dance, and Geronimo, with approximately 60 warriors, again fled to Mexico. The Apache under Geronimo reentered the United States in April 1882, attacking reservation policemen at San Carlos and enabling several hundred Apache to flee to Mexico. This daring raid set off the APACHE WAR along the border of the United States and Mexico and led to reciprocal agreements between the United States and Mexican governments to join forces against the Apache. After several years of battles in both Mexico and the United States, including broken deals and bungled negotiations, Geronimo accepted a deal to relocate the Apache to Florida for two years before being allowed to return to the West.

To whites, Geronimo became the most well-known Apache, appearing at the St. Louis World's Fair in 1904 and in President Theodore Roosevelt's inaugural parade in 1905. However, Geronimo never was allowed to return to the Southwest and died in Oklahoma on February 17, 1909.

Further reading: Angie Debo, *Geronimo* (Norman: University of Oklahoma Press, 1976).

— Scott Sendrow

Ghost Dance War See Sioux wars

Gibbs, Josiah Willard (1839–1903)

Born in New Haven, Connecticut, on February 11, 1839, Willard Gibbs, an outstanding physicist, was the son of a distinguished philologist and Yale professor of sacred literature. The boy's interests, however, ran to technology and mathematics. Gibbs entered the Sheffield Scientific School at Yale in 1858, earning the nation's second Ph.D. in science (or first in engineering) with a thesis on gear design. After patenting a railroad-car brake, Gibbs spent the years 1866–69 studying mathematics and physics in Paris, Berlin, and Heidelberg. In 1871 he was appointed professor of mathematical physics at Yale College. For nine years the position carried no salary, but Gibbs, a lifelong bachelor with simple needs who lived with his sister's family, got by somehow. In 1873 he turned down a paying job at Bowdoin College. What mattered to him was his complete freedom at Yale to teach what and when he wanted in three or four lectures a week to one or two students. His interest in engineering problems turned him toward thermodynamics in 1872, but he went far beyond the merely practical. The half-dozen years that followed were the most brilliantly and intensely creative of his illustrious career.

Gibbs's great work in thermodynamics began with two relatively short papers on plane and solid graphical representations, published in the Connecticut Academy of Arts and Sciences's *Transactions* in 1873. They were masterful and illuminating. The great Scottish physicist James Clerk Maxwell was entranced by them, and his enthusiastic public notice initiated Gibbs's rise to fame in international scientific circles (though not among the public at large). Gibbs's truly epochal paper, "On the Equilibrium of Heterogeneous Substances," appeared in *Transactions* in two parts, one of 141 pages in 1876 and another of 182 pages in 1878. No one on the Academy's publication committee could understand them, but the committee accepted them anyway on faith in Gibbs. Maxwell immediately grasped their importance and spread the word. Gibbs himself sent copies to nearly all of the world's mathematicians, astronomers, physicists, and chemists likely to appreciate them, 507 in all, including some in India, Brazil, China, and Japan. In America, Henry Rowland and Gibbs quickly recognized the importance of the work. On its strength, Willard Gibbs was elected to the National Academy of Sciences in 1879 and offered a Johns Hopkins professorship at $3,000 in 1880. Yale held him, however, on the basis of sentiment, loyalty, and—at last—a $2,000 salary.

The famous "equilibrium" paper, unlike the first two, was almost entirely analytical rather than graphical in its approach. Fundamental yet strikingly original, powerfully and flawlessly logical, it formed a completed whole from which most subsequent developments in the broad fields it covered derived naturally and inevitably. From its prime equation, which produced the theory of chemical equilibrium, could be deduced all the thermal, mechanical, and chemical properties of a complex system. It virtually engendered the field of physical chemistry. Its celebrated "phase rule" yielded manifold applications in metallurgy, mineralogy, and petrology, as well as in theoretical chemistry. Another segment of the paper played a large role in the electrochemical industry. The paper's contributions to an understanding of entropy have shaped ideas of the universe and its future. Gibbs's very methods were so fundamental and so logically irrefutable that they survived the revolution in 20th-century physics and continued to generate ideas and solutions even in quantum mechanics. Gibbs died in New Haven on April 28, 1903.

Further reading: Lynde Phelps Wheeler, *Josiah Willard Gibbs: The History of a Great Mind* (Woodbridge, Conn.: Ox Bow Press, 1998).

— Robert V. Bruce

Gibson Girl See illustration, photography, and the graphic arts

Gilded Age: A Tale of Today, The (1873)

This novel by MARK TWAIN (Samuel Langhorne Clemens) and Charles Dudley Warner gave its name to an era. Thanks in part to *The Gilded Age,* American society in the final third of the 19th century would forever be known for its unbridled greed, unmerited fortunes, tasteless opulence, cynical politics, and corrupt governance. Working from recent headlines (the scandals of the Grant administration, the stealings of Boss Tweed of TAMMANY HALL, and revelations that Senator Samuel Pomeroy of Kansas had tried to purchase his reelection by bribing state legislators), the authors employed satire, melodrama, parody, and reportage to depict an age of excess. Although not a major contribution to American literature, *The Gilded Age* is in a class with two other contemporary critiques of American politics, Walt Whitman's *Democratic Vistas* (1871) and HENRY ADAMS's *Democracy* (1880).

The political aspect of the novel hinges on three land schemes, two of which depend upon government largess and influence peddling. The other, by way of contrast, comes down to honest dealing, hard work, sacrifice, and commitment. In elaborating these episodes, Twain and Warner explored the full range of Gilded Age venality, including financial finagling, railroad and mining scams, and the buying and selling of legislation.

The authors offered little hope that the "best people" would put an end to the greed and corruption, or even rise above it. Twain and Warner identified three distinct aristocracies: The Antiques are "cultivated, high-bred old families" whose ancestors had been "great in the nation's councils and its wars from the birth of the republic downward." In the world of *The Gilded Age,* the Antiques still enjoyed social prominence but no longer set the tone for politics. (Henry Adams personified this class in the real world of Washington, but he has no significant counterpart in *The Gilded Age.*) The Parvenus are newly rich, ostentatious, opportunistic, and amoral. They call the tune in Washington, New York, and wherever else power and money can generate more power and money. Twain and Warner find much to admire in the third group of aristocrats, the Middle Group. These are people of learning, taste, and honor. In *The Gilded Age,* they are the Boltons of Philadelphia and the Montagues of New England. But for all their merits, such people are no match for the Parvenus. Sharp operators regularly dupe the generous but gullible Mr. Bolton. For his part, the high-minded Squire Montague maintains an admirable household where "there was always so much talk . . . of the news of the day, of the new books and of authors, of Boston radicalism and New York civilization, and the virtue of Congress." But for all their fine talk and head shaking, men like the good Squire remain aloof from the unseemly nexus of money and power and so have no positive effect on public affairs.

Civic life may have been irredeemable, but individual goodness is not entirely absent from *The Gilded Age.* Readers could take heart from the spontaneous kindness of Squire and Mrs. Hawkins, who take in a distraught small boy whose mother has recently died and a young girl who has lost her parents in a steamboat accident; from Ruth Bolton's attempt to elevate her gender and serve humanity by studying medicine; from Alice Montague's selfless devotion to friends; and from Philip Sterling's dedication and honesty.

Although known principally for its satirical treatment of politics, *The Gilded Age* contains other elements, including stories of passion and unrequited love, a melodramatic murder complete with sensational trial (all the better to ridicule the judiciary), and a disastrous steamboat race. Twain and Warner occasionally rely on Dickensian touches, not least of which is the novel's most interesting and amusing character, the Micawber-like Colonel Sellers, whose grandiose but unfounded (and unfunded) schemes are usually, but not always, harmless.

The Gilded Age is set in Tennessee, Missouri, Philadelphia, New York City, New England, and the nation's capital. Tennessee is a place of backwardness and false hopes, while Missouri is a virgin land sullied by rapacious financial interests. Philadelphia is grand and almost good; New York is grand and bad. New England is high-minded, cultured, and venerable. As for Washington, it is not the city of hallowed traditions and monuments, but a den of wheeler-dealers whose brazenness would make the most disreputable frontier boomtown seem prim by comparison.

The response to *The Gilded Age* was mixed. It sold well, but critics were divided. Some newspapers that were allied with the persons and interests that Twain and Warner had excoriated accused the authors of seeking to profit from the misfortune of others. Neutral critics found it noteworthy that two popular humorists had turned to satire. A few were disappointed in the results; others were delighted by the authors' new seriousness.

Whatever its strengths and weaknesses, *The Gilded Age* is noteworthy as Mark Twain's first attempt at writing a novel, albeit in collaboration. That Charles Dudley Warner was an easterner and Twain a westerner may account for the fault line between the regions in their story. In *The Gilded Age* the East is urban, sophisticated, and (except for people like the Montagues and Boltons), corrupt; the West is rural, simple, and innocent—ripe for exploitation. Even the shameless self-promoting Missourian, Colonel Sellers, seems a mere bumpkin compared to the oily lobbyists and politicians of Washington. In general, Dudley Warner developed the eastern scenes and characters (Philip Sterling, the Boltons, and the Montagues), while Colonel Sellers, the Hawkins family, and the Missouri setting are unmistakably Twain's work. For the story line about the Hawkins's land holdings, Twain tapped the experience of his wife's family, which had inherited undeveloped land in Tennessee. For the book's delineation of congressional skullduggery, Twain drew on his own brief and unsatisfactory experience in Washington as personal secretary to Senator William Stewart of Nevada. Current events inspired other characters and incidents. Senator Samuel Pomeroy was the model for the sanctimonious and corrupt Senator Dilworthy. The charming but doomed Laura Hawkins is the fictional counterpart of Mrs. Laura Fair, the defendant in a much-publicized murder trial.

The Gilded Age collaboration extended beyond Twain and Warner. The novel features unique chapter headings consisting of arcane mottoes in a variety of foreign languages. The noted scholar J. Hammond Trumbull suggested the mottoes and provided translations at the end of the narrative. In addition, the book included illustrations by Augustus Hoppin. (Political cartoonist THOMAS NAST, Boss Tweed's arch-enemy, declined the commission.)

The Gilded Age had a complex afterlife. In 1874 playwright George Densmore staged an unauthorized adaptation of the novel. After Twain sued Densmore, the two litigants collaborated on a reworked version that was produced in New York as *The Gilded Age.* Subsequently, Twain, this time with Charles Dudley Warner, created yet another stage adaptation, this time calling it *Colonel Sellers.* Twain and WILLIAM DEAN HOWELLS wrote a sequel that they called *The American Claimant* (1887). The New York production flopped, but Twain published a novelization in 1892. Compared with *The Gilded Age,* it seems less a sequel than an afterthought.

See also LITERATURE.

Further reading: Philip Fisher, *Still the New World: American Literature in a Culture of Creative Destruction* (Cambridge, Mass.: Harvard University Press, 1999); Morey French, *Mark Twain and The Gilded Age: The Book That Named an Era* (Dallas: Southern Methodist University Press, 1965); Justin Kaplan, *Mr. Clemens and Mark Twain: A Biography* (New York: Simon & Schuster, 1966); Alan Trachtenberg, *The Incorporation of America: Culture and Society in the Gilded Age* (New York: Hill & Wang, 1982); Mark Twain and Charles Dudley Warner, *The Gilded Age,* foreword by Shelley Fisher Fishkin, introduction by Ward Just, afterword by Gregg Camfield (New York: Oxford University Press, 1996).

— William Hughes

Gladden, Washington (1836–1918)

Born in Pottsgrove, Pennsylvania, on February 11, 1836, Washington Gladden was a notable early voice of the SOCIAL GOSPEL movement. He rejected the orthodox Calvinism of his youth and believed that salvation was achieved not through doctrinal beliefs but by accepting the love of God and living it every day. Beginning in 1860 Gladden ministered to various Congregational churches in New York and Massachusetts, but especially in Columbus, Ohio, from 1883–1918.

Gladden's emphasis on the commandment of Jesus to love God and one's neighbor led him to confront the social, economic, and political problems engendered by rapid industrialization and urbanization. With his conviction that the churches had to do more than target personal sin and had to help solve social problems, Gladden took up the moral torch carried by the abolitionists and became the first voice of what became known as the Social Gospel. Aware that workers were not getting their fair share of profits, Gladden was an early advocate of labor unions. At first he thought strikes were counterproductive, but in time the intransigence of capitalists made him more militant. He was a firm believer in government regulation of industry and ownership of utilities, but he opposed SOCIALISM as too bureaucratic and too stifling of individual enterprise. He was an urban reformer favoring municipal home rule and worked to establish social services and cultural opportunities in Columbus. Two of his books, *Social Salvation* (1902) and *The Church and Modern Life* (1908), effectively sum up the Social Gospel. Gladden supported virtually every reform encompassed by PROGRESSIVISM IN THE 1890s and early 20th century, and his death on July 2, 1918, during World War I, quite coincidentally marked the demise of both the Progressive Era and the vogue of the Social Gospel.

Further reading: Jacob H. Dorn, *Washington Gladden: Prophet of the Social Gospel* (Columbus: Ohio State University Press, 1967).

— W. Frederick Wooden

Godkin, Edwin Lawrence (1831–1902)

An influential newspaper man, Edwin Godkin established new standards for American journalism by using his sharp wit and stronger pen in support of political reform. He was born in Ireland on October 2, 1831, and was the eldest child of Reverend James and Sarah Lawrence Godkin. Although his parents were English, Godkin's father allied himself early on with home rule for Ireland and was a prolific controversial writer, a dissenting clergyman who often served as a correspondent for the London *Times.*

Edwin was sickly as a child, but he was sent to England, near Leeds, for his schooling. He returned to Ireland to earn an undergraduate degree from Queen's College, Belfast, in 1851. Shortly after graduation, Godkin decided to study law in London, but anxious to utilize his training in history, economics, and political theory, he abandoned law for political journalism. He joined the staff of John Cassell's radical magazine, *The Workingmen's Friend,* and supported the recent Hungarian revolution in a series of articles that Cassell in 1853 published in book form as *The History of Hungary and the Magyars.* In 1854 he traveled to Hungary and was warmly received by revolutionaries. For two years (1853–55) he served as a correspondent for the London *Daily News* during the Crimean War, gaining a grasp of military theory and a hatred of war that often showed in his scathing language about it throughout his life.

Godkin immigrated to the United States in 1856 and continued to send letters to the *Daily News.* A tour of the South confirmed his antislavery views, and during the Civil War he edited the *Sanitary Commission Bulletin* as well as contributed to the *New York Times.* After the war Godkin, with his transatlantic reputation as a journalist and writer, accepted a position as the first editor (1865–1900) of the NATION, a weekly magazine. Although its founders wanted the *Nation* to improve the condition of former slaves, Godkin soon ignored them and denounced as corrupt the black, carpetbagger, and Reconstruction governments in the South. Consistent with his 19th-century liberalism, Godkin believed in economic individualism and laissez-faire and opposed any government involvement in social causes. No longer "the workingmen's friend," he opposed labor unions. Under his reign the *Nation,* with its stinging prose, assailed POLITICAL CORRUPTION in President Ulysses S. Grant's Republican administration and in New York City under the control of the Democratic party's Tammany Hall. He was an ardent advocate of CIVIL SERVICE REFORM and, in keeping with his laissez-faire philosophy, supported a tariff to raise revenue but not to protect industry and also favored a currency based on the gold standard.

In 1881 Godkin accepted a larger journalistic opportunity as editor of a daily newspaper, the *New York Evening Post.* Editing both publications, Godkin combined selected editorial content from the *Nation* with the *Evening Post* and handled large issues independently without favoring any political party. Because of his broad interest in history, economics, and political theory, his influence upon the press and public opinion was strong and persuasive. Although his publications never had more than 35,000 subscribers, he was read by the clergy, lawyers, and college professors, who disseminated his views to wider publics. Godkin was often considered a "voice of reason." In 1898, for example, when other newspapers were urging the United States to go to war with Spain, Godkin was stalwart in his belief that the war would be wrong. The war, which did occur, added to the growing pessimism he expressed in three books published in the 1890s: *Reflections and Comments* (1895), *Problems of Modern Democracy* (1896), and *Unforeseen Tendencies of Democracy* (1898).

Always writing with indignation and a strong affinity for prosaic language, Godkin cared more for the editorial than the news pages of his publications. He often said he did not try to compete with other newspapers of the day but chose instead to be known for opinion and activist reform. Ill health forced Godkin to step down from his post in 1900, but he continued to write articles for the *North American Review,* the *Atlantic,* and *Scribner's* among other magazines. He died in Brixham, England, on May 21, 1902.

Further reading: William M. Armstrong, *E. L. Godkin: A Biography* (Albany: State University of New York Press, 1978); William M. Armstrong, ed., *The Gilded Age Letters of E. L. Godkin* (Albany: State University of New York Press, 1974).

— Ellen Tashie Frisina

gold and silver mining

See mining: metal and coal

gold reserve

See currency issue

Gold Standard Act (1900)

See currency issue

Gompers, Samuel (1850–1924)

Born on January 27, 1850, in London, England, labor leader Samuel Gompers attended school for four years before getting a job to supplement his family's income. He tried shoemaking for a short time before deciding to become a cigarmaker. In 1863 Gompers moved with his family to America, where they settled in New York City. Although he attended lectures at the Cooper Union, his greatest exposure to ideas was in the workplace; cigar makers broke the monotony of their jobs by hiring someone to read to them while working. A fellow worker, Ferdinand Laurrel, introduced him to SOCIALISM but cautioned him to avoid the trap of ideology. Gompers carried this admonition with him all his life, consistently measuring issues by how they would affect the union and not against an ideological orthodoxy.

A union member in England, Gompers joined a New York local of the Cigarmakers International in America, but he was an apathetic member until the early 1870s. The cigar mold, which allowed nonskilled workers to form the filler or interior of the cigar, was being adopted in New York, and skilled cigarmakers were losing their jobs. Initially, the union did not organize the unskilled workers, with the result that by 1872 Gompers's local union had less than 50 members.

Gompers and a friend, Adolph Strasser, began to rebuild the union by accepting the mold (arguing that it was efficient and inevitable) and by recruiting the unskilled cigarmakers. By 1875 they recruited 245 members, making it the largest union of cigarmakers in the United States. Two years later, however, the union suffered a major defeat. Manufacturers switched production from shops to tenements, where immigrant families made cigars on a contract basis under deplorable conditions. In 1877 the exploited and unorganized tenement cigarmakers went on strike. Against the wishes of their leaders, the local's membership voted to support them. The strike failed after exhausting the union's treasury, but Gompers learned from the experience.

Also in 1877 Strasser and Gompers gained control of the Cigarmakers International and began a reorganization based on the lessons of the recent strike and upon Gompers's experience with English trade unions. Only workers in the trade could become members. Membership carried sick and death benefits. Central officers were supreme, and all strikes required their prior approval. If necessary, the union would break unauthorized walkouts. The union charged high dues to pay the benefits and build a sizable reserve fund to cushion economic recessions. Other trade unions adopted this successful model and recognized their debt to Gompers in 1886 by electing him president of the AMERICAN FEDERATION OF LABOR (AFL), a position he held, with the exception of one year, until his death on December 13, 1924.

Samuel Gompers *(Dover Publications)*

Gompers used his presidency of the AFL as a pulpit for expounding his philosophy of wage-conscious unionism. Labor unions, he argued, should only be concerned with the economic conditions of their members, not with creating utopias, forming political parties, organizing producers cooperatives, or reforming society. Collective bargaining, strikes, and boycotts conducted by businesslike unions were the only means of improving wages and working conditions. The AFL made no attempt to organize unskilled workers, but Gompers argued that unorganized unskilled workers often benefitted from the better wages, hours, and working conditions won by union labor.

Further reading: Harold C. Livesay, *Samuel Gompers and Organized Labor in America* (Boston: Little, Brown, 1978).

— Harold W. Aurand

Gould, Jay (1836–1892)

Jay Gould was the most important and the most notorious financier of the Gilded age. Born Jason Gould on May 27, 1836, in Roxbury, New York—the son of Mary More and John Gould, a farmer and storekeeper—Jay Gould studied in local schools before going to work as a clerk in his father's store at age 16. An unusually serious and ambitious youth, he invented a mousetrap before he was out of school, and by the time he was 17 he had taught himself surveying and formed his own company to practice it. He made maps, which he sold at a reasonable price, and at the age of 19 wrote a 426-page history of Delaware County that a century and a half later was still recognized as the definitive work on the early history of his region of New York. From 1856 to 1859 Gould and partners operated a tannery in Pennsylvania, but disagreements followed by the suicide of one of the partners led Gould to abandon tanning and take up finance on New York's Wall Street.

Gould quickly mastered the intricacies of finance and was phenomenally successful. Arriving at Wall Street with almost nothing to invest, according to a contemporary source, he made himself a millionaire long before the end of the Civil War. In 1863 he married Helen Day Miller, with whom he had six children and lived in exemplary domestic harmony until her death in 1889. He loved books and flowers, especially orchids.

Gould had a particular passion for RAILROADS. In 1867 he joined Jim Fisk and Daniel Drew on the board of directors of the Erie Railroad and frustrated the monopolistic attempt by CORNELIUS VANDERBILT of the New York Central Railroad to control it. But in doing so Gould and Fisk allied themselves with the spectacularly corrupt TWEED RING, issued $8 million in watered stock for the Erie in defiance of a restraining order, and spent a reported $1 million bribing the New York legislature to legalize the action. In 1868 Gould became president and treasurer of the Erie and had grand schemes for its expansion, but the Tweed Ring was destroyed, Fisk was murdered, and Gould in 1872 was ousted from control of the Erie. In 1869, in a move linked to his ambitious plans for the Erie, Gould (with Fisk) attempted to corner the gold market on "Black Friday," precipitating a Wall Street panic and reputedly sharing profits of $11 million with Fisk.

Gould's participation in the Erie War and the Black Friday scheme caused him to be reviled as a "robber baron," but ironically his subsequent career was more constructive, more responsible, than his earlier corrupt, dishonest rise. Gould was a talented, efficient administrator and a man of vision. From 1874 to 1878 he controlled the Union Pacific Railroad, which he improved during those years. Yet he forced the Union Pacific to buy at par the Kansas Pacific, which he controlled, netting him $10 million that he used to build a railroad empire in the Southwest, including the Missouri Pacific and the Texas & Pacific. By 1880 he controlled more than 8,000 miles of railroad, more than any other individual in the world, and in 1881 he gained control of the Western Union telegraph system and the Manhattan elevated transit system, all of which he administered very carefully. Nevertheless, when he died on December 2, 1892, he had not lived down his reputation as the most hated man in America, and he remains the most widely reviled capitalist in American history.

Further reading: Maury Klein, *The Life and Legend of Jay Gould* (Baltimore: Johns Hopkins University Press 1986).

— Dennis Wepman

graduate education See education, higher

Grady, Henry See New South

Grand Army of the Republic (GAR)

The Grand Army of the Republic (GAR) was formed after the Civil War as a fraternal organization for veterans of the Union army. It was first organized in the spring of 1866 by a group of veterans in Springfield, Illinois, led by Dr. Benjamin F. Stephenson. GAR posts were established in several states, and their first National Encampment (the GAR's version of a national convention) was held in November at Indianapolis, Indiana. Initially, the GAR grew slowly, but between 1881 and 1882 its membership rose from approximately 87,718 to 131,900; by 1890 membership in the GAR reached 409,489, making it the largest and most powerful veterans' organization in the United States.

Although it originally avoided political involvement, the GAR became a major political force, influencing several elections with its financial support and partisan electioneering for Republican candidates. The principal goals of the GAR were to increase pensions and other benefits for veterans and their families and to remember those who died in the war. The GAR was instrumental in securing the observance of Decoration Day (currently observed as Memorial Day, commemorating all war dead) in 1868 to honor those who gave their lives for the Union during the Civil War. The GAR successfully pressed for the 1879 Pension Arrears Act, which provided for back pensions (to the date of discharge) for disabled Union veterans. In 1887 Congress passed the Dependents Pension bill, granting a pension of $12 a month to all Union veterans suffering from any disability that prevented them from earning a living and gave the same pension to the dependent parents and widows of a deceased veteran. Although the GAR had lobbied Congress for many years to pass such a bill, President GROVER CLEVELAND vetoed it, earning for himself the enmity of the GAR. In the 1888 presidential election, the GAR supported BENJAMIN HARRISON, the Republican candidate. Harrison not only triumphed but the Republicans also carried both houses of Congress. In 1890 Congress passed and President Harrison signed the Dependents Pension Act, which embodied many of the same features of the earlier bill. The law doubled the number of pensioners from 490,000 to 966,00 and ensured that the GAR would remain a virtual wing of the Republican Party.

Further reading: Mary Dearing, *Veterans in Politics: The Story of the G.A.R.* (Baton Rouge: Louisiana State University Press, 1952); Stuart McConnell, *Glorious Contentment: The Grand Army of the Republic, 1865–1900* (Chapel Hill: University of North Carolina Press, 1992).

— Phillip Papas

grandfather clause (1895–1910)

Most AFRICAN AMERICANS were not permitted to vote in the United States until they were enfranchised in the former Confederacy by the act of March 2, 1867, and in the rest of the nation in 1870 by the Fifteenth Amendment to the U.S. Constitution. Following the end of Reconstruction, white southerners used various means to disfranchise black voters such as literacy tests, good-character requirements, and poll taxes. The grandfather clause, however, exempted impoverished and illiterate whites from these restrictions. Beginning with South Carolina in 1895, seven states used the grandfather clause, which declared that those who voted prior to January 1, 1867, and their lineal descendants were exempt from property, educational, or tax requirements for exercising the franchise. Following

South Carolina, Louisiana (1898), North Carolina (1900), Alabama (1901), Virginia (1902), Georgia (1908), and Oklahoma (1910) adopted the grandfather clause. Although the grandfather clause was applicable for a limited period (except in Oklahoma), its effect in disfranchising black voters was devastating and lasting. For example, in Louisiana the already low African-American voter registration dropped from 130,734 in 1896 to 1,324 in 1904. Apart from Oklahoma, where blacks composed only 7 percent of the population, the states that employed the grandfather clause to suppress the black vote disfranchised either a majority or a substantial minority of their citizens and created a "lily white" electorate. The percentage of blacks in those states ranged from 58 percent in South Carolina to 33 percent in North Carolina.

The permanent grandfather clause was challenged in Oklahoma after election judges denied an African American the privilege of voting. They were indicted and convicted for conspiring to deny a citizen his constitutional rights under federal statutes. The U.S. Supreme Court heard the case of *Guinn v. United States* in 1913 and decided unanimously in 1915 that the grandfather clause obviously violated the Fifteenth Amendment and struck it down. The decision, however, had little practical effect, since the grandfather clause in other states had already disfranchised African Americans and had lapsed, and the small number of blacks in Oklahoma were disfranchised by other devices.

Further reading: Loren Miller, *The Petitioners: The Story of the Supreme Court of the United States* (Cleveland: Meridian Books, 1967).

— William Seraile

Granger laws

See railroads

Granger movement

See Patrons of Husbandry

Great Strike of 1877

The Great Strike of 1877 was a series of spontaneous railroad strikes between July 16 and August 5 that collectively involved the largest number of people in a labor conflict in the 19th century. Four years of layoffs and wage deductions as high as 35 percent had angered railroad workers. The workers' frustration slowly boiled over when the major eastern RAILROADS announced another round of wage cuts during the early summer of 1877.

On July 16 a small group of workers on the Baltimore and Ohio Railroad (B&O) refused to move trains at Camden Junction, Maryland. Local authorities dispersed the strikers and restored traffic on the line. Two days later, however, B&O trainmen at Martinsburg, West Virginia, refused to work. Finding local authorities unable or unwilling to end the strike, management asked Governor Henry M. Mathews to send in state troops to suppress the crowd. Discovering the militia ineffective, the company persuaded Mathews to request federal troops. With some misgiving President RUTHERFORD B. HAYES accepted the governor's definition of the strike as a domestic insurrection and sent in the army to keep the peace. But by this time the strike was spreading throughout the country, stopping the flow of railroad traffic at Pittsburgh, Chicago, St. Louis, San Francisco, and many smaller cities.

Violence also escalated as unemployed men and boys joined the strikers and rioters. In Pittsburgh, for example, local elements of the state militia would not prevent the mob from looting and burning the property of the hated Pennsylvania Railroad (PRR). Authorities then ordered in the militia from Philadelphia, Pittsburgh's eastern rival. Crowds stoned the troops' train as it traveled westward. At Pittsburgh the Philadelphians fired into the crowd, killing 26 people. The angry mob forced the troopers into a roundhouse, set it on fire, and drove them out of town. In Reading, Pennsylvania, one militia company threatened to fire into another if it continued to harass strikers. Small detachments of federal troops were dispatched to Pittsburgh and elsewhere to restore order. Universally respected, the U.S. Army neither fired any shots at rioters nor were they fired upon. By August 5 most strikes were over.

The Great Strike was a traumatic experience for the American public. It was a spontaneous upheaval that smacked of European-style class warfare. Together with the recent MOLLY MAGUIRES episode, the Great Strike justified for some the notion that labor protest was sinister and un-American. As a result, states built armories in their industrial centers, and some enacted conspiracy laws that could be used against labor. But the Great Strike also made the public aware of the real grievances railroad workers had against management. The *New York Times* recognized that "beneath the vicious elements which produced the riots, the country traces evidence of hardship, of suffering, of destitution to an extent for which it was unprepared." Indeed, even railroad managers conceded that the cut in pay was more costly than an increase would have been and began restoring the wage cuts that caused the strike.

Although Hayes has been accused of breaking the Great Strike, he did not. He sent in troops only when properly requested by state and local officials, ordering them to protect government and private property and not "to quell the strikers or run the trains" and refusing the demands of THOMAS A. SCOTT of the PRR to use the pretext of obstruction of the mails for intervention, a tactic adopted by President GROVER CLEVELAND in the 1894 PULLMAN STRIKE.

Hayes, however, did enforce injunctions issued by federal courts acting as receivers for bankrupt railroads. After the Pullman Strike, the injunction was also used to protect solvent corporations and would become a powerful tool to break strikes.

Government action during the strike temporarily thrust labor into politics. In New York, Pennsylvania, and Ohio, Workingmen's Parties attracted a significant number of votes during the fall elections. In 1878 some labor leaders attended the founding convention of the GREENBACK-LABOR PARTY, which enjoyed some success that year. But despite the name, it appealed primarily to farmers and not to workingmen.

Further reading: Robert V. Bruce, *1877: Year of Violence* (Indianapolis: Bobbs-Merrill Company, 1959); Gerald G. Eggert, *Railroad Labor Disputes: The Beginnings of Federal Strike Policy* (Ann Arbor: University of Michigan Press, 1967).

— Harold W. Aurand

Greeley, Horace See Volume V

Greenback-Labor Party

During the crisis of the Civil War the federal government had issued $450 million of fiat paper money (not backed by gold) called greenbacks, which depreciated in value and drove gold out of circulation. After the war the number of greenbacks was reduced to under $400 million. While conservative banking and creditor interests applauded contraction and deflation, agrarian and many business interests were alarmed and succeeded in stopping the contraction. During the second administration of President Ulysses S. Grant (a hard-money man), the United States plunged into a serious depression following the PANIC OF 1873. Debtor groups pressed the government to increase the number of greenbacks in circulation, while supporters of "sound money" wanted a currency based on the gold standard.

The greenback question became one of the primary points of contention in the post–Civil War period, and CONGRESS reacted inconsistently. In April 1874 Grant vetoed its bill that would have increased greenbacks to $400 million; in June 1874 Congress placed a $382 million ceiling on greenbacks; and in January 1875 it passed the Specie Resumption Act, calling for the reduction of greenbacks to $300 million and their redemption with gold dollars by January 1, 1879. But the Specie Resumption Act also required that for every $80 in greenbacks retired, $100 in national bank notes had to go into circulation. However, the amount of national bank notes issued did not meet expectations, and the contraction of greenbacks stopped at $347 million. The overall result of the legislation was to appreciate the value of greenbacks.

Reacting to the Specie Resumption Act, the advocates of greenbacks ("soft money") conferred in Cleveland and Cincinnati, Ohio; held a convention in May 1876 in Indianapolis, Indiana; and organized a National Independent (Greenback) Party. These Greenbackers—including farmers, labor reformers, and some businessmen—called for the repeal of the Specie Resumption Act and nominated for president the 85-year-old philanthropist Peter Cooper, who polled less than 1 percent of the popular vote (82,000 votes). While all Greenbackers wanted an increase in the number of greenbacks, most were not in favor of a runaway inflation but, rather, a managed currency that would better reflect the needs of the economy. Following the labor strife of the late 1870s, several workingmen's groups joined the Greenback movement. The new coalition came to be known as the Greenback-Labor Party. Thereafter, the Greenbackers not only supported currency inflation but also promoted an eight-hour workday, the creation of a government labor bureau, and the restriction of Chinese immigration. Primarily agrarian, but bolstered by labor support, the party candidates fared better in the 1878 midterm elections as 15 Greenbackers were elected to the U.S. House of Representatives and countless others to state and local offices. In 1880 the Greenback-Labor presidential candidate General James B. Weaver of Iowa gained 300,000 votes, but in the 1884 election Greenbacker Benjamin F. Butler of Massachusetts received only 175,000 votes.

By the middle 1880s the Greenback-Labor Party had all but collapsed. Subsequently, the Greenbackers joined the advocates of FREE SILVER to agitate for currency expansion. Although it had only limited political success, the Greenback-Labor Party did encourage voters to act independently of the two major parties and trained some of the leaders of the PEOPLE'S PARTY (Populists).

See also CRIME OF '73; CURRENCY ISSUE; POLITICAL PARTIES, THIRD.

Further reading: Walter T. K. Nugent, *Money and American Society, 1865–1880* (New York: Free Press, 1968); Robert P. Sharkey, *Money, Class, and Party: An Economic Study of the Civil War and Reconstruction* (Baltimore: Johns Hopkins University Press, 1959); Irwin Unger, *The Greenback Era: A Social and Political History of American Finance, 1865–1879* (Princeton, N.J.: Princeton University Press, 1964).

— Phillip Papas

H

Half Breeds See Republican Party

Hanna, Marcus Alonzo (1837–1904)
Marcus Hanna, perhaps the most successful political organizer in the Gilded Age, was born in New Lisbon, Ohio, on September 24, 1837, entered the family wholesale grocery business in Cleveland, and in 1862 he became a partner upon his father's death. Two years later he married the daughter of a coal and iron industrialist, eventually controlling that company, had interests in a bank, a newspaper, and in streetcars. He was a generous, paternalistic employer, made it his business to get along with his workers, and in time accepted labor unions.

By 1880 substantial contributions to the Republican Party won him a place on that party's state committee. Sharing with WILLIAM MCKINLEY the views that large corporations were the wave of the future and that the protective tariff benefitted both capital and labor, Hanna became his chief promoter and identified Bill McKinley with the high-tariff 1890 McKinley bill. Hanna helped elect McKinley governor of Ohio in 1891 and launched a McKinley-for-president campaign, gaining him some support in 1892 and succeeding in 1896. Hanna did so by carefully marshaling the support of both business and political leaders.

Named chairman of the Republican National Committee, Hanna managed McKinley's presidential campaign with great success. The 1883 PENDLETON CIVIL SERVICE REFORM ACT prohibiting assessments of civil servants had dried up that source of campaign funds, but Hanna assessed corporations and amassed an unprecedented $3.5 million. He was aided in part because of McKinley's views and in part because the inflationary Free-Silver ideas of the Democratic nominee WILLIAM JENNINGS BRYAN were perceived as dangerous (see FREE-SILVER MOVEMENT), although Hanna was largely responsible for that perception. Hanna shrewdly used the corporate money to project the image of McKinley as the advance agent of prosperity, stability, and harmony. McKinley's triumph was Hanna's triumph; and Hana, perhaps more than anyone else in American history, deserves the title of "president maker."

Hanna advised, but did not attempt to dominate, President McKinley. Neither was he a dominating force after he was appointed to the Senate from Ohio in 1897 and elected to a full term in 1898. He reluctantly supported the war with Spain and the acquisition of the Philippines and in 1900 was unable to prevent the nomination of Theodore Roosevelt as McKinley's running mate. After Roosevelt became president following McKinley's assassination, Hanna had little use for his progressive policies, but could not thwart them. He died in Washington on February 15, 1904.

Further reading: Thomas Beer, *Hanna* (New York: Knopf, 1929); Herbert Croly, *Marcus Alonzo Hanna: His Life and Work* (New York: Macmillan, 1912); Lewis L. Gould, *The Presidency of William McKinley* (Lawrence: University Press of Kansas, 1980).

Harlan, John Marshall (1833–1911)
John Marshall Harlan, the great dissenting SUPREME COURT judge, was born on June 1, 1833, in Boyle County, Kentucky, the son of James Harlan and Eliza Shannon Davenport. A graduate of Centre College in Danville, Harlan attended law school at Transylvania University in Lexington and completed his studies in his father's law office in Frankfort, Kentucky. In 1853 Harlan was admitted to the Kentucky bar, and from 1854 to 1856 he served as the city attorney for Frankfort. In 1856 he married Malvina French Shanklin of Evansville, Indiana, with whom he had six children. From 1858 to 1861 he served as a judge of the Franklin County Court.

Although at first a supporter of the Whig Party, its demise in the 1850s led Harlan into the Know-Nothing Party. In the 1860 presidential election, Harlan endorsed the Constitutional Union Party ticket of John Bell and

Edward Everett. During the Civil War, he recruited the 10th Kentucky Volunteer Regiment for the Union army and served as its colonel until he resigned in 1863.

From 1863 to 1867 Harlan served as the attorney general of Kentucky. Although a supporter of the Union, he was a critic of the Lincoln administration and in 1864 endorsed the Democratic presidential candidate George B. McClellan. When the Thirteenth Amendment abolishing slavery in the United States was proposed in 1865, Harlan opposed it on the grounds that it violated state sovereignty. Following the war, Harlan joined the Republican Party and reversed his initial position on the Thirteenth Amendment. He also supported the Fourteenth and Fifteenth Amendments as well.

Harlan ran unsuccessfully as the Republican candidate for governor of Kentucky in 1871 and 1875. He led the Kentucky delegation at the 1876 Republican National Convention, where he initially supported the candidacy of his law partner Benjamin H. Bristow. Harlan, however, switched his support and led his delegation behind the candidacy of RUTHERFORD B. HAYES, who went on to win the Republican nomination and subsequently the PRESIDENCY. In April 1877 President Hayes named Harlan to the Louisiana Electoral Commission, which was established to finesse the departure of federal troops from Louisiana. In October 1877 Hayes nominated Harlan for a seat on the U.S. Supreme Court.

During his long career on the Court, Harlan became known for his dissenting opinions. He supported the extension of rights to AFRICAN AMERICANS and was an advocate for government regulation of industry. In the *United States v. E. C. Knight Company* (1895), Harlan strongly dissented from the Court's ruling that the creation of the Sugar Trust did not violate the SHERMAN ANTITRUST ACT (1890). He dissented from the Court's decision in the CIVIL RIGHTS CASES (1883) that equality of rights in public accommodations was not enforceable under the Fourteenth and Fifteenth Amendments. Harlan was also the sole dissenter from the Court's decision in *PLESSY V. FERGUSON* (1896) that upheld racial segregation by embracing the so-called separate-but-equal doctrine. Harlan argued that the Thirteenth Amendment barred not only slavery but also segregation, which is a "badge of slavery," and declared the "Constitution is color-blind, and neither knows nor tolerates classes among citizens."

In 1892 he was appointed by President BENJAMIN HARRISON to represent the United States in its arbitration case with Great Britain over the BERING SEA DISPUTE. Harlan also taught constitutional law at George Washington University. He died on October 14, 1911, in Washington, D.C.

Further reading: Lauren P. Beth, *John Marshall Harlan: The Last Whig Justice* (Lexington: University of Kentucky Press, 1992); Tinsley E. Yarbrough, *Judicial Enigma: The First Justice Harlan* (New York: Oxford University Press, 1995).

—Phillip Papas

Harrison, Benjamin (1833–1901)

Benjamin Harrison, the 23rd president of the United States, was the grandson of William Henry Harrison, the ninth president. Although Ohio born and educated (Miami University, 1852) and trained in the law, Benjamin Harrison moved in 1854 to Indianapolis, Indiana, with his bride of one year, Caroline Lavinia Scott. A deeply religious Presbyterian, Harrison by dint of hard work became a successful lawyer, and by possessing both strong moral feelings about slavery and stump speaking skills, he became a leading member of the Republican Party. But while he could move a multitude, he was cold and aloof in small groups and with individuals. During the Civil War he helped raise the 70th Indiana regiment, was appointed its colonel by Governor Oliver P. Morton, fought effectively in General William T. Sherman's 1864 Atlanta campaign, stumped effectively in Indiana's 1864 political campaign, and emerged from the war a brigadier general with bright political prospects. He could have won a seat in CONGRESS, but his wife objected to further absences from home and he returned to his law practice in Indianapolis. He prospered and by campaigning vigorously for others remained a prominent Republican.

In 1876 Harrison agreed to run for governor and lost a close race to James Douglas (Blue Jeans) Williams, but in 1881 the Indiana legislature elected Harrison to one term in the U.S. Senate. There his probity preserved his purity and his aloofness ensured his lack of influence while he worked for pensions for union veterans and a protective tariff. These qualities enhanced Harrison's "availability" for the 1888 Republican presidential nomination when coupled with the certainty that he could carry Indiana, an important swing state. When JAMES G. BLAINE, the most popular Republican of that era, decided not to run, the available candidate—the least offensive to all factions—to run against the incumbent GROVER CLEVELAND proved to be Harrison. Although Cleveland won more popular votes, Harrison, with his votes more strategically located, won a majority in the electoral college and was elected president.

Although his orderly, lawyerly mind made him a good administrator, Harrison's frigid personality made him an inept politician. He managed to offend Republican congressmen even while awarding them with patronage. As everyone expected, he made Blaine his secretary of state but appeared reluctant to do so. Initially, they worked well together, but in time they drifted apart. Harrison succeeded in offending both civil service reformers and spoilsmen. When his assistant postmaster general quite legitimately replaced Democratic postmasters who were not covered by CIVIL SERVICE REFORM rules, reformers objected, and when Harrison's most prominent civil service commissioner Theodore Roosevelt frustrated spoilsmen, *they* howled. But despite Harrison's support, Roosevelt dismissed him as "a coldblooded, narrow-minded, prejudiced, obstinate, timid old psalm-singing Indianapolis politician." That most unfair characterization was belied, for example, by Harrison's consistent support on moral grounds of a Federal Elections bill that would enforce the Fifteenth Amendment and enable African Americans to vote. Southern Democrats secured the support of westerners anxious to pass inflationary silver legislation, thus blocking passage in 1890 of what they called the Force bill.

Policies and legislation adopted during Harrison's administration wiped out the $100 million surplus of revenue over expenditures. His commissioner of pensions for six months, "Corporal" James Tanner, exclaimed "God help the surplus!" as he arbitrarily raised disability payments before being forced out of office, but Congress in 1890 passed the Dependent and Disability Pension Act for Union veterans, which raised the appropriation for pensions from $81 million to $135 million. In that same year the "Billion Dollar Congress" passed the MCKINLEY TARIFF, which raised already protective rates to new heights, but it also included a reciprocity feature both Blaine and Harrison fought for. To secure western votes for the McKinley Tariff, anti-inflationary easterners agreed to the Sherman Silver Purchase Act (1890), which required the U.S. Treasury to purchase 4.5 million ounces of silver monthly with notes redeemable in gold or silver. By redeeming these notes in gold, the Harrison administration kept the United States on the gold standard but began to erode the Treasury's gold reserve. At Harrison's request and to redeem an 1888 campaign pledge, Congress also passed the SHERMAN ANTITRUST ACT (1890), which outlawed combinations in restraint of trade. But vague wording, lax enforcement, and judicial hostility made the Sherman Act ineffective over the next decade, while mergers and monopolies proliferated.

Contrary to expectations, Harrison was not dominated by Blaine (whose health declined) in the conduct of a vigorous FOREIGN POLICY. Harrison favored a strong navy, an Isthmian canal, and the acquisition of naval bases (securing a protectorate in SAMOA in 1889). He supported the first modern Pan-American Conference (1889), negotiated eight reciprocity agreements under the Mckinley Tariff, and managed to open European markets previously closed to American pork. Harrison was aggressive in the BERING SEA DISPUTE with Great Britain; chauvinistic when American sailors were killed in Valparaiso, Chile; and not overly disturbed by Italy's outrage when a New Orleans mob lynched alleged members of the Mafia. Harrison's biggest foreign policy disappointment was his last-minute failure to secure Senate approval of a treaty annexing HAWAII.

Benjamin Harrison *(Library of Congress)*

The legislation of the billion-dollar Congress, especially the McKinley Tariff, resulted in a Democratic landslide in 1890. Despite the coolness of Blaine and other leading Republicans, Harrison was renominated in 1892 and defeated by Cleveland. Prior to the death of his wife just before that election, Harrison had an affair with her niece Mary Lord Dimmick, whom he married in 1896. After the presidency, Harrison represented Venezuela in the VENEZUELA BOUNDARY DISPUTE and helped frustrate Great Britain's ambition to control the mouth of the Orinoco River. He died on March 13, 1901, in Indianapolis.

See also CHILEAN-AMERICAN RELATIONS; MAFIA INCIDENT; and TARIFF ISSUES.

Further reading: Harry J. Sievers, *Benjamin Harrison, Hoosier President: The White House and After* (Indianapolis: Bobbs-Merrill, 1968); Homer E. Socolofsky and Allan B. Spetter, *The Presidency of Benjamin Harrison* (Lawrence: University Press of Kansas, 1987).

Hatch Act (1887) See education, federal aid to

Hawaii

Great Britain, France, and the United States became interested in Hawaii after its discovery by Captain James Cook in 1778. American missionaries arrived in 1820, and treaties of friendship and commerce with the Kingdom of Hawaii were signed by the United States in 1826, Britain in 1836, and France in 1839. The U.S. Senate did not ratify its treaty, but Hawaii abided by its provisions, and in 1842 the United States recognized Hawaii's independence. American whalers used Hawaii as a base, and with American acquisition of Oregon and California a few years later, Hawaii's importance for the defense of the West Coast became apparent. In 1851 when France had designs on Hawaii, the United States warned that it would not permit its annexation by a European power.

It was in the Gilded Age that America solidified its influence in Hawaii. More for strategic than for economic reasons, the United States in 1875 entered into a reciprocity agreement with the Hawaiian kingdom whereby both nations agreed to drop tariffs on a long list of products, the main one being sugar. Within a year American capital began to flood the island, and sugar production by American growers skyrocketed. In 1887 the reciprocity treaty was extended, and the United States was permitted to establish a naval base at Pearl Harbor.

Since the royal family was capricious, Americans in Hawaii generally favored annexation by the United States to protect their property. But after the MCKINLEY TARIFF of 1890 put foreign sugar on the free list (depriving Hawaii of its favored position) and gave domestic sugar a two cent per pound subsidy, they became ardent annexationists. In addition Queen Liliuokalani, advocating "Hawaii for the Hawaiians," set aside the Constitution of 1887 that favored whites and promulgated an autocratic constitution in 1893. American planters, with the connivance of U.S. minister John L. Stevens and aided by a contingent of marines, ousted Queen Liliuokalani and declared a republic, but they immediately agreed to a treaty of annexation with the United States in the closing days of Republican president BENJAMIN HARRISON's administration. The Senate, however, failed to ratify the treaty before the incoming Democratic president GROVER CLEVELAND, an anti-imperialist, took office. Cleveland, suspicious of Stevens's actions, withdrew the treaty and sent Georgia congressman James H. Blount to Hawaii to investigate. After a thorough investigation Blount concluded that Stevens and the American military had actively abetted the coup. Contrary to dispatches from Stevens, marines from the cruiser USS *Boston* were not called out to protect American lives but were strategically placed across from the royal palace, which was far away from the consulate or any American property.

After reading the report, Cleveland and his secretary of state Walter Q. Gresham wished to regain the throne for the queen and amnesty for the rebels. The queen, however, insisted that the coup leaders be beheaded as Hawaiian custom dictated, while Sanford Dole, president of the provisional republic of Hawaii, would not resign and said that the United States could either annex Hawaii or respect its independence. Unable to work out a solution, Cleveland placed the problem in the lap of CONGRESS in December 1893 and stated that he would execute whatever solution it devised. After much partisan wrangling, Congress neither annexed the islands nor attempted to disturb Dole's provisional government. On July 4, 1894, the provisional government became the Republic of Hawaii, and a month later Cleveland acquiesced and recognized the white minority government.

Cleveland was succeeded in 1897 by Republican WILLIAM MCKINLEY, who was more aware of the islands' strategic value and less troubled by the illegitimate birth of the Republic of Hawaii. Accordingly, in June 1897 a new treaty of annexation was signed, but strong Democratic opposition prevented ratification. Annexation, however, became imperative following Admiral GEORGE DEWEY's stunning victory at Manila Bay and the need to "bridge the Pacific." That victory also emphasized the perception of Admiral ALFRED THAYER MAHAN that Hawaii was the "key to the Pacific." In July 1898, during the SPANISH-AMERICAN WAR, the United States annexed Hawaii by a joint resolution of Congress with McKinley's approval.

Further reading: William A. Russ Jr., *The Hawaiian Revolution* (Selinsgrove, Pa.: Susquehanna University Press, 1959); William A. Russ Jr., *The Hawaiian Republic: 1894–1898* (Selinsgrove, Pa.: Susquehanna University Press, 1961).

— Timothy E. Vislocky

Hay, John Milton (1838–1905)

John Milton Hay capped his distinguished literary and diplomatic career by serving as secretary of state from 1898 to 1905. Born in Salem, Indiana, on October 12, 1838, Hay grew up in Illinois, graduated from Brown University, and by 1860 was back in Illinois studying law in the office of his uncle in Springfield. Friendship with Abraham Lincoln's secretary, John Nicolay, enabled Hay to become assistant personal secretary to the new president in 1861. The youthful presidential aide won the confidence of his chief and also amused him with his storytelling ability. After the Civil War, from 1865 to 1870, Hay received brief diplomatic postings to Paris, Vienna, and Madrid, where he despised European aristocrats and sympathized with radical democrats. He achieved fame in 1871 as a poet with the publication of *Pike County Ballads and Other Pieces*, and from 1870 to 1875 he wrote editorials for the *New York Tribune*. In 1874 he married Clara Stone the daughter of Cleveland railroad builder and financier Amasa Stone, and from 1878 to 1881 Hay served as assistant secretary of state. Disturbed by the GREAT STRIKE OF 1877, Hay had become conservative and anonymously published in 1883 an antilabor novel, *The Bread-winners,* and in the 1880s he wrote with Nicolay a 10-volume biography of Lincoln.

Having married wealth, Hay was a heavy contributor to the Republican Party and in 1897 was delighted to be appointed by WILLIAM MCKINLEY as ambassador to Great Britain. As an ardent Anglophile, Hay facilitated the rapprochement between London and Washington and encouraged British support of the United States in the SPANISH-AMERICAN WAR. Soon after hailing it as the "splendid little war," Hay in August 1898 became secretary of state, and although he had earlier opposed IMPERIALISM, he favored the acquisition of the Philippines (with their proximity to China) at that war's end and defended the American suppression of the subsequent FILIPINO INSURRECTION. In the OPEN DOOR NOTES of 1899 to 1900, Hay sought to prevent the dismemberment of China and to preserve equal access there for American investors and missionaries at a time when other foreign powers were acquiring spheres of influence. In the Caribbean, Hay obtained British acquiescence to an American-fortified isthmian canal across Central America in 1901; negotiated a treaty with Colombia for a canal zone in its province of Panama, which that government rejected; and then in 1903 negotiated similar concessions from Panama following its successful (with American help) revolt against Colombia. In his last year in office Hay played a lesser role in FOREIGN POLICY as President Theodore Roosevelt essentially became his own secretary of state. Hay died on July 1, 1905.

Further reading: Kenton J. Clymer, *John Hay: The Gentleman as Diplomat* (Ann Arbor: University of Michigan Press, 1975); Howard I. Kushner and Anne Hummell Sherrill, *John Hay: The Union of Poetry and Politics* (Boston: Twayne, 1977).

— Bruce Abrams

Hayes, Rutherford B. (1822–1893)

Born in Delaware, Ohio, on October 4, 1822, three months after his father died, Rutherford Birchard Hayes, 19th president of the United States, had a happy, although sheltered childhood and found a role model in his uncle Sardis Birchard, who prospered as a merchant and land speculator. Hayes was a good student, graduating from Kenyon College as valedictorian of his class in 1842 and from Harvard Law School in 1845. Admitted to the Ohio bar that year, he then spent five unchallenging years in Lower Sandusky (later Fremont), the home of his uncle Sardis.

Hayes moved to Cincinnati, the largest city in the West, on Christmas Eve 1849 to make his mark or fail. His practice grew slowly but picked up as he gained a reputation as a defender of murderers. He also enjoyed the cultural advantages and social life of a large city and fell in love with Lucy Webb, whom he married on December 30, 1852. Lucy, a strong believer in Methodism, abstinence from alcoholic beverages, and abolition, influenced but did not radically change Hayes. He never joined a church but in time attended services regularly; he drank temperately but, as president, he became a teetotaler; and after marriage he abandoned his tepid antislavery stance and became a noted defender of runaway slaves. He opposed the extension of slavery into western territories and helped establish the Republican Party in Ohio. When the Civil War broke out in 1861, Hayes enthusiastically supported the Union cause, was commissioned in June as a major in the 23rd Ohio Voluntary Infantry, was wounded five times while serving for four years, and emerged from the war a major general and a popular war hero.

Elected to and a member of CONGRESS from 1865 to 1867, Hayes supported Radical Republican Reconstruction measures before he resigned to make the first of three successful runs for governor of Ohio. While in that office (1868–72, 1876–77), he fought successfully for passage of the Fifteenth Amendment (voting rights for blacks) to the U.S. Constitution, for the establishment of Ohio State University, and for the nonpartisan administration of asylums and prisons. His gubernatorial victory in 1875, despite a resurgent Democratic Party (capitalizing on a severe economic depression and POLITICAL CORRUPTION in the Ulysses S. Grant administration), made Hayes a candidate for the 1876 Republican presidential nomination. He proved to be more "available" than other contenders, since he combined a distinguished military career with a radical record on Reconstruction issues, a reform record as governor, and the capacity to carry a big swing state. Republicans nominated Hayes in hopes that he would unite the party and prevent defections to the Democrats.

Hayes and the Republicans had an uphill fight. Not only was the party identified with hard times and sleaze, but the Democrats also nominated Governor SAMUEL J. TILDEN of New York, who was renowned as a reformer and as a political organizer. The Republican tactic of identifying the Democrats with treason during and persecution of black Americans after the Civil War had lost its appeal to those who yearned for prosperity and political purity. Tilden had a majority of votes cast, but violence and intimidation in the South kept thousands of AFRICAN AMERICANS from the polls and enabled Republicans to void Democratic votes and claim that not Tilden but Hayes had carried South Carolina, Louisiana, and Florida, giving him a majority of one electoral vote (185 to 184) and the presidency. But Democrats, who controlled the House of Representatives and a majority in the joint session of Congress in whose presence the electoral votes would be counted, accused the Republicans of fraud and claimed those states and victory for Tilden. This disputed election was finally resolved in Hayes's favor on March 2, 1877, two days before Grant's term expired.

When Hayes took office, Republican Reconstruction governments existed only in South Carolina and Louisiana, and these governments held sway only in the vicinity of the state capital buildings, where small detachments of federal troops upheld their authority. Extralegal Democratic governments, supported ardently and violently by the white minority, controlled the rest of those states, and Republican authority could only be restored by sizable armies of occupation, which neither northern public opinion nor the House of Representatives would condone. Reinforcement was not a realistic option. Hayes himself had no faith in military coercion as a long-range cure for the South's problems and would rely instead on the school and the vote for blacks, the goodwill of the "better class" of whites, and erasing the color line in politics. Using his eroding bargaining position, Hayes extracted pledges from South Carolina and Louisiana Democrats to respect the civil rights of black and white Republicans before he ordered the troops to cease

Rutherford B. Hayes *(Library of Congress)*

their support of the Republican governments. White southerners, including the so-called better people, reneged on those pledges by the next election, and the solid white-supremacy Democratic South became a reality.

Having settled on a southern policy, Hayes turned next to CIVIL SERVICE REFORM. His cabinet appointments, especially that of reformer CARL SCHURZ, offended Republican spoilsmen in Congress who were using federal patronage to maintain their hold on local party organizations. Hayes believed that the so-called senatorial courtesy of allowing senators and representatives to dictate who should be appointed politicized the civil service, reduced its efficiency, and deprived the president of his power to be an effective administrator. In June 1877 Hayes prohibited forced political contributions (assessments) by civil servants and forbade their management of party organizations and political campaigns. Feeling that CHESTER A. ARTHUR, head of the New York customhouse, was not sympathetic to reform, Hayes succeeded in removing him after a long struggle with his political patron, ROSCOE CONKLING, over senatorial courtesy. Hayes then insisted that the merit system of appointing on the basis of competitive examinations be introduced in the customhouse, and its success in what was the largest federal office in the land helped secure the PENDLETON CIVIL SERVICE REFORM ACT of 1883.

The severe economic depression with its wage cuts and layoffs led to the GREAT STRIKE OF 1877. Beginning on the Baltimore & Ohio Railroad, it quickly spread to other roads and industries. As unemployed men and boys joined strikers, unprecedented riots, violence, and arson broke out, especially in Pittsburgh and Baltimore. Hayes did not break the strike, and he dispatched federal troops (who never fired a shot) only at the call of state and local officials. Despite the begging of THOMAS ALEXANDER SCOTT of the Pennsylvania Railroad, Hayes would not order troops to run the trains on the pretext that the strike interfered with the U.S. mail. Although Hayes favored an eight-hour day for industrial workers, he disliked labor agitators. He also disliked railroad moguls and favored federal regulation of railroads.

Hard times also led to demands for currency inflation, which Hayes adamantly opposed on moral and practical, but certainly not political, grounds. Believing that inflation was dishonest and that fears of it prolonged the depression, Hayes insisted the United States return to the gold standard in 1879 (as scheduled by Congress in 1875) and opposed the popular 1878 BLAND-ALLISON ACT, which allowed the limited coinage of silver dollars at the ratio of 16 to one part of gold and which passed over his veto. The stunning business revival that accompanied the resumption of specie payments confirmed for Hayes his monetary orthodoxy.

Having offended spoilsmen and inflationists in his own party while failing to attract "better" southerners, who later also turned out to be racists, Hayes saw the Republican

Party lose control of the Senate as well as the House in 1878. Ironically, the Democrats helped Hayes reunite Republicans and made possible their victory in 1880. Realizing that Hayes would veto any direct attempt to repeal the election laws designed to enforce the civil- and voting-rights principles of the Fourteenth and Fifteenth Amendments, the Democrats attached riders to necessary appropriations bills that they thought Hayes would be forced to sign lest the government be shut down. They were wrong; Hayes relished this "battle of the riders," vetoed appropriations bills, and rallied public opinion and his party behind him with his stirring messages. Realizing the Democrats wished to stuff ballot boxes in northern cities and to intimidate southern blacks at the polls, Hayes argued for the sanctity of the ballot and defended executive power by maintaining that the riders unconstitutionally deprived the president of his veto power.

Hayes was a precursor of modern 20th-century presidents. He rallied public opinion to his side with his well-publicized vetoes and the short speeches he made while traveling extensively. By shrewdly expounding principles, exploiting issues, enhancing executive power, and introducing modern bureaucratic procedures, Hayes stressed the politics of reform that presidents have come to embrace. Ironically, Republican congressmen, wedded to the politics of organization, thought Hayes an inept politician, but his presidency illustrated his belief "that he serves his party best who serves his country best."

After leaving office, Hayes campaigned tirelessly for social causes. His major emphasis was on EDUCATION, which was for him a panacea for society's ills. He served on the boards of three universities in Ohio but was especially committed to the education of disadvantaged black and white children in the South. He was on the boards of the philanthropic Peabody and Slater funds and campaigned vigorously, but unsuccessfully, for distributing federal funds to impoverished school districts throughout the nation. He believed that education was the key to economic improvement, and for African Americans, economic improvement was the key to civil rights. He advocated industrial education for all children, whether their parents were rich or poor. If politicians and capitalists knew what it was like to work with their hands, they would understand labor's demands and industrial strife would be mitigated. Hayes also believed education could rehabilitate criminals and was president of the National Prison Reform Association. As governor and president he had been generous with pardons and in time opposed the death penalty. He thought poverty caused crime and that wealth should be more evenly distributed through confiscatory inheritance taxes. He also saw the growing power of the corporation as a threat to the government and "the Standard Oil monopoly . . . a menace to the people." In his remarkably active retirement, Hayes was a precursor of the Progressives. He died on January 17, 1893.

Further reading: Ari Hoogenboom, *Rutherford B. Hayes: Warrior and President* (Lawrence: University Press of Kansas, 1995).

Haymarket riot (1886)

The Haymarket tragedy is rooted in the Eight-Hour movement. The drive, beginning in 1865, to legislate an eight-hour workday had not succeeded, but the idea remained very popular. In 1884 the trade unions, organized in 1881 as the Federation of Organized Trades and Labor Unions of the United States, revived the idea by calling a nationwide strike for the eight-hour day on May 1, 1886.

In Chicago, anarchists saw the strike call as an excellent propanganda opportunity. Unfortunately, their revolutionary rhetoric combined with intense grassroots support for a shorter workday convinced many that Chicago was on the brink of a violent social upheaval. On May 1, 1886, a large number of people, led by prominent anarchists Albert Parsons and August Spies, peacefully marched up Michigan Avenue in support of the eight-hour day. But rather than allay fears of violence, the parade contributed to the general apprehension.

Two days later an unrelated incident touched off the anticipated violence. Earlier, on February 16, workers at the McCormick Harvesting Machine Company had gone on strike over the issue of hiring nonunion people. The company responded by shutting down the plant and then hiring replacements. Although production had not regained its former levels, it became obvious by late April that McCormick had secured enough strikebreakers to defeat the union. To maintain its union-busting strategy, the company even granted its workers an eight-hour day when many refused to work on May 1. On May 3 union picketers attacked the strikebreakers as they left work. The Chicago police intervened by shooting into the crowd, killing two.

August Spies, a speaker at a nearby mass meeting in support of the eight-hour day, rushed to the scene and witnessed the carnage. Returning to the office of the anarchist newspaper he edited, Spies issued a pamphlet urging workers to arm themselves and attend a protest meeting the following evening at Haymarket Square. About 3,000 people braved the miserable weather to hear Spies and his fellow anarchists Parsons and Samuel Fielden. Despite the rhetoric of the so-called revenge circular, the meeting was peaceful and began to break up when police entered the square. Someone threw a bomb among the police, killing one officer outright and fatally injuring others. The police then opened fire. The bomb and the bullets killed

12 people (eight police and four civilians) and wounded at least 90 others.

The episode appeared to confirm the widespread fear of revolution. The press and a large cross section of the community demanded that radicalism be smashed. Police arrested known radicals, searched their homes, and tried to induce false testimony. As a result of this investigation eight people—Parsons, Spies, Fielden, Eugene Schwab, Adolph Fischer, George Engel, Louis Lingg, and Oscar Neebe—all anarchists, were tried and convicted.

Although the prosecution could not link them directly to the bomb throwing, the jury obeyed Judge Joseph Gary's instructions to find them guilty if it determined that they had ever advocated violence. Neebe received a 15-year sentence, and the seven others were sentenced to death. Lingg committed suicide during the appeals process, and Parsons, Spies, Engel, and Fischer were executed on November 11, 1887. Fielden and Schwab, whose death penalties were commuted to life imprisonment, were, with Neebe, pardoned in 1893 by Governor JOHN P. ALTGELD.

Further reading: Paul Avrich, *The Haymarket Tragedy* (Princeton, N.J.: Princeton University Press, 1984).

— Harold W. Aurand

Hepburn v. Griswold (1870) See currency issue

Herbert, Victor August (1859–1924)

Victor Herbert is remembered for his operettas, which enjoyed immense popularity from the 1890s through World War I. He was one of the finest cellists, conductors, and composers of his generation and was an important advocate for composers' rights.

Herbert was born on February 1, 1859, in Dublin, Ireland, the son of Edward Herbert and Fanny Lover. Edward died while Victor was still an infant, and he spent his early childhood in England at the home of his maternal grandfather, noted Irish painter, novelist, and songwriter Samuel Lover. In 1866 Herbert's mother married a German doctor, and the family settled in Stuttgart, Germany. Victor enrolled at the local gymnasium and began music studies, at first piano and flute before settling on the cello. He left the gymnasium at age 15, and from 1874 to 1876 he studied cello with Bernhard Cossmann.

In 1876 he began his professional career as a cellist, performing with orchestras throughout Europe. Around 1880 he spent a year in Vienna with the orchestra of Eduard Strauss, where he gained a familiarity with the Viennese operetta and lighter classical music that was to greatly influence his own work. In 1881 he returned to Stuttgart to play in the court orchestra; in 1883 he appeared as soloist with the orchestra in his first large-scale composition, the Suite for Cello and Orchestra, op. 3, and in 1885 he appeared as soloist in his First Cello Concerto, op. 8. During these years he studied composition with Max Seifritz at the Stuttgart Conservatory. In 1886 Herbert married Therese Forster (1861–1927), a distinguished Viennese soprano who had been engaged by the court opera in 1885. She was offered a contract with the Metropolitan Opera Company of New York, and it was arranged that Herbert would be offered a position as first cellist with the opera orchestra. The couple sailed for New York in the autumn of 1886.

In New York, Herbert quickly became a leading figure in the musical life of the city. In addition to playing in the opera orchestra, he found work as a conductor, teacher, chamber musician, and cello soloist. In 1889 he was appointed to the faculty of the National Conservatory, where Antonín Dvořák served as director from 1892 to 1895. Although he left the conservatory in 1893, he developed a warm personal relationship with Dvořák. He was appointed director of the 22nd Regiment Band of the New York National Guard in 1893. That band, known as "Gilmore's band," was founded in 1861 by Patrick S. Gilmore and was considered one of the finest bands in the nation. The reputation of the band declined following Gilmore's death in 1892, but Herbert quickly reestablished it as a leading organization and toured widely with it for the next seven years. In 1898 he was appointed conductor of the Pittsburgh Symphony Orchestra, and he succeeded in raising it to the level of the finest American orchestras. In 1904 he founded the Victor Herbert Orchestra, which achieved national fame and popularity by performing light orchestral music.

Herbert was active and successful as a composer from his arrival in America. In 1894 he introduced his Second Cello Concerto with the New York Philharmonic. His tone poem *Hero and Leander* (1901) reflects the influence of Wagner and Liszt, yet he composed and arranged many marches and lighter works for band and orchestra. He composed two operas, *Natoma* (1911) and *Madeleine* (1914), and wrote one of the first scores for the classic full-length film *The Birth of a Nation* (1916). But it was as a composer of operettas that he had his greatest success. His first operetta, *Prince Ananias,* was produced in New York in 1894 by the Bostonians, a popular theater company. The work was only a modest success, but the following year saw the production of *The Wizard of the Nile,* the first of a string of hits that would last for the next 30 years. *The Serenade* (1897) and *The Fortune Teller* (1898) were major successes, and in 1899 he had three more shows in production on Broadway. In all, Herbert wrote more than 40 operettas, the most notable being *Babes in Toyland* (1903), *Mlle. Modiste* (1905), *The Red Mill* (1906), *Naughty Mari-*

etta (1910), *Sweethearts* (1913), and *Eileen* (1917). These shows reflect the influence of Viennese operetta but also owe a debt to Gilbert and Sullivan and Tin Pan Alley. Many of the most popular songs of the era came from these works, including "Kiss Me Again," "Italian Street Song," "Ah, Sweet Mystery of Life," "Streets of New York," and "Because You're You."

Herbert was a leader in the fight for composers' rights. His testimony before Congress was influential in the passage of the copyright law of 1909 that secured composers' royalties on the sale of recorded cylinders, discs, and piano rolls. He was also one of the founders of the American Society of Composers, Authors, and Publishers (ASCAP), and he served as a vice president and director from 1914 until his death on May 26, 1924. He recognized the importance of sound recording and made many early recordings as a cellist and conductor.

Further reading: Edward N. Waters, *Victor Herbert: A Life in Music* (New York: Macmillan, 1955).

— William Peek

Hill, James J. (1838–1916)

James Jerome Hill, the builder of the Great Northern Railway, was born on September 16, 1838, in Rockwood, Ontario, Canada, to farmers James Hill and Alice Dunbar. James J. Hill left school at age 14 and worked as a grocery-store clerk. In 1856 he moved to St. Paul, Minnesota, where he held a variety of jobs as a clerk and agent of companies involved in river and railroad transportation. In 1866 he established his own company, specializing in the transfer and warehousing of freight, and in 1867 he contracted to supply the St. Paul & Pacific Railroad with fuel. Poorly managed, that railroad went bankrupt in 1873, and Hill, recognizing the importance of rail transportation to the future of the Northwest, acquired it in 1878 with the support of three Canadian investors. Hill extended the St. Paul & Pacific line to link St. Paul with Winnipeg, Manitoba, Canada, in 1878, and the next year he reorganized it as the St. Paul, Minneapolis & Manitoba Railway. He also built west through the Dakotas and Montana to Great Falls by 1887. In contrast to the jerry-built Northern Pacific Railroad (NP), Hill's road was carefully surveyed, well constructed, and efficiently managed. In 1890 Hill united all his railroad holdings in to the Great Northern Railway Company, a vast network that in 1893 reached Seattle, Washington, and for a time ran steamships to China and Japan.

While dedicated to the expansion of his rail empire, Hill was implacable in defending and promoting his financial interests and in eliminating competition. Hill and financier J. PIERPONT MORGAN in 1896 gained control of the NP, and in 1901 they acquired the Chicago, Burlington & Quincy Railway Company (CB&Q), thus gaining access to Chicago. Edward H. Harriman, the dominant figure in southwestern railroads, and who was backed by financier Jacob Schiff, also wanted the CB&Q and challenged Hill and Morgan for control of the NP, which had half-interest in the CB&Q. The bidding for NP stock was so intense that Wall Street was shaken, but the rivals made an uneasy peace later that year by forming the Northern Securities Company, with Hill as president. Serving as a holding company for the Great Northern, the NP, and the CB&Q systems, the Northern Securities Company was dissolved in 1904 when the SUPREME COURT declared it to be in violation of the SHERMAN ANTITRUST ACT of 1890. Despite the Court's action, the NP remained strongly influenced by Hill. Ironically, in 1970 the Interstate Commerce Commission approved the merger of the Great Northern, NP, and the CB&Q.

Hill was widely regarded as an "empire builder." To generate traffic for the Great Northern, he promoted the settlement and development of the Northwest. He encouraged immigration, sought to improve farming methods, and by keeping freight rates and passenger fares affordable along his right of way, earned a reputation for concern for the welfare of the pioneers in the region. Hill had the clear vision to see that their prosperity was the source of the Great Northern's strength and his fortune. He died in St. Paul on May 29, 1916.

Further reading: Michael P. Malone, *James J. Hill: Empire Builder of the Northwest* (New York: Oxford University Press, 1996); Albro Martin, *James J. Hill and the Opening of the Northwest* (New York: Oxford University Press, 1976).

— Dennis Wepman

Hoar, George F. (1826–1904)

Born in Concord, Massachusetts, on August 29, 1826, George Frisbie Hoar, a distinguished reform-minded U.S. senator, came from an eminent family. His grandfather Roger Sherman had signed the Declaration of Independence and the Constitution; his father Samuel was a conspicuous antislavery man driven from South Carolina by a mob in 1844; his older brother Ebenezer Rockwood was Ulysses S. Grant's attorney general; and his sister Elizabeth was noted for her brilliance among the outstanding intellectuals of their town. Hoar graduated from Harvard College and Harvard Law School, practiced in Worcester, Massachusetts, entered politics as a Free-Soiler, and joined the Republican Party in 1856. From 1856 to 1857 he worked with the free-state element in Kansas. After several years in the Massachusetts legislature, Hoar served in the U.S. House of Representatives from 1869 to 1877 and from then on in the Senate until his death in Worcester on September 30, 1904.

While always loyal to the Republican Party, Hoar neither forgot its reform origins nor his own heritage of conscientious public service. Honest, upright, decent, and forthright, Hoar had an independent streak, and when aware of wrongdoing, he would expose the misdeeds and oppose the policies of fellow Republicans if he thought them wrong. He helped investigate the Credit Mobilier scandal (implicating the vice president and members of Congress for taking bribes), opposed the so-called Salary Grab Act (1873) (retroactively raising congressmen's salaries), and in 1876 was a manager of the impeachment of Grant's secretary of war (for selling Indian-post traderships) even after he had resigned.

Having begun his career as an antislavery reformer, Hoar consistently supported civil rights for all (the Fourteenth Amendment); voting rights for African Americans (the Fifteenth Amendment, which he thought was "the crowning measure of Reconstruction"), and for women (for which he wrote pamphlets); and the rights of Chinese immigrants and American Indians. He also worked to purify politics and to improve the machinery of government. He supported the 1883 PENDLETON CIVIL SERVICE REFORM ACT, which required that civil servants be appointed on the basis of open competitive examinations, and he wrote the 1887 repeal of the Tenure of Office Act as well as the 1886 Presidential Succession Act. The growth of monopoly disturbed Hoar, who was an architect of the 1890 SHERMAN ANTITRUST ACT and who later sought to regulate corporations more effectively by licensing those engaged in interstate commerce.

In the twilight of his career Hoar denounced IMPERIALISM as contrary to the ideals of the founders of the Republican Party, the principles of the Declaration of Independence, and the morality of the Golden Rule. Urging that the United States promote self-determination, he strongly favored Cuban independence and opposed the annexation of the Philippines and Puerto Rico. The anti-imperialist crusade failed: CUBA, nominally independent, became an American protectorate; Puerto Rico became a colony; and the Philippines were conquered and annexed. Self-determination was ignored, but a generation after Hoar's death the United States found that self-determination was preferable to imperialism.

Further reading: Richard E. Welch Jr., *George Frisbie Hoar and the Half-Breed Republicans* (Cambridge, Mass.: Harvard University Press, 1971).

holding companies

See trusts

Homer, Winslow (1836–1910)

Winslow Homer is credited with originating an American vein of realism in depictions of genre scenes, the landscape, and the seascape. His was a muscular realism that celebrated the paint surface.

Born in Boston on February 24, 1836, Homer had a two-year apprenticeship with a lithographer, almost his only formal training. In 1857 he began supporting himself as a freelance illustrator for magazines and newspapers, work he continued for 20 years. His images of the Civil War, which focused on the soldiers' everyday camp life instead of the battlefield, received wide circulation. In 1866–67 he traveled to Paris, where he probably saw the work of early modernists such as Edouard Manet and Gustave Courbet. The color theorist Eugene Chevreul and Japanese art also influenced Homer. In the 1860s and 1870s he was an active figure in the New York art world, and his oils and watercolors found a ready market. Always an active outdoorsman, Homer chose, after 1884, to live much of his life in the relative isolation of Prout's Neck, Maine, where he died on September 29, 1910.

Homer found his first success as a painter with genre scenes expressed in a distinctly American idiom. A series depicting public education included *Snap the Whip* (1872, Butler Institute of American Art, Youngstown, Ohio), which shows boys playing that game in front of a one-room rural school house. The painting was widely exhibited and frequently engraved. Among the paintings derived from his work as a war correspondent was *Prisoners from the Front* (1866, Metropolitan Museum of Art, New York), which depicts a young Union officer inspecting three Confederate captives, the dress, posture, and facial expressions of each conveying their rank and character. A decade later Homer revisited the South and perceptively painted recently freed slaves at work, *The Cotton Pickers* (1876, Los Angeles County Museum of Art), and at leisure, *Sunday Morning in Virginia* (1877, Cincinnati Art Museum).

Homer often turned his attraction to dramatic landscapes and dramatic events in the landscape rendered dispassionately. He painted the sporting life in the Adirondacks: deer frantically swimming away from hunters, a fighting trout at the end of a line, and the rugged guides who made such scenes accessible to Homer and his patrons. Winters spent in Bermuda, Florida, and other warm places resulted in vivid watercolors. Some of his oils distill these outdoor experiences; for example, in *The Fox Hunt* (1893, Pennsylvania Academy of the Fine Arts, Philadelphia), two crows and their quarry, a fox, are silhouetted against the snow; the canvas quotes Japanese prints as well as real life.

Homer is perhaps most well known for his seascapes. Many earlier genre scenes included the water; for example, *Breezing Up* (1876, National Gallery of Art, Washington,

The Unruly Calf, by Winslow Homer, 1875 *(Library of Congress)*

D.C.), shows a group on a small sloop experiencing the exhilaration of a sail full of wind. From a 20-month stay in Cullercoats on the North Sea coast in England came many iconic depictions of fisherwomen and the sea. As time went on, his seascapes became stripped down to depictions of waves, rocks, and sky. Although works such as *Northeaster* (1895, Metropolitan Museum of Art, New York) fit comfortably into an international vogue for marine painting, Homer's paintings were seen as being especially American in their vigor.

Further reading: Nicolai Cikovsky, Jr., and Franklin Kelly, *Winslow Homer* (Washington, D.C.: National Gallery of Art; New Haven, Conn: Yale University Press, 1995).

— Karen Zukowski

homesteading

The effect of the Homestead Act, which gave settlers free farms under certain conditions, has been exaggerated. After years of agitation, the Homestead Act passed CONGRESS on May 20, 1862. It provided that any American citizen or alien 21 years of age who filed papers declaring his or her intent to become a citizen could settle on 160 acres (a quarter of a section) of public land and, after residing on and cultivating it for five years, would gain title to that land. Since a married couple could only obtain 160 acres and a single man and a single woman could each obtain 160 acres, some delayed marriage and lived in a home straddling the dividing line of their adjourning properties.

Advocates of the Homestead Act hoped it would provide homes in the West for poor urban laborers and tenant farmers in the East. They were disappointed; it did not provide relief for the needy. Most of the land available for homesteads was located west of the Mississippi, and the cost of moving a family hundreds or thousands of miles was prohibitive for workers and tenants who could hardly provide for their families and had no savings. Once on the land, shelter had to be built, draft animals and implements had to be acquired, and two or three years of "sod busting" had to be done before the land would yield crops sufficient to support a family. On top of these difficulties, most urban workers knew nothing about farming, and much of the available land was arid and suitable only for grazing. To raise cattle successfully, 160 acres was entirely too small. Younger sons of middle-income farmers were better equipped to succeed at homesteading, but even they found it difficult; before 1890 two-thirds of all homesteaders failed.

The overwhelming majority of settlers purchased their land from either RAILROADS or land speculators, because they owned the land most fertile and closest to transportation. Railroads had received huge land grants to encourage their construction in sparsely settled areas and had grabbed the best land, while speculators using dummy settlers took advantage of loopholes in the Homestead Act and engrossed large amounts of desirable land. Probably only one-eighth and possibly only one-tenth of the family farms established from 1870 to 1900 were acquired by genuine settlers under the terms of the Homestead Act. The cost of land was not exorbitant: Since the railroads wanted settlers producing freight along their right of way, they sold their land relatively cheaply, and land speculators to remain competitive did the same. Given the expense of establishing a farm, it made economic sense to buy productive land rather than cultivate poor, albeit free, land. Nevertheless, the dream of providing free farms to settlers was largely frustrated while land speculators and railroads made a profit.

Further reading: Fred A. Shannon, *The Farmer's Last Frontier: Agriculture, 1860–1897* (New York: Holt, Rinehart and Winston, 1945).

Homestead Strike (1892)

The Homestead Strike, or technically lockout, was a struggle between the most powerful union in the AMERICAN FEDERATION OF LABOR (AFL) and Carnegie Steel, one of the largest enterprises in America. When ANDREW CARNEGIE purchased the Homestead Mill in 1889, he attempted to lower costs by announcing a 25 percent decrease in wages, but the Amalgamated Association of Iron, Steel and Tin Workers forced him to rescind the pay cut and sign a three-year contract. Since Carnegie was not one to share control of the workplace, it was a pyrrhic victory for the Amalgamated.

In 1892 Carnegie instructed his chairman, HENRY C. FRICK, to remove the union from Homestead. Frick prepared for a confrontation with the union by increasing production and constructing a 12-foot-high stockade around the plant. In April, Frick demanded that the union accept a 22 percent cut in wages and gave the union until June 24 to accept his terms. On June 9, the day before the contract expired, he closed the mill.

To keep the company from replacing its members, the Amalgamated organized a 24-hour watch to prevent anyone from entering the plant. Frick asked local authorities to protect company property, but finding little sympathy in the community, he turned to outside support. On July 6, a steamer towed two barges containing 300 armed Pinkerton detectives from Pittsburgh up the Monongahela River toward Homestead. Despite efforts at secrecy, strikers and their sympathizers knew the PINKERTONS were coming. The strikers, most carrying weapons, broke through the stockade around the plant and were on hand at the landing near the pump house when the barges arrived. A shot followed by a volley killed one detective and wounded five as they attempted to disembark. The Pinkertons returned the fire, killing three and wounding 30. The battle continued sporadically throughout the day, claiming a total of 16 dead and 60 wounded. Finally the Pinkertons surrendered, and an angry crowd assaulted them as they were marched to the railroad station.

Although peace returned to Homestead after the battle, Governor Robert Pattison ordered the Pennsylvania National Guard into the steel community. Under the command of General George Snowden, the troops protected strikebreakers and allowed the plant to reopen. Public opinion at first was solidly aligned against Carnegie Steel, but the bungled attempted assassination of Frick on July 23 by anarchist Alexander Berkman eroded this support. Nevertheless the union continued its fight until November 20, when, with its treasury exhausted and its stockpile of supplies depleted, the Amalgamated called off the strike. Carnegie Steel, however, rehired only a few of the strikers and blacklisted their leaders. The defeat at Homestead virtually eliminated effective trade unionism in the steel industry for more than 40 years.

Further reading: Leon Wolff, *Lockout: The Story of the Homestead Strike of 1892: A Study of Violence, Unionism and the Carnegie Steel Empire* (New York: Harper & Row, 1965).

— Harold W. Aurand

Hooker, Isabella Beecher (1822–1907)

Isabella Beecher Hooker was a radial, eccentric suffragist. Born on February, 22, 1822, in Litchfield, Connecticut, Hooker was the daughter of the distinguished Calvinist minister Lyman Beecher, and she was the half sister of HENRY WARD BEECHER, the preacher. Catharine Beecher, the educator; and Harriet Beecher Stowe, the author. Educated largely in schools founded by Catharine, Isabella in 1841 married John Hooker, a lawyer, but having observed the "radical defect" in the marriages of her brothers, she did so with the understanding that she and John would be partners. They ultimately settled in Hartford, prospered, and raised three children. Although she desired domestic equality, Isabella Hooker was not attracted to the WOMEN'S RIGHTS movement until the 1860s, when she read the English philosopher John Stuart Mill on the enfranchisement of women.

Hooker, who had longed for some kind of significant public activity, found her avocation. She met SUSAN B.

ANTHONY and Elizabeth Cady Stanton and in 1868 joined OLYMPIA BROWN in establishing the New England Woman Suffrage Association. In that same year she published "A Mother's Letters to a Daughter on Woman's Suffrage" in *Putnam's Magazine.* In 1869 Hooker joined the National Woman's Suffrage Association (NWSA) and was the chief organizer of the Connecticut Woman Suffrage Association. John Hooker, with the support of Isabella, drafted a married-woman's property bill that in 1870 was introduced in the Connecticut state legislature; the Hookers lobbied vigorously for the bill until it passed in 1877. Isabella Hooker played a prominent role in NWSA meetings, testified at congressional hearings, and also published arguments for women's rights, including *Womanhood: Its Sanctities and Fidelities* (1873). Drawing upon her own life, Hooker argued that a woman's job supervising children and running a household gave her ample experience to participate in government.

Hooker had radical and bizarre ideas. Her preacher relatives were not happy that she agreed with Anthony and Stanton that marriage and divorce laws needed reform to give women equal rights. Her Beecher relations were made even more unhappy by Hooker's support of VICTORIA WOODHULL, a suffragist, spiritualist, and an adventurer whom she befriended after Woodhull addressed the January 1871 Washington Convention that Hooker had organized. In November 1872 Woodhull published in *Woodhull and Claflin's Weekly* the scandalous tale of Henry Ward Beecher's adulterous affair with a parishioner, Elizabeth Tilton. While the Beechers supported Henry, Hooker was the exception and was ostracized by her family. She obviously thought him guilty and deplored the double standard that exonerated her brother. The Beechers, for their part, accused her of mental instability.

The alienation and accusations of her family took their toll on Hooker. In 1874 she and John went to Europe for two years, and they found some solace in spiritualism, to which Woodhull had introduced them. Upon her return in 1876 she got the idea that she was destined to lead a matriarchal government of the United States and then of the world. With local Hartford mediums present on New Year's Eve 1876, she expected to receive the call, but it did not come. Hooker abandoned her fantastic notion (but not spiritualism) and continued to work for women's rights. After the National American Woman Suffrage Association (NAWSA) (1890) emphasized state campaigns, she backed Olympia Brown's Federal Suffrage Association (1892), but her activities tapered off. She died in Hartford on January 25, 1907.

Further reading: Milton Rugoff, *The Beechers: An American Family in the Nineteenth Century* (New York: Harper & Row, 1981).

Hoosac Tunnel

The Hoosac Tunnel, one of the great engineering feats of the 19th century, had its inception in the early years of what the historian George Rogers Taylor has called the "transportation revolution." The westward movement across the Appalachians after the War of 1812 created a demand for easier and faster transport of people and goods to the Ohio Valley and other points west. In 1819 a canal tunnel was proposed to run under the Berkshire Mountain Range, 136 miles west of Boston. In 1826, soon after the Erie Canal opened in New York, surveys were made for the Berkshire canal. However, plans changed when the RAILROAD age began in the 1830s. In 1848 the Troy & Greenfield Railroad was chartered, and in 1850 surveys were made for a railroad tunnel.

Work began in 1851 on what would be known as the Hoosac Tunnel. It was finally completed in 1874, and the first train passed through in the following year. The statistics were staggering for that period. The tunnel ran for four and three quarter miles and cost, in 1874 dollars, $21, 241, 342. The rock excavation was 24 feet wide and 20 feet high, requiring the removal of 2 million tons of rock. Half a million pounds of nitroglycerin were used, the first commercial use of that powerful and unstable explosive. In 1865 a British inventor devised the rock drill, in which steam or compressed air powered a hammer tool to drill holes for the explosive. The pneumatic drill was used for the Mont Cenis tunnel in the Swiss Alps, eight and a half miles long, which when opened in 1871 was the longest tunnel in the world. It was also used in the Hoosac Tunnel, which became the second longest tunnel in the world when it opened and remained the longest tunnel in North America until 1916. It is still the longest tunnel east of the Rocky Mountains.

The Hoosac Tunnel cost more than sweat and dollars. Its toll in lives has been variously estimated but appears to have approached 200. The chief causes of death among construction workers were "tunnel sickness" due to heat, foul air, explosives, and rock falls. But in the 19th century such deaths were accepted as the unavoidable price of progress.

Further reading: Edward C. Kirkland, *Men, Cities and Transportation: A Study in New England History 1820–1900,* 2 vols. (Cambridge, Mass.: Harvard University Press, 1948).

— Robert V. Bruce

horse racing

During the 1860s, several newly made millionaires revived the sport of horse racing. The troubled sport had been on the verge of collapse for the previous two decades because of inconsistent patronage from the nation's wealthiest classes, national economic problems, and charges of gambling, chicanery, and commercialism. Wealthy patrons, however, ushered horse racing into a new golden age, building new tracks, providing large stakes, reducing corruption, and shortening racing distances. John Morrissey, a former boxing champion and TAMMANY HALL politician, opened a race track at Saratoga Springs, New York, in August 1863 and persuaded New York socialites Leonard Jerome, the American grandfather of Sir Winston Churchill, and William Travers to join him in the venture. He earned considerable profits with an extensive August racing season that attracted notables. Previously, race meetings usually had lasted just one or two days. Morrissey arranged the first stakes races, named after the aristocratic Travers family, and offered generous purse money.

In 1866 Leonard Jerome, enlisting the support of Travers, August Belmont, and other wealthy New Yorkers, founded the American Jockey Club as a central governing board. The American Jockey Club reestablished racing on a firm basis in New York, building Jerome Park on more than 200 acres of land in Westchester County. The nation's most lavish course, it contained a luxurious clubhouse, barred the sale of liquor, and discouraged professional gamblers. The Belmont Stakes, the oldest of the Triple Crown races, was held at Jerome Park from 1867 to 1888 and shifted to Morris Park in 1889. Ruthless, ridden by J. Gilpatrick, captured the first Belmont Stakes in 1867. Jim McLaughlin rode six Belmont Stakes winners between 1882 and 1888, missing only in 1885. Morris Park opened in August 1889 and sponsored races through 1904. The American Jockey Club, whose wealth and social status extended well beyond New York City, led the movement to replace the old three- or four-mile heats with shorter dashes that emphasized speed over stamina and permitted the running of several daily races. The Travers Stakes, Belmont Stakes, and other large permanent prizes brought greater excitement and stability to horse racing.

Race tracks were built in 1870 at Monmouth Park in New Jersey and at Pimlico in Baltimore, Maryland; in 1873 at the Fair Grounds in New Orleans, Louisiana; and in 1875 at Churchill Downs in Louisville, Kentucky. The Preakness Stakes at Pimlico and the Kentucky Derby at Churchill Downs soon joined the Belmont Stakes as Triple Crown races. George Barbee triumphed aboard Survivor in the inaugural Preakness Stakes in 1873 and aboard Shirley in 1876, while Lloyd Hughes rode three Preakness winners in 1875, 1879, and 1880. In 1875 Oliver Lewis captured the initial Kentucky Derby aboard Aristides for a $2,850 prize. Isaac Murphy, a black jockey, rode three Kentucky Derby winners: Buchanan in 1884, Riley in 1890, and Kingman in 1891. Willie Simms followed suit with Ben Brush in 1896 and Plaudit in 1898. Other tracks opened in Chicago, Cincinnati, Memphis, Boston, and Springfield, Massachusetts, and more Thoroughbreds were imported from England.

Murphy and Edward "Snapper" Garrison were the era's most dominant jockeys. In addition to his three Kentucky Derby wins, Murphy in June 1890 guided Salvator to a half-head victory over Garrison's Tenny at Sheepshead Bay in Brooklyn, New York, in a widely publicized, exciting race. Murphy rode nearly every famous American horse and triumphed in every major race except the Futurity Stakes at Belmont Park, compiling 628 victories in 1,412 mounts. Garrison, one of the first jockeys to use the short stirrups and monkey crouch, usually lagged behind and then thrilled crowds with spectacular, breathtaking finishes. From 1880 to 1896, he won more than $2 million in nearly 700 races.

Racing lacked national governing control until the 1890s, with each racing association operating under its own rules. The Jockey Club, incorporated by 50 industrial and financial giants in February 1894 and headquartered in New York, adopted uniform national racing rules, appointed officials, licensed jockeys, and set national racing dates. Bookmakers from Great Britain made their first appearance on American tracks in 1873 and broadened gambling to the small-time bettor. At that time, bookmaking was the only form of wagering allowed on New York tracks. Horse-racing authorities turned to machine politicians in New York, New Orleans, Chicago, and elsewhere to obtain the repeal (or exemption from enforcement) of laws restricting racing and gambling. Political leaders in New York and other horse-racing centers were willing to help and maintained close connections with track officials.

Further reading: Tom Biracree and Wendy Insinger, *The Complete Book of Thoroughbred Horse Racing* (Garden City, N.Y.: Doubleday, 1982); Roger Longrigg, *The History of Horse Racing* (New York: Stein & Day, 1972); William H. P. Robertson, *The History of Thoroughbred Racing in America* (Englewood Cliffs, N.J.: Prentice Hall, 1964).

— David L. Porter

housing

The major housing need between 1870 and 1900 was simply to provide dwellings for the nation's exploding population, which doubled from 38.6 to 76 million. This task was particularly challenging in cities, since the urban population more than tripled, from 9.9 to 30.2 million, during these years. In these three decades 6.4 million new urban housing units were built for 20.3 million new urban residents, a ratio of 3.2 new residents per new unit. By way of comparison, nationwide there were five persons per dwelling unit in 1890 and 4.8 in 1900. Between 1880 and

1900 the number of dwellings increased at a faster rate than the number of inhabitants in 18 of the 28 largest cities.

Housing came in a wide variety of types, sizes, configurations, and materials. The diverse housing stock comprised millionaires' mansions along Cleveland's Euclid Avenue and on Beacon Hill in Boston, as well as lavish suburban estates far from urban congestion and pollution; sharecroppers' shacks in the rural South; tenements in New York City; apartments above commercial buildings everywhere; balloon-frame, wooden two- and three-story houses in new subdivisions on city outskirts; wooden upstairs-downstairs duplexes in midwestern industrial cities; and the endless streets of brick rowhouses—three- and four-story narrow, attached single-family residences—in Baltimore and Philadelphia.

The single-family residence was the norm not only in rural and small-town settings but also in the nation's large cities. In 1890 at least 75 percent of the housing stock in two-thirds of the 28 largest cities was single family; in Denver, Indianapolis, New Orleans, Omaha, Philadelphia, and San Francisco, single-family residences constituted more than 90 percent of total dwellings. Only in New York City did single-family houses comprise less than half of the dwellings.

Home ownership was an important goal for many households, both as a form of investment and as a means of gaining greater control over a family's housing destiny and higher status. Housing tenure was first measured systematically in the census of 1890, so earlier estimates are somewhat episodic. Both the 1890 and 1900 censuses showed national ownership rates of 47 percent. In these years there was a substantial gap between ownership in rural and urban areas: The rural rate was 65 percent ownership, as compared with only 37 percent in urban areas, which also had widely varying ownership rates.

Obtaining financing was a major obstacle to purchasing one's own house, especially in urban areas. Despite the growth of building and loan associations, individuals still accounted for more than half of all home loans in the last decade of the century, and land contracts were more prevalent than mortgages. Repayment schemes were not well developed, so buying homes required large down payments and short mortgages or contracts. Most borrowers made regular payments only on the interest, so they had to repay the entire loan at the end of the two-to-three-year contract, which meant they had to obtain a new loan and hopefully, but not always, reduce the amount of the loan. Under these conditions, home lending was a risky business and less attractive to lenders than loans for rental properties, a factor that increased the costs and risks for home buyers.

While the increase in quantity of new housing exceeded the increase in population, the quality of that housing was uneven at best. The poignant, stark photographs of immigrant families in New York City by JACOB RIIS published in the mid-1880s and his classic book *How the Other Half Lives* (1890) constitute the most enduring and widespread images of housing in late-19th-century urban America, leaving the impression that all immigrants and working-class city dwellers lived in dark, windowless, airless, unsanitary, overcrowded, tiny tenement apartments. However, outside New York City most working-class city dwellers lived in single-family houses at much lower densities. But in all cities shoddy construction resulted in inferior dwelling units. Primitive technology and the enormous expense of providing infrastructure for explosive urban growth created neighborhoods with few amenities, many liberally strewn with animal and human refuse and with streets that became quagmires and virtual cesspools when it rained.

Homes of the poorer classes, Chattanooga, Tennessee *(Library of Congress)*

Reformers linked the problem of housing to the problem of slums, a much more comprehensive issue. Attempts to address the physical issues of the house centered on creating a code of minimum standards for space, light, direct access, plumbing, materials, and the like. New York, Boston, and Milwaukee had such codes enacted in the late 1860s. But they were difficult to enforce and tended to make housing even more costly. The work of late 19th-century reformers laid the foundation for the later adoption of stronger regulations in all cities, beginning with the landmark New York Tenement House Law of 1901.

Further reading: Robert G. Barrows, "Beyond the Tenement: Patterns of American Urban Housing, 1870–1930," *Journal of Urban History* 9, no. 4 (1983): 395–420; Clifford Edward Clark, Jr., *The American Family Home, 1800–1960* (Chapel Hill: University of North Carolina Press, 1986); Michael J. Doucet and John C. Weaver,

"Material Culture and the North American House: The Era of the Common Man, 1870–1920," *Journal of American History* 72, no. 3 (1985): 560–87; Sam B. Warner, Jr., *Streetcar Suburbs: The Process of Growth in Boston, 1870–1900* (Cambridge, Mass.: Harvard University Press, 1962).

— J. Paul Mitchell

Howells, William Dean (1837–1920)

A leading realistic novelist of the Gilded Age, William Dean Howells was also its most distinguished literary critic. The son of Mary Dean and William Cooper Howells, a printer and journalist, William Dean Howells was born on March 1, 1837, in Martin's Ferry, Ohio, but his family moved to Hamilton, 20 miles from Cincinnati, when he was three. His father was an idealistic, abolitionist editor of a Whig newspaper who sacrificed the family's prosperity for his egalitarian radicalism. Young Howells had almost no formal education and was working as a typesetter in his father's shop by the age of nine. The family moved repeatedly as the elder Howells tried to restore his fortunes with a variety of unsuccessful newspapers, and at the age of 19 Howells began reporting on the state legislature for a Cincinnati paper. Two years later, in 1858, he became editor of the *Ohio State Journal* at Columbus. In 1860 his campaign biography of Abraham Lincoln earned him enough to visit the cultural center of the country, Boston. There he met such luminaries as Ralph Waldo Emerson, Nathaniel Hawthorne, and James Russell Lowell. Howells's biography impressed the newly elected Lincoln enough to bring him an appointment as consul at Venice, a post he held from 1861 to 1865. In 1862 he married Elinor Mead, a gifted artist, with whom he had three children. Within a year of his return to Boston, he joined the staff of the *Atlantic Monthly*, of which he became editor in 1871. During his ten years in that position, his essays made him one of the most influential critics in the country, and he published six novels of his own, developing a distinctive literary voice of objective psychological and social realism.

With his seventh novel, *A Modern Instance* (1882), Howells emerged as the leader of the realistic school in America, portraying the average American with sensitivity to the interaction of character and social conditions. His best-known work, *The Rise of Silas Lapham*, published four years later, wittily contrasts the Boston aristocracy of Beacon Hill with a self-made man who tries to rise in genteel society, loses his fortune, and rises above his defeat by strength of character. In Lapham, Howells created a classic American type, his vulgarity and pushiness offset by his scrupulous moral rectitude. In *A Hazard of New Fortunes* (1890), Howells examined the effect of industrialism on the common person and demonstrated his growing engagement with social issues. Influenced by Tolstoy, he dealt increasingly with issues of poverty and suffering and the need for more humane values in the capitalist age. He became one of literature's leading voices for liberal causes, taking a courageous stand for the anarchists condemned as a result of the HAYMARKET RIOT of 1886, helping found the National Association for the Advancement of Colored People (NAACP) in 1909, and supporting labor in the PULLMAN STRIKE of 1894.

Howells wrote the Editor's Study column for *Harper's Monthly* from 1886 to 1891 and the Editor's Easy Chair from 1900 until his death. A forum for his socialist ideas and modernist literary opinions, these influential posts enabled him to promote the reputations of EMILY DICKINSON and his close friend HENRY JAMES, introduce the work of several Russian novelists to America, and encourage such emerging realist writers as HAMLIN GARLAND, STEPHEN CRANE, and Theodore Dreiser. Much honored in his later years, he became known as the dean of American letters. He was the president of the American Academy of Arts and Letters from its founding in 1904 until his death on May 11, 1920.

Further reading: Kenneth Schuyler Lynn, *William Dean Howells: An American Life* (New York: Harcourt Brace Jovanovich, 1971).

— Dennis Wepman

Hunt, Richard Morris See art and architecture

Hunt, William Morris See painting

I

illustration, photography, and the graphic arts

In their daily lives, Americans at the end of the 19th century encountered more images than any other culture had yet experienced. Trends converged to produce an explosive growth in illustrated media of all types: America's rising population became increasingly literate. The introduction of a second-class postal rate and improved railroad networks meant faster and wider distribution of printed goods. America's expanding manufacturing capabilities spawned a consumer economy buoyed by mass communication, especially ADVERTISING. Images captured attention and conveyed information, and they were put to the service of this new economy. Newly minted professionals—commercial artists, illustrators, photographers, and graphic designers—supplied these images.

In the 1880s and 1890s, important advances were made in the technologies used for the mass reproduction of images. By 1876 the Webb press could print 15,000 large-format sheets per hour, and Mergenthaler's linotype machine, in use at the *New York Tribune* by 1886, was one of several devices that mechanized typesetting. Wood engraving, the staple of the illustrated media at mid-century, was supplanted by various methods of photoengraving, especially the halftone. By this process any image could be photographed through a screen that converted it into a set of dots that were then transferred mechanically, via acid, to a printing plate. Although printing plates were often improved by hand, the halftone process eliminated the need for large corps of engravers. Professional photographers flourished as the dry-plate process, accessory lenses, and handheld cameras made photography less cumbersome and complex. Amateur photography boomed after 1888 when the Kodak camera was introduced, with its slogan "you push the button and we do the rest." Chromolithography, used for color images, became more industrialized and less costly. In short, the production of images became a profession separate from the production of other printed matter, and images could be created much faster and at a much lower cost.

A wide variety of media incorporated images. In 1865, 700 periodicals were published in America, but by 1900 the number was 5,000. Illustrated MAGAZINES and NEWSPAPERS were published daily, weekly, and monthly and were aimed at the most general and the most specialized audiences. Among those that owed their success to their illustrations were *Scribner's, Century, Harper's Weekly, Leslie's Weekly, Ladies' Home Journal, Popular Science,* and *Life.* Publishing conglomerates were formed; Harper's, for example, published four major magazines in addition to their books. Novels and children's books were commonly illustrated. Advertising and promotional media proliferated, and trade cards, posters, and packaging were often produced in vivid color chromolithography. Illustration pervaded every aspect of life through ephemeral and miscellaneous materials such as sheet-MUSIC covers, stock certificates, wallpapers, billheads, and receipts. Portrait photography came within the reach of most households. Large photographic companies commissioned depictions of subjects of public interest: foreign countries, the American West, celebrities, and newsworthy events such as world's fairs. These images were published as stereographs, cabinet cards, and in portfolios that were commonly sold through bookstores. With the improved printing methods, photography in magazines, newspapers, and reports also became commonplace.

All these images were supplied by artists who often straddled the worlds of fine art and commercial art. Prominent painters, among them Edwin Austin Abbey, Howard Pyle, and FREDERIC REMINGTON, also produced oils intended as book and magazine illustrations. The Gibson Girl, introduced in 1890, became a vehicle for social synopsis, and its creator, Charles Dana Gibson, was a celebrated art editor, publisher, and painter.

Illustrations could be a force for social change; JACOB RIIS's photographs of slum images in *How the Other Half Lives* (1890) prompted housing reform. In 1878 Eadweard Muybridge first used stop-action photography to document a horse trotting, and his continued work advanced the scientific study of animal and human locomotion. Mainly, though, illustration illuminated or decorated. Will Bradley introduced the art nouveau style to American audiences through his posters and magazine covers. While fine engravings produced in limited editions by JAMES MCNEILL WHISTLER, WILLIAM MERRITT CHASE, and MARY CASSATT entered the collections of connoisseurs, high-quality chromolithographs, such as William Michael Harnett's *The Old Violin* and Daniel Ridgway Knight's *Hailing the Ferry,* decorated middle-class houses.

Editors and publishers, such as Charles Parsons at *Harper's,* Cyrus H. K. Curtis of the *Ladies' Home Journal,* and Louis Prang, maker of chromolithographs and greeting cards, shaped America's visual culture.

The history of American late-19th-century illustration is still largely unwritten. Because so many artists worked freelance and anonymously, their accomplishments remain untraceable except through the initials they incorporated within their illustrations.

Further reading: Michele H. Bogart, *Advertising, Artists and the Borders of Art* (Chicago: University of Chicago Press, 1995); Susan E. Meyer, *America's Great Illustrators* (New York: Galahad Books, 1978); Martha A. Sandweiss et al., *Photography in Nineteenth-Century America* (Fort Worth, Tex.: Amon Carter Museum; New York: Harry N. Abrams, 1991); Ellen Mazur Thomson, *The Origins of Graphic Design in America, 1870–1920* (New Haven, Conn.: Yale University Press, 1997).

— Karen Zukowski

immigration

The United States is a nation of immigrants and their children. From the earliest migrants who walked from Asia over an isthmus at what is now the Bering Strait many thousand years ago, peoples have come to America in waves. The main flow of immigration to the United States in 1870 has come to be known as the "Old Immigration," and it began just after the Napoleonic Wars. Between 1820 and 1880 more than 10 million immigrants entered the country. More than 90 percent of the newcomers were from northern and western Europe: England, Scotland, Wales, Ireland, Germany, Holland, and Scandinavia, with Irish and German migrants predominating. The remainder came from eastern and southern Europe, China, Japan, and the Americas. In 1870, for example, out of 387,000 immigrants, 329,000 came from Europe, and of those, 118,000 came from Germany, 104,000 from Great Britain, 57,000 from Ireland, 31,000 from Scandinavia, 9,000 from other northwestern European countries, and a mere 10,000 immigrated to the United States from the remaining central, eastern, and southern European countries. The number of immigrants from Ireland had dropped considerably from 221,000 in 1851, and those from Scandinavia had risen dramatically from the 2,000 to 3,000 that came in the 1850s.

Virtually all of the 1870 immigrants were from rural areas, where most owned little or no land and lived in poverty, and almost all were lured to the United States by cheap land and a dynamic economy. The Irish were among the poorest immigrants and settled mostly in northeastern cities such as Boston and New York City, formed tight-knit communities, and supported the political machines associated with the DEMOCRATIC PARTY in those cities. Although a large number of middle-class German intellectuals migrated to America following the failure of the liberal revolutions of 1848, by 1870 the typical German immigrant was a small farmer or skilled artisan seeking improved economic conditions. Many of the German arrivals came with enough money to move to the Midwest, where they purchased land and established farms or opened businesses in cities such as Chicago, Milwaukee, Cincinnati, and St. Louis. Those who arrived with skills quickly found work as craftsmen. Like the Irish in the Northeast, those Germans who settled in the cities of the Midwest formed their own ethnic communities and gave their support to the Democrats. Scandinavians tended to settle on farms in Minnesota, the Dakotas, and Nebraska, although many found employment as skilled carpenters. Migrants from Great Britain (England, Scotland, and Wales) usually carried skills with them and found work in industry. Welsh coal miners, for example, settled in the anthracite regions of Pennsylvania.

Approximately 70 percent of all immigrants arriving in America landed in New York City. Until the early 1890s immigrants at New York were processed at Castle Garden at the foot of Manhattan Island, but in 1892 the federal Bureau of Immigration established Ellis Island in New York harbor as a new point of entry for immigrants. At Ellis Island, federal medical and nonmedical immigration officials enforced the minimal restrictions on immigration and turned back paupers, criminals, polygamists, the mentally deficient, the contagiously ill, and contract laborers. From 1864 to 1885 these laborers—who agreed to a maximum of one year's work in return for passage to the United States—were admitted, but CONGRESS, which had originally authorized the practice of CONTRACT LABOR, forbade it in 1885. Only about 2 percent of those who wished to enter were turned back at Ellis Island. Officials recorded the names of those who passed, made sure they paid an entry tax, and put them on the ferry that landed them at the lower tip of New York City. As at Ellis Island, federal inspectors operated landing stations in Boston, Philadelphia, and Baltimore on the east coast, New Orleans in the South, and on Angel Island in San Francisco.

By 1900 sufficient changes among newcomers had occurred to speak of a "New Immigration." In that year

449,000 persons immigrated to the United States, of whom 425,000 were from Europe. However, compared with 1870, there was a sharp drop in immigrants from northern and western Europe and a spectacular rise in those who came from eastern, central, and southern Europe. Emigrants from Germany fell to 19,000, from Great Britain to 13,000, and from Ireland to 36,000, but almost the same number—a bit more than 31,000—came from Scandinavia. Those from other northwestern European countries fell to 6,000. In contrast, 98,000 came from eastern Europe, 115,000 from central Europe, and 108,000 from southern Europe.

These new immigrants were pushed from their homelands and pulled to the United States. Several forces drove these immigrants from their homes: the undermining of subsistence farming by commercial agriculture; the shift away from household production because of industrialization; the steady growth in population that brought a shortage of available farmland; oppressive taxes; famine and disease; and religious and political persecution. America's growing economy and its demand for workers held great promise for the new immigrants. With the exception of those from eastern Europe, virtually all of the immigrants in 1900 came to the United States to better their economic position, and some would return to their homelands having earned enough to buy land, houses, or set up businesses. Most of the immigrants from eastern Europe were Jews fleeing persecution (pogroms) in the Russian Empire.

The decision to migrate often occurred through social networks of people linked by kinship, place of residence, friendship, and work experience. These "migration chains," extending from one's homeland to specific destinations in America, helped migrants cope with the considerable risks entailed by their long journey. In addition, letters from those who had already migrated often gave glowing reports of the opportunities enjoyed by newcomers and raised the expectations of and excited potential migrants.

New technologies such as the railroad, telegraph, and steamship also added to the appeal of America by making communications and travel cheaper, safer, and quicker. Whereas it once took sailing ships from one to three months to travel across the Atlantic, by the 1880s new steam-powered ships were making the trip in one to two

This cartoon places the blame for "anarchy, socialism, the Mafia, and such kindred evils" on the liberal immigration policy of the time, 1891. *(New York Public Library)*

weeks. Major steamship lines such as Cunard, Holland-America, and White Star competed for passengers. Immigrants who chose to pay the cheapest fares were quartered deep in the bowels of the vessel in the filthy, crowded "steerage" section.

Most migrants from central, eastern, and southern Europe were very poor. One-third of the immigrants that came through Ellis Island could afford to go no further than New York City or its environs. Coming from rural backgrounds, most of the "new" immigrants were unskilled mechanically and did backbreaking labor on construction and railroads, as well as in coal mines, steel mills, and factories. Ironically, in the needle trades, where some skills were required, immigrants were exploited in sweat shops. The hardest, dirtiest, lowest paying jobs in industry were known as "foreign" jobs. For most immigrants, the work was harder, the hours longer, and the pay better than in their homeland, and in the last respect America kept its promise.

Although America utilized immigrant brawn, many of its native-born citizens did not welcome the immigrant presence. Immigrants are strangers in a strange land, but the new migrants from central, eastern, and southern Europe were even more strange in—and estranged—from America than the "old" migrants from northern and western Europe. Upon arriving in America, the newcomers' inability to speak the language and unfamiliarity with American customs led many to seek people who spoke their language, shared their cultural values, and practiced their religion. Ethnic communities emerged in areas where large numbers of immigrants concentrated, and these communities helped immigrants make the transition from their homelands to America. They were places where the newcomers could learn about the traditions of their new homeland while retaining their own cultures.

In America's cities, new immigrant communities took the form of densely populated ghettos. Overcrowded tenements, poor sanitation, and inadequate health services made many immigrant communities unhealthy places to live. The new immigrants, most of whom were not Protestant in religion, also confronted a brand of NATIVISM that viewed them as a threat to traditional American values and customs. American reformers attempted to remedy the situation in the immigrant communities and assist in the process of assimilation by operating various social and educational programs for the newcomers. The SETTLEMENT HOUSE movement, started in the United States by Jane Addams and Ellen Gates Starr, the cofounders of Hull-House in Chicago (1889), offered an important source of help for immigrants. The success of Hull House was followed by similar projects in most major American cities, especially New York, Boston, and Philadelphia. The settlement-house workers provided immigrants with medical services, emergency relief, citizenship courses, counseling or vocational training, assistance in getting a job, and lessons in cooking, hygiene, and English. These services were designed not only to improve the living conditions within immigrant communities, but also to provide the newcomers with the means and knowledge to assimilate into American culture and to become good citizens.

The urban immigrant communities also developed a mutually beneficial relationship with the local political "boss." Many urban political machines, especially TAMMANY HALL in New York City, relied on the immigrant vote for electoral success, and immigrants felt they could turn to the boss when they needed help, which indeed they often did. In exchange for immigrant votes, the boss would provide jobs, emergency relief, legal assistance, or housing accommodations. Since the Democratic Party dominated much of the urban political landscape, many immigrants became loyal Democratic partisans.

See also AMERICAN PROTECTIVE ASSOCIATION; IMMIGRATION RESTRICTIONS; PLUNKITT, GEORGE WASHINGTON; PROGRESSIVISM IN THE 1890S; RIIS, JACOB A.; STATUE OF LIBERTY.

Further reading: John Bodner, *The Transplanted: A History of Immigrants in Urban America* (Bloomington: Indiana University Press, 1985); Oscar Handlin, *The Uprooted: The Epic Story of the Great Migrations that Made the American People* (Boston: Little, Brown, 1951); Alan M. Kraut, *The Huddled Masses: The Immigrant in American Society, 1880–1921* (Arlington Heights, Ill.: Harlan Davidson, 1982).

— Phillip Papas

immigration restrictions

During the late 19th century, increasing immigration to the United States from southern and eastern Europe—as well as smaller numbers from China and Japan—provoked the rise of NATIVISM and demands for restricting immigration. Nativist and anti-Catholic groups such as the Immigrant Restriction League and the AMERICAN PROTECTIVE ASSOCIATION (APA), labor union leaders, and several American intellectuals called on the federal government to rethink its open-door immigration policies and implement a program of more selective immigration.

The movement to restrict the number of immigrants entering the United States had first emerged in the 1870s. The roots of the restrictionist movement were grounded in the social and economic changes taking place in America following the Civil War. These changes had produced a more stratified society where class tensions and labor conflicts abounded. Many Americans saw the new immigrants as the source of the nation's social and economic problems. Restrictionists argued that the newcomers promoted radical or un-American interests, were mentally and physically inferior, corrupted politics by selling their votes, were prone to crime and poverty, undermined the standard of living of American workers, and posed a threat to traditional American values.

Among the earliest proponents of restrictions on immigration were labor unions, with the bitterest opposition focused on the Chinese of California. The Workingmen's Party of California blamed unemployment and low wages on Chinese immigration. Supported by labor organizations in the East, western labor leaders lobbied CONGRESS to pass restrictive measures aimed at reducing the number of Chinese immigrants entering the United States. As a result, Congress passed the CHINESE EXCLUSION ACT in 1882, which prohibited the immigration of Chinese (except teachers, students, merchants, tourists, and officials) for 10 years. This law was renewed in 1892 and extended indefinitely in 1902. In addition, the influx of Japanese labor in the 1890s eventually led to a series of "gentlemen's agreements" with Japan beginning in 1900, with Japan agreeing to limit the emigration of unskilled workers bound for the United States. Unions opposed the importation of laborers from Europe as well as from Asia. Both the KNIGHTS OF LABOR and the AMERICAN FEDERATION OF LABOR (AFL) called for the end of recruiting contract laborers overseas. In 1885 Congress passed a CONTRACT-LABOR law that prohibited the importing of workers under contract.

Religious bigotry was another source of restrictionist sentiment. Nativist groups in America, of which the APA was most prominent, were fearful of a "Catholic menace" and called for the restriction of immigrants from predominantly Catholic nations. Although the APA as an organization declined after 1896, anti-Catholicism continued to inspire opponents of immigration.

The third major restrictionist group was made up of American intellectuals based primarily in New England. Affected by a loss of status in the new social order emerging in late-19th-century America, they regarded themselves as the guardians of traditional American values. Their nationalist sentiments led them to credit American achievements to Anglo-Saxon superiority and traditions. They also accepted pseudoscientific SOCIAL DARWINISM, with its belief that the immigrants were mentally and physically inferior and therefore would corrupt America's superior Anglo-American stock; by barring new immigrants from entering the United States, traditional American values and Anglo-Saxon superiority would be preserved.

Apart from excluding Chinese (1882) and Japanese (1900) laborers, restriction made little headway in the 19th century. Restrictionists embraced literacy tests as the first step toward achieving their goal, and although Congress passed such a measure in 1896, President GROVER CLEVELAND vetoed it. As the 20th century began, more and more migrants sought freedom and opportunity in the United States, and the restrictionist movement continued to gain strength.

See also IMMIGRATION; PROGRESSIVISM IN THE 1890S.

Further reading: Thomas J. Curren, *Xenophobia and Immigration, 1820–1930* (Boston: Twayne, 1975); John Higham, *Strangers in the Land: Patterns of American Nativism, 1860–1925* (New Brunswick, N.J.: Rutgers University Press, 1955).

— Phillip Papas

imperialism

Imperialism in late 19th-century America involved both territorial and economic expansion, but not necessarily at the same time or in the same place. Imperialism was an international phenomenon, but the Americans, who had a whole continent to provide raw materials and domestic markets, had little compulsion to acquire more territory; in contrast, the Europeans and Japanese had an entirely different attitude toward imperialism. The United States, during the years 1870 to 1900, added 125,000 square miles, while Germany and Great Britain gained 1 million and 4.7 million square miles, respectively.

With the acquisition in 1898 of Spanish-held islands and HAWAII, the United States embraced overseas imperialism. Earlier efforts to acquire territory in the Caribbean and the Pacific had been frustrated in large part because of beliefs that territorial acquisitions should become states and that tropical islands with their nonwhite populations should not become states. Strategic, political, economic, and ideologic considerations undermined these ideas, opening the door for American imperialism.

Strategic concerns were straightforward. The surest way to thwart the imperialist ambitions of potentially threatening powerful, industrial nations was to acquire territory before they did. With a growing awareness of its need for an isthmian canal, the United States wanted to reduce the presence of European powers in the Caribbean, and it was obvious that Hawaii in the possession of a hostile power would threaten the safety of the West Coast. The United States also was plagued by social and political unrest in the 1890s. A severe economic depression with widespread unemployment, violent strikes, low farm income, and a divisive debate over the currency attracted politicians to an imperialist venture that would divert attention from sectional and class tensions at home.

Unlike political and strategic concerns, the economic factors affecting American imperialism were more complex, less compelling, and did not necessarily require annexation of territory. European imperialists desired colonies for their raw materials, their markets, their investment opportunities,

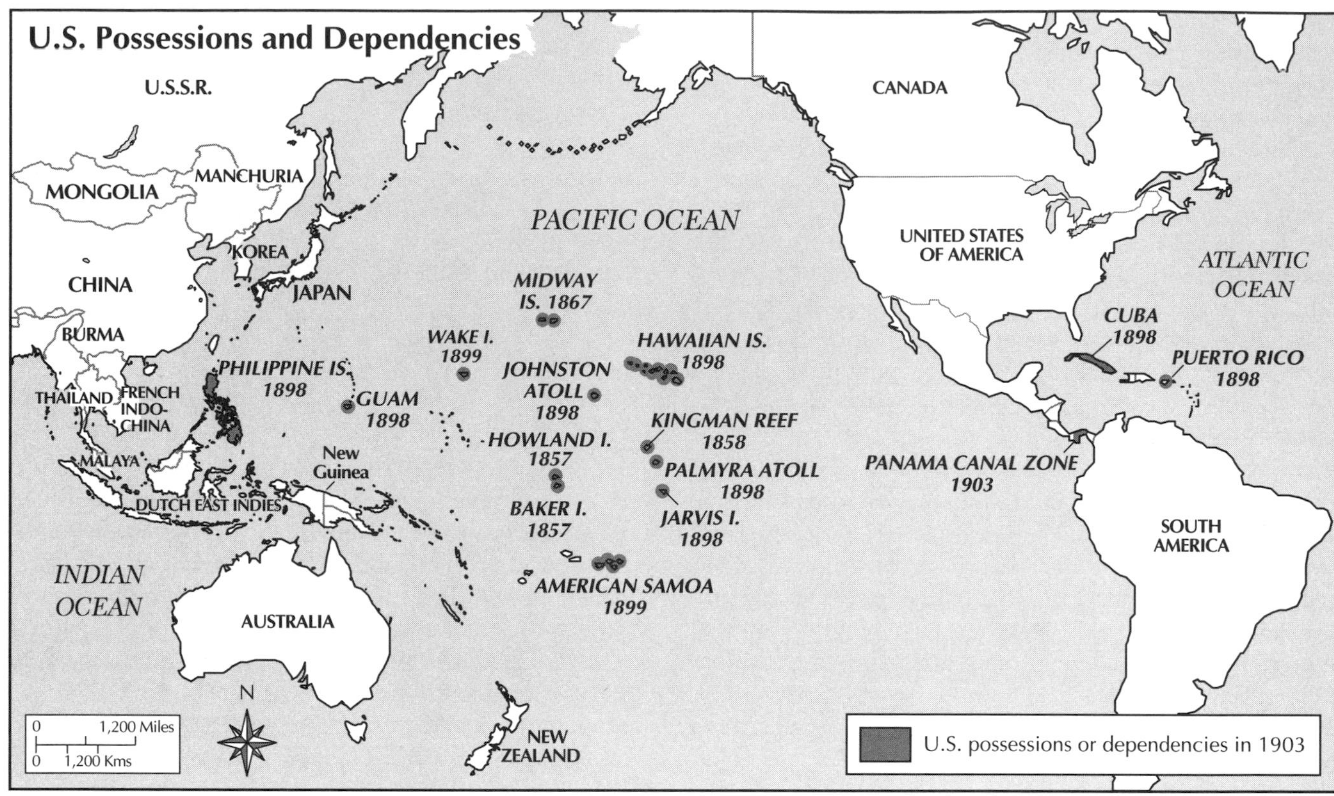

and their capacity to absorb surplus population. The United States, however, lacked few raw materials, sold most of its manufactured goods at home, had ample outlets for its capital in its own railroads and factories, and attracted thousands of immigrants from Europe. Economic factors did not compel the United States to dominate noncontiguous lands, but advocates of imperialism stressed that the nation needed markets for growing surpluses of agricultural crops, raw materials, and manufactured goods to avert disastrous downturns in the BUSINESS CYCLE like the one that began in 1893. Although exports accounted for less than 7 percent of the gross national product and Europe (the most economically advanced continent) bought more than three-fourths of American exports from 1870 to 1900, promoters of imperialism optimistically argued that trading agreements bringing less well-developed lands into the American economic orbit would be a substantial benefit.

The imperialists of 1898, however, openly advocated war and annexation. Guided by the ideology of Manifest Destiny, the United States had appropriated the land of Native Americans and of Mexico. Manifest Destiny, which imbued Americans with a sense of inevitable triumph and with its assumption of American superiority, was simply a rationale for imperialism. But by the 1890s it had acquired the pseudoscientific gloss of SOCIAL DARWINISM, which applied Charles Darwin's ideas of biological evolution (especially the survival of the fittest) to society. With nationalistic pride in American democratic institutions and in American enterprise mixed with notions of American cultural and racial superiority, American imperialists felt they were not only fit to survive, but among the fittest nations to dominate the world. In 1885 a Congregational missionary society published Reverend JOSIAH STRONG's *Our Country* in which, among other things, he predicted the ultimate triumph of English-speaking Protestant peoples throughout the world, with the United States taking the lead. Secretary of State JOHN HAY believed that peace and order in the world depended on its domination by Anglo-Saxons. Impatient for the inevitable triumph, American imperialists at the end of the 19th century advocated an aggressive FOREIGN POLICY lest their country be left behind in the scramble for colonies and spheres of influence. Ironically, many anti-imperialists agreed that the United States was a superior nation, but to keep it that way they opposed the incorporation of additional nonwhite peoples within its borders.

Imperialists succeeded in taking advantage of opportunities created by the SPANISH-AMERICAN WAR in 1898. Just as Congress ruled out the acquisition of CUBA in its war resolution that April, most Americans did not think of the war as one of conquest. But once the Philippines were occupied, President WILLIAM MCKINLEY felt compelled to keep them rather than allow them to fall prey to Germany, Russia, or Japan. Fears that a totally independent Cuba would tempt foreign powers also led McKinley to insist on the 1901 Platt Amendment, which made Cuba an American protectorate.

Possession of the Philippine Islands made the United States a Far Eastern power and gave it a base at Manila for enlarging its minuscule (2 percent) trade with China. (Many Americans also thought of it as a base for missionary activities.) But other industrial powers were already carving China up into spheres of influence and threatening it with dismemberment. To arrest these trends, Secretary of State John Hay in 1899 and 1900 circulated the OPEN DOOR NOTES among the great powers, advocating equal commercial opportunity for all within the various spheres of influence and upholding China's administrative and territorial integrity. A stalemate born of mutual fears rather than Hay's notes preserved China, but he enunciated an American policy that lasted 40 years and by renouncing territory (albeit for trade) gave it a moral flavor. Indeed, the lust for overseas territory was short-lived, but American imperialism—with its mix of uplift, mission, and trade—differed merely in emphasis from that of contemporary great-power nationalism. Generally, Americans preferred to hold the door open to their missionaries and products without formal annexation. Thus, informal empire was the lasting legacy of American imperialism.

Further reading: Michael H. Hunt, *Ideology and U.S. Foreign Policy* (New Haven, Conn.: Yale University Press, 1987); Ernest R. May, *American Imperialism: A Speculative Essay* (New York: Atheneum, 1968).

— Bruce Abrams

Indian Affairs, Office of (Indian Bureau)

The Office of Indian Affairs dates back to 1824, when it was established by Secretary of War John C. Calhoun to over-

A cartoon criticizing the corruption of the Office of Indian Affairs *(Library of Congress)*

see white-Indian relations and administer programs to "civilize" NATIVE AMERICANS. The office was formally endorsed by CONGRESS in 1832 and received full authorization in 1834, empowering the president to appoint a commissioner of Indian Affairs. Initially the office was lodged in the War Department, but in 1849 the Office of Indian Affairs was transferred to the newly created Department of the Interior and was primarily engaged in moving Native Americans to the West in order to open their lands for white settlers. The military presence in the Office of Indian Affairs continued until 1870, when Congress prohibited the appointment of military personnel to positions on the reservations that the government had begun to establish following the Civil War.

In 1871 Congress decided that Indian tribes would no longer be regarded as independent nations with whom treaties were made, in effect decreeing that Indian affairs would be conducted by the federal government without the consent of Native American nations, tribes, or bands. With occasional broad guidelines from Congress, the president, and the secretary of the interior, the Office of Indian Affairs implemented Indian policy.

By the 1870s the Office of Indian Affairs was renowned for its corruption. Its crucial work was performed by approximately 70 Indian agents appointed by the president for four-year terms. These agents administered Indian reservations, some as large as Connecticut, and often cheated both the government and the Native Americans under their jurisdiction. Since removing Indians to reservations usually deprived them of their livelihood, the distribution of annual subsidies from the federal government ($5.9 million in 1880, for example) provided ample opportunities for graft. Agents, aided by approximately 750 employees—about 11 per reservation—were expected to keep the peace and to help the Native Americans become law-abiding, economically productive people. A typical agency might hire from outside the reservation a farmer, a blacksmith, a carpenter, a teacher (who occasionally was a woman), and a miller and from the tribe itself an interpreter, a herder, a teamster, and a laborer. Apart from schools on reservations, the Office of Indian Affairs also established off-site boarding schools (the most famous was at Carlisle, Pennsylvania) that worked to assimilate young Native Americans by separating them from their homes and culture.

Aimed at assimilating Indians into the larger Euro-American society, the Office of Indian Affairs' programs worked to destroy the Indian way of life. On reservations, hunting had to be abandoned and agriculture adopted, but it proved inadequate and necessitated food rations, which kept the tribes dependent on the government. The agency also administered the distribution of land following the DAWES SEVERALTY ACT of 1887, which conferred land ownership to individual members of tribes, thus breaking a long tradition of collective ownership within each tribe. The Office of Indian Affairs remained a paternalistic force in Indian culture until the 1930s, when the agency became more concerned with protecting Native American culture and heritage and promoting self-determination among the tribes.

Further reading: Frederick E. Hopie, *A Final Promise: The Campaign to Assimilate the Indians, 1880–1920* (Cambridge: Cambridge University Press, 1984); Francis Paul Prucha, *The Great Father: The United States Government and the American Indians* (Lincoln: University of Nebraska Press, 1986).

— Scott Sendrow

Indian Rights Association

Founded in 1882, the Indian Rights Association was the first major advocacy organization for NATIVE AMERICANS. As a lobbying power and shaper of public opinion, the Indian Rights Association raised consciousness about the plight of Native Americans as it worked to enact reforms and ameliorate conditions for Indians.

The Indian Rights Association was founded in large part by Herbert Welsh, an upper-middle-class Philadelphian. Welsh and his colleague Henry S. Pancoast traveled with an Episcopal mission to the Dakota Territory in the spring of 1882 and spent four weeks visiting Sioux agencies. Welsh returned and published his proposals for reform in a pamphlet called *Four Weeks among Some of the Sioux Tribes.* By the end of the year, he and Pancoast had established the Indian Rights Association to secure political and civil rights for Native Americans and to act as a watchdog group to ensure that their treaties with the U.S. government were enforced.

Association members were affluent, and Welsh tapped Philadelphia high society for support. Welsh spent the next year meeting with influential patrons in the East, doing speaking engagements and raising funds. By 1885 the Association had a home office in Philadelphia and a lobbyist in Washington, D. C. Welsh and the Indian Rights Association worked on behalf of the Sioux tribes, in particular, in the organization's first years and lobbied for the DAWES SEVERALTY ACT of 1887, which distributed tribal lands to individual Indians, a measure designed to acculturate and "civilize" Indians. As the latter goal suggests, the Indian Rights Association was paternalistic in its approach, and Welsh initially looked to assimilate the tribes and replace their customs with Christianity, a system of laws and education, and a Protestant work ethic. Welsh worked to increase educational opportunities for Native Americans, which tended to break the fabric of Indian culture rather than encourage it. Ultimately, Welsh trusted the concept of federal oversight of tribes, and the Indian Rights Association worked within the federal OFFICE OF INDIAN AFFAIRS (Indian Bureau) to guarantee fair dealings between the government and the tribes.

True to its name, the Indian Rights Association promoted Indian rights in the Sioux land dispute during the 1880s, the APACHE WAR in the late 1880s, the GHOST DANCE WAR in 1890, and the attempted removal of the Ute Indians from Colorado in the 1890s. Welsh relinquished direct control of the organization in 1904, which, despite its paternalism and its efforts to acculturate Indian Society, had ameliorated the treatment of Native Americans.

Further reading: William T. Hagan, *The Indian Rights Association: The Herbert Welsh Years, 1882–1904* (Tucson: University of Arizona Press, 1985).

— Scott Sendrow

Indians

See Native Americans

industrial revolution, second

While the first American industrial revolution occurred primarily in the manufacture of textiles, the second, or new, industrial revolution occurred in steel, petroleum, and electrical industries. The revolution in textiles began in the late 18th century and made Great Britain the manufacturing center of the world; the second revolution began roughly about 1870 and resulted in American primacy among industrial powers. Indeed, during the Gilded Age the United States experienced the greatest surge of increased productivity the world has ever witnessed. American success resulted in part from American advantages. The United States was a huge country with abundant raw materials. It possessed the most extensive RAILROAD network in the world, one that moved raw materials and finished products at high speeds and low costs, allowing a quick return on invested capital. Its relatively prosperous population, growing from natural increase and immigration, provided both an adequate labor supply and an expanding home market. Capital was in short supply, but Europeans—especially the British—invested heavily in the United States. Finally, the American government was stable and encouraged industry with a protective tariff (see TARIFF ISSUE).

No matter what index of production is used, industry's rate of growth in the Gilded Age was prodigious. Robert E. Gallman has calculated that the value added by manufacturing multiplied almost six times from 1869, when it was $1,078 million, to $6,252 million in 1899, while Edwin Frickey's index of manufacturing production multiplied four times from 1870 to 1900. Rapid growth also resulted from American ingenuity. Manufacturers were quick to adopt technological innovations because labor was expensive and labor-saving devices cut costs significantly. Some of the largest companies established laboratories and employed scientists, especially chemists, to improve processes. Americans were inventive, but the concepts of interchangeable parts and the division of labor were basic to American productivity. In addition, manufacturers began to embrace the "scientific management" advocated by Frederick W. Taylor, who made time and motion studies of workers and instituted piecework to induce them to move faster and more efficiently. Perhaps the entrepreneurs themselves were the most important factor in the surge of American production; both John D. Rockefeller and ANDREW CARNEGIE, for example, were talented organizers and administrators, picked able associates, and worked hard. Rockefeller's attention to detail down to the minuscule cost of barrel bungs and Carnegie's obsession with efficiency were legendary.

Virtually all industries experienced rapid growth in the Gilded Age, but the most spectacular developments were in STEEL, OIL, and electricity. With the introduction of the BESSEMER PROCESS, the steel industry took off and with it the MINING of the iron ore and bituminous coal necessary for its production. Steel (an alloy of iron and carbon that is strong and malleable) had been produced in small quantities for swords and armor for centuries and, since the 18th century, in slightly larger amounts in crucibles. The Bessemer converter, which made steel quickly and in large batches, was invented in Great Britain in the 1850s, but large-scale production of American steel began in the 1870s. In 1870 only 68,750 long tons were produced; by 1880 1.2 million; by 1890 4.3 million; by 1900 10.2 million; and in 1913, on the eve of World War I, 31.3 million long tons of American steel were manufactured. By then the United States produced more steel than Germany, Britain, and France combined.

The production of nonferrous metals, although only a fraction of steel output, was significant and grew rapidly in the Gilded Age. Copper production in 1870 was 14,112 tons, doubled to 30,240 tons in 1880. It took off to 129,882 tons in 1890 and 303,059 tons in 1900. Lead production rose steadily from 17,830 tons in 1870 to 367,773 tons in 1900, while zinc went from 5,400 tons in 1870 to 123,886 tons in 1900. Aluminum production, beginning with minuscule amounts in 1886, reached 23,000 long tons in 1900, but its importance would grow in the 20th century.

Unlike railroading, coal mining, and steelmaking, the petroleum industry began in America. Edwin L. Drake drilled the first successful oil well in 1859 near Titusville, Pennsylvania. Drake invented, but failed to patent, the drive pipe that essentially is still used in drilling wells and made little money from his discovery. The impact of his discovery was instantaneous, since petroleum could be refined (distilled) inexpensively into superior lubricants and kerosene, which provided excellent lamplight. In 1861, two years after Drake's discovery, more than 2 million barrels of crude oil were produced, and by 1870 production had increased to 5.3 million barrels and continued to grow to 63.6 million barrels in 1900.

Although virtually all factories were powered by steam engines in the Gilded Age, electricity was of great importance. Instantaneous COMMUNICATION—by the telegraph and the telephone—over great distances were made possible by electrical devices. Illumination by the electric lightbulb invented by THOMAS A. EDISON in 1879 was superior to that given off by a kerosene lamp and demand for it led to the development of a central power station on Pearl Street in New York in 1882 and to the rise of electric utilities. By 1889 electric power stations were producing 260,000 horsepower, which by 1900 increased to 2.4 million horsepower. The early Edison power stations generated direct current, which could be transmitted only short distances, but George Westinghouse (who in 1869 invented the railroad air brake) utilized a transformer in 1885 to raise the voltage of an alternating current (AC) and succeeded in transmitting it a significant distance. Although AC could light bulbs, there was no AC motor. NIKOLA TESLA, an independent electrical inventor who associated briefly with both Edison and Westinghouse, developed AC generators, transformers, and—most important—motors. Tesla sold his patents to Westinghouse in 1888. Thanks to Tesla's inventions and despite Edison's opposition, AC triumphed, especially after Westinghouse put on a spectacular exhibit at the 1893 WORLD'S COLUMBIAN EXPOSITION at Chicago. Tesla's motors installed on trolley cars and ELEVATED RAILROADS (els) revolutionized urban transport and enabled cities to add an outer ring heretofore unreachable by horsecar. Tesla's work also had a great impact on industry. The electric motor, powering individual machines, provided flexibility and was particularly advantageous for the small factory. Although only 2 percent of factories in 1900 were powered by electric motors, they were clearly the wave of the future.

The spectacular economic development of the late 19th century was largely accomplished by corporations. The corporation, consisting of many shareholders, had great advantages over individual ownership or partnerships: The liability of investors in a corporation is limited to the shares owned, shares can easily be sold, the corporation has a life of its own, and large amounts of capital can be raised by a corporation through the sale of stocks and bonds. To function—to acquire a life of its own—a corporation required a charter that, in the early years of the republic, required a special act of incorporation, but by the 1870s usually were acquired through general incorporation laws.

Gilded Age corporations, to eliminate competition (which their managers abhorred while praising it in public), combined with one another to form what became known as TRUSTS. Initially pools, or informal agreements, were used to eliminate competition. Railroads used pools to set rates, divide freight, and apportion receipts until the Interstate Commerce Act made them illegal. The chaotic oil industry and competition by railroads for its freight led to the notorious but short-lived South Improvement Company pool. The carriers divided freight on a percentage basis, and refiners—among which Rockefeller's Standard Oil Company was the most prominent—apportioned their shipments, on which they received a rebate, among the railroads. Pools functioned best in flush times but easily collapsed when business fell off and cheating increased. In addition to their generally short duration, pools could not be enforced.

Although Rockefeller and other refiners organized a subsequent pool, an association, that allotted crude oil to its members, he and his associates (who refined 90 percent of the nation's oil) were unhappy with pooling arrangements. His lawyer, S. C. T. Dodd, suggested that a trust agreement among the associates would provide order and authority. Accordingly, 41 stockholders of Standard Oil of Ohio signed a trust agreement that gave them trust certificates for their property, which they turned over to a board of nine trustees. The trust was so obviously monopolistic that the Ohio courts dissolved it in 1892.

The Standard Oil trustees had already incorporated the Standard Oil Company of New Jersey. That state's incorporation laws did not prevent the creation of a holding company, which in effect was the corporation that combined the individual corporations. In 1899 Standard Oil of New Jersey became a true holding company by increasing its stock from $10 million to $110 million and exchanging that stock for the stock of 40 companies in the Standard group.

Consolidation also characterized the iron and steel industry. Almost 1,000 iron companies were combined in the late 19th century into a few large companies, of which Carnegie Steel was the largest. Since the early 1870s with the opening of his J. Edgar Thompson Steel Works, Carnegie had dominated the steel industry. He assembled a vertical combination controlling iron ore and coal mines, transport facilities, steel mills, and fabrication plants. Carnegie Steel, however, was a limited partnership, not a corporation, for much of its existence. Yet disputes with partners, especially HENRY CLAY FRICK, and Carnegie's desire to retire required that he convert his partnership into a corporation, which he did in 1900. Unlike the oil business where virtually no competition existed, there were other formidable steel combinations, especially Elbert H.

Gary's Federal Steel, a holding company established in 1898 with which Carnegie was willing to compete. Gary did not wish to compete and with the blessing of J. P. MORGAN asked Carnegie to name his price. The $480 million asked was immediately accepted, and in 1901 U.S. Steel became a billion-dollar holding company controlling 60 percent of the industry, with Carnegie Steel as its largest component.

Consolidations occurred in electrical industries. Western Union had long dominated the telegraph business. American Telephone & Telegraph (AT&T) was established in 1885 by American Bell to institute long-distance service, and in 1907, following its reorganization by J. P. Morgan, AT&T began aggressively acquiring independent telephone companies in its quest for one nationwide system. Morgan also supported HENRY VILLARD's consolidation in 1892 of Edison and other electrical companies into the General Electric Company. Four years later Westinghouse and General Electric, the only major manufacturers of electrical equipment, agreed to pool their patents covering light bulbs, motors, dynamos, and street railway equipment. Despite the pooling of information, the two electrical giants remained surprisingly competitive. Nevertheless, the overall trend of mergers and consolidations was the elimination of competition, the adjustment of supply to match demand, and a certain rigidity in price that repealed the law of supply and demand.

Further reading: Alfred D. Chandler, Jr., *The Visible Hand: The Managerial Resolution in American Business* (Cambridge, Mass.: Harvard University Press, 1977); Samuel Haber, *Efficiency and Uplift: Scientific Management in the Progressive Era, 1890–1920* (Chicago: University of Chicago Press, 1964); Edward C. Kirkland, *Industry Comes of Age: Business, Labor, and Public Policy, 1860–1897* (New York: Holt, Rinehart and Winston, 1961).

Internal Revenue taxes

The first income tax in the United States was levied to help finance the Civil War. In August 1861 Congress approved a tax of 3 percent on incomes above $800; by 1864 it had graduated to 10 percent on incomes in excess of $10,000. In addition, excise taxes on virtually every raw and manufactured material were levied by Congress in July 1862. By 1865 these internal revenue taxes provided the bulk of federal tax receipts. Congress removed most of the excise taxes from 1866 to 1870 (distilled liquors was one of the exceptions) and the income tax in 1872. During the Ulysses S. Grant administration, the "whiskey ring" of Internal Revenue officers and distillers defrauded the federal government of excise tax revenues.

In the late 19th century the income tax received wide support. Such tax legislation would improve the government's revenue base while securing more tax dollars from corporations and the wealthier individuals. The idea of a graduated or progressive income tax that would require people with higher incomes to pay a higher percentage than those with less income was supported by several agrarian and labor organizations. The GREENBACK-LABOR PARTY, the PEOPLE'S PARTY (Populists), the KNIGHTS OF LABOR, and several members of the DEMOCRATIC PARTY endorsed the graduated income tax. By the 1890s the movement for a federal graduated income tax was taken up by the Progressive reformers.

Efforts to enact federal income tax legislation encountered a major constitutional obstacle over the question of whether the federal government could levy direct taxes on individuals instead of apportioning them out to the states according to their respective populations. In 1894 Congress included in the Wilson-Gorman Tariff a 2 percent tax on all incomes above $4,000. It was the first direct tax on Americans during peacetime. The constitutionality of the income tax was immediately challenged in the U.S. SUPREME COURT, and in the case of *Pollock v. Farmers' Loan and Trust* (1895) the income tax was ruled unconstitutional. The Court held that it constituted a direct tax and hence was subject to the constitutional requirement of apportionment among the states according to population.

Despite the Supreme Court's ruling in the *Pollock* case, the demand for a federal income tax did not go away. As the Progressive movement gained momentum in the early 20th century, so did the push for a federal income tax. Progressive reformers argued that an income tax was the best and fairest means of raising revenue for the federal government. In 1913 the Sixteenth Amendment was ratified, permitting a federal income tax.

Further reading: W. Elliot Brounlee, *Federal Taxation in America: A Short History* (New York: Cambridge University Press, 1996); Morton Keller, *Affairs of State: Public Life in Late Nineteenth Century America* (Cambridge, Mass.: Harvard University Press, 1977); Sidney Ratner, *Taxation and Democracy in America* (New York: Norton, 1967).

— Phillip Papas

Interstate Commerce Commission See railroads

inventions and technology

Between 1870 and 1900, the United States experienced an explosion in innovation. Independent American inventors such as THOMAS EDISON and ALEXANDER GRAHAM BELL and Serbian-born NIKOLA TESLA dominated technological advancement, in some cases building large empires around

An interior section of the Electricity Building at the Chicago's World's Fair of 1893. The Westinghouse electrical systems and Tesla motor were on display. *(Smithsonian Institution)*

their innovations. Edison was perhaps the best-known inventor of this time period; his expansive laboratory in West Orange, New Jersey, established in 1887, employed dozens of men who worked to produce more than 1,000 patents for new inventions. Electrical inventions—the greatest innovations of the era—and a host of smaller inventions laid the foundation for the economic boom that improved the quality of life for Americans in the 20th century.

Theories on electricity were first developed in Europe in the early 1800s, and early electric engines, called "dynamos," evolved there in the 1870s. Meanwhile, the development of electric lighting in the United States sparked the wider use of electric power in all aspects of technology. Charles F. Brush was one of the first Americans to adapt arc lighting, an early 19th-century technology utilizing an electric arc between carbon rods, for use in homes and businesses. During the 1870s Brush developed a cheaper arc-lighting system, which began to supplant gas-powered lamps, especially when used for outdoor lighting. Brush experimented with high-voltage dynamos and central stations that transmitted electricity in a large-scale system (rather than using them for small independent circuits). The first central electric station to power arc lighting appeared in San Francisco in 1879. By the following year similar operations were established in New York, Philadelphia, and Boston. In subsequent years Elihu Thomson (1853–1937) founded the Thomson-Houston Electric Company and became a leader in the arc-lighting industry, developing better dynamos and other techniques that increased efficiency.

In 1878 Thomas Edison began to develop incandescent lighting, refining the technology of the lightbulb and cutting down on expensive copper wiring to make the technology less expensive. On New Year's Eve 1879 Edison demonstrated 150 bulbs that used carbonized cotton thread in Menlo Park, New Jersey. Edison's first test of electricity for wider uses came in 1882 in New York City, when he laid underground wiring as part of a direct current (DC) system in a small section of New York's financial district, thus establishing a prototype of the modern power grid. In 1885 the electric transformer was invented to facilitate the transmission of electricity. Edison established one of the first power companies, the Edison Electric Illuminating Company, to provide consumers with the power to run electric lights. By 1888 Edison had established electric companies in eight major cities, and he had founded other subsidiaries that built conductors, generators, and lamps while continuing to dominate the market for incandescent lighting. However, in 1886 George Westinghouse (1846–1914) developed an alternating current (AC) lighting method that became a viable challenger to Edison's DC empire. Alternating-current technology, capable of higher voltage, had an advantage over direct current in carrying electricity over long distances efficiently.

Electricity proved useful in other applications, including public transportation. Pollution-causing horse-drawn trolleys were common until the mid-1880s, when steam and electric-powered trains began to be used. Again, Thomas Edison was at the forefront of early efforts to use electrical power with streetcars. These early attempts, however, were unsuccessful and dangerous, and his low-power DC motors were ill-equipped to handle large streetcars. During the mid-1880s Frank J. Sprague, who worked with Edison's company, began to develop better DC motors, which were used in electric cars. In 1887 the municipality of Richmond, Virginia, awarded Sprague the contract to build the first electric train line; by 1903 nearly all streetcar lines in the United States were electrified. The Pullman Car Company constructed an electric freight-hauling locomotive in 1888, although steam-powered trains continued to dominate long-distance train traffic well into the 20th century.

Because of its high energy use, direct current was less economical than steam power. Realizing that alternating current used less electricity than direct current and was therefore cheaper, George Westinghouse began experimenting with AC for use in motors. Westinghouse then tapped Nikola Tesla, who had discovered the rotating electromagnetic field in 1882, to create an AC motor using his discovery. Tesla invented an AC motor in 1888, and Westinghouse immediately bought the patents. Tesla continued to advance electricity technology, inventing the Tesla coil in 1891, which supplied a high-frequency, high-voltage current that would later reach wide use in radios and televisions. Meanwhile, Edison had recognized the limitations of DC and wanted to begin working with AC. Patent laws forced Edison to merge in 1892 with Thomson-Houston, the Westinghouse rival that also had patents on AC technology. The merger created General Electric, which survives to this day. General Electric developed its own AC motor technology in 1894 and eventually pooled patents with Westinghouse for a period of time in order to refine electric technology. The market for electricity expanded in the 1890s after Westinghouse built the first hydroelectric turbogenerator at Niagara Falls in 1896, which harnessed nature to generate power on a large scale.

The development of the telephone and its wide-scale use began with Alexander Graham Bell in the mid-1870s, although its rudimentary technology predated his patent. Bell expanded on experiments first undertaken by Italian inventor Antonio Meucci and submitted an application for telephone technology in 1876. Western Union, the telegraph company, began to utilize telephone technology in 1877, leading Bell to file a patent-infringement lawsuit. In the end, however, Western Union's patent infringement had the positive effect for Bell of greatly expanding phone use in the country. Western Union ended up selling its 56,000 phones to Bell in 1879 after settling their dispute; only a few hundred phones had been in use in 1877, and Western Union's wide use of phone technology ultimately helped precipitate the decline of telegraph technology. Bell began to use central exchange systems to expand telephone use, eliminating the need for an abundance of unsightly wires. By the early 1880s Bell began to implement a system of underground wires, eventually developing telephone connections between Boston and New York in 1884 and expanding them to Washington, D.C., and Chicago in 1893, thus solidifying his monopoly on long-distance telephone service for years to come.

American life was transformed by new building materials such as concrete, iron, and steel during this time period. SKYSCRAPERS built of iron and steel consolidated increasingly large business operations in central locations and contributed to the density of urban centers like New York and Chicago. The first skyscrapers were built following the CHICAGO FIRE of 1871, which devastated the central part of the city. The first tall structure was the 10-story Montauk Building in Chicago, made from cast-iron. The first true skyscraper, using a steel frame, was Chicago's 10-story Home Insurance Building, which was constructed in 1883. The invention of the electric elevator in 1889, using technology pioneered by Elisha Otis (1811–61), and the escalator in 1891 hastened the era of the skyscraper.

Industry benefited greatly from technology developed during this period. Arc lighting and eventually incandescent bulbs lit even the deepest mine shafts, made possible by the new application of dynamite and nitroglycerine. Miners used steam-powered air drills instead of picks and shovels to pull ore out of the ground, and the refining process itself became more efficient through the use of new machines. The logging industry also was helped by steam power and machines, and both industries greatly increased production as a result of new technology. RAILROADS, which played a key role in the expansion of both the logging and MINING industries, were improved through the systemization of rail gauges across the country, more powerful locomotive engines, the invention of the air brake (by Westinghouse), and the use of steel in rails and bridges.

Other smaller inventions made life and commerce easier. These included the electric dental drill (1875), Louis Waterman's fountain pen (1884), the ballpoint pen (1888), William Burrough's adding machine (1888), and King Gillette's safety razor (1895). The first punch-card "computer" technology was developed in 1888 and used in the 1890 U.S. census.

Many of the inventions and patents from this period were more fully developed in the 20th century. The patent on the gasoline-powered car was obtained by George Selden (1846–1922) in 1895, and Henry Ford (1863–1947) constructed his first car in 1896. Edison developed primitive motion-picture technology during this period, and celluloid photographic film—invented in 1887—expanded both still- and motion-picture technology. The first publicly screened motion picture was shown in New York City in 1896. GEORGE EASTMAN (1854–1932) advanced photographic technology with several major inventions during the 1880s and 1890s, including the Eastman Kodak box camera, which used roll film and opened up the world of photography to amateurs. Edison's early phonograph, which used tinfoil cylinders to record sounds, was more fully realized in later years by the recording industry. Together with motion-picture technology, Edison's inventions helped transform American POPULAR ENTERTAINMENT. Orville and Wilbur Wright's work on the airplane, which would revolutionize transportation and warfare, capped a burst of innovation on par with one of civilization's greatest eras of achievement.

Further reading: Ruth S. Cowan, *A Social History of American Technology* (New York: Oxford University Press, 1997); Alan I. Marcus and Howard P. Segal, *Technology in America: A Brief History* (San Diego: Harcourt Brace Jovanovich, 1989).

— Scott Sendrow

investments, American, abroad

American investments abroad were negligible before the Civil War. As a debtor nation, (more foreign capital was invested in the United States than American capital was invested abroad), the United States was chronically short of capital. Americans invested in domestic enterprises that utilized the country's abundant natural resources and had little interest in doing business elsewhere.

In the late 19th and early 20th centuries, American manufacturers, insurance companies, utility operators, and mining companies found it advantageous to develop a foreign presence. Most of these enterprises, like the Singer Manufacturing Company, which opened a sewing machine plant in Scotland in 1882, were launched to distribute their products to foreign markets. A variety of factors converged to encourage American businesses to establish operations in foreign countries: high tariffs in Canada after 1879 and Japan in 1899; restrictions on the use of electrical patents in France and Germany; and deposit requirements for insurance businesses in Germany, Austria, and Switzerland. Nevertheless, in these enterprises American firms were able to attract foreign capital, managers, and even technology.

American businessmen preferred investing funds in neighboring North American countries. In Mexico, the country with the largest American investments before the Mexican Revolution began in 1910, the dictatorship of Porfirio Díaz created a climate favorable to foreign investment. Canada was second in favor as a location for American investment. In CUBA and elsewhere in the Caribbean, American investments increased after the SPANISH-AMERICAN WAR. After the depression from 1893 to 1897, American businesses eagerly sought opportunities to develop markets by operating abroad, and the United States became a net exporter of capital during the period from 1898 to 1901.

Further reading: Mira Wilkins, *The Emergence of Multinational Enterprise: American Business Abroad from the Colonial Era to 1914* (Cambridge, Mass.: Harvard University Press, 1970).

— Bruce Abrams

investments, foreign, in the United States

Although the American economy had matured considerably by 1870, development was still largely dependent on infusions of foreign capital. Prior to the Civil War the British had already invested in bonds to finance the construction of turnpikes, canals, and railroads, but the railroad boom in the late 19th century created an almost insatiable demand for capital from abroad. American bankers such as George Peabody amassed a fortune by selling American securities while living in England. Declining interest rates from 6 percent to 4 percent made American entrepreneurs even more anxious to sell their bonds abroad. Foreign investments in the United States, which totaled $1.5 billion in 1869, grew to $3.4 billion in 1897 and $6.4 billion in 1908.

The large value of American exports, especially of agricultural products, over that of imports was sufficient to meet growing interest payments and keep trade in balance. But by the mid-1890s American business leaders became concerned that the large infusions of foreign capital would require greater exports, especially in manufactured goods, to prevent the outflow of gold to pay foreign investors. Thus, the search for overseas markets became a factor in popular opinion on foreign policy issues. World War I, however, abruptly changed the patterns of international investment. European capital invested abroad shrank and the United States—with its enormous productivity and high rate of savings—suddenly was transformed from a debtor to a creditor nation.

Further reading: Ron Chernow, *The House of Morgan: An American Banking Dynasty* (New York: Simon & Schuster, 1990); Mira Wilkins, *The History of Foreign Investments in the United States to 1914* (Cambridge, Mass.: Harvard University Press, 1989).

— Bruce Abrams

J

Jackson, Helen Hunt (1830–1885)

The author Helen Hunt Jackson became the most eloquent Indian-rights advocate of the Gilded Age. Born on October 15, 1830, in Amherst, Massachusetts, Helen Maria Fiske was a close lifelong friend of EMILY DICKINSON, but for years she gave little indication of her own literary talent. She did have an independent spirit that rejected the puritanism of her parents, was reasonably well educated for a woman of her day, and was witty and vivacious. Attending a ball given by Governor Washington Hunt of New York, she attracted the attention of his brother Lieutenant Edward Bissell Hunt, an army engineer, and they married in 1852. Over the next 11 years they led a nomadic life, but she met the editor Thomas Wentworth Higginson in Newport, Rhode Island, and made valuable contacts in Washington. In 1863, however, her husband accidentally died in New York harbor while trying to develop a torpedolike device, and in 1865 her only surviving child died of diphtheria. Helen Hunt worked her way out of her despair by writing poetry, which began to appear in the *NATION* and the *New York Evening Post,* and turned to Higginson to help her hone her writing skills. By the 1870s she was a successful writer not only of poetry but also of travel books, reviews, and anonymous novels, including a roman à clef about Dickinson, whose talent she recognized and whom she urged to publish. In 1873 Hunt sought relief from a sore throat in the Rockies, where she met William Sharpless Jackson, a wealthy railroad promoter. They married in 1875 and settled in Colorado Springs, but she regularly visited California (which she loved) and the East Coast to maintain her publishing contacts.

Ironically, it was not in Colorado or California but in Boston where she became aroused by the plight of the NATIVE AMERICANS. There in 1879 she heard the Ponca chief Standing Bear and Bright Eyes, a young Omaha woman (the Omaha were closely related to the Ponca), protest the removal of the Ponca from their reservation to the Indian Territory (present day Oklahoma). Although Jackson previously had shown little interest in reform, she became an ardent advocate of Indian rights and in 1881 published *A Century of Dishonor,* which condemned the federal government for its treatment of the Indians.

The Interior Department, rather than ignoring Jackson, asked her along with Abbot Kinney to investigate the condition of the Mission Indians of California. When their report, which appeared in 1883, had no obvious effect on CONGRESS, Jackson resolved to write a novel that she hoped would affect Indian rights the same way her friend Harriet Beecher Stowe's *Uncle Tom's Cabin* had affected the abolitionist movement. *Ramona,* published in 1884, was an immediate success and has gone through more than 300 printings. Ramona, a half-breed young woman raised by an old Spanish California family, falls in love with an Indian forced off his land by whites. Jackson was disappointed that although her book was enormously popular and her readers enjoyed her romantic tale, they did not seem to get the underlying message of the ill treatment of Native Americans. A year later, on August 12, 1885, Jackson died of cancer in San Francisco.

Further reading: Evelyn I. Banning, *Helen Hunt Jackson* (New York: Vanguard Press, 1973); Valerie Sherer Mathes, *Helen Hunt Jackson and Her Indian Reform Legacy* (Norman: University of Oklahoma Press, 1997).

James, Henry (1843–1916)

The son of Henry James, the heir of a prosperous entrepreneur, and Mary Robertson Walsh, novelist Henry James was born on April 15, 1843, in New York City. Brought up in an intensely intellectual household—his father wrote several books on religious philosophy and his older brother WILLIAM JAMES was to become an influential philosopher and psychologist—James was tutored at home, where family friends included Nathaniel Hawthorne and Ralph Waldo Emerson. Between 1855 and 1860 his parents broadened his cultural horizons by bringing him to England, Switzerland, France, and Germany, where he continued to study with private tutors, and at the age of 19 he followed his brother to Harvard. After a semester in law school, he returned to New York and devoted himself to writing, publishing both fiction and literary criticism by the age of 21.

Still hungry for a deeper cultural perspective than he felt the materialistic American intellectual climate provided, James returned to Europe in 1869 and settled at last in London in 1872. Except for brief visits to the United States, he remained there until his death on February 28, 1916, becoming a British subject in 1915. The most famous American literary expatriate of his time, he befriended the leading authors of Europe, including French and Russian realists Gustave Flaubert, Émile Zola, and Ivan Turgenev and such British intellectuals as Herbert Spencer and Thomas Henry Huxley.

In 1875 he published his first collection of stories, *The Passionate Pilgrim,* foreshadowing his recurring themes of nostalgia for an older culture and the confrontation between the innocent American and the sophisticated European. His novel *Roderick Hudson,* serialized that year in the *Atlantic Monthly* (then edited by his close friend WILLIAM DEAN HOWELLS), recounted the story of an American sculptor studying in Italy and disillusioned by Old World cynicism. He repeated the theme explicitly in his 1877 novel *The American,* in which an American millionaire is defeated in his pursuit of European culture by the conventions of French aristocracy, and in his 1878 novella *Daisy Miller,* the tale of a spontaneous American girl in conflict with European codes of behavior in Florence. James reflected America's expanding cultural horizons in his use of foreign settings, but in the 1880s he interrupted the creation of "international novels," with which his fiction had become associated, and turned to the American scene. His *Washington Square* (1880) was a poignant psychological novel dealing with the effects of circumstance on character in New York, and *The Bostonians* (1886) was a satire of American bluestockings and suffragists.

James lived a remote personal life and never married. Always a detached realist, he was indifferent to politics and business in his fiction as in his life. His characters were upper class and his settings elegant—it has been observed that there are no bathrooms in James's fiction—but his stories analyzed primal emotions with keen, sometimes clinical, insight, and if he did not deal with the everyday reality of the common person, like Howells and HAMLIN GARLAND, his themes were universal. The novels, novellas, and short stories that flowed from his pen grew increasingly subtle, and his prose style grew increasingly complex and ambiguous in his later years, influencing a whole generation of modern writers that included D. H. Lawrence, Edith Wharton, Joseph Conrad, and James Joyce.

Further reading: Leon Edel, *Henry James,* 5 vols. (Philadelphia: Lippincott, 1953–1972).

— Dennis Wepman

James, William (1842–1910)

An outstanding psychologist and philosopher, William James, the brother of novelist HENRY JAMES, was born in New York City on January 11, 1842, the son of Henry James, a prosperous entrepreneur influenced by the mysticism of Emanuel Swedenborg. Since inherited wealth enabled his family to travel widely, James's preparatory education included schools and tutors in Europe, making him fluent in French and German. His fragmented schooling inspired him to become either a painter or a scientist. A year spent in the studio of William Morris Hunt convinced James that he could not become a first-rate artist. He therefore entered the Lawrence Scientific School at Harvard in 1861, where he studied chemistry and physiology, and Harvard Medical School in 1864. Further travel necessitated by poor health postponed his medical degree until 1869. Hampered by poor eyesight and a weak back and beset by doubts and fears, James soon fell into a deep and severe depression, almost losing the will to live (although he continued to read voraciously). He was rescued from the illness by a newfound and passionate belief in the freedom and power of individual will that was to characterize his thinking as a psychologist and philosopher. Embracing free will meant rejecting scientific, theological, and metaphysical determinism.

In 1872 James joined the Harvard faculty as an instructor in physiology, which as a branch of biology immersed him in the theory of evolution, while the physiology of the nervous system pushed him into psychology. In 1890, after years of study and association with European psychologists, James published his *Principles of Psychology.* He was an empiricist, believing the mind was shaped by experience, but he opposed the biological and environmental determinism of WILLIAM GRAHAM SUMNER and Herbert Spencer. He believed the mind was active, engaged, interested, and free to experiment with and alter some of life's circumstances. To the question "Are we automata?," he gave an emphatic "no," as he rejected scientific materialism. *The Principles of Psychology* was enormously popular as much for its readability as for its ideas. James was adept at utilizing illustrations, metaphors, humor, and plain language to present complex ideas clearly.

With wide exposure came great influence. An abridged textbook version of *Principles of Psychology* was published in 1892, and in 1898 James brought out *Talks to Teachers on Psychology.* Both books were used extensively by future teachers in colleges of education. James knew that children needed knowledge and skills, but he believed that the specific skills, the manner of learning, and the pace and sequence of instruction should be determined by the special nature of both childhood and the individual child. James, however, did not advocate that children should determine what, when, or how they learned, but rather that sensitive teachers should be aware of many simultaneously occurring instincts in children. They should seize these instincts, such as pride or desire for personal gain, and build lessons that would lead to powerful and positive habits. After reading the *Principles of Psychology,* John Dewey was convinced that creative intelligence could change the world, and when this progressive thinker gathered like-minded educators about him at the University of Chicago, James exclaimed, "*A real School,* and *real Thought.* Important thought, too!"

In 1880, since psychology was regarded as a branch of philosophy, James joined that department. He acknowledged the relationship between the two (although he believed that the science of psychology was a separate discipline) and maintained an interest in both studies. After the *Principles of Psychology* appeared, James's attention turned more to religion and philosophy, and in 1897 he changed his title to professor of philosophy. His interest in religion was psychological, not theological and not in doctrines but in the phenomena of religious experience. Approaching religion as an empiricist, James concluded that although life after death was unproved (his attempts at psychic research yielded no positive results), the record of religious experience—the fruitful moral effects of the practice of religion—pointed to the existence of God. His *Varieties of Religious Experience* (1902) was extremely popular, largely because its scientific approach reassured those who adhered to a mystical faith.

James, however, is chiefly renowned as the philosopher of PRAGMATISM. He first used the term in 1898 when, while lecturing at the University of California at Berkeley, he argued that the meaning of all ideas are in their consequences, and over the next decade he elaborated on this theme. He observed that we deal not with the reality of truth but with our changing perceptions of the reality of truth, that truth is relative, workable, unfolding, and advancing. Ideas should be judged not by their relationship to moral absolutes like truth or goodness but by their consequences. James's pragmatism was implicit in his empiricism and stress on experience, his belief in free will and rejection of determinism, and his hostility to absolutes and embrace of a pluralistic universe. The subtitle of his book *Pragmatism: A New Name for Old Ways of Thinking* (1907) was appropriate.

James's pragmatism was easily accepted in a rapidly evolving, growing, competitive American society. His philosophy rejected prejudiced or fixed views and promoted the analysis of experience in determining what worked in personal lives and social institutions. Solving problems and answering human needs took precedence over traditional beliefs and practices, and pragmatism became the tool for achieving goals. An antidogmatic philosophy, James's pragmatism has not become a rigid doctrine, but it has encouraged the development of new, original ideas. He died on August 26, 1910.

William James *(Library of Congress)*

Further reading: Gay Wilson Allen, *William James: A Biography* (New York: Viking Press, 1967); R. W. B. Lewis, *The Jameses: A Family Narrative* (New York: Farrar, Strauss and Giroux, 1991).

— Harry Stein

Jefferson, Joseph, III (1829–1905)

Actor Joseph Jefferson III was born on February 20, 1829, in Philadelphia, Pennsylvania, the son of Joseph Jefferson II and Cornelia Frances Thomas Burke, actors. His grandfather, the first of that name, was a noted comic actor who immigrated to the United States in 1795, and his father worked as a manager and scene painter as well as an actor. Jefferson made his first appearance on stage at the age of three in a crowd scene and the next year performed in a minstrel show in Washington, D. C. His education was limited entirely to his apprenticeship in the theater, accompanying his family on tours throughout the South and into Mexico. After his father died in 1842, the family continued performing, but Jefferson returned to Philadelphia alone and joined a stock company at the age of 17. Three years later he made his first appearance in New York. In 1850 he married Margaret Clements Lockyer, who died in 1861 after bearing four children.

Jefferson worked steadily as an actor and a stage manager in Philadelphia and several southern cities. In 1858 he had a major success starring in Tom Taylor's comedy *Our American Cousin*, a vehicle in which he helped eliminate the theatrical stereotype of the boorish Yankee. After his wife's death, he traveled to California and then worked for several years in Australia. In 1865 he toured South America and England.

It was in London that he resumed a professional connection with the popular American playwright Dion Boucicault and proposed a new dramatization of Washington Irving's classic *Rip Van Winkle.* In collaboration, the two produced a version that provided Jefferson with a role that he was to play for the rest of his life. A hit in London, the play traveled to New York in 1866 and found a warm welcome. The next year he remarried. His second wife, Sarah Warren, was the daughter of a popular comic actor, William Warren. The couple had three children.

Jefferson's dedication to his craft impelled him to undertake a variety of roles. In 1875 he and his family traveled to England, where they spent two and a half years and where he created a memorable interpretation of Bob Acres in Richard Brinsley Sheridan's 18th-century play *The Rivals.* His limber frame and mobile face enabled him to run the gamut from tragic melodrama to broad physical comedy, but his reputation was solidly based on his restrained and easygoing portrayal of Irving's archetypal ne'er-do-well Rip. His performance of that role is credited with marking a turning point in American theatrical style, from the formalism of the 19th century to the relaxed naturalism of the modern era. In 1890 Jefferson published his *Autobiography,* which discussed his craft in perceptive detail and has become a classic of stage history.

Jefferson earned a large fortune and owned homes in Massachusetts, Florida, and Louisiana. In his spare time, he was also an avid and skilled impressionist painter and exhibited at the Pennsylvania Academy of Fine Arts in 1868 and the National Academy of Design in 1890. Honored both professionally and socially, he was made president of the Players Club in 1893 and did much to elevate the status of the acting profession. Jefferson died on April 23, 1905, in Palm Beach, Florida.

Further reading: Arthur W. Bloom, *Joseph Jefferson: Dean of the American Theater* (Savannah, Ga.: Frederic C. Beil, 1999).

— Dennis Wepman

Jim Crow laws

Segregation (or Jim Crow, after a racially stereotyped minstrel show character) existed prior to the Civil War, but it was not systematic. Many hotels excluded blacks, and most churches had balconies or separate pews for AFRICAN AMERICANS. With the emancipation of slaves following the Civil War, the custom of segregation continued as communities formed dual school systems to maintain the status quo. The CIVIL RIGHTS ACT (1875) did not try to integrate schools, but it did call for the integration of public facilities. The voiding of that desegregation law by the U.S. SUPREME COURT in the 1883 CIVIL RIGHTS CASES in effect encouraged discrimination. Nevertheless, Jim Crow—segregation—laws were rare in the South before the 1890s and became prevalent at the turn of the century. Indeed, Virginia did not separate the races on the state's railroads prior to 1900. Nor were the state's streetcars segregated by race, and despite discrimination, blacks generally were not barred from or segregated in bars, waiting rooms, theaters, or other public venues. Excepting churches, schools, and railroad cars, most areas in the South did not practice either de facto or de jure segregation prior to 1897.

The *PLESSY V. FERGUSON* Supreme Court case in 1896 set into motion the concept of legally separating the races in public arenas. The Court upheld the 1890 Louisiana Jim Crow law requiring that railroads provide "equal but separate accommodations for the white and colored races." Not all southern whites demanded Jim Crow laws: South Carolina resisted establishing Jim Crow cars before 1898, and the conservative editor of the Charleston *News and Courier* considered such a law absurd. He noted sarcastically that a Jim Crow car would logically call for Jim Crow railroads, passenger boats, waiting rooms, eating halls, jury boxes, as well as a Jim Crow Bible for court procedures and even two or three Jim Crow counties for blacks. But in time his sarcastic absurdities became realities as nearly all his examples were adopted by southern legislatures. In 1898 South Carolina enacted a Jim Crow car for first-class coaches and two years later amended the law to include second-class coaches. Jim Crow streetcars were established by North Carolina and Virginia (1901); Louisiana (1902); Arkansas, South Carolina, and Tennessee (1903); Mississippi and Maryland (1904); Florida (1905); and Oklahoma (1907). Other Jim Crow statutes separated whites and other races in public facilities such as libraries, concert halls, parks, and railroad and bus terminals. Eventually, Jim

Crow was applied to churches, housing, employment, sport teams, hospitals, orphanages, cemeteries, funeral homes, morgues, and places of entertainment, and throughout the South, "white only" or "colored only" signs were strictly enforced.

These signs were particularly humiliating to African Americans and liberals. Beginning in the 1950s, civil rights activists protested against Jim Crow laws by sitting in at lunch counters, wading in at swimming pools, and supporting economic boycotts of businesses that supported Jim Crow enforcement. These odious laws remained in effect until the passage of the 1964 Civil Rights Act, which prohibited discrimination in all public facilities.

Further reading: C. Vann Woodward, *The Strange Career of Jim Crow,* 3d rev. ed. (New York: Oxford University Press, 1974).

— William Seraile

jingoes

In the late 19th century, the descriptive term *jingoes* applied to those who displayed an intense, unquestioning patriotism while advocating an aggressive FOREIGN POLICY. In 1878 the term was used in England to describe the followers of Prime Minister Benjamin Disraeli, who sought to use the British fleet to check the Russian advances in the Black Sea. The group adopted a theme song whose refrain went:

> We don't want to fight, but, by jingo, if we do,
> We've got the ships,
> We've got the men,
> We've got the money, too.

The "jingo" tag soon began to be used pejoratively in the United States for aggressive imperialists who would go to war to acquire overseas territories and naval bases. The opponents of the jingoes thought them manic, impulsive, possessed of limited intelligence, and oblivious to the consequences of war.

— Timothy E. Vislocky

Johnstown flood (May 31, 1889)

On May 31, 1889, the South Fork Dam in western Pennsylvania broke, pouring 20 million tons of water downstream, inundating Johnstown 15 miles below, and killing approximately 2,200 people. The flood and its aftermath demonstrate dominant themes of the Gilded Age: The doctrine of laissez-faire, very much in vogue, discouraged government inspection or regulation of the dam. Belief in individualism enabled people to do as they wished with their property, even to the point of endangering others. Casualness bordering on callousness was rampant. The owners of the poorly maintained South Fork Dam were wealthy and prominent Pittsburghers who were never held accountable for their carelessness. But when the disaster struck, ordinary people proved to be heroes, and a spirit of cooperation prevailed as almost everyone put aside their personal losses and cared for the injured, buried the dead, and cleared the debris. Warmhearted people from all over—even other countries—contributed more than $3.7 million and trainloads of provisions.

Originally part of Pennsylvania's Main Line canal system, the South Fork Dam had been built to supply the canal west of Johnstown with water during the dry summer months. It was soon rendered obsolete by the Pennsylvania Railroad, fell into disrepair, and was in 1879 acquired and inadequately patched up by the South Fork Fishing and Hunting Club (among its members were ANDREW CARNEGIE and HENRY CLAY FRICK).

Following an extremely heavy rainfall, the dam broke and water cascaded down the narrow valley, devastating Johnstown in 10 minutes. Houses were swept off their foundations and split apart; their inhabitants hurled about or clinging to the debris that lodged in a massive jam at the stone railroad bridge on the downstream side of town. More than 500 people who had not been drowned or crushed were tangled in the debris. Rescue work proceeded slowly because few tools were available, and that evening the debris caught fire and as many as 80 men, women, and children perished.

Those who survived the flood and the fire awoke on June 1 to a dismal day but coped with the disaster. Rafts were built to aid in rescue operations, and committees were formed to bury the dead and care for the injured. The next day a relief train arrived from Pittsburgh, and by that night more than 1,000 doctors, undertakers, workmen, and newspapermen had come. Clara Barton and her newly organized Red Cross soon arrived and remained for five months rendering aid to people in need. Andrew Carnegie also came and characteristically promised Johnstown a new library. Life in time returned to normal. Not one cent, however, was realized from the damage suits that followed the flood.

Further reading: David G. McCullough, *The Johnstown Flood* (New York: Simon & Schuster, 1968).

Joseph, Chief

See Nez Perce War

Judaism

Jews and Judaism have played an important role in American history since the colonial period, but the last third of the 19th century was a time of great growth and change. In 1850 a "dignified orthodoxy"—established by the early Sephardic communities—prevailed in American Judaism, but by then the German Ashkenazim were in a majority. IMMIGRATION swelled their numbers enormously in the next decade as the Jewish population rose from 50,000 to 160,000. Immigrants escaped from oppressive societies, but they also left their close-knit, traditional religious communities to spread out in a land of toleration where they were more susceptible to change.

Indeed, change was already in the air in Europe. Paralleling the 18th-century Enlightenment, the Haskala, or Jewish Enlightenment, arose in Germany, and from it Reform Judaism emerged as a movement. Its 19th-century proponents, eager to encounter modern life, were either looked to by the American-German Jewish community for guidance or personally came to America to try out their ideas. Of these, David Einhorn and Isaac Mayer Wise were the most prominent. Einhorn, who served as leader of the new movement in Germany and Hungary, came to Baltimore, Maryland. With his arrival in 1855, the new Reform ideas—which approached Judaism from a scientific viewpoint, rejected ceremonial law (dietary restrictions, for example), and interpreted moral law by contemporary standards—spread rapidly. Within a generation, largely due to the efforts of Isaac Mayer Wise, the overwhelmingly Sephardic orthodox culture of Judaism had become just as overwhelmingly German reform.

Wise came to the United States in 1846. During his first rabbinate in Albany, New York, his liturgical changes divided the congregation, and in 1854 he began his rabbinate in Cincinnati. There he turned to publishing (two magazines and many books) to promote his radical religious ideas and to organize their adherents. In 1873 he founded the Union of American Hebrew Congregations, which by 1880 was the closest any group ever got to dominating American Judaism. Wise served as president until his death in 1900. The high-water mark of Reform Judaism came in 1885 with the 18-point Pittsburgh platform, which Einhorn heavily influenced and Wise called "the Jewish Declaration of Independence." The platform laid out the principles of Reform Judaism that endured through the late 20th century.

Judaism shifted again near the end of the 19th century, owing chiefly to the next wave of immigration from the eastern European Ashkenazic community. With renewed persecution in Russia, Poland, and the surrounding areas, the resulting immigration doubled the number of synagogues in the United States between 1880 and 1890. These Jews were far more sequestered from the world than the German Jews two generations before, and they brought a whole culture with them. With their Yiddish language and a folk piety formed within the shtetls of the pale—often Hasidic or tinged with Hasidism—these Jews did not connect with the Reform Jewish community. Indeed, their presence led to a resurgence of Orthodox Judaism.

While these immigrants clung vigorously to their culture, their children were often eager to assimilate in American society. Growing secularism, beginning in Europe and growing in America, led to Zionism, which was a nonreligious Jewish response to anti-Semitism, although it was a Reform rabbi, Stephen Wise, who founded the Federation of American Zionists in 1898. These same secular forces strengthened the Ethical Culture movement, a nontheistic religious organization founded by Felix Adler in 1876, which had its intellectual and cultural origins in Judaism but dissociated itself from that tradition almost entirely.

In 1900, when Isaac Mayer Wise died, Judaism was about to become tripartite in form: Orthodox, Reform, and Conservative. In the space of merely 50 years, the most ancient faith of Abraham, Isaac, and Jacob had changed more than any other religion in America.

Further reading: Michael Meyer, *Response to Modernity: A History of the Reform Movement in Judaism* (New York: Oxford University Press, 1988); Sefton D. Temkin, *Creating American Reform Judaism: The Life and Times of Isaac Meyer Wise* (Portland, Oreg.: Littman Library of Jewish Civilization, 1998).

— W. Frederick Wooden

K

kindergarten

The origins of the kindergarten movement of the late 19th century derive from a fundamental change in how Europeans envisioned and understood young children. The traditional view—that children were tainted by the original sins of Eve and Adam and thus were depraved and best governed by strict authority—was attacked by John Amos Comenius (1592–1670), John Locke (1632–1704), Jean-Jacques Rousseau (1712–1778), and Johann Pestalozzi (1746–1827). These humane philosophers and educators argued that children are innocent, impressionable, and capable of being educated without harsh discipline by skillful teachers who understand their intelligence and emotional capabilities. Children are thus best prepared for school in homes where love rather than unwavering discipline prevails. In 1837 Pestalozzi's pupil Friedrich Froebel (1782–1852) established in Germany a kindergarten for little children that emphasized games, social activities, art, music, and physical movement. Froebel and like-minded early-childhood educators believed that literacy skills and arithmetic were more effectively introduced between the ages of six and eight.

Inspired by Froebel, Margaretha Schurz (wife of reformer CARL SCHURZ) in 1857 started a kindergarten in Watertown, Wisconsin, and others soon sprang up. Between 1870 and 1900 kindergarten classes were established in many publicly supported urban and rural schools, but they usually failed to realize Froebel's ideas. In rural one-room schools with 10–20 students, the five-year-old kindergartners were thrown in with all ages and grades (up to 14–16-year-old eighth-graders) and were often ignored while the teacher prepared older students in demanding subjects for state examinations. Teacher turnover was high, with 90 percent spending less than five years in any one school, and teachers normally were young and inexperienced, with only two or three years of education beyond the eighth grade. They were hired by local school boards and were occasionally observed and evaluated by state officials. In urban schools or towns large enough to operate a graded school, the kindergarten children were assigned their own teachers (whom principals evaluated frequently) and had special rooms and learning materials.

When parents sent children to public kindergarten, they took the first step in a transition from family-controlled to state-controlled education. Henceforth, while parents retained the responsibility of feeding, clothing, and maintaining the health of their children, the schools would try to educate them according to their merit for independent, self-reliant behavior. Indeed, if families failed to develop proper health habits or instill moral training in their children, the schools at least would get them off the streets, rid their heads of lice, improve their posture through scoliosis inspection, and develop their characters while teaching them basic skills. In the late 19th century, kindergartens were the beginning of eight to 10 years of schooling for the typical child, 95 percent of whom then went out to work for the rest of their lives.

Further reading: Lawrence Cremin, *The American Common School: A Historical Conception* (New York: Teachers College Press, 1951); Barbara Finkelstein *Governing the Young: Teacher Behavior in Popular Primary Schools in the Nineteenth Century* (New York: Falmer Press, 1989); Wayne, Fuller. *The Old Country School: The Story of Rural Education in the Midwest* (Chicago: University of Chicago Press, 1982).

— Harry Stein

King, Clarence (1842–1901)

Clarence Rivers King—American geologist and founder-leader of federal surveys—was born in Newport, Rhode Island, on January 6, 1842. King's mother raised and educated him after his father died at Amoy in 1848 while in the China trade. With his stepfather's aid, King attended Yale (Ph. B., 1862). From 1863 to 1866 he worked throughout

California with Josiah Whitney's state-sponsored geological survey until he became solely responsible for his twice-widowed mother, two stepsiblings, and eight other persons. In 1867 King returned east and won approval for his U.S. Geological Exploration of the 40th parallel sponsored by the Army Corps of Engineers. By 1872 King and his men had mapped and assessed the geology and mineral resources of a 100-mile swath of land flanking the transcontinental railroad between California's Sierra Nevada and Colorado's Front Range. In 1872 King earned national renown by exposing a cunning "diamond hoax" in Colorado and publishing *Mountaineering in the Sierra Nevada,* a volume of stories real and imagined based on his years with Whitney. King's episodic interpretations of geologic history and organic evolution (1877) clashed with the gradualist views of his friend and collaborator, Yale paleontologist OTHNIEL CHARLES MARSH.

In 1878 King completed *Systematic Geology,* his synthesis of the 40th-parallel studies, and strove to establish a national federal survey that would consolidate the missions of his organization, one led by JOHN WESLEY POWELL, and two others also examining the public domain. As a member (1876) of the National Academy of Sciences (NAS), King advised Marsh's NAS committee, which was charged by CONGRESS to plan for reforming the federal mapping and scientific surveys. At Interior Secretary CARL SCHURZ's request, King cowrote legislation based on the NAS plan. King and Powell promoted its passage by Congress on March 3, 1879; a month later, King became director of the new U.S. GEOLOGICAL SURVEY (USGS). He and Powell also served on the Public Lands Commission, authorized by the same statute.

Congress and President RUTHERFORD B. HAYES established the USGS principally as a bureau of practical science to help the mineral industry aid the nation's reviving economy by eliminating shortfalls in gold and iron production. Although the USGS's initial appropriation was only two-thirds of that of the three surveys it replaced, King immediately launched the new agency on a scientific program of applied economic geology (as mandated) and supporting basic studies (to provide new discoveries to apply). He also cofunded and participated in cooperative investigations for the 10th census.

While leading the USGS, King continued to display professional brilliance, personal magnetism, a natural style of command, and a genuine sympathy for everyone who worked for him. He intended to remain as director, however, "only long enough to appoint its staff, organize its work, and guide the force into full activity." The agency's ethics clauses prevented King from mining investments or consulting within the United States, activities that would yield the larger income he needed to support his family and his lifestyle. In March 1881, after recommending Powell as his successor, King resigned as director. Soon, as King noted with dismay, Powell deemphasized practical science and turned the USGS into an agency for topographic mapping and general geology.

King returned to New York City, his professional and social base, where he had been a spellbinding raconteur in the Century Club since 1876. Thereafter, with mixed success, King promoted mines in Mexico, ranches in Wyoming, a bank in Texas, and other ventures. King returned often to Washington, where he, Marian and HENRY ADAMS, and Clara and JOHN MILTON HAY sometimes convened their informal "Five of Hearts Club." From 1888 King also led a second life in Brooklyn in a loving but clandestine common-law marriage to Ada Todd, a black nursemaid who bore him five children. In 1893 King published his estimate of the Earth's age, but a nervous breakdown ended his hope of resuming leadership of the USGS. The financial panic later that year destroyed King's resources, leaving him hopelessly in debt to Hay. King refused continued offers from academe or additional help from Hay and resumed active work as a mining consultant. These efforts increasingly damaged his health. Tuberculosis forced King to California and then to Arizona, where he died on December 24, 1901.

Further reading: Thurman Wilkins, *Clarence King: A Biography* (Albuquerque: University of New Mexico Press, 1988).

— Clifford M. Nelson

Klondike gold rush

The gold rush era in the United States began in California in 1848 and continued through 1900. Although miners searched for the valuable metal well into the 20th century, the Klondike gold rush, from roughly 1897 to 1900, was the last of the major rushes to occur where independent prospectors flocked to a region in the hopes of "striking it rich." The epicenter of the Klondike gold rush was up the Yukon River just over the Alaskan border in Canada, and close to Dawson City; to reach it, hopeful prospectors opened up the Alaskan frontier.

The United States acquired Alaska in 1867, but it was basically unknown and unsettled until the late 1890s, when large numbers of prospectors poured into it in search of gold. Although the town of Juneau, Alaska, was established in 1880 after gold was found there (and in the Canadian Yukon in the mid-1880s), the major "strike" occurred in August 1896, when the son a California forty-niner found gold while panning in Rabbit Creek, which soon became known as "Bonanza Creek."

Prospectors from the Canadian Yukon rushed up to Bonanza Creek and began staking claims along the creek

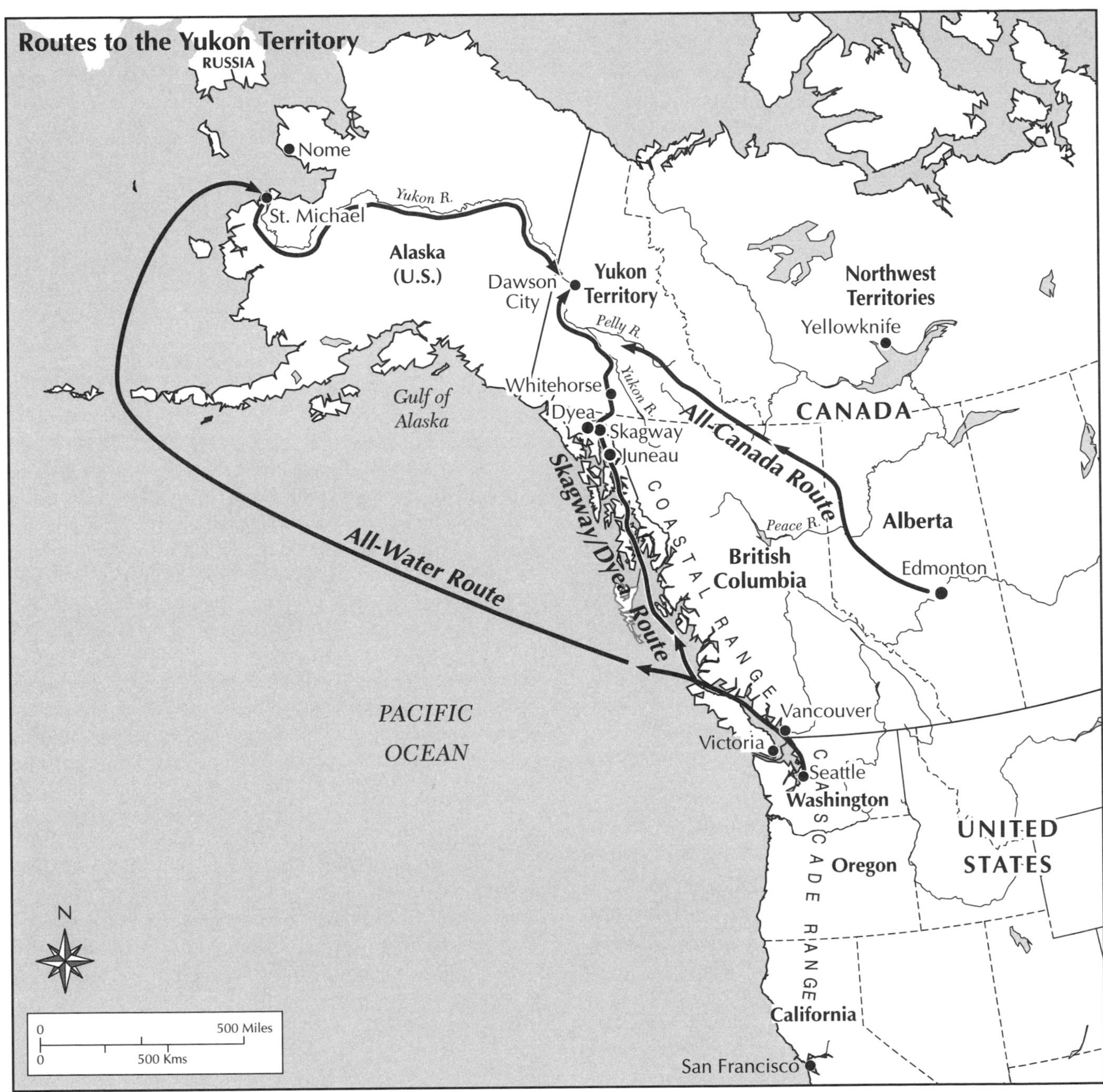

and in the surrounding area. Several prospectors during this initial period enjoyed gold yields that brought them more than $1 million. News about the gold did not reach the West Coast and the outside world until the summer of 1897, precipitating a gold rush that followed the pattern of the California gold rush of 1849. Large numbers of men without women gave rise to vice and violence, vastly inflated prices for necessities that were brought in with difficulty, and the tendency for some prospectors to settle in the area permanently. Mining activity created Dawson City, and by September 1897 6,000–8,000 prospectors were already in the area near the head of the Yukon River.

Depressed economic conditions following the PANIC OF 1893 heightened interest in the new gold fields, and by the end of 1897 thousands of hopefuls were on their way to Alaska. Many boarded transcontinental railroads for Seattle, Washington, the closest major city, to catch a vessel heading up the coast to Alaska. By 1898 Seattle was full of miners waiting for a steamship that would take them 2,000 miles northwest to the mouth of the Yukon River in the

Bering Sea, then 1,300 miles up the Yukon to Dawson City. A late-arriving steamer in 1897 actually became stuck in the ice and had to wait until the following season to make it to Dawson City. Others took a boat to Juneau and then attempted the treacherous land route north, braving avalanches, crevasses, and the 1,500-square-mile Malaspina Glacier; many of these prospectors died.

Driven by rumors of gold elsewhere, many prospectors scattered across the vast expanses of the Alaskan tundra in search of the metal, moving as far north as the Arctic Circle in some instances. Historians estimate that 100,000 people journeyed to the Dawson City area in search of gold. In the summer of 1899 prospectors discovered gold in the sand on the beach near Nome, Alaska (an isolated area near the Bering Strait), which began another Alaskan gold rush. Steamers from Seattle were unable to penetrate the ice that had already formed late in the summer, and eager miners were forced to wait until the next season. Nome's population expanded to 18,000 by the time the gold rush ended. The Klondike gold rush, and to a lesser degree the rush to Nome, succeeded in opening up the "last frontier" (Alaska's nickname) of the United States and was the final opportunity for the amateur prospector to claim "poor man's gold."

Further reading: Paula Mitchell Marks, *Precious Dust: The American Gold Rush Era: 1848–1900* (New York: William Morrow, 1994).

— Scott Sendrow

Knights of Labor

A group of Philadelphia garment workers led by Uriah Stephens organized the first local assembly of the Noble Order of the Knights of Labor (Knights) in 1869. They cloaked the society in rituals and secrecy (abolished in 1881 to placate opposition from the Roman Catholic hierarchy) to protect its members from discharge and blacklisting. At first, growth was slow, with a number of local assemblies forming district assemblies without much effort to coordinate activities. A rapid influx of members following the GREAT STRIKE OF 1877, however, necessitated the formation of a national organization.

In January 1878 delegates from the various district assemblies meeting in Reading, Pennsylvania, created the general assembly as the order's national legislative body and elected Stephens its executive director, or "grand master workman." The Knights opened membership to all productive people over the age of 18, including women and AFRICAN AMERICANS, but excluded saloonkeepers, bankers, lawyers, and stockbrokers. The inclusive membership was necessary, for the Knights' overarching goal was social reform. The organization lobbied for the abolition of CONTRACT LABOR and favored weekly pay laws and worker safety laws. It also called for government ownership of RAILROADS and telegraph lines and established producers' cooperatives. TERENCE V. POWDERLY, who replaced Stephens as grand master workman in 1879, and other leaders emphasized arbitration instead of strikes, which they dismissed as knee-jerk reactions that could do little or nothing to ameliorate the condition of workers.

Ironically, the Knights grew and died by the strike. Membership increased from 100,000 to more than 700,000 after two successful strikes against the southwestern railroads in 1885, but the Knights lost more than 100,000 members after the same railroads defeated them in a strike the following year. Membership continued to decline, as the order was unable to win another important strike over the next two years. The order lost additional prestige among workers when it became known that Powderly, true to antistrike philosophy, refused to support the eight-hour movement sponsored by the trade unions.

Trade union hostility also contributed to the demise of the Knights. Skilled workers resented the Knights' organizational scheme of geographically based local units in which they were outvoted by unskilled workers and unable to dominate a trade. The Knights met these objections by permitting the formation of district assemblies based upon occupation, but skilled workers further resented Powderly's refusal to support strikes and began joining the resurgent trade unions of the AMERICAN FEDERATION OF LABOR (AFL). Soon open warfare between the two organizations (with each breaking the strikes of the other) substantially weakened the Knights. By 1890 the producer cooperatives sponsored by the order, upon which it had pinned so much hope, had disappeared and many of its remaining members joined the Populist movement.

It would be a mistake, however, to write off the Knights as a failure. As a reform organization it achieved such significant legislation as the prohibition of imported contract labor, the creation of the Federal Bureau of Labor, and, in some states, the abolition of convict labor.

Further reading: Robert E. Weir, *Beyond Labor's Veil: The Culture of the Knights of Labor* (University Park: Pennsylvania State University Press, 1996).

— Harold W. Aurand

Ku Klux Klan cases (1884)

The Ku Klux Klan began in 1866 in Pulaski, Tennessee, as a secret social club of former Confederate veterans. It derived its name from the Greek word *kyklos,* which means "circle." The Klan opposed Radical Republican Reconstruction by intimidating former slaves and their white supporters with threats, beatings, and murders. Spreading rapidly, the Klan by 1867 had become "the invisible empire of the South," led by former Confederate general Nathan Bedford Forrest. The Klan was a formidable organization that helped restore white rule in North Carolina (1870) and Georgia (1871). In 1871 CONGRESS passed the Ku Klux Enforcement Act, which provided President Ulysses S. Grant with the authority to suspend the writ of habeas corpus, to suppress disturbances by armed force, and to fine terrorist groups.

The SUPREME COURT, however, severely limited the effect of the Enforcement Act of 1871 as well as that of 1870. In *United States v. Cruikshank* (1876) it emphasized that the Fourteenth Amendment limited the actions of states but not the acts of individuals. That same year in *United States v. Reese,* the Court would not uphold the Enforcement Acts in local and state elections. The Court further reduced the effect of the Ku Klux Enforcement Act in *United States v. Harris* (1883) by holding that Congress did not have the power to legislate against crime within states.

The Court, however, did uphold the Ku Klux Enforcement Act in *Ex parte Yarbrough* (1884). Joseph Yarbrough and others were indicted under two sections of the Enforcement Act of 1871 for whipping and conspiring to prevent Barry Saunders from exercising a constitutional right to vote for a member of Congress. Yarbrough questioned the constitutionality of the law, but although the Supreme Court had emasculated the Enforcement Acts, *Ex parte Yarbrough* dealt with an individual denying a person the right to vote in a federal election. The Supreme Court ruled that Congress had the right to protect persons who vote for members of Congress from intimidation or violence and to punish as a crime the interference by any individual with another person's right to vote in federal elections. Based on this decision, Yarbrough and others were denied a writ of habeas corpus and were sent back to jail. The *Yarbrough* case, however, was exceptional and had no effect on the intimidation of black voters in the South by white supremacists.

Further reading: David M. Chalmers, *Hooded Americanism: The History of the Ku Klux Klan,* 3d ed. (Durham, N.C.: Duke University Press, 1987); Loren Miller, *The Petitioners: The Story of the Supreme Court of the United States* (Cleveland: Meridian Books, 1967).

— William Seraile

L

labor, child

The number of children under age 16 working in nonagricultural pursuits doubled between 1890 and 1900. Children that age composed 13 percent of the cotton industry's workforce in 1900. Boys under 16 almost exclusively filled three occupations—slate picker, door tender, and mule driver—in the anthracite coal mining industry. Children worked in canneries, glass factories, and most other industries. Some worked in the streets selling newspapers and shining shoes. Others, particularly immigrants, worked with their families in sweatshops that often doubled as their living quarters.

Employers hired children because they were cheap labor. A slate picker in the anthracite mines earned between six and 10 cents an hour. Canneries paid children less than 14 years of age 2.5 cents an hour. When paid, youngsters in sweatshops received between one and two cents an hour. Cotton mills might pay an "experienced" 12-year-old five cents an hour. Some mills would give kids the opportunity to gain experience by allowing them to work without pay for a probationary period of up to six weeks. At the end of the period they would often be fired and replaced by another batch of eager learners.

Children worked long hours for their meager pay. A workday of 14–16 hours was common in the sweatshops. Canneries worked at least 12 hours during peak season. The workday varied between 10 and 12 hours in other industries. Supervisors kept the children working constantly though the day with shouts, curses, and, if necessary, corporal punishment. Some overseers held smaller children by their feet out of a window, threatening to drop them unless they behaved; other overseers simply beat the children with a rod or whip.

Children often resisted oppressive behavior. On an individual level they would throw stones or spit on abusive bosses when they were not looking. Supervisors were targets of practical jokes. Some were not above sabotaging machines to gain time to rest or play. Children also participated in concerted activities. Anthracite breaker boys, for example, would quit work collectively to go sleighing or swimming. The boys at a colliery in Moosic, Pennsylvania, refused to return to work until an objectionable boss was replaced. In 1899 newsboys refused to sell copies of the *New York Journal* and the *New York World* when the publishers increased the wholesale cost of their papers by 10 cents per 100 without a corresponding increase in the retail price. The strike ended with a compromise after two

Young boys were often a source of cheap labor in the mining industry. *(Library of Congress)*

weeks: The new wholesale rate remained, but the publishers agreed to refund the price of all unsold copies. A strike of New York messenger boys earlier that year, however, failed because of poor organization.

With the exception of the United Mine Workers of America, which organized boys into separate local unions, trade unions did not attempt to recruit children, whom they regarded as cheap competition. Consequently, unions did join with reform groups in lobbying for laws that would make the employment of children cost prohibitive.

One reform tactic was to increase the number of years of compulsory EDUCATION. As with many reforms, compulsory education addressed several concerns: It would Americanize immigrant children by teaching them English and giving them "correct" values while keeping children out of the workplace. But although the public schools proved effective instruments of acculturation, compulsory education failed to end child labor. Yielding to pressure from employers, school districts established special night schools for working children.

Labor unions and reformers also lobbied for laws restricting the hours a child could work. By 1900 eight states prohibited children from working at night. Most northern states mandated a 10-hour day and 60-hour work week for children. Many states also established a minimum age for industrial work.

The minimum-age laws, however, had little effect. Seeking cheap labor, employers did not inquire too closely into the ages of young people applying for work, and children lied about their ages with the blessings of their parents. Economic necessity forced many parents to make their children work. Wages were so low that most working-class and lower-middle-class families could not subsist on one income.

Technology, not laws, forced a decline in child labor. In the 1890s, mechanical devices began eliminating the need for door boys and slate pickers in anthracite coal mining, and the adoption of electric haulage locomotives eliminated the need for mules and their drivers. But children continued to work in industries where machinery could not perform their normal tasks. As late as 1938, many southern cotton mills employed children under the age of 16.

Further reading: Walter I. Trattner, *Crusade for the Children: A History of the National Child Labor Committee and Child Labor Reform in American* (Chicago: Quadrangle Books, 1970).

— Harold W. Aurand

labor, radical

Labor radicals wanted to transform the Gilded Age society from one based on economic individualism to one based upon common ownership of property managed for the

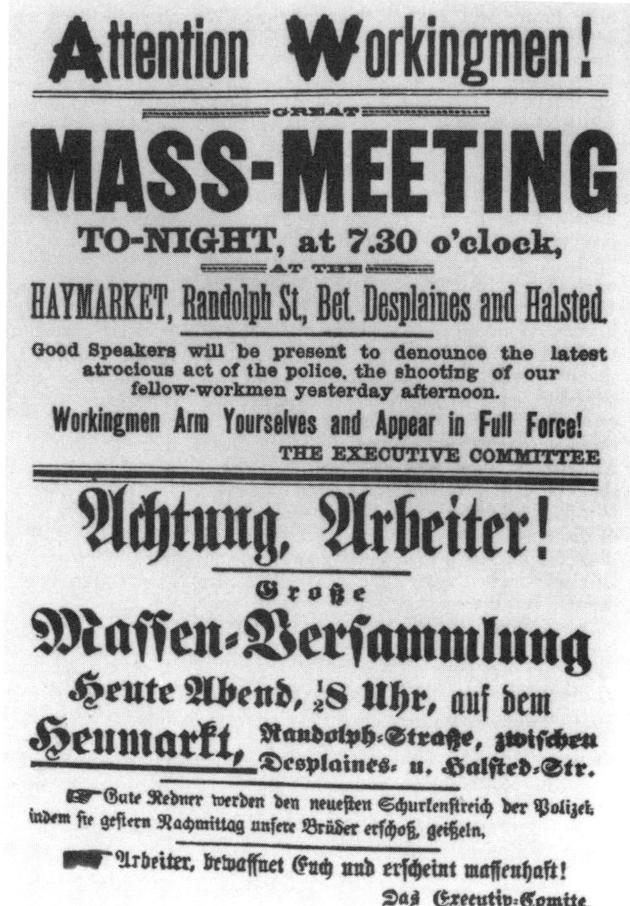

Reproduction of anarchist handbill distributed prior to the Haymarket Riot of 1886 *(Library of Congress)*

common good. However, radicals disagreed on strategy and tactics. Socialists realized that political power would be necessary to eradicate private property, but they disagreed over how to gain control of the state. One group adhered to the principles of the German socialist, Ferdinand Lassalle, which held that manhood suffrage would permit workers to gain control of the state through the electoral process. Until then, the Lassalleans would use the electoral process to win immediate goals such as the eight-hour day and low-interest loans to establish cooperatives.

The followers of Karl Marx argued that a government reflected the social order it was designed to protect, so workers could not gain control of the bourgeois state through the ballot. Their only alternative was to destroy it and replace it with a "dictatorship of the proletariat" before they could establish communism. Although the Marxists used electoral politics for agitation and propaganda purposes, they emphasized organizing workers into revolutionary unions. But Marxists could not agree on tactics. Should they capture existing labor unions, or should they establish their own? Marxist trade-union leaders such as Peter J. McGuire of the carpenters wanted to "bore within" the AMERICAN FEDERATION OF LABOR (AFL) to convert it and its affiliated members to socialism. However, SAMUEL GOMPERS, president of the AFL and a firm believer in pure and simple unionism, defeated their efforts. Socialists in 1893 also failed to capture the KNIGHTS OF LABOR. Although they dominated District Assembly 49 in New York, they only succeeded in electing James P. Sovereign, a farm editor from Iowa, as president of the Knights. Frustrated by the failure of the "boring within" tactic, Daniel De Leon, leader of the SOCIALIST LABOR PARTY (SLP), in 1895 launched a purely Marxist union, the Socialist Trade and Labor Alliance. De Leon also ordered SLP members not to accept offices in other trade unions, but that tactic forced many trade unionists to join the Lassallean SOCIALIST PARTY.

Another radical group, the anarchists, disagreed with both the Marxists and Lassalleans. They maintained that all government had to be destroyed before a true communal society could be established. American socialists with anarchist tendencies formed the Social Revolutionary Party in 1881. The following year they acquired a powerful spokesman, Johann Most. Expelled from the German Socialist Party for his radicalism, Most immigrated to America, where he became editor of the weekly New York *Freiheit.* Most's editorials condoned "propaganda by deed," or terrorism, including assassination, as a way of galvanizing the working masses into revolutionary action. In 1887 Most played an important role in the formulation of the so-called Pittsburgh Manifesto, which denounced the state as an instrument of tyranny and dismissed political action as an exercise in futility. The Pittsburgh meeting also created the American section of the International Working People's Association, the "Black International" (black being the color of anarchism and red the color of socialism), which soon claimed 8,000 members. In addition to the *Freiheit,* the anarchist press in America consisted of the Chicago *Arbeiter Zeitung* and later the *Alarm,* the Boston *Anarchist,* and the St. Louis *Voice of the People.*

The Chicago anarchists tended to be anarcho-syndicalists, or those anarchists who favored the creation of labor unions (syndicates) as the primary instruments of revolution. In 1884 they helped form the Central Labor Union, which preached open rebellion against capitalists. It quickly became embroiled in a fight for control of Chicago's labor movement with the central body of the trade unions, the Amalgamated Trades and Labor Assembly. Both sides embraced the eight-hour-day issue as an organizing device. The violent rhetoric on its behalf by the anarchists directly contributed to the HAYMARKET RIOT and the subsequent antiradical witch hunt that led to the execution of four anarchists in 1887.

Five years later another violent act increased American abhorrence toward anarchism. Angered by the HOMESTEAD STRIKE, a New York anarchist, Alexander Berkman, aided by Emma Goldman, decided to assassinate HENRY C. FRICK. The assassination attempt failed, but this propaganda by deed turned public opinion against the Homestead strikers. Ironically, Johann Most did not approve of Berkman's action, and for that repudiation he was horsewhipped by Emma Goldman, his former lover and Berkman's current one.

Further reading: John M. Laslett, *Labor and the Left: A Study of Socialist and Radical Influences in the American Labor Movement* (New York: Basic Books, 1970).

— Harold W. Aurand

labor: strikes and violence

The history of American labor-management disputes is the most violent in the world. Labor violence can best be understood when placed within the context of rights. Workers believed that by joining a union and conducting strikes, they were exercising their right to improve themselves and protect their families. Managers, on the other hand, regarded the demand that employees be granted some control over their working conditions as an invasion of their property rights.

Management employed different strategies to keep a union off its property: It could compel workers to sign a "yellow dog contract" stating they would never join a union as a condition of employment. Or, it could hire private detective agencies to spy on workers and identify labor agitators so they could be fired before organizing a union.

The Pinkerton Detective Agency was the best-known and most feared antilabor force in America during the last third of the 19th century. Founded in 1850 by Allen Pinkerton, the agency amassed the world's largest collection of mug shots by 1870 and supplemented the pictures with a large database on criminals and their activities. Pinkerton agents infiltrated a company's workforce with the goal of identifying discontents and sowing discord in established unions. These "Pinkertons" were involved as labor spies, agent provocateurs, or guards in the Anthracite Strike of 1875, the Iron Moulders Lockout of 1883, the Burlington Railroad Strike of 1888, the New York Longshoremen's Strike of 1887, the COEUR D'ALENE Strike of 1892, the HOMESTEAD STRIKE of 1892, as well as in other strikes.

Local authorities not only quelled labor disturbances but also attacked peaceful demonstrations. On December 11, 1887, New York police attacked and brutally beat members of an unarmed crowd of 7,000 as they prepared to parade through the city to demand jobs for the unemployed. In 1897 a sheriff's posse shot into a crowd of more than 200 unarmed miners as they peacefully marched down a public highway in Lattimer, Pennsylvania, killing 19 people, most of whom were shot in the back as they ran away.

However, management could not always trust local authorities, who often were elected by workers. During the GREAT STRIKE OF 1877, officials of the Lackawanna Coal and Iron Company, fearful that the city police would sympathize with the strikers, had the mayor of Scranton deputize 40 of its trusted employees as a special police force. Armed by the company and instructed by its commander, the company superintendent, "to shoot low and shoot to kill," the Special Police fired into a crowd, killing six and wounding 55. The creation of a special police force in Scranton actually was unnecessary, for in 1869 the Pennsylvania legislature gave railroad and coal companies the power to maintain their own police forces. The coal and iron police used deadly force, wounding nine, in a confrontation with strikers in Shenandoah, Pennsylvania, in 1887.

Soldiers represented the last line of employer defense. Governors willingly dispatched their militia or National Guard to strike scenes. Both the state militia and federal troops helped break the PULLMAN STRIKE of 1894. In 1896 mine operators in Leadville, Colorado, broke a strike by insisting that strikebreakers be enlisted in the Colorado National Guard and be issued weapons to defend themselves and company property.

In fact, strikers often vented their frustration against strikebreakers and company property. During the Leadville Strike, for example, a group of strikers attacked the Coronado mine and dynamited its oil storage tank. Strikers reserved most of their rage for strikebreakers, whom they denounced as scabs and blacklegs. Strikebreakers were stoned and beaten, and many were killed. Strikers justified this violence by arguing that strikebreakers were taking their jobs. The strikers believed that in going out on strike they were not quitting their jobs but, rather, they were temporarily withdrawing from work to better their pay or working conditions.

Racism also ignited labor violence. On September 2, 1885, a group of white coal miners attacked Chinese workers in Rock Springs, Wyoming, killing 28 and wounding 15 more. This massacre was rooted in racial prejudice, since it exacerbated the fear that the Chinese miners would keep wages low and sharpened the memory that 10 years earlier the Chinese had broken a strike.

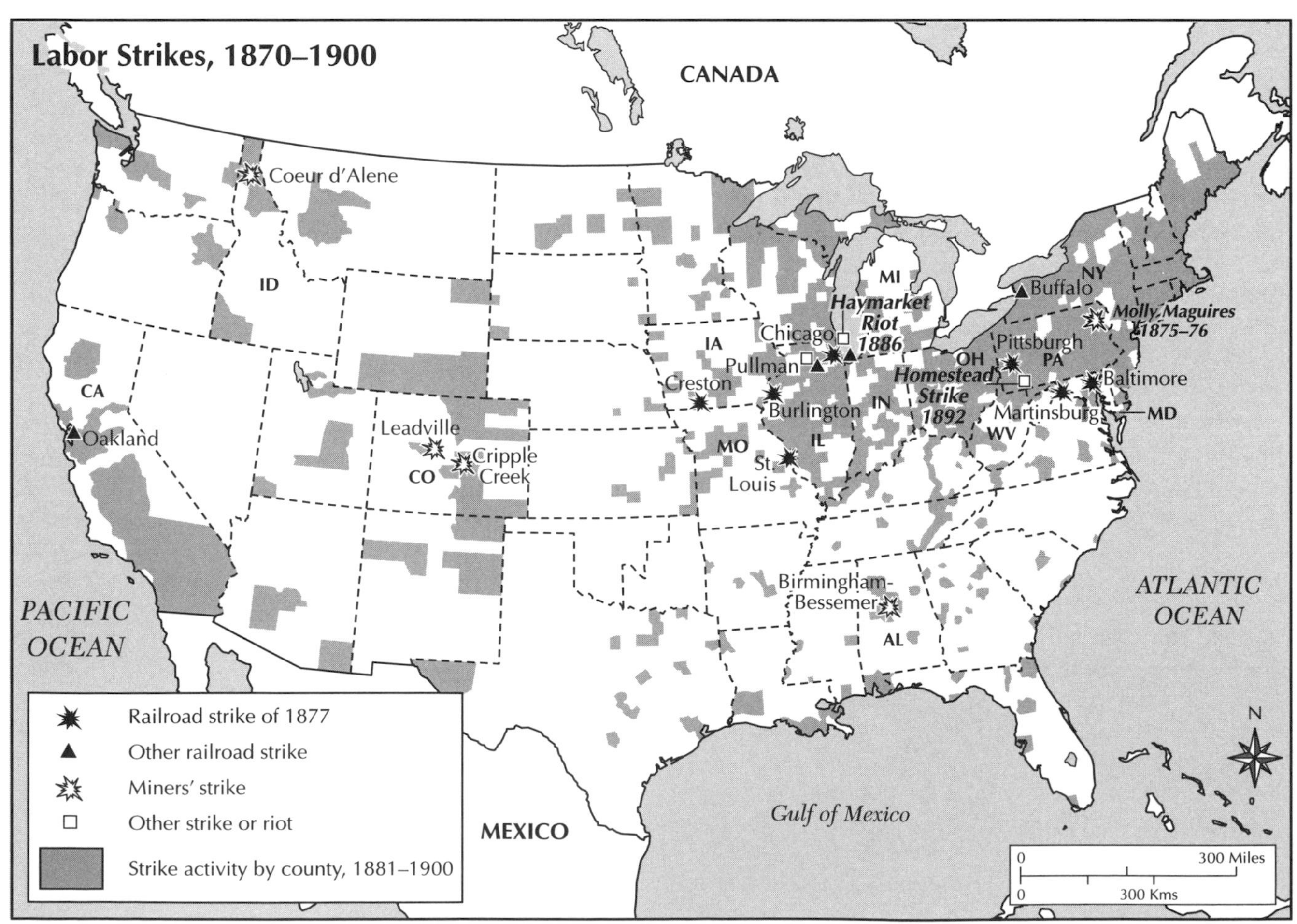

Further reading: P. K. Edwards, *Strikes in the United States, 1881–1974* (New York: St. Martin's Press, 1981); Ronald L. Filippelli, *Labor Conflict in the United States: An Encyclopedia* (New York: Garland Publishing, 1990).

— Harold W. Aurand

labor, woman

The number of women working outside the home dramatically increased between 1870 and 1900. Textile factories were among the largest employers of females, but women also found work in the expanding food-preparation, garment, and shoe industries, among others. More respectable nonmanufacturing employment opportunities also increased. The introduction of the typewriter created more than 400,000 office jobs for women. The number of females in retail sales increased nearly 20 times (from 7,462 to 142,265) between 1880 and 1900. Young single females filled most of the jobs, but after 1880 an increasing number of women either entered or remained in the labor market after marriage.

Several factors explain the trend of married women working for an income. One was the increase of jobs in retail clerking, office work, and COMMUNICATIONS (telegraph and telephone) that appealed to middle-class women. But economic necessity was the primary motive. Most working-class and lower middle-class families could not subsist on one income. The declining birth rate, particularly in nonimmigrant families, left fewer children to provide that income while freeing women from years of child-rearing responsibilities.

The working woman's contribution to her family's income was not substantial, since women suffered from wage discrimination. In 1900 male factory workers' average earnings were 75 percent more than those paid to women. The so-called respectable occupations paid even less; a female factory worker could earn two to three times as much as a retail clerk. Low wages tempted many into the nation's flourishing sex industry. In 1894 the Chicago Vice Commission investigation found that a prostitute could earn at least four times as much as a woman working in a factory.

Women attempted to improve their conditions by joining labor unions. Perhaps the best-known female trade union was the Daughters of Saint Crispin (shoemakers), founded in 1871, which conducted several successful strikes. But most trade unions ignored women. Male shoemakers, for example, belonged to the Knights of Saint Crispin. The KNIGHTS OF LABOR (Knights), however, encouraged female membership. More than 200 local assemblies were exclusively female, with the largest one, located in Cincinnati, having at least 1,000 members. Many local assemblies were gender diversified. In 1887 the Knights hired Leonora Marie Barry as its general instructor and director of women's work. Barry's investigation of working conditions of women helped shape the Pennsylvania Factory Inspection Act of 1899.

Middle-class reform groups also took an interest in improving the conditions for working women. Many reformers desired to protect them from evil influences that might tempt them into prostitution, but several addressed economic needs. The Working Women's Protective Union of New York, for example, collected unpaid wages for thousands of cheated women. Reform societies also lent their support to the passage of a variety of laws that limited the hours per week a woman could work and setting sanitation standards. But the laws were rarely enforced strictly.

Further reading: Alice Kessler-Harris, *Out to Work: A History of Wage-Earning Women in the United States* (New York: Oxford University Press, 1982).

— Harold W. Aurand

labor organizations

During the last third of the 19th century, labor organizations fell into two categories: trade unions focusing on job-related issues and reform unions seeking basic social change. Most trade unions recruited members from a single craft, such as iron molders, machinists, or carpenters. A small number organized on an industrial basis, admitting all those working in a particular industry.

Proponents of both trade and reform unions agreed on the eight-hour day. As early as 1866, representatives of trade unions, eight-hour leagues, and other reform groups founded the National Labor Union (NLU). Although it spearheaded an organizational drive that established several national trade unions, the NLU sought a better world based upon cooperatives, and it embraced the idea of a cheap currency to finance those cooperatives. In 1872 the NLU transformed itself into the Labor Reform Party, causing it to lose the support of many trade unionists. A disaster at the polls and the onslaught of the depression of 1873 caused the NLU to disintegrate. Federated into decentralized national organizations, nearly three-fourths of the trade unions existing in 1870 did not survive the economic depression of 1873–79.

The KNIGHTS OF LABOR (Knights) inherited the NLU's reform mantel. Although founded in 1869, the Knights did not become a significant organization until its membership vastly expanded as a result of the GREAT STRIKE OF 1877. It, like the NLU, envisioned the wage system being replaced by a cooperative society, and it emphasized arbitration rather than strikes. The Knights, as an inclusive union, organized all "productive people" into local assemblies that were grouped into larger district assemblies. Its general assembly and grand master workman (president) provided direction at the national level.

The disastrous 1873–79 depression forced trade-union leaders to rethink their organizational plans. One of the influential leaders of this "new unionism" was SAMUEL GOMPERS of the cigar makers. Drawing on his experience in the British trade union movement, Gompers centralized control at the national level and charged high dues to build a reserve fund and a strike fund and to cover operating expenses. Many unions also provided their members with life insurance plans, disability insurance programs, or both.

But the primary purpose of the trade union was the improvement of wages and working conditions through collective bargaining supported by the strike and boycott. The strategy required each union to exclusively control its segment, be it craft or industry, of the labor market or jurisdiction. As a result "dual unionism" (two or more unions operating in the same occupational niche) was denounced as an abomination while unions also attempted to expand their jurisdictions.

Resolution of jurisdictional disputes, combined with the need to present a united front on political issues, required a coordinating body. Citywide federations of labor unions first appeared in the 1830s, but to centralize power a national organization was necessary. In November 1881 more than 100 delegates meeting in Pittsburgh created the Federation of Organized Trade and Labor Unions of the United States and Canada (FOOTALU). The new federation was not a success; only 19 delegates attended its second convention. In an effort to revive its fortunes, FOOTALU resurrected agitation for an eight-hour day and called for a general strike on May 1, 1886, if the shorter day had not been achieved. That call resulted in the tragic HAYMARKET RIOT and failed to resuscitate the FOOTALU.

It was possible for a worker to belong to both the Knights and a trade union without an apparent conflict of interest as long as the local assembly of the Knights drew its membership from a number of occupations. But when local assemblies represented members of only one craft, they became a dual union. Soon craft assemblies and trade-union locals began raiding each other for members. The raids led to the dissolution of the weak FOOTALU and the formation of the AMERICAN FEDERATION OF LABOR (AFL) in 1886. The AFL then demanded that the Knights refuse membership to anyone working in the jurisdiction of an established trade union.

The Knights refused and ordered its single-craft locals to withdraw from their district assembly and join one of the 22 newly formed national trade assemblies. Open warfare soon broke out, with AFL unions and the Knights supplying workers to break the strikes of the other's organization. But the Knights were ill-prepared to fight such a war; its leadership was philosophically opposed to strikes, and the creation of national trade assemblies caused many trade unionists, especially those in mixed assemblies, to leave the order.

The AFL's defeat of the Knights enabled "pure and simple unionism" to prevail among labor organizations by 1900. It was pure because only working people were permitted to join and simple because it focused on economic issues, but since virtually all its members were skilled craftsmen, it was also exclusive and elitist.

Further reading: Melvin Dubofsky, *Industrialism and the American Worker, 1865–1920,* 2d ed. (Arlington Heights, Ill.: Harlan Davidson, 1985); David Montgomery, *The Fall of the House of Labor: The Workplace, the State, and American Labor Activism, 1865–1925* (New York: Cambridge University Press, 1987); Irwin Yellowitz, *Industrialism and the American Labor Movement, 1865–1900* (Port Washington, N.Y.: Kennikat, 1977).

— Harold W. Aurand

labor trends

Four major trends—loss of control over the workplace, labor conflict, rapid geographic mobility, and increasing diversity— shaped the development of American labor during the last third of the 19th century. In 1870 skilled artisans working in small shops in which they exerted a great deal of control over the productive process dominated the American industrial landscape. But the reduction of skills, already well underway, combined with mechanization to transform the shops into large impersonal factories. Diminution of skills began with the subdivision of a process into minute tasks and assigning one person to each task. At some point the reduction procedure suggested a mechanical means of replacing or supplementing human effort. The machines, mostly driven by steam, but increasingly by electricity from the late 1880s, were grouped into large factories. By 1899 two-fifths of the 512,191 industrial establishments in the United States were factories.

Mechanization dramatically increased per capita productivity; the average worker in the 1890s produced twice as much as his or her counterpart in the 1860s. But the worker lost control over the job in the factory. The machine, not the employee, set the pace of work. Deprived of the knowledge of how the productive process worked, the unskilled worker became dependent upon instructions from management. It became apparent that just as machines could be redesigned to increase efficiency, so could the worker. Frederick W. Taylor, the father of "modern management," began his scientific analysis of work behavior at the Midvale Steel Company during the 1880s. Through his and the efforts of others, the term *human engineering,* with all its questionable implications, came into vogue.

As laborers became viewed as cogs in a machine they lost their ability to determine their income. The diminution of skills rendered apprenticeship obsolete. But apprenticeship was more than an educational system that taught the novice the mysteries of a craft: It was the gate used by artisans to control entry into the job market. Moreover, workers had only their time to sell as demand for their skills declined. Without any real bargaining power in a highly competitive market, the individual worker was at the mercy of the employer.

Workers joined unions to improve their bargaining power and used the strike to enforce their demands. The number of strikes per year, of course, varied, but the pronounced trend in the Gilded Age was toward more strikes involving more people and lasting a longer period of time. There were twice as many strikes in 1895 as in 1893. In 1896 a total of 183,813 workers went on strike. Three years later, 308,267 strikers walked the picket line. Labor-management disputes often degenerated into armed conflict, as in the HOMESTEAD STRIKE. Reprisals followed strikes as employers blacklisted or identified strike leaders as unsuitable employees, forcing many to leave their communities.

Geographic mobility rates soared as workers, suffering from unemployment or looking for better jobs, moved from town to town. Waltham, Massachusetts, and Hazleton, Pennsylvania, illustrate the rapid population changes that most American communities experienced during the era: Only 17 percent of adult males living in Waltham in 1870 resided in that city in 1890. Less than half the people residing in Hazleton, Pennsylvania, in 1884 were living there in 1890. The out-migration in both cities did not indicate a population loss. Waltham's population increased from 9,065 to 11,512 between 1870 and 1890, while Hazleton's population doubled between 1880 and 1890.

IMMIGRATION fueled a large part of the population growth. More than 9 million people immigrated to the United States between 1870 and 1890. The ethnic composition of the immigrants also changed. Prior to 1870 most immigrants were from northern Europe. After 1870, however, people from eastern and southern Europe began to arrive in increasing numbers. Only 55,759 Italians came to America during the 1870s, for example, but 651,893 made the trip between 1891 and 1900.

American workers feared the "new immigrants" as cheap labor and potential strike breakers. Trade unions, dismissing them as unorganizable, sought to restrict immigration or drive them out of their job jurisdictions. In 1897 the United Mine Workers of America lobbied successfully for a law (later declared unconstitutional) that taxed anthracite coal mine operators for every alien they hired. Ethnic prejudice against Slavic, Jewish, and Italian immigrants helped taint all industrial workers as inferior and, perhaps, un-American. Racism also victimized AFRICAN-AMERICAN industrial workers. Women who were entering the workforce in increasing numbers also suffered wage discrimination.

Further reading: Melvyn Dubofsky, *Industrialism and the American Worker, 1865–1920,* 3d ed.(Wheeling Ill.: Harlan Davidson, 1996).

— Harold W. Aurand

Langston, John Mercer (1829–1897)

John Mercer Langston—lawyer, educator, and militant reformer—was born on December 14, 1829, in Louisa County, Virginia, the son of Ralph Quarles, a white planter, and Lucy Langston, his freed slave. After his parents died in 1834, Langston was raised by a white couple in Ohio and in 1844 entered the preparatory department at Oberlin College, an antislavery hotbed. There he became active in the antislavery cause, receiving his bachelor's degree in 1849 and in 1853 a graduate degree in theology. Langston did not enter the ministry (largely because the churches had failed to oppose slavery), choosing instead to read law under the tutelage of Philemon Bliss, and in 1854 he was admitted to the Ohio bar.

Langston in 1854 also helped establish the Republican Party in the Western Reserve in northeastern Ohio and married Caroline Matilda Wall, whom he had met at Oberlin. The following year he was elected town clerk in Brownhelm, Ohio, becoming the first of his race elected to office in the United States by popular vote. Technically, Langston was considered "white" because Ohio's law considered those with at least 51 percent Caucasian "blood" to be white. Langston, however, choosing to be black, optimistically wrote to Frederick Douglass that his victory "argues the steady march of the antislavery sentiment, and augurs the inevitable destruction and annihilation of American prejudice against colored men." Langston added that more black voters were needed to have political influence, for it represented "the bridle by which we can check and guide to our advantage the selfishness of American demagogues."

Langston was a militant reformer. He helped maintain Ohio's "underground railroad" for runaway slaves and in 1858 defied the Fugitive Slave Act of 1850 by participating in the rescue of John Price. In 1858 he organized and served as president of the all-black Ohio State Anti-Slavery Society. Langston also protested discrimination at home. Although Ohio's racist "black laws" had been repealed in 1848–49, AFRICAN AMERICANS still could not vote and did not have the "bridle" Langston knew they needed. Like many of his abolitionist contemporaries, Langston was an advocate of WOMEN'S RIGHTS and temperance. During the early 1850s he supported emigration and black separatism, but he changed his view after attending the 1854 Cleveland Emigration Convention and devoted his life to a vigorous defense of integration. Langston conspired with John Brown but did not participate in the latter's ill-fated 1859 raid on the federal arsenal at Harpers Ferry to arm slaves in Virginia.

Langston saw the Civil War and its aftermath as an opportunity to destroy American slavery and achieve equality for African Americans. He was a chief recruiter in the West for the Union during the war years, and from 1864 to 1868 he served as president of the all-black Equal Rights League. The Reconstruction period was both a time of opportunity and of peril for former slaves. As an inspector for the Freedmen's Bureau, Langston toured the South in 1867, urging the freedmen and women to seek education, political equality, and economic justice. In Washington, D.C., he organized Howard University's law department in 1869, and from 1873 to 1875 he served as that institution's acting president, only to resign in disappointment when he was not named its permanent president.

Langston was a leading Republican spokesman for African Americans and served that party in various capacities. As the legal officer of the District of Columbia's Board of Health (1871–77), he drew up Washington's sanitation code. He also helped Senator Charles Sumner draft the CIVIL RIGHTS ACT (1875). From 1877 to 1885 he was consul general and resident minister to Haiti. Upon returning to the United States in 1885, Langston assumed the presidency of Virginia Normal and Collegiate Institute at Petersburg, but within two years Democratic pressure forced him to resign. Langston turned to politics and decided to represent Virginia's mostly black Fourth Congressional District, but General William Mahone, a former Confederate general and Republican leader, opposed having a black man in CONGRESS. Langston ran as an independent and won a bitterly fought campaign in 1888, but the results were contested. Langston was finally admitted to Congress in 1890 but was defeated in his bid that year for reelection, serving out his "lame duck" session until March 1891.

Langston then returned to Washington where he practiced law. In 1894 he published his autobiography, *From the Virginia Plantation to the National Capitol.* When Langston died in Washington on November 15, 1897, he had—despite the current rampant disfranchisement and segregation—faith that "in the courts, by the law" African Americans would achieve the equality that was their right as citizens.

Further reading: William Cheek and Aimee Lee Cheek, *John Mercer Langston and the Fight for Black Freedom, 1829–1865* (Urbana: University of Illinois Press, 1989); Maurine Christopher, *America's Black Congressmen* (New York: Thomas Y. Crowell, 1971).

— William Seraile

Lassallean socialists

See labor, radical

Latter-day Saints, Church of Jesus Christ of

See Mormon Church

Lazarus, Emma (1849–1887)

The daughter of Moses Lazarus, a wealthy sugar merchant, and Esther Nathan Lazarus, Emma Lazarus renowned for her poem celebrating America as the refuge for the oppressed, was born in New York City on July 22, 1849, where she grew up in a cultured upper-class household. Her family descended from one of the oldest Jewish families in New York City and belonged to a Sephardic aristocracy that moved easily in wealthy Christian circles; her father joined the Vanderbilts and Astors in founding the elite Knickerbocker Club and built a fashionable summer house in Newport, Rhode Island. She received a sound classical education at home and was proficient in French, German, and all the attainments of her class.

Lazarus was devoted to literature from her childhood and began to write poetry in her early teens. Her proud father published her first collection, *Poems and Translations Written between the Ages of Fourteen and Sixteen,* in 1866, and she sent a copy of it to Ralph Waldo Emerson in 1868. Although her youthful efforts were strained and imitative, the Sage of Concord responded warmly and entered into a long-standing correspondence with her. When her second volume was commercially published in 1871, it met with excellent reviews in both the United States and England, and her 1874 novel based on the life of Goethe won praise from the eminent Russian author Turgenev. She was later to receive encouragement from such literary notables as the naturalist John Burroughs and the novelist HENRY JAMES, and during her 1883 visit to Europe she became a friend of William Morris and Robert Browning.

Lazarus, like her family, had never been observant of religious laws or rites, although in her writing she had occasionally drawn on her Judaic heritage. In her early 30s, however, she became increasingly aware of the persecution of Jews in czarist Russia and the flood of Jewish immigrants to the United States. Turning from classical topics and Teutonic legends for themes, she began to write both poetry and essays in support of her people. As anti-Semitism spread through eastern Europe, she became a spokesperson for the Jewish community, protesting its mistreatment both at home and abroad. In a series of articles entitled "An Epistle to the Hebrews" that appeared in 1882–83 in *American Hebrew,* she called on American Jews to recognize their rights, and in 1882 she published a collection of poetry entirely devoted to Jewish themes, *Songs of a Semite.*

Writing was not her only contribution to the cause. She worked actively for the Hebrew Immigration Aid Society, helped establish the Hebrew Technical Institute for Vocational Training, and in 1883 founded the Society for the Improvement and Colonization of East European Jews, calling for the establishment of a Jewish homeland in Palestine 13 years before the term *Zionism* came into use.

In 1882 Lazarus wrote the sonnet "The New Colossus" for an auction in support of the Bartholdi Pedestal Fund. Contrasting the welcoming female figure of *Liberty Enlightening the World* with the militaristic sculpture of antiquity, the poem presents America as a nurturing force, "Mother of Exiles," and helped define America's image as a haven for the oppressed in that period of open IMMIGRATION. Her best-known work, it was engraved on a plaque on the base of the STATUE OF LIBERTY in 1903. Lazarus died in New York City on November 19, 1887.

Further reading: Bette Roth Young, *Emma Lazarus in Her World: Life and Letters* (Philadelphia: Jewish Publication Society, 1995).

— Dennis Wepman

Lease, Mary Elizabeth Clyens (1850–1933)

Mary Elizabeth Lease, a stirring Populist orator, was born in Ridgeway, Pennsylvania, on September 11, 1850, to Irish immigrant parents. Her father, two brothers, and an uncle died in the Civil War, leaving the family impoverished. Friends sent her to St. Elizabeth's Academy in Allegany, New York, from which she graduated in 1868. She taught in McKean County, Pennsylvania, schools until 1870 when, having failed to unionize fellow teachers, she took a position in a Catholic girls school in Osage Mission, Kansas. In 1873 she abandoned Catholicism and married Charles L. Lease, a local druggist. Together they farmed in Kansas and Texas for 10 lonely, dreary, unsuccessful years and then settled in Wichita, Kansas, where Charles Lease resumed his career as a druggist and, to make ends meet, Mary Elizabeth—while raising four children—took in washing. The following year, in 1884, Lease, who was very bright, began studying law at home and later claimed she was admitted to the Kansas bar in 1885.

Lease was committed to egalitarian reforms and organized a women's group, the Hypatica Society, to discuss issues. She was a gifted orator with a gorgeous, moving, contralto voice, and in 1885 she began her public-speaking career by raising funds for the Irish National League and later that year advocated woman suffrage in an address to the Union Labor Party state convention. That party, a remnant of the GREENBACK-LABOR PARTY, was supported by debt-ridden Kansas farmers with whom Lease identified. By 1888 she not only spoke widely for the Union Labor Party but also edited the *Union Labor Press*. Lease joined the KNIGHTS OF LABOR and in 1891 was elected master workman (president) of a large local assembly in Kansas. By 1890 she had also stumped Kansas for the FARMERS' ALLIANCES. She spoke extemporaneously; was vehement, charismatic, prone to exaggerate; and often could not recall precisely what she said. Although renowned for telling farmers to "raise less corn and more hell," she denied having said those words, but in that spirit she aroused farmers by heaping invective upon RAILROADS, bankers, and landlords.

Although a political force, Lease was more an agitator than a politician. She seconded the nomination of James B. Weaver for president at the 1892 POPULIST PARTY convention and joined him in his campaign in the West and South. Hostile Democrats, however, made the tour of the South unsuccessful and heightened her hatred (originating during the Civil War) of that party. The Populists secured the governorship of Kansas in 1893, and Lease was appointed president of the State Board of Charities. In that same year she opposed, without success, the fusion of Populists and Democrats in the legislature. The governor, who was a fusionist, removed her in 1894 when she refused to appoint Democrats and called him a corruptionist. She sued and triumphed in the state supreme court, but for 30 years she received no restitution from the state. A leading antifusionist Populist, Lease opposed to no avail the nomination of WILLIAM JENNINGS BRYAN at the 1896 Populist convention and actually supported WILLIAM MCKINLEY. When the *New York World* hired Lease to cover the Bryan campaign and then kept her on, she left Kansas (much to the delight of her former compatriots).

Prior to Lease's defection to the Republicans, she published *The Problem of Civilization Solved* (1895). It called for a strong leader who would promote IMPERIALISM, hemispheric free trade coupled with protection, socialism, FREE SILVER, and enable the people to force the consideration and enactment of legislation, particularly the initiative and referendum. Settling in New York with her children, Lease divorced, embraced theosophy, and supported Theodore Roosevelt and progressive reforms, including woman suffrage, prohibition, and especially birth control. She died on October 29, 1933, at Callicoon, New York.

Further reading: O. Gene Clanton, *Kansas Populism: Ideas and Men* (Lawrence: University Press of Kansas, 1969); Walter T. K. Nugent, *The Tolerant Populists: Kansas Populism and Nativism* (Chicago: University of Chicago Press, 1963); Richard Stiller, *Queen of the Populists: The Story of Mary Elizabeth Lease* (New York: Crowell 1970).

legal-tender cases (1870, 1871) See currency issue

Liberal Republican Party (1872)

Ulysses S. Grant, the taciturn Civil War hero, unified the various elements in the Republican Party and triumphed in the 1868 presidential campaign. Since his views were unknown, spoils politicians, patrician reformers, merchants, manufacturers, and farmers—all with their differing interests—could hope and even surmise that he would be sympathetic to issues close to their hearts. Perhaps no group surmised more optimistically than the liberal reformers who had embraced a cluster of beliefs, including CIVIL SERVICE REFORM, free trade, the gold standard, reconciliation with the South, and anti-IMPERIALISM. Their ideal was a laissez-faire government staffed by experts, rather than political operatives, and headed by a first-rate administrator and leader who could achieve their goals. Grant, who as a general had picked able subordinates, seemed to liberal reformers to be superbly equipped for the presidency.

Grant, however, disappointed reformers. His cabinet included some reformers but also some spoils politicians, some cronies, and some wealthy men who had entertained Grant. Disappointment turned to disillusionment when his appointments to office favored the candidates of party leaders in the Senate and House, who almost invariably strengthened their political organizations and slighted the cultivated gentlemen of distinguished families who belonged to the reform wing of the party. Grant proved to be a passive leader and a weak administrator who neither dominated his cabinet nor led CONGRESS.

Worse, when he did become involved, he either was duped into supporting a scheme to corner the gold market or became obsessed with the idea of annexing Santo Domingo. For his part, Grant was not only infuriated by the reform opposition to annexation but also by the willingness of liberal reformers, despite increasing violence against blacks in the South, to ally themselves with ex-Confederates and overthrow regular Republicans in border states like Missouri. By 1871 Grant—appreciating party regularity more than independence—eliminated liberal reformers from his cabinet and their sympathizers from the civil service, allied himself with Senate spoilsmen like ROSCOE CONKLING and called for tough Ku Klux Klan legislation to protect southern black Republicans.

The Liberal Republicans—strongly supported by major urban newspapers and the intelligentsia, but also joined by a number of disgruntled spoils politicians whom Grant had ignored and alienated—moved to form their own party and to nominate a candidate acceptable to the Democrats for 1872. Meeting in Cincinnati, the Liberal Republican convention, with CARL SCHURZ presiding, endorsed civil service reform and attempted to attract white southerners and Democrats by attacking Radical Reconstruction, but did not take a strong stand on the TARIFF ISSUE.

Schurz and other reformers, along with their newspaper allies, had expected to nominate Charles Francis Adams, the son and grandson of presidents and the distinguished minister to England during the Civil War, but to their dismay the convention was stampeded into nominating HORACE GREELEY, editor of the *New York Tribune*. That nomination was ludicrous, since Greeley was hostile to civil service reform, favored a protective tariff, and was easily lampooned as the advocate of a variety of reforms, causes, and fads, ranging from abolition and utopian socialism to spiritualism and vegetarianism. Rather than support Greeley, some liberal reformers voted for Grant, others supported neither, while still others like Schurz, after much anguish, campaigned for Greeley. The Democrats "swallowed" Greeley, whom for decades they had despised, but many of them stayed home on election day. Greeley broke with tradition and spoke effectively as he campaigned vigorously, but his words could not dispel the unmerciful caricatures of THOMAS NAST in *Harper's Weekly*. Grant decisively defeated Greeley who, brokenhearted by that loss and the recent death of his wife, died within a month of the election. With its members divided and demoralized, the Liberal Republican party evaporated.

Further reading: Earle Dudley Ross, *The Liberal Republican Movement* (Seattle: University of Washington Press, 1970); John G. Sproat, *"The Best Men": Liberal Reformers in the Gilded Age* (New York: Oxford University Press, 1968).

Liberia, immigration to

In the 1820s Liberia began as a colony of the American Colonization Society, a private organization composed of whites who believed that the black race's destiny was in Africa and not in the United States. Liberia became a republic in 1847 and ranked with Haiti and Ethiopia as the world's only independent black-ruled nations. The existence of Liberia provoked a heated debate among AFRICAN AMERICANS prior to the Civil War. Emigrationists advocated a return to Africa, where they hoped to have a life free of racism and discrimination. In contrast, anti-emigrationists believed that it was their duty to remain and fight not only for greater inclusion in American life but also to eradicate slavery. Before 1860, the majority of emigrants to Liberia were slaves who were freed on the condition that they leave the country. During the Civil War, Edward W. Blyden, who emigrated years earlier from the Danish West Indies to Liberia, visited the United States and encouraged immigration to that land. But interest in emigration waned during the war and its aftermath, as many hoped that emancipation would lead to the attainment of civil and political rights.

Those hopes, however, ebbed as Radical Reconstruction gradually ended and white supremacists gained control of the South. The desire to emigrate to Africa was spurred by intimidation and atrocities perpetrated against former slaves by southerners determined to deprive blacks of the civil and political rights acquired during Reconstruction. The Liberian Exodus Joint Stock Steamship Company was organized in 1877 by Martin Delany and others in Charleston, South Carolina, but its ship—captained by an incompetent white—made only one voyage and in 1878 was seized for the payment of debts.

Interest in African emigration increased during the 1890s because of the proliferation of JIM CROW LAWS and the denial of the vote to African Americans. HENRY M. TURNER, a bishop in the African Methodist Episcopal (AME) Church, championed a back-to-Africa movement. He argued that Africa and specifically Liberia was the home of the American black and that life there would restore the dignity of African Americans. He viewed American democracy as hypocrisy and even considered the U.S. Constitution "a dirty rag, a cheat, a libel" that "ought to be spit upon by every Negro in the land." Turner believed that a limited emigration of 5,000–10,000 persons a year was feasible, and his visit to Africa in 1891 on behalf of the AME Church resulted in a series of glowing, optimistic reports on Africa's potential for immediate development by American blacks. While Turner persuaded many, his scheme was widely criticized by blacks such as BENJAMIN TUCKER TANNER. When Turner issued a call in November 1893 for a national convention to meet in Cincinnati to discuss repatriation outside of the United States, the majority of the delegates opposed emigration.

Despite the rosy views, migrants faced difficulties in getting to, and prospering in, Africa. Transportation was costly (approximately $100 per passenger), and schemes to provide it cheaply were often abortive, ill planned, and fraudulent. In 1890 Democratic senator Matthew Butler of South Carolina proposed a bill to provide free transportation for all blacks who departed the South to become citizens of another country. Although the bill had support among southern conservatives it never had any chance of passing CONGRESS. The all-black Afro-American Steamship and Mercantile Company was formed in 1893 to operate steamship service to Liberia, but it was soon dissolved, since few blacks were either able or willing to purchase $10 shares. Investors were reluctant because hustlers constantly cheated trusting African Americans into buying bogus tickets to Liberia for three dollars or some other ridiculously low price. In Arkansas, ignorant but hopeful emigrants gave thousands of dollars to two anonymous preachers who put 410 individuals on a train to Brunswick, Georgia, to meet a nonexistent ship. In 1895 would-be emigrants to Liberia were stranded in Florida waiting for free transportation. In Louisiana, defrauded persons were promised transportation to Africa for one dollar. In 1894 four whites formed the International Migration Society to capitalize on black southern interest in Liberia. Potential emigrants would pay a one-dollar membership fee and one dollar monthly until they contributed $40 to pay for steamship passage and provisions. Most of the Society's income came from forfeited payments, but it did at least transport some passengers to Liberia.

Even after successfully securing transportation to Liberia, there was no guarantee that settlers could expect success as pioneers. Charles H. J. Taylor, who was a U.S. diplomat in Liberia for four months, was so negative that he—with some exaggeration—suggested there ought to be a law imprisoning for 10 years anyone who encouraged immigration to the "black land of snakes, centipedes, fever, miasma, . . . ignorance, poverty, superstition and death." Taylor's bleak words seems appropriate for the shipload of passengers that arrived in Monrovia, Liberia, in 1895 under the auspices of the International Migration Society. No one knew that they were coming, no provisions were available for them in Monrovia, and several died soon after their arrival. In addition, there was political unrest because the dominant "mulatto clique," as the dark-skinned Edward W. Blyden termed it, was resented by "pure Negroes." Indeed, Blyden, convinced that mulattoes were troublemaking "vipers" and realizing that they would be a part of any African-American migration, renounced his earlier stand and concluded that "no greater evil could befall Africa or the Negro . . . than an exodus of Negroes from the United States."

A few other voyages to Liberia in the late 1890s repeated the failures of previous voyages. Many died from diseases or were quickly disillusioned by their pioneer experience. The International Migration Society folded in 1899 only to be followed in the 20th century by other back-to-Africa proposals, including Marcus Garvey's Universal Negro Improvement Association's aborted effort to repatriate African Americans to Liberia in the 1920s.

Further reading: Hollis R. Lynch, *Edward Wilmot Blyden:Pan-Negro Patriot, 1832–1912* (London: Oxford University Press, 1967); Floyd J. Miller, *The Search for a Black Nationality: Black Emigration and Colonization, 1787–1863* (Urbana: University of Illinois Press, 1975): Edwin Redkey, *Black Exodus: Black Nationalists and Back to Africa Movements, 1890–1910* (New Haven, Conn.: Yale University Press, 1969).

— William Seraile

libraries, public, growth of

In the late 19th century, urban public libraries developed into major repositories of scholarly books and learned journals and were at the core of the intellectual life of the nation. Apart from Harvard and Yale, universities did not possess libraries of note until the 20th century. Some of the greatest public libraries were in fact mixed enterprises based on private as well as public resources. The vast holdings of the Library of Congress, the national library of the United States, began with Thomas Jefferson's books, and the New York Public Library—the greatest city library in the world—was established in 1895 by consolidating the private Astor and the Lennox Research Libraries, which although rather snobbish were open to the public, with the bequest of SAMUEL JONES TILDEN.

During the Gilded Age, the collection of research materials documenting developments in contemporary society was regarded as the responsibility of the public library and not the university. The public libraries of wealthy cities were urged to collect "everything" including "silly, and even immoral, publications" to enable future historians to reproduce the life of the past. The earliest library aiming to fulfill that mission was the Boston Public Library, established in 1848 in part to provide that city with research facilities similar to New York's Astor Library. It was freely open to all. Justin Winsor, the head of Boston Public Library from 1868 to 1877, urged the collection of newspapers, periodicals, pamphlets, local historical materials, and genealogical records. Public libraries in Cleveland, Philadelphia, Detroit, and St. Louis also expanded their general collections and added to their research holdings during the Gilded Age. The Chicago Public Library—established shortly after the disastrous fire of 1871 and headed by William F. Poole, an outstanding bibliographer—did not achieve his hope that it would become the immense Midwestern research center, but it did acquire some scholarly resources and in 1897 established a working arrangement with two private research libraries (the Newberry, specializing in the humanities, and the John Crerar, specializing in science and technology).

By 1900 several huge public library buildings had either been completed recently or were under construction. The new building of the Boston Public Library opened its doors in 1895. The new home for the Library of Congress, completed in 1897, was the largest and most expensive library building in the world. In 1897 the Chicago Public Library also moved into its new building, and the contract was signed for the construction for the great marble repository of the New York Public Library. The development of great library collections, accessible to all and housed in monumental temples, reflected the economic wealth, cultural aspirations, and democratic values of American society.

Further reading: Phyllis Dain and John Y. Cole, *Libraries and Scholarly Communication in the United States: The Historical Dimension* (New York: Greenwood Press, 1990); Phyllis Dain, *The New York Public Library: A History of Its Founding and Early Years* (New York: New York Public Library, 1972).

literature

The last third of the 19th century saw the emergence of mass literature in America along with profound shifts in the style and content of serious writing. MAGAZINES were the principal purveyors of literature for the masses. At midcentury, most fiction and poetry appeared first in the leading magazines, but after the Civil War new magazines proliferated, increasing 10-fold by 1900 as new modes of distribution enabled them to reach a larger audience. Book publication also expanded significantly, though prior to 1891 many titles were by foreign authors, largely because the absence of international copyright protection enabled American publishers to reprint cheap editions of foreign works without paying for the rights. The International Copyright Law of 1891 ended that practice and enlarged the market for American authors.

American popular literature during the middle and late years of the 19th century was rigidly gendered. Women, who took the greatest interest in literature, generally preferred sentimental romances full of melodramatic incidents and moral uplift, and book publishers and magazine editors catered to their tastes. Men usually preferred DIME NOVELS depicting the heroic (and often violent) activities of detective Nick Carter, frontiersman Buffalo Bill (WILLIAM F. CODY), and other adventurers.

In the realm of serious literature, most American fiction in the years between 1870 and 1900 conformed to one or another of three major paradigms: the genteel tradition, realism, and naturalism. The genteel tradition, which upheld the traditional values associated with VICTORIANISM, prevailed in the 1870s. During the 1880s realists launched a literary revolution with their controversial but authentic depictions of the people, places, and circumstances that genteel writers preferred to ignore. Realism, by focusing attention on the dilemmas and hardships of common Americans, prepared the way for the naturalism of the 1890s, with its emphasis on socioeconomic or biological determinism in the struggle for survival.

The genteel tradition was the literary standard during the second half of the 19th century; respectability was its hallmark. Originally, such writing was mostly by and for white Anglo-Saxon Protestants, especially those of the eastern establishment. It reflected their notions of art, propriety—even reality. Genteel culture was cosmopolitan and Anglophile (Victorian) in taste and Germanic (Idealist) in philosophy. Through quality magazines such as *The Century, The North American Review, Harper's Monthly,* and *The Atlantic Monthly,* elite literary preferences infiltrated the cultured elements of the middle class. Editors of those magazines—Richard Henry Stoddard, George Boker, Richard Watson Gilder, Edmund Clarence Stedman, and Thomas Bailey Aldrich—were guardians of the genteel tradition and arbiters of literary taste. Indeed, Aldrich, as novelist, poet, and editor of *The Atlantic Monthly* from 1881 to 1890, was the acknowledged master of the genteel style and, for a time, the nation's most esteemed author. Thanks to Aldrich and other leading editors, American literature was no longer the exclusive domain of literary ladies and gentlemen of the eastern elite; it had become a profession. Readers came to expect literature that was well-crafted, traditional in form, high-minded in content, and full of highly selective, even idealized, depictions of reality, whether the setting was American or, as it often was, international.

Even during the 1870s, however, the genteel tradition came under attack. It had grown formulaic, effete, and out of touch with a nation experiencing turbulent social, economic, and technological changes. This apparent indifference to contemporary issues merely masked anxieties about social and cultural pluralism. Try as they might to preserve the ideal of a unified culture, literary traditionalists could not hold back the tide. An emerging generation of writers and critics called for a new fiction, something distinctly American in style and content, a literature that would portray the nation in all its specificity and diversity. This critique of the genteel tradition heralded the rise of realism.

Although scholars have found realistic elements in the literature of the 1850s, realism did not become a vital force until the 1880s. American realism of the late 19th century was the product of philosophical materialism, the influence of French novelists Gustave Flaubert and Emile Zola, and the unwillingness of the genteel writers and editors to face the realities of American life. Unlike genteel writers, who idealized their subjects, realists valued objectivity. They tried to render "lifelike" or "factual" accounts of ordinary people in the varied circumstances and settings that constituted the new America. Rarely, if ever, had American writers been so responsive to social, political, and economic issues as during the last two decades of the 19th century. HELEN HUNT JACKSON depicted mistreatment of NATIVE AMERICANS. Albion W. Tourgee, George Washington Cable, and Charles W. Chesnutt, the first important AFRICAN-AMERICAN novelist, reconnoitered the racial divide. Tourgee and John W. DeForest explored sectional reconciliation in the aftermath of the Civil War. DeForest, HENRY ADAMS, Charles Dudley Warner, and MARK TWAIN (Samuel Langhorne Clemens) detailed the corrupt ways of politicians. Charlotte Perkins Gilman, Elizabeth Stuart Phelps, and Kate Chopin challenged conventional views of domesticity, while Mary Wilkins Freeman chronicled strong-willed women who faced adversity with courage and independence. JOHN HAY and Henry F. Keenan presented opposing perspectives on labor unrest. HAMLIN GARLAND and Harold Frederick chronicled "the ugliness, the drudgery, and the loneliness" of farm life on the Great Plains. Abraham Cahan wrote of the immigrant experience. WILLIAM DEAN HOWELLS delineated issues of class, especially the phenomenon of upward mobility in an age of new fortunes.

Howells was the pivotal figure in the realistic movement. Despite his strong ties to the major authors and editors of the genteel tradition, Howells used his prestige as editor of *The Atlantic Monthly* during the 1870s and columnist for *Harper's Monthly* during the 1880s to promote the new literary aesthetic. Howells's novels—*A Modern Instance* (1882), *The Rise of Silas Lapham* (1885), and *A Hazard of New Fortunes* (1890)—bridged the genteel and realist traditions. As a leading critic he encouraged realists to democratize American literature by including characters of various classes, regions, occupations, and ethnic backgrounds. Above all, he advanced the careers of innovative and talented realists, including Mark Twain, Henry James, and STEPHEN CRANE, who would remake American literature.

Twain emerged as the foremost practitioner of regional realism, which introduced readers to the distinctive natural environments, customs, folklore, and dialects of provincial America. Sarah Orne Jewett's Maine, George Washington Cable's New Orleans, Hamlin Garland's Middle Border, E. W. Howe's country town, Joel Chandler Harris's rural Georgia, and Bret Harte's mining frontier are notable examples of regional realism. Twain's masterpiece, *The Adventures of Huckleberry Finn* (1884), drew on the author's experiences along the great Mississippi River. In Twain's hands, this seemingly innocuous genre, which was sometimes merely quaint, humorous, or nostalgic, became a medium for exposing the self-deceptions and distortions of reality that perpetuated racism.

Henry James did not invent international realism, but he perfected the genre. In *Roderick Hudson (1876), The American (1877), Daisy Miller* (1878), and other novels, he isolated aspects of the national character by placing his Americans in foreign social settings. Because James wrote almost exclusively about the genteel classes, he sometimes is mistakenly associated with the genteel tradition. But in his greatest works, such as *The Portrait of a Lady* (1881), he subtly but mercilessly deconstructed the self-serving myth of genteel society—that propriety is a hallmark of good moral character.

Stephen Crane is best known for the poetic images and psychological realism of his great Civil War novel, *The Red Badge of Courage* (1895), but no less important was his classic of urban realism, *Maggie: A Girl of the Streets* (privately printed in 1893, published in 1896). Like many early realists, Crane was a newspaperman. He drew upon his knowledge of New York City's slums to write his powerful and shocking account of a fragile young woman's degradation and death. Crane's use of violent incidents and street language, as well as his references to prostitution, broke new ground in American fiction but at the cost of offending critics and readers.

Though it often went beyond the bounds of social propriety, realism did not rule out virtue or self-determination in human affairs. Naturalism, which in many ways resembled realism, had no place for morality or free will. Grounded in the ideas of Herbert Spencer and Charles Darwin, naturalism posited a deterministic universe in which people are at the mercy of inexorable socioeconomic or natural forces. Frank Norris's *McTeague* (1899) and Theodore Dreiser's *Sister Carrie* (1900) are classics of the genre.

Two idiosyncratic but indispensable authors wrote as if realism and naturalism were nonexistent. Ambrose Bierce's tall tales and stories of war and horror were experiments in improbability, the very antithesis of realism. Herman Melville's *Billy Budd* was a true anomaly: set in 1797; written in Melville's rich 1850s manner; composed between 1888 and 1891; and left unfinished at his death, only to be recovered and published in the 1920s. His tale of innocence and evil, justice and order, has layers of allusion and meaning that make all but the best realism and naturalism seem constricted and superficial.

Also outside realism and naturalism were the utopian novelists. Troubled by the social discord that they attributed to contemporary capitalism's plutocratic power structure, its unseemly scramble for wealth, and its economic inequities, many authors were moved to create projections of a better society. The second half of the 19th century saw the publication of no fewer than 48 utopian novels, nearly all of which preached that collectivism and futuristic technologies could bring about economic justice and social harmony. EDWARD BELLAMY'S *Looking Backward, 2000–1887* (1888) spawned a movement to nationalize industry. *A Traveler from Altruria* (1894) by William Dean Howells was a socialist tract. *Caesar's Column* (1890), Ignatius Donnelly's strange futuristic novel, projected apocalyptic destruction as the necessary prelude to a better world.

Unlike the fiction of the period, which by and large was committed to finding new ways to depict contemporary reality, poetry was generally traditional in form and content. American poetry typically conformed to British models and appeared indifferent to the issues that energized contemporary fiction. Poets of the well-entrenched genteel tradition (classical, formalist, idealist, elitist, and cosmopolitan) frequently treated their own time and place by indirection, reconstructing legendary tales and classical symbols to illuminate moral or spiritual dilemmas. Sidney Lanier, the most highly regarded poet of the age, glorified the chivalric tradition. He was a supreme technician who infused his work with musicality and sensory imagery. Other notable traditionalists were George Cabot Lodge, Richard Hovey, and three Harvard poets—Trumbull Stickney, William Vaughn Moody, and George Santayana (though Santayana later criticized the genteel tradition for being "grandmotherly" and "sedate").

Genteel poetry coexisted with a Whitmanesque strain that was less formal, more passionate, democratic in spirit, and regional in outlook. Joaquin Miller was a self-promoting poet who fancied himself the Walt Whitman of the West. He had the manner, but not the talent, as *Song of the Sierras* (1871) revealed. Whitman himself survived into this era (he died in 1892) but wrote no major poetry in his last years. His most important contribution to the literature of the Gilded Age was a work of prose, *Democratic Vistas* (1871).

Most Americans favored neither genteel nor Whitmanesque poems, but some version of popular poetry. It was usually brief, simple in form, and humorous or sentimental in tone. James Whitcomb Riley, America's best-selling poet, was the master of the genre. His *The Old Swimmin' Hole and 'Leven More Poems* (1883) is a representative collection.

Three noteworthy poets elude categorization. Stephen Crane, in *The Black Riders* (1895) and *War Is Kind* (1899), experimented with parable and free verse to attack conventional religious faith, uplift, and optimism. His iconoclastic tone and precise imagery anticipated the modernists of the first quarter of the 20th century. Herman Melville (1819–91), virtually unknown during these years, nevertheless wrote the most ambitious poem of the era. *Clarel* (1876), a spiritual epic about a pilgrimage to the Holy Land, explored the major philosophical and theological concerns of the latter 19th century. EMILY DICKINSON, nearly all of whose work was published posthumously during the 1890s and neglected from about 1900 to World War I, had little effect on her contemporaries, though she is today the best-known poet of her age. Deceptively simple but powerful in image and emotion, Dickinson's lyrics are a remarkable record of emotions, insight, and observation. Notwithstanding the poems of Crane, Melville, and Dickinson, the great periods of American poetry were in the recent past (the American renaissance of the 1850s) and the immediate future (modernism).

The legacy of fiction was more substantial. At the level of individual talent, it produced three writers of genius and originality: Crane, James, and Twain. Realism and naturalism generated a vivid fictional record of a pluralistic nation in turbulent times. The topical novels of the period documented the decline of Victorianism and the emergence of modern attitudes about race, class, gender, marriage, and morality, while Edward Bellamy's utopianism profoundly influenced American notions of the good society. And Melville, the forgotten man of the American Renaissance, left behind a remarkable "buried treasure" to be unearthed by future generations. Add to these accomplishments the poetry of Emily Dickinson, and it would not be unreasonable to assert that from 1870 through 1900 American writers brought forth a body of work that was unsurpassed by any other period in the nation's literary history.

Further reading: Philip Fisher, *Still the New World: American Literature in a Culture of Creative Destruction* (Cambridge, Mass.: Harvard University Press, 1999); Howard Mumford Jones, *The Age of Energy: Varieties of American Experience, 1865–1915* (New York: Viking Press, 1971); Jay Martin, *Harvests of Change: American Literature, 1865–1914* (Englewood Cliffs, N.J.: Prentice-Hall, 1967); David E. Shi, *Facing Facts: Realism in American Thought and Culture, 1850–1920* (New York: Oxford University Press, 1995); Eric J. Sundquist, *To Wake the Nations: Race in the Making of American Literature* (Cambridge, Mass.: Harvard University Press, 1993).

— William Hughes

Lloyd, Henry Demarest (1847–1903)

Henry Demarest Lloyd, a social reformer, was born in New York City on May 1, 1847, the son of Aaron Lloyd and Marie Christie Demarest. A graduate of Columbia College (1867) and Columbia Law School (1869), Lloyd was admitted to the New York bar and then became involved in reform causes. From 1869 to 1872 he was assistant secretary of the American Free Trade League and a member of the Young Men's Municipal Reform Association.

In 1872 the *Chicago Tribune* hired Lloyd as its literary editor. A year later, he married Jessie Louise Bross, with whom he had four children. In 1874 Lloyd became the paper's financial editor and in 1880 was promoted to the position of chief editorial writer. Much of Lloyd's editorial work for the *Tribune* was concerned with the growth of TRUSTS and monopolies and the problems faced by the burgeoning labor movement. In 1881 the *Atlantic Monthly* published Lloyd's article "The Story of a Great Monopoly," in which Lloyd exposed the advantageous rates (rebates) the Standard Oil Company, with its huge shipments, secured from the Pennsylvania Railroad. This article was a great success and earned Lloyd a reputation as "the first muckraker." His subsequent articles revealed Lloyd to be a relentless champion of government regulation, independent competition, consumer rights, social reform, and the American worker.

In 1885 Lloyd resigned from the *Tribune* to work full time for social reform. Following the 1886 HAYMARKET RIOT and the conviction of anarchists (accused of throwing a bomb that killed police officers), he became involved in a clemency movement that succeeded in commuting the death sentences of two anarchists. Throughout the 1890s, Lloyd's interest in the labor-industrial conflicts of the day intensified. In 1893 he became an unofficial organizer of the Milwaukee streetcar workers and defended the actions of Eugene V. Debs and the American Railway Union during the PULLMAN STRIKE of 1894. Lloyd's involvement with the American labor movement led to the publication of his *Wealth against Commonwealth* (1894), denouncing monopolies and their socially destructive practices. Lloyd also became actively involved in the PEOPLE'S PARTY (Populist Party) and ran unsuccessfully for CONGRESS in 1894 on a Chicago Labor-Populist fusion ticket. That loss and the eventual absorption of the Populists by the DEMOCRATIC PARTY led Lloyd to abandon his plan of bringing about social reform through national politics. Embracing "social democracy," Lloyd supported cooperatives as alternatives to monopolistic corporations, advocated municipal ownership of utilities, and favored compulsory collective bargaining in labor management disputes. Lloyd died in Chicago on September 28, 1903.

See also PROGRESSIVISM IN THE 1890s.

Further reading: Chester Destler, *Henry Demarest Lloyd and the Empire of Reform* (Philadelphia: University of Pennsylvania Press, 1963); Richard Digby-Junger, *The Journalist as Reformer: Henry Demarest Lloyd and Wealth against Commonwealth* (Westport, Conn.: Greenwood Press, 1996); E. Jay Jernigan, *Henry Demarest Lloyd* (Boston: Twayne, 1976).

— Phillip Papas

lobbies and pressure groups

Lobbies and pressure groups conjure up images of smooth operators either corrupting or bullying sleazy or hapless members of CONGRESS to secure legislation profiting their clients at the expense of the commonwealth. The images are not completely fair, since there are interest groups whose main concern is the commonwealth and, for that matter, lobbyists representing selfish interests may rely on attractively packaged information rather than on bribes or strong-arm tactics. In any event, whether fair or foul means are relied upon, lobbies and pressure groups are an informal, but genuine, part of the legislative process, and they achieved significance during the Gilded Age.

After the Civil War, the federal government encouraged the building of RAILROADS, protected industries, and rewarded veterans. Bills to accomplish these objectives originated in an inexperienced Congress that was scarcely equipped to deal with them. Most congressmen served only a few terms, if that many, and had no staff to research the ramifications of pending legislation except for the clerks of the committees on which they served. Lobbyists were only too glad to educate legislators. For example, the Pacific Railway Act of 1862, with its generous land grants and loans to the Union Pacific and Central Pacific

Railroads, was essentially written by Theodore D. Judah, a railroad engineer and a lobbyist for the Central Pacific whose expertise had secured him the positions of secretary of the Senate Committee and clerk of the House Committee on Railroads.

The power of the lobby can be overstated. Judah could shape the Railway Act because Congress wanted a transcontinental railroad. The efforts of the supposedly powerful Texas & Pacific Railroad lobby to secure a land grant by resolving the 1876–77 disputed election in favor of RUTHERFORD B. HAYES neither affected the outcome (despite what some historians believe) nor secured a land grant. The Democrats dared not extend their filibuster and plunge the nation into chaos, while Hayes was not interested in giving any more public lands to railroads. The most celebrated lobbyist of the Gilded Age, Samuel Ward, apparently was hired by railroads, steamship lines, and manufacturers to secure land grants, subsidies, and favorable tariff rates, and he had the good business sense to encourage his reputation as the "King of the Lobby." The extent of his influence, however, can only be surmised, since he had all his papers relating to lobbying destroyed.

Lobbyists were effective, but only in details of policies Congress had embraced. Thus, James M. Swank, the arch-protectionist lobbyist of the American Iron and Steel Association, did influence tariff legislation by issuing millions of tariff tracts beginning in 1876. Swank was a statistician who relied on education, but John E. Searles Jr., lobbyist for the Henry O. Havemeyer sugar trust, did more than inform Senator Nelson W. Aldrich, who took care that the tariff schedules reflected the interests of eastern sugar refiners: The sugar trust lent Aldrich enough money to acquire the street railways in Providence, Rhode Island, and made him a wealthy man. Aldrich was not purchased, since in any event he would have manipulated the tariff to benefit eastern manufacturers, but he profited in a corrupt fashion from his powerful position.

Lobbyists also tried to influence executive departments and represented humble people. For example, a major portion of BELVA LOCKWOOD's law practice in Washington, D.C., dealt with representing veterans in presenting pension claims.

Further reading: Lately Thomas, *Sam Ward: "King of the Lobby"* (Boston: Houghton Mifflin, 1965); Margaret Susan Thompson, *The "Spider Web": Congress and Lobbying in the Age of Grant* (Ithaca, N.Y.: Cornell University Press, 1985).

Lockwood, Belva Ann Bennett McNall
(1830–1917)

Born in Royalton, New York, on October 24, 1830, Belva Ann Lockwood was the first woman allowed to practice before the U.S. SUPREME COURT. She began teaching in local schools at the age of 15 and in 1848 married Uriah H. McNall, a sawmill operator who died accidentally five years later. To support herself and their daughter, she returned to teaching and furthered her own education by attending Genesee College. After graduating with honors in 1857, she became the principal of the Lockport, New York, Union school. An innovative educator and a believer in WOMEN'S RIGHTS (she met SUSAN B. ANTHONY), Lockwood broadened the curriculum for women with liberating courses in public speaking and gymnastics. After teaching in other New York schools, Lockwood moved to Washington, D.C., in 1866 and established one of its first coeducational schools. Two years later she married Ezekiel Lockwood, who took over the administration of her school while she pursued her ambition to become a lawyer.

Lockwood overcame great obstacles in that pursuit. Her applications to law schools were rejected (one because she would divert the attention of male students from their studies) until 1871, when the newly established National University Law School admitted her and some other women. In 1873, however, that school tried to deny a diploma to her and to another woman who had completed her training, since the male graduates did not want to graduate with women. Lockwood appealed to President Ulysses S. Grant, the ex-officio president of the school, who not only saw that the women received their degrees but also that Lockwood was immediately admitted to the District of Columbia bar. She began her practice of law only to have the federal Court of Claims refuse to allow her to plead a case before it, and her petition to practice before the SUPREME COURT was denied in 1876 on the grounds that women traditionally did not practice before it. Undeterred, Lockwood lobbied CONGRESS and in 1879, with the support of Senators Aaron A. Sargent and GEORGE FRISBIE HOAR, it passed an act entitling women to practice before the Supreme Court. In that same year, Lockwood became the first woman allowed to practice law before the Supreme Court.

While advancing the rights of women in her profession, Lockwood also fought for the rights of all women. In 1867 she helped organize the Universal Franchise Association in Washington, and in the 1870s she was especially active in the National Woman Suffrage Association (NWSA). By circulating petitions, she helped secure legislation guaranteeing equal pay for female federal employees.

Lockwood believed that independent political action by women was the best way to achieve equal rights. Accordingly, she spoke in favor of VICTORIA WOODHULL's presidential candidacy in 1872, and when that collapsed she supported the LIBERAL REPUBLICAN candidate Horace Greeley. In 1884 Lockwood made Anthony and other suffragists in the NWSA who were working through the

Republican Party unhappy when she accepted the presidential nomination of the Equal Rights Party on a platform of equality for all, woman suffrage, uniform marriage and divorce laws, CIVIL SERVICE REFORM, veterans pensions, prohibition, and peace. Although she polled only a little more than 4,000 votes, she and her cause received much publicity, and in 1888 she ran again for the Equal Rights Party. Indeed, her law practice, which concentrated on pension claims, prospered as a result of her candidacies.

Lockwood never gave up on woman suffrage, but her candidacies had soured her relations with the suffragists, and she began to concentrate her energies on world peace through the arbitration of disputes. She belonged to the Universal Peace Union, was a delegate to international peace congresses, and served on the nominating committee of the Nobel Peace Prize. In her final year she campaigned for Woodrow Wilson because he had kept the United States out of war. She died in Washington on May 19, 1917, one month after the United States entered World War I.

Further reading: Madeleine Stern, *We the Women: Career Firsts of Nineteenth-Century America* (Lincoln: University of Nebraska Press, 1962).

lynching

The popular image of lynching, which occurred with great frequency in the Gilded Age, includes a white mob, a black victim, and a rope for hanging. In reality, lynching is more complicated and more consequential. Stripped down to basics, lynching is murder—killing outside the law, destroying a life without due process. It involves, in historian Leon Litwack's words, the "slow, methodical, sadistic, often highly inventive forms of torture and mutilation." Historically, it almost always included a mob—a loosely organized, emotionally aroused group of white men from all walks of life (occasionally with women and children cheering from the sidelines)—pursuing a black man alleged to have committed a crime or shown disrespect to whites. Mob leaders and participants came together to uphold the standards of society as they saw them; from a more objective perspective, the allegations were unproved, the standards discriminatory, and the objective the denigration of human beings of a different skin color.

While lynching generally meant murder by hanging, white mobs also used guns, whips, fire, and other methods to kill and torture their prey. Most victims were AFRICAN-AMERICAN men, but sometimes a white man or woman was lynched. Most lynchings took place in the South, but occasionally lynch mobs north of the Mason-Dixon line mobilized for the slaughter. The statistics on lynching do not include unreported lynching events; as a result, the available data document what was presumably only a fraction of violent black deaths at the hands of whites.

Most lynching victims were African-American men, such as the one in this photograph. *(Library of Congress)*

Early in 1882 the *Chicago Tribune* began to publish what became its annual accounting of lynchings. It is the initial source of reported lynchings; other sources appeared later, but reports of lynchings prior to 1882 are reconstructed and not contemporary accounts. After the Civil War, the Ku Klux Klan held their lynching parties well before the *Tribune* started counting. By the end of Reconstruction, southern whites, again in control of their states, saw lynching as a positive pressure to keep blacks subordinated and disciplined. By that time, a recent study concluded, the familiar imagery of organized night-riding terrorists was succeeded, at least in part, by the passionate violence of lynch-mob justice. The *Chicago Tribune*'s first tabulation recorded 44 southern lynchings; 34 of the victims were black. The numbers grew in a jagged sequence, reaching highs in the four years between 1891 and 1894 (121, 129, 116, 117). The occasional lynchings outside of the 10 southern states are not recorded.

One analysis suggests that there were four distinct types of lynching: Small mobs of less than 50 persons can be classified as either terrorist or private. The terrorist mob, like the Ku Klux Klan or night riders, specialized in flogging victims, burning their homes, and chasing them out of town. Death was a frequent side effect. Private mobs ranged in numbers from a very few up to 50, and their object was vengeance for real or imagined acts. Death was an invariable consequence. Neither of these two mob types pretended that they were supporting the law.

A third type was the posse, a familiar feature of early western movies. In the South, a lynching posse could number from a handful of people to hundreds. They hunted their victims down in the belief that they were upholding the law and then stepped over the line by killing their victim without a trial. A fourth type was the mass mob, consisting of anywhere from 50 persons to, on rare occasions, thousands. Generally, their pursuit was brief, a day or less, brutal, and sometimes marked with great ceremony. The bodies of victims were often dismembered and the parts—a finger or an ear, for example—claimed by lynchers and onlookers as mementos of the chase.

Determining the causes of irrational acts of lynching has intrigued historians and social scientists for generations, but the explanations are still inconclusive. Lynchers often boasted that their act would deter other black Americans from breaking the law or the white-established social code. On a more analytical level, many white workers and white planters feared that African Americans offered competition in the labor market and the voting booth, and lynchings reminded black Americans to stay in their place. African Americans who struggled out of the pit of poverty to own land and a small farm threatened the status of lower-class whites who were less successful economically or socially. The coincidence of lynching to cotton prices and production is demonstrable. More lynchings in the 1880s and 1890s took place in states heavily dependent upon cotton when its prices were sliding, but it is difficult to verify a cause-and-effect relationship.

Lynching was a grim exposure of white apprehensions. It is clear that as a general rule after the end of slavery, whites deemed that a strict structure of social control was essential to keep African Americans a servile, voteless, laboring underclass. Until disfranchisement and a rigid segregation were securely in place by the beginning of the 20th century, maintaining control could be nerve-wracking. It is more than coincidental that when those controls were firmly fixed, the number of lynchings began a slow decline. Nevertheless, it is perplexing to unravel the intricate and complex motivations that led mobs of men to murder.

Given the overwhelming numbers of whites and the fear that the lynching process generated, it was impossible for family and friends to protect an intended victim or to retaliate. In 1892, however, a young African-American woman editor of a weekly paper in Memphis had had enough killing and lashed out in her paper about "a town which will neither protect our lives and property, nor give us a fair trial in the courts, but takes us out and murders us in cold blood when accused by white persons." IDA B. WELLS-BARNETT was chased out of Memphis for her verbal attack and her newspaper office destroyed. She settled in the North and became the leading and loudest voice to attack lynching and its perpetrators in speeches, newspaper articles, and pamphlets, even traveling to England to stir antilynching sentiment across the Atlantic. Six years later, when a changing Wilmington, North Carolina, political situation depended on racial cooperation, whites used their greater numbers to instigate a riot that killed an estimated 300 African Americans, caused thousands to flee for their lives, and introduced an intransigent segregated society. Hopelessly outnumbered, black Americans tried to fight back against insurmountable odds. Whether or not the Wilmington battle set a precedent, African Americans have since that time increasingly stood up for their rights despite riots, lynchings, segregation, and other forms of racism. It was this growing strength of resistance that helped to limit lynching and call attention to more subtle forms of racism.

The first year of the new millennium continued the renewed interest in the study of lynching. *Witness,* a dramatic photographic exhibit, was mounted in New York City, and *Without Sanctuary,* a book of photographs and essays, was published and praised. What should people take away from the exhibit?, the gallery owner was asked. "Questions," he replied. "Questions about our culture, our history, our times." What did one reviewer think of the book? It was, she said, "the gift of knowledge, the chance for greater consciousness and caring."

Further reading: W. Fitzhugh Brundage, *Lynching in the New South: Georgia and Virginia, 1880–1930.* (Urbana: University of Illinois Press, 1993); Stewart E. Tolnay and E. M. Beck, *A Festival of Violence: An Analysis of Southern Lynchings, 1882–1930* (Urbana: University of Illinois Press, 1995).

— Leslie H. Fishel jr.

M

MacDowell, Edward Alexander (1860–1908)

In his own time, Edward MacDowell was considered to be the first great American composer, and he was the first American-born composer whose works were published and widely performed in Europe. MacDowell was born in New York City on December 18, 1860, the third son of Thomas and Frances Knapp McDowell. (MacDowell changed the spelling of the family name in the late 1870s.) He began piano lessons at the age of eight with Juan Buitrago, a Colombian violinist who was a boarder in the McDowell home. He also took occasional lessons from the young Venezuelan pianist Teresa Carreo, who later became a champion of his music. Showing exceptional promise, at the age of 16 he moved to Paris with Buitrago and his mother to continue his studies. He won a scholarship and full admission to the Paris Conservatory in 1877. In 1879 he entered the Hoch Conservatory in Frankfort, where he studied composition with conservatory director Joachim Raff. He left the conservatory after one year but remained in Germany, composing, teaching, and performing until 1888. In 1884 he was married to Marian Nevins in New York, after which the couple returned to Germany and settled in Wiesbaden. He was strongly encouraged by Franz Liszt, who recommended his works for performance and publication. During these years in Germany, he composed prolifically, completing many works for piano, songs, part-songs, two piano concerti, the *Romanz* for cello and orchestra, and three orchestral tone poems.

In 1888 MacDowell and his wife returned to the United States and settled in Boston, where his reputation was quickly established. Within a year, he had performed his Second Piano Concerto, op. 23, with the Boston Symphony Orchestra under Wilhelm Gericke and in New York with an orchestra under the direction of Theodore Thomas. During his years in Boston, he continued to compose, teach, and perform, and his music was heard frequently in American concert halls. In 1896 MacDowell moved to New York City to accept appointment as the first professor of music at Columbia University. For the next eight years he devoted himself tirelessly to the creation of a music department. In addition to his academic responsibilities, he conducted the Mendelssohn Glee Club, a prominent New York men's chorus. From 1899 to 1900 he served as president of the newly formed Society of American Musicians and Composers. MacDowell resigned his position at Columbia in 1904 following a dispute with the university president, Nicholas Murray Butler. By 1905 he was showing signs of the mental illness that plagued him during his last years. He died of paresis (general paralytica) in New York City on January 23, 1908.

Although MacDowell was an American composer, his music was firmly within the late romantic European tradition. Some of his best-known works, such as *Indian Sketches* and *From Puritan Days*, celebrated American themes. Yet his compositional style reflected the influence of Schumann, Liszt, Wagner, and Greig. He resented concerts of exclusively American music and at times refused to participate in such events. He disliked being categorized as an American composer, preferring to be recognized as a composer whose nationality happened to be American. Today, with the exception of a few pieces, MacDowell's music is infrequently performed. Among American composers active before 1900, William Billings, Louis Moreau Gottschalk, and Stephen Foster, all of whose music is more idiosyncratic and uniquely American, if less refined than that of MacDowell, are more celebrated.

Further reading: Alan H. Levy, *Edward MacDowell: An American Master* (Lanham, Md.: Scarecrow Press, 1998); John Fielder Porte, *Edward MacDowell: A Great American Tone Poet, His Life and Music* (Boston: Longwood Press, 1978).

— William Peek

machine politics

Political leaders preferred to think that they headed organizations, but their opponents referred to them pejoratively as "bosses" and their disciplined followers as "machines." In fact, fielding candidates and winning elections necessitated the formation of organized political parties. American parties are decentralized and comprise local units that are built from the ground up. In the Gilded Age, political organizations were fine-tuned to the point that, in many urban areas and in some states, they achieved machinelike efficiency.

The Democratic machine in New York City, TAMMANY HALL, and the Republican machine in Pennsylvania are the most renowned, but they were not alone, since virtually all politicians attempted to organize their supporters.

The basic element in all political machines was the worker in direct contact with voters. In cities it was the precinct captain who knew everyone and their problems, offered them help when needed, and made sure they got to the polls. Above the precinct captain was the ward boss and above him the district leader and, ultimately, the urban boss. Since no one working 10 hours a day for six days a week could find the time or energy to be in such close contact with the electorate, the political leader in whose interest they worked found them jobs in the municipal, state, and federal civil service where they put in less than a full day for a good salary. With their livelihood dependent on victory at the polls (since the opposition, if triumphant, would replace them with its party hacks), political workers did their utmost for the machine.

Political machines were most difficult to overthrow in the Gilded Age because direct primary elections for candidates were rare. The first mandatory primary law was adopted in 1903 in Wisconsin, and the passage of similar laws in other states hampered the activity of political machines in the 20th century. In the late 19th century, however, nominations for local, state, and national offices were made by conventions whose delegates were also selected by conventions. Hence, local conventions would nominate local candidates and also select delegates to the county convention and so up the line to the quadrennial national convention. To overthrow a boss, reformers had the daunting if not impossible task of gaining control of local conventions, which were often held in saloons and occasionally in bordellos.

Machines were occasionally overthrown and often threatened, but they were either repaired or prevailed. Their operators were tenacious, while reformers—as GEORGE WASHINGTON PLUNKITT of Tammany Hall observed—faded like morning glories. But political bosses, while clinging to power, accomplished little beyond running their machines. The Republican machine in Pennsylvania had a remarkably long life, but its operators—Senators Simon and Donald Cameron, Matthew Quay, and Boies Penrose—had virtually no legislative impact. They were able men, but when not dealing with major revolts by local Philadelphia or Pittsburgh machines or by reformers, they were consumed by the minutiae involved in balancing the demands of minor politicians in every small town in the state.

Further reading: James A. Kehl, *Boss Rule in the Gilded Age: Matt Quay of Pennsylvania* (Pittsburgh, Pa.: University of Pittsburgh Press, 1981); Joel Arthur Tarr, *A Study in Boss Politics: William Lorimer of Chicago* (Urbana: University of Illinois Press, 1971).

Mafia incident (1891)

A diplomatic controversy between the United States and Italy in 1891 grew out of the LYNCHING of Italian nationals by a New Orleans mob. In the 1890s New Orleans was plagued with criminal gang violence that was blamed on supposed members of the Sicilian Mafia among the recent flood of immigrants from southern Italy. Police superintendent David C. Hennessy launched a campaign against the gang warfare but was assassinated just before he was to testify in court on October 15, 1890. Nineteen men were arrested and charged with murder, but a trial of nine resulted in no conviction. On March 14, 1891, a mob calling itself the Committee of Fifty murdered 11 of those in custody, among whom were three Italian citizens.

The Italian minister to the United States, Baron Francesco Saverio Fava, demanded that the members of the mob be punished and an indemnity be paid. Secretary of State JAMES G. BLAINE informed Baron Fava that the federal government could not punish the lynch mob because it had no jurisdiction in the case. Italians were outraged. Unable or unwilling to understand the workings of federalism, the Italian government called Fava back to Italy in protest. Thereafter, President BENJAMIN HARRISON recalled the U.S. minister from Rome and refused to discuss the incident as long as the Italian minister was absent. In fact, most Americans, given their ethnic prejudices and their tolerance for lynching, remained unfazed by the Mafia incident.

Although it was disturbed, the Italian government did not want war. In a conciliatory gesture, Italy dropped its ban on the importation of American pork. In December 1891 Harrison announced in his annual address that the lynching was a deplorable act, but he reiterated that he would only discuss the matter if the Italian minister returned to Washington. Italy was ready to send Fava back when the United States agreed to the principal of an indemnity, but Harrison, feeling that he had done so already in his annual address, refused to do anymore. Secretary of State Blaine, who had just recently returned to work after an extended illness, informed the president that drawing out the negotiations over a minor point was more embarrassing than having to pay damages. He also reminded Harrison that since Italy would appoint an arbitrator to the international panel empowered to resolve the BERING SEA DISPUTE with Britain, it was in the nation's best interest to be reconciled with Italy. Harrison understood, and in March 1892 he sent the American minister back to Rome. One month later the United States paid Italy an indemnity of $24, 330.90, and Italy sent Baron Fava back to Washington.

Further reading: Charles S. Campbell, *The Transformation of American Foreign Relations, 1865–1900* (New York: Harper & Row, 1976); Edward P. Crapol, *James G. Blaine: Architect of Empire* (Wilmington, Del.: Scholarly Resources, 2000).

— Timothy E. Vislocky

magazines

In the years following the Civil War, there was a surge of magazines appearing in the United States. The number of periodicals published grew from 700 in 1865 to 3,300 by 1885, and magazines began to target specific reading populations. Americans had more leisure time for reading because of the technological advances of the Industrial Revolution. Machines produced vast quantities of goods, created great wealth, and revolutionized COMMUNICATIONS. Americans began to travel both within their own country and to Europe at a greater rate. Magazines, the most important source of literary pleasure, reflected these changes and focused on entertainment, leisure, travel, and fashion. As Americans lost interest in the issues of Civil War and Reconstruction, they sought diversion. Established monthly magazines like *Harper's, Scribner's,* and the *Atlantic* continued to concentrate on short stories, serialized novels, and poetry, but other journals became "niche" publications marketed to an increasingly professionalized American society with special needs.

Magazines began accepting advertisements, and their style of writing changed to lighter, less-serious prose. Articles now ran with bylines rather than anonymously. Magazines for women increased in number, but most of them surprisingly opposed woman suffrage. As a result, smaller journals spoke for women's rights, including the very outspoken *Woodhull and Claflin's Weekly* (1870–76). At the same time women's fashion magazines including *Harper's Bazaar* (1867 to present) flourished, but the first magazine to reach 1 million subscribers, the *Ladies' Home Journal* (1883 to present), celebrated domesticity. Founded by Cyrus H. K. Curtis and initially edited by his wife, Louisa Knapp, the *Ladies Home Journal* flourished under his son-in-law Edward W. Bok and had 5 million subscribers by 1900.

Specialized magazines grew enormously during the Gilded Age, with new periodicals focusing on the sciences, engineering, manufacturing, and mechanics. Professional journals for physicians and teachers sprang up, agriculture and farm journals proliferated, sports magazines began publishing, and a number of monthly magazines for children appeared. Weekly magazines devoted to news and commentary included popular journals with their woodcut illustrations like *Harper's Weekly* (among its featured artists were WINSLOW HOMER and cartoonist THOMAS NAST) and *Frank Leslie's Illustrated Newspaper* and the era's most outstanding journal of opinion, *THE NATION,* edited by EDWIN L. GODKIN. Several publications devoted to humor (preeminently *Puck,* 1877–1918) and illustrations (mainly *Life,* 1883–1936) appeared. *Puck* was distinguished by a double-page cartoon in the centerfold, printed in color and drawn by artist Joseph Keppler. *Life* was known for outstanding black-and-white drawings, especially by Charles Dana Gibson, who invented a "look" for an entire generation of young women with his stunning and sophisticated GIBSON GIRLS. Local and regional magazines took hold, including the "city weekly" best exemplified by *Rolling Stone* (1894–95) edited in Austin, Texas, by William Sydney Porter (O. Henry). These magazines mixed politics, entertainment, society chit chat, and light literary fare.

In the last third of the century, the larger national magazines increased their circulation because the advent of second-class postage in 1879 and rural free delivery in the 1890s enabled them to reduce their cost generally to 20 cents per issue. Some, like *Munsey's Magazine* and *Godey's Lady's Book,* charged only a dime, and the *Ladies' Home Journal* went on sale for a nickel. These price cuts were helped along by cheaper paper, lower printing costs, and halftone engraving.

At the turn of the new century, popular magazines were heavily illustrated and fiction had been deemphasized in favor of politics, history, and economics. Magazine publishers recruited writers from other magazines instead of from NEWSPAPERS, as in the early 1800s. Magazines in America were becoming, like their older newspaper siblings, a moneymaking business, with national circulation. Their tone had changed from polite to frank, and they were ready to wield enormous influence as "muckrakers," exposing corrupt politicians and monopolistic TRUSTS and paving the way for progressive reforms.

Further reading: Frank Luther Mott, *A History of American Magazines,* 5 vols. (Cambridge, Mass.: Harvard University Press, 1930–68).

— Ellen Tashie Frisina

Mahan, Alfred Thayer (1840–1914)

Alfred Thayer Mahan's influential books argued that seapower, accompanied by a flourishing merchant marine, was essential for world power, and that maritime nations that established, exploited, and retained colonies—in peace and war—were blessed with strong economies. Born on September 27, 1840, Mahan graduated from the U.S. Naval Academy in 1859, and although a veteran of the Civil War, he was more scholar than sailor. Beginning in 1884 he taught at the Naval War College in Newport, Rhode Island, and wrote two histories of naval warfare, *The Influence of Sea Power upon History, 1660–1783* (1890) and a sequel covering the French Revolution and Napoleonic war (1892). His writings, appearing when industrial powers either were carving or were preparing to carve colonies out of Africa and Asia, inspired imperialist policy makers abroad in Great Britain, Germany, Japan, and elsewhere. At home, expansionists like Theodore Roosevelt, JOHN HAY, and Henry Cabot Lodge—who advocated a large, modern, steel navy to promote exports abroad—regarded Mahan as their prophet, but they extrapolated more from his writings than he intended.

Mahan's IMPERIALISM was limited by his concept of the strategic defensive perimeters of the United States. Those perimeters extended south to include the Caribbean Sea and Central America and stretched west into the Pacific Ocean 3,000 miles from San Francisco. In that area he wanted the navy to be paramount, and to maintain its strength, he wanted the United States to annex HAWAII and to control an isthmian canal and its approaches. Unlike his expansionist American disciples, he was not anxious to acquire territory or to thwart the designs of other nations beyond his perimeters. He was reluctant to take the Philippines, since they would be difficult to defend in a war with Japan, and he thought that trying to maintain the OPEN DOOR in remote China was unwise, since the United States had neither the will nor the capacity to wage war in defense of either China's territory or its minuscule trade with America. Mahan even doubted the wisdom of enforcing the Monroe Doctrine south of the Amazon River.

Prior to Mahan, other naval officers had advocated increased spending on the fleet and the acquisition of an interoceanic canal and naval bases, but unlike Mahan, they lacked a popular audience. Although today his writings are better known than read, in the 1890s he profoundly influenced the public, policy makers, and scholars. Indeed, his esteem among historians was such that he was elected president of the American Historical Association in 1902. Mahan died on December 1, 1914.

Further reading: Robert Seager II, *Alfred Thayer Mahan: The Man and His Letters* (Annapolis, Md.: Naval Institute, 1977).

— Bruce Abrams

mail-order houses

A nationwide rail system created a national market in place of local and regional markets and gave rise to mail order houses. Efficient express companies, utilizing widespread rail facilities, could speed packages to villages throughout the country and could serve most of the populace. The U.S. Post Office reduced rates and began rural free delivery in 1896, but it did not inaugurate parcel post service until 1913. In 1879, however, CONGRESS aided rural Americans and mail-order houses when it provided that packages of up to four pounds could be mailed throughout the country at the flat rate of one cent an ounce. Mail-order houses existed prior to the Civil War, but they stocked only a few items and their market was limited by inadequate transport.

In 1872, the year after the great CHICAGO FIRE, Aaron Montgomery Ward began his mail-order business in Chicago, a rail hub. To keep his prices low, he would buy in bulk with cash and eliminate middlemen by selling and shipping directly to the rural consumer for cash. He established close ties to the GRANGER MOVEMENT and claimed to be "The Original Grange Supply House," selling goods to Grange cooperative stores and to members of that farm organization. He further cultivated the good will of his customers with the slogan "satisfaction guaranteed, or your money back." In 1889, with sales at $2 million and profits at $115,000, Ward and his partners established Montgomery Ward & Company, and by the 1890s its catalog—the "wish book" containing 24,000 items—had brought the DEPARTMENT STORE into the home and changed forever the buying habits of rural Americans.

In 1891 Richard Warren Sears and his associate in retailing watches, Alvah Curtis Roebuck, formed a partnership that became Sears, Roebuck and Company to compete with Montgomery Ward. Sears took great risks, expanded during the depression of the 1890s, bought out the nervous Roebuck, and in 1895 acquired Aaron Nusbaum (who pulled out in 1901) and his brother-in-law Julius Rosenwald as partners. With Sears, who was a gifted salesman with a knack for advertising, handling the merchandising and Rosenwald, a brilliant organizer, conducting the rest of the business, Sears, Roebuck took off, passed Montgomery Ward, and grossed $10 million in 1900. In competition with Ward, Sears did not innovate but met Ward head on, claiming lower prices, superior goods, better guarantees, more selections, and simpler order forms. Although Sears, Roebuck advertised widely, its best advertisement was its catalog—a larger wish book than Montgomery Ward's—that by 1908 had 100,000 items, including automobiles. But in that year Sears's risk taking was more than Rosenwald could stand and he forced Sears to resign as president.

Further reading: Boris Emmet and John E. Jeuck, *Catalogues and Counters: A History of Sears, Roebuck and Company* (Chicago: University of Chicago Press, 1950); Cecil C. Hoge Sr., *The First Hundred Years Are the Toughest: What We Can Learn from the Century of Competition* *between Sears and Ward* (Berkeley, Calif.: Ten Speed Press, 1988).

Maine, Remember the (1898)

The battle cry of the SPANISH-AMERICAN WAR, coined by the jingo (see JINGOES) press, whipped up war sentiment after the USS *Maine* was destroyed in an explosion while anchored in Havana harbor. The sinking served as the cause for the United States to declare war on Spain. The battleship *Maine* arrived in CUBA, ostensibly for a "friendly" naval visit, at 11:00 A.M. on January 25, 1898. With Spain involved in a vicious colonial war with Cuban rebels, such visits had been avoided since 1895, but as American sympathy for the rebels grew, so too did anti-American sentiment among Spanish loyalists in Havana. Rioting in Havana on January 12, 1898, worried the American consul, Fitzhugh Lee, who cabled that "ships may be necessary later but not now." Although Havana calmed down, the McKinley administration on January 24 ordered the *Maine* to Havana.

The *Maine* was a second-class battleship, weighing 6,682 tons and with a maximum speed of 17 knots. Although Spanish officials would rather the *Maine* were elsewhere, they were cordial and the city was calm. Nevertheless, Captain Charles D. Sigsbee did not allow his sailors liberty for fear of an incident. Security on the ship was high. The ship's watch was greatly enlarged and sentries were armed. Both boilers were kept going—a departure from the usual practice of operating a single boiler—in case the ship was called to immediate action, and shells were kept near all of the *Maine*'s guns.

At 9:40 on the evening of February 15 an explosion ripped through the *Maine* and sent it to the bottom of the Havana harbor. With the entire forward part of the vessel destroyed, 260 men were killed (out of a crew of 355). NEWSPAPERS immediately attributed the explosion to Spanish treachery and called for war. A naval court of inquiry concluded on March 20 that an underwater mine sank the *Maine,* although responsibility for laying the mine could not be determined. The Spanish offered to send the matter to arbitration in order to settle the cost of the damage and even agreed to an armistice (to last as long as the commanding general in Cuba thought prudent) in the war on the Cuban rebels. But the United States was in no mood for arbitration or for negotiations.

President WILLIAM MCKINLEY had experienced the carnage of war firsthand as an officer during the Civil War. He hoped that the report's inability to blame the Spanish for the sinking would leave open an opportunity to negotiate a peaceful settlement of the sinking and of the political status of Cuba. But public sentiment was not with him. Reports of Spanish atrocities in Cuba both real and imagined and the

The U.S. battleship *Maine* *(Library of Congress)*

mass starvation produced by Spain's military policies created great sympathy for the Cuban rebels. The publication a few weeks before the explosion of the *Maine* of the DE LÔME LETTER, in which the Spanish minister had made derogatory remarks about the president, abetted the growth of war fever in the United States. Bowing to pressure, McKinley on April 11, 1898, asked CONGRESS for the authority to use the armed forces to intervene in Cuba. Congress debated for a week before agreeing on April 19 by joint resolution. McKinley signed it the following day and the war began.

Seventy-eight years later a study, using the latest naval technology, by Rear Admiral Hyman Rickover of the U.S. Navy concluded that an internal explosion occurring in one of the coal bunkers had caused the sinking of the *Maine*.

Further reading: Ivan Musicant, *Empire by Default: The Spanish-American War and the Dawn of the American Century* (New York: Henry Holt and Co., 1998); G. J. A. O'Toole, *The Spanish War: An American Epic, 1898* (New York: Norton, 1984).

— Timothy E. Vislocky

Manifest Destiny See imperialism

Marsh, Othniel Charles (1831–1899)

Lockport, New York, the place of Othniel Charles Marsh's birth on October 29, 1831, influenced his eventual distinguished career as a paleontologist. Fields, woods, and the fossil-rich Erie Canal excavations near his father's farm turned him toward the study of nature. His advanced schooling came late, but money held in trust for him since his mother's death enabled him to attend Phillips Andover Academy in Massachusetts during his early 20s, and his maternal uncle George Peabody, a leading international financier, paid for his study at Yale College during his late 20s. At Yale, which was especially strong in science, he studied under James D. Dana, the foremost American geologist in those years. He graduated with honors in 1860, earned a master of arts degree in 1862, and with his uncle's support studied abroad with leading German scientists. In 1866 his uncle's endowment of the Peabody Museum at Yale led to Marsh's appointment as curator and as the first professor of paleontology in the United States. Upon his uncle's death in 1869 Marsh received a substantial inheritance that enabled him to forgo a Yale salary until 1898 and thereby avoid the chore of teaching.

The fossil riches of the West were beginning to capture the public imagination, as were the evolutionary theories of Charles Darwin. Marsh caught the rising tide. In 1868 on his first trip west, his train stopped briefly at Antelope Station, Nebraska, where Marsh poked through the diggings of a nearby well and turned up a major find: the bones of a small primordial horse that proved to be a missing link in the evolution of the modern horse and therefore a crucial piece of evidence in support of Darwin's theory. Between 1870 and 1873 Marsh returned to the West four times with parties of Yale seniors. Thereafter, Marsh used his ample financial resources to send out scores of diggers in the field while he remained at Yale classifying their finds—30 freight-car loads in all. As paleontologist of the U.S. GEOLOGICAL SURVEY, 1882–92, he had federal money to support his collectors and the laboratory staff and artists at his museum. Darwin's chief apostle, Thomas Huxley, was delighted with Marsh's fossil parade of evolving horses and promoted Marsh's reputation in Europe. During his career Marsh published more than 270 papers and books, naming 496 fossil species. Awards and prizes attested to his worldwide reputation, and he served as president of the National Academy of Sciences from 1883 to 1895.

Marsh's chief rival was Edward Cope, a fiercely pugnacious Philadelphia Quaker. Marsh himself was stern, stocky, and aggressive. In 1871 Cope poached on what Marsh considered his own dinosaur-hunting preserves in Wyoming. Each man accused the other of unscrupulous tactics, and both were right. Their escalating war was marked by cloak-and-dagger secrecy and spying, false trails, subverting of each other's hired collectors, and public accusations of lying, theft of specimens, and false dating of papers. The struggle raged for two decades. With the weight of his money, connections, and towering reputation, Marsh prevailed. But the battle had stirred Cope into writing a mammoth compilation of his own researches that established him as one of the world's great naturalists. Marsh died on March 18, 1899, and, never having married, bequeathed his estate to the Peabody Museum, the National Academy of Sciences, and Yale University.

Further reading: Mark J. McCarren, *The Scientific Contributions of Othniel Charles Marsh: Birds, Bones, and Brontotheres* (New Haven, Conn.: Peabody Museum of Natural History, Yale University, 1993); Charles Schuchert and Clara LeVene, *O. C. Marsh: Pioneer in Paleontology* (New Haven, Conn.: Yale University Press, 1940); Elizabeth Noble Shor, *The Fossil Feud between E. D. Cope and O. C. Marsh* (Hicksville, N.Y.: Exposition Press, 1974).

— Robert V. Bruce

Marxian socialists See labor, radical

McKim, Charles Follen See White, Standford

McKinley, William (1843–1901)

Born in Niles, Ohio, on January 29, 1843, William McKinley, the 25th president of the United States, attended

Allegheny College and taught school before enlisting in the 23rd Ohio (RUTHERFORD B. HAYES's regiment) for the duration of the Civil War. His efficiency as a commissary sergeant at the Battle of Antietam made him an officer, and at the war's end he was a major. He then studied law and in 1867 began practicing in Canton, Ohio. There in 1871 he married Ida Saxon, to whom he remained devoted despite the onset of epilepsy and neurotic behavior following the loss of their two infant daughters. In 1876 he was elected as a Republican to CONGRESS and served from 1877 to 1883 and 1885 to 1891 (losing only in the Democratic landslide years of 1882 and 1890); he became the most conspicuous champion of protectionism and the author of the MCKINLEY TARIFF of 1890, which jacked up rates but also provided for the novel feature of reciprocal trade agreements.

McKinley shrewdly gave protectionism a plausible populistic nationalistic spin, ascribing to it the prosperity of American workers and farmers by creating jobs and domestic markets. While usually successful, that argument was rejected on the national level by voters in 1890 and 1892, but it was again embraced by them following the PANIC OF 1893 and it enhanced McKinley's reputation. He won the Ohio governorship in 1891 and 1893 and in 1896, aided by his political lieutenant, MARCUS ALONZO HANNA, easily won the Republican presidential nomination. Having rejected its incumbent president, GROVER CLEVELAND, the DEMOCRATIC PARTY, led by WILLIAM JENNINGS BRYAN, was discredited, demoralized, and divided by the depression following the Panic of 1893. Bryan wished to inflate the currency with the unlimited coinage of silver, while McKinley stressed that the gold standard and protection would promote prosperity and warned that an inflated dollar would destroy the real wages of workers. Both Bryan and McKinley spoke constantly, Bryan as he toured the country and McKinley as he stood on his front porch receiving hundreds of delegations. Hanna raised $3.5–4 million for the campaign, while the Democrats had only one-seventh that amount to spend. McKinley triumphed decisively with 271 electoral votes to Bryan's 176.

McKinley was often underestimated by his contemporaries, and many historians have followed their lead. His amiable, pragmatic, and compromising nature—combined with his ability to maneuver unobtrusively while pursuing his goals—have masked his strength of character, his capacity to deal with Congress, and his domination of advisers. Indeed, JOHN HAY dismissed as "idiots" those who thought Hanna would "run" McKinley. He began his presidency by calling a special session of Congress to raise the tariff, and it obliged with the Dingley Tariff (1897). Far from doctrinaire on the monetary issue, McKinley favored international BIMETALLISM (basing currency on gold and silver), but when the British rejected that idea he signed the Gold Standard Act (1900).

William McKinley *(Library of Congress)*

War and empire, not the tariff and the currency, dominated the McKinley administration. In 1895 CUBA again revolted for its independence, and Spain soon resorted to harsh measures to preserve its colony. Outraged by newspaper accounts of Spanish atrocities, many Americans clamored for a war of liberation in Cuba. Using diplomacy and the threat of military intervention, McKinley secured some concessions from Spain, but when it would not free Cuba, he reluctantly asked for and received from Congress a declaration of war. The SPANISH-AMERICAN WAR (1898) was of short duration, and McKinley not only directed the war effort but also, to the dismay of the anti-imperialists, made the decisions that gave the United States Puerto Rico in the

Caribbean and the Philippine Islands in the Pacific. Ironically, his administration suppressed the FILIPINO INSURRECTION against American rule using the same tactics that Spain had employed to put down the Cuban revolution, and Cuba, though nominally independent, was made an American protectorate. Increased Caribbean interests made an isthmian canal under American control an imperative objective of the McKinley administration, and in the Hay-Pauncefote Treaties (1900, 1901) with Great Britain, the Clayton-Bulwer Treaty (1850) was superseded and the United States could proceed unilaterally with a canal between the Atlantic and Pacific Oceans. After gaining possession of the Philippines, American interest in trading with China was heightened, which led to circulating the OPEN DOOR NOTES (1899, 1900) to oppose its dismemberment and the dispatching of troops to help suppress its Boxer Rebellion (1900). By enhancing the power and prestige of the presidency, McKinley was a forerunner of modern 20th-century chief executives. McKinley, for example, justified sending troops to China on the basis of his war powers even though there was no war.

McKinley was renominated in 1900, and, with a popular vice presidential running mate, Theodore Roosevelt, he triumphed for a second time over Bryan. But his plans for his second term to moderate the protective tariff through reciprocity treaties were not realized. McKinley was shot by an assassin on September 6, 1901, in Buffalo, New York, and died on September 14.

Further reading: Lewis L. Gould, *The Presidency of William McKinley* (Lawrence: University Press of Kansas, 1980); H. Wayne Morgan, *William McKinley and His America* (Syracuse, N.Y.: Syracuse University Press, 1963).

McKinley Tariff (1890) See tariff issue

meatpacking

The combination of the technologies of railroading and refrigeration resulted in the refrigerator car ("reefer"), introduced in 1870 but perfected in 1881, which in turn cre-

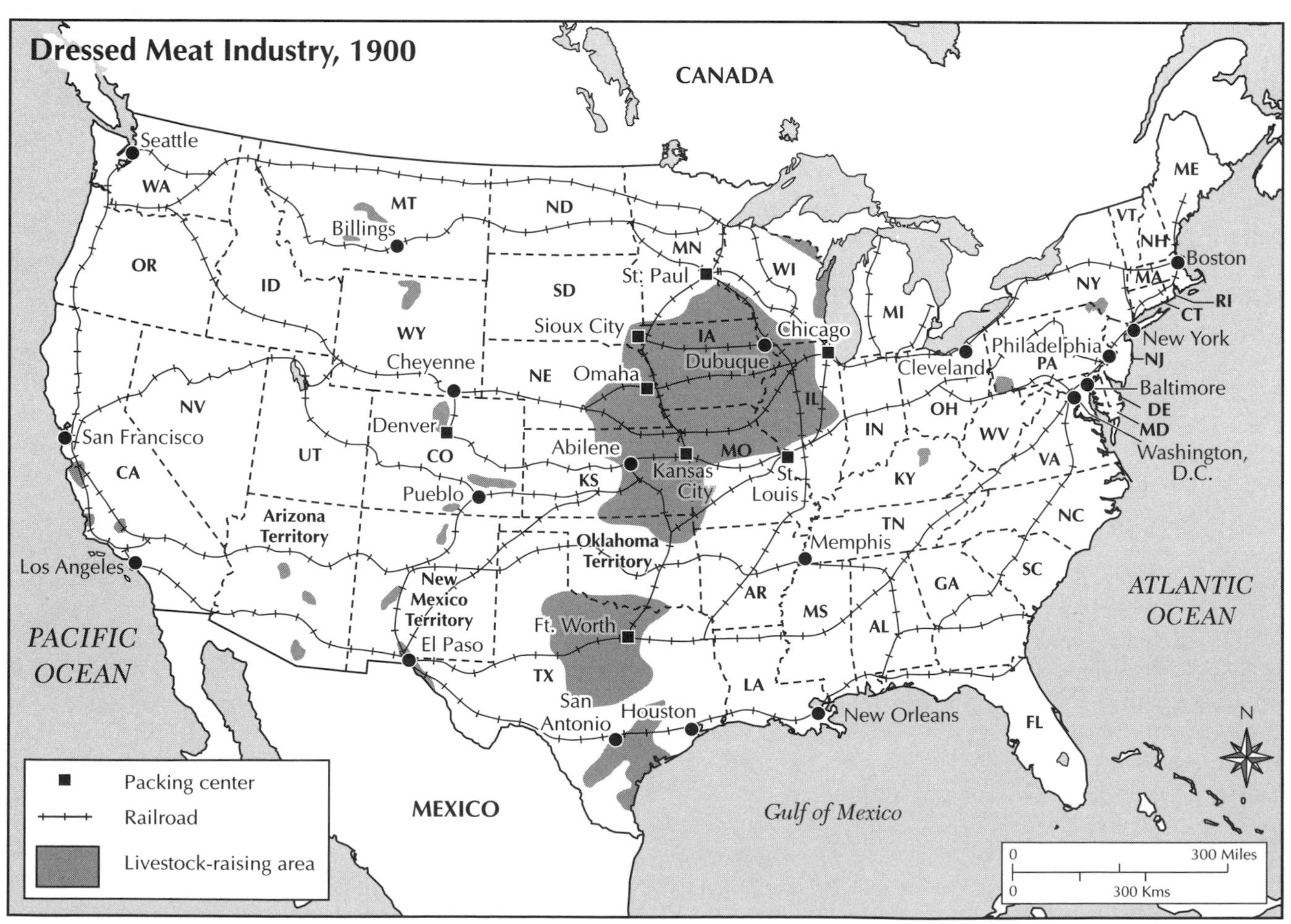

ated the major industry of meatpacking. Prior to the Gilded Age, meatpacking utilized animals raised in the Midwest; was restricted to curing hams, salting pork (Cincinnati, the major center, was called "Porkopolis"), and some corning of beef; and could be done only in cold weather so as to retard spoilage. Fresh meat had to be butchered locally, and cities had their slaughterhouse districts. By 1870 the penetration of the West by railroads brought western cattle to packing centers like Chicago (its Union Stock Yards opened in 1865), and efficient reefers after 1881 enabled packers like Philip D. Armour and Gustavus F. Swift to aggressively market their dressed beef in eastern cities. To break down eastern consumer hostility against western beef, Swift established East Coast branches and refrigerated warehouses. Their success was such that shipments of dressed beef to urban centers replaced those of live animals to small slaughterhouses at those points. Most of the nation's butchers no longer butchered; instead, they cut up carcasses slaughtered hundreds of miles away. In the early 1890s six large-scale firms—Armour, Swift, Cudahy, Morris, Hammond, and the kosher meat dealer Schwartzchild & Sulzberger—dominated the meatpacking industry. The Big Six, following Swift's leadership, were integrated companies with their own purchasing units, packing plants, refrigerator cars, and branch houses.

The Big Six preferred cooperation to competition and, with Swift and Armour leading out, created an informal pool in 1893 with weekly allocations designed to produce a profit for all. By 1902 this "Beef Trust" was, with the antitrust movement underway, vulnerable. The Big Six managed, however, to continue their monopolistic practices that year when Armour, Swift, and Morris bought into the National Packing Company, which Hammond and some smaller companies had formed; although Cudahy and Schwartzchild & Sulzberger remained independent, they following its leadership in pricing and production quotas. By 1910 the meatpackers had abandoned National Packing at the behest of the Justice Department, but the Big Six understood each other so well that without any formal arrangement they simply continued to follow the prices set by Swift and Armour.

Further reading: Alfred D. Chandler Jr., *The Visible Hand: The Managerial Revolution in American Business* (Cambridge, Mass.: Harvard University Press, 1977).

medicine and public health

American medicine and public health lagged behind European countries during the 19th century, in part because of the country's largely rural character at the beginning of the period. Cities spread disease, and it was not until late in that century that population shifts transformed the United States into an urban nation (see CITIES AND URBAN LIFE). From 1870 to 1900 the United States made modest progress in the field of sanitation with the establishment of health agencies at the municipal level. Advances, however, were even more modest in medicine and surgery.

Until the 1890s, the most able American doctors were trained in Europe, particularly in Germany (see EDUCATION, HIGHER). Whereas gaining acceptance to medical schools in the 21st century is notoriously difficult, 19th-century American schools accepted most applicants for study. Moreover, American medical schools relied on lectures and provided little clinical training. An 1867 graduate of New York's College of Physicians and Surgeons who received a prize for his thesis on the "Fatty Degeneration of the Liver" later criticized his training by noting that he had never seen a liver that had undergone fatty degeneration, nor had he seen a patient who had suffered from such a liver. Furthermore, medical schools sponsored virtually no research. Consequently, graduates were handicapped by having little hands-on experience and little knowledge of the emerging field of bacteriology, which was critical in understanding disease in urban centers. Although Joseph Lister first practiced antiseptic surgery in 1865 in England, for much of the Gilded Age doctors were ignorant of those procedures, with fatal consequences for many of their patients. For example, scrupulously cleanly conditions would have saved many women who died of puerperal (childbed) fever after giving birth. The first significant body of medical research was undertaken not by a school of medicine but by the U.S. Department of Agriculture, which enlisted Dr. Theobald Smith to study Texas cattle fever and resulted in Smith's discovery in 1891 of how ticks transmit disease; this finding played a key role in understanding diseases like malaria, typhus, and Lyme disease.

There were however, some attempts in the Gilded Age by medical schools to raise their standards. Recognizing that standards varied widely from state to state, leaders in the medical profession attempted to revise curricula at medical institutions, and some even advocated a national medical school supported by federal funding. Northwestern University in Illinois was the first to address curricular reform by instituting a three-year graded program as early as 1859. No other institution, however, followed their lead until 1871, when Harvard University began a three-year program, adding the prerequisite of an academic degree. The University of Pennsylvania and Syracuse University improved their curricula in 1877, with Yale and the University of Michigan following suit in 1880. The University of Pennsylvania supplemented its medical education program by establishing its University Hospital, which provided on site faculty-supervised clinical training. The founding of

Johns Hopkins Medical School in 1893 (with clinical training at the Johns Hopkins Hospital) further raised the bar by patterning its medical education program after German universities and buttressing the curriculum with top-notch facilities, laboratories, and a large endowment to help fund medical research.

The Gilded Age also witnessed the early attempts to professionalize and improve American medicine. These efforts focused on self-policing by professional organizations and accreditation bureaus and, to a lesser extent, the establishment (and in some cases reestablishment) of state licensing boards. Toward the end of the century, the American Medical Association (AMA) attempted to create medical standards in the field of education that exceeded government regulations. An accrediting agency to ensure standards, the American Medical College Association (AMCA), was established in 1876 but was shortly disbanded after several colleges withdrew because of its stringent requirements. In 1890 the AMCA reorganized with more success, becoming the Association of American Medical Colleges; although it lacked licensing power, the body soon developed revised standards, including a three-year program, instruction in chemistry and pathology, and a graded curriculum. By the end of the century, most states had established medical licensing boards, and during the first years of the 20th century the AMCA, with a stronger AMA, had succeeded in closing down substandard medical programs. The rigorous reform of American medical schools occurred only after Abraham Flexner's damning 1910 report recommended closing 120 out of 155 medical schools in the United States and Canada.

American doctors were behind the curve in adopting and improving upon European advances in anesthesia and antiseptic surgical practices, although by the 1890s—especially after some improvement in medical education—American medicine began to catch up with Europe. In that decade the United States was home to several notable medical firsts, including the world's first open-heart surgery in 1893 and the first appendectomy in 1894. Some American doctors were instrumental in the field of anesthesiology as well, including Dr. William S. Halsted (1852–1922), who experimented with uses of cocaine, especially on himself (his self-administered injections contributed to a lifelong addiction to the drug).

In the area of public health, officials built on discoveries in Europe by focusing on eliminating infectious disease and safeguarding water systems. In the United States the field of public health grew as a result of growing cities and their endemic unsanitary conditions. Early municipal health officials inspected sewer systems with the goal of providing clean living conditions in socially disadvantaged neighborhoods. In practice this was difficult; rudimentary sewer systems proved inadequate, and drinking water tended to be polluted in rapidly expanding cities. True reform in the area of public health—such as vaccinations, bathhouses, modern sewer systems, and slum clearance programs—would not come until the start of the 20th century. Efforts, however, were made: The founding of the American Public Health Association in 1872 signaled within the medical profession a new awareness of this specialized field, as municipalities and states began establishing boards of health; by 1900 most states had boards of health. The federal government tended to stay out of health issues, although CONGRESS passed a national quarantine law in 1893 to attempt to stop the spread of infectious diseases carried by immigrants from other countries.

Further reading: John Duffy, *From Humors to Medical Science: A History of American Medicine,* 2d ed. (Urbana: University of Illinois Press, 1993); John Duffy, *The Sanitarians: A History of American Public Health* (Urbana: University of Illinois Press, 1990).

— Scott Sendrow

merchant marine

The merchant marine was one sector of the otherwise booming Gilded Age economy that was in decline. In the 1850s more than 70 percent of American exports and imports were shipped in American vessels, but by 1897 only 15 percent of the value of imports and 8 percent of the value of exports were carried by American ships. The decline began in 1863, during the Civil War, and steadily continued thereafter. By 1870 American ships totaling approximately 2.5 million tons entered and cleared American seaports, as compared with a tonnage for foreign vessels of about 3.8 million. By 1900 American tonnage entering and clearing U.S. seaports was 4 million, while foreign tonnage leaped to 19.6 million.

The most obvious reason for the decline is the Civil War, which is indeed when it first set in. Confederate raiders sank about 800,000 tons of American ships, which jacked up insurance rates and prompted owners to sell an even larger tonnage to foreigners to be operated under neutral flags. But in the past seafaring nations have suffered depredations to their commerce and have rebuilt their merchant marine in times of peace to reclaim their share of the carrying trade. The Civil War is partly responsible but probably not even the major reason for the long-term decline.

By the time of the Civil War technological innovations were fundamentally altering ships. Canvas sails and wooden vessels were being supplanted by steam engines in iron and later steel hulls. The change did not occur overnight because, where speed was not of critical importance, sailing vessels remained cost effective throughout the Gilded Age in shipping bulky goods like coal or timber. But as time went on, steam engines improved in efficiency, taking up less space, producing more power, and burning less coal; steel hulls provided more capacious holds; and the industrial world demanded celerity, punctuality, and predictability.

With an ample supply of timber, Americans had excelled in constructing wooden sailing ships. Their clipper ships of the 1850s were the fastest sailing vessels afloat. American shipbuilders were on the cutting edge of wood and sail, but not of iron and steam. During the Gilded Age American shipbuilders did build iron- and steel-hulled steamships, but their labor costs were significantly higher than those of British shipbuilders. The efficiency that made Americans preeminent as STEEL producers was absent in their shipyards, where vessels were not mass-produced. American shipowners did not buy foreign-built ships because by law only American-built ships could be registered as American. Not only were American ships more expensive to build than foreign vessels, but they also were more costly to operate. Lower costs for operators of foreign ships meant lower freight rates than those Americans charged and resulted in steadily increasing shipments in foreign bottoms.

The decline of the merchant marine rankled patriotic Americans, who sensed that "effeminacy" and "decadence" would surely follow. To reverse the trend CONGRESS provided subsidies in the form of lucrative mail contracts and in 1891 passed a Merchant Marine Act that gave bounties per mile on certain outward-bound routes. Subsidies, however, were ineffective in stemming the drift to shipping in foreign vessels, and Americans, who supported an indirect subsidy in the form of a protective tariff, were reluctant to provide significant direct support to the American shipowners.

Further reading: K. Jack Bauer, *A Maritime History of the United States: The Role of America's Seas and Waterways* (Columbia: University of South Carolina Press, 1988); Andrew Gibson and Arthur Donovan, *The Abandoned Ocean: A History of United States Maritime Policy* (Columbia; University of South Carolina Press, 2000); Edward C. Kirkland, *Industry Comes of Age: Business, Labor, and Public Policy, 1860–1897* (New York: Holt, Rinehart and Winston, 1961); Benjamin W. Labaree, *America and the Sea: A Maritime History* (Mystic, Conn.: Mystic Seaport, 1988).

mining: metal and coal

American mining production increased by a factor of five during the last 30 years of the 19th century. The discovery of new deposits in part drove the increase. In 1872 Jordan Nelson opened the first commercial coal mine in the rich Pocahontas, West Virginia, bituminous coal field. Gold was discovered in the Black Hills of Dakota in 1876. Copper mining began in the Tombstone, Arizona, district in 1879, and the Copper Queen mine opened near Bisbee, Arizona, the following year. The Coeur d'Alene silver-lead mining district of Idaho began operations in 1883, and the first shipment of iron ore from the Mesabi Range in Minnesota occurred in 1892.

Individual prospectors continued to discover new deposits. But government-sponsored geological surveys greatly expanded the fund of knowledge concerning the nation's mineral resources. In 1870, for example, Pennsylvania conducted a second geological survey that focused on petroleum and updated previous findings on coal. In 1879 the federal government established the U.S. GEOLOGICAL SURVEY as a permanent bureau in the Department of the Interior.

Mining consists of several distinct operations. The first is gaining access to the resource. Gold was often discovered in streams at "placers," or deposits laid bare by erosion or weathering. Placer mining was a simple operation of swirling material in a pan or a larger rocker until the heavier metal settled on the bottom. Other minerals were easily quarried at their outcrops or where they penetrated the surface. Open-pit mining extracted the resource by removing the overburden where deposits lay near the surface. By the 1890s steam-powered shovels working in open pits extracted anthracite coal in Pennsylvania and iron ore in Minnesota's Vermillion and Mesabi Ranges. Hydraulic mining used powerful water canons to uncover shallow deposits of gold and other precious metals.

Three types of entry gained access to deposits located deep below the surface: The shaft was a vertical hole sunk through rock strata to the deposit. A slope was an inclined plane following the strata's dip, while the drift was driven on an upward angle. Wherever possible, mine operators drove drifts and slopes through the mineral's seam or vein. Tunnels were driven horizontally from the side of a mountain to the deposit.

The second step in mining is freeing the material from the earth. At first, miners used hand-powered drills and augers to bore holes into the deposit, filled the holes with explosives, and then blasted the material free. Several technological changes improved productivity at this stage of mining. In western hard-rock mines, jackhammers powered by compressed air began to replace the hand augers in drilling rock in the 1870s. The use of undercutting and other mining machines were used in bituminous coal mining by the 1890s. Dynamite, invented in 1867, gradually replaced black powder as the explosive of choice.

The third procedure in the mining process, moving the freed material to the surface, consisted of loading and

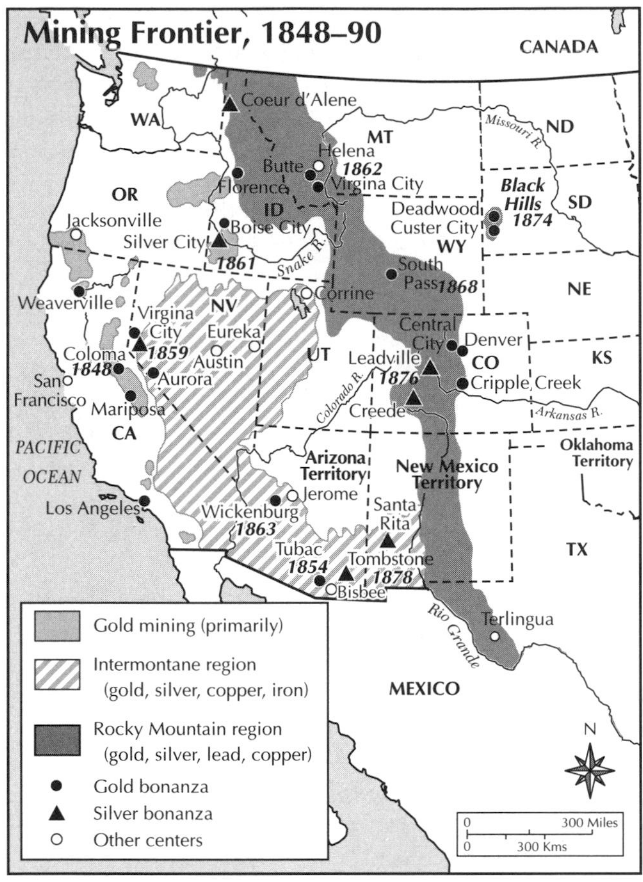

transporting. Although some mines utilized mechanical loading devices, hand loading, either by shovel or the manual adjustment of chutes, remained dominant circa 1900. At first, mules provided the motive power for hauling loaded cars through gangways. As early as 1867 anthracite mining companies experimented with small steam locomotives inside the mines. Although they proved cost effective, they created a pollution problem. In 1891 the Susquehanna Coal Company installed the industry's first compressed-air locomotive, which proved very effective, but it began to give way to electric locomotives by the turn of the century.

Mastery of the increasing technological complexity of mining required specialized knowledge. Columbia University established the nation's first School of Mines in 1864. Other institutions began offering mining engineering degrees. In 1871 both the formally educated and practically trained engineers formed the American Institute of Mining Engineers as a forum for the exchange of ideas and to enhance the status of their occupation. Most mining engineers, however, were content to become corporate bureaucrats rather than entrepreneurs.

Opening deep mines, keeping them dry and well ventilated, and procuring the latest technology required more capital than an individual could afford. As a result, the entrepreneurial order quickly gave way to corporate control in hard-rock as well as in coal mining. By 1914 the Guggenheim family, for example, had expanded their initial hard-rock holdings in Leadville, Colorado, into the greatest mining empire in the world, with facilities in the West, Mexico, Alaska, Chile, and the Congo extracting, smelting, and marketing copper, silver, gold, and lead. Corporate consolidation was also pronounced in the anthracite coal industry, where seven carrier-operators controlled 90 percent of the productive capacity.

Further reading: Priscilla Long, *Where the Sun Never Shines: A History of America's Bloody Coal Industry* (New York: Paragon House, 1989); David W. Pearson, *This Was Mining in the West* (Atglen, Pa.: Schiffer, 1996); Clark C. Spence, *Mining Engineers and the American West: The Lace Boot Brigade, 1849–1933* (New Haven, Conn.: Yale University Press, 1970).

— Harold W. Aurand

Minor v. Happersett (1875) See women's rights

Mitchell, Maria (1818–1889)

Maria Mitchell, the first woman professor of astronomy in the United States, was born on August 1, 1818, into a Quaker family of 10 children on Nantucket Island in Massachusetts. Her father believed that girls, like boys, should be educated to the extent of their abilities. She was a precocious child and exhibited a special talent for arithmetic. Her father was interested in astronomy and navigation, and at the age of 14 she assisted him in his work of rating nautical chronometers.

Mitchell taught school briefly and then, beginning in 1836, served for 20 years as librarian of the Nantucket Atheneum. In that position she had enough free time to study mathematical and scientific treatises and to indulge with her father in their shared interest in astronomy. When, also in 1836, he became the cashier of the Pacific Bank in Nantucket, he installed a four-inch telescope in a small observatory on the roof of his family's living quarters adjoining the bank. Maria and her father used this telescope at night, making accurate stellar observations that attracted the attention of the Harvard College Observatory and the U.S. Coast Survey.

On October 1, 1847, Maria Mitchell discovered a comet (subsequently named for her) that could be seen only with a telescope. Her feat earned her an international reputation, and the king of Denmark awarded her a gold medal. In 1848 she became the first woman elected to the American Academy of Arts and Sciences in Boston (apparently the only woman until 1943, almost a century later). Appointed as a computer in 1849 for the *American Nautical Ephemeris and Almanac,* she did calculations on the positions of Venus. On the recommendation of Louis Agassiz, in 1850 she became the first woman voted into a membership in the American Association for the Advancement for Science. Having given up her librarianship, she toured Europe in 1857 to 1858 meeting distinguished scientists and visiting the Greenwich and Vatican Observatories.

Mitchell was both a feminist and a feminist heroine who was living proof that women were the intellectual equals of men. Consequently, she was interested in Matthew Vassar's plans for a women's college in Poughkeepsie, New York, that would be comparable to the best men's colleges in the country. She accepted Vassar's invitation and joined the college in 1865 as its first woman professor, and although she had no higher education, she was the only faculty member with a national reputation. As a woman, however, she was paid less than her less distinguished male colleagues. Vassar baited his invitation with the promise, which he kept, of an observatory with a 12-inch telescope. Mitchell was a gifted teacher who imparted her love of astronomy to her students, as well as and also her distrust of authority and her love of independence. She disliked compulsory attendance of classes and of chapel. She believed in God and that God is good but rejected all dogma beyond that. She urged her students to question everything and to observe carefully for themselves, and several, including ELLEN SWALLOW RICHARDS, did achieve academic distinction. Mitchell also continued her research as an astronomer with the 12-inch telescope and contributed to the understanding of the nature of sunspots.

Mitchell leaned toward the moderate rather than the militant wing of the suffragists. She was a friend of LUCY STONE and invited her to speak on behalf of woman suffrage at Vassar. Mitchell was one of the founders in 1873 of the Association for the Advancement of Women, serving as its president from 1875 to 1876. After more than 20 years at Vassar, Mitchell, in poor health, retired in 1888 and died on June 28, 1889, in Lynn, Massachusetts.

Further reading: Helen Wright, *Sweeper in the Sky: The Life of Maria Mitchell, First Woman Astronomer in America* (New York: Macmillan, 1949).

— Alfred Kohler

Molly Maguires (ca. 1855–1877)

Benjamin Bannan, Whig editor of the Pottsville, Pennsylvania, *Miners' Journal,* established the notion that a secret Irish society operated in Schuylkill County's anthracite coal fields during the 1850s. Hoping to drive a wedge between Irish and German Democrats, he editorially attacked the Irish as an ignorant group of drunkards whose behavior was easily manipulated. He alleged that a secret society, aligned with the "liquor interests," controlled Irish votes for insidious and criminal purposes. Later, he identified this secret society as the Molly Maguires, implying that they were the offshoot of a violent antilandlord society of the same name that operated in Ireland during the 1840s.

Violent protests against the Civil War gave some credence to Bannan's anti-Irish tirades. In July 1862, for example, John Kehoe, an Irish antiwar Democrat, spit upon the American flag during a public meeting in Audenried, Pennsylvania. F. W. Langdon admonished Kehoe and later was found so badly beaten that he died the next day. The following month a large group of men stopped a train of draftees so those who wished to do so could go home. Bannan, now a Republican, was quick to note that these outrages occurred in areas heavily populated by Irish.

But Bannan was not the only person speaking about a secret criminal society. A serious crime wave, including more than 50 murders, broke out in Schuylkill County during the war, and most of the murders were unpunished. The county's district attorney, Franklin B. Gowen, blamed his failure to prosecute on a secret society that could produce alibis at will. Gowen did not name the secret society, but everyone understood that it was the Molly Maguires. After the Civil War, however, rumors of a criminal society in Schuylkill County receded.

Gowen resurrected the notion in 1871. Appearing before a legislative committee investigating a strike of coal miners, Gowen, now president of the Philadelphia & Reading Railroad, implied that a secret society killed anyone who disobeyed the union's strike call. Two years later he hired the PINKERTON Detective Agency to investigate the alleged secret society. The agency sent five operatives into the coal fields. Four infiltrated the union (the Workingmen's Benevolent Association), but they failed to link it with a criminal society.

The fifth detective, James McParlan, tried the Irish connection. He infiltrated the Ancient Order of Hibernians (AOH), a secret, benevolent fraternal organization, which he stated in a preliminary research paper was the American branch of the infamous Molly Maguires of Ireland. Although he uncovered two other criminal groups in his initial investigation, McParlan remained focused upon the AOH. He soon learned that there was indeed a secret inner terrorist circle within the secret AOH. According to him, the AOH lodge's bodymaster heard grievances and (without the knowledge of the lodge as a whole) arranged a proper retaliation, be it a beating or a killing, by securing men from a different community. As the level of violence increased, McParlan gathered information on several incidents, resulting in the arrest a number of AOH members.

During the "great Molly Maguire trials" in 1876, the prosecution not only tried to convict individuals but also the entire AOH by telling juries that membership in that society alone was sufficient evidence for conviction. Furthermore, the AOH was connected to Civil War violence when John Kehoe, an AOH bodymaster, was tried for the murder of F. W. Langdon. Although 14 years had passed since the crime was committed, the prosecution discovered witnesses to the event. Despite their conflicting testimony, Kehoe was found guilty and was hanged. Indeed, a total of 20 so-called Molly Maguires were executed.

The evidence supporting the existence of the Molly Maguires—McParlan's testimony corroborated by witnesses granted immunity—is suspect. McParlan began his investigation with a preconceived notion of the Molly Maguires that he then applied to the bodymasters of the AOH. That is not to say that the murders he investigated did not occur or that all of the executed were innocent. But it is doubtful that the well-organized, violent, secret criminal society that McParlan described actually existed. It is more likely, given the motives for murder, that McParlan stumbled upon a loose-knit group of men acting out the agrarian tradition of retributive justice.

The Molly Maguire trials, however, gave credence to Benjamin Bannan's fulminations about the Irish and to Franklin B. Gowen's false innuendoes that Molly Maguire terrorists dominated the Workingmen's Benevolent Association, which in turn convinced many that organized labor was both violent and criminal. Ironically, many still believe Gowen's innuendoes and perversely applaud mythic Molly Maguires as martyrs of the labor movement.

Further reading: Kevin Kenny, *Making Sense of the Molly Maguires* (New York: Oxford University Press, 1998).

— Harold W. Aurand

monetary policies See currency issue

Moody, Dwight Lyman (1837–1899)

Few people so characterize their age and time as did Dwight Lyman Moody. Born on February 5, 1837, in Northfield, in rural Massachusetts, he went to Boston at age 17 to work as a salesman in his uncle's shoe business with the equivalent of a fifth-grade education. Two years later Moody experienced a religious conversion and awakening (he had joined the Boston Young Mens Christian Association [YMCA]) and soon thereafter moved to the then-rowdy and uncertain Chicago. Again working as a shoe salesman he also "sold" religion and filled the four pews he rented at Plymouth Congregational Church. His interests, however, were not narrowly denominational, and, besides working for the YMCA, he established in 1859 the North Market Sabbath School, which recruited its students from surrounding slums. To fund this burgeoning "congregation," he recruited men of wealth, including George Armour, Cyrus McCormick, and especially Charles Farwell, a rich merchant.

Although successful, Moody gave up secular business in 1860 to devote himself entirely to his urban missionary activities. During the Civil War he served in the United States Christian Commission ministering to Union soldiers, but between trips to the front, he worked in Chicago and in 1863 established a nondenominational church for his Sunday school congregation. He became president of the Chicago YMCA in 1866, and, thanks to his zeal, he was renowned as a "circuit rider in the urban wilderness."

After the CHICAGO FIRE of 1871 destroyed both his church and the YMCA building, Moody decided to become an evangelist. He had visited and preached in England in 1867 and in 1872, and when invited back in 1873 he

Dwight Lyman Moody *(Library of Congress)*

launched a two-year evangelist campaign there. He took with him Ira Sankey, whose musical gifts had already augmented his preaching in Chicago. The response to Moody and Sankey in Britain was tremendous, and Moody remained a full-time evangelist. Although a religious conservative who believed literally in the Bible and that Christ would come again, Moody was a layman neither trained nor interested in theology or doctrines. Rather, he stressed "God's love for sinners," which appealed to and reassured his listeners in a period of industrial and urban change. Returning to America, Moody and Sankey held equally successful meetings in cities from Brooklyn to San Francisco from 1875 to 1881.

Moody and Sankey reinvented the religious revival, taking it from its antebellum style and substance into the urban industrial age. With the skills and cunning of a salesman, with fresh and singable sentimental hymns, and with a message of divine love and salvation, Moody brought hope and comfort to millions and changed lives for the better. Moody was attuned to the individualism of his time, telling converts to join a church not of his but of their choice and to do good because it is the consequence of an inward, personal faith. Despite his meager education and conservative religious outlook (the term *fundamentalism* was not used during his lifetime), he numbered university professors, religious liberals, and ecumenically minded clergymen among his friends and supporters. When Moody died on December 22, 1899, he had become a major influence on the popular culture and spirituality of American Protestantism.

Further reading: James F. Findlay Jr., *Dwight L. Moody: American Evangelist, 1837–1899* (Chicago: University of Chicago Press, 1969).

— W. Frederick Wooden

Morgan, John Pierpont (1837–1913)

J. P. Morgan was the preeminent financier of the Gilded Age. Born on April 17, 1837, in Hartford, Connecticut, the son of international banker Junius Spencer Morgan and Juliet Pierpont, daughter of a Unitarian minister, John Pierpont, Morgan was educated at public schools in Hartford and Boston. Upon graduating from high school in 1854, he went on to study in Europe. In 1857, when his father relocated in London, he began his career in finance with Duncan, Sherman & Company in New York and in 1861 established his own private bank, J. P. Morgan & Company, becoming his father's agent in New York. During the Civil War he avoided conscription in the Union Army by hiring a substitute and profiteered by speculating in gold and by purchasing defective carbines from the War Department and reselling them to the government at a high profit. His father reined him in by pairing him in 1864 with Charles Dabney in Dabney, Morgan & Company, and in 1871 (again at his father's urging) Morgan merged with Philadelphia's Drexel & Company to form Drexel, Morgan & Company. In 1895, after the death of Anthony Drexel in 1893, the firm became J. P. Morgan & Company. From the start Morgan was the leading spirit in these firms.

Morgan's main business was underwriting (selling) new issues of bonds and stocks of RAILROADS and other enterprises. Since railroads and industry were expanding rapidly and in constant need of capital, they were compelled to listen to Morgan who, to protect the investments of his clients, sought to eliminate wild speculation and cutthroat competition. As a result, Morgan emerged as the major force in organizing, integrating, and stabilizing American railroads and industry in the Gilded Age. In the early 1880s, for example, the New York Central (NYC)—in which Morgan was deeply interested—and the Pennsylvania Railroad (PRR) engaged in rate wars and invasions of each other's territory. The PRR backed the construction of the West Shore line up the Hudson opposite the NYC's main line, while the NYC was constructing the South Pennsylvania paralleling the PRR's main line. In July 1885 Morgan invited representatives of the PRR and the NYC to meet with him on board his yacht the *Corsair* on the Hudson River. With his guidance the railroads agreed to cease their rate wars: The NYC got the West Shore line and the PRR received the South Penn, which it abandoned. (A half century later the Pennsylvania Turnpike utilized the South Penn's route and tunnels.) Neither the PRR nor the NYC reneged on their agreement, since Morgan could punish them by making their future financing difficult.

In the 1880s and 1890s Morgan reorganized many bankrupt railroads (including the Reading, the Chesapeake & Ohio, the Southern, and the Erie) and saw to it that dependable allies would sit on their boards of directors and vote against rate wars and overbuilding, which so often had caused their failures. Morgan came to dominate a vast transportation network with more than 55,000 miles of rail, but he had no influence over the systems of both JAY GOULD (whom he never trusted) and Edward H. Harriman (who reminded him of Gould). Harriman was backed by Jacob Schiff of Kuhn, Loeb, & Company. Morgan and his ally JAMES J. HILL clashed in 1901 with Harriman over control of the Chicago, Burlington & Quincy (CB&Q), which connected Chicago to both St. Paul, Minnesota, and Omaha, Nebraska. Hill and Morgan controlled the Great Northern (GN) and the Northern Pacific (NP), which came no further east than St. Paul, while Harriman controlled the Southern Pacific and the Union Pacific, which got no closer to Chicago than Omaha. Their struggle panicked Wall Street, but Morgan and Schiff caught themselves and compromised, with Harriman getting a share in the management of the CB&Q. The deal was solidified by establishing the Northern Securities Corporation, which owned the GN, NP, and CB&Q. To Morgan's disgust it was dissolved by the Supreme Court in 1904, but a community of interest had been established.

As industrial corporations began to dominate the American economy in the 1890s, J.P. Morgan & Co. became a leader in their consolidation and reorganization, financing many of the country's greatest industrial developments. In 1892 Morgan financed the organization of General Electric, and in the following years he financed American Telephone and Telegraph (AT&T) and International Harvester. Morgan's greatest merger occurred in 1901, when he merged ANDREW CARNEGIE's steel company with other firms in the STEEL industry to form the first billion-dollar corporation, United States Steel ("Big Steel").

In his later years Morgan collected art and rare books as compulsively as he had collected railroads, accumulating by the time of his death what was estimated as the largest private collection of paintings, sculpture, manuscripts, and jewelry in history. He became the president of the Metropolitan Museum of Art in New York, to which he left the bulk of his collection of art, and his personal library was made public after his death. He was also a major benefactor of the New York Public Library and the Cathedral of St. John the Divine. Morgan took a strong public stand for moral rectitude and assisted ANTHONY COMSTOCK in establishing the New York Society for the Suppression of Vice in 1873. Nevertheless, though married in 1865 to Frances Louisa Tracy, with whom he had four children, he had a mistress and was widely criticized for marital infidelity.

For the last 20 years of his life, Morgan was the most powerful financial figure in America. Indeed, his power was so great that during two notable crises presidents followed his lead and enabled Morgan to play a statesmanlike role for a price. In 1895 GROVER CLEVELAND was failing in his efforts to keep the nation on the gold standard as its gold reserves dwindled. Morgan, however, organized a loan to the federal government of $62 million in gold, which restored confidence, stanched the outflow of gold from the treasury, saved the gold standard, and netted his firm a $295,000 profit. In 1907, in the absence of a central bank, Morgan's arbitrary and effective actions (for which he was harshly criticized) reduced the effect of the Panic of 1907, but he used that crisis to extract from the TRUST-busting Theodore Roosevelt approval of United States Steel's acquisition of Tennessee Coal, Iron, & Railroad Company, which under normal circumstances Roosevelt never would have agreed to. Morgan was not the richest man in America, but his influence exceeded that of men like John D. Rockefeller and Andrew Carnegie, who were far wealthier than he. Morgan died on March 31, 1913, in Rome.

Further reading: Vincent P. Carosso, *The Morgans: Private International Bankers, 1854–1913* (Cambridge, Mass.: Harvard University Press, 1987); Ron Chernow, *The House of Morgan* (New York: Simon & Schuster, 1990), Jean Strouse, *Morgan: American Financier* (New York: Random House, 1999).

— Dennis Wepman

Mormon Church

The Church of Jesus Christ of Latter-day Saints, founded by Joseph Smith (1805–44) in 1830, was unique and American. Smith said he translated the *Book of Mormon* (1830), which he claimed was the sacred record of North American contemporaries among whom Jesus lived and taught following the Resurrection. Regarded as a prophet, Smith rapidly gained adherents who sought the purity of early Christianity. They coalesced about him but were persecuted and hounded from place to place as much for their formidable presence as for their beliefs. In 1841 Smith embraced the shocking doctrine of eternal marriage, which included polygamy. In 1844 he announced his candidacy for the presidency and later that year was lynched at Carthage, Illinois. Led by Brigham Young (1801–77), the Mormons fled west to build their Zion; they prospered in the valley of the Great Salt Lake. Politically, their Zion (Utah) was a theocracy, with Young at its head. Its economy was mixed, with families working their plots of land, herds communally owned, and milling, mining, transporting, banking, and merchandizing enterprises owned by the Mormon Church.

Mormon theocracy and polygamy caused problems with the federal government. The Mormons applied for statehood in 1849, but Congress in 1850 created the Utah Territory and President Millard Fillmore appointed Young as governor. Other federal appointees, however, were hostile to the politically powerful and economically dominant Mormon Church, and in 1857 President James Buchanan replaced Young as governor and dispatched troops to uphold federal authority. Fearing that the army was bent on destroying their Zion, Young resisted and the Mormon militia destroyed supplies for the troops. The hysteria led Mormons to join Paiute Indians in the September 7, 1857, massacre of 120 Arkansas and Missouri migrants (sparing 17 children) at Mountain Meadows in southern Utah. By June 1858 the "Utah War" ended. Young did not want to fight the U.S. Army, and Buchanan promised amnesty if Young and the Mormons submitted to federal authority. Although Young was no longer governor, he remained, as head of the church, the dominant political force in Utah.

The federal government, however, gradually increased pressure on the Mormons. CONGRESS in 1862 passed a law banning polygamy that in 1879 was upheld by the SUPREME COURT. Although there were more arrests for polygamy following the Edmunds Act of 1882, the Mormon Church did not give up the practice until 1890, after the Supreme Court upheld the 1887 Edmunds-Tucker Act, which threatened Mormon institutions by dissolving the church as a corporate entity. With the Mormon Church no longer sanctioning polygamy, Utah became a state in 1896. The communitarian aspect of Mormonism gave way to the vigorous individualism of America at large. Perhaps the largest dissenting Euro-American social order in the 19th century, Mormonism in the 20th century ironically became a bastion for conservative American cultural values.

Further reading: Leonard J. Arrington, *Brigham Young: American Moses* (New York: Knopf, 1985); Stanley P. Hirshson, *Lion of the Lord: A Biography of Brigham Young* (New York: Knopf, 1969).

— W. Frederick Wooden

Morrill Land Grant Act (1862) See education, federal aid to

mugwumps (1884)

The mugwumps, Republican advocates of CIVIL SERVICE REFORM, were distressed when their party, at its 1884 national convention, nominated JAMES G. BLAINE for the presidency. Blaine was not only hostile to their pet reform but also favored a protective tariff, IMPERIALISM, and worst of all was a corruptionist. (Years before, when serving as Speaker of the House of Representatives, he sold to the Union Pacific Railroad—which was anxious to retain his friendship—some nearly worthless Little Rock & Fort Smith Railroad bonds for $64,000). When the Democrats nominated the anti-TAMMANY HALL governor of New York, GROVER CLEVELAND, many reform Republicans, including former Secretary of the Interior CARL SCHURZ and editors EDWIN L. GODKIN and George William Curtis, bolted and supported Cleveland. Loyal Republicans derisively called them mugwumps— apparently Algonquian for "great men"—since the bolters unabashedly thought of themselves as "the best men."

The mugwump defection was disastrous for Blaine. It was especially strong in New York, and Blaine lost that state and therefore the election by a handful of votes. If 600 New York mugwumps had voted for Blaine instead of for Cleveland, Blaine would have been elected.

While the term *mugwumps* has particular relevance for the election of 1884, those men so-labeled had behaved independently in the past and would do so in the future. Several of them, including Schurz and Godkin, had participated in establishing the 1872 LIBERAL REPUBLICAN PARTY in opposition to President Ulysses S. Grant. Cleveland as president pleased mugwumps by his support of civil service reform and by trying to reduce tariff rates, and most of them supported him for president again in 1888 and in 1892. But they revered the gold standard and abhorred FREE SILVER, and in 1896 they voted for Republican WILLIAM MCKINLEY and against the Democrat WILLIAM JENNINGS BRYAN. The mugwumps, however, were anti-imperialists, and in the twilight of their careers opposed the acquisition of the Philippines by the McKinley administration.

Further reading: Gerald W. McFarland, *Mugwumps, Morals and Politics, 1884–1920* (Amherst: University of Massachusetts Press, 1975).

Muir, John (1838–1914)

John Muir was the leading naturalist and conservationist in the Gilded Age. Born on April 28, 1838, in Dunbar, Scotland, Muir migrated with his family to Wisconsin in 1849. His father worked him unmercifully hard on the family farm, stunting his growth (so Muir thought) but also developing his phenomenal capacity for endurance. Early each morning Muir read whatever books he could get hold of, since his father forbade reading in the evening. In addition, Muir was a talented whittler, had a creative mind, and fashioned mechanical contrivances, including an ingenious clock that woke him up early to do his reading. He exhibited his inventions in 1860 at the State Fair at Madison, and, impressed by their quality plus his general knowledge, the University of Wisconsin admitted Muir. Limiting his studies to subjects that interested him—chemistry, geology, and botany—Muir left in 1863 without earning a degree and began taking walking tours that became the passion of his life. Tramping through Wisconsin, Iowa, Illinois, Indiana, and into Canada, Muir kept journals recording and picturing what he had seen each day. Later, he would draw upon these records for his writings.

In 1867, while working in a wagon factory in Indianapolis, Muir injured an eye and "bid adieu to mechanical inventions" to study "the inventions of God." He walked 1,000 miles from Indianapolis to Florida and then went to California in 1868 and walked from San Francisco to the Yosemite Valley, where he lived for the next six years. While there he concluded that it had been shaped by eons of glacial activity, thus earning the derision of both California State geologist Josiah D. Whitney and the future head of the U. S. GEOLOGICAL SURVEY, CLARENCE KING; ultimately, though, Muir's views and not their ideas were accepted by geologists. Muir also explored Nevada, Utah, and the Pacific Northwest before marrying in 1880 Louie Wanda Strenzel, the daughter of a Polish patriot who fled Poland after the abortive Revolution of 1830, settled in Martinez, California, in 1849, and became a leading horticulturist.

John Muir *(Library of Congress)*

After visiting Alaska in 1881 (where he discovered and described glaciers, one of which is named for him), Muir purchased a portion of his father-in-law's land, lavished his attention upon it, and, like his father-in-law, became an outstanding horticulturist. By 1891—having sold or leased his land—Muir was able to pursue his avocation as a naturalist and conservationist.

Muir had contributed numerous articles on the natural beauty of the West to *Scribner's Monthly* and to the *Century Magazine.* He took Robert Underwood Johnson, the *Century* editor, on a camping trip in the Yosemite region, showing him its grandeur and the damage wrought by grazing sheep ("hooved locusts" Muir called them). Together they launched a campaign to create Yosemite National Park. Muir's earlier articles had aroused considerable interest in preserving beautiful areas, and, with popular support quickly building, CONGRESS in October 1890 created YOSEMITE NATIONAL PARK. The following year Congress empowered the president to create forest reserves, and in 1896 a Forestry Commission was created. Muir accompanied it on its investigative tour, and GROVER CLEVELAND in the waning days of his administration set aside 13 forest reservations. Lumber interests, however, succeeded by 1898 in undoing all but those in California. Muir wrote impassioned articles, again aroused public opinion, and the forest lands were reserved anew. In this work Muir was aided by the SIERRA CLUB, which he founded in 1892 and which has since become the leading advocacy group for the CONSERVATION of resources and the preservation of nature. With the presidency of Theodore Roosevelt, whom Muir in 1903 took camping in Yosemite, conservation had a warm friend in the White House. Roosevelt added 148 million acres to forest reservations and created 16 national monuments (including Muir Woods) and national parks (including Sequoia National Park). Muir, however, lost his last battle to prevent the flooding of Yosemite's Hetch Hetchy Valley for a San Francisco reservoir. He died in Los Angeles on December 24, 1914.

Further reading: Michael P. Cohen, *The Pathless Way: John Muir and the American Wilderness* (Madison: University of Wisconsin Press, 1984); Stephen Fox, *John Muir and His Legacy: The American Conservation Movement* (Madison: University of Wisconsin Press, 1985).

Munn v. Illinois See railroads

music: art, folk, popular

Art Music

The years following the Civil War saw the emergence of a national identity in the United States. One aspect of this was the gradual emergence of an American artistic identity. In the case of art music, there was a sense that America should develop a musical life of a quality equal to that of the European nations. William Mason (1829–1908)—pianist, composer, and the son of Lowell Mason—spoke for many of his generation and class when he encouraged the cultivation of refined musical taste in America. The 19th century saw the establishment of New York, Boston, and Philadelphia as the primary American cultural centers, but the arts were gaining a foothold in growing cities throughout the country. Symphony orchestras, choral societies, and other musical organizations were founded in many American cities.

In the first half of the century, organizations such as the Handel and Haydn Society in Boston (1815) and the New York Philharmonic Society (1842) were semiprofessional, offering individual concerts or a short season. The late 19th century saw the founding of professional organizations in many cities, including the New York Symphony Orchestra (1878), the Boston Symphony Orchestra (1881), the Chicago Symphony (1891), the Cincinnati Symphony Orchestra (1895), and the Philadelphia Orchestra (1900). Theodore Thomas (1835–1905), a German-born violinist, was the most influential conductor and promoter of symphonic music. In 1865 he founded the Theodore Thomas Orchestra, a New York–based organization that set a standard of excellence in orchestral music and was rivaled only by the finest European orchestras. Thomas also brought distinction to other orchestras he served as director, including the Brooklyn Philharmonic, the New York Philharmonic, and from 1891 until his death, the Chicago Symphony Orchestra.

Art music in the second half of the 19th century was dominated by a group of composers known as the "Boston classicists," or the second New England school (the first being William Billings and the "singing school" composers of the 18th and early 19th centuries). Most of the representatives of this school studied in Germany and considered the music of Haydn, Beethoven, and other German masters as models. Their approach to composition was academic and, indeed, as it was not possible to earn a living as a composer, many of them held appointments at recently founded conservatories and universities that were establishing music departments.

John Knowles Paine (1839–1906) could be considered the "father" of the New England school. Paine was born in Portland, Maine, studied organ and composition in Berlin, and was the first professor of music at Harvard. His orchestral works were highly regarded in his lifetime and received frequent performances. George W. Chadwick (1854–1931) was a composer whose orchestral music marked the beginning of an American style. Born in Lowell, Massachusetts, he studied at the New England Conservatory and in Germany with Josef Rheinberger. He taught at the New England Conservatory from 1882 until shortly before his death. Chadwick's orchestral style was firmly rooted in German romanticism and demonstrated colorful orchestration, yet was also marked by a distinctly American "tunefulness" and accessibility. It could be said that American orchestral composers of the 20th century, from Hollywood composers working in the 1930s to composers such as Aaron Copland, were his artistic descendants.

AMY MARCY CHENEY BEACH (Mrs. H. H. A. Beach) was the first important American woman composer and one of the finest composers of the second New England school. Born in Henniker, New Hampshire, Beach was mostly self-taught as a composer, in part because opportunities for formal study were not available to women. Beach was an internationally acclaimed concert pianist, and her compositions included chamber music, songs, many works for piano, and a small number of significant orchestral works.

EDWARD MACDOWELL (1860–1908) was the most celebrated composer of this generation. Although he was born in New York and lived much of his life there, he lived and worked in Boston from 1888 to 1896 and shared many characteristics with his New England contemporaries. His formative years of study were spent in Germany, and his work is within the German romantic tradition. He was professor of music at Columbia University from 1896 to 1904, and he was hailed in his lifetime, both in the United States and Europe, as the first great American composer. Other important members of the second New England school included Arthur Foote (1853–1937), organist at the First Unitarian Church of Boston, and Horatio Parker (1863–1919), professor of music at Yale University. Charles Martin Loeffler (1861–1935), assistant conductor of the Boston Symphony Orchestra for more than 20 years, was born in Alsace but lived most of his life in Medfield, near Boston. He studied in Paris and was the first American composer whose music exhibited the influence of French impressionism more than German romanticism. Dudley Buck (1839–1909), a contemporary of Paine, was one of the leading organists, choral directors, and composers of sacred music. He held positions in Hartford, New York, Chicago, and Boston.

In 1892 Antonín Dvořák came to the United States to serve as director of the National Conservatory of Music in New York. He encouraged American composers to make use of American folk music as source material for their compositions, as he had done with Bohemian folk music in his own compositions. He especially encouraged the use of American Indian music, as he felt this was the true indigenous music of America, and African-American music, which he found very beautiful and thoroughly American. His Symphony No. 9 *(From the New World)* employs themes inspired by African-American melodies. Many leading composers, including Chadwick, MacDowell, and Beach, did use folk melodies in their compositions. Arthur Farwell (1872–1952) was a leader of the "Indianist" movement. He made extensive use of NATIVE AMERICAN themes in his compositions and in 1901 founded the Wa-Wan Press, which published arrangements and compositions by some 37 composers based on Native American music.

Folk Music

One result of the growing appreciation of American culture was the first serious studies of Native American music. In 1882 Theodore Baker (1851–1934), an American music historian, published the first scholarly study of Native American music, *Uber die Musik der Nordamerikanischen Wilden* (On the Music of the North American Indians), as his doctoral dissertation at Leipzig University. It was from this work that MacDowell drew his themes for his *Indian Suite,* op. 48. The works of Alice Fletcher (1838–1923) and, later, Frances Densmore (1867–1957) were not only of great importance in the field of Indian studies but were pioneering in the field of ethnomusicology. Fletcher, an anthropologist and ethnologist, published *A Study of Omaha Indian Music* (1893), *Indian Story and Songs* (1900), and *Indian Games and Dances with Native Songs* (1915). Densmore, who studied composition and piano at Oberlin Conservatory and was strongly influenced by Fletcher, did landmark studies of the music of the Chippewa and tribes of the Plains and the Southwest.

A man plays the fiddle while a family dances in this lithograph by James Queen, 1872. *(Library of Congress)*

Africans brought to the New World as slaves between the 17th and 19th centuries brought with them music and dance traditions that were an integral part of their lives. In the isolation of the plantations, many elements of these traditions were preserved for generations. Yet as the slaves were exposed to Anglo-Saxon Protestant society and its music, they gradually incorporated elements of that music into their own. By the beginning of the 19th century, a distinctive African-American music had formed. The music was communal and functional, and it included religious songs, work songs, and various types of recreational or play songs. *Slave Songs of the United States* (1867) was the first published collection of African-American folk songs. It was the work of three Northern antislavery activists, William Francis Allen, Charles Pickard Ware, and Lucy McKim Garrison, and contained mostly sacred music. The compilers describe different varieties of sacred songs, including the "shout," a type of ring dance accompanied by largely improvisational singing, and the "spirituals," which were more closely related to Protestant hymns. In the late 1860s, George L. White organized a small choir at Fisk University, a school for AFRICAN AMERICANS in Nashville, Tennessee. The repertoire of this choir consisted mostly of arrangements of African-American spirituals. In 1871 White took the choir on tour to raise money for the school. After attracting the support of HENRY WARD BEECHER in Brooklyn, New York, the Fisk University Jubilee Singers became an international sensation, concertizing widely in the United States and Europe. After severing connection with the university in 1878 and becoming an independent organization, the Jubilee Singers spent more than six years touring the world, including India, China, Japan, and Australia. The choir can be credited with introducing the world to African-American sacred music.

Following the end of the Civil War, substantial African-American communities were established in the South, and in these communities there evolved forms of African-American secular music that would have a profound influence on American music of the 20th century. The "blues," a form that probably originated in the Mississippi Delta, traces its ancestry to the work songs and "hollers" of the slaves. But where that music was communal, the blues was personal. Each singer expressed his or her own personal sorrow, pain, and joy in song. The blues was characterized by use of a "blues scale," which included a flattened third and seventh degree. Blues often involved an exchange between voice and instruments, typically banjo and guitar. Gradually, a strophic form evolved, which typically employed a 12-bar chord progression (tonic: four bars, subdominant: two bars, tonic: two bars, dominant: one bar, subdominant: one bar, tonic: two bars). The verse often consisted of a line of text that was repeated and then followed by a third line that answered and rhymed with the first two lines. New Orleans has been considered the birthplace of jazz. It is thought that the style had its origins in the music played by dance bands and marching bands formed for parades and funeral processions. Although the term *jazz* was not used until after 1910, these ensembles were developing a new style of music that featured syncopation and improvisation by the 1890s.

The predominant culture in the eastern United States was of British origin, and much "American" folk music has British roots. The 19th century saw the arrival of millions of European immigrants who brought with them the music of their homelands. European musical traditions were preserved in many immigrant communities. Irish communities in Chicago and Boston, Jewish and Italian communities in the Middle Atlantic states, German and Scandinavian in the Midwest, Slavic and Polish in Pennsylvania, all preserved music of their homelands and contributed elements to American popular music.

Popular Music

American popular music between the end of the Civil War and the turn of the 20th century traces its inspiration and origins to a variety of sources. British broadside ballads and folk songs, Irish and Scottish songs, melodies from Italian opera, and the hybrid music of the immensely popular blackface minstrel shows were all parts of antebellum popular song style. This style found its culmination in the songs written by Stephen Foster between 1844 and 1864, and the style of Foster was to profoundly influence all future American popular songs. Postwar popular music saw the increasing influence of German musicians and music, from the songs of Franz Schubert to melodies from the musical dramas of Richard Wagner. Yet in many ways, postwar popular songs seemed to try to recapture a perceived naivete and innocence of prewar society, and many of the most popular were simple, sentimental songs that expressed a longing for the past.

"Silver Threads among the Gold" (1873) by Hart Pease Danks, "Grandfather's Clock" (1876) by Henry Clay Work, "I'll Take You Home Again, Kathleen" (1876) by Thomas Paine Westendorf, and "Carry Me Back to Old Virginny" (1878) by James Bland were typical of their day and reveal a stylistic debt to Foster. One new trend in American popular music was the publication of songs of the American West, such as "Home on the Range" (1876). The evangelical revivalist movement of the 1860s and 1870s produced a new style of "gospel" hymnody. Ira Sankey, Philip P. Bliss, Robert Lowry, and others wrote hymns that shared much in style with the popular music of the day. Lowry's "Beautiful River" and Joseph P. Webster and S. Fillmore Bennett's "Sweet By and By" are well-known examples of this genre.

The postwar years saw the rise of musical theater and the emergence of New York City as its most important center. In 1866 *The Black Crook* was produced in New York. The show incorporated a troupe of 100 French female dancers in a melodrama about a man who made a pact with the devil. This musical extravaganza, which combined sex appeal, elaborate stage effects, and popular music, had a run of 16 months and enjoyed frequent revivals through the turn of the century. Its success encouraged other extravaganzas such as *Humpty Dumpty* (1868) and *Evangeline* (1874), a parody of Longfellow's poem that was billed as a "musical comedy."

In 1878 Gilbert and Sullivan's *H.M.S. Pinafore* received its first American performance in New York in a pirated edition, and in 1879 Gilbert came to America to direct the first authorized performances. The operettas of Gilbert and Sullivan were enormously successful, and soon comic operas and operettas were in vogue in New York. French and Viennese operettas were produced, and American composers tried to duplicate the success of Gilbert and Sullivan. JOHN PHILIP SOUSA composed and produced several operettas in the 1880s, but he had his greatest theatrical successes with *El Capitan* (1895), *The Bride Elect* (1897), and *The Charlatan* (1898).

The 1870s saw the beginnings of vaudeville, a new form of entertainment that would enjoy great popularity for the next 50 years. Vaudeville had its roots in the blackface minstrel shows, which had been a leading form of entertainment earlier in the century. However, the vaudeville of the 1870s was conceived as a more respectable form of entertainment, one that women could enjoy. Tony Pastor (1837–1908), a singer and comedian, opened his "New Fourteenth Street Theater" in the 1870s. His shows featured singers, dancers, instrumentalists, comedy, and skits, and his theater quickly became a great success. Ned Harrigan (1844–1911) and Tony Hart (1855–91) developed shows that interspersed spoken dialogue with songs and dances and that featured ethnic humor and satire. *The Mulligan Guard Ball* (1879) was their first major success, which was followed by a string of hits in the 1880s.

Harrigan and Hart worked with Dave Braham, an English songwriter who wrote their most popular songs. Harrigan and Hart hits such as "The Babies on Our Block," "Paddy Duffy's Cart," and "The Widow Nolan" were among the most popular songs of the 1880s.

The last decade of the century witnessed the first attempts to establish African-American professional theater in New York. The first productions such as *The Creole Show* (1889) and *Black America* (1895) were linked to minstrelsy. *Clorindy; or, the Origin of the Cakewalk* (1898) was the first successful African-American musical. The music was composed by Will Marion Cook (1869–1944), a gifted musician who attended Oberlin Conservatory, the National Conservatory in New York, and studied violin with Joseph Joachim in Berlin. Cook entered theater music because, as an African American, that was one of the few avenues open to him.

The success of musical theater in New York City led its establishment as the center of a new kind of music industry. Many music publishing houses, including Thomas B. Harms (1881), Willis Woodward (1883), and M. Witmark & Sons (1885), were founded in the 1880s and 1890s. Most of these companies had offices on 28th Street between Fifth Avenue and Broadway, and the street became known as "Tin Pan Alley," a term that would later be applied to the industry in general. Publishers employed songwriters who concentrated their efforts on producing songs that would be commercially successful and earn money for the publisher. The publishers also employed song "pluggers" who would work to get new songs performed in vaudeville and musical theater. The songs of Tin Pan Alley were almost all in major keys, and many were in waltz time. They usually include a brief piano introduction followed by verses alternating with a chorus. Among the most popular were "After the Ball" (1892) by Charles K. Harris, "Daisy Bell" (1892) by Harry Dacre, "Sidewalks of New York" (1894) by Charles B. Lawlor and James W. Blake, "The Band Played On" (1895) by John E. Palmer and Charles B. Ward, "Sweet Rosie O'Grady" (1896) by Maude Nugent, and "When You Were Sweet Sixteen" (1898) by James Thornton. Each of these sold more than 1 million copies and remain popular and familiar today.

The 1890s saw the publication of the first songs in a new style known as "ragtime." By 1898 ragtime songs were being performed on the New York musical stage, and a national ragtime craze had begun. The style evolved in the saloons and brothels of St. Louis, but in the music of its greatest artist, Scott Joplin, it attained a level of sophistication that has led to its being considered the first African-American art music. Joplin's "Maple Leaf Rag" (1899) sold more than 1 million copies, a remarkable amount for a difficult piano solo.

Concert bands were popular throughout the 19th century, and the last decades of the century saw the rise of some very successful and popular professional bands. Although John Philip Sousa achieved success as a composer of theater music, his greatest success was as a band leader. Sousa directed the United States Marine Band and in 1892 formed his own band, which achieved worldwide fame and had a great impact on American musical taste.

Perhaps the greatest contribution of the 19th century to the history of music was an invention. In 1877 Thomas Edison produced the first sound recordings. While commercial recordings were not widely available until the turn of the century, this invention profoundly affected the way music was created and consumed, setting the stage for the musical world of the 20th century.

Further reading: Gilbert Chase, *America's Music: From Pilgrims to the Present* (Urbana: University of Illinois Press, 1992); Richard Crawford, *America's Musical Life: A History* (New York: Norton, 2001); Ronald L. Davis, *A History of Music in American Life: The Gilded Years, 1865–1920* (Huntington, N.Y.: Krueger, 1980); John Tasker Howard, *Our American Music* (New York: Thomas Y. Crowell, 1954).

— William Peek

Nast, Thomas See Volume V

Nation, The

The first weekly journal of opinion to achieve long life and wide influence, the *Nation* was founded in 1865 by EDWIN L. GODKIN as a 16-page paper filled with literary criticism and commentary on American political and social life and problems. The list of the contributors to the *Nation* from 1865 to 1900 encompassed most of the famous American and many of the well-known British scholars and thinkers of that period. Godkin concentrated his efforts on political and social commentary and developed an avid nationwide following among the educated and professional classes. *The Nation*'s circulation never reached more than 12,000, but it was read by influential people—lawyers, ministers, and college professors—who from pulpit and lectern spread the opinions fostered in it. Although the *Nation* has been identified with progressive causes in the 20th century, under Godkin in the 19th century it adhered to the classic liberal doctrine of laissez-faire and advocated small government, CIVIL SERVICE REFORM, a revenue (not protective) tariff, and the gold standard for money. Among adherents of those views, like the English poet and critic Matthew Arnold and British historian JAMES BRYCE, the *Nation* was the best weekly in America and possibly the world.

Further reading: William M. Armstrong, *E. L. Godkin: A Biography* (Albany: State University of New York Press, 1978); William M. Armstrong, ed., *The Gilded Age Letters of E. L. Godkin* (Albany: State University of New York Press, 1974).

— Ellen Tashie Frisina

National American Woman Suffrage Association (NAWSA) See women's rights

national banking system (1863–1913)

Ever since President Andrew Jackson orchestrated the destruction of the Second Bank of the United States in 1832, Whig and later Republican political leaders had wanted to establish some type of national banking system. During the antebellum period, the principal form of currency in the United States had been notes issued by state-chartered banks. With the dismantling of the Second Bank of the United States, which had kept state banknotes in check, the number of different banknotes in circulation dramatically increased. When the Civil War began, the advocates of a national banking system were given the chance to remedy the situation. Several southern Democrats who had favored state-chartered banks and opposed any form of centralized banking system left CONGRESS, thereby giving the Republicans a majority. Salmon P. Chase, the secretary of the treasury in the Lincoln administration, also argued that a national banking system would provide a more stable, uniform paper currency and would help finance the Union war effort by providing a large market for government bonds.

Congressional legislation in 1863, 1864, and 1865 created a new national banking system that existing or newly formed banks could join if they had enough capital and were willing to invest one-third of it in federal bonds. The national banknotes were to be uniform in design and backed by federal bonds that the banks would buy and deposit with the Comptroller of the Currency (a new division within the Treasury Department) in return for the notes. If a national bank should fail, the bonds would then be liquidated and the note holders compensated without loss.

Although the idea sounded feasible, it did not work out as planned. Note-issuing banks did not give up their state charters and join the national banking system, as was anticipated, until 1865 when legislation placed a prohibitive 10 percent tax on state banknote issues. Existing banks found the new laws more restrictive than the ones they had been operating under. These restrictions included bond purchase requirements, a limitation on the amount of notes any one national bank could issue to 90 percent of the market value of the bonds it deposited with the Comptroller, and a limit of $300 million on the total number of national banknotes issued for the nation. The new legislation also set minimum capital requirements for national banks that were too high to make joining the system profitable for banks in small towns. They also prohibited the popular practice of extending loans on the basis of real estate collateral, a major drawback in rural, agricultural areas, where land is the major asset possessed by many of the people. Faced with these operating restrictions, many existing banks chose not to give up their state charters and did not join the national banking system. The goal to make all banks national banks during the Civil War was not achieved, but by the end of 1865 there were 1,600 national banks, mostly former state banks, located primarily in the Northeast.

The shortcomings of this policy had a tremendous effect on the nation's economy in the late 19th century. The national banking system with its many restrictive policies never flourished in the nation's small towns and rural areas and as a result remained a mostly urban and northeastern institution. Furthermore, the state banks (which were favored by many Americans living in rural, agricultural parts of the country) were nearly destroyed by the 10 percent tax Congress placed on state banknotes. The idea behind this tax was to force all banks (state-chartered and private) to join the national system. The system soon earned the reputation in rural America as the tool of the wealthy industrialists and financiers of the urban Northeast.

Another problem that plagued the national banking system in the post–Civil War years was its susceptibility to financial panics. It was unable to do anything about the periodic shortages of cash and credit that are a natural part of the BUSINESS CYCLE. The system was based on cash reserves, and the total amount of cash could not be quickly altered because the system lacked a central institution that could hold the reserves of the commercial banks and, most importantly, could increase those reserves to meet demand. The politics of banking eventually became intertwined with the CURRENCY ISSUE as financial panics and industrial depressions struck the nation in 1873, 1884, and 1893. Those Americans most affected by the economic downturns, the farmers, targeted the national banking system and the government's reliance on the gold standard for their most vocal attacks.

Members of the FARMERS' ALLIANCES and later the PEOPLE'S PARTY (Populists) called for currency inflation in the form of either an increase in the amount of greenbacks (fiat money issued during the Civil War) in circulation or the free and unlimited coinage of silver (FREE SILVER). They also advocated the abolition of the national banking system and the creation of a subtreasury system to take its place. In 1913 the more flexible, decentralized Federal Reserve System would replace the national banking system as the central banking institution of the United States in 1913.

Further reading: Morton Keller, *Affairs of State: Public Life in Late Nineteenth-Century America* (Cambridge, Mass.: Harvard University Press, 1977); Edward C. Kirkland, *Industry Comes of Age: Business, Labor, and Public Policy, 1860–1897* (New York: Holt, Rinehart and Winston, 1961); Sidney Ratner, James H. Soltow, and Richard Sylla, *The Evolution of the American Economy: Growth, Welfare, and Decision Making* (New York: Basic Books, 1979).

— Phillip Papas

national parks

See conservation

National Woman Suffrage Association (NWSA)

See women's rights

Native Americans

From 1870 to 1900 Native Americans lost significant amounts of land and power to the U.S. government, which already had begun to remove and in some cases force Indian tribes onto reservations, making them wards of the government. Major tribes were assigned reservations in which to live, often far from their original homes and sometimes alongside enemy tribes. Wars on the Great Plains and in the Southwest, often brutal, eventually defeated hostile Indian tribes by attrition. Significant federal legislation, such as the well-intentioned DAWES SEVERALTY ACT of 1887, dissolved tribes as legal entities and distributed communal lands to individual Indians, which greatly reduced the land owned by Native Americans. Further, the EXTERMINATION OF THE BUFFALO took away the Plains Indians' way of life and economy, forcing nomadic tribes to adopt a settled farming lifestyle. Although humanitarian Easterners established reform groups to aid Native Americans, these organizations tended to be paternalistic and worked to further separate Indians from their traditional ways of life and assimilate them into the larger white society.

The wars against Native Americans waged by the U.S. government subdued Indian tribes and opened up their lands for white settlement in the frontier regions of the plains, the Southwest, and the Pacific Northwest. After the Civil War the government was successful in relocating various bands of the Sioux Nation (RED CLOUD was their most conspicuous leader) on reservations as a result of the SIOUX

WARS. Several bands, however, most notably the Oglala, Hunkpapa, and Miniconjou, resisted government efforts to relocate. In the War for the Black Hills (1876–77), the federal government aimed to remove Sioux tribes and clear the way for mining interests, but at the Battle of the Little Bighorn (June 25, 1876), General GEORGE ARMSTRONG CUSTER's troops were annihilated by SITTING BULL and CRAZY HORSE (Custer's Last Stand).

Tragically, the 1877 NEZ PERCE WAR was fought by the army against a people who could not be characterized as hostile to white settlers and who were protesting their removal from land in Oregon on which they clearly had a right to remain. Led by Chief Joseph, the Nez Perce's incredible 1,700 mile retreat through Idaho and Montana, during which they continually fought off the U.S. Army, ended with their surrender within a few miles of the Canadian border. Despite assurances that they could remain in the Northwest, they were shipped off to the Indian Territory (present-day Oklahoma), although ultimately they were allowed to return to reservations in Idaho and Washington.

The APACHE WAR, marked by frequent skirmishes and battles along the border between the United States and Mexico, lasted from the early 1870s into the 1880s. During the struggle the military, intent on bringing peace to a region plagued by frequent Apache raids, focused on securing the area for copper-mining interests after settlers began to mine copper ore. The government tried to subdue the disparate bands of Apache by consolidating them at the San Carlos Reservation in eastern Arizona, succeeding only after GERONIMO's renegade fighters were resettled in Florida in 1886.

The last of the Sioux Wars, indeed the last of all the Indian wars, came in late 1890. Sioux Indians adopted a movement that had started in the West 20 years earlier called Ghost Dancing, which involved communing with ancestors via a trancelike dance. The practice of Ghost Dancing unnerved the agents in charge of the Pine Ridge Reservation, where it had become popular, and in 1890 the U.S. Army moved in to monitor the situation. Reservation agents killed Sitting Bull, who had joined in the movement and whom they suspected was stirring up trouble, while trying to arrest him. Fearing an uprising, the army on December 29, 1890, massacred at Wounded Knee Creek a group of Miniconjou Sioux suspected of planning to revolt with their Sioux brethren at the Pine Ridge Reservation. The massacre united the Sioux, who ambushed military personnel the next day. Outnumbered, the Sioux surrendered on January 15, 1891, a date that historians have called the end of the Indian wars.

Federal legislation, backed by humanitarian reformers in the INDIAN RIGHTS ASSOCIATION, aimed to acculturate Indian customs and tradition and to assimilate Native Americans into the dominant Euro-American society. The Dawes Severalty Act of 1887, which opened western lands to individual ownership and broke the Native American tradition of collective landholding, allotted reservation lands to each tribal member. The act formed the basis of federal policy toward Native Americans until the 1930s. Western interests, including railroad companies, tended to support the act, since it would put surplus lands formerly held by tribes for sale, opening Indian lands to free-market forces. Reformers believed that passage of the law would help Native Americans realize the benefits of land ownership and therefore help them become full U.S. citizens. Over time, the long wait (25 years) for full title to land was considered an impediment and after 1906 could be shortened by the secretary of the interior. The Dawes Act decreased the size of Indian landholdings dramatically; by the 1930s Indian landholdings were only a bit more than one-third of what they were at the time the Dawes Act was passed, and two-thirds of Native Americans had no land at all. The Indian Rights Association's goals of assimilation mirrored the federal government's objectives in subduing the Indian tribes, as both worked to replace Indian religious traditions, social organizations, and cultural attitudes with Christianity, codified systems of laws, western-style schools, and a Protestant work ethic.

The OFFICE OF INDIAN AFFAIRS (often referred to as the Indian Bureau), attempted to carry out federal Indian policy. During the Gilded Age it established a few off-site

Photograph of a Sioux village taken in 1891, one month before the events at Wounded Knee *(Library of Congress)*

boarding schools (the most famous Indian school was founded in 1879 at Carlisle, Pennsylvania) that worked to assimilate young Native Americans by separating them from their homes and culture. The Office of Indian Affairs was charged with the task of overseeing the Indians on reservations and carving up those reservations under the Dawes Act. Shrinking landholdings forced Native Americans to abandon hunting and adopt farming, for which they had little inclination, on land that was not productive, with the result that food rations were needed, which in turn kept tribes dependent on the federal government. The Office of Indian Affairs remained a paternalistic force in Indian culture until the 1930s, when the agency became more concerned with protecting Native American culture and heritage and promoting self-determination among the tribes.

The extermination of the buffalo, which occurred throughout the course of the 19th century, culminated in a 10- to 15-year period of intense slaughter during the 1870s and 1880s, when the animal was nearly hunted to permanent extinction. The disappearance of the buffalo destroyed Plains Indians' culture and economy, made them dependent on grazing and farming, and broke their resistance to the invasion of white settlers. By 1880 all the wild buffalo in the southern plains had been killed. In the northern plains, extinction was delayed by the war with the Sioux for the Black Hills, but by 1879 the species was extinct in Wyoming and eastern Nebraska and by 1883 in Montana and the Dakotas. The extinction of the buffalo coincided with the removal of the Plains Indians to reservations.

Some Native Americans, after resisting the army and the hordes of white settlers, ceased their opposition. Red Cloud, a most formidable Sioux warrior during the War for the Bozeman Trail in 1866, negotiated a treaty at Fort Laramie in 1868 and adopted a peace stance in future wars. He was either hailed as a realistic statesman who understood the futility of further resistance or mistrusted as a sellout co-opted by the U.S. government, although he never received much from it for his cooperation. Other prominent Native American warriors became part of a sideshow in American popular culture during the 1890s, after all of the hostile western tribes had been successfully subdued. Geronimo became the most well-known Apache to whites, appearing at the St. Louis World's Fair in 1904 and in President Theodore Roosevelt's inaugural parade in 1905. Sitting Bull, after being imprisoned by the U.S.

government from 1881 to 1883 for conspiring during the War for the Black Hills, toured with WILLIAM FREDERICK (Buffalo Bill) Cody's Wild West Show between 1885 and 1886, performing with luminaries such as the sharpshooter Annie Oakley.

The reduction of Indian landholdings accelerated toward the end of the Gilded Age. Even Oklahoma's Five Civilized Tribes (the Cherokee, Choctaw, Chickasaw, Creek, and Seminole), who were considered the most "sovereign" Native American tribes, and the Osage were in 1898 no longer exempt from the Dawes Act, with the result that their lands were sharply reduced to accommodate white settlers. Western lands that in 1870 were almost exclusively occupied by Indians, like Montana and the Dakotas, were in 1889 granted statehood. By the end of the 19th century, tribal sovereignty had ended, and most Indians were on the way to becoming U.S. citizens. But rather than being integrated into the larger society, Native Americans were marginalized economically and physically on its fringes.

Further reading: Dee Brown, *Bury My Heart at Wounded Knee: An Indian History of the American West* (New York: Henry Holt, 1970); Francis Paul Prucha, *The Great Father: The United States Government and the American Indians* (Lincoln: University of Nebraska Press, 1986); Richard White, *A New History of the American West* (Norman: University of Oklahoma Press, 1991).

— Scott Sendrow

nativism

Prior to the Civil War the influx of large numbers of Roman Catholic immigrants, primarily from Ireland but also from Germany, aroused fears that produced an organized nativist, or anti-immigrant, movement in the United States. Nativists argued that the newcomers (who tended to join the Democratic Party) corrupted politics by selling their votes and robbed native workers of their jobs by working for low wages, but at the core of this xenophobia was anti-Catholicism. The nativists organized the American Know-Nothing Party, which upon the demise of the Whig Party in 1854 showed surprising strength on the state level, but antislavery quickly eclipsed anti-Catholicism and the American Know-Nothing Party disappeared.

After the Civil War ended in 1865, the pace of IMMIGRATION quickened, and by the 1880s it had become more cosmopolitan. (Chinese and Japanese laborers, for example, were attracted to California.) Between 1880 and 1924 almost 27 million immigrants came to the United States, but unlike earlier arrivals, most of them were from southern and eastern Europe. This "new" immigration was accompanied by a revival of nativism that stressed the old fears: anti-Catholicism, widespread unemployment, and wage reductions. However, this wave of nativism latched on to a new, apparently scientific justification for xenophobia. Nativists such as Madison Grant and others popularized a pseudo-Darwinian belief that the new immigrants were mentally and physically inferior and would corrupt America's superior northern European stock. Arguments were also made that the newcomers would promote radical or un-American ideas, were prone to crime and poverty, and posed a threat to traditional American customs and values.

Nativist groups such as the AMERICAN PROTECTIVE ASSOCIATION (APA) and the Immigration Restriction League (which advocated a literacy test for immigrants) sprang up throughout the United States. They used anti-Catholic, anti-Semitic, and anti-Asian rhetoric to promote a backlash against the newcomers. Later, in the 1920s, members of the revived Ku Klux Klan often resorted to violence and intimidation to dissuade immigrants from settling in certain communities. In that decade, nativists successfully called on the federal government to rethink its open-door immigration policies and adopt IMMIGRATION RESTRICTIONS that would limit the number of immigrants from each country allowed to enter the United States.

Further reading: Thomas J. Curran, *Xenophobia and Immigration, 1820–1930* (Boston: Twayne, 1975); John Higham, *Strangers in the Land: Patterns of American Nativism, 1860–1925* (New Brunswick, N.J.: Rutgers University Press, 1955).

— Phillip Papas

New South

The term *New South* was used to describe the post-Reconstruction economic development of the former Confederate states. In the years following Reconstruction, many southern leaders viewed the agriculture-based economy of the antebellum South as no longer viable and argued that the Confederacy had lost the Civil War because its economy had been unable to compete with the industrialized North. They believed that the future of their region lay in economic diversification and industrialization. Among those who advocated a modernized southern economy was Henry W. Grady, editor of the Atlanta *Constitution.* By the mid-1880s, Grady had become the leading spokesman of the New South ideology.

Several southern politicians and businessmen joined Grady and others to introduce a new spirit of enterprise into southern life. Lacking capital, southern leaders actively pursued northern and European economic investment. Capital from these sources poured into the South, helping to develop the region's RAILROADS, cotton textile mills, tobacco factories, and iron and STEEL industries. As a result, many southern industries came to be controlled by directors who lived outside the region and made decisions that affected the South's economy.

Railroads and steel were two New South industries that were especially attractive to northern and foreign investment. During the 1880s railroad construction in the South outplaced the national average, with more than 180 new railroad companies appearing in the region. Southern railroad mileage increased from 16,605 miles in 1880 to 39,108 in 1890. In 1886 southern railroads changed the gauge of their tracks to correspond with the national standard, thus bringing the southern rail lines into the national transportation network. The economic depression of 1893–97 led to the reorganization and consolidation of several southern railroads, giving more economic power to northern bankers and financiers. Expansion of the South's iron and STEEL industries was fueled by the discovery of great iron deposits in Tennessee and northern Alabama, the proximity of coal and limestone deposits, the rapidly developing transportation system, and the influx of northern and English capital. Between 1880 and 1890 Southern production of pig iron more than doubled. By the late 1890s, Birmingham, Alabama, had become one of the world's largest producers of pig iron.

Another southern industry that witnessed a rapid growth in the years following Reconstruction was cotton textile manufacturing. Between 1880 and 1900 textile production in the South increased from 5 percent to 23 percent. Initially, southerners provided the capital for this expansion; by the 1890s investors came increasingly from the North as New England mill owners began to recognize the benefits of relocating their businesses to a region with a ready supply of cheap, nonunion labor; abundance of water power; and low taxes. And finally, the rapid expansion of the tobacco industry in North Carolina and Virginia resulted from the introduction of new machinery, northern investment, and an increased demand for cigarettes.

Although several southern leaders called for the development of a New South based on the growth of new industries, others were hostile, and nostalgia for the Old South lingered. The myth of the "lost cause" permeated nearly every aspect of southern life, portraying the Confederacy's struggle against the North as a noble effort to preserve the

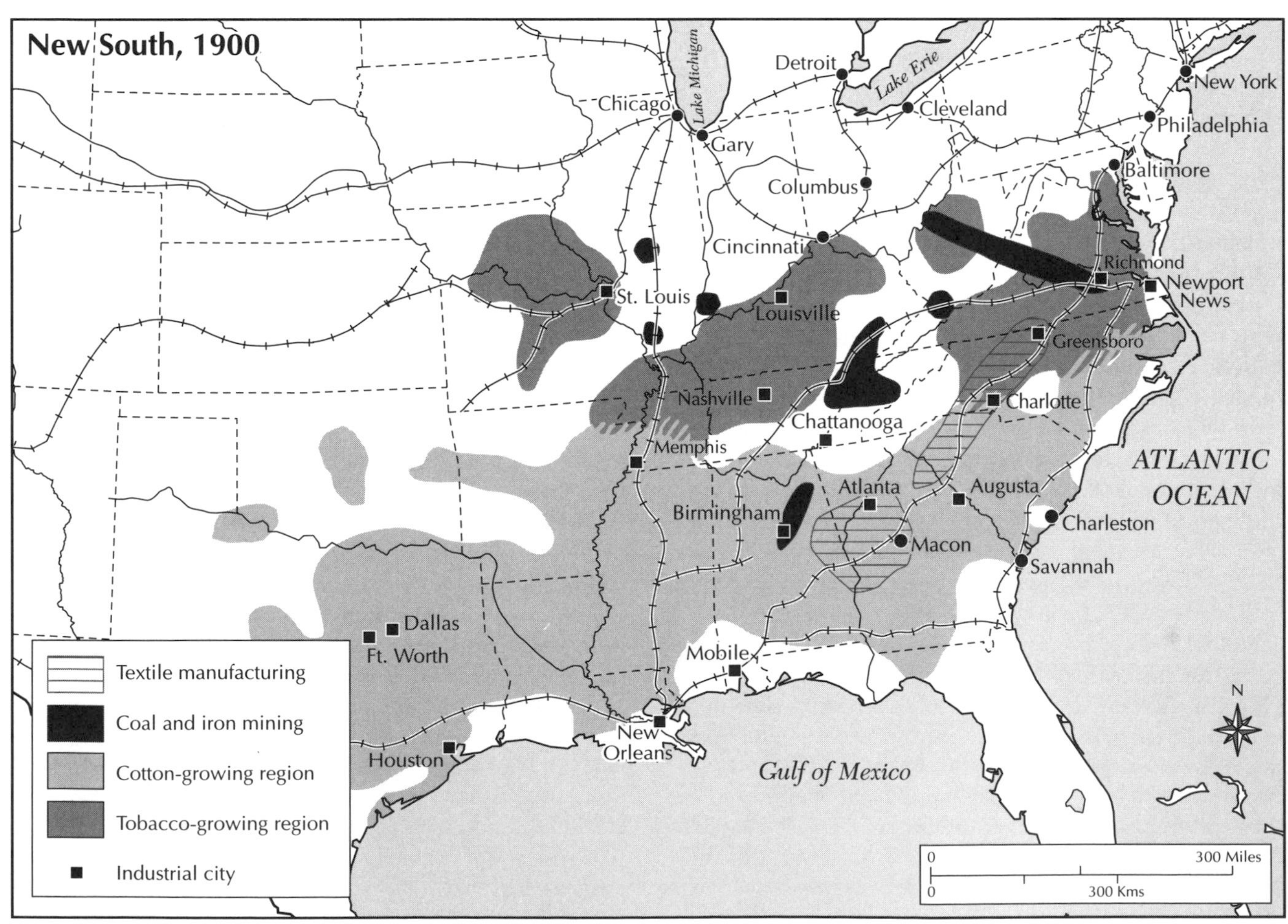

values of the antebellum South. Also, southern agrarians attacked the New South, blaming industrialism—especially northern bankers and capitalists—for the breakdown of the family farm and the movement away from traditional southern values.

Further reading: C. Vann Woodward, *Origins of the New South, 1877–1913* (Baton Rouge: Louisiana State University Press, 1951).

— Phillip Papas

newspapers

During the last third of the 19th century, a number of changes took place in the United States that greatly impacted newspapers. After the Civil War they reflected a landscape changed by rapid urban growth and the SECOND INDUSTRIAL REVOLUTION. Although preoccupied before the war with slavery, newspapers now confronted social issues including labor unrest, WOMEN'S RIGHTS, and civil rights for freed blacks as well as economic issues like the TRUSTS, the TARIFF ISSUE, and the CURRENCY ISSUE. Newspaper circulation grew as population and literacy rates increased among blacks and whites. (In 1870 the literacy rate for whites was 88.5 percent and for blacks 20.1 percent, both rising a decade later to 92.3 percent for whites and 30 percent for blacks.) Technological changes affected both newsgathering and the printing of newspapers; reflecting trends in other businesses, publishing a metropolitan paper became a big business dependent on infusions of capital and subject to acquisition by a "chain." The entire nation had changed, and what affected society affected the American press.

Some newspapers stepped up their collection of news and strengthened their financial base through increased ADVERTISING. New York City took the lead as the economic and political center of the nation, and its newspapers—already known for their complete coverage during the war—maintained their circulation and revenue figures. At the same time that advertising strengthened a paper's survival, editors and publishers began to think a bit more independently of party lines, since those newspapers most independent of party affiliation were most apt to survive.

A new generation of editors took over after the deaths or retirements of publishing giants like Horace Greeley, Henry Raymond, James Gordon Bennett, and William Cullen Bryant during the 1870s. The new editors—Whitelaw Reid, EDWIN L. GODKIN, Charles A. Dana, James Gordon Bennett, Jr., and JOSEPH PULITZER, among the most prominent—were poised to cover and comment on a new world.

Reid, who took over the *New York Tribune* from Greeley, was consistently loyal to the Republican Party but exposed corruption in both major parties. Within the Republican Party he opposed ROSCOE CONKLING and supported his archenemy JAMES G. BLAINE. Reid aimed to make the *Tribune* a respectable, conservative paper written by gentlemen for gentlemen and avoiding the radicalism of his predecessor Greeley and the sensationalism indulged in by other contemporary papers.

The *New York Sun,* edited by Dana, gained prominence through his concept of putting news first as well as its crisp writing and photography. The *Sun* hired college graduates at adequate salaries and gave them the freedom to write as they chose. Although the *Sun,* like most of its competitors, focused on crime and scandal, Dana told his staff to stress the human-interest angles and the emotional impact of stories. (Dana is chiefly remembered for assuring Virginia that there is a Santa Claus.) The *Sun* was often referred to as "the newspaperman's newspaper."

The *Sun's* closest competitor was the *New York Evening Post,* edited by Godkin, who was less interested in the news pages than the editorial pages. His eminently respectable and fiercely independent paper was peppered with intelligent, forceful commentary from a laissez-faire perspective.

The most flamboyant and erratic editor in these decades was James Gordon Bennett, Jr., who inherited his father's newspaper, the *New York Herald.* When he took over its management in 1867 it was the largest and most profitable paper in the nation. Ostracized from society for unseemly behavior (when drunk, he once urinated in mixed company), Bennett moved to Paris but closely supervised the *Herald.* Although Bennett maintained the *Herald's* sense of decadence and sensational news, for years it remained the nation's leading paper in its thoroughness of news coverage. It also "created" news. For example, it financed Henry Stanley's search in Africa for missionary/physician David Livingstone. Undisciplined absentee control, however, took its toll, and by 1900 the *Herald* was in decline.

While the *Herald* declined, the *New York World* became enormously prosperous, under the leadership of Pulitzer, whose formula for success was to mix sensational stories on crime and scandal with civic crusades. Perhaps the best known of his crusades was the campaign for schoolchildren's pennies to pay for the base of the STATUE OF LIBERTY, since CONGRESS was too stingy to appropriate the necessary funds.

The change to the independent (rather than party affiliated) press came largely as a result of the Industrial Revolution. The daily newspaper in the Gilded Age was produced at large industrial plants; gone were the days when the owner-editor could finance his business by selling his opinions. A split between ownership and editorship ensued, with editors often becoming "hired help." Newspapers became moneymaking business enterprises, not forums for personal opinion. Publishers sold stock to raise capital, causing editors to lose financial control of their papers. Advertising support became increasingly important and surpassed circulation income. By 1879 nearly 54 percent of all newspaper income was derived from advertising. And as journalists responded to changes in society, advertisers influenced the press in ways that would incense today's newspaper owners. Many advertisers believed they had a right to influence the editorial or news pages of papers that carried their ads, and they often boycotted newspapers because of the stories they covered or editorial positions they took.

While business pressures increased, political influence declined. As independents, newspaper editors were free to criticize their own political parties and look more objectively at world events and their impact on society. Editors began to adopt a different set of news values that conformed to the newspaper's role as holding up a mirror for society to view itself. That trend made it difficult to tell whether news or editorials shaped public opinion or whether the press reflected the public's opinion.

During the late 19th century, blacks broke into journalism and women played a more prominent role in newspapers. The first AFRICAN AMERICAN to be hired as a reporter was T. Thomas Fortune, who began writing for the *New York Sun* in 1887. He went on to publish his own paper, the New York *Age*. Other former slaves, such as Frederick Douglass, purchased newspapers, and the U.S. census for 1880 estimated that there were 31 black-owned newspapers, all weeklies. Although women had always worked on newspapers covering weddings and society events, these decades saw the beginning of the hiring of a handful of women who covered national politics (before they had the right to vote), including Mary Clemmer Ames (New York *Independent*) and Emily Briggs (Philadelphia *Press*). The most famous woman reporter of the day was the *New York World*'s Nellie Bly, who pioneered investigative reporting by feigning insanity to get herself committed to New York's Women's Lunatic Asylum and then writing a sensational exposé of conditions there. She is best remembered for making in 1889 the fastest (and most publicized) trip around the world, completing the journey in just 72 days.

The greatest changes affecting newspapers in the last 30 years of the 19th century came about because of technology. The invention of the telephone in 1876 permitted reporters in the field to phone in their stories, speeding up the process of getting news events into print and creating a more informed world at a faster pace. At the same time, technological advances made it possible to decrease the cost of publishing a newspaper and increase the distribution, so that the news traveled faster than ever before. The world was growing smaller, thanks to submarine telegraph cables, the invention of a completely automatic (rather than manual) printing press, and the creation of a national rail system. In 1875 the Pennsylvania Railroad began running fast mail trains seven days a week. A train originated in New York City loaded with the morning's newspapers, delivered them within hours to Philadelphia, and then delivered New York and Philadelphia newspapers to Chicago by the next morning.

The "new journalism" of the mid-1880s is renowned as the golden age of journalism. The number of newspapers published increased at a roaring pace. Between 1870 and 1900, some 1,200 newspapers began operating in the United States. Printing technology had advanced (the linotype was in wide use by the 1890s), and paper produced from wood pulp made newsprint cheaper than ever before. Screen printing was perfected, and, through a halftone process invented by Stephen Horgan in the late 1890s, photographs in newspapers were clear and crisp and began to surpass the use of engraved illustrations.

In the 1890s two opposing trends in newspapers became apparent. Adolph Ochs, a successful newspaper owner in Tennessee, purchased the *New York Times* in 1896 and proclaimed that it would be devoted to "all the news that's fit to print." In doing so he countered the popular sensational YELLOW JOURNALISM of Pulitzer and William Randolph Hearst, which at that moment dominated the New York newspaper scene and helped bring on the SPANISH-AMERICAN WAR. In addition, the influence of newspaper "chains" like those of Hearst and the Scripps family—with papers in several major cities—was growing. With Hearst and E. W. Scripps strongly influencing the editorial policies of their papers, individual newspapers were no longer the personal vehicle of the idiosyncratic editor and publisher. "One-man rule" gave way to a corporate style of management as newspapers became an industry. Competitors merged, and trade associations, such as the American Newspaper Publishers Association (founded in 1887), dealt with wide-ranging issues like unscrupulous advertising or biased reporting. The old-fashioned newspaper, led and dominated by dynamic and opinionated individuals, had entered a new world in the 20th century, with distinct jobs and philosophies for reporters, editors, publishers, advertising managers, and circulation managers.

Further reading: Frank Luther Mott, *American Journalism: A History, 1690–1960,* 3d ed. (New York: Macmillan, 1962).

— Ellen Tashie Frisina

Nez Perce War

The ancient home of the Indian bands that constituted the Nez Perce Nation was in the mountainous region where

Oregon, Washington, and Idaho meet. The Nez Perce, like other Native Americans, deified their ancestral land, and renouncing it was the equivalent of giving up their religion. In 1855 the federal government had guaranteed their title to their land, but in 1860 gold was discovered there. Miners rushed in and then remained to raise cattle and crops, despite the fact that they were trespassing. Federal Indian agents in 1863 bribed and coerced the chiefs of some bands to agree to a treaty moving them to Lapwai, Idaho, but other Nez Perce chiefs would not agree to the treaty and remained on their land. Among those was Chief Joseph (ca. 1840–1904), whose band lived in the Wallowa Valley of Oregon. President Ulysses S. Grant in June 1873 ordered that Joseph's band be given a reservation in part of the Wallowa Valley. Subsequent protests by white settlers, the governor, and the Oregon congressional delegation led to a reexamination of the case by the OFFICE OF INDIAN AFFAIRS (Indian Bureau) and a decision by Grant on January 6, 1877—two months before leaving office—that the 1863 treaty obligated all Nez Perce to remove to Lapwai.

Joseph and his fellow nontreaty Nez Perce chiefs, Looking Glass and White Bird, hoped to reason with the Indian Bureau and the U.S. Army. But at a council on May 14, 1877, General O. O. Howard told them that if they did not move in 30 days he would drive them off their land. To avert war, the chiefs agreed to move to Lapwai. Beyond the pain of eviction, moving required the difficult task of rounding up thousands of horses and cattle. Some animals were abandoned to settlers and others were lost while fording the swollen Snake River on the way to Lapwai. Smoldering with resentment, the Nez Perce camped 10 miles from the reservation on June 2, and Joseph and his brother Ollokot used their last days of freedom to go hunting.

In their absence, young braves from White Bird's band, to avenge a murder two years earlier, murdered four whites and then went on a rampage with 17 other warriors, killing more than a dozen other settlers. When Joseph and Ollokot returned they tried to persuade all to await the army, surrender the guilty braves, and avert punishment for everyone, but they failed. The Nez Perce moved to a defensible position on White Bird Creek and hoped that Howard would send emissaries to talk and avoid further bloodshed, but that did not happen. The pursuing cavalry and volunteers sent no one to talk and attacked at dawn on June 17, 1877, but suffered a disastrous defeat, with 34 men killed while the Nez Perce had only three men wounded. With Howard in pursuit, Joseph crossed the Salmon River to a new defensible position. "No general," Howard remarked, "could have chosen a safer position, or one that would be more likely to puzzle and obstruct a pursuing foe." Despite his admiration, Howard relentlessly pursued the Nez Perce, who were encumbered by the old and infirm, women and children, possessions, and livestock. Throughout the summer and into the fall the Nez Perce outfought and, despite encumbrances, outmaneuvered the army on a 1,700-mile retreat that is a classic in military history. In October Colonel Nelson A. Miles and 400 men cornered the Nez Perce at Bear Paw Mountain in Montana, just short of the Old Woman's Country—Queen Victoria's Canada—where they hoped to find refuge. After a five-day battle in which both sides suffered heavy losses and Howard reinforced Miles, Joseph surrendered with the understanding that the Nez Perce could return to the Pacific Northwest. With his clothes riddled with bullet holes, Joseph gave his rifle to Miles, turned to Howard, and declared, "I am tired of fighting. Our chiefs are killed. . . . It is cold, and we have no blankets. The little children are freezing to death. . . . Hear me, my chiefs! I am tired. My heart is sick and sad. From where the sun now stands I will fight no more forever."

To the dismay of Miles, who remained an advocate of the Nez Perce to his death, his promise to Joseph was ignored by Generals Philip Sheridan and William T. Sherman (who wanted to hang Joseph), and the Nez Perce were sent to the Indian Territory (present-day Oklahoma) where 68 died in their first year of captivity. In 1879 Joseph was allowed to go to Washington to plead for the return of his people to Idaho, but Secretary of the Interior CARL SCHURZ was afraid to allow them to return, since indictments were still out for the murders that began the war. In the 1880s the Nez Perce were allowed to return to the Pacific Northwest, but most of them, including Joseph, were kept at Colville, Washington. In 1899 and again in 1900 Joseph visited his beloved Wallowa Valley, but white settlers there would not sell him a small piece of land that had belonged to him and his ancestors. Joseph died in Colville on September 21, 1904.

Further reading: Alvin M. Josephy Jr., *The Nez Perce Indians and the Opening of the Northwest* (New Haven, Conn.: Yale University Press, 1965).

oil

The petroleum industry originated in America in 1859 when Edwin L. Drake drilled the first successful oil well at Titusville, Pennsylvania. The small amounts of petroleum that previously had seeped to the surface were bottled for medicinal purposes. Drake invented (but neglected to patent) the drive pipe that is still used today. He also neglected to secure oil leases on adjourning lands and thus made very little from his momentous discovery. Others rushed in, however, for its impact was instantaneous. Petroleum could be easily distilled (refined) into superior lubricants and especially into kerosene, which when burned in a lamp provided superior lighting and was far cheaper than whale oil. The crude oil initially was transported in barrels by wagons and barges to RAILROADS, but railroads extended their lines into the western Pennsylvania oil fields and by 1865 had developed tank cars. A short pipeline was constructed in that same year, and by 1881 a long-distance pipeline connected the oil region with the eastern seaboard. By 1870, 5.3 million barrels, of crude oil were produced; in 1880, 26.3 million barrels; in 1890, 45.8 million barrels; and in 1900, 63.6 million barrels. Pennsylvania remained a significant producer of petroleum throughout the Gilded Age, but in the 1880s both Ohio and West Virginia were in production, and in the 1890s Wyoming, California, and Texas had oil wells. The great Spindletop Strike in Texas, however, did not come until 1901.

Initially chaotic, the oil industry was monopolized quickly by John D. Rockefeller and his associates. Indeed, it was more completely monopolized in the Gilded Age than when major oil fields outside Pennsylvania and the Old Northwest subsequently opened up. In 1865 Rockefeller began refining oil in Cleveland, Ohio, formed a partnership with other refiners in 1867, and in 1868, to compete in eastern markets, secured a rebate (reduced freight rate) from the New York Central Railroad. In 1870 his associates and others formed the Standard Oil Company of Ohio, bought out oil companies in Cleveland and elsewhere, and controlled the largest refineries in the world, enabling Rockefeller to boast, "The oil business is mine."

Building upon his great volume, Rockefeller secured further rebates with the object of destroying his competitors. In 1872, with THOMAS A. SCOTT of the Pennsylvania Railroad, Rockefeller revived the South Improvement Company to allocate the oil shipments of its 13 members (10 of whom were in the Standard group) among the New York Central, Erie, and Pennsylvania Railroads. The railroads doubled their oil freight rates but allowed the 13 members a 50-percent rebate plus drawbacks that would give 50 percent of their competitors' freight rates to the South Improvement Company. Facing ruin, independents sold out to Rockefeller. The outcry against the South Improvement Company was such that the Pennsylvania legislature withdrew its charter, but Rockefeller continued to try to eliminate competition by rebates, underselling, creating tank-car and barrel shortages, and forming pools to fix prices and control production. By 1878 Rockefeller controlled well over 90 percent of the nation's refining capacity.

Pools enlarged the Standard group, but they were unwieldy and, as Rockefeller said, "ropes of sand." In 1882 the 41 stockholders of the Standard Oil Company signed a TRUST agreement that placed control of all the Standard group into the hands of nine trustees. This arrangement was so obviously monopolistic that the state of Ohio dissolved it in 1892. The Standard group's monopoly, however, was hardly shaken, since it remained intact and in 1898 refined 83.7 percent of the nation's oil. It also reorganized. The Standard trustees had already secured a charter for Standard Oil of New Jersey, which in 1899 was converted into a holding company by increasing its stock from $10 million to $110 million and exchanging this stock for the stock of the 40 members of the Standard group. Significantly its board of directors, headed by Rockefeller, was essentially the same group of men who had dominated the oil industry since the 1870s.

Oil well in California, 1898 *(Library of Congress)*

Further reading: Ralph W. Hidy and Muriel E. Hidy, *Pioneering in Big Business, 1882–1911: History of the Standard Oil Company (New Jersey)* (New York: Harper and Brothers, 1955); Harold F. Williamson and Arnold R. Daum, *The American Petroleum Industry: The Age of Illumination, 1859–1899* (Evanston, Ill.: Northwestern University Press, 1959).

Omaha platform (1892)

In July 1892 the PEOPLE'S PARTY (Populist Party) held its first national convention in Omaha, Nebraska, and adopted one of the most memorable party platforms in American history. With a stirring preamble written by Ignatius Donnelly of Minnesota, it proposed reforms dealing with transportation, land, and finance. The Omaha platform called for a graduated federal income tax; the nationalization of the transportation system; the Australian, or secret, ballot; the free and unlimited coinage of silver (see FREE-SILVER MOVEMENT); a flexible currency system of at least $50 per capita; laws to discourage large-scale land speculation and alien ownership of land; IMMIGRATION RESTRICTIONS; the eight-hour work day; the direct election of U.S. senators; a constitutional amendment that would limit the president and vice president to one term; and the initiative that would enable the public to compel the legislature to consider a proposal and the referendum that would allow the voters to approve or turn down a measure.

This platform was not hastily assembled. As the FARMERS' ALLIANCES spread throughout the South and Middle West between 1887 and 1890, they prepared the way for the People's Party and the Omaha Platform by contributing ideas and leadership. At a meeting in Ocala, Florida, in 1890, representatives of the farmers' alliance discussed the option of fielding a national political party in the upcoming 1892 elections. It was at this meeting that the Ocala demands were issued and became the cornerstone of the Alliance movement for as long as it existed. First and foremost, the Ocala demands called for the creation of "sub treasuries" that would allow farmers to store their crops in government warehouses. In return, they could claim Treasury notes for up to 80 percent of the market value of their crops. This loan was to be repaid when the crops were sold. The idea was to allow farmers to keep their crops in storage until market prices were more favorable. At the same time, the low-interest government loans on the value of the crops would help farmers pay their annual debts. Furthermore, the Ocala demands urged the free and unlimited coinage of silver; a graduated federal income tax; an end to protective tariffs and the NATIONAL BANKING SYSTEM; the direct election of U.S. senators; and effective government regulation and, if necessary, control of all RAILROADS and public utilities. Thus, several of the reforms embodied in the Ocala demands reappeared in the Omaha platform, which in turn shaped the ideological core of the Populist movement. Although the Populists were defeated, most of the Omaha platform was subsequently enacted by the major parties.

Further reading: Lawrence Goodwyn, *Democratic Promise: The Populist Moment in America* (New York: Oxford University Press, 1976); John D. Hicks, *The Populist Revolt: A History of the Farmers Alliance and the People's Party* (Lincoln: University of Nebraska Press, 1961).

— Phillip Papas

Open Door notes (1899–1900)

America's China policy at the turn of the century, called the Open Door, aimed to guarantee the free and equal access to Chinese markets and to prevent imperial powers from carving the "celestial kingdom" into a contentious patchwork of spheres of influence and special concessions. On September 6, 1899, Secretary of State JOHN HAY circulated a note to the capitals of Britain, France, Germany, Italy, Russia, and Japan requesting that they agree to allow equal commercial opportunity in each other's spheres of influence in China. Only Italy, which had no sphere of influence, agreed wholeheartedly, while the others equivocated to varying degrees. Nevertheless, on March 20, 1900, Hay audaciously proclaimed that all the powers agreed, but it was essentially an American policy and binding on no nation.

The Boxer Rebellion that spring, which led to an international expedition of imperialist powers to rescue their besieged legations in Beijing, immediately threatened Hay's Open Door policy. Concerned that the great powers would utilize the presence of their troops to expand their spheres of influence, Hay on July 3, 1900, circulated a new note stating that the United States stood for the territorial integrity of all China and commercial equality for all throughout the land. Hay, however, had merely announced a policy that the United States had neither the means nor the moral fortitude to enforce. In the late summer of 1900, Russia occupied Manchuria, using the large number of troops that it had mobilized to help quell the Boxer uprising. When queried by the Japanese as to what the United States planned to do to prevent its annexation by Russia, Hay admitted that the United States would not resort to armed force to make Russia abide by the Open Door. Furthermore, in November 1900, Hay himself was negotiating with China for rights to a naval station in Samsah Bay, which was within the Japanese sphere of influence.

Not surprisingly, the good will and the presumption of American honesty that were the policy's binding force quickly dissipated, and the policy was viewed abroad henceforth as mere empty rhetoric. What territorial and administrative integrity China retained resulted not from the forbearance of the great powers but from the stalemate produced by their fears of each other.

Further reading: Michael H. Hunt, *The Making of A Special Relationship: The United States and China to 1914* (New York; Columbia University Press, 1983); Akira Iriye, *Across the Pacific: An Inner History of American East Asian Relations* (New York: Harcourt, Brace & World, 1967).

— Timothy E. Vislocky

P

painting

Late 19th-century American painters adopted a cosmopolitan outlook in their lives and an introverted focal point on their canvases, in contrast to the nationalist, extroverted stance of the prior generation. European training, especially that offered in Paris by the École des Beaux-Arts and affiliated ateliers, supplanted native schools. American painters entered the world stage, not only by exhibiting abroad but often by expatriating, especially to France and England. Subjects that had dominated canvases—confident Americans and marvels of the landscape—were replaced by quieter, reflective people and places. Sophisticated technique became at least as important as subject matter.

This change was especially apparent in landscape painting. While Albert Bierstadt, Jasper Cropsey, and other Hudson River school painters continued to produce huge, minutely detailed canvases celebrating America's scenic wonders, the next generation chose to paint the poetry of place rather than delineate its particulars. French painters of the Barbizon school who forged a humble realism were important influences for Americans. The landscapes of George Inness, John Francis Murphy, and Alexander Helwig Wyant depicted circumscribed territories, such as glades, fields, and streams. Subsets within landscape painting developed, such as the tonalist canvases of Birge Harrison, the dreamscapes of Albert Pinkham Ryder, and the "glare aesthetic" of William Lamb Picknell. By the end of the century a decorative form of French impressionism came to dominate, with light-filled landscapes depicted in broad brush strokes and brilliant color. The canvases of Childe Hassam, Julian Alden Weir, Theodore Robinson, John Twachtman, and WILLIAM MERRITT CHASE were especially prominent.

Genre painting, or canvases with a narrative, which formerly had comprised only a small proportion of the American output, grew and diversified. Americans studied history painting, the highest art in the European canon, and from it learned how to paint the human figure and how to construct a story line. Like their European peers, Americans favored scenes of distant lands and remote times. Painters researched their subject through travel and reading and became experts in the topics. Orientalist artists such as Edwin Lord Weeks and Frederick Bridgman painted India and the Near East. George Hitchcok and Gari Melchers painted Dutch peasants, while George Boughton and Francis Davis Millet painted Puritans and colonists. Henry Ossawa Tanner, a successful African-American painter, produced symbolist biblical scenes. Religious, patriotic, and erotic subtexts were common in genre painting.

As the ranks of American's wealthy class swelled, so did the numbers of portraitists. While capturing a likeness was the basic measure of competency, elegance and refinement were also demanded. JOHN SINGER SARGENT and William Merritt Chase dominated the field, but many able painters thrived, among them Cecilia Beaux, Charles Courtney Curran, Julius L. Stewart, and Irving R. Wiles.

With the proliferation of civic and religious buildings, opportunities for mural painting grew. By 1876 John La Farge was put in charge of a team decorating Trinity Church in Boston, providing a model for future large, collaborative projects. Well-known easel painters such as Elihu Vedder and Will Low produced murals, while others, such as Edwin Howland Blashfield and Kenyon Cox, became specialists in the field. Murals were meant to instruct and inspire, so they depicted paragons and paradigms (saints, historical figures, and allegorical scenes). They were an integral element in the American Renaissance.

American painting became a viable profession in the late 19th century. Having familiarized them with the European art world throughout their training abroad, American painters sought to establish sustaining networks in their own country. They exhibited in established institutions, such as the National Academy of Design in New York City and the Pennsylvania Academy of the Fine Arts in Philadelphia. Their works were showcased in a string of international expositions: the PHILADELPHIA CENTENNIAL EXPOSITION of 1876, the Universal Exposition of 1889 in Paris, the WORLD'S COLUMBIAN EXPOSITION of 1893 in Chicago, and the Universal Exposition of 1900 in Paris. The painters formed professional organizations to exhibit and sell their work, including the Society of American Artists and the Ten American Painters. American painters became scholars, writers, collectors, and connoisseurs, thus differentiating themselves from tradespeople. Commonly, painters kept elaborately furnished studios filled with works of art, antique furniture, and exotic objects. Many painters worked in more than one genre; landscapists populated their scenes with figures, genre painters took portrait commissions, and so on. The boundaries between easel painting, mural painting, interior design, and the production of the decorative arts became quite permeable. JAMES MCNEILL WHISTLER produced remarkable interiors, while LOUIS COMFORT TIFFANY abandoned painting for interior designs and glass-making. As painters became more professional and their numbers grew, and as artistic endeavour became a popular topic in the media, more Americans interacted with art.

See also ART AND ARCHITECTURE; CASSATT, MARY.

Further reading: Brooklyn Museum, *The American Renaissance 1876–1917* (New York: Brooklyn Museum, 1979); Carolyn Kinder Carr et al., *Revisiting the White City: American Art at the 1893 World's Fair* (Washington, D.C.: National Museum of American Art and the National Portrait Gallery, 1993); Diane P. Fischer, ed., *Paris 1900: The American School at the Universal Exposition* (New Brunswick, N.J.: Rutgers University Press; Montclair, N.J.: Montclair Art Museum, 1999); H. Barbara Weinberg, *The Lure of Paris: Nineteenth-Century American Painters and Their French Teachers* (New York: Abbeville, 1991).

— Karen Zukowski

Pan-American Union

The Pan-American Union was established at a joint conference held in Washington in 1889–90, and since 1948 it has served as the secretariat of the Organization of American States. Although the 1826 Panama Congress—called by the South American revolutionary hero Simon Bolívar and enthusiastically backed by American secretary of state Henry Clay—was a fiasco, the idea of a hemispheric organization was revived in 1881 by Secretary of State JAMES G. BLAINE, who was anxious for closer commercial relations with Latin America. However, the assassination of President JAMES A. GARFIELD led to Blaine's resignation, and his unimaginative successor cancelled the invitations Blaine had sent for an International American Conference. By 1888 the value of hemispheric cooperation became apparent, and the GROVER CLEVELAND administration called for a conference in Washington to discuss an ambitious agenda to preserve peace and promote prosperity. Among the proposed items of discussion were avoiding war through arbitration, a customs union with common regulations, uniform weights and measures and a common silver coin, the protection of patents and copyrights, and the improvement of COMMUNICATIONS.

Appropriately, Blaine had returned to office as BENJAMIN HARRISON's secretary of state when, in 1889, representatives of 17 nations gathered in Washington as the First Inter-American Conference and elected Blaine as its presiding officer. As its leading spirit, he tried mightily to develop machinery to arbitrate disputes and to secure a customs union that would mutually lower tariffs and serve the economic interests of the United States. Both efforts failed, largely because Latin Americans feared that the power of the United States would be dominant in these economic and political arrangements. European traders, with their strong presence in Latin American, encouraged those fears because their interests would suffer if an American customs union were established. Blaine's other proposals of mutual coinage and transportation links met with lukewarm responses among the Latin American delegates. The conference, however, did suggest the appropriateness of reciprocal trade agreements, did consent to the arbitration of monetary claims, and did establish the Pan-American Union.

ANDREW CARNEGIE, one of the American representatives at the conference, in 1907 donated funds for the Pan-American Building, the organization's permanent headquarters in Washington. Meeting at irregular intervals at various capitals, the conferences accomplished little until 1910 at its fourth meeting, when it protected copyrights and patents. While the United States intended that the Pan-American Union promote its hemispheric hegemony, Latin Americans used it in the 1920s as a forum to protest intervention in Caribbean affairs by the United States and by 1933 secured a resolution, to which the United States agreed, condemning intervention.

Further reading: Walter LaFeber, *The New Empire: An Interpretation of American Expansion, 1860–1898* (Ithaca, N.Y.: Cornell University Press, 1963).

— Bruce Abrams

Panic of 1873 See business cycles

Panic of 1893 See business cycles

Patrons of Husbandry

In 1867 the Patrons of Husbandry, better known as the Granger movement, was founded in Washington, D.C. Its strength was among farmers in the upper Mississippi Valley, who joined it to better their economic position and to enhance their social life. Led by Oliver H. Kelley, the organization originally had secret rituals that included songs, flags, costumes, and passwords and admitted both men and women to membership. Each local chapter was known as a "grange," and in many farming communities across the United States it became the center of social activity.

The Granger movement spread rapidly where farmers experienced the greatest hardships. In the years immediately following the Civil War, wheat and corn prices made farmers on the Great Plains optimistic. Unfortunately, the PANIC OF 1873 coupled with severe blizzards, droughts, and grasshopper infestations dashed their dreams. Furthermore, faced with growing competition from Argentina, Australia, Canada, India, and Russia, farmers in the South and Middle West began to experience declining prices for their grains and cotton. Many of the nation's farmers were on the brink of bankruptcy, and many of them believed that only through collective action through the grange could their economic condition improve. They began to join the Granger movement en masse. In 1875, spurred on by the publication of Ignatius Donnelly's influential weekly, the *Monopolist* (1874–79), membership in the National Grange of the Patrons of Husbandry reached a peak of 858,050.

Promotional print for Grange members showing scenes of farming and farm life *(Library of Congress)*

Grangers blamed bankers, railroad operators, eastern land companies, and the manufacturers of farm equipment for compounding their sudden economic hardship. They complained, for example, that farm supplies and equipment were being sold at exorbitant prices, forcing many farmers to borrow money and incur debts averaging twice that of other Americans. Banks and eastern land companies charged farmers unusually high interest, making it difficult for farmers to pay off their mortgages. Grangers also complained to lawmakers about the price-fixing policies of grain wholesalers, warehouse owners, and grain elevator operators. Furthermore, they attacked RAILROADS for their discriminatory shipping rates that commonly charged farmers (who had no alternative means of transportation) more to ship their crops short distances than shippers (where competition existed) paid for long hauls. Grangers believed that the monopoly held by the railroads over travel and freight should be regulated for the good of the public.

Between 1871 and 1874, the Grangers became very active in politics and scored major legislative victories in several midwestern states. The Granger movement gained a political boost from independent farmers' parties that had been organized in nine midwestern states and in California and Oregon. As a result, so-called Granger laws were enacted in Illinois, Iowa, Minnesota, and Wisconsin. In 1871 the Illinois legislature prevented railroads from charging less for a long than for a short haul. In 1874 the legislatures of Wisconsin and Iowa began to regulate interstate railroad freight rates. Just a year earlier, the Illinois legislature enacted the Warehouse Act, which established maximum storage rates for grains and other crops.

The constitutionality of the Granger laws was soon challenged in the U.S. SUPREME COURT. In Granger cases, the most famous of which was *Munn v. Illinois* (1877), the Court upheld the Illinois Warehouse Act on the grounds that states had the authority to regulate private property when it was used in the public interest. The Court denied that Illinois violated the DUE PROCESS CLAUSE of the Fourteenth Amendment or, in the absence of federal legislation, the commerce clause of the U.S. Constitution.

Along with its political program, the Granger movement also established cooperative enterprises for both the purchase of supplies and the marketing of crops. They opened retail stores, operated local grain elevators, and manufactured their own farm equipment. A few of the local granges even ran banks and fraternal life and fire insurance companies.

The deepening economic depression of the 1870s, however, dealt the Granger movement a severe blow as several of its cooperatives were driven out of business. By 1880 membership in the Patrons of Husbandry had dropped to 124,420 members. In addition, the Supreme Court in *WABASH V. ILLINOIS* (1886) overturned its earlier decisions in the Granger cases. The Court declared that under the commerce clause of the Constitution, states could not regulate railroad rates on interstate shipments. This regulatory void led CONGRESS in 1887 to pass the Interstate Commerce Act. Although membership in the Patrons of Husbandry declined nationwide, the grange survived as a center of rural, small-town life in New England and a few Middle Atlantic states. Despite these setbacks, the Granger movement increased public awareness of the monopolistic practices of the nation's railroads and set an example for farmer cooperation and political action that would influence agrarian protests for the rest of the 19th century.

See also FARMERS' ALLIANCES.

Further reading: Solon J. Buck, *The Granger Movement: A Study of Agrarian Organization and Its Political, Economic, and Social Manifestations, 1870–1880* (Cambridge, Mass.: Harvard University Press, 1913); George Miller, *Railroads and the Granger Laws* (Madison: University of Wisconsin Press, 1971); Dennis S. Nordin, *Rich Harvest: A History of the Grange, 1867–1900* (Jackson: University Press of Mississippi, 1974).

— Phillip Papas

Pendleton Civil Service Reform Act (1883) See civil service reform

pensions, veterans See Grand Army of the Republic

People's Party (Populist Party) (1892–1908)

The People's, or Populist, Party was formed in response to the declining agricultural prices, rising operating costs, and high interest rates for agricultural credit that southern and western farmers confronted during the late 19th century. The strength of the People's Party lay in the South, Middle West, and Far West. It developed out of the National FARMERS' ALLIANCES, which was composed of the Southern and Northwestern Farmers' Alliances. The Alliance movement provided the Populists with membership, leaders, and ideas. Members of the Alliance movement made their initial foray into party politics during the 1890 elections when they aligned themselves with the DEMOCRATIC PARTY in the South and various independent farmers parties in the West. In 12 states, candidates supported by Alliance members won partial or complete control of the legislature. Alliance-supported candidates also won six governorships, three seats in the U.S. Senate, and 50 seats in the U.S. House of Representatives. These results encouraged several Alliance members to contemplate the creation of a third national party that would focus on the demands of the nation's agrarian interests.

Between 1890 and 1892 the support for a third party grew rapidly within the Alliance movement. In December 1890 the Alliance held a national meeting at Ocala, Florida, and issued the so-called Ocala demands that put forth the following objectives: the direct election of U.S. senators; a graduated federal income tax; the free and unlimited coinage of silver; the establishment of federal "subtreasuries" (warehouses) for the storage of surplus crops, with government loans at 2 percent interest secured by those crops; and effective government regulation and, if necessary, ownership of the RAILROADS and public utilities. The Ocala demands represented radical ideas for that time. Anticipating that the Democrats and Republicans would resist endorsing the Ocala demands, many members of the Alliance movement were eager to form a party of their own. It seemed as if the two-party system would not or could not respond to the growing problems facing America's farming and laboring classes. Sentiment for a third party was strongest among western agrarians, but several southern leaders, such as Thomas E. Watson of Georgia and Leonidas L. Polk of North Carolina, also supported the idea.

Alliance leaders discussed plans for a national third party in meetings held at Cincinnati (May 1891) and St. Louis (February 1892). These meetings were attended by many Northwestern Alliance members as well as leaders of the Southern Farmers Alliance and representatives from the dying KNIGHTS OF LABOR. In July 1892 more than 1,000 delegates met at Omaha, Nebraska, for the first National Convention of the People's Party. The platform adopted at the convention, largely written by Ignatius Donnelly of Minnesota, became known as the OMAHA PLATFORM and called for the Australian or secret ballot; a graduated federal income tax; the nationalization of the transportation system; the free and unlimited coinage of silver; a flexible national currency; inexpensive loans for farmers; laws to discourage large-scale acquisition of land; the direct election of U.S. senators; and the initiative which would enable the public to compel the legislature to consider a proposal and the referendum which would allow voters to adopt or reject a measure. Although the new political organization's name was the People's Party, the larger movement it belonged to was known as Populism.

In 1892 the Populists ran James B. Weaver, a former Union general and Greenbacker from Iowa, as their presidential candidate. For vice president they chose James G. Field, a former Confederate from Virginia. The Weaver-Field ticket won slightly more than 1 million popular votes and received 22 electoral votes. Weaver did very well in Colorado, Idaho, Kansas, Nevada, North Dakota, and Oregon. The Populists also elected five U.S. senators, 10 congressmen, and three governors, and nearly 1,500 Populist candidates won election to seats in state legislatures. Although the Populists had great success in the West, the party did very little in the Northeast. It also failed to gain much support in the South, where Populist strategy sought to build on the close relationship between African-American farmers and the mostly white local alliances that existed in the region. To do this, Populists stressed the common economic problems faced by all farmers and demanded fair elections. This strategy, however, was undermined by the prevalent racism in the region, ingrained Democratic loyalties, distaste for a presidential ticket headed by a former Union general, and widespread voter fraud and intimidation. The Populists' failure in the South ended any hope for an interracial agrarian reform movement.

Where the Populists won statewide elections, they established impressive reform records that included railroad and banking legislation, increased funding for public schools, and the exposure of corrupt business and political practices. Yet, despite its impressive record on state and local levels of government, the People's Party suffered from internal conflicts that prevented it from achieving a nationwide political base. It was also undermined by the two major parties, each of which incorporated some Populist programs into their platforms.

By 1896, the demand for Free Silver became an increasingly powerful force in America. The Populists had scheduled their 1896 national convention after those of the two major parties, assuming that both parties would be dominated by supporters of the gold standard. The Republican presidential candidate was WILLIAM MCKINLEY of Ohio, who was nominated on a platform that endorsed the gold standard. The Democrats, however, nominated WILLIAM J. BRYAN of Nebraska, who ran on a platform that emphasized stricter federal regulation of railroads and TRUSTS and supported Free Silver. When the Populists met in St. Louis, some believed that if they supported Bryan they risked losing their party identity, while others felt that if the party nominated its own candidate, they would ensure a McKinley victory in November. Ultimately, the Populists decided to nominate Bryan for president but named their own vice presidential candidate, Thomas E. Watson. Several Populists hoped in vain that the Democrats would drop their vice presidential candidate Arthur M. Sewall, a Maine businessman, from the ticket in favor of Watson.

Although the Bryan-Watson fusion ticket appeared on many state ballots, some states refused to include Watson and listed only the Democratic Bryan-Sewall ticket. Throughout the 1896 campaign Bryan ignored Watson. Consequently, many Populists ended up voting for the Democratic ticket instead of their own. McKinley easily defeated Bryan, collecting 271 electoral votes to Bryan's 176. The Republican candidate also received 7,036,000 popular votes to the Democrats' 6,468,000. The results of the 1896 election sent the People's Party into decline.

Although it continued to nominate candidates until 1908, the People's Party was effectively absorbed by the Democrats. The main contribution of the Populists was the eventual acceptance of their proposals by the two major parties. Their calls for reform of the banking system and national monetary policy, commodity exchanges, and new electoral procedures had a significant impact on American politics. Yet, lingering sectional and racial biases from the Civil War hampered the People's Party. Class bias also existed against a party supported almost exclusively by small farmers. The Populist position of maintaining private property and economic competition for small producers while demanding federal regulation of the national economy was met with derision by large-scale farming interests and the business community. Despite attempts to transform itself into a nationwide political phenomenon, Populism remained a predominantly rural, sectional movement with some power on the local level. In the end the Populists represented the last major agrarian protest movement against an increasingly urban and industrial America.

See also BIMETALLISM; CURRENCY ISSUE; FREE-SILVER MOVEMENT; PATRONS OF HUSBANDRY; SIMPSON, JERRY.

Further reading: Lawrence Goodwyn, *Democratic Promise: The Populist Moment in America* (New York: Oxford University Press, 1976); John D. Hicks, *The Populist Revolt: A History of the Farmers Alliance and the People's Party* (Minneapolis: University of Minnesota Press, 1931); Robert C. McMath, Jr., *American Populism: A Social History, 1877–1898* (New York: Hill & Wang, 1993).

Philadelphia Centennial Exposition (1876)

Running from May to November, the Philadelphia Centennial Exposition—a celebration of the nation's first 100 years—was attended by 8 million people. It took place in Fairmount Park, where 236 acres were enclosed for what was officially called the United States International Exhibition. The center of the exhibition was the great Corliss engine, whose geared flywheel and two huge walking beams dominated Machinery Hall. It powered 13 acres of machines spinning cotton, printing newspapers, and pumping water, and it symbolized the nation's industrial growth. WILLIAM DEAN HOWELLS, the novelist, called it "an athlete of steel and iron" and observed that "America is voluble in the strong metals and their infinite uses." Technological innovations especially impressed visitors. These included the new typewriter on which for 50 cents one could have a letter written, a lamp burning electricity rather than gas or oil, and ALEXANDER GRAHAM BELL's telephone. Besides Machinery Hall there were halls devoted to agriculture and horticulture, 24 state buildings, and 37 representing foreign countries. Memorial Hall, a permanent granite building that is now part of the Philadelphia Museum of Art, exhibited paintings and sculptures, including nudes that shocked yet fascinated puritanical Americans.

There was also a Woman's Pavilion. In it, shortly after the Corliss engine was set in motion, a six-horsepower engine powered looms and other machines and printed a weekly magazine, *The New Century for Woman.* Women not only tended the machines but also were responsible for everything exhibited, from Queen Victoria's etchings to articles of clothing.

The centennial committee planned a special celebration on the Fourth of July at Independence Square. Emboldened by the success of the Woman's Pavilion, suffragists asked to present, but not to read, their special Declaration of Independence for Women. They were turned down, but five suffragists with press cards resolved to read their declaration. Before 150,000 people jammed in the square and following the reading of the Declaration of Independence, SUSAN B. ANTHONY, MATILDA GAGE, and three companions stunned the crowd by marching up to the podium, introducing their declaration, distributing copies, and then proceeding to the musicians' platform, where Anthony read it while Bayard Taylor recited his National Ode from the speaker's platform. Most men present saw no connection between Thomas Jefferson's declaration and that of the women, but for women who could not vote and had difficulty keeping property after marriage, the connection was obvious.

The Centennial Exhibition demonstrated for all the world that America had come of age industrially. It also reminded Americans that although women were more emancipated in their country than elsewhere, they still lacked fundamental political rights and would demand, as effectively as possible, WOMEN'S RIGHTS.

Further reading: Dee Brown, *Year of the Century: 1876* (New York: Scribners, 1966); Robert W. Rydell, *All the World's a Fair: Visions of Empire at American & International Expositions, 1876–1916* (Chicago: University of Chicago Press, 1984).

Pinkertons See labor: strikes and violence

Plessy v. Ferguson (1896)

After the U.S. SUPREME COURT ruled in 1883 that the CIVIL RIGHTS ACT of 1875 was unconstitutional, various southern municipalities began to establish separate facilities for whites and AFRICAN AMERICANS. Eight states between 1887 and 1891 enacted laws requiring RAILROADS to maintain separate facilities for the races. Louisiana's version of this statute, enacted in 1890, outraged blacks, who organized a committee to test the constitutionality of the separate-car law the following year. In 1892 Homer Plessy, an African American, purchased a first-class ticket and occupied a seat in the "white" car. Arrested and convicted, Plessy appealed his case in the Louisiana courts and ultimately the U.S. Supreme Court. Albion Tourgee, a Radical Republican and a major supporter of equal rights, defended Plessy. Tourgee argued that denying his client the right to sit in a first-class car was a violation of his rights under the Thirteenth Amendment, which prohibited involuntary servitude, and the Fourteenth Amendment, which guaranteed "equal protection of the laws." Although six of the Supreme Court justices were former attorneys for railroads or corporations closely allied with railroads (and separate cars meant more trouble and expense for the roads), the Court ruled seven to one against Plessy and legitimized the "separate but equal" doctrine not only on railroads but in schools as well.

Justice Henry B. Brown delivered the majority opinion. He noted that the Fourteenth Amendment did not abolish distinctions based on color and was not meant to force social equality between the races. Brown added that separation laws did not stamp the badge of inferiority on blacks because whites were also separated, which did not make them inferior. Brown concluded the majority opinion with the observation that social equality between races was "the result of natural affinities, a mutual appreciation of each other's merits, and a voluntary consent of individuals. . . . Legislation is powerless to eradicate racial instincts or to abolish distinctions based on physical differences" and would only prove counterproductive.

JOHN MARSHALL HARLAN was the dissenting voice. Harlan, a former slave owner and Union officer, leaned on Tourgee's brief and insisted that the "Constitution is colorblind and neither knows nor tolerates classes among citizens," that the Thirteenth Amendment eliminated the "badge of servitude" as well as slavery itself, that the so-called "equal" accommodations was a "thin disguise" misleading no one, and that laws "which in fact proceed on the ground that colored citizens are so inferior and degraded that they cannot be allowed to sit in public coaches occupied by white citizens" will certainly create distrust and "arouse race hate." Harlan concluded that the Louisiana statute was "inconsistent with the personal liberty of citizens, white and black, in that state, and hostile to both the spirit and letter of the Constitution of the United States."

Southern states would within a few years enact additional JIM CROW (segregation) LAWS to effectively separate the races in schools, playgrounds, concert halls, railroad and bus terminals, movie theaters, opera houses, streetcars, and virtually every form of public facilities. Those laws prevailed in the South until the Civil Rights movement of the 1950s and 1960s forced CONGRESS in 1964 to pass the Civil Rights Act that eliminated the concept of "separate but equal."

Further reading: Paul Finkelman, ed., *The Age of Jim Crow, Segregation from the End of Reconstruction to the Great Depression* (New York: Garland Publishing, 1992); Charles A. Lofgren, *The Plessy Case: A Legal Historical Interpretation* (New York: Oxford University Press, 1987).

— William Seraile

Plunkitt, George Washington (1842–1924)

George Washington Plunkitt, ward boss of New York's Hell's kitchen, was born on "Nanny Goat Hill" on the Upper West Side of Manhattan to Irish immigrant parents. He had little formal education, quitting school at the age of 11, but in time he became smart enough to make politics his profession and shrewd enough to make it pay handsomely. By 1876 he had worked his way up through the ranks to become the Democratic ward leader of the New York 15th Assembly District in Hell's Kitchen on Manhattan's West Side. For nearly 50 years Plunkitt dominated the politics of the 15th Assembly District to the point that he once simultaneously held the public offices of magistrate, alderman, supervisor, and state senator.

TAMMANY HALL, arguably the most powerful "political machine" during the Gilded Age, was the Democratic organization that dominated New York City politics throughout the 19th century. Plunkitt supported every Tammany boss from William M. Tweed to Charles F. Murphy. He became well known for conducting business and talking with the press while perched majestically on the bootblack stand at the New York County courthouse.

Speaking frequently in 1905 with a local journalist, William L. Riordon, Plunkitt defended political machines against attacks by reformers, whom he dismissed as quick-fading morning glories. These interviews, which Riordon probably embellished, originally appeared as "Very Plain Talks on Very Practical Politics" in the *New York Evening Post;* they were subsequently published as *Plunkitt of Tammany Hall* and have achieved the status of a political classic. In them, Plunkitt described in amusing detail how he succeeded in politics and accumulated a fortune. The key to Plunkitt's success was winning and keeping the loyalty of the voters in his district. To do so he attended every wake, wedding, christening, and picnic and provided needy constituents with groceries, a bucket of coal on cold days, legal support, a place to live, or a job. Plunkitt used his access to patronage to find work for the unemployed in city agencies, within the political organization itself, or in local businesses anxious to stay on his good side. Plunkitt became wealthy not by stealing but by what he called "honest graft." Plunkitt made money by acting on inside information about proposed public improvements to which he was privy.

See also MACHINE POLITICS; TWEED RING.

Further reading: William L. Riordon, *Plunkitt of Tammany Hall: A Series of Very Plain Talks on Very Practical Politics,* ed. Terence J. McDonald (Boston: Bedford, 1993).

— Philip Papas

political parties, third

Two major parties—the REPUBLICAN PARTY and the DEMOCRATIC PARTY—have dominated American politics. Third parties, however, have occasionally been organized by advocates of an issue or group they feel the major parties have ignored. No third-party candidate has ever won the presidency, although a few have been elected to the Senate and the House of Representatives, and more have had success at the state and local level. More significantly, third parties, by playing the part of the spoiler, force their agendas (although often watered down) onto the platforms of either the Democrats or the Republicans, who are anxious to prevent the defection of key constituencies.

In the late 19th century, third parties formed around issues related to political reform, agrarian discontent, class conflict, and prohibition. The LIBERAL REPUBLICAN PARTY was organized prior to the 1872 election by Republicans who were disturbed by the course of the Ulysses S. Grant administration. They favored low tariffs, wanted CIVIL SERVICE REFORM, were anti-inflation, and had soured on Radical Reconstruction. The Liberal Republican movement did not survive the election of 1872. In part it self-destructed due to the ludicrous nomination of Horace Greeley—a high tariff, anti–civil service reform man—for the presidency, but also because Grant and the Republican CONGRESS undercut the Liberals by adopting both tariff reductions and civil service reform before the election and then abandoning them in 1875.

The most notable Gilded Age third parties were born of agrarian discontent and focused on the CURRENCY ISSUE. The GREENBACK-LABOR PARTY (National Independent Party) was organized in the 1870s and promoted the expansion of the currency by issuing more paper money ("greenbacks") and rejecting the gold standard in order to ease the financial burdens of farmers and industrial workers. The Greenbackers were succeeded in the 1890s by the PEOPLE'S PARTY (Populists), which promoted currency expansion through the unlimited coinage of silver at a 16-to-1 ratio with gold (see FREE-SILVER MOVEMENT). The Populists also advocated low interest rates to farmers based on crops stored in "subtreasuries" (warehouses), favored government ownership of RAILROADS and utilities, a graduated income tax, an end to the NATIONAL BANKING SYSTEM, and the direct election of U.S. senators. The Democratic Party, however, adopted Free Silver in 1896 and forced the Populists to choose between maintaining their party or fusion with the Democrats. They chose fusing and their party survived a few years in the Midwest before expiring. The Populists ultimately succeeded in that most of the reforms they advocated were adopted by the Progressives and the New Deal in the 20th century.

Among the other third parties to emerge at the end of the 19th century was the PROHIBITION PARTY, which sought the enactment of legislation outlawing the manufacture and sale of alcoholic beverages. It was the spoiler for the Republican Party in 1884 when enough upstate New York Republicans deserted to vote the Prohibitionist ticket, enabling the Democratic candidate, GROVER CLEVELAND, to win the state and with it the presidency. By the early 20th century politicians in both parties supported Prohibition. Some third parties like the SOCIALIST LABOR PARTY, established in 1874, were so small that the major parties could and did ignore them.

See also BIMETALLISM; OMAHA PLATFORM; SIMPSON, JERRY; WATSON, TOM.

Further reading: Steven J. Rosenstone, Roy L. Behr, and Edward H. Lazarus, *Third Parties in America: Citizen Response to Major Party Failure* (Princeton, N.J.: Princeton University Press, 1984).

— Phillip Papas

population trends

The population of the United States almost doubled from 40 million in 1870 to 76 million in 1900. Its growth was rapid during the Gilded Age, but not as fast as in previous 30-year periods. Although overall growth was beginning to level off, the late 19th century was a period of enormous population shifts in the United States. The influx of immigrants from Europe, among whom there were a large number of young single males, accounts for the fact that in 1870 there were virtually the same number of males and females, but in 1900 there were more than 1.5 million more men than women in the United States. European IMMIGRATION also accounts for the percentage decline of nonwhites from 13.7 percent in 1870 to 12 percent in 1900. The annual number of immigrants fluctuated with economic conditions. Large numbers came in prosperous years (788,992 in 1882) and fewer in hard times (138,469 in 1878).

Within the United States two major trends occurred simultaneously: the move west that more than doubled the number of farms from 2.7 million in 1870 to 5.7 million in 1900, and a nationwide move from farms to cities. In 1870 for each city dweller there were three persons living in rural areas, but by 1900 there were two city dwellers for three persons living in rural America. Urban population tripled from 9.9 million to 30.2 million, while rural population grew from 28.7 million to 45.8 million. Major established cities like New York more than doubled in population, and newer cities like Chicago multiplied more than five times from over 300,000 in 1870 to 1.7 million in 1900. States west of the Mississippi from 1870 to 1900 gained approximately 11.4 million people born east of the Mississippi, and during the same period 1.4 million southerners took up residence in the North. Most of those southerners who headed north were white, since the black population of the North increased by only 428,000 from 1870 to 1900. The enormous black migration from southern farms to northern cities came in the 20th century.

Americans were also a restless people constantly on the move. Quite apart from moving a long distance west or north, there was enormous geographic mobility within regions and between and within cities. Those who were unsuccessful would move a relatively short distance to a different farm or to another town in search of a better job. In places as different as Newburyport and Boston, Massachusetts, Omaha, Nebraska, and Poughkeepsie, New York, workers moved with great frequency, with as many as half of the unskilled moving in a 10-year period. There was also an enormous amount of moving within cities as tenants found better housing. With many leases in New York City expiring on May 1, it was called "moving day" and was a holiday of sorts, since the streets and sidewalks were so jammed with carts, wagons, and possessions that normal business could hardly be conducted. A remarkable number of Gilded Age Americans, especially those without real estate, were on the move.

Further reading: Raymond A. Mohl, *The New City: Urban America in the Industrial Age, 1860–1920* (Arlington, Heights, Ill.: Harlan Davidson, 1995); Walter T. H. Nugent, *structures of American Social History* (Bloomington: Indiana University Press, 1981); Stephan Thernstrom, *Poverty and Progress: Social Mobility in a Nineteenth Century City* (Cambridge, Mass.: Harvard University Press, 1964); Stephan Thernstrom, *The Other Bostonians:*

Poverty and Progress in the American Metropolis, 1880–1970 (Cambridge, Mass.: Harvard University Press, 1973); U.S. Bureau of the Census, *Historical Statistics of the United States* (Washington, D.C.: U.S. Bureau of the Census, 1975).

populism

See People's Party

Populist Party

See People's Party

Powderly, Terence Vincent (1849–1924)

Terence Vincent Powderly, a labor leader, was the 11th of 12 children born to Terence and Margery Powderly. After his birth on January 22, 1849, he was raised in Carbondale, Pennsylvania, and he quit school in 1862 to become a switchman for the Delaware & Hudson Railroad. Four years later he became an apprentice machinist for the same company. Laid off immediately after he finished his three-year apprenticeship, he took a job with the Delaware, Lackawanna, & Western Railroad Company (DL&W) in nearby Scranton, Pennsylvania.

While at the DL&W he joined the Machinists and Blacksmiths International Union and quickly became an officer of his local. Although he was not militant, he was fired and blacklisted in 1873 for his union activities. Unable to find work in Scranton, he took advantage of his union's job-referral service to secure a position in Oil City, Pennsylvania. While in Oil City he became involved in the broader labor reform movement. He returned to Scranton the following year, where he helped organize the local GREENBACK-LABOR PARTY. In 1878 he began the first of three consecutive terms as mayor of Scranton.

The following year Powderly succeeded Uriah Stephens as grand master workman (president) of the KNIGHTS OF LABOR (Knights), a position he would hold for 14 years. In his vision, the Knights would serve as an educational vehicle destined to replace the wage system with producer cooperatives. He advocated government ownership of public utilities, the abolition of child labor, workplace safety laws, and the exclusion of Chinese immigrants. Once a member of the Father Mathew Total Abstinence and Benevolent Union, he denounced alcohol as a major contributor to working-class poverty. He opposed strikes, believing that immediate concerns such as wages and working hours could be resolved best through arbitration. He issued a secret circular directing his members to withhold their support of the general strike called in support of the eight-hour working day. Avoiding the appearance of radicalism, he twice opposed resolutions expressing sympathy for the anarchists convicted of the Haymarket bombing at the Knights General Assembly in 1886. Yet he privately believed they were unjustly condemned.

Nevertheless, the Knights declined rapidly following the HAYMARKET RIOT. As a result, Powderly reached out to agrarian reformers. He and other leaders of the Knights attended the convention of the Southern Farmers Alliance, where they agreed to coordinate lobbying activities in Washington and support alliance candidates, but he was reluctant to ally the Knights with the PEOPLE'S PARTY (Populist Party) in 1892. The following year, disappointed agrarians joined with members of the SOCIALIST LABOR PARTY to remove him as grand master workman, and in 1894 he was expelled from the Knights.

That year, Powderly, who had previously studied law, was admitted to the Lackawanna County bar at Scranton. In 1897, having campaigned for WILLIAM MCKINLEY, he was appointed U.S. commissioner general of IMMIGRATION, but he was removed by Theodore Roosevelt in 1902 because of corruption on Ellis Island. Roosevelt, however, in 1906 gave him a position in the Department of Commerce and Labor, shifting him the next year back to the Bureau of Immigration, where he served until his death on June 24, 1924.

Further reading: Craig Phelan, *Grand Master Workman: Terence V. Powderly and the Knights of Labor* (Westport, Conn.: Greenwood Press, 2000).

— Harold W. Aurand

Powell, John Wesley (1834–1902)

Powell, an American ethnologist, geologist, and leader of federal mapping and scientific surveys, was born in Mount Morris, New York, on March 24, 1834. The son of a Methodist preacher and farmer, Powell moved with his family to the Midwest, where he developed a taste for natural history. Although educated intermittently at colleges in Illinois and Ohio, without earning a degree, Powell pursued his avocation. He collected specimens widely and, on the eve of the Civil War, was secretary of the Illinois Society of Natural History. Powell led Union artillery units at Shiloh (where he lost his right arm below the elbow), in the Vicksburg and Atlanta campaigns, and at Nashville before resigning on disability as a major in January 1865.

Powell then began teaching geology and natural history at Illinois Wesleyan University and resumed his curatorial work for the natural history society. Summers spent in the central Rocky Mountains with his wife and cousin Emma Dean, whom he had married in 1862, led to real exploration. On May 24, 1869, Powell and his nine-man team, supplied in part by army rations, began a daring exploration by boat down the Green and Colorado Rivers that ended successfully on August 30 below the Grand Canyon, except for three men who did not return. With funds from CONGRESS, Powell and a new team made a second, more scientific voyage downriver in 1871. His account of these twin adventures, published in 1875, merged events from both trips.

During the 1870s Powell, expanding on his river explorations, surveyed areas on and near the Colorado Plateau, first under the auspices of the Smithsonian Institution and then within the Department of the Interior. From 1877, Powell's U.S. Geographical and Geological Survey of the Rocky Mountain region operated south of the 42nd parallel as part of the Interior Department's work to map and assess the West's lands and resources by triangulation surveys that used a rectangular system, uniform scale, and contour topography. By 1879 Powell and his colleagues had contributed significantly to understanding the development of mountains and valleys, to ethnology, and to classifying the public lands by their nature and use. Their interpretations of canyons as "antecedent," "consequent," or "superimposed" reflected the dynamic relations between rivers and the geologic structures they crossed. Powell also supported a more rational use of the West's lands and limited waters and a wiser, humane policy toward its native peoples.

In the debates after 1873 about improving the federal mapping and scientific surveys of the public lands in the West, Powell favored consolidation under civilian control. In March 1879 Congress and President RUTHERFORD B. HAYES terminated Powell's and the two other competing western surveys. They established in their place the U.S. GEOLOGICAL SURVEY (USGS) to scientifically classify the public lands and to aid mineral industries and the nation's economy by examining the geology, minerals, and products of the national domain. Powell successfully supported CLARENCE (RIVERS) KING for USGS director. Powell moved back to the Smithsonian to lead the Bureau of Ethnology (BE), established by the same legislation; served with King on the Public Lands Commission; and was elected to the National Academy of Sciences. When King resigned in March 1881, he recommended Powell as his successor.

Powell's goals and methods in science and its administration differed widely from King's. Powell, who represented an older, less-specialized, and often self-taught tradition in science in America, believed that everything possible must be learned about a subject before the information gained could be applied to solving problems. This view paralleled his looser approach to management, one that allowed the USGS staff to choose their own subjects for study. In 1882, to advance the national geologic map sought by King, Congress authorized USGS activities nationwide. Under this rubric, Powell remade the USGS into a bureau of topographic mapping and basic research in geology, but this change came at the expense of the mandated studies of mineral resources. Congress increased USGS funding in the 1880s, until the legislators and their constituents grew dissatisfied with the paucity of practical results useful in meeting the nation's economic and educational needs and pressed Powell to reform. That drive culminated in the early 1890s after the USGS failed to respond to a renewed monetary crisis and Powell's Irrigation Survey (IS) refused to recommend sites whose selection would have reopened the public lands to entry and released federal-dowry lands to six new states. Congress and President BENJAMIN HARRISON discontinued the IS and selectively slashed the USGS budget, reducing Powell's salary and forcing him to fire some of its best geologists. Powell resigned in 1894.

Powell then underwent a needed operation on the stump of his arm; recovering, he remained chief of the BE. He continued to promote the reclamation of arid lands by wise irrigation and land use and to recommend that counties in new states be organized by drainage districts. Powell summarized his philosophy in *Truth and Error or the Science of Intellection* (1898). He died at his retreat in Haven, Maine, on September 3, 1902, less than three months after the passage of the National Reclamation (or Newlands) Act and the establishment of the Reclamation Service within the USGS.

Further reading: W. C. Darrah, *Powell of the Colorado* (Princeton, N.J.: Princeton University Press, 1951); W. E. Stegner, *Beyond the Hundredth Meridian: John Wesley Powell and the Second Opening of the American West* (Boston: Houghton Mifflin, 1954); Donald Worster, *A River Running West: The Life of John Wesley Powell* (New York: Oxford University Press, 2001).

— Clifford M. Nelson

pragmatism

Pragmatism is a philosophy that significantly influenced education and social reform movements in the period from 1870 to 1900 and beyond. Actually, some scholars contend that pragmatism is not a philosophy but rather a way to think about a problem, create possible solutions, and then test or evaluate them against their consequences. Pragmatism was a response to the seemingly fixed and fatalistic evolutionary determinism of Herbert Spencer and WILLIAM GRAHAM SUMNER. Rather than accept and adjust to their rigid concept of evolution, pragmatists used the language of evolution and argued that humans were "organisms" who lived in and could change their environment. People were not helpless and passive in the throes of a master law; rather, through their minds and behavior they could alter their circumstances and use knowledge for reform and progress. Pragmatists saw the world as dynamic, full of possibilities, and not governed by eternal, cosmic moral laws with fixed behavioral standards. There was no final analysis, for all analyses are continuously criticized and revised. This belief system won favor with many Americans living through the last three decades of the 19th century as the American landscape and its beliefs were drastically affected by industrialization, urbanization, the growth of a national integrated market and COMMUNICATION system, and unprecedented large waves of IMMIGRATION.

Charles Peirce (1839–1914) was a very influential pragmatist philosopher. Trained as a mathematician and astronomer, he emphasized the presence of chance and possibility in nature. Writing in 1878, he argued that our ideas become clearer when people understand that their knowledge comes from human experience and activity. The meaning of an idea did not come from an ancient, ethical, or moral belief but rather came from our understanding and giving value to its practical, immediate effects. Truth was derived from experience and could be best approached by rigorously testing hypotheses with the tools of logic. He had, in his words, a "laboratory habit of mind." Peirce, however, was difficult to understand and had little direct influence on the public at large.

In contrast, WILLIAM JAMES, who was influenced by Peirce, wrote with clarity and popularized pragmatism. Reflecting his training as a psychologist, James emphasized the role of the human will and the personal and emotional satisfaction that ideas gave the individual. Ideas—even religious beliefs—were true if they worked. People should judge ideas by their factual results. But by that test, what is true at one time and for one person may not be true for another person at another time. Essentially, ideas and truths are on trial and subjected to constant evaluation and reshaping. James perceived that the universe was open and an "unfinished experiment," and he believed that people should not follow abstract, previously agreed upon solutions to problems. If truth was the goal, truth was what reality brought to an idea. The idea's value came from its utility. Threaded through his beliefs was the central theme that humans, through their intelligence, could be actively involved in creating and managing their lives. They simply had to carefully learn from their daily experiences and constantly test their behavior against its results. If one way of doing something did not work, then change was called for. If one result did not satisfy, then one should recognize the situation and find other experientially tested means to meet personal or organizational goals. This philosophy made sense in a society whose credo was that self-made individuals, through hard work and a bit of luck, could achieve their dreams.

While James's stress was on the personal and emotional, John Dewey, a late 19th- and early 20th-century educational philosopher and teacher-educator, applied pragmatic principles to social issues. Since society was unfinished, the experimental method should be utilized to solve social problems. Study the history of a problem, research solutions, try them out, and adjust them to make them work. Dewey's influence in the classroom was and still is enormous. He taught that teachers should always know the needs and interests of students. They should not impose morals, knowledge, or skills on children. While children had to learn reading, writing, computing, and civics, they needed to construct a path of learning from their own circumstances to these unknown skills and beliefs. If children in school learned how to solve problems, as adults they might transfer these experiences into political life and reform institutions.

In other applications of pragmatism, educators in universities conducted research on reforming electoral systems, civil services, taxation, and governmental services. Specialists in agriculture carried their research from universities into the villages and fields of American farmers, showing families how they could raise productivity and improve their lives. For many Americans, politics, government actions, and human relationships were not determined by unchangeable economic and social laws or absolute moral standards. For them, human needs and the best methods for fulfilling them were informed by pragmatic ethics.

Further reading: Bruce Kuklick, *The Rise of American Philosophy: Cambridge, Massachusetts, 1860–1920* (New Haven, Conn.: Yale University Press, 1977); David W. Marcell, *Progress and Pragmatism: James, Dewey, Beard, and the American Idea of Progress* (Westport, Conn.: Greenwood, 1974); Louis Menand, *The Metaphysical Club: A Story of Ideas in America* (New York: Farrar Straus Giroux, 2001).

— Harry Stein

presidency, the

The powers exercised by presidents increased in the late 19th century. In 1870 the Whig concept of a passive chief executive (a reaction to the vigorous presidency of Andrew Jackson) prevailed. The president was expected to follow the lead of CONGRESS and simply execute the laws it made. He could suggest but not dictate legislation, and he should resort to the veto only in extraordinary cases. Indeed, members of Congress interfered with the administrative responsibilities of the president by dictating whom he should appoint as the department heads that formed his cabinet as well as civil servants in their districts and states. The president was to be dignified and above the sordid business of politics. Neither the Civil War nor

Reconstruction appreciably changed the presidency. Necessity forced Abraham Lincoln to expand presidential war powers temporarily, but he deferred to Congress in other matters, while Andrew Johnson not only lost the battle with Congress over reconstructing the Union but also damaged the prestige of his office.

Yet, whatever political experience, theoretical ideas, or personality traits presidents possess, they all make some effort, with varying success, to defy Congress and enhance their power. Ulysses S. Grant, upon taking office in 1869, selected his cabinet without consulting Republican congressional leaders, but soon, at their behest, he replaced the conspicuous political independents with pliant party men. On the other hand, Grant influenced the Senate to depose Charles Sumner, chairman of the Senate Foreign Relations Committee, when he challenged Grant's control of FOREIGN POLICY, and in 1874 Grant obeyed his hard-money conscience and vetoed the Inflationary bill (which actually had very little inflation in it).

RUTHERFORD B. HAYES, however, consistently tried to enhance the power of the executive. His choice of a cabinet outraged party leaders, and his attack on "senatorial courtesy" succeeded to the point that members of Congress suggested but did not dictate appointments. Hayes also, in the "battle of the riders," preserved the executive veto power by vetoing several appropriations bills with additions that were designed to force his acceptance of unwanted legislation. The veto messages, as Hayes wished, aroused public opinion. Hayes also travelled widely, spoke frequently on policies but not politics, and identified his presidency with issues as contrasted with the congressional orientation toward party organization. JAMES A. GARFIELD after long service in Congress was inclined to defer to his former colleagues, but to control his appointments to office he fought and again defeated senatorial courtesy. The adoption of CIVIL SERVICE REFORM during the CHESTER A. ARTHUR administration reduced the men and money available for political parties and would in time enhance the control of issue-oriented presidents over their party.

Presidential power did not grow during GROVER CLEVELAND's first term. Immersed in the minutiae of office, he specialized in scrutinizing and vetoing private pension bills. Although in 1887 he signed the Interstate Commerce Act and the DAWES SEVERALTY ACT, he shaped neither, and while he called for tariff revision he did not fight effectively for it. In contrast, his successor BENJAMIN HARRISON did influence much of the legislation passed by the "billion dollar Congress," including the SHERMAN ANTITRUST ACT (1890) and the reciprocal feature of the MCKINLEY TARIFF (1890). And the economic depression following the PANIC OF 1893 inspired Cleveland in his second term to convince a reluctant Congress in 1894 to repeal the Sherman Silver Purchase Act of 1890.

WILLIAM MCKINLEY, much like his Civil War commander Rutherford B. Hayes, was not dominated by Congress on either domestic or foreign policy issues and cultivated public opinion. Responding to his wishes, Congress raised rates and included the reciprocity feature in the Dingley Tariff (1897). He was not stampeded into a declaration of war against Spain in 1898; he personally directed the war effort; and he made the decisions that acquired overseas possessions in the Pacific and the Caribbean and paved the way for the construction of an isthmian canal. In his relations with Congress, his conduct of foreign policy, his enlarged White House staff, and his use of the press, McKinley paved the way for powerful 20th-century presidents.

Further reading: H. Wayne Morgan, *From Hayes to McKinley: National Party Politics, 1877–1896* (Syracuse, N.Y.: Syracuse University Press, 1969).

presidential campaigns (1872–1900)

Just as THE PRESIDENCY was evolving during the Gilded Age, so, too, were presidential campaigns. In the 1860s candidates for president were supposed to be above participating in the campaign, even though most of them had devoted a lifetime to securing the nomination from their party's national convention. Republican candidates needed a simple majority, but Democrats had to have a two-thirds majority to get the nomination. In trying to identify their candidate with the selflessness and purity of the legendary Cincinnatus, who abandoned the plow to heed the call to save the Republic of Rome, conventions would send a delegation to the nominee's home to inform him of his selection. The candidate would respond with a letter of acceptance stressing those planks in the party's platform (which the convention also adopted) that the candidate wished to be identified with and on which he believed the campaign should be run. From that point on the nominees remained in virtual seclusion and were restricted to giving behind-the-scenes advice. Campaigns were financed by assessing civil servants (whose jobs depended on the outcome of the election) a percentage of their annual salary, and they were relied upon to get out the vote. National committees were nominally in charge of the campaign, but because they had limited funds and were weak, virtually independent state committees ran the campaign in their states. Campaigns were enormously entertaining, with spellbinding speakers, roasted oxen at barbecues, brass bands, songs, chants, brawls, and torchlight parades with illuminated windows along the right of way. No sporting or theatrical event could match the spectacle of a Gilded Age political campaign.

Election statistics show that usually the major parties were evenly matched:

Year	Candidate	Party	Popular Vote (%)	Electoral Vote
1872	Ulysses S. Grant	Republican	3,596,745 (55.6)	286
	Horace Greeley	Democratic	2,843,446 (43.9)	66
1876	Rutherford B. Hayes	Republican	4,036,572 (48.0)	185
	Samuel J. Tilden	Democratic	4,284,020 (51.0)	184
1880	James A. Garfield	Republican	4,449,053 (48.3)	214
	Winfield S. Hancock	Democratic	4,432,035 (48.2)	155
1884	Grover Cleveland	Democratic	4,874,986 (48.5)	219
	James G. Blaine	Republican	4,851,981 (48.2)	182
1888	Benjamin Harrison	Republican	5,444,337 (47.8)	233
	Grover Cleveland	Democratic	5,540,050 (48.6)	168
1892	Grover Cleveland	Democratic	5,554,414 (46.0)	277
	Benjamin Harrison	Republican	5,190,802 (43.0)	145
	James B. Weaver	People's	1,027,329 (8.5)	22
1896	William McKinley	Republican	7,035,638 (50.8)	271
	William J. Bryan	Democratic	6,467,946 (46.7)	176
1900	William McKinley	Republican	7,219,530 (51.7)	292
	William J. Bryan	Democratic	6,356,734 (45.5)	155

Compared with the 1860s, presidential candidates in 1900 were more active; national committees were more effective; contributions of money and time by civil servants were greatly diminished; and the donations and influence of big business were greatly increased in campaigns. In 1872 Grant did not campaign against his opponent; Horace Greeley, editor of the *New York Tribune,* however, broke tradition and delivered speeches to large audiences, but to no avail. Although nominated by Liberal Republicans who were disillusioned with Grant and Democrats who realized that Greeley was their only hope to defeat Grant, neither group gave him wholehearted support. He was not enough of a reformer for many Liberal Republicans, and many Democrats could not forgive him for his previous attacks on their party.

Because of hard times following the PANIC OF 1873, corruption in the Grant administration, and the ebbing of Civil War passions, Republicans in 1876 had an uphill battle. They nominated Hayes, a war hero with a reform reputation, while the Democrats nominated Tilden, who had fought the corrupt TWEED RING in New York City. The campaign was conducted in a conventional manner until the late hours of election day. Although Tilden seemed on his way to victory, Daniel Sickles at Republican headquarters calculated that if Hayes could carry Louisiana, Florida, and South Carolina—states where Republicans controlled the election machinery—he would win the election by one electoral vote. He dispatched telegrams to Republicans to hold those states for Hayes. Republican election boards in these states, as well as in other states, determined the official vote and could disqualify returns where people were prevented from voting. Threats and violence did occur, and the Republican-dominated returning boards threw out enough votes, some fraudulently, to carry those states for Hayes.

With Republican fraud countering Democratic violence, it is impossible to tell who would have won in a fair election. Republican governors certified the votes of Republican electors, but Democrats also claimed to have carried the three disputed states and sent their electoral votes to Washington. The Constitution requires that the electoral votes be counted by the president of the Senate in the presence of a joint session of CONGRESS. Since the presiding officer of the Senate was a Republican and the Democrats controlled the House of Representatives and, with that, a majority in a joint session, Congress deadlocked over who would decide what votes to count. It resolved that question with a compromise most congressmen both disliked and favored.

The Electoral Commission Act (1877) created a 15-member commission to make the difficult decision. It was designed to be composed of seven Republicans and seven Democrats and one independent, but simultaneously with its passage, the independent—Justice David Davis—was elected to the Senate with Democratic votes, disqualified himself, and a Republican took his place. The commission decided by a partisan eight-to-seven margin not to question the official certified returns and awarded the disputed states to Hayes.

By recessing, the Democratic House delayed the count and threatened to plunge the nation into chaos with no president on inauguration day. The Democrats hoped to force the withdrawal of troops supporting Republican state governments in the South and, to a lesser extent, to gain railroad subsidies for the South. There were negotiations, but no concessions were made beyond what Hayes promised in his letter of acceptance. He would withdraw the troops when the civil and voting rights of black and white Republicans were respected. The count was completed on March 2, 1877, not because of a negotiated bargain but because the high-handed rulings of the Democratic Speaker of the House Samuel J. Randall choked off the filibuster. Randall was willing to use the threat of chaos in an attempt to gain concessions but not to risk the actual chaos of no president on inauguration day. To avoid any future wrangling by Congress over electoral votes, it passed the 1887 Electoral Count Act, which required it to accept the certified returns from the states and, in effect, ratified the decision of the 1877 electoral commission.

In 1880 with the Republican convention deadlocked by STALWART supporters of Grant, so-called HALF-BREED supporters of James G. Blaine, and supporters of JOHN SHERMAN, it turned to a dark horse, James A. Garfield. The Democrats ran a distinguished Civil War general, Winfield Scott Hancock, whose political views were unknown. Relying on party organization rather than issues, Garfield's letter of acceptance was equivocal and retreated on CIVIL SERVICE REFORM, and during the campaign he encouraged the assessment of civil servants. Garfield calculated correctly that to win he had to carry New York, and to activate ROSCOE CONKLING's New York Republican machine, he journeyed to New York, met with Conkling's lieutenants and other leading Republicans, and, at his ambiguously agreeable best, motivated them with vague promises of patronage. The machine carried New York for Garfield and with it the election, although his plurality over Hancock was razor thin.

In 1884 the Republicans did choose Blaine, while the Democrats picked Cleveland as their nominee. Blaine, popular with rank-and-file Republicans, had identified himself with the protective tariff and a vigorous foreign policy. Cleveland lacked the qualities associated with a successful politician; he was brutally honest, frugal with public money, undramatic, ungracious, obstinate, admired for his enemies rather than his friends, not a Union veteran, and a bachelor. His contrariness attracted reformers and political independents, who helped elect him governor of New York in 1882, and the Democrats hoped they would help make him president. The 1884 campaign was vituperative and close. It pitted the personal morals of Cleveland (he was possibly the father of an illegitimate son) against the public morals of Blaine, who had accepted $64,000 from the Union Pacific Railroad for some worthless bonds. Blaine broke with tradition and campaigned vigorously, but MUGWUMP reformers

Poster showing the Democratic nominees, Grover Cleveland for President and Thomas Hendricks for vice president, in the 1884 elections *(Library of Congress)*

deserted the Republicans, and Cleveland carried New York by 1,100 votes and won the election.

In 1888 Cleveland, calling for tariff revision, ran for reelection, but although he had a plurality of popular votes he lost New York and was defeated in the electoral college by Benjamin Harrison. In 1892, however, Cleveland decisively defeated Harrison in a campaign that again stressed the tariff.

The severe depression following the Panic of 1893 ended the near equilibrium between Republicans and Democrats and realigned the major parties. The shock of hard times was so severe that the Democrats repudiated Cleveland and his hard-money views and in 1896 nominated William Jennings Bryan on a platform that stressed the inflationary free (unlimited) coinage of silver at a 16-to-1 ratio with gold. The Republicans nominated McKinley on a platform that stressed a protective tariff and remaining on the gold standard. Unlike past contests, both candidates campaigned effectively, if differently. Bryan travelled 18,000 miles by rail and spoke to hundreds of thousands of voters, while McKinley stayed at home but spoke to almost as many who arrived in several delegations daily at his front porch. To each group he gave a short speech tailored for them, extolling the virtues of protectionism and the dangers of Free Silver (see FREE-SILVER MOVEMENT). Republicans raised millions of dollars largely from big businessmen and blanketed the country with 250 million pamphlets, while the Democrats could raise only thousands of dollars. McKinley won handily; the Republicans had become the dominant party and would remain so for three decades. The 1900 campaign featured the same two candidates, and the results confirmed the profound shift that had taken place. McKinley, riding the crest of popularity as a result of returned prosperity and a victorious war, triumphed even more decisively over Bryan, who had embraced anti-IMPERIALISM.

Further reading: Robert D. Marcus, *Grand Old Party: Political Structure in the Gilded Age, 1880–1896* (New York: Oxford University Press, 1971); H. Wayne Morgan, *From Hayes to McKinley: National Party Politics, 1877–1896* (Syracuse, N.Y.: Syracuse University Press, 1969).

progressivism in the 1890s

The late 19th century was a period of increased industrialization, urbanization, and IMMIGRATION in America. These economic and social changes resulted in inequities and, at their worst, evils that produced tensions within American society. Between 1889 and the First World War, a large number of middle-class, college-educated Americans were aware that for many the "promise" of America was not realized, and they embraced the ideas that became known as progressivism. They shared in the belief that a new response was needed to address the economic and social problems facing American society in the late 19th century. Far from having a hard-and-fast program, progressivism was a diverse collection of reform movements, each aimed at renovating or restoring American society, its institutions, and its values.

The influx of new immigrants into the United States as well as a general rural-to-urban population trend during the 1880s and 1890s placed a great burden on the nation's major cities. Overcrowded tenements, poor sanitation, and inadequate health services made many immigrant communities unhealthy places to live. In the 1890s the SETTLEMENT HOUSE movement, begun in the United States by Jane Addams and Ellen Gates Starr, the cofounders of Hull House (1889), was at the vanguard of progressive reform aimed at bettering the lives of the nation's immigrant populations. The settlement-house workers were mostly college-educated, middle-class women who provided immigrants with medical services, citizenship courses, counseling or vocational training, emergency relief, assistance in finding employment, and lessons in cooking, hygiene, and English. These services were designed not only to improve the immigrants' living conditions but also to provide them with the means necessary to assimilate into American society and become participating citizens. In addition, Alfred T. White, with his model tenement HOUSING in Brooklyn, and JACOB RIIS, with his reporting on slum conditions, began a housing reform movement.

Another aspect of the progressivism of the 1890s was moral reform. The crusades against prostitution and alcohol consumption reached a new level of intensity in the 1890s. Those involved in the anti-prostitution and Prohibition movements were a diverse group of business leaders, politicians, social workers, feminists, and the clergy. Prostitution was seen as a product of the increased poverty found in many of the nation's overcrowded cities, but the demand for it owed much to the large percentage of young men among immigrants. Prostitution was connected to drunkenness and the saloon culture that perpetuated it. Other problems connected to it were unemployment, industrial inefficiency, a large number of work-related accidents, violence, health problems, urban poverty, and political corruption. To combat these related evils, progressives advocated the prohibition of the manufacture and sale of alcoholic beverages.

Progressives in the 1890s also advocated political reform on all levels of government. Progressive reformers grew despondent over what seemed to them a government system controlled by corrupt bosses and party hacks that used politics to enrich themselves at the expense of the public. On the local and state levels, progressives led efforts to reform the structure of municipal government, increase accountability of city officials, reduce transit fares, obtain government regulation of public utilities, and implement the secret ballot. They also argued for the right of citizens to initiate legislation as well as nominate and recall judges. At the national level, the progressives supported antitrust laws, federal conservation measures, lower tariffs, a federal graduated income tax, woman suffrage, the direct election of U.S. senators, and a reform of the NATIONAL BANKING SYSTEM that would eventually lead to the creation of the Federal Reserve System.

See also INTERNAL REVENUE TAXES; PROHIBITION PARTY; TARIFF ISSUE.

Further reading: Allen F. Davis, *Spearheads for Reform: The Social Settlements and the Progressive Movement, 1890–1914* (New Brunswick, N.J.: Rutgers University Press, 1984); Steven J. Diner, *A Very Different Age: Americans in the Progressive Era* (New York: Hill & Wang, 1998); Arthur S. Link and Richard L. McCormick, *Progressivism* (Arlington Heights, Ill.: Harlan Davidson, 1983).

— Phillip Papas

Prohibition Party

Efforts to prevent the consumption of alcohol have generated intense political conflict in the United States. Temperance had been a major reform movement in the antebellum years, mobilizing large numbers of Americans in a crusade to persuade individuals to give up alcohol and, through legislation, prevent them from drinking. Prior to the Civil War, slavery eclipsed the temperance/prohibition issue, but during the 1870s it experienced a major resurgence. The public was concerned over the large number of saloons, their unwholesome influence in local politics, and their links to gambling, prostitution, public drunkenness, and violence. In 1873 the "Women's war" broke out across the nation as thousands of women marched to saloons and demanded that saloon keepers give up their businesses. Individual reformers such as Carry Nation lobbied public officials for temperance and prohibition. But it was the Prohibition Party, the Anti-Saloon League (ASL), the WOMEN'S CHRISTIAN TEMPERANCE UNION (WCTU), and several influential religious organizations that stood at the forefront of the prohibition campaign in the late 19th century.

Under zealous and determined leaders, prohibition groups worked hard to end the production, sale, and consumption of alcoholic beverages. Drinking was held responsible for some of the problems facing American society in the last two decades of the 19th century. Women were at the forefront of the Prohibition movement because of the large number of drunkards who abused their wives and children. Business owners blamed alcohol for industrial inefficiency and the high rate of work-related accidents. Employees often missed time because of drunkenness or came to work intoxicated and performed poorly at their tasks. Drunkenness and the saloon culture that perpetuated it were linked to violence, unemployment, health problems, urban poverty, and the corrupt practices of big-city political machines. Prohibition was viewed as a major step toward moral reform in America.

Currier and Ives print (1874) showing a young woman as a warrior for temperance *(Library of Congress)*

The Prohibition Party provided a voice for temperance and prohibition in national electoral politics. Its members called for the enactment of legislation outlawing the manufacture and sale of alcoholic beverages. The party was founded in September 1869 by delegates from 20 states at a national meeting held in Chicago. It drew its support mostly from Protestant, native-born, small-town, rural Americans. But some native-born, middle-class Protestants living in the nation's major cities also joined the party. In the main, its members were recruited from the Republican Party. In its crusade against alcohol, the Prohibition Party played upon the prevalent antiurban and anti-immigrant prejudices in late 19th-century America. The saloons in the slums were an inviting and fruitful target. Prohibitionists often associated urban and immigrant life with a weakening of morals that could eventually threaten American democracy.

In 1872 the Prohibition Party participated in a presidential election for the first time, but its candidate received only 5,600 votes. In 1884, however, the party's presidential candidate John P. St. John garnered 150,369 votes, enabling the Democrats to triumph, and in 1888 Clinton B. Fisk received nearly 250,000 votes. The Prohibition Party polled its highest vote total of 264,133 in the presidential election of 1892 when it ran John Bidwell, a former congressman, as its candidate. Although the Prohibition Party never acquired numerical strength on the national level, its candidates did win election to several state and local offices. Furthermore, one of the party's major effects on American politics was that it necessitated more careful scrutiny of a candidate's character.

The WCTU was formed in 1873 to focus attention on the problems associated with drunkenness. Under the leadership of FRANCES WILLARD, it became involved in social work, prison reform, public health, child nurseries, and the woman suffrage campaign. However, the Anti-Saloon League (ASL) had a much narrower focus. The ASL was founded in 1893 and organized local campaigns across the nation against the sale and consumption of alcoholic beverages. In effect, the ASL was a single-issue pressure group whose members called for the legal abolition of saloons. The ASL used a network of local and state chapters and its presses in Westerville, Ohio, to publicize the role of alcohol consumption and the saloon in health problems, family disorder, poverty, political corruption, and workplace inefficiency. Gradually, its assault on the neighborhood saloon grew to include a call for a nationwide prohibition of the sale and manufacture of alcoholic beverages.

The Prohibition Party, the Anti-Saloon League, and the Women's Christian Temperance Union convinced the nation to try prohibition. In 1919 the Eighteenth Amendment was ratified, banning the manufacture, sale, and transportation of intoxicating beverages in the United States. Although it did indeed cut alcohol consumption in the 1920s, it also led to excessive lawlessness, and the Prohibition Amendment was repealed in 1933 by the Twenty-first Amendment.

See also NATIVISM; PROGRESSIVISM IN THE 1890S; POLITICAL PARTIES, THIRD.

Further reading: Jack S. Blocker, *Retreat from Reform: The Prohibition Movement in the United States, 1890–1913* (Westport, Conn.: Greenwood Press, 1976); John Kobler, *Ardent Spirits: The Rise and Fall of Prohibition* (New York: Putnam, 1973); Roger C. Storms, *Partisan Prophets: A History of the Prohibition Party, 1854–1972* (Denver, Colo.: National Prohibition Foundation, 1972).

— Phillip Papas

protectionism

See tariff issue

public health

See medicine and public health

Pulitzer, Joseph (1847–1911)

Although his highly successful *New York World* printed its share of scandal and gossip, Joseph Pulitzer is better known for the annual prizes bearing his name that are awarded for excellence in journalism, history, biography, literature, and music. Born in Hungary on April 10, 1847, Pulitzer arrived in the United States at age 17. He served briefly in the Union army, moved to St. Louis, Missouri, and in 1868 became a reporter for CARL SCHURZ's German-language *Westliche Post.* The next year Pulitzer, a Republican, ran for the state legislature in a heavily Democratic district and, having campaigned seriously, won. In the legislature he fought graft and corruption and in 1872 was appointed as one of three police commissioners in St. Louis. He joined Schurz in the LIBERAL REPUBLICAN movement and attended its 1872 national convention, which nominated fellow journalist Horace Greeley for president. After Greeley, who also had the Democratic nomination, lost, Pulitzer became a Democrat.

Industrious and ambitious, Pulitzer bought the bankrupt St. Louis *Dispatch* in 1878 and merged it with the St. Louis *Evening Post* to form the *Post-Dispatch.* In the *Post-Dispatch* he launched crusades against gamblers and tax dodgers and ran a number of successful drives to improve St. Louis streets though repairs and cleaning. In 1883, at age 36, he purchased the ailing *New York World* and made it a success by combining sensationalism with public service. Beginning in 1895 Pulitzer engaged in a circulation war with William Randolph Hearst, who that year acquired the *New York Journal.* The two newspapers—and their publishers—created YELLOW JOURNALISM as they went head-to-head in trying to best the other with stories featuring entertaining gossip, prurient scandal, and sensational crime. In the early part of his career, Pulitzer had vowed to "expose all fraud and sham, fight all public evils and abuses" and disdained large headlines. However, in his circulation battle with Hearst's *Journal,* he changed his outlook and went to ever-larger headlines and type to attract readers to his stories. He defended this course by saying that people needed to know about crime in order to combat it, and he claimed that there was no contradiction in his paper's lurid news pages and its thoughtful, literate editorial pages. After a few years he ceased trying to out-Hearst Hearst, and the *World* in the early years of the 20th century became a responsible public-service newspaper with high journalistic and moral standards.

Believing that journalism should be more than a trade and that journalism education could elevate the job to a profession, he offered Harvard University a large sum of money to open a journalism school in his name. Harvard turned down Pulitzer's offer, and he instead provided $2 million to Columbia University to establish the graduate school of journalism and the annual Pulitzer Prizes. He died aboard his yacht *Liberty* in the harbor of Charleston, South Carolina, on October 29, 1911.

Further reading: W. A. Swanberg, *Pulitzer* (New York: Scribners, 1967).

— Ellen Tashie Frisina

Pullman Strike (1894)

The Pullman Strike of 1894 began as a rebellion against greedy paternalism. George M. Pullman, the railroad sleeping-car mogul, built a "model town" (named after himself) complete with a park, playgrounds, and a library for his employees. But Pullman was not acting as a philanthropist; he made a profit on his investment by deducting rents and fees from the workers' wages. During the depression of 1893 Pullman cut wages by as much as 25 percent without lowering rents in the company town. When he fired members of the workers' committee that asked him to either restore the wage cut or lower rents, his employees walked off their jobs.

The strikers knew that they would fail if they could not stop Pullman's primary source of revenue, which was from RAILROADS using his cars. As members of the American Railway Union (ARU), an industrial union recently formed by Eugene V. Debs, they appeared at the organization's first convention begging for help. Flushed by a victory over the Great Northern Railroad, the convention delegates ignored Debs's advice and instructed him to order a boycott if Pullman refused to negotiate. Pullman refused, and Debs in June 1894 instructed his membership to stop moving the sleeping cars.

The General Managers Association, an organization of the 24 railroads serving Chicago, used the boycott as an opportunity to destroy the militant ARU. The railroads precipitated a general strike by firing workers who refused to move Pullman cars. The managers then appealed to Washington for help. Attorney General Richard Olney, a former railroad attorney, responded by appointing another railroad lawyer, Edwin Walker, as special assistant to the federal attorney in Chicago, instructing him to use all legal means to break the strike. One legal recourse was obvious; it was against the law to obstruct the movement of the mail, which most passenger but few freight trains carried. To secure the movement of the freight trains, Walker appealed to the courts to enforce the SHERMAN ANTITRUST ACT prohibiting conspiracies in restraint of trade. On July 2, 1894, the courts complied by issuing an injunction forbidding interference with any railroad activity and ordering Debs and anyone else to stop inducing workers to strike. The following day a U.S. marshall requested troops to help enforce the injunction. And on July 4 President GROVER CLEVELAND ordered the army into Chicago and other railroad centers, much to the dismay of Illinois governor JOHN PETER ALTGELD, who believed the troops were not needed.

Debs appealed to other unions for financial and moral support, but the request was largely ignored. The railroad brotherhoods were happy to see the upstart ARU disappear, and the AMERICAN FEDERATION OF LABOR (AFL) opposed industrial unions. Realizing the strike was doomed, Debs offered to call it off if the railroads promised to rehire the strikers. Management did not respond, and the strike disintegrated. The victorious railroads blacklisted strike leaders, and the ARU collapsed. Arrested for contempt of court, Debs was sentenced to six months in prison, and in the landmark case *In re Debs* (1895), the SUPREME COURT upheld the use of the injunction against striking labor unions.

Further reading: Stanley Buder, *Pullman: An Experiment in Industrial Order and Community Planning, 1880–1930* (New York: Oxford University Press, 1967).

— Harold W. Aurand

R

racism See African Americans; imperialism; nativism; Social Darwinism

ragtime See music: art, folk, popular

railroad regulation See railroads

railroads

The Gilded Age was the golden age of railroads. Railroad mileage almost quadrupled from 54,000 in 1870 to 193,000 in 1900. Four major trunk lines (New York Central, Erie, Pennsylvania, and Baltimore & Ohio) connected the eastern seaboard with the Midwest, and railroads penetrated the trans-Mississippi West. The East and West Coasts were first linked across the continent in 1869 when the Union Pacific met the Central Pacific along the central route; the connection was further solidified by the later completion of transcontinentals to the north (the Northern Pacific in 1883 and the Great Northern in 1893) and to the south (the Southern Pacific [1883] and the Santa Fe [1884]). Shorter feeder lines were acquired or constructed by trunk lines, creating large systems that crisscrossed the nation with a grid of rails, giving the United States the most extensive rail system in the world.

While railroad mileage almost doubled in the 1870s and the 1880s, only 30,000 miles of track were added in the 1890s. By then the roads concentrated less on expansion and more on improving existing lines and making them more efficient. Railroads were rebuilt, eliminating curves, reducing grades, replacing iron bridges with stronger steel structures, widening tunnels, retracking with heavier steel rails and better ties, double tracking in areas of great density, introducing more sophisticated signaling systems, enlarging freight yards, and building beautiful passenger stations. More powerful locomotives, attractive passenger cars, and capacious freight cars equipped with automatic couplers and air brakes were also introduced. With these improvements railroads by 1900 were able to reduce the cost of moving a ton of freight one mile (a ton mile) to three-quarters of one cent.

The impact of railroads, with their enormous and efficient carrying capacity, on the American economy and society can hardly be exaggerated. Railroads made possible the rapid settlement of the West and the spectacular growth of cities in the late 19th century. Railroads transported bulky products of mines, forests, and fields cheaply to smelters and mills for processing and refining, then to manufacturers, and finally to consumers in rural and urban areas. Railroads facilitated the phenomenal growth of large-scale factories by supplying them with materials, distributing finished goods far and wide, and by giving food to their workers and families. The railroad network converted mid-19th-century regional economies into a national economy. For example, cheaper factory goods from the East caused less efficient California manufacturers to cut labor costs by using underpaid Chinese laborers, touching off racist riots. At the same time, superior California pears ruined Pennsylvania pear growers. Easy and rapid transportation also bound the nation closer, bringing outlying areas nearer to the mainstream. Trips that earlier in the 19th century were arduous, hazardous, and literally took months could be completed in a few days in comfortable sleeping cars during the Gilded Age.

By 1870 railroads had developed into the largest business enterprises the nation had seen. Major railroads built or acquired thousands of miles of track stretched over several states. They required enormous investments of capital in their rights of way, rolling stock, freight-handling facilities, and passenger stations. And they were built and operated by a labor force the size of an army and whose strikes were among the most spectacular of the era (the GREAT STRIKE OF 1877, the KNIGHTS OF LABOR in 1885–86, and the 1894 PULLMAN STRIKE). Although railroads were private corporations, their construction (especially of western

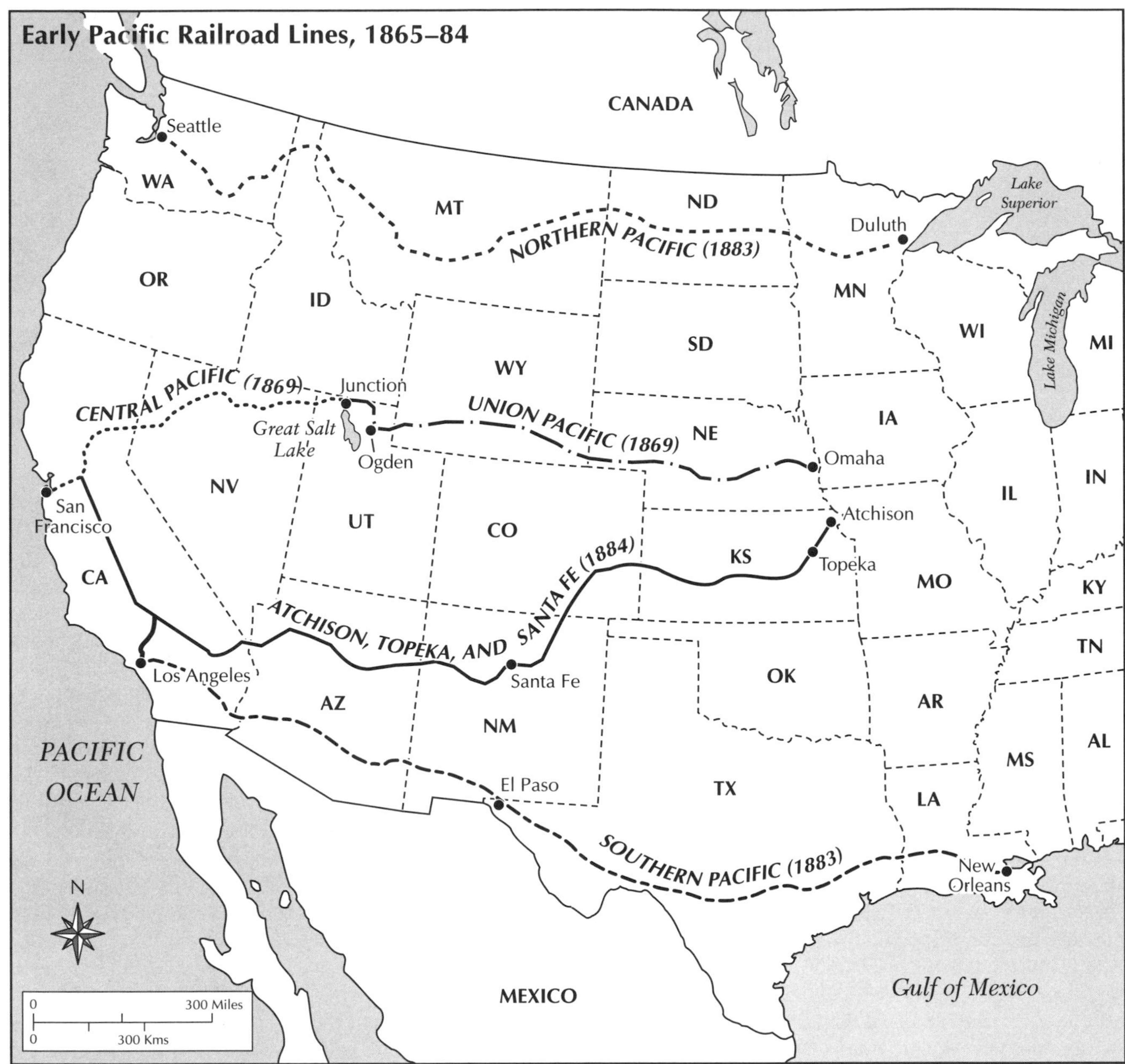

roads in sparsely populated areas) was financed in part by the federal land grants and by outright gifts from communities anxious for rail service. American and foreign, especially British, investors bought railroad bonds and financed most of their construction.

In 1870 some railroads were controlled by dishonest, corrupt managers who cheated their investors and bribed legislators. The construction companies they created (like the Credit Mobilier) to build the road (like the Union Pacific) would pad costs and pay the insiders enormous dividends, leaving the road—which they would abandon—deeply in debt and overcapitalized. This was accomplished by "watering" the stock, i.e., by selling more securities than the real worth of the railroad. In the late 1860s, because federal loans financed construction of the Union Pacific, the Credit Mobilier used some of that money to bribe members of CONGRESS. JAY GOULD of the Erie Railroad spent $1 million bribing the New York State legislature to legitimize the fraudulent issuing of stock. Overcapitalization took its toll. After Gould abandoned the Erie Railroad, it went bankrupt four times. Following the PANIC OF 1893, railroads controlling one-third of the nation's mileage were bankrupt.

By 1900, however, investment bankers like J. PIERPONT MORGAN had reorganized bankrupt roads and squeezed most of the "water" out of railroad indebtedness. Morgan (among others) also worked to consolidate railroads into ever-larger systems. His efforts culminated in the 1901 Northern Securities Company, which controlled the Northern Pacific, Great Northern, and the Chicago Burlington & Quincy, thus monopolizing territory from Chicago to Seattle. This led to the 1904 *Northern Securities* case, wherein the SUPREME COURT dissolved that holding company as a violation of the SHERMAN ANTITRUST ACT (1890).

From their beginning, railroads had been subject to government regulation. Chartered by states as common carriers, railroads were forbidden to discriminate among their customers. But railroads were competitive at some points (usually cities served by other railroads or water transportation) and monopolistic over long stretches of their tracks (usually rural areas), and these facts encouraged them to discriminate. To boost the volume of freight carried between competitive points, railroads would offer large shippers like Standard Oil "rebates" (a refund of part of the published rate), charging them less for a long haul than they charged for a short haul along routes where they had a monopoly. Railroads preferred not to give rebates and occasionally attempted to create pools among themselves, dividing up tonnage or revenues and thus avoiding ruinous rate wars between competitive points.

Farmers, merchants, communities, and even regions were outraged by discrimination and by monopolistic pools, and in the 1870s they turned to politics and formed the Granger movement (PATRONS OF HUSBANDRY) to seek redress in government regulation. Responding to their demands, state legislatures in the Midwest passed legislation setting rates and eliminating the long-haul/short-haul abuse, and in 1876 the Supreme Court in *MUNN V. ILLINOIS* upheld state regulation of railroads even if involved in interstate commerce. Ten years later, the Court reversed itself in *WABASH V. ILLINOIS* (1886), holding that states could not regulate interstate commerce and triggering demands in the West and South for federal action. Congress responded in 1887 with the Interstate Commerce Act, which was too strong for the railroads and too weak for reformers. Railroads were disturbed when pools were outlawed, but there was a loophole in the clause that prevented long-haul/short-haul discrimination, so while railroads had to adhere to published rates, the law did not specifically provide for rate regulation. It did provide for the Interstate Commerce Commission (ICC) to administer the act. The ICC was effective until 1897, when the Supreme Court specifically outlawed its power to set rates (*Maximum Freight Rate* decision) and so interpreted the long-short haul clause to render it useless (*Alabama Midland* case). The ICC was reduced to collecting statistics, and effective railroad regulation was postponed until the Progressive Era.

An engraving showing two express trains leaving the station *(Library of Congress)*

Further reading: Alfred D. Chandler, Jr., ed., *The Railroads: The Nation's First Big Business* (New York: Arno, 1981); Thomas C. Cochran, *Railroad Leaders, 1845–1890: The Business Mind in Action* (Cambridge, Mass.: Harvard University Press, 1953); Ari Hoogenboom and Olive Hoogenboom, *A History of the ICC: From Panacea to Palliative* (New York: Norton, 1976); Albro Martin, *Railroads Triumphant: The Growth, Rejection, and Rebirth of a Vital American Force* (New York: Oxford University Press, 1992).

Reconstruction, end of See Hayes, Rutherford B.

Red Cloud (Mahpiya Luta) (ca. 1822–1909)

An Oglala Sioux war leader, Red Cloud was one of their fiercest warriors, rivaling fellow Oglala CRAZY HORSE. However, once Red Cloud recognized the futility of further warfare, he became one of the "statesmen" of the Sioux people, traveling to Washington, D.C., to broker peace deals and establish reservations in the Dakotas.

Red Cloud was born along the North Platte River in modern-day western Nebraska. After his father died, he was raised by his maternal uncle, Chief Smoke. Red Cloud earned a reputation as a skilled warrior while fighting rival tribes such as the Pawnee, Crow, Ute, and Shoshone. He sided with his uncle in an Oglala dispute, which prevented him from becoming chief of the tribe at that time, but by the 1860s he was considered one of the war leaders of the Oglala.

In the spring of 1865 Red Cloud's forces began attacking whites who encroached on Oglala land on their way to gold mines in Montana. After failed negotiations with the U.S. government, Red Cloud's warriors and other Lakota, in the War for the Bozeman Trail (1866–68), forced the army to abandon its Bozeman posts. That war is notable as the one western engagement decisively won by Indian forces. Red Cloud negotiated a treaty at Fort Laramie in 1868 establishing the Great Sioux Reservation in South Dakota, but several bands refused to accept the treaty and move to that reservation and criticized him for pursuing diplomacy. Although he was a great warrior, Red Cloud in subsequent SIOUX WARS consistently advocated peace. He traveled to New York and Washington, D. C., in 1870 and settled on the reservation in 1871. The move of white settlers onto Sioux lands following the discovery of gold in the Black Hills led to the War for the Black Hills (1876–77). Red Cloud opposed that war and encouraged Crazy Horse to surrender in 1877, but the army suspected Red Cloud of having secretly supported his fellow Sioux in the campaign culminating in General GEORGE A. CUSTER's disaster at the Battle of Little Bighorn, where indeed his son had fought. General George Crook denounced Red Cloud and tried unsuccessfully to depose him as chief.

Following Crazy Horse's surrender, the Oglala Sioux were confined on the Pine Ridge Agency in western South Dakota, and Red Cloud was regarded as their chief by the Oglala and the federal government. Red Cloud soon ran into difficulty with Valentine T. McGillicuddy, the government agent in charge of the reservation, who regarded him as a nonprogressive opponent of acculturation. Red Cloud petitioned for McGillicuddy's removal and fought to preserve the Great Sioux Reservation. Red Cloud opposed the DAWES SEVERALTY ACT of 1887, which redistributed reservation land to members of Native American tribes, replacing communal ownership with individual ownership and reducing the size of reservations. Red Cloud continued to oppose individual ownership and only in 1905, feeble and nearly blind, did he accept his allotment. Nevertheless, he remained a man of peace. During tensions stemming from the Ghost Dance movement in 1890, Red Cloud again tried unsuccessfully to prevent bloodshed. Although opposed to acculturation, he made it a two-way street by mingling Lakota and Christian religious ideas, and prior to his death on December 10, 1909, he was baptized as a Roman Catholic.

Further reading: Robert W. Larson, *Red Cloud: Warrior-Statesman of the Lakota Sioux* (Norman: University of Oklahoma Press, 1997).

— Scott Sendrow

Reed, Thomas Brackett (1839–1902)

Thomas Brackett Reed, the powerful Speaker of the House of Representatives, was born on October 18, 1839, in Portland, Maine, the son of Thomas Brackett Reed Sr. and Mathilda Prince Mitchell. Following his graduation from Bowdoin College (1860), Reed taught school and began to study law in California. In 1863 he returned to Portland and was appointed in 1864 as an acting assistant paymaster in the navy, serving to the end of the Civil War. After his discharge from the navy, Reed resumed his legal studies in Portland and in 1865 was admitted to the Maine bar. In 1870 Reed married Susan Merrill Jones, with whom he had two children.

Reed was a member of the REPUBLICAN PARTY. From 1868 to 1869 he served in the lower house of the Maine state legislature and in 1870 in the state senate. Elected as the attorney general of Maine in 1870, he served from 1871 to 1874 but failed to be renominated, and from 1874 to 1877 he served as city attorney for Portland. Elected to the U.S. House of Representatives in 1876, Reed assumed the seat vacated by JAMES G. BLAINE when he was elected to the Senate.

In the House, Reed quickly distinguished himself. In 1878, as a minority member of the Clarkson Potter Committee investigating the disputed presidential election of 1876, Reed uncovered evidence of fraud and violence in Louisiana and discredited several Democratic witnesses. As a congressman, he favored federal policies that would secure voting rights for AFRICAN AMERICANS in the South, advocated protective tariffs, supported the gold standard, and opposed greenbacks, BIMETALLISM, and FREE SILVER. He voted against the BLAND-ALLISON ACT of 1878 and in 1893 supported President GROVER CLEVELAND's demand for the repeal of the Sherman Silver Purchase Act of 1890.

In 1889, when the Republicans regained control of the House, Reed was chosen Speaker and moved to expedite business. Opposition members had paralyzed the House by refusing to answer the roll call and preventing the quorum necessary to legislate. As Speaker, Reed achieved a quorum by counting as present members who refused to answer the roll call. He then forced the adoption of the so-called Reed rules, strengthening the Speaker's control over floor procedures, and by so doing was called "Czar Reed." Using his power as Speaker, Reed enabled the 51st Congress ("billion dollar Congress") to enact such legislation as the MCKINLEY TARIFF and the SHERMAN ANTITRUST ACT (1890). However, when the Democrats returned to power after the 1890 elections, they restored the old rules in the 52nd and 53rd Congresses.

The Democrats lost control of Congress in 1894, and the Republican majority reelected Reed to the speakership and reinstated his rules. In 1896 Reed was mentioned as a possible Republican presidential candidate. A powerful but acerbic figure in Congress, he could not attract national support. The Republicans instead nominated the far more affable WILLIAM MCKINLEY for the presidency. After the Republican victories in the 1896 elections, Reed was again elected to the speakership. Reed pushed the Dingley Tariff (1897) through the House but unsuccessfully opposed going to war with Spain in 1898 and the acquisition of colonial possessions. Disgusted with IMPERIALISM, Reed resigned from Congress in 1899 and entered private law practice in New York City, where he resided until his death on December 7, 1902.

Further reading: Ronald M. Peters, *The American Speakership: The Office in Historical Perspective* (Baltimore, Md.: Johns Hopkins University Press, 1990); William A. Robinson, *Thomas B. Reed, Parliamentarian* (New York: Dodd, Mead, 1930).

— Phillip Papas

religion

Religious diversity has always characterized the United States because it is both a land of freedom and a nation of immigrants. With everyone enjoying liberty of conscience, the various religions brought by migrants have often fractured, leading to the emergence of new religions and sects. And within each religion, challenges posed by the changing social order demanded new and frequently unsettling responses. The quickening pace of life in America during the last third of the 19th century posed great challenges and added significantly to the diverse religious scene. Four general trends affected American religion between the Civil War and 1900. These developments involved adjusting to the results of the Civil War, confronting the urban-industrial challenge, dealing with the intellectual-scientific challenge, and the growth of non-Protestant religions. The roots of these trends existed beforehand, and their effects remained long after, but all matured during the Gilded Age.

Prior to the Civil War the antislavery issue divided the Baptists, Methodists, and Presbyterians into northern and southern denominations. The war further accentuated their differences, and although the hierarchal churches (Roman Catholic, Lutheran, and Episcopal) retained their traditional structure, regionalism also stamped their nature. These differences gave rise to the cultural identity attached to southern Protestantism. The churches that defended the Confederacy during the war became bastions for old-time life and old-time religion. Southern Protestant churches, never doubting the literal authenticity of the scriptures, were among the most vigorous in resisting the theological challenges of Darwinism and the new scholarship. Finally, postbellum America, especially in the South, segregated the faiths by establishing AFRICAN-AMERICAN CHURCHES and denominations. In part, separation was the work of white churches that banished blacks, but disenfranchised black communities also wanted to form their own institutions. The black church in the South became the center of power for the black community, and by the end of the century the church comprised the single largest category of property and assets in that community.

Perhaps the most serious challenge to late 19th-century religion was the rapid industrialization and urbanization of the nation. Not only had native-born Americans abandoned the churches in their small, close-knit, rural communities for the anonymity of large impersonal cities, but those cities were also flooded by immigrants from abroad. Protestantism's first response was to save souls lost in the urban wilderness with Sunday schools for adults as well as for children and with revival meetings. DWIGHT L. MOODY was the most successful evangelist of the Gilded Age, converting literally thousands in revival meetings in the major cities. Moody and those who followed him were generic Protestants, noncreedal evangelicals, emphasizing God's love and that salvation was more an inner personal matter not dependent on church doctrine or community approval. While the evangelists were immensely popular in their time, the power of revivalism peaked soon after Moody died in 1899. He also had promoted adult Sunday schools, having organized a thriving one among the poor in Chicago at the beginning of his career. B. F. Jacobs, encouraged by Moody, and John H. Vincent of the Sunday School Union gave the American Sunday School movement structure, uniformity, and vitality. The movement in turn helped meet the needs of a new urban generation for structure, community, and connection in an unpredictable world. The CHAUTAUQUA MOVEMENT with its adult educational program was a direct outgrowth of the Sunday School movement.

Large cities and the publicity available there made the rise of the preacher/celebrity possible. While Moody the revivalist had the greatest national exposure, there were preachers who were not revivalists and yet achieved high visibility in their pulpits and preached to huge congregations. Most famous and infamous of these was HENRY WARD BEECHER of the Brooklyn, New York, Plymouth Congregational Church, who embraced reforms as well as his female parishioners (see BEECHER-TILTON SCANDAL). In Boston, Phillips Brooks achieved an almost equal stature as rector of Trinity Episcopal Church. Like Beecher and other urban pastors, Brooks was a broad-church man, speaking not to or for Episcopalians but to a wide cross section of Americans as one family. With one foot in an older world, with its romantic optimism and traditional moralism, and another in the modern world of industry and science, Brooks and Beecher both straddled the intellectual and spiritual divide, trying to harmonize the dissonant features that others considered hopelessly discordant.

In contrast to the stress of revivalists on achieving eternal life in the next world, the advocates of the SOCIAL GOSPEL stressed achieving a decent standard of living in this world. They believed that religion from a practical, intellectual, and spiritual point of view had to address the problems spawned by industrialism and urbanism. Inspired by the thought of WASHINGTON GLADDEN and organized by the work of JOSIAH STRONG, the Social Gospel saw the church's mission in the city as more than just saving souls; the church also had a duty to comfort the afflicted and afflict the comfortable and to encourage government to play a larger role in regulating industry, protecting labor, and eradicating poverty.

While the growth of factories and the rise of cities caused people to drift away from their churches, the intellectual challenge of 19th-century science appeared to erode the very basis of Judeo-Christian religions. Scientific methods, discoveries, and theories in geology, biology, and history questioned the literal text of the Bible. Charles Lyell's three-volume *Principles of Geology* (1830–33) raised disturbing questions about the age and development of the earth, but when Charles Darwin's *On the Origin of Species* (1859) theorized (on the basis of evidence) that plants and animals had evolved over eons through natural selection—and were not created by God in a few days—the effect was revolutionary. At the same time biblical scholars (higher critics) in Germany, analyzing language and applying rules of evidence, questioned the authorship and dates of various books of the Bible.

Christians divided into liberal and orthodox groups. The liberals accommodated their theology to the new scholarship, while the orthodox adhered to their faith that the Bible was literally the word of God. For liberals, John Fiske's *Outlines of Cosmic Philosophy* (1874) reconciled theism and evolution by arguing that there was no conflict between science and religion. He relegated religion to what the leading apostle of evolution, Herbert Spencer, called "the unknowable." Indeed, liberals came to view evolution as God's plan. Henry Ward Beecher associated evolution and progress with Christianity and civilization. By 1900 preachers were citing evolution as a proof of Christianity rather than a challenge to it. In a similar adjustment, Charles A. Briggs, a distinguished higher critic, while rejecting as idolatrous the idea that the Bible was literally without error argued that higher criticism was in the spirit of the Reformation and promoted a better understanding of God through a better understanding of his word.

The extent of liberal acceptance of the implications of Darwinism and higher criticism varied. Some saw religion as a natural phenomenon and Christianity merely as one expression of that impulse, subject to the same tests of integrity as any other faith or, for that matter, any secular idea, but most liberals still believed that Christianity was special and not just one among many valid religions. By 1900 the seminaries and urban ministers of the major Protestant denominations were comfortable with an evolutionary philosophy that apparently confirmed the superiority of Christianity because it seemed to be the "most" evolved of the world's religions. Ironically, Darwinism, initially perceived as a threat by Protestants, was a generation later used by some, like Josiah Strong, to sustain a belief in American Protestant Anglo-Saxon superiority and, inspire missionary activity.

Orthodox Protestants, who tended to be rural and working class, also varied their responses as they rejected evolution, higher criticism, and the Social Gospel. The entire South was orthodox, while in the North, mainstream Protestant denominations had orthodox and liberal wings or factions. For example, the overwhelmingly conservative leadership of the Presbyterians in 1893 suspended Briggs from the ministry for the heresy of higher criticism, although New York Presbyterians disagreed and did not think him a heretic. The acceptance of Darwinism and of higher criticism in scholarly seminaries and in fashionable churches led to a resurgence of millennialism within mainstream churches and the establishment of new denominations. The emphasis on prophesies of the imminent second coming (advent) of Christ and the end of the world led to an emphasis on the literal, not the metaphorical, truth of the Bible.

Adventism originated with William Miller, who mistakenly predicted the coming of Christ in 1844. Although bitterly disappointed, Ellen Gould Harmon White began having prophetic visions that Christ would soon come, gathered supporters about her, and in 1863 with her husband James organized the Seventh-Day Adventist Church at Battle Creek, Michigan. Under her leadership Adventists emphasized fidelity to the Bible and, because of her infirmities, health and diet. Her protegé, John Harvey Kellogg, as head of the Battle Creek Sanitarium, realized her principles and developed his ideas, and in so doing he gave the world corn flakes and peanut butter.

Another distinct Adventist group is the Jehovah's Witnesses, founded in the 1870s by Charles Taze Russell (1852–1916). He differed from other Adventists in believing that Christ had begun to return spiritually in 1874 and that by 1914 God's kingdom would take over the world. The onset of World War I in that year raised hopes that it would lead to the Battle of Armageddon and the beginning of God's kingdom. Following Russell's death the Witnesses, led and considerably altered by Joseph Franklin Rutherford (1869–1942), endured.

Adventism was also embraced by those in mainstream churches who reacted against modernity. Orthodox scholars organized two prophecy conferences (in 1878 and 1886) and also an annual Niagara Bible Conference to share in recognizing signs of the end and also to uphold a literal belief in the Bible. Through their Bible study they decided that God had ordained a system of "dispensations," or eras, following upon each other and ending with the last days. A close associate of Dwight L. Moody, Cyrus Ingerson Scofield (1843–1921), was its chief advocate. Scofield, a Congregational minister, consolidated the dispensational scheme into seven ages, concluding with the Great Sabbath or the Millennium of Christ ushered in by the Second Coming and the End of Days. His work endures today in the popular *Scofield Reference Bible* (1909). Vital to the dispensational analysis of history and the Bible is the need to assert the literal and infallible authority of the Bible; from that need, the 20th-century Fundamentalist movement developed.

The most important religious trend of the late 19th century was the growth of faiths apart from the major Protestant denominations of Methodists, Baptists, Presbyterians, Congregationalists, and Episcopalians. The numbers of Roman Catholics and Jews—and, among Protestants, Lutherans—were augmented by the enormous volume of IMMIGRATION in the Gilded Age. Other non-Protestant groups such as the Eastern Orthodox, Islam, and Asian faiths were known in America, but they did not achieve visibility beyond their own communities until the 20th century. In addition, there were Mormons, Spiritualists, Theosophists, and the religions of indigenous NATIVE AMERICANS (Indians). Increasing diversity led to the religious pluralism of the 20th century.

The rise of ROMAN CATHOLICISM was rapid. There were 200,000 Catholics in 1829, 3 million in 1860, 7 million in 1880, and 10 million in 1900. Migrants, especially from Ireland, accounted for much of this growth, making the American Catholic Church quite Irish in character. Roman Catholicism grew also by virtue of the nation's conquest of Mexican territory in the Southwest and by attracting dissatisfied Protestants. The most notable converts were Isaac Hecker, who founded the Paulist order of priests, and Orestes Brownson, who in a distinguished publishing career defended both Americanism and Catholicism.

Hostility with strong racist overtones dogged the Roman Church. Anti-Catholic nativists, who formed political parties in the 1840s and 1850s, and the AMERICAN PROTECTIVE ASSOCIATION (APA) in the 1880s and 1890s combined religious bigotry with ethnic hostility to Irish and eastern and southern European immigrants. The nativists suspected that the Catholic Church was clandestinely working to undermine both the American state and Protestant values.

In fact, the opposite was true. The Americanism of late 19th-century American Catholicism caused problems with Rome and precipitated within the church the Americanism crisis. In essence, it was a culture war, since the Roman Catholic hierarchy was authoritarian and reactionary and America was democratic and progressive. In 1895 Pope Leo XIII's encyclical to the American Church, *Longinqua Oceani*, lamented the separation of church and state and admonished the faithful to be obedient to their bishops and to associate mostly with other Catholics. His additional pronouncement in 1899 warned American bishops and others of the risk of heresy in adopting American values too thoroughly. That the Church later called the whole group of issues "modernism" reveals the real issue: America was the wave of the future, while the Church looked to the past. Leo's fears, however, were misplaced, since the liberalism of American Catholics was social and political, not doctrinal or institutional, and they were not about to become heretics or revolutionaries. But Leo effectively silenced liberal thought, making the American Catholic Church between 1900 and the Vatican II Council (1962–65) a very cautious body.

The rise of JUDAISM was also rapid in the late 19th century, but in contrast to Catholicism it experienced an institutional transformation. Orthodox Judaism prevailed early in the 19th century, but on the eve of the Civil War the ferment of radical religious reform that resulted from the Jewish enlightenment in Germany spread to the American Jewish community. In 1846 Isaac Mayer Wise and in 1855 David Einhorn, both influential reform-minded rabbis, arrived in the United States from Germany. Arriving in Baltimore, David Einhorn dispensed with Hebrew and the ceremonial (including dietary) laws, and Wise in 1853 began his rabbinate in Cincinnati, where he founded two magazines and wrote many books to promote reform. In 1873 Wise helped found the Union of American Hebrew Congregations, the Reform Jewish association of synagogues. By 1880 it claimed the overwhelming majority of synagogues in the United States. In 1885 Reform Judaism proclaimed an 18-point platform that Einhorn heavily influenced and Wise called "the Jewish Declaration of Independence," spelling out principles of Reform Judaism that endured until the late 20th century.

At that same moment, though, Judaism began shifting again in response to the wave of immigration from the Ashkenazic Jews of eastern Europe, which doubled the number of synagogues in the United States between 1880 and 1890. With the Yiddish language and a subculture created by oppression, these Jews were unresponsive to reform ideas and responsible for the resurgence of Orthodox Judaism. By 1900 Judaism was on the verge of becoming the familiar trinity of Orthodox, Reform, and Conservative. In two or three generations, the most ancient western faith had become, in part, one of the most modern.

Although Protestant, Lutherans were like Jews and Catholics in that they comprised strong ethnic communities for whom faith was part of their identity. Loyal to their German and Scandinavian cultures, Lutherans were not truly a part of the broader Protestant milieu. Three million Lutherans immigrated to the United States between 1869 and 1918. Most came to escape rural poverty and had no quarrel with Lutheran liturgy and doctrines, and many, especially among the Scandinavians, went to the Midwest and plains states. Lutherans formed local synods (at one point there were 66 independent church organizations), but there remained a general unity of faith and practice. A series of mergers and connections in the late 19th century brought most, except a few orthodox groups, into some sort of union in all but name.

The MORMON CHURCH—Church of Jesus Christ of Latter-day Saints, founded by Joseph Smith (1805–44) in 1830—was an American original. Smith claimed the *Book of Mormon,* which he published in 1830, was a sacred record of contemporaries of Jesus in North America, among whom he lived and taught following his resurrection. Smith and his adherents were persecuted and hounded from place to place as much for their formidable presence as for their beliefs, which included polygamy. He was lynched in 1844, but the Mormons, led by Brigham Young (1801–77), fled west to the valley of the Great Salt Lake. The Zion they built was politically a theocracy, with Young at its head, and economically a mixed system with family-owned and family-worked plots of land, cooperatively owned herds, and church-owned milling, mining, transporting, banking, and merchandizing enterprises.

Mormon theocracy and polygamy caused problems with the federal government. Congress in 1850 created the Utah Territory, and Young initially served as governor, but other federal appointees were hostile to the politically powerful and economically dominant Mormon Church, and Young was removed in 1857. Troops were dispatched to uphold federal authority, to which Young submitted in 1858 after the Mormons were promised amnesty. Although Young was no longer governor, he remained, as head of the church, the dominant political force in Utah. The federal government, however, gradually increased pressure on the Mormons. CONGRESS in 1862 passed a law that banned polygamy, which in 1879 was upheld by the SUPREME COURT. Two subsequent federal laws brought political and economic sanctions into play, in 1890 the church renounced plural marriage, and in 1896 Utah became a state. The communitarian aspect of Mormonism gave way to the vigorous individualism of America at large. Perhaps the largest dissenting Euro-American social order in the 19th century, Mormonism in the 20th century ironically became a bastion of conservative American cultural values.

Spiritualism arose in the "burned over district" of western New York State in 1848 by way of Margaret Fox (ca. 1833–93) and her sister Catherine (ca. 1836–92). They interpreted strange rappings first in their home and then elsewhere as contact with the spirits of the dead. They gave public demonstrations, and Horace Greeley, who had recently lost his five-year-old son, believed in them and publicized them. As other "mediums" appeared and gave "seances," spiritualism grew rapidly. Many who were religious, especially Quakers and Swedenborgians, embraced spiritualism because it confirmed the existence of the immortal soul. It also gave comfort to the bereaved, like the Greeleys and Abraham Lincoln's wife Mary. In 1870 spiritualism reached its greatest acceptance and size, claiming 11 million "believers." Although the Fox sisters became alcoholics, with Margaret in 1888 creating a sensation when she demonstrated at New York's Academy of Music that the rappings were a fraud, true believers in spiritualism said she was under the influence of alcohol. Later Margaret, in need of money, recanted and once again held seances. When she died in 1893, the National Spiritualism Association was organized on a loose congregational basis.

Closely related and yet distinct from spiritualism, the Theosophical Society was first organized in New York City in 1875 by Helena Petrovina Blavatsky (1831–91) and

Helena Petrovna Blavatsky, the spiritual teacher and cofounder of the Theosophical Society in New York City, 1875 *(United Lodge of Theosophists)*

Henry Steel Olcott (1832–1907), who were drawn together by their interest in the spirit world. Blavatsky, the major influence on the movement, arrived in New York in 1872 with a reputation for esoteric wisdom gained from ancient "mahatmas" of India and Tibet. Though ultimately denying spiritualism itself, Blavatsky based Theosophy on her communion with and illumination by Hindu and Buddhist masters past and present. Blavatsky and Olcott moved to India in 1878 and set up the international headquarters of the Theosophical movement; Olcott served as president in India, and William Quan Judge became the leader of American Theosophists. After Blavatsky died in 1891, Olcott and Judge (who in the 1890s believed his body was occupied by an Indian yogi) had differences, and the American followers of Judge seceded in 1895 and fragmented the Theosophists. The movement, however, survived with Annie Wood Besant (1847–1933) as its major force, and in the 1960s, with the interest in occult and eastern religions growing, Theosophy flourished.

Among NATIVE AMERICANS, the Ghost Dance—their most significant religious development in the late 19th century—had tragic results. The Ghost Dance had different phases in 1870 and 1890, and both originated in the Walker River Country of Nevada. The Ghost Dance of 1870 initially prophesied the arrival of material goods for Indians and later the destruction of all but Indians. The more significant 1890 Ghost Dance originated with its prophet Wovoka, a Northern Paiute, who was also known as Jack Wilson. With his people plagued by disease in 1887, he had a vision in 1888 in which God gave Wovoka control over the weather and told him that the people should dance upwards of five days. At first Wovoka's message was one of peace and brotherhood and aimed at curing the sick, but during the 1889 eclipse of the Sun he had an apocalyptic vision that eruptions and floods would kill the whites; that the Messiah would come and save the believers, heal the sick, and raise the dead; and that all things would return to their pre-Columbian state. Wovoka prescribed that believers should dance every three months and predicted the Messiah would come during the winter of 1890–91. Convinced that Wovoka brought rain to drought-ridden Nevada in 1889, believers spread the word, and the Ghost Dance movement spread rapidly eastward, including to the Sioux in South Dakota. The Indian agent at the Pine Ridge Agency panicked, called for troops, and before the Ghost Dance War (1890–91) was over, SITTING BULL had been killed and 200–300 Indians were massacred at Wounded Knee. After the Messiah did not appear, and anxious to avoid a repetition of the SIOUX WAR, Wovoka ceased to predict a date and counseled Native Americans to take up farming and adopt white ways. Ghost Dances continued but apparently ceased by 1930. A syncretic religion, the Ghost Dance of Wovoka combined elements of Christianity and Native American culture that simultaneously accommodated, preserved, and cut across tribal lines.

Further reading: Sydney Ahlstrom, *A Religious History of the American People* (New Haven, Conn.: Yale University Press, 1972); George Marsden, *Fundamentalism and American Culture: The Shaping of Twentieth Century Evangelicalism, 1870–1925* (New York: Oxford University Press, 1980); Francis P. Weisenburger, *Ordeal of Faith: The Crisis of Church-Going America, 1865–1900* (New York: Philosophical Library, 1959).

— W. Frederick Wooden

Remington, Frederic (1861–1909)

Through his paintings, sculpture, and illustrations, Frederic Remington was a key figure in creating a conception of the vanishing American West. Born in Canton, New York, on October 4, 1861, Remington took his first trip west in 1881 and spent a few peripatetic years as a sheep rancher and co-owner of a saloon and a hardware store, while making drawings.

In 1886 four of his illustrations appeared in various magazines published by Harper's, and Remington committed himself to a career in art. He quickly became a celebrity as an illustrator of life in the western states and commanded large sums for his work. Simultaneously, he exhibited paintings in prestigious New York City venues and won a silver medal at the 1889 Universal Exposition in Paris. He settled into a pattern of travel interspersed with months of work at home in his studios in New Rochelle, New York, and, after 1900, at a 16-acre compound on the St. Lawrence River. He went to CUBA in January 1897 on assignment for William Randolph Hearst to cover the Cuban Revolution. When the artist found all quiet, Hearst is said to have cabled back: "You furnish the pictures and I'll furnish the war." The famous comment, probably apocryphal, exemplified not only the power of Hearst's publishing empire but the bellicose IMPERIALISM of the nation. Remington did indeed furnish illustrations of the SPANISH-AMERICAN WAR. In the last decade of his life, Remington produced fewer illustrations and more paintings, finally turning to pure landscapes. In 1898 he also took up sculpture. A rotund, affable but opinionated man, Remington died in New Rochelle of peritonitis from a ruptured appendix on December 26, 1909.

Remington depicted rugged men and animals: cowboys and cattle, Indians, miners, cavalry soldiers, canoeists, hunters and their dogs. His studios were filled with written notes, sketches, photographs, models, and especially artifacts, such as Apache baskets, lariats, saddles, and pewter drinking mugs. His art usually contained human figures in action, often in violent conflict. In *A Dash for the*

Timber (1889, Amon Carter Museum, Fort Worth, Texas) cowboys rush at breakneck speed into the foreground of the canvas, a large band of Indians in pursuit. By mid-career, many compositions feature a few figures set against a high horizon and a limited if brilliant palette. Typical is *Fight for the Waterhole* (1903, Museum of Fine Arts, Houston, Texas), which shows cowboys, rifles to shoulders, ringing the rim of a waterhole while riders advance. This pared-down aesthetic strategy was consonant with his work in illustration. Remington's thousands of published illustrations included images for Theodore Roosevelt's *Ranch Life and the Hunting Trail* (1888) and nearly 400 images for an 1891 edition of Longfellow's *Song of Hiawatha.*

Remington's art depicted the white man in a heroic struggle against untamed forces; the protagonists became symbols of the frontier's demise. Some modern historians see Remington's art as infiltrated with the era's anxiety over race and IMMIGRATION, empire-building, and the wane of masculine power, but for many his stature in crafting icons of the American West is undiminished.

See also ILLUSTRATION, PHOTOGRAPHY, AND THE GRAPHIC ARTS.

Further reading: Peter H. Hassrick and Melissa J. Webster, *Frederic Remington: A Catalogue Raisonné of Paintings, Watercolors and Drawings.* (Cody, Wyo.: Buffalo Bill Historical Center; Seattle: University of Washington Press, 1996); Alexander Nemerov, *Frederic Remington & Turn-of-the-Century America* (New Haven, Conn.: Yale University Press, 1995); Michael Edward Shapiro et al., *Frederic Remington: The Masterworks* (Cody, Wyo.: Buffalo Bill Historical Center; New York: Harry N. Abrams, 1988).

— Karen Zukowski

Republican Party

The election of Ulysses S. Grant to the presidency in 1868 and 1872 by substantial majorities of the popular vote and huge majorities in the electoral college obscures the transient nature of the Republican Party's popular base. Grant was an exceptionally popular military hero, but as the passions of the Civil War era receded, the appeal of lesser heroes declined. In addition, Republican strength in the South, based on disfranchising former Confederates and enfranchising former slaves, eroded rapidly with pardons for rebels, their intimidation of black voters, and the consequent replacement of black Republican Reconstruction state governments with white-supremacy Democratic regimes. In the aftermath of the 1876 election the Republicans lost control of their last three southern states and for generations to come would have to contend with a "solid" Democratic South. In presidential elections from 1876 to 1892 (except for 1880) the Democrats won more popular votes than the Republicans, and in 1880 the Republican plurality was a mere 7,000 votes. The Republicans, however, with their votes more strategically located, won three of those five elections in the electoral college.

The Republican Party was a loose alliance of state organizations, as was the DEMOCRATIC PARTY. They got together every four years in a national convention to nominate candidates for the PRESIDENCY and vice presidency, and their successful candidates for the Senate and House of Representatives would caucus and, if in a majority, organize those bodies. They would cooperate, but not at the expense of their constituents. As long as a senator or congressman had a secure base he could defy the president or the caucus. The decentralized nature of American parties fostered factionalism. In one sense, there were as many factions in the Republican Party as there were state organizations, but they formed loose and often shifting alliances within the party. These alliances often identified with an attractive personality like Grant or JAMES G. BLAINE. There also were party members who felt more strongly about specific issues like CIVIL SERVICE REFORM, the CURRENCY ISSUE, or the TARIFF ISSUE than about loyalty to an organization or devotion to a personality.

From the 1870s to the early 1880s Grant's supporters, led in particular by ROSCOE CONKLING, proudly thought of themselves as Stalwarts, but that faction, so cohesive at the 1880 convention, disintegrated shortly thereafter when Conkling committed political suicide by resigning from the Senate. Throughout the 1870s and 1880s the followers of Blaine, who was very popular, formed another faction—called Half Breeds by their enemies—which with the political demise of Conkling (who hated and opposed Blaine) became dominant. Reformers, with more strength in the press than in party organizations, formed a third and undependable faction. They were hostile to corruption, wished to reform the civil service, and wanted to lower the tariff. Reacting against Grant, his policies, and his appointments, many of them bolted in 1872 and formed the LIBERAL REPUBLICAN PARTY. They returned to the Republican fold to support RUTHERFORD B. HAYES in 1876 and JAMES A. GARFIELD in 1880, but as MUGWUMPS in 1884 they deserted to the Democrats and voted for GROVER CLEVELAND rather than vote for Blaine, whom they regarded as corrupt.

By the 1890s Republican factionalism subsided. With the rapid industrialization of the United States, the protective tariff became the dominant and unifying Republican issue and WILLIAM MCKINLEY its most prominent spokesman. Cleveland, meanwhile, identified the Democrats with a low-revenue tariff and had the misfortune to win a decisive victory in 1892. The PANIC OF 1893 and a severe depression followed, discrediting Cleveland, the Democrats, and the revenue tariff and making the Republican party the majority party for the next three decades. When the Democrats repudiated Cleveland and embraced inflation in 1896, McKinley, who had easily won the Republican nomination, triumphed on a gold-standard, protectionist platform and confirmed the profound political shift that had begun in 1894. The 1898 SPANISH-AMERICAN WAR and the acquisition of an overseas empire added to the popularity of the Republicans as the 20th century began.

Further reading: Stanley P. Hirshson, *Farewell to the Bloody Shirt: Northern Republican and the Southern Negro, 1877–1893* (Bloomington: Indiana University Press, 1962); Robert D. Marcus, *Grand Old Party: Political Structure in the Gilded Age, 1880–1896* (New York: Oxford University Press, 1971); George H. Mayer, *The Republican Party, 1854–1966,* 2d ed. (New York: Oxford University Press, 1967); H. Wayne Morgan, *From Hayes to McKinley: National Party Politics, 1877–1896* (Syracuse, N.Y.: Syracuse University Press, 1969).

Richards, Ellen Henrietta Swallow (1842–1911)

Born near Dunstable, Massachusetts, on December 3, 1842, Ellen Henrietta Swallow Richards, a chemist and home economist, graduated from the coeducational Westford Academy and taught school. She returned home to nurse her ill mother and to keep the books of her father's store and became very unhappy until her parents agreed to let her enter Vassar College in 1867. She was mature (25 years old), entered with advanced standing, and studied astronomy and chemistry under the celebrated scholar MARIA MITCHELL. Upon graduation in 1870, she failed to find work as a chemist, so she applied for admission and was accepted by Massachusetts Institute of Technology (MIT), which waived her tuition for the sexist reason that it did not want a woman on its rolls. Nevertheless, she became the first woman to earn a degree from MIT, getting her bachelor of science in 1873 and, having submitted a thesis on mineralogy to Vassar, received in the same year a master of arts. She wished to earn her doctorate in chemistry at MIT but was discouraged, since the institute did not want its first chemistry Ph. D. to be a woman. She stayed on at MIT as a laboratory assistant and in 1875 married Robert H. Richards, an MIT professor of mining and metallurgy.

At MIT Richards, who possessed enormous drive, pursued her career in chemistry and pioneered a new field that became known as "home economics"; at the same time, she encouraged other women to secure an education in science. In 1876 she set up a women's laboratory at MIT, and in 1882 she helped found the American Collegiate Association, which became the American Association of University Women. She encouraged MIT to admit women on an equal basis with men, which it did in 1883, and she always functioned as the unofficial counselor for women at MIT.

In 1884 MIT appointed Richards instructor of sanitary chemistry, but despite her accomplishments never promoted her. She conducted the first scientific tests of drinking water in America—40,000 samples from Massachusetts—in 1887 to 1888. Earlier in the women's laboratory she had begun to apply scientific principles to daily life in the home and especially in the kitchen. In 1880 she published *The Science of Cooking and Cleaning,* in 1885 *Food Materials and Their Adulterations,* and in 1893 she set up a model kitchen at the WORLD'S COLUMBIAN EXPOSITION in Chicago. To establish home economics as a field of study—an academic discipline—Richards organized a series of summer Lake Placid conferences (1899–1907), which resulted in the establishment in 1908 of the American Home Economics Association, with Richards as its first president. Departments of home economics were established at colleges and universities but, because of the opposition of Bryn Mawr's M. CAREY THOMAS, not at prestigious women's colleges and, despite the presence of Richards, not at MIT. Richards died on March 30, 1911.

Further reading: Robert Clarke, *Ellen Swallow: The Woman Who Founded Ecology* (Chicago: Follett, 1973); Sarah Stage, "From Domestic Science to Social Housekeeping: The Career of Ellen Richards," in *Power and Responsibility: Case Studies in American Leadership,* eds. David M. Kennedy and Michael E. Parrish (San Diego, Calif.: Harcourt Brace Jovanovich, 1986).

Richardson, Henry Hobson (1838–1886)

A larger-than-life figure, H. H. Richardson popularized a muscular, rusticated stone architecture that became known, even in his own day, as Richardson Romanesque. A doorway with a low-sprung arch composed of huge voussoirs is a hallmark of the style. Born on September 29, 1838, on a sugar plantation north of New Orleans, Louisiana, Richardson graduated from Harvard in 1859. He trained in the private atelier of Jules Andre at the École des Beaux-Arts and traveled extensively in Europe. In 1865 he opened an office in New York City, and after 1874 he worked primarily out of his home in Brookline, Massachusetts. Throughout his career he gathered talented draftsmen around him, including STANFORD WHITE and Charles F. McKim, opening his large library and photograph collection to them all. A man of Falstaffian appetites, his magnetic personality charmed clients and many confessed that their buildings grew larger under the force of his personality. Richardson died at home at age 47 (April 27, 1886) of Bright's disease; several of his most important commissions were completed posthumously, and long after his death Richardson Romanesque remained popular.

In response to a country that was urbanizing and suburbanizing, Richardson developed new architectural forms, especially for public buildings. Trinity Church (1877, Boston), a free rendering of the French Romanesque ecclesiastical architecture of Auvergne, served as an auditorium for the spellbinding preacher Phillips Brooks. This landmark of the American AESTHETIC MOVEMENT, with stained glass by John La Farge, William Morris, and others, as well as a mural program directed by La Farge, set a pattern for highly collaborative projects. Richardson went on to develop commuter train stations, public libraries, and civic halls, many of them built in the Boston vicinity. The Oakes Ames Memorial Hall (1881, North Easton, Mass.), a large, turreted, dormered lecture hall, uses asymmetrical massings to take advantage of a steep hillside site. The Allegheny County Buildings (1888, Pittsburgh, Penn.) comprise a courthouse and a jail, the two connected by a "bridge of sighs." The courthouse, with a campanile modeled after medieval urban civic buildings, is organized around a courtyard, while the jail uses contemporary ideas of penal reform in its design of three radial cell blocks surrounded by a wall.

Richardson Romanesque was not a slavish historicism but rather an elaboration and adaptation of the northern European architecture of the 11th and 12th centuries, especially Norman and British vernacular buildings. Richardson achieved picturesque effects and pragmatic space provisions through polychromatic stone massings; brick, wood, and other materials were also used. The Glessner House (1887, Chicago) presents severe, regular facades to the street, but its interior court is composed of a series of brick turrets arranged around a garden. Richardson's emphasis on structural elements, while perfectly in line with Ruskinian demands for truth in architecture, was championed by 20th-century critics writing as modernism took hold. Thus, his Marshall Field Wholesale Store (1887, Chicago), a huge stone warehouse composed of stacked arches of descending height and width, is cited as a landmark protomodernist structure.

Further reading: Margaret Henderson Floyd, *Henry Hobson Richardson: A Genius for Architecture* (New York: Monacelli Press, 1997); James F. O'Gorman, *Living Architecture: A Biography of H. H. Richardson* (New York: Simon & Schuster, 1997).

— Karen Zukowski

riders, battle of the

See Hayes, Rutherford B.

Riis, Jacob A. (1849–1914)

Jacob August Riis, housing reformer, was born on May 3, 1849, in Ribe, Denmark, the son of Niels Edward Riis and Carolina Lundholm. In 1870 Riis immigrated to the United States. For several years he wandered about the Northeast, but he eventually settled in New York City. In 1877 the *New York Tribune* hired him. After just one year at the *Tribune,* Riis moved on to the *New York Sun* where for the next 11 years he worked as the paper's police reporter. Riis was twice married: first to Elizabeth Nielsen (1876), with whom he had six children, and in 1907 to Mary Phillips, with whom he had one child that died in infancy.

As a police reporter, Riis knew the abject poverty among the immigrants on New York's Lower East Side and especially in the overcrowded, disease-ridden tenements they were forced to live in. Using photography and his skills as a reporter, Riis produced his most influential book, *How the Other Half Lives* (1890), documenting life in the slums and influencing a whole generation of urban reformers. The popularity of *How the Other Half Lives* allowed Riis to leave his job at the *Sun* and devote all of his time to writing and lecturing on the horrors of tenement life and the need for better HOUSING regulations.

Although landlords and several politicians opposed him, Riis did gain the support of Theodore Roosevelt, who served as New York's police commissioner from 1893 to 1895. Roosevelt had read *How the Other Half Lives* and assisted Riis in his work. The two men became close friends and for 20 years collaborated on several projects. In 1902 Riis dedicated his book *The Battle with the Slum* to Roosevelt.

In his autobiography *The Making of an American* (1901), Riis retold his experience as he assimilated into American society. He argued that the cure for the ills of immigrant life in America's cities was the promotion of housing reform, the construction of municipal parks, the expansion of public education, and the implementation of neighborhood improvement programs. Riis was also an ally of the SETTLEMENT HOUSE movement. Among his other works were *The Children of the Poor* (1892), *Out of Mulberry Street* (1898), *A Ten Years' War* (1900), *Children of the Tenements* (1903), and *The Old Town* (1909). Riis lived the last decade of his life in failing health but still maintained a grueling schedule of lecturing and writing in the interests of reform. He died on May 26, 1914, in Barre, Massachusetts.

See also IMMIGRATION; PROGRESSIVISM IN THE 1890S.

Further reading: Alexander Alland, *Jacob A. Riis: Photographer and Citizen* (Millerton, N.Y.: Aperture, 1974); James B. Lane, *Jacob A. Riis and the American City* (Port

Washington, N.Y.: Kennikat Press, 1974); Louise Ware, *Jacob A. Riis: Police Reporter, Reformer, Useful Citizen* (New York: D. Appleton-Century, 1938).

— Phillip Papas

Roman Catholicism

In the late 19th century Protestant Americans viewed Roman Catholicism, although the earliest European Christian church, as both an interloper and a latecomer—it was neither. In Florida and in the Southwest its roots in the New World were deeper than those of Protestants, and Catholics were among the first settlers of Maryland in 1634, since it was founded by a Catholic for Catholics. The Catholic Church grew rapidly in the 19th century. There were 200,000 Roman Catholics in the United States in 1829, 3 million in 1860, 7 million in 1880, and 10 million in 1900. Migrants from Ireland and later from eastern and southern Europe accounted for this startling growth. While the church grew, so too did its problems from without and from within. In the 1840s virulent anti-Catholic nativists rioted in Philadelphia and elected a mayor of New York, and their Know-Nothing Party reached its zenith in 1854 and 1855 but disintegrated after 1856. The party disappeared, but Protestant hostility to Catholics remained, surfacing in controversies over public aid for parochial schools raised by the AMERICAN PROTECTIVE ASSOCIATION (APA) in the 1880s and 1890s.

There were also differences between American Catholics and their authorities in Rome. Since Catholics were suspected of loyalty to a foreign potentate (the pope), American Catholic leaders from the birth of the United States publicly and eagerly embraced their nation and its democratic values. But Pope Pius IX (1792–1878, elected 1846), as his temporal power eroded, issued his reactionary encyclical *Quanta Cura* (1864) with its "Syllabus of Errors" that attacked "progress, liberalism, and contemporary civilization," rejected liberty of conscience and toleration of other religions, and asserted church control of science, culture, and education. Liberal Catholics, who had embraced religious liberty and democracy, were dismayed, and American Catholics did their best to affirm American principles at their 1866 second plenary council in Baltimore. Pius, however, at the nadir of his temporal power in 1870 triumphed at the Vatican Council, which proclaimed the dogma of papal infallibility. But that victory led to struggles with the governments of Germany, France, and elsewhere.

Contending forces beset Roman Catholicism during the Gilded Age. It was ruled by a reactionary authority abroad, it existed in the most democratic country in the world, and it acquired millions of disparate new members from Ireland, Germany, Italy, and Poland. As IMMIGRATION expanded the church, ethnic divisions were apparent among the laity and clergy, with the Irish resenting the French dominance of the hierarchy early in the century and, later, the Germans resenting the Irish. The Germans, for example, resisted Irish efforts to require English in all parochial schools.

The ideas of Pius IX also clashed with those of the laity, who wholeheartedly participated in the American democratic process, and with the thoughts of two prominent American converts to Roman Catholicism. Orestes Brownson (1803–76) had moved from Calvinism to Universalism to Unitarianism to Transcendentalism—becoming committed to radical social causes including SOCIALISM, abolitionism, and WOMEN'S RIGHTS along the way—before embracing Roman Catholicism in 1844. From then until his death he worked at reconciling his Catholicism and his natural rights as an American. Only Catholicism, he believed, could discipline the American people sufficiently to make democracy work and to achieve the radical social reforms he continued to hold dear. For Brownson, America and Catholicism were not in conflict and actually were spiritual siblings.

Isaac Hecker (1819–88), the child of German immigrants, who with his brothers owned a prosperous bakery and flour mill, met Brownson in 1841 and under his influence sojourned among Transcendentalists for a year and in 1844 also converted to Roman Catholicism. He studied abroad for the priesthood, was ordained in 1849, returned to the United States as a Redemptorist missionary, and wrote *Questions of the Soul* (1855) and *Aspirations of Nature* (1857). In them he merged romantic Transcendentalism with Catholicism, arguing that while basic human aspirations transcended experience, they were reflected in the sacraments of the Catholic Church. Hecker, a proselytizer at heart, recognized that the Redemptorist order, composed primarily of German immigrants, would convert more Protestants if a thoroughly American branch of the order were established. His German superior disagreed, and when in 1857 Hecker went to Rome to plead his case he was tossed out of the order. Pius IX, however, allowed Hecker in 1858 to found the Society of Missionary Priests of St. Paul the Apostle in New York. The Paulists were American and had as their object the conversion of American Protestants, and they used American culture as a positive force conducive to the true Catholic faith. Hecker's last book *The Church and the Age* (1887) argued that the church was not at odds but rather at home with modernity.

Another sign of American independence was the creation of the Catholic University of America in 1889 so that American priests seeking advanced study would not have to go abroad. For conservatives, this move entailed the risk of disconnecting priests from traditional and dependable orthodox European authorities. A papal delegate returned from America to Rome in 1892 with a sobering report to the Pope on the state of the church.

The reactionary Pope Pius had been succeeded by Leo XIII (1810–1903, elected 1878), who was conciliatory by nature and is renowned for his *Rerum Novarum,* which applied Christian principles to the relations between capital and labor, but he was not a liberal. Besieged by nationalism in Italy and beset by anticlericalism in France, Leo perceived that modernism was a threat to the authority of Rome. Quite understandably he found the teachings of Brownson and Hecker disturbing and recognized that the new American university might encourage a drift from Rome. Consequently Leo's encyclical, *Longinqua Oceani* (1895), cautioned the American church against attributing its strength to American ideas instead of to God's mysterious design, lamented the separation of church and state, and admonished Catholics to be more cohesive and obedient. In 1899 following the SPANISH-AMERICAN WAR, in which the United States defeated a Catholic power, Leo issued *Testem Benevolentiae,* attacking Hecker's ideas, Americanism, and modernism directly, warning that they were a mix of heretical notions and that it was wrong to "desire a church in America different from that which is in the rest of the world." To Leo the tumult of change was a danger, while to Brownson and Hecker in America it was an opportunity. Trusting its long history and durability, Rome chose to stay its usual course and demanded that America heel to. As a result, the American hierarchy became conservative in the first half of the 20th century. And yet while doctrinally and institutionally conservative, there was a pragmatic liberal strain in the American Roman Catholic Church. Isaac Hecker's belief that America and American culture were ideal situations for the natural growth of Catholicism propelled many liberal Catholics. And the thinking of Hecker, far more than that of Pius IX or Leo XIII, influenced the liberalizing Second Vatican Council (1962–65).

Further reading: Robert D. Cross, *The Emergence of Liberal Catholicism in America* (Chicago: Quadrangle, 1968); Andrew M. Greeley, *Catholic Experience* (Garden City, N.Y.: Doubleday, 1967); Thomas T. McAvoy, *Americanist Heresy in Roman Catholicism, 1895–1900* (Notre Dame, Ind.: University of Notre Dame Press, 1963)

— W. Frederick Wooden

Rough Riders

The First Cavalry Regiment during the SPANISH-AMERICAN WAR, commanded by Theodore Roosevelt, was informally known as the Rough Riders and became famous for its charge up Kettle Hill during the Santiago campaign in CUBA. The volunteers who gathered at San Antonio for this mounted regiment were diverse and a bit exotic. Cowboys, bookkeepers, college boys, policemen, Indians, and Mexicans all signed up to fight Spain. Theodore Roosevelt, the future president but then the assistant secretary of the navy, resigned his post to join the unit. In an uncharacteristic act of humility he refused command because he felt unqualified, having only served three years with the New York National Guard. Roosevelt recommended his friend Colonel Leonard Wood, an army surgeon and physician, to Secretary of War John Long. Roosevelt was made second in command. Unlike the rest of the army, the Rough Riders were outfitted with private funds provided by many of the soldiers themselves, thus assuring that they had the best equipment, such as Krag-Jorgenson rifles and smokeless powder cartridges.

Because of monumental confusion at the point of embarkation, the Rough Riders arrived at Daiquiri, Cuba, on June 22 without their horses. Forced to travel on foot, they distinguished themselves by their speed of advance. At the battle of Las Guasimas the swift-marching Rough Riders stormed and took Spanish entrenchments, thus opening up the road to Santiago before the infantry arrived.

On July 1 the Rough Riders, commanded by Roosevelt (Wood had moved up to command a brigade), would charge their way into history. The San Juan Heights was the key to taking Santiago, and on San Juan and Kettle Hills, the Spanish were in trenches and protected on their flanks by blockhouses. As the Americans attacked, they were pinned down by Spanish rifle fire with little protection other than tall jungle grass. In the ensuing confusion, regiments became mixed up. Roosevelt felt that they would all be killed if they remained in the grass, and finding himself the highest ranking officer, he ordered his Rough Riders and the other cavalry regiments to charge up Kettle Hill. When officers of the other regiments refused to do so without orders from their own commanding officers, Roosevelt told them to step aside and let his Rough Riders through. Roosevelt, riding one of the few horses to make it to Cuba, led his soldiers up the hill. The other regiments, fearing they would be seen as cowards, fell in with the Rough Riders. The further the men advanced the faster they marched. The Spanish quickly retreated in the face of this mass of galloping, horseless cavalry. The Americans suffered many casualties taking the blockhouses, but by 1 P.M. Roosevelt and his men had taken Kettle Hill. Roosevelt paused for a few minutes and then joined in the successful charge up San Juan Hill.

At the end of the war the First Volunteer Cavalry unit was disbanded. Roosevelt returned home to a hero's wel-

Colonel Roosevelt and his Rough Riders atop the hill they captured, Battle of San Juan Hill, 1898 *(Library of Congress)*

come, was soon elected governor of New York, and would in a few years be president of the United States. And yet he knew that July 1, 1898, was "the great day of my life" and also realized that he would "talk about the regiment forever."

Further reading: Edmund Morris, *The Rise of Theodore Roosevelt* (New York: Coward, McCann & Geoghegan, 1979).

— Timothy E. Vislocky

S

Saint-Gaudens, Augustus (1848–1907)
Augustus Saint-Gaudens, arguably America's preeminent sculptor in the late 19th century, was known both for his monumental public SCULPTURE and smaller private commissions. A major figure in the American Renaissance, Saint-Gaudens introduced an appealing naturalism in a sculptural lineage stretching back to classical antiquity. Of French and Irish extraction, born on March 1, 1848, in Dublin, the son of a shoemaker, Saint-Gaudens moved to America as an infant. He apprenticed for three years as a cameo cutter in New York City. In 1866 he entered the National Academy of Design in New York City, and in 1868 he enrolled in the studio of Francois Jouffroy of the École des Beaux-Arts in Paris. In 1877 he married Augusta Homer, from a prominent Boston family. The artist also kept a mistress, Davida Clark, a model whose features can be traced in many sculptures.

When in 1876 he won the commission for the *Farragut Monument* (1880, Madison Square Park, New York), Saint-Gaudens became a leading figure in public sculpture. Most of his work focused on the human figure and was executed in marble or bronze. Saint-Gaudens often collaborated with his friend, architect STANFORD WHITE, in the design and setting of monuments. Among his most prominent public works were the *Shaw Memorial* (1891, Boston Common), *Abraham Lincoln* (1906, Grant Park, Chicago), and *Diana* (1891), which stood atop the spire of the original Madison Square Garden but is now at the Philadelphia Museum of Art. He was instrumental in many organizations, including the Society of American Artists, the American Academy in Rome, and the sculptural commissions for the WORLD'S COLUMBIAN EXPOSITION of 1893 and the Library of Congress.

Once awarded a contract for a major sculpture, Saint-Gaudens took a long time to complete it. He began with numerous drawings and proceeded to small-scale clay maquettes. He often retained these for years, examining, adjusting, and sometimes radically reworking his original conception. In studios in New York City, Paris, and later Aspet, his country home in Cornish, New Hampshire, Saint-Gaudens gathered congenial assistants, who produced the large-scale clay and plaster models used to cast the completed works. Many of Saint-Gauden's sculptures exist in different versions and scales; they represent various stages in the process from conception to casting. On August 3, 1907, Saint Gaudens died at Aspet, which is a now a museum of his work.

Saint-Gaudens's genius lay in uniting the real and the ideal. His numerous bas-relief portraits, such as *Mariana Griswold Van Rensselaer* (1888, Metropolitan Museum of Art), are charming in their immediacy and delicate realism. He was capable of startling synthesis in his allegorical works. The *Adams Memorial* (1891, Rock Creek Cemetery, Washington), a funerary monument commissioned by historian HENRY ADAMS after the suicide of his wife, used both Buddhist literature and Michelangelo's Sibyls as sources. Describing the heavily draped, meditative figure, Adams wrote: "The whole meaning and feeling of the figure is its universality." *The Sherman Monument* (1903, Grand Army Plaza, New York) successfully quotes venerable antique sculpture while expressing the vitality of the Civil War commander. The *Shaw Memorial* (1897, opposite the State House, Boston) commemorates the sacrifice of Robert Gould Shaw and conveys the determination of his men of the 54th Massachusetts Infantry as they fought.

Further reading: John H. Dryfhout, *The Work of Augustus Saint-Gaudens* (Hanover, N. H.: University Press of New England, 1982); Burke Wilkinson, *Uncommon Clay: The Life and Works of Augustus Saint-Gaudens* (San Diego: Harcourt Brace Jovanovich, 1985).

— Karen Zukowski

The Shaw Memorial, Boston, Mass., sculpted by Augustus Saint-Gaudens, 1891 *(Library of Congress)*

Samoa

Located in the South Pacific, the islands that make up Samoa are of little economic importance, but they do have strategic value. They are near shipping lanes and, with the fine harbor of Pago Pago, are suitable for a naval base. By the 1880s a three-way competition between Great Britain, Germany, and the United States for Samoa led to a confrontation between the United States and Germany. In 1878 the United States signed a treaty with a six-foot, four-inch "tattooed prince" of Samoa. The treaty allowed the United States to develop a naval station at Pago Pago but committed it to support the native government should it have problems with foreign powers. Within a year the British and Germans also secured trading rights and agreed to respect the independence of Samoa. But American, British, and German consular agents were, with reason, suspicious of the annexationist intrigues of each other, and over the next decade the islands were in a state of constant turmoil.

Germany was more aggressive than either Britain or the United States. The newly united German Empire had embarked on a policy of catch-up colonialism to secure what it believed to be its rightful place among the great powers of Europe, and it wanted Samoa. Early in 1887 Germany sought to install a more compliant monarch on the Samoan throne. A subsequent tripartite conference in Washington did little to relieve the resultant political tensions, nor did it deter the Germans from their plans. German naval vessels arrived in Apia harbor, Western Samoa, soon after and proclaimed an island chief by the name of Tamaese as the new monarch. Fortified with 6,000 warriors, a rival chief named Mataafa rose up against Tamaese and his German backers and took over most of the islands, killing 20 and wounding 30 of the 140 German naval guards who participated in the struggle.

In an attempt to block what he saw as an unjust attempt to annex the islands and to placate public opinion that had been whipped up by the imperialist Republican press, President GROVER CLEVELAND sent three warships to Apia, where the British corvette HMS *Calliope* and three German warships were anchored in that small and rather unprotected harbor. With a trans-Pacific cable still years away, news from Samoa took 10 to 20 days to reach the United States. Rumors abounded in the press about battles in Apia harbor and the sinking of American ships. War fever grew unabated. The new CONGRESS talked of spending $50 million to refit the navy to raid German commerce.

Actually, the ships were in a tense standoff that was broken on March 16, 1889, when a furious typhoon struck Apia and sank or drove on shore all the vessels except the *Calliope,* which made it out to the open sea and safety. The magnitude of the tragedy and the eerily equitable distribution of the casualties (50 sailors were killed) ended war talk in the press and made the powers more amenable to compromise. An 1889 conference in Berlin resolved that Mataafa would be king of the islands and Germany, Britain, and the United States would act as protectors of Samoa's independence. Shared responsibility was the equivalent of no responsibility. Once again jealousy and intrigue became the order of the day, and Americans and Germans in particular annoyed each other. Finally, in 1899 the three powers met again and negotiated a treaty that allowed Germany to annex the western half of the islands while the United States acquired the eastern end, with Britain withdrawing entirely from Samoa.

Further reading: Edwin P. Hoyt, *The Typhoon That Stopped a War* (New York: David McKay Company, 1968); Richard O'Connor, *Pacific Destiny: An Informal History of the U.S. in the Far East* (Boston: Little, Brown, 1969).

— Timothy E. Vislocky

sanitation

See medicine and public health

Santo Domingo, proposed annexation of

The annexation of Santo Domingo, now the Dominican Republic, was a major FOREIGN POLICY initiative of President Ulysses S. Grant, it failed because it was opposed by the chairman of the Senate Foreign Relations Committee, Charles Sumner. With his nation bankrupt and in revolt against his dictatorship, President Buenaventura Baez—the "great citizen" of Santo Domingo—was willing to have it annexed to the United States if its debts were assumed. A combination of speculators anxious for profits and naval officers anxious for a base on the Bay of Samana convinced Grant that annexation was not merely desirable but necessary. Grant's personal secretary Orville Babcock, armed with instructions from Secretary of State Hamilton Fish, arrived in Santo Domingo and negotiated two treaties by November 1869. The first provided for complete annexation, while the second leased Samana Bay to the United States with the right to purchase should the first treaty fail in the Senate. While Grant wished to gratify greedy friends and naval strategists, he also wanted to find a haven for freedmen in a land ruled by descendants of Africans.

Grant spoke with Sumner and thought he had enlisted his support for annexation, but Sumner after study and reflection opposed it as the project of a mercenary dictator, unscrupulous adventurers, and ambitious naval officers. In Sumner's view, the project would be the opening wedge leading to the acquisition of the black republic of Haiti and the rest of the West Indies. As chairman of the Foreign Relations Committee, Sumner adversely reported the annexation treaty in March 1870 and argued that instead of being absorbed by the United States, Santo Domingo should take its place in an independent Caribbean federation ruled by blacks protected by the United States. Grant was outraged, and although he used his influence to the utmost, the Senate in June rejected the annexation treaty by a split 28 to 28 vote (well short of the required two-thirds majority) and did not consider the Samana Bay lease. When the next CONGRESS organized in March 1872, the Grant administration vengefully convinced Republican senators to remove Sumner from his committee chairmanship, but in April even Grant conceded that the annexation of Santo Domingo was dead.

Further reading: David Donald, *Charles Sumner and the Rights of Man* (New York: Knopf, 1970); William S. McFeeley, *Grant: A Biography* (New York: Norton, 1981).

— Bruce Abrams

Sargent, John Singer (1856–1925)

The ultimate cosmopolitan expatriate, John Singer Sargent was acclaimed as America's most successful portrait painter, professionally and aesthetically. Born in Florence, Italy, on January 12, 1856, Sargent lived a nomadic childhood in Europe with his American expatriate family. He received little formal education, yet he played the piano well and was fluent in French, Italian, and German in addition to English. In 1874 he was accepted as a student in the private atelier of Carolus-Duran in Paris, and he matriculated at the École des Beaux-Arts later that year. He was equally adept in oils and watercolors, and he often worked on a large scale. Until 1886 he lived primarily in Paris, then primarily in London, but he often traveled in Europe and visited America nine times. He exhibited frequently at the Royal Academy in London, the Paris Salon, and with the Society of American Artists in New York City. A reserved and cultivated man, his friends were many of the era's leading literary and artistic figures, including the actress Ellen Terry, the writers Edmund Gosse and HENRY JAMES, as well as several leading painters of the day.

Sargent succeeded to the British grand-manner portrait tradition of Van Dyke and Gainsborough. His patrons were the wealthy industrialists of America and the noble families of England, whose social status was brilliantly conveyed on canvas through posture, clothing, and carefully selected props. Psychological penetration was not his strong suit; while he always captured a likeness, many of his sitters wear the same expression of apprehensive dignity. Instead, Sargent's abundant technical abilities allowed him to achieve maximum visual impact by means of fluid brushwork and a few startling notes of color. Family portraits, such as *The Daughters of Edwin D. Boit* (1882, Museum of Fine Arts, Boston), show the relationships among people by ingenious compositions. Sargent's best-known work is probably *Madame X* (1884, Metropolitan Museum of Art, New York), an uncommissioned portrait of Madame Pierre Gautreau, a beauty known for her audacious choices in makeup, clothing, and lovers. Sargent used a highly unconventional pose: face in profile, nose tilted up, her body—in a severe black dress—twisted toward the viewer.

By 1909, with 500 portraits completed, Sargent virtually abandoned the genre, turning instead to landscape painting and themes from religious history and modern life. Throughout his career Sargent had painted harsh, dramatic, and fleeting lighting conditions. His *El Jaleo* (1882, Isabella Stewart Gardener Museum, Boston) shows a flamenco dancer in footlights, while *Carnation, Lily, Lily Rose* (1886, Tate Gallery, London) shows children lighting paper lanterns in the midst of a flower garden at dusk. Sargent's landscapes, whether depicting Capri, Venice, or the Tyrolean Alps, stretched the limits of representation through expressive stroke and color. Monumental works engrossed him at the end of his career, including a series of murals for the Boston Public Library tracing the history of Western religion and several huge canvases depicting World War I themes. Sargent died in London on April 15, 1925.

Further reading: Patricia Hills et al., *John Singer Sargent* (New York: Whitney Museum of American Art and Harry N. Abrams, 1987); Richard Ormond and Elaine Kilmurray, *John Singer Sargent* (New Haven, Conn.: Paul Mellon Center for Studies in British Art and Yale University Press, 1998).

— Karen Zukowski

Schurz, Carl (1829–1906)

Political reformer Carl Schurz was born in Liblar (near Cologne), Germany, on March 2, 1829. He attended the University of Bonn, where he imbibed the Democratic ideas of Gottfried Kinkel, participated in the Revolution of 1848, gained fame by rescuing Kinkel from a Spandau jail, and fled abroad for his life. He taught and practiced journalism in England and France, but his fortunes improved in 1852 when he married and migrated. His wife was Margarethe Meyer, a wealthy heiress, and the newlyweds settled in Philadelphia, Pennsylvania.

Four years later the Schurzes moved to Watertown, Wisconsin, where she opened the first KINDERGARTEN in the United States (she had trained under its originator Friedrich Froebel) and he dabbled in real estate, journalism, and especially in politics. Hostile to slavery, Schurz campaigned effectively for the REPUBLICAN PARTY in two languages and was appointed to its national committee by 1860 and influenced German Americans to vote for Abraham Lincoln. He was rewarded in 1861 with the ministry to Spain. With the outbreak of the Civil War, Schurz came home, secured a brigadier generalship, and was promoted to major general and commander of the 11th Corps (composed largely of German Americans), but ill luck plagued his corps, and neither Schurz nor his men emerged from the war with an enviable military reputation.

Schurz, nevertheless, retained his political clout. In the summer of 1865 he toured the South at the request of President Andrew Johnson and, finding its rebellious spirit unabated, recommended the radical position that African-American suffrage should be a condition for readmission to the Union. Returning to journalism, he was by 1867 editor and part owner of the St. Louis *Westliche Post,* but his keynote address at the 1868 Republican National Convention revealed a drift away from Radical Republicanism. Elected to the Senate from Missouri, Schurz took office in 1869 and soon broke with the Grant administration over patronage and principles. Deprived by Grant of appointments ("spoils") in Missouri, he embraced CIVIL SERVICE REFORM. In addition, he denounced Grant's pet scheme to annex SANTO DOMINGO and Schurz was willing to sacrifice black Republicans to conciliate and woo the former Confederates. He led in the formation of the LIBERAL REPUBLICAN PARTY of 1872 but was chagrined when its convention nominated Horace Greeley, who was neither the civil service nor tariff reformer Schurz desired. Schurz nevertheless supported Greeley, as did the Democrats, but he was decisively defeated by Grant. Schurz continued to oppose Grant in the Senate until 1875, when he lost his seat, ironically, because the former Confederates he had conciliated replaced him with a Democrat.

In 1876 Schurz supported the reform-minded Republican presidential nominee RUTHERFORD B. HAYES, and upon his election Hayes made Schurz his secretary of the interior. Serving from 1877 to 1881, Schurz introduced civil service reform principles in his department, cleaned out a corrupt Indian Bureau (OFFICE OF INDIAN AFFAIRS) ring, promoted the CONSERVATION of forests, and, although slow to do so, ended the policy of removing NATIVE AMERICANS from their lands to reservations.

From 1881 to 1883 Schurz coedited the *New York Evening Post* with EDWIN L. GODKIN and Horace White, but he and Godkin did not get along and Schurz had to resign. He made ends meet by lecturing and writing (publishing a two-volume biography of Henry Clay in 1887 and writing editorials for *Harper's Weekly* from 1892 to 1898) and by serving as the American representative of the Hamburg American Steamship Company.

Although he never again held public office after leaving the Interior Department, Schurz remained an independent force in politics, advocating civil service reform, sound money, and anti-IMPERIALISM. Accordingly he was a leading MUGWUMP supporter of the reform Democrat GROVER CLEVELAND rather than the Republican candidate JAMES G. BLAINE in 1884. In 1896, however, he supported Republican WILLIAM MCKINLEY and the gold standard instead of WILLIAM JENNINGS BRYAN and FREE-SILVER MOVEMENT. Schurz soon opposed McKinley and the annexation of the Philippines, and in 1900 and 1904 he switched his support to the Democrats on that issue. Schurz died in New York City on May 14, 1906.

Further reading: Hans L. Trefousse, *Carl Schurz: A Biography* (Knoxville: University of Tennessee Press, 1982).

science

While the United States was a world leader in patenting inventions, developing new technologies, and utilizing scientific discoveries in industrial processes, it was not on the cutting edge of the advance of science itself in the late 19th century. The frontiers of science were advanced primarily in Germany, Britain, and France. Nevertheless, individual American scientists made significant contributions in geology, paleontology, chemistry, physics, and astronomy.

The sciences of geology and paleontology were encouraged by the federally funded U.S. GEOLOGICAL SURVEY as well as by state-supported geological surveys. Lawmakers generally intended the geological surveys to identify deposits of minerals of practical value to industry and society, but some geologists were more interested in researching the science of geology as distinct from economic geology. The first director of the U.S. Geological Survey, CLARENCE (RIVERS) KING, was an advocate of economic geology, while his successor JOHN WESLEY POWELL pushed basic research. Those interested in research on both the state and national level made important discoveries.

Thomas C. Chamberlin (1843–1928), who initially became interested in glaciation research during his work with the Wisconsin Geological Survey, was appointed by Powell to head the glacial division of the U.S. Geological Survey. Chamberlin moved on to become president of the University of Wisconsin and later headed the Geology Department of the then-new University of Chicago, but he remained the outstanding authority on glaciers. That expertise on cold climates in the distant past led him to question the widespread idea that the earth had been a molten mass that was gradually cooling. With a University of Chicago astronomer and mathematician, Forest R. Moulton, he posited a new "planetesimal" hypothesis that the earth coalesced from small particles in orbit about the sun and had a much cooler climate, which would account for evidence of early glaciation.

OTHNEIL CHARLES MARSH in 1866 became America's first professor of paleontology at Yale University. In 1882 Powell appointed Marsh the U.S. Geological Survey's first vertebrate paleontologist, and while serving in that capacity he amassed a huge collection of almost 500 species. Marsh was an expert in constructing the skeletons of extinct animals, and he identified 80 forms of dinosaurs. His work gave significant support to Charles Darwin's hypothesis of evolution by discovering birds with teeth and especially by finding a sequence of American fossil horses. Marsh's arch enemy, Edward Drinker Cope, with whom he engaged in an unseemly feud over who found what first, was also a paleontologist of note who described many new species and did important work on reptiles and fish. Cope, however, was hasty in his work, abrasive in his personal relations, and received no help from the Geological Survey after Marsh became its chief paleontologist.

The greatest American scientist of the Gilded Age was JOSIAH WILLARD GIBBS, whose theoretical papers fundamentally influenced chemistry, physics, and mathematics. His most renowned publication was "On the Equilibrium of Heterogeneous Substances," which provided a theoretical basis for all possible chemical reactions and the mathematics to calculate the energy expended and the heat gained or lost. In that paper he reformulated the second law of thermodynamics and essentially established the discipline of physical chemistry. Mathematics was at the core of much of Gibbs's work. His notes on mathematical representation were published as *Vector Analysis,* which he preferred to think of as "multiple algebra." He was interested in the speed of light, electricity, and magnetism, and he believed that light was electromagnetic. Another chemist of note, Ira Remsen (1846–1927), suggested the experiments that developed saccharin and headed the graduate program in chemistry at Johns Hopkins University.

Americans excelled in astronomy. MARIA MITCHELL had discovered a comet in 1847 and in the Gilded Age was professor of astronomy at Vassar College. In 1882 Henry Draper (1837–82) photographed the Orion Nebula, and in

1891 astrophysicist George Ellery Hale (1868–1938) used his spectroheliograph to photograph the sun's prominences (clouds of gas high above the sun's surface). The aviation pioneer Samuel P. Langley (1834–1906) was also an astrophysicist, who in 1878 invented the bolometer to detect temperature differences on the sun. The bolometer was an electric thermometer so sensitive that it could measure variations in temperature of up to one-millionth of a degree. Asaph Hall at the U.S. Naval Observatory in Washington discovered in 1873 the two moons of Mars, and in the early 1890s James E. Keeler (1857–1900) discovered that Saturn's rings were not solid but rather were composed of small particles, with each ring having its own orbit about the planet.

During the Gilded Age, the day of the gifted amateur—the dilettante—scientist was passing, and the university with its faculty was becoming the center of research. In 1870 only Harvard and Yale could claim to be institutions of research as well as of teaching. They were joined by Johns Hopkins, which from its founding in 1876 became a center of research. By 1900, however, state and other private universities were building significant libraries and laboratories, promoting research, and laying the foundation for the enormous contributions of America to science in the 20th century.

Further reading: A. Hunter Dupree, ed., *Science and the Emergence of Modern America, 1865–1916* (Chicago: Rand McNally, 1963); A. Hunter Dupree, *Science in the Federal Government: A History of Policies and Activities* (Baltimore, Md.: Johns Hopkins University Press, 1986).

Scott, Thomas Alexander (1823–1881)

Railroad manager Thomas Alexander Scott was born on December 28, 1823, at Fort Loudon, Pennsylvania. He went to work at the age of 11 and held a variety of clerkships until 1850, when he became station agent for the Pennsylvania Railroad (PRR), at Duncansville, Pennsylvania. Able, energetic, handsome, and gregarious, Scott advanced rapidly in that organization. In 1852 he became the superintendent of the PRR's division west of Altoona (hiring ANDREW CARNEGIE as his personal telegrapher and secretary), in 1858 its general superintendent, and in 1860 its first vice president. With the outbreak of the Civil War (the first railroad war) in 1861 the War Department called Scott to Washington to organize the transportation of men and munitions from northern cities to the front lines; in August he was appointed assistant secretary of war. Scott resigned in June 1862 but returned to the War Department in September 1863. The administration of RAILROADS by Scott and others rapidly moved troops and enabled the North to overcome the South's advantage of shorter distances (interior lines) between fronts.

After the war Scott continued his meteoric rise in the PRR and branched out. In 1871 he was named president of the Pennsylvania company that operated the PRR system west of Pittsburgh and in 1874 became president of the PRR. Scott, however, was a man of grandiose visions whose interests included more than the PRR. In 1871 he obtained controlling interest in the Union Pacific (which he sold to Vanderbilt interests in 1872) and in 1872 in the Texas & Pacific (T&P), which he wished to build into a transcontinental road. The PANIC OF 1873 and the ensuing depression frustrated Scott's dreams for the T&P. He lobbied Congress assiduously, but unsuccessfully, for a land grant for the T&P. Apparently, his lobby also worked during the 1877 electoral college count for the selection of RUTHERFORD B. HAYES (on the dubious assumption that Hayes would be more likely to approve a land grant than SAMUEL J. TILDEN), but Scott's lobbyists had no appreciable effect on the outcome, and Hayes did not support a land grant. Hayes disappointed Scott further during the GREAT STRIKE OF 1877, which Scott—in collusion with other railroad presidents—precipitated with carefully coordinated wage cuts. Hayes refused to call up volunteers to suppress the strike as Scott demanded and used the army sparingly to keep the peace. Although Scott managed the PRR conservatively, his bold, risky efforts to create a transcontinental system during an economic downturn failed and took a toll on his health. In 1880 he resigned as president of the PRR and sold the T&P to JAY GOULD in 1881. Shortly thereafter, Scott died at Darby, Pennsylvania, on May 21, 1881.

Further reading: Edwin P. Alexander, *On the Main Line: The Pennsylvania Railroad in the 19th Century* (New York: C.N. Potter, 1971), George H. Burgess, and Miles C. Kennedy, *Centennial History of the Pennsylvania Railroad Company, 1846–1946* (New York: Arno, 1976).

sculpture

The mainstream, high-style sculpture of late 19th-century America, largely public monuments and architectural embellishments, was an important chapter in the story of the American Renaissance. Commissioned mainly by government and other corporate bodies, sculpture advanced civic virtues. The formal neoclassicism of Rome that had dominated sculpture at mid-century was replaced by the freer, yet still academic, Beaux-Arts classicism of France. The human figure, executed in marble and bronze, was the dominant subject matter. A degree of immediacy and naturalism was thus injected into the long heritage of Greco-Roman statuary.

Most of the prominent sculptors trained in Paris, either at the École des Beaux-Arts or in affiliated ateliers. Americans returned home to establish their own ateliers for the production of large-scale sculpture. With drawings and clay maquettes, the artist conceived the basic form; then specialized assistants, working in the studio, the foundry, and the marble yard, enlarged it in plaster and cast or carved it. Professionalism was furthered by the exhibition of maquettes and finished works in national and international exhibitions and with the founding of the National Sculpture Society in 1893.

Ambitious buildings of the era included elaborate sculptural programs. Alexander Milne Calder supervised sculpture, which encompassed figural groups as well as capitals and pilasters, for the Philadelphia City Hall, built from 1871 to 1881. Daniel Chester French, a master at personifying abstract concepts, kept a large workshop busy for decades; his important commissions included the Minnesota State Capital in Saint Paul and the U.S. Customs House in New York City. An important subset of architectural sculpture was ephemeral, constructed from a plaster and straw mixture known as staff and erected at world's fairs and other celebrations. At the WORLD'S COLUMBIAN EXPOSITION of 1893 in Chicago, millions saw the colossal *Republic* and *Barge of State* by French and Frederick MacMonnies, respectively, which decorated the central lagoon, while virtually every building in the fair was adorned with sculpture.

Civil War memorials and life-size bronzes depicting honored native sons were commissioned for countless public squares. While too many of these were formulaic, many incorporated an expressive naturalism. Among the best was John Q. A. Ward's *HENRY WARD BEECHER* (1891, Borough Hall Square, Brooklyn). Collaborative works with architects were common; monuments by architect STANFORD WHITE and sculptor AUGUSTUS SAINT-GAUDENS were among the style-setters. The pairing of French and Henry Bacon produced the *Lincoln Memorial* (1922, Washington, D.C.).

A smaller percentage of the era's sculpture was concerned less with memorializing and more with the exploration of form, surface, and psychological insight. Herbert Adams's polychromatic busts were derived from early Renaissance sculpture, while FREDERIC REMINGTON'S bronzes celebrated the American cowboy. George Gray Barnard's *Struggle of the Two Natures in Man* (1894, Metropolitan Museum of Art, New York) owed a debt to the expressive innovations of Auguste Rodin. Occasionally, sculpture was controversial, especially the nude. In 1893 temperance and women's groups protested that MacMonnies's *Bacchante and Infant Faun* was licentious; in opposition, the Metropolitan Museum of Art gave it a home, and the Luxembourg Museum of Paris ordered a replica.

See also AESTHETIC MOVEMENT; ART AND ARCHITECTURE.

Further reading: Michele H. Bogart, *Public Sculpture and the Civic Ideal in New York City, 1890–1930* (Chicago: University of Chicago Press, 1989); Wayne Craven, *Sculpture in America*, 2d ed. (Newark: University of Delaware Press; New York: Cornwall Books, 1984); Lorado Taft, *The History of American Sculpture*, rev. ed. (New York: Macmillan, 1924).

— Karen Zukowski

secret ballot See elections, conduct of

settlement houses

Settlement houses first appeared in the United States in the late 1880s as a response to the poverty, drabness, and dehumanization so obvious in the poor working-class neighborhoods of large industrial cities. Their founders were women and men of higher education who believed they could bring hope and the benefits of higher culture by extending the university atmosphere of intellectual exchange, artistic opportunity, and social reform to working-class people. They proposed to achieve this by establishing a physical facility within needy neighborhoods and moving there to live, thereby creating an outpost of education, culture, service, and friendship available to residents.

The initial model for the settlement movement was Toynbee Hall, founded in East London in 1884 by Samuel Barnett, vicar of the "worst parish in London." Part of Barnett's inspiration came from the teachings of John Ruskin, who held that industrialization and urbanization separated people—whether university educated or factory toilers—from meaningful work, culture, and beauty. Thus, poverty of spirit was as deadly as poverty of bread and shelter.

By 1891 there were six settlement houses in the United States: University Settlement in New York City's Lower East Side was reorganized by Charles B. Stover and Edward King after the Neighborhood Guild founded by Stanton Coit in 1886 collapsed. Jane Addams and Ellen Gates Starr began Hull-House on Halsted Street in Chicago in 1889. In 1887 Vida Scudder and two of her Smith College classmates founded the College Settlement Association, which in 1889 established College Settlements in New York City and Philadelphia and opened Denison House in Boston in 1892. In 1893 Lillian Wald and Mary Brewster started a Visiting Nurse Service for Lower East Side tenement residents in New York, and two years later they moved into their own building, thereby creating the Henry Street Settlement. By 1900 there were more than 100 settlement houses, heavily concentrated in the large industrial cities of the Northeast and Midwest.

Settlement houses provided a meaningful occupation for idealistic college graduates, especially women, who were convinced that their minds, education, and talents could be put to good use addressing the social problems of urban slums. The pioneers and settlement workers in the 1890s were motivated by strong religious beliefs, which impelled them to serve but not to convert. Unlike in England, settlement houses in the United States took pains to avoid direct religious proselytizing and distanced themselves from charity organizations and their approach. Settlement houses were deeply committed to serving, befriending, and empowering their clients, most of whom were recent immigrants.

Settlement houses adjusted to the needs of the people they served. They shifted their emphasis from art, music, lectures, and general intellectual stimulation to providing instruction in English, skilled trades, and homemaking. Hull House offered women and children child care, KINDERGARTEN, playgrounds, and instruction in sewing, a skill valuable for generating in-home supplemental income. As was the case with other settlements, Hull-House gradually became a center for political activism to improve HOUSING, public education, and other public services. Later, some settlements worked for electoral reform and engaged in labor organizing to improve working conditions and wages.

Further reading: Allen F. Davis, *Spearheads for Reform: The Social Settlements and the Progressive Movement, 1890–1914* (New Brunswick, N.J.: Rutgers University Press, 1984).

— J. Paul Mitchell

Anna Howard Shaw *(Library of Congress)*

Shaw, Anna Howard (1847–1919)

One of the most powerful orators of the woman suffrage movement, Anna Howard Shaw was born on February 14, 1847, in Newcastle-on-Tyne, England; at age four she moved with her family to Massachusetts. When she was 12 her father moved her, her mother, and her younger siblings to a homestead in Michigan while he returned East. As a result, Shaw carried more than her fair share of family responsibilities and became a teacher at the age of 15.

Eventually seeking more education, Shaw enrolled in high school at age 23 and entered Albion College at 26. In 1876 she enrolled in the divinity program at Boston University, graduated in 1878, and became the pastor of a Methodist Church in East Dennis, Massachusetts. When she applied for ordination, however, the New England Conference of the Methodist Episcopal Church refused to ordain a woman. She then applied to the Methodist Protestant Church and was ordained in 1880, becoming that denomination's first woman minister.

While she continued her pastoral work, she enrolled in medical school at Boston University. She also began to deliver speeches on temperance and woman suffrage. By the time she graduated from medical school in 1886, she had begun to believe that the best way she could serve women would be by pushing for the removal of the stigma of disfranchisement. In 1887 she began an independent career as a lecturer. She also became active in the WOMEN'S CHRISTIAN TEMPERANCE UNION (WCTU), and from 1888 to 1892 she was the superintendent of its national Franchise (or suffrage) Department.

Shaw's sermon before the International Council of Women in 1888 caught the attention of SUSAN B. ANTHONY. Shaw, who was already involved with the American Woman Suffrage Association (AWSA) became, at Anthony's behest, involved in the National Woman Suffrage Association (NWSA) as well, and when the organizations merged in 1890 she became a national lecturer for the National American Woman Suffrage Association (NAWSA). When Anthony became the NAWSA president in 1892, Shaw became vice president.

Shaw wanted to follow Anthony as president of the NAWSA, but Anthony chose the more politically astute Carrie Chapman Catt as her successor. Shaw continued as vice president. When Catt resigned the presidency in 1904, Shaw became president. Her talents, however, did not fit the demands of the job. She was an ineffective administrator, she did not deal well with people who disagreed with her, and she had little talent for strategic thinking. So while the momentum for woman suffrage continued to grow, she was unable to give it direction. In 1915, after disaffected members persuaded Catt to challenge Shaw for the NAWSA presidency, Shaw announced that she would not seek reelection, but she remained on the board and continued to contribute her oratory to the cause.

After the United States entered World War I, Shaw chaired the Woman's Committee of the U.S. Council of National Defense. She had planned to return to lecturing for woman suffrage after the war, but she put it off when she was asked to join a speaking tour to rally support for the Treaty of Versailles and the League of Nations. She collapsed with pneumonia during that tour and died three days later on July 2, 1919.

See also WILLARD, FRANCES; WOMEN'S RIGHTS.

Further reading: Eleanor Flexner, *Century of Struggle: The Women's Rights Movement in the United States,* rev. ed. (Cambridge, Mass.: Harvard University Press, 1975).

— Lynn Hoogenboom

Sherman, John (1823–1900)

Born in Lancaster, Ohio, on May 10, 1823, able and effective politician John Sherman served Ohio in the U.S. Senate for most of the Gilded Age. Sherman practiced law in Mansfield after admission to the bar in 1844 and paid little attention to politics until the 1854 Kansas Nebraska Act threw open to slavery territories that had been free soil since the 1820 Missouri Compromise. Elected to CONGRESS as an anti-Nebraska man, Sherman in 1855 participated in the formation of the Ohio REPUBLICAN PARTY and served in the House from 1855 to 1861 and the Senate from 1861 to 1877. From 1877 to 1881 Sherman was secretary of the treasury in the RUTHERFORD B. HAYES administration and then in 1881 returned to the Senate, where he remained until 1897, when he became WILLIAM MCKINLEY's secretary of state. He resigned in 1898 and died in Washington on October 22, 1900.

During his long career in Congress and the Treasury Department, Sherman was identified with public finance. He supported the protective tariff and opposed inflation, but he was not doctrinaire, adjusting to political pressure, and compromising in the interest of harmony. As befits a political leader from an industrial as well as agrarian state, he was a moderate, adept at balancing diverse interests. He supported the inflationary 1862 Legal Tender Act, which issued greenbacks, as an essential war measure, but in 1875 he was the main architect of the Resumption Act, which called for the return to the gold standard in 1879 by redeeming greenbacks in gold. While serving as treasury secretary under Hayes, Sherman secured enough gold to accomplish that feat. He participated in the CRIME OF '73 demonetizing silver, but with increasing demands for Free Silver, Sherman recognized that some limited silver coinage was politically necessary, and with the passage of the Sherman Silver Purchase Act of 1890, the government began to coin 4.5 million ounces monthly (see FREE-SILVER MOVEMENT).

While Sherman thought that the government should encourage railroad and industrial development through subsidies and the protective tariff, he also favored government regulation, in moderation, of large-scale enterprises. He wanted to regulate interstate commerce but did not wish to determine railroad rates, and the 1890 SHERMAN ANTITRUST ACT prohibiting combinations in restraint of trade was sufficiently vague as to minimize its impact during the Gilded Age.

Sherman yearned to be president, but although he had solid support at the 1880 and 1888 Republican National Conventions he failed to get the nomination. His cold manner (he was known as "the Ohio Icicle") was no help, and despite ability and moderation, his identification with many issues gave voters too much to react against. In 1888 Hayes consoled Sherman with "the reflection that . . . the man of great and valuable service . . . must be content to leave the Presidency to the less conspicuous and deserving." Sherman remained in politics too long. As McKinley's secretary of state he did not favor IMPERIALISM, but he could do nothing to prevent either war with Spain or the acquisition of colonies overseas. Tired and ignored, he resigned.

Further reading: H. Wayne Morgan, *From Hayes to McKinley: National Party Politics, 1877–1896* (Syracuse, N.Y.: Syracuse University Press, 1969); David J. Rothman, *Politics and Power: The United States Senate, 1869–1901* (Cambridge, Mass.: Harvard University Press, 1966).

Sherman Antitrust Act (1890)

The last two decades of the 19th century were marked by widespread discontent among farmers, workers, and small businessowners toward the monopolistic practices of the RAILROAD, OIL refining, lead, sugar, and MEATPACKING industries. Although a number of states had enacted antitrust laws, state legislation had little or no impact on huge TRUSTS engaged in interstate commerce. Increasing demand for national regulatory legislation forced CONGRESS to act. In 1887 it passed the Interstate Commerce Act, creating a commission to regulate railroads, and in 1890 passed the Sherman Antitrust Act to regulate monopolies. These laws, designed to protect small business owners, farmers, and consumers, were largely ineffective in the Gilded Age.

Introduced by Senator JOHN SHERMAN, an Ohio Republican, the Sherman Antitrust Act declared that any "combination in the form of trusts or otherwise, or conspiracy, in restraint of trade or commerce among the several states, or with foreign nations" was illegal. Vagueness, however, weakened the Sherman Act. It did not clearly define what it exactly meant by a trust, a combination, or restraint of trade. Between 1890 and 1893, the government lost seven of eight cases involving the Sherman Antitrust Act that were brought before federal courts.

The most important case involving the Sherman Antitrust Act was *United States v. E. C. Knight Company* (1895). Since the Knight Company controlled virtually all sugar refining in the United States, the federal government argued it violated the Sherman Act.

The SUPREME COURT, however, in an 8 to 1 decision (JOHN MARSHALL HARLAN was the lone dissenter) ruled against the government's claim. The majority distinguished between commercial and manufacturing enterprises and declared that manufacturing was not commerce, did not restrain trade, and therefore did not fall under the jurisdiction of the Sherman Antitrust Act. The justices reasoned that manufacturing was essentially intrastate, even if the goods produced were sold across state lines. The E. C. Knight decision was not only a major setback to the antitrust movement in the United States, but it also restricted the application of the Sherman Antitrust Act to such a degree that it virtually became a dead letter until Theodore Roosevelt resuscitated it a decade later.

See also PROGRESSIVISM IN THE 1890S.

Further reading: Edward C. Kirkland, *Industry Comes of Age: Business, Labor, and Public Policy, 1860–1897* (New York: Holt Rinehart and Winston, 1961).

— Phillip Papas

Sherman Silver Purchase Act (1890) See currency issue

Sierra Club See conservation; Muir, John

Simpson, Jerry (1842–1905)

The Populist orator Jerry Simpson was born on March 31, 1842, in Westmoreland County, New Brunswick, Canada. Between 1848 and 1852 he resided in several towns near the Great Lakes in both Canada and the United States. Except for a few years of home schooling, Simpson had almost no formal education. At age 14 he became a cook on a lake freighter and ultimately rose to the rank of ship captain. In 1861 Simpson enlisted in the Union Army. However, he was mustered out after just three months because of poor health. Simpson married Jane Cape on October 12, 1870. They had two children.

In 1879 the Simpsons moved to Holton, Kansas, where he owned and operated a farm and sawmill. Taking advantage of high prices, Simpson sold out and invested his profits in a cattle ranch near Medicine Lodge in southwestern Kansas, but the severe winter of 1886 wiped out his herd and left him in debt. Having dabbled in politics, he was lucky to secure an appointment at $40 a month as the marshall of Medicine Lodge. He also became involved in local politics. Originally a Republican, Simpson twice ran unsuccessfully for the state legislature as a Greenbacker (1886) and as a Union Labor Party candidate (1888). Between 1888 and 1889, Kansas plunged further into agricultural depression, and farmers throughout the state began to join the FARMERS' ALLIANCES in an effort to find a solution to their pressing economic problems. In 1890 the Farmers' Alliances joined with local reform elements in Kansas to create the PEOPLE'S PARTY (Populist Party). Simpson's attraction to reform-based politics made him an active member of the new party, which nominated him for a seat in the U. S. House of Representatives.

During the campaign, his opponents disparaged him as "Sockless Jerry," but Simpson shrewdly turned the intended insult to his advantage. He conveyed the Populist message in a folksy political style that endeared him to audiences. Not only was Simpson a tireless champion of political and economic reform, but he was also an advocate of the "single tax" plan popularized by HENRY GEORGE. Both Kansas Populists and Democrats endorsed Simpson, and he was elected to Congress in 1890, 1892, and 1896. As a leader of the fusion wing of the People's Party, Simpson supported the Populist nomination of WILLIAM JENNINGS BRYAN in 1896 and urged the Populists to support Democratic candidates whenever possible. His promotion of fusion (without which he could not have been elected) made many leading Populists resent him.

As a congressman, Simpson delivered few speeches and introduced few bills. Yet, he was well known for his sharp, shrewd wit and was a leader among House Populists. Simpson fought for currency inflation (he preferred greenbacks but accepted Free Silver [see FREE-SILVER MOVEMENT]), disliked the autocratic rule of Speaker THOMAS B. REED, and opposed IMPERIALISM.

In 1898 Simpson lost his bid for reelection. He then moved to Wichita, where he began to publish *Jerry Simpson's Bayonet.* Following his failure to secure the Populist nomination for the Senate in 1900, Simpson retired from active political life. In 1902 he moved to Roswell, New Mexico, where he took up ranching and became a land-grant agent for the Santa Fe Railroad. He died on October 23, 1905, in Wichita.

Further reading: O. Gene Clanton, *Kansas Populism, Ideas and Men* (Lawrence: University Press of Kansas,

1969); Lawrence Goodwyn, *Democratic Promise: The Populist Moment in America* (New York: Oxford University Press, 1976).

— Phillip Papas

single tax

See George, Henry

Sioux wars

The Sioux (Lakota) Indians fought three wars against the U.S. Army. From 1866 to 1868 the Sioux, led by RED CLOUD, opposed the building of the Bozeman Wagon Road and the army posts along it, since they encroached on Sioux hunting grounds. The Sioux resistance was successful, the army withdrew from its posts, and after protracted negotiations Red Cloud and some Sioux chiefs agreed to the 1868 Treaty of Fort Laramie, which created the Great Sioux Reservation in western South Dakota, including the Black Hills. Several bands, however, most notably the Oglala, Hunkpapa, and Miniconjou, would not relocate on a reservation no matter how large and refused to accept the treaty.

In the early 1870s nontreaty Sioux warriors mounted raids against white settlers who had moved into Montana, Wyoming, and Nebraska, but the second Sioux war broke out as a result of the BLACK HILLS GOLD RUSH. In 1874 miners accompanying an expedition led by General GEORGE A. CUSTER discovered gold in the Black Hills. The news spread quickly and thousands of whites poured into the Black Hills, trespassing on the Great Sioux Reservation, in search of the valuable metal. After the government tried unsuccessfully to purchase the Black Hills, which were sacred to the Sioux, federal officials in December 1875 ordered the uncooperative Sioux to relocate to reservations in six weeks (an impossibility in winter) or come under attack.

In March 1876 the army, previously hampered by severe winter weather, opened hostilities against the nontreaty Sioux, who turned out to be most formidable. The Oglala were headed by renowned warrior CRAZY HORSE, and the Hunkpapa, led by SITTING BULL, defeated General George Crook on June 17, 1876, at the Battle of the Rosebud and annihilated Custer and his troops eight days later at the Battle of the Little Bighorn.

The army eventually prevailed in the spring of 1877, and Crazy Horse surrendered and apparently was prepared to live quietly on the reservation. General George Crook, however, believing rumors that Crazy Horse was planning to escape and lead another uprising, ordered his arrest, and the warrior was bayonetted in that process. Sitting Bull fled to Canada with approximately 2,000 Hunkpapa, Oglala, Miniconjou, Sans Arc, and Blackfoot Sioux; he returned to the Dakota Territory to surrender in 1881 after several difficult Canadian winters. After two years in prison Sitting Bull was relocated to the Standing Rock Agency on the border between North and South Dakota. There, he tried farming and actually toured one season with WILLIAM FREDERICK (Buffalo Bill) CODY's Wild West Show, but he did not particularly wish to assimilate and did not get along with the federal agent in charge of the reservation.

Sitting Bull became interested in the Ghost Dance religious movement that had started in the West around 1870 and was being revived on the Sioux reservations in 1889. Ghost Dancing, which involved communing with ancestors via a trancelike dance, unnerved the agents in charge, and in 1890 the army under General Nelson A. Miles moved in to monitor the situation. When Sitting Bull joined in the Ghost Dancing movement, the federal Indian agent in charge demanded that he be removed from the reservation. As Sitting Bull was being arrested, a fight ensued, and he was shot and killed.

After Sitting Bull's death, General Miles moved to stop what he saw as a potential uprising. On December 28, Miles confronted a group of Miniconjou Sioux at Wounded Knee Creek led by Chief Big Foot, whom he mistakenly thought were joining their Sioux brethren at the Pine Ridge Agency to revolt. As the military were disarming the Miniconjou, a gun discharged, which set off a fight. A total of 153 Miniconjou, including Chief Big Foot, were killed at Wounded Knee, and another 150 or 200 died later of wounds. In retaliation the Sioux ambushed the Seventh Cavalry on December 30, but Miles's Ninth Cavalry joined the Seventh in support. Outnumbered, the Sioux surrendered on January 15, 1891, which marked the end of the Indian Wars.

Further reading: Edward Lazarus, *Black Hills, White Justice: The Sioux Nation versus the United States, 1775 to the Present* (New York: HarperCollins, 1991).

— Scott Sendrow

Sitting Bull (ca. 1831–1890)

Born in what is now South Dakota, Sitting Bull became a renowned Sioux warrior, Wichasha Wakan (holy man), and chief of the Hunkpapa Sioux tribe. His father, a Hunkpapa chief named Sitting Bull, first called him Jumping Badger, knowing that he would earn a more appropriate name at some point in his life. (Early on, he also was known as Hunkesni, or "Slow.") He was reared by his father and uncles in the traditions of war and hunting buffalo and killed his first buffalo at age 10. When he became part of the Hunkpapa warrior society at 14, his father gave him his name and he became Sitting Bull. Sitting Bull was married for the first time in 1851 and became a Hunkpapa war chief in 1857. Following his father's death in 1859, Sitting Bull's standing within the tribe grew, and he soon became onc of the leaders of the Hunkpapa band of the Teton branch of Sioux.

Sitting Bull *(National Archives of Canada)*

His first battles with U.S. forces occurred in 1863 when troops went after the Minnesota Sioux tribes and pushed into the Dakota Territory. Sitting Bull and his warriors fought against the army in the Battle of Killdeer Mountain on July 28, 1864, and continued to fight as the army built posts on the upper Missouri River. Sitting Bull did not sign the 1868 Treaty of Fort Laramie, which established the Great Sioux Reservation, and his standing among the nontreaty, resisting factions of the Sioux tribes (the hostiles) was such that in 1869 they designated him as their supreme war chief. In contrast, RED CLOUD, who had led the Sioux resistance, signed the treaty, accepted reservation life, and advocated peace. As a consequence, Red Cloud has been called the Sioux "statesman" and Sitting Bull the Sioux "patriot."

The Great Sioux Reservation encompassed the land west of the Missouri River in the Dakota Territory and included the Black Hills. Prospectors suspected that the Black Hills region held gold, and in July 1874 an expedition under General GEORGE A. CUSTER (supposedly exploring the route for a road) happened to have prospectors along who found that there was indeed gold in those hills. The BLACK HILLS GOLD RUSH ensued, with thousands of miners pouring into that area and trespassing on Sioux lands. The federal government tried to purchase or lease the Black Hills, but the Sioux, buttressed by the nontreaty Sioux, refused. The U.S. government countered by ordering in December 1875 the nontreaty Sioux onto reservations in six weeks, which, even if they wished to comply, was in winter an impossibility. The army began the second of the SIOUX WARS in the spring of 1876. But in June 1876 Sitting Bull and the Oglala Sioux chief CRAZY HORSE defeated General George Crook at the Battle of the Rosebud and annihilated Custer, making his "last stand," at the Battle of the Little Bighorn. Shocked and aroused, the army relentlessly pursued the warring Sioux until in 1877 Crazy Horse surrendered; Sitting Bull fled to Canada with about 2,000 followers. As the number of buffalo dwindled, so too did his followers, and Sitting Bull in 1881 returned to the Dakota Territory to surrender to the army.

Sitting Bull was imprisoned until May 1883, when he moved to a reservation where he even attempted farming, although he resisted assimilation. Between 1885 and 1886 Sitting Bull toured with BUFFALO BILL CODY's Wild West Show with sharpshooter Annie Oakley, a peculiar twist in American popular culture. In 1890 Sitting Bull, who was a holy man as well as a warrior, embraced the Ghost Dance RELIGION and was its leader on his reservation. Since the Ghost Dance religion had led to unrest on other reservations, authorities feared the worst and ordered Sitting Bull's arrest. When Indian policemen attempted to arrest him on December 15, 1890, his followers resisted, and in the melee Sitting Bull was shot and killed.

Further reading: Robert M. Utley, *The Lance and the Shield: The Life and Times of Sitting Bull* (New York: Ballantine Books, 1993).

— Scott Sendrow

skyscrapers

The elevator and the STEEL frame were the necessary technological developments for construction of the first tall office buildings, which engineers, architects, and real estate developers pioneered in New York and Chicago in the 1880s and 1890s. The conditions motivating construction of the first skyscrapers were, however, economic in nature and derived from two key trends: the phenomenal increase in city populations after the Civil War due to IMMIGRATION from farms and foreign countries, and the industrialization and bureaucratization of work that concentrated more and more activities downtown. These developments increased the value of downtown land, which then stimulated an increase in the number of stories in individual buildings, tentatively in the first iron-frame structures and then decisively with the introduction of steel framing in 1888 in Chicago's Tacoma Building.

Tall office buildings then stimulated further increases in the value of the ground under these buildings, the office rents charged within them, and the number of floors necessary to ensure profits for the developers. This continuous spiral quickly increased the height of tall office buildings from the 10–15 stories of the earliest buildings to the 20 and 30 stories more readily associated with skyscrapers, a word first used in the early 1890s. New York skyscrapers tended to emphasize the theatrical possibilities of historical, largely neoclassical forms. The major architectural firms in Chicago tended to design skyscrapers that expressed the underlying steel frame.

No sooner had the steel frame been introduced than the first race to achieve supreme height occurred in Chicago. Between 1890 and 1891 the Masons and the Odd Fellows strove to acquire not just bragging rights for owning the tallest office building in the world but also the higher rents or the greater resale value that this added prestige would bring with it. The Odd Fellows failed to get their project off the ground, so Chicago's Masonic Temple—designed by Burnham and Root to be an innovative mixture of shops, offices, and Masonic parlors grouped around a 20-story atrium and topped by a roof garden complete with flower shows, tea service, and music recitals—became the first of the world's tall office buildings to be highly touted as such, as well as the source for the vaunting skyscraper rhetoric that surrounded similar rivalries in the 20th century.

Photograph of the Flat Iron Building, New York City, and the area surrounding the junction of Broadway and 5th Avenue. The Flat Iron Building was completed in 1902 and was the first building in New York with a steel frame. *(Library of Congress)*

No matter how high they rose, however, the primary concern in first-class office buildings was to provide amenable working environments. This imperative meant maximizing the amount of natural light in all offices during a period when electric light bulbs ran on low wattages. It also meant lining the corridors and vestibules of these buildings with the mosaics, marbles, plate glass, and glazed bricks that reflected or admitted the maximum amount of natural light into the offices. Light-hued luxurious materials also validated or reinforced Victorian propriety in new work situations where men and a growing number of female clerks and secretaries mixed more freely with one another than they did elsewhere.

Further reading: Sarah Bradford Landau and Carl W. Condit; *Rise of the New York Skyscraper 1865–1913* (New Haven, Conn.: Yale University Press, 1996); Carol Willis, *Form Follows Finance: Skyscrapers and Skylines in New York and Chicago* (New York: Princeton Architectural Press, 1995).

— Edward W. Wolner

slaughterhouse cases (1873) See due process clause

Social Darwinism

Those who embraced Social Darwinism applied a convincing biological hypothesis to the workings of society. Charles Darwin's *On the Origin of Species,* published in England in 1859 and in the United States a year later, presented evidence that animals and plants evolve into new species through a process of natural selection that enabled those that best adjusted to the environment (the fittest) to survive. Americans were preoccupied with slavery, Civil War, and Reconstruction in the 1860s, but by the 1870s their main intellectual preoccupation had become evolution or, as it was frequently called, *Darwinism.* It quickly converted the scientific community, and secular-minded intellectuals—influenced especially by John Fiske (for whom evolution confirmed his optimistic belief in progress)—soon followed suit. Christian churches, however, regarded Darwinism as an assault on RELIGION, since it denied that God created the world and all in it—including humans in his own image—in six days; substituted for the fall of man from innocence to sin the ascent of man; and suggested that all was accomplished not by God's orderly plan but by haphazard, accidental mutations. Yet, the Darwinian hypothesis was so compelling that theologians of mainstream Protestant denominations and subsequently ministers of fashionable urban churches like HENRY WARD BEECHER accepted evolution as God's plan and Darwinism as compatible with theism.

Darwin's ideas triumphed not merely because of his evidence but also because his notions of competition and progress resonated strongly with the outlook of Gilded Age business owners, politicians, and intellectuals. The term *Social Darwinism* gave their ideas the sanction of science. Herbert Spencer, the most outstanding Social Darwinist, was enormously popular in the United States. Beecher said he expected to meet Spencer in heaven as proof of the survival of the fittest, and ANDREW CARNEGIE understandably enough was his most prominent American disciple. Spencer argued that competition led to progress; that the fit (the rich and powerful) should be free to eliminate the unfit; and that government attempts to protect the unfit (the weak and poor) from the strong impeded progress, violated scientific law, and would in the long run fail. Spencer's laissez-faire ideas aimed to discourage any intervention on the part of government in the economy and also to paralyze the humanitarian reform spirit that would aid the weak.

WILLIAM GRAHAM SUMNER was Spencer's most consistent American disciple. A Yale sociologist, Sumner combined elements of the Protestant ethic—industry, frugality, temperance—with laissez-faire and Darwin's natural selection through competition. He regarded himself not as an apologist for wealthy businessmen but as a spokesman for the forgotten in the middle class who had to get by on their own wits. Sumner insisted that while laissez-faire should not protect the weak, it also meant no special governmental favors like the protective TARIFF for manufacturers. Sumner was a determinist who believed that the mores of a society evolved over time, uncontrolled by people and uninfluenced by government action, and he is renowned for his observation that you cannot legislate morality.

Social Darwinists not only saw a figurative jungle in the unbridled competition between and crass exploitation of individuals prevailing in Gilded Age America but also applied the concept of natural selection to nations and peoples. Although Americans had been convinced by historian George Bancroft that God had watched over the United States, John Fiske argued that America and Americans were the fittest nation and the most superior people in the world. In the hands of Fiske and other historians as well as clergymen like JOSIAH STRONG, Darwinism provided a scientific rationale for racist ideas and IMPERIALISM, while English and German scholars stressing Teutonic and Anglo-Saxon superiority did the same.

Darwinism (evolution), however, is a neutral concept and above all is not static. Competitive ideas arise that challenge and overthrow prevailing ideas, including those of the social Darwinists. LESTER FRANK WARD in *Dynamic Sociology* (1882) challenged the Social Darwinism of Spencer and Sumner with reform Darwinism. Ward's basic argument is that while the environment transforms animals, people transform the environment, and people can therefore control the evolutionary process. The Social Darwinists failed to appreciate the power of the human mind. Cutthroat competition and government inaction resulted from people's decisions, and if those practices harmed society, then people could through government regulate competition. Ward's ideas were not popular during the Gilded Age, but they were followed by reformers in the ensuing Progressive Era. Notions of racial and national superiority lost all intellectual underpinning in the 20th century with the rise of the Nazis in Germany and the post-World War II decline of imperialism.

Further reading: Robert C. Banister, *Social Darwinism: Science and Myth in Anglo-American Social Thought* (Philadelphia: Temple University Press, 1979); Richard Hofstadter, *Social Darwinism in American Thought,* rev. ed. (Boston: Beacon Press, 1955).

Social Gospel

A religious movement affecting mainstream Protestant denominations, the Social Gospel stressed the commandment of Jesus to love thy "neighbor" and confronted the deleterious effects on American society of industrialization and urbanization. Its American roots were in Puritanism, utopianism, and abolitionism, but its intellectual foundation was notably in the English Christian Socialism of Charles Kingsley and John Ruskin and the ideas of German theologians such as Albrecht Ritschl and Adolf von Harnack. The Social Gospel arose in the 1880s, became coherent in the 1890s, and was passé by 1918, the year in which its earliest voice, WASHINGTON GLADDEN, and its most eloquent voice, Walter Rauschenbusch, both died. And it paralleled, reflected, and reinforced the Progressive movement of which it was in many respects a religious manifestation. It was distinct from the urban ministries of the Young Mens Christian Association (YMCA) and the Salvation Army, which served the poor in the cities to save souls but not to end poverty or injustice. The Social Gospel in large part gave PROGRESSIVISM its strong religious overtones and its moral fervor.

The first phase of the Social Gospel was intellectual, marked by efforts to create a coherent vision of both the issues raised by industrialism and urbanization and the role of Protestant Christianity in addressing those issues. Gladden laid the groundwork by forging a liberal theology that addressed social needs. Other voices at this time were Francis Greenwood Peabody, Unitarian clergyman and Harvard

Divinity School professor; economist Richard T. Ely; and sociologist Albion W. Small. With others, they formed the conceptual apparatus that combined theology with the emerging disciplines of sociology and economics that would propel the next phase of the Social Gospel movement.

The second phase was dominated by JOSIAH STRONG, who organized the movement and was its most dynamic leader. He was renowned in his time (and notorious in ours) for his book *Our Country: Its Possible Future and Its Present Crisis* (1885). Modern readers are offended by his assumptions of Anglo-Saxon superiority and his paternalistic embrace of IMPERIALISM, but Strong's contemporaries regarded *Our Country* as a call for social reform at home and for Americans to promote peace, prosperity, and justice abroad through service, not political domination. *Our Country* was the most influential book to come out of the Social Gospel movement, but Strong's major contribution to the movement was organizing its disparate elements as general secretary of the Evangelical Alliance (1886–90), as leader of the American Institute for Social Service (1898–1916), and in 1908 helping create the Federal Council of Churches. These organizations backed legislation and programs to improve working conditions, combat social evils like drunkenness, eliminate political corruption, and improve the lives of the urban poor.

While both Gladden and Strong advocated state-regulated capitalism and were not socialists, Walter Rauschenbusch carried the social implications of Christianity further. This son of a German immigrant family began serving a Baptist congregation in New York's Hell's Kitchen in 1886. Struck by "an endless procession of men out of work, out of clothes, out of shoes, and out of hope," Rauschenbusch was soon deep into the social ministry. Acquainted with HENRY GEORGE and JACOB RIIS, familiar with the writings of Karl Marx, EDWARD BELLAMY, and English Fabian Socialists, Rauschenbusch coalesced his ideas into his 1907 book *Christianity and the Social Crisis,* which defined the role of the church in a society that had the resources and the technology to provide all with a decent standard of living. Specifically, he advocated legislating public ownership of utilities and transportation, fair wages and better working conditions, and the redistribution of land to provide workers with decent housing. In 1917 he published *A Theology for the Social Gospel,* which provided a theological base for Progressive Christian beliefs just as progressivism was in decline.

Further reading: Susan Curtis, *A Consuming Faith: The Social Gospel and Modern American Culture* (Baltimore, Md.: Johns Hopkins University Press, 1991); Peter F. Frederick, *Knights of the Golden Rule: The Intellectual as Christian Social Reformer in the 1890s* (Lexington: University of Kentucky Press, 1976); Robert T. Handy, ed., *The Social Gospel in America, 1870–1920* (New York: Oxford University Press, 1966); Charles Howard Hopkins, *The Rise of the Social Gospel in American Protestantism, 1865–1915* (New Haven, Conn.: Yale University Press, 1940).

— W. Frederick Wooden

socialism

Socialists believe that a society based upon public ownership of property and its management for the common good (goods and services would be distributed according to need) is superior to one founded on private property and administered for individual profit. The concept of communal property is old and widespread; early Christians as well as NATIVE AMERICANS practiced it. But the modern socioeconomic-political doctrine denoted as socialism was a response to the major social changes wrought by industrialization.

Although writers such as Saint-Simon, Charles Fourier, Robert Owen, and Ferdinand Lassalle contributed to the theory, Karl Marx exerted the greatest influence over its development. Believing that economics was the dominant force in shaping history, Marx posited a class struggle between workers (the proletariat) and capitalists. The conflict would inevitably result in the establishment of socialism.

German immigrants carried socialist ideas with them to the United States prior to the Civil War, but it was not until the 1870s that the doctrine gained attention beyond ethnic communities. The activities of two flamboyant sisters, Tennessee Claflin and VICTORIA WOODHULL, however, created discord within the movement. The two worked as clairvoyants in the Midwest before moving to New York, where Claflin became a close friend of railroad tycoon CORNELIUS VANDERBILT. Vanderbilt made them stockbrokers and ensured their success with inside information. Despite this connection, the sisters joined Section 12 of the Marxist International Workingmen's Association (IWA), better known as the First International. They also published a newspaper, *Woodhull and Claflin's Weekly,* which advocated free love, abortion, and spiritualism as well as socialism. Fearful that the *Weekly* exposed socialism to ridicule, the European leaders expelled Section 12 in 1872. The expulsion caused a split, with "Americans" forming the American Confederation, which eventually lost its membership, and the German-Americans creating the North American Federation. Doctrinal disputes soon split the Germans into the Lassalleans, who favored political action, and the marxists, who emphasized the organization of labor unions, and the IWA died in 1876. The two factions, however, came together in 1876 to form what became the SOCIALIST LABOR PARTY (SLP). The SLP suffered numerous schisms until 1892, when Daniel De Leon became its undisputed leader.

EDWARD BELLAMY's book *Looking Backward* (1888) provided the basis of an American version of socialism. Set in the year 2000, *Looking Backward* projected a socialistic society that voluntarily evolved. The lack of revolutionary conflict appealed to the many who joined Nationalist Clubs to promote the abolition of private property. But both the European and American forms of socialism had little impact.

It is ironic that Gilded Age America, rapidly industrializing and experiencing labor violence, did not embrace socialism. Several explanations for this apparent paradox have been advanced. One argues that the constant dissension and schisms within the socialist movement made it seem ridiculous. Another suggests that socialism was too closely identified with immigrants to be accepted by Americans. Still another notes that American labor unions, seeking immediate economic gains, rejected socialism. One further holds that the anticlericalism of most socialists alienated them from their ethnic communities, which tended to revere the church. Perhaps the best explanation is that the American promise of upward mobility, so attractive to immigrants, negated the appeal of socialism.

Further reading: Seymour Martin Lipset and Gary Marks, *It Didn't Happen Here: Why Socialism Failed in the United States* (New York: Norton, 2000); Howard Quint, *Forging of American Socialism* (Columbia: University of South Carolina Press, 1953).

— Harold W. Aurand

Socialist Labor Party (SLP)

The history of the Socialist Labor Party (SLP) is one of dissension and schism. Meeting in Pittsburgh in 1876, representatives of the two major divisions among socialists—the Lassalleans (who favored using the electoral process to capture the existing state) and the Marxists (who wanted to organize the working class for the revolutionary destruction of the state)—called for a "Unity Congress." Assembling in Philadelphia in July 1876, the congress established the Workingmen's Party of the United States (WPUS). Although the delegates elected a Lassallean, Philip Van Patter, as national secretary of the WPUS, they demonstrated their Marxist leanings by prohibiting electoral politics except at the local level and then only when conditions appeared extremely favorable.

Convinced by the GREAT STRIKE OF 1877 that political action was expedient, the 1877 WPUS convention, boycotted by most militant Marxists, repealed the stricture against entering politics and changed its name to the Socialist Labor Party (SLP). The SLP supported the candidates of the GREENBACK-LABOR PARTY in the 1880 presidential election, but disenchanted by defeat, the 16 delegates attending the party's 1883 convention adopted the policy of using electoral politics only for propaganda purposes. Agitation for the eight-hour workday, however, encouraged the Lassallean leadership to reenter politics in 1886 by joining a number of local third parties. Although that effort was a disaster, the party ran its slate of presidential electors in New York during the 1888 election only to be badly defeated. The dismal returns reignited the internal debate over the role of electoral politics and ended in 1889 when the Lassalleans, known as the W. L. Rosenberg or Cincinnati group, bolted from the party to form the Social Democratic Federation.

The SLP's marxist tendency became more pronounced with the rise of Daniel De Leon to power, although he, like the Lassalleans, also wanted to participate in electoral politics. In 1892 De Leon, a Columbia University law professor, became the SLP's dominant voice as editor of its newspaper, *The People*, and the SLP regularly participated in presidential campaigns, receiving, for example, 36,000 votes in 1896. But the SLP directed most of its attention to capturing the labor union movement by "boring within," or placing its members in key union positions. This tactic resulted in the temporary replacement of SAMUEL GOMPERS as president of the AMERICAN FEDERATION OF LABOR (AFL) and the permanent removal of TERENCE V. POWDERLY as grand master workman (president) of the KNIGHTS OF LABOR. But both organizations repulsed the SLP's bid for control. Angered, De Leon launched another SLP organization, the Socialist Trade and Labor Alliance. The creation of a dual (competing) union caused a group of trade unionists (called either the Kangaroos or the Rochester SLP) led by Morris Hillquit to leave the SLP in 1900. After a series of legal battles, the minuscule De Leon faction retained the name SLP, while the Kangaroos joined the SOCIALIST PARTY. In the early 20th century the SLP, led by the doctrinaire and divisive De Leon, had virtually no influence on the socialist movement and absolutely none on American society.

Further reading: Frank Girard and Ben Perry, *The Socialist Labor Party, 1876–1991: A Short History* (Philadelphia: Livra Books, 1991).

— Harold W. Aurand

Socialist Party

The Socialist Party was the product of Eugene Victor Debs's disillusionment following the PULLMAN STRIKE and schisms within the SOCIALIST LABOR PARTY (SLP). In 1897 Debs dissolved the American Railway Union and reconvened it as the Social Democracy of America. In addition to railroaders, two other distinctive groups joined the new organization. One, largely composed of recent immigrants, based their SOCIALISM upon the writings of Karl Marx and other European theorists. Victor Berger and his followers comprised the largest group in this wing. Emigrating from Austria, Berger settled in Milwaukee where he founded the Wisconsin *Vorwarts* and advocated political action to achieve immediate goals. Disciples of the Lassallean W. L.

Rosenberg, who left the SLP in 1889, and a New York faction recently expelled from the SLP completed the "European" wing of the party. The other wing, most of whom were born in America, consisted of former KNIGHTS OF LABOR, disgruntled agrarian radicals, and those who drew their inspiration from EDWARD BELLAMY's *Looking Backward* (1888), a novel describing a futuristic socialist society.

Reflecting its utopian basis, the Social Democracy committed itself to a colonization scheme. According to this plan members of the party would move into a western territory, where they would establish a socialist commonwealth. Once established, the commonwealth would fulfill Bellamy's prophesy and would be the example that the country would emulate and copy. Within a year Berger and others, however, convinced Debs that the colonization dream was unrealistic. Unable to convince the 1898 convention that it should remove the colonization plank from its platform, Debs, Berger, and others seceded from the Social Democracy to form the Social Democratic Party. After electing two representatives to the Massachusetts legislature in 1898, the new party attracted more followers.

Another schism within the SLP in 1900 altered the Social Democratic Party's fortunes. Opposed to the SLP's creation of a dual (competing) union, the Socialist Trade and Labor Alliance—a group of SLP trade unionists led by Morris Hillquit—withdrew and conducted their own convention in Rochester, New York. After nominating a presidential ticket of Job Harriman and Max Hayes, the SLP dissidents and the Social Democratic Party discussed a merger, and although negotiations languished, the Social Democratic convention created a fusion ticket of Debs for president and Harriman for vice president. Both groups supported the fusion ticket, which received 97,000 votes, outpolling the SLP by a factor of three. Encouraged by the vote, both factions met in Indianapolis in 1900 and formed the Socialist Party of America, which at its high point in 1912 and with Debs at its head, attracted almost 1 million voters.

Further reading: Ray Ginger, *The Bending Cross: A Biography of Eugene Victor Debs* (New Brunswick, N.J.: Rutgers University Press, 1949).

— Harold W. Aurand

sod houses

The scarcity of timber in the West meant that settlers could not easily or cheaply build a typical log cabin. The sod house, an austere dwelling built out of the earth itself,

Sod school house *(National Archives)*

supplanted the log cabin in the West and became a symbol of the hardscrabble existence of the Western settler. These settlers staked their claim on land, and then built homes made of the land.

The first sod houses appeared in Kansas during the 1850s. To make a sod house, a settler simply plowed the ground and used the furrowed sod to make bricks. The bricks, similar to the adobe clay bricks found in some Southwestern dwellings, were a yard long, 12 to 18 inches wide, and three inches thick. Roofs were crafted using layers of brush and grass and a final layer of sod, with the grass side down; a more expensive version used lumber or tar paper in place of the grass or brush. Some interiors featured plaster covering the sod walls, but windows and window frames proved to be a luxury, so sod houses usually had little light or ventilation. A one-room house used approximately a half-acre of sod.

Sod houses were either free standing or built into a hill. The dugout variety involved excavating the side of a hill or ravine and building a front wall out of sod bricks. Dugout homes lasted only a season or two and generally served as interim dwellings until a four-wall sod house could be built. A regular sod house was expected to last about six or seven years. The structures looked like grass huts, as the organic sod bricks sprouted grass as well as insects and vermin. Although the sod protected homes against fire and were easy to repair, leaking tended to be a problem, and its inhabitants constantly checked walls and ceilings that were in danger of caving in. Successful settler families eventually built traditional homes, although they continued to use "soddies" for livestock or outhouses.

Further reading: Everett Dick, *The Sod-House Frontier, 1854–1890* (New York: D. Appleton-Century, 1937).

— Scott Sendrow

Solid South

The term *Solid South* refers to the political dominance of the DEMOCRATIC PARTY in the states of the former Confederacy. During the Reconstruction period, conservative, white-supremacy, Democratic governments gradually replaced the Radical Republican governments set up under the First Reconstruction Act (1867). Virginia and Tennessee were "redeemed," as the Democrats put it, in 1869, North Carolina in 1870, Georgia in 1871, Texas in 1873, Alabama and Arkansas in 1874, Mississippi in 1875 after a most violent election, and Florida, South Carolina, and Louisiana in 1877. The triumph of the Democratic Party in the South can be ascribed to a combination of amnesty that enfranchised former Confederates, intimidation of black voters who were invariably Republican, and racial politics that identified the REPUBLICAN PARTY with AFRICAN AMERICANS and thus united the white race in its opposition. The final withdrawal of federal troops supporting Republican governments in South Carolina and Louisiana in 1877 by President RUTHERFORD B. HAYES was foreordained by Democratic control of the House of Representatives and with it army appropriations, by the preoccupation of the North with the problems of a severe economic depression, and more fundamentally by the North's apathy over the civil rights of blacks. After 1877 the former Confederate states sent practically solid Democratic congressional delegations to Washington and until 1928 consistently supported Democratic presidential candidates.

Further reading: William Gillette, *Retreat from Reconstruction, 1869–1879* (Baton Rouge: Louisiana State University Press, 1979); J. Morgan Kousser, *The Shaping of Southern Politics: Suffrage Restriction and the Establishment of the One-Party South, 1880–1910* (New Haven, Conn.: Yale University Press, 1974); C. Vann Woodward, *Origins of the New South, 1877–1913* (Baton Rouge: Louisiana State University Press, 1951).

— Phillip Papas

Sooners

In the latter half of the 19th century, expansion rapidly filled the western territories. By the 1880s the states surrounding the Indian Territory (Oklahoma) were far more populous than the territory, which had less than two inhabitants per square mile. The federal government was under pressure to open the fertile triangle in the center of the Indian Territory that was not assigned to any tribe. "Boomers" from Kansas, Texas, and Arkansas desired that land, as did the RAILROADS. The most notorious Boomer, David L. Payne, anticipated that the government would eventually open the unassigned lands ("Old Oklahoma") and surreptitiously surveyed land, going so far as to sell lots (without actually owning any of the land) in what is now modern-day Oklahoma City.

Bowing to pressure, CONGRESS authorized the opening of the unassigned lands to homesteaders in 1889. After the land was surveyed, as many as 20,000 people assembled at the borders of the district to claim land. At noon on April 22, 1889, homesteaders rushed forth on various modes of transportation to stake claims on land, and in one chaotic afternoon 1.9 million acres of land were claimed and Oklahoma City had a population of 10,000. The settlers acquired the land for free under the Homestead Act (1862), and the term *Sooners* refers to those who had sneaked past guards to get a head start on claiming the most desirable land. By the end of 1889 the Old Oklahoma District was home to more than 60,000 people. On September 16, 1893, a second major Boomer rush occurred in Oklahoma when the "Cherokee Outlet" was opened for settlement. Eventually, the chaos caused by the land rush led to the establishment of an application and lottery process.

The DAWES SEVERALTY ACT of 1887 made more Oklahoma land available for settlement. It provided for the redistribution of reservation land to members of Indian tribes and made land unclaimed by NATIVE AMERICANS available to white settlers at a cost of $1.25 an acre, a modest price for the time. (The cost served to recoup money paid out by the government to Indian tribes.) In addition, in 1898 the Osage tribe and the Five Civilized tribes (the Cherokee, Choctaw, Chickasaw, Creek, and Seminole) were no longer exempt from the Dawes Act, and their surplus lands ultimately were for sale. Oklahoma became a state in 1907.

Further reading: Frederick Merk, *History of Western Movement* (New York: Knopf, 1978).

— Scott Sendrow

Sousa, John Philip (1854–1932)

Famous throughout the world as a band director and composer of marches, John Philip Sousa was born on November 6, 1854, in Washington, D.C., to immigrant parents (his father was Portuguese and his mother was Bavarian). His musical ability was evident early, and as a child he studied violin at a local MUSIC school. Sousa's father was a trombonist in the U.S. Marine Band, and when John Philip was 13, his father arranged to have him enlisted as an apprentice. He served in the Marine Band until 1875. During these years he also studied theory, harmony, and composition with George Felix Benkert, a Washington orchestral conductor and pianist. In 1876 he moved to Philadelphia, where he played first violin in Jacques Offenbach's orchestra for the PHILADELPHIA CENTENNIAL EXPOSITION. He remained in Philadelphia for four years, working as a theater violinist, teaching, arranging, conducting, and composing. He found work as a director of musical theater, including a production of Gilbert and Sullivan's *H.M.S. Pinafore* and a show titled *Our Flirtations* for which he composed, compiled, and arranged the score.

In 1880 Sousa was appointed conductor of the U.S. Marine Band. During the next 12 years, he developed the band into a first-rate musical ensemble. In 1889 he composed *The Washington Post March,* which brought him international fame, and by 1891 he was known as the March King.

In 1892 he resigned to form his own band, Sousa's Band, which achieved an extraordinary level of excellence and worldwide fame. The Sousa Band was a band unlike any that had preceded it; its repertoire included, in addition to Sousa's own marches, movements from popular operas and arrangements of popular music, including ragtime. Concerts by the band usually featured a performance by an attractive female vocal or instrumental soloist. Performances by virtuoso members of his band were also featured. Some of the most notable soloists were Arthur Pryor on trombone (Pryor also served as assistant conductor and arranger), Herbert L. Clarke on cornet, and E. A. Lefebre on saxophone. The Sousa Band flourished for nearly four decades, touring North America annually except during World War I. During the war, Sousa served in the navy, organizing band units and directing a navy band of more than 300. The Sousa Band made four European tours between 1900 and 1905 and a world tour in 1910–11. The band was finally dissolved in 1931 due to difficulties brought on by the Great Depression and Sousa's declining health. He died on March 6, 1932, in Reading, Pennsylvania, while preparing for a guest-conducting appearance.

Sousa's contributions to American music were many. From the time of his appointment to the Marine Band until after World War I, Sousa was the most prominent national musician. He composed and performed music for virtually every significant national event or celebration, from the WORLD'S COLUMBIAN EXPOSITION at Chicago in 1893 to the Liberty Loan Drive of 1917. Known throughout the world, Sousa is best remembered as a composer of marches. Among the best and most popular were *El Capitan* (1896), *Semper Fidelis* (1888), *The Stars and Stripes Forever!* (1896), and *United States Field Artillery* (1917). Some marches, such as *The Washington Post,* were popular for dancing in the United States and Europe. He developed a standard form for the march that has been widely adopted and imitated. A typical Sousa march has a brief introduction, strains A and B, both repeated, a brief interlude (called the "break"), and then a trio that is usually in a key a 4th above the opening tonic. The trio is most often repeated with a countermelody. Repeats of the trio are sometimes separated by brief dramatic episodes. The marches are in brisk 2/4 or 6/8 time. This form was borrowed and adapted by many ragtime composers.

Sousa's operettas were very successful and popular in their time. Between 1882 and 1915 he completed 12 operettas, of which the most successful were *El Capitan* (1895), *The Bride Elect* (1897), and *The Charlatan* (1898). Inspired by Gilbert and Sullivan, they pointed the way for the development of musical THEATER in the 20th century. Sousa contributed the sousaphone, a bass tuba that encircles the body with a widely flared bell, to the family of brass instruments. He had the first built to his specifications in the 1890s. Sousa objected to recorded music (he is credited with originating the term *canned music* in an article in *Appleton's Magazine,* September 1906). However, his band made many recordings, the earliest usually under the direction of Arthur Pryor. Sousa was also a prolific author. He published three novels, an autobiography, *Marching Along* (1928), numerous newspaper and magazine articles, and many other works. He was a shrewd businessman and a fighter for composers' rights. He was a founding member of the American Society of Composers, Authors, and Publishers (ASCAP) in 1914 and served as a director and vice president of the society from 1924 until his death in 1932.

Further reading: Paul E. Bierley, *John Philip Sousa: American Phenomenon* (Columbus, Ohio: Integrity Press, 1986).

— William Peek

Spanish-American War (1898)

The four-month Spanish-American War, fought primarily on the island of CUBA, marked the arrival of the United States as a world power and brought an end to Spain's empire in the Americas. The immediate cause of the war was Spain's brutal, yet failing, strategy to quell a revolt in Cuba, which along with Puerto Rico, the Philippines, some Pacific islands, and a few African possessions was all that remained of the Spanish empire. The revolution began in Cuba in 1895, and Americans viewed it as a fight by a ragtag army of insurrectionists for freedom from a bloated and corrupt monarchy and equated the struggle with their own fight a century earlier against England. Egged on by Cuban exiles living in the United States, Americans began to smuggle weapons to the Cubans.

Americans also had strong commercial interests in Cuba. The widespread devastation caused by Spain's pacification strategy threatened American investments in Cuban railways and sugar plantations. In addition, with the frontier of continental North America effectively closed by the 1890s, expansionists preached the need for the United States to expand its economic power and export its surplus production into the Americas and the Pacific. Beyond Cuba's economic value was its strategic usefulness in defending an envisioned Central American isthmian canal that would permit the eastern American ports to exploit allegedly rich markets of the Orient.

In 1873 the United States had almost intervened in an earlier Cuban Revolution following the *VIRGINIUS AFFAIR*, but by 1898 IMPERIALISM—driven by economic ambitions, strategic concerns, and humanitarian impulses heightened by a sensationalist press—made war far more likely. In February 1898 the *New York Journal* published the DE LÔME LETTER in which the Spanish minister to the United States made disparaging remarks about President WILLIAM MCKINLEY. This insult was followed on February 15, 1898, by the explosion in Havana harbor that sank the American battleship *Maine* and killed 260 sailors and marines. The American press immediately blamed Spanish treachery and called for war, but a naval court of inquiry—while concluding that an underwater mine sank the *Maine*—could not determine responsibility. Although the Spanish government was the least likely culprit, it offered to have the questions of responsibility and reparations arbitrated and even agreed to an armistice (to last as long as the commanding general in Cuba thought prudent) in the war on the Cuban rebels. But the United States was in no mood for arbitration or for negotiations. McKinley, who had experienced the carnage of war, reluctantly gave in to pressure and on April 11, 1898, asked CONGRESS for the authority to use the armed forces to intervene in Cuba. Congress debated for a week before agreeing on April 19 by joint resolution, which McKinley signed the following day, and the war began.

A few days after the declaration of war, Commodore GEORGE DEWEY steamed with the American Asiatic Squadron to the Philippines to stop a decrepit Spanish fleet from voyaging halfway around the globe to reinforce Spanish naval forces at Cuba. Off Cavite in Manila Bay on the morning of May 1, the American fleet put the Spanish fleet of 10 ships out of action and forced its supporting shore batteries to surrender. While Dewey awaited troops, the Filipinos revolted for their independence and cooperated with the American army when it arrived to besiege Manila. American-Filipino relations deteriorated after Spanish authorities surrendered Manila on August 13, 1898, to American forces and the Filipino insurgents were frozen out. When it became apparent that the American goal was annexation of the Philippines and not independence, a bloody war called the FILIPINO INSURRECTION broke out.

The campaign for Cuba, plagued by logistic and transportation problems, got underway on June 22 with the landing of soldiers and marines at Daiquiri. Only after five days would all the troops be deployed and the beachhead be secured. The American strategy in Cuba was for the navy to blockade the island and cut off supplies for the Spanish while the army stormed the port of Santiago from the land. The navy soon had the Spanish fleet trapped at Santiago Bay. The army meanwhile fought its way through dense jungle from the coast to the San Juan Heights overlooking the city. At the Battle of San Juan Hill, Theodore Roosevelt drove the Spanish from their trenches atop Kettle Hill with his ROUGH RIDERS by brazenly charging up the slope in the face of heavy fire. With Santiago certain to be captured, the Spanish fleet on July 3 risked destruction in an attempt to escape. Led by Admiral Pascual Cervera's flagship the *Infanta Maria Theresa,* the fleet steamed out the narrow mouth of the harbor to be destroyed by the American fleet. Faced with the probability of being shelled by land and sea, Governor General Ramón Blanco y Erenas surrendered his troops on July 17, 1898.

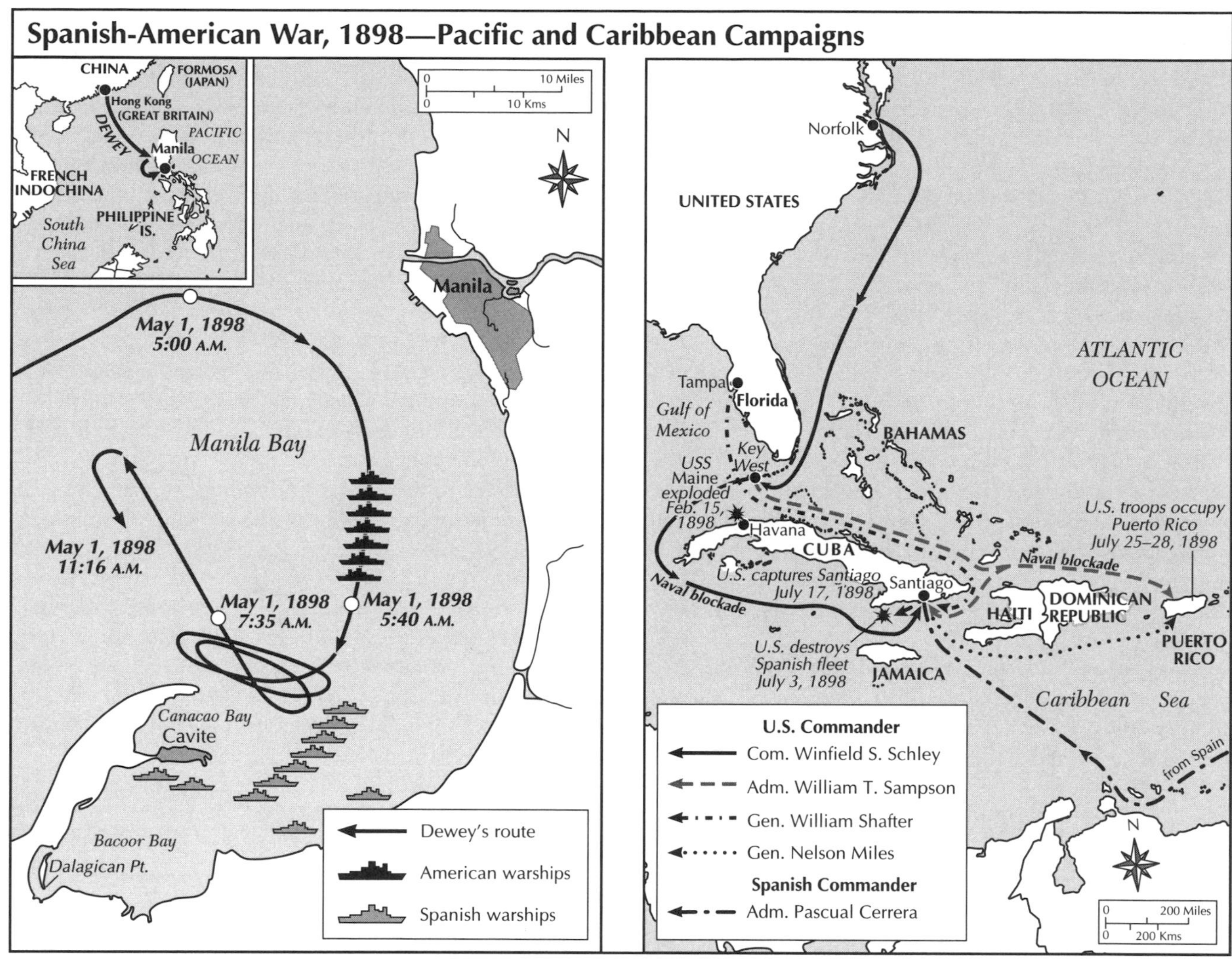

The peace treaty signed on December 10, 1898, gave the United States the Philippines, Puerto Rico, and Guam. Cuba became independent, since the Teller Amendment to the declaration of war specifically forbade its annexation by the United States. Cuba's independence, however, was nominal, since in 1901 it was forced to write into its constitution the Platt Amendment, which gave the United States the right to intervene in its affairs.

See also *MAINE*, REMEMBER THE; YELLOW JOURNALISM.

Further reading: Ernest R. May, *Imperial Democracy: The Emergence of America as a Great Power* (New York: Harper & Row, 1961); Ivan Musicant, *Empire by Default: The Spanish-American War and the Dawn of the American Century* (New York: Henry Holt & Co., 1998); G. J. A. O'Toole, *The Spanish War: An American Epic, 1898* (New York: Norton, 1984).

— Timothy E. Vislocky

specie payments, resumption of

See currency issue

spiritualism

See religion

spoils system

See civil service reform

sports and recreation

Several sports, including tennis, golf, and basketball, developed in the Gilded Age. Outdoor tennis, invented in Great Britain, came to the United States via Bermuda in 1874. There, the vacationing Mary Outerbridge of Staten Island, New York, liked tennis so well that she embarked for home with net, rackets, and balls that, upon her landing, perplexed customshouse officers. In spring 1874 she designed the first American tennis court at the Staten Island Cricket and Baseball Club. Courts were built at Lakewood, New Jersey; Tuxedo Park, New York; and Newport, Rhode Island. By 1880 more than 30 eastern clubs had laid out tennis courts. The first important tennis tournament was held in 1880 on Staten Island.

The U.S. Lawn Tennis Association (USLTA), formed in 1881, sponsored a challenge-round tournament at Newport from 1881 to 1915. Richard Sears won the first seven USLTA tournaments. The sport was played mainly by wealthy easterners, and the early champions often came from Harvard University. Robert Wrenn, Frederick Hovey, and Malcolm Whitman won the singles championships from 1893 through 1900, while Holcombe Ward and Dwight Davis captured consecutive doubles titles from 1899 through 1901. Harvard students modernized tennis by using a twist overhand service, the passing shot, and the lob and by rushing to the net. Tennis gained popularity in 1900 when Davis donated a cup for annual competition among all nations, but in particular the Davis Cup stimulated competition between the United States and Great Britain. The Americans, led by Whitman, Davis, and Ward, upset the British, 5–0, in 1900.

Golf appeared in the United States by the 1880s. The leisurely sport appealed to wealthier, older people and was dominated by the British. Robert Lockhart purchased a set of golf clubs and two dozen guttie balls (rubberlike balls made from the gum of the gutta-percha tree) in Dunfermline, Scotland, in 1887 and brought them back to his Yonkers, New York, home. John Shotts, a Yonkers butcher, permitted golfers to hit balls around his 30-acre lot. In November 1888, Scotsman John Reid established St. Andrews, the first permanent American golf club. The six-hole St. Andrews course was built on Shotts's property and shifted locations several times over the next decade.

Scottish professional Willie Dunn in 1891 built Shinnecock Hills, the nation's first true golf course, at Southampton, New York. Dunn and 150 Indians from the Shinnecock Reservation cleared 4,000 acres of thick brush and laid out a 12-hole seaside golf links. After incorporating, Shinnecock Hills built a clubhouse and opened in 1892 with 70 club members.

In 1893 the Chicago Golf Club built the nation's first 18-hole course. Charles Macdonald, the club's best player, won the U.S. Golf Association's (USGA) first amateur championship in 1895 at the Newport Golf Club in Newport, Rhode Island. The USGA also sponsored the initial U.S. Open golf tournament in 1895. The Open was increased from 36 holes to 72 holes in 1898. Foreign-born golfers won every U.S. Open tournament from 1895 to 1910. American John McDermott prevailed with a winning

Advertisement for a lawn-tennis equipment manufacturer, 1882 *(Library of Congress)*

307 in 1911 at the Chicago Golf Club in Wheaton, Illinois. Golf grew rapidly from 50 clubs in 1895 to 1,040 by 1900.

In 1893 the Shinnecock Hills Golf Club designed a nine-hole course for women. Within two years, other courses for women were built at Morristown, New Jersey, and Yonkers, New York. Holland Ford, by 14 strokes, won the first women's tournament, held in October 1894 on the seven-hole Morristown course. In 1896 Beatrix Hoyt captured the first USGA-sanctioned amateur championship by two holes, with one hole left to play, at Morris County Golf Club in Convent, New Jersey. She won the next two USGA women's amateur titles by wider margins.

Basketball, the only major sport purely American in origin, was invented by Dr. James Naismith, who taught physical education at YMCA Training College in Springfield, Massachusetts (now Springfield College). Dr. Luther Gulick, physical education department head, asked Naismith to conduct an indoor activity for students. Naismith invented basketball, in which participants scored by shooting soccer balls into peach baskets suspended at each end of the school's gymnasium. In January 1892 Naismith wrote 13 basketball rules. Since his class had 18 students, Naismith assigned nine players to each side. Each team fielded three forwards, three centers, and three guards. Two centers tipped the ball at mid-court to start the game. Players committing fouls were put in a penalty box until the next basket was made. To speed the game, Naismith removed the bottom from the peach basket. The game was called "Springfield ball" and "triangle ball" before student Frank Mahan named it basketball. Basketball initially was considered a YMCA exercise rather than a serious sport. Geneva, Yale, Pennsylvania, Wesleyan, Trinity, Chicago, Iowa, Stanford, Nebraska, and Kansas soon fielded men's varsity basketball teams, while Smith, Vassar, Wellesley, Newcomb, and Bryn Mawr had women's basketball teams. Columbia, Cornell, Harvard, Princeton, and Yale formed the Eastern Intercollegiate League in 1901.

Further reading: Parke Cummings, *American Tennis: The Story of a Game* (Boston: Little, Brown, 1957); Donald V. Mrozek, *Sport and American Mentality, 1880–1910* (Knoxville: University of Tennessee Press, 1983); Bernice Larsen Webb, *The Basketball Man: James Naismith* (Lawrence: University Press of Kansas, 1973); Herbert Warren Wind, *The Story of American Golf*, 3d rev. ed. (New York: Knopf, 1975).

— David L. Porter

stalwarts See Republican Party

Standard Oil See oil

star route frauds

Special postal routes, designated on lists by three stars for "certainty, celerity, and security," were mostly in the West and depended on horses for transportation. Marauders, topography, and climate made them difficult and dangerous. In 1878 there were 9,225 star routes (some handling only three letters a week), for which $5.9 million was appropriated. Between 1878 and 1880, Second Assistant Postmaster General Thomas J. Brady and his accomplices furnished sham petitions requesting that service be expedited on 93 of these routes. Improved service jumped annual operating costs from $762,858 to $2,723,464 and required a deficiency appropriation that aroused the suspicions of CONGRESS and President RUTHERFORD B. HAYES, but the Post Office Department claimed that increased service was needed and the money was appropriated. Hayes, however, insisted that no new star route liabilities be incurred without a review by himself.

In 1881, less than two months after Hayes left office, President JAMES A. GARFIELD's postmaster general, Thomas L. James, exposed the star route frauds and revealed them as the source of some of the money that had financed Garfield's election. Stephen W. Dorsey, the secretary of the Republican National Committee, through his connection with Brady, was able to engineer Garfield's crucial victory in Indiana with star route money. Dorsey's brother, his brother-in-law, and a former partner controlled 24 contracts that had been worth $55,246 but were increased to $501,072. A small part of the increase went for additional service; the rest was put to private and political use. Dorsey later made the preposterous claim that he had spent $400,000 in Indiana, but the Republicans were well funded in that state.

Garfield's assassination interrupted the investigation of the frauds, but the CHESTER A. ARTHUR administration persisted and eventually brought Brady and Dorsey to trial. After protracted litigation both were acquitted.

Further reading: Ari Hoogenboom, *Rutherford B. Hayes: Warrior and President* (Lawrence: University Press of Kansas, 1995); Allan Peskin, *Garfield: A Biography* (Kent, Ohio: Kent State University Press, 1978).

Statue of Liberty

The Statue of Liberty symbolizes America as a haven for those seeking freedom from oppression and the opportunity to better their lives. It has been a beacon of hope to millions of immigrants, welcoming them to the United States. The French historian and statesman Edouard de Laboulaye was the first to come up with the idea for the Statue of Liberty. The statue was to commemorate the Franco-American alliance during the American Revolution

Statue of Liberty, Bedloe (later Liberty) Island, New York, 1890 *(Library of Congress)*

as well as the idea of liberty embodied in America. The eminent French sculptor Auguste Bartholdi was entrusted with designing the monument. Bartholdi chose Bedloe's Island (now Liberty Island) in the Upper New York Bay as the site for the statue.

In 1875 fund-raising campaigns began in both France and the United States. The French were to raise money to pay for the statue, and the Americans would contribute to the cost of its pedestal. By 1881 the French campaign had managed to raise $400,000. The American public, however, was not as enthusiastic. By 1885 the American Committee for the Statue, which was composed largely of members from the Union League Club, had raised only half of the $100,000 needed for the pedestal. To supplement the funds already raised by the committee, JOSEPH PULITZER, the publisher of the *New York World,* took up the campaign and in less than five months raised the rest of the money.

Bartholdi began construction on the statue in 1875. More than 300 sheets of copper (which appropriately, given the origin of many immigrants, came from Norway) were hammered into shape on wooden molds and then riveted together. Gustave Eiffel, to whom the design of the statue's internal steel and wrought iron framework was entrusted, began his work in 1879. The 151-foot Statue of Liberty was assembled and displayed in Paris before being shipped in parts to New York. Richard Morris Hunt, who was the first American to study at the École des Beaux-Arts in Paris, designed the 98-foot pedestal. Hunt had also designed the *New York Tribune* Building and the Lenox Library in New York City. The Statue of Liberty was officially presented to the United States in Paris on July 4, 1884, and was accepted on behalf of the American people by the U.S. minister to France, Levi P. Morton. The American dedication took place on October 28, 1886, with President GROVER CLEVELAND in attendance.

The Statue of Liberty soon became one of the most widely recognized landmarks in the entire world. It stood as a symbol of the opportunity American offered for those in pursuit of freedom and new lives. In 1903, when EMMA LAZARUS's poem "The New Colossus" was inscribed on a bronze tablet and mounted on its pedestal, the Statue of Liberty became forever associated with the hopes and dreams of the millions of immigrants who have entered the United States.

See also IMMIGRATION.

Further reading: Barbaralee Diamonstein, *The Landmarks of New York: Part II* (New York: Harry N. Abrams, 1988); Walter Huggins, *Statue of Liberty National Monument: Its Origins, Development, and Administration* (Washington, D.C.: U.S. Department of the Interior, National Park Service, 1958).

— Phillip Papas

steel

Steel is an alloy of iron and carbon (up to 1.7 percent) that is malleable, light, and strong compared to cast iron, which has a higher carbon content. Steel had been made in small quantities for swords and armor for centuries and in slightly larger amounts in crucibles since the 18th century. The discovery of the BESSEMER PROCESS in 1856 meant that steel could be produced inexpensively by blowing cold air through molten iron in a pear-shaped converter. This British discovery marked the beginning of the SECOND INDUSTRIAL REVOLUTION, which was born around 1870. In addition to Bessemer's contribution, an international collaboration between a German living in Britain and brothers in France had earlier developed the Siemens-Martin open-hearth method for making steel in 1858. It employed a shallow-bowled reverberatory furnace from which samples of the molten metal could be taken so that the refining could be stopped when the desired quality of the steel was obtained. The open-hearth furnace, however, was much slower than the Bessemer process, in which the proper carbon content was judged by the color of the converter's flame.

Bessemer steel was first made in the United States in 1864 and open-hearth steel in 1868. Because of the time lag between a discovery and its widespread application, the Civil War was fought with iron rather than steel, and large-scale inexpensive steel production was not realized until the 1870s. Initially, American manufacturers preferred the speed and guesswork of the Bessemer converter—especially in meeting the enormous demand for rails—but later when more alloys were added to steel, precision was required and the open-hearth furnace became more popular. The production of open-hearth steel did not overtake Bessemer steel until 1908. Overall steel production jumped from 68,750 long tons in 1870, to 1.2 million in 1880, 4.3 million in 1890, and to 10.2 million long tons in 1900. In 1880 open-hearth steel production was one-tenth that of Bessemer steel, in 1890 it was one-seventh, but by 1900 it was almost seven-tenths.

The technology of steelmaking was expensive and led to large-scale business organization. Smaller iron-producing companies were consolidated into large steel-producing corporations. Ironically, ANDREW CARNEGIE—colorful, controversial, contradictory, and the most successful steel producer—neither used the corporate form (Carnegie Steel was a limited partnership) nor depended on the protective TARIFF to build his empire of steel. Carnegie was an optimist who expanded during the depressions following the Panics of 1873 and 1893 (see BUSINESS CYCLES) when costs were low, picked talented men to be his partners, and was an excellent organizer. By 1900 Carnegie Steel—a vertical combination that owned iron and coal mines, transportation facilities, iron and steel plants, and fabricating mills—was producing between 25 and 30 percent of the nation's steel, and its profits were $40 million, of which Carnegie's personal share was $25 million. Carnegie's ambitions, however, transcended moneymaking, and in 1901 his company became the backbone of United States Steel ("Big Steel"), a $1.4-billion corporation organized by J. P. MORGAN. It comprised 149 steel plants, 84 blast furnaces, 1,000 miles

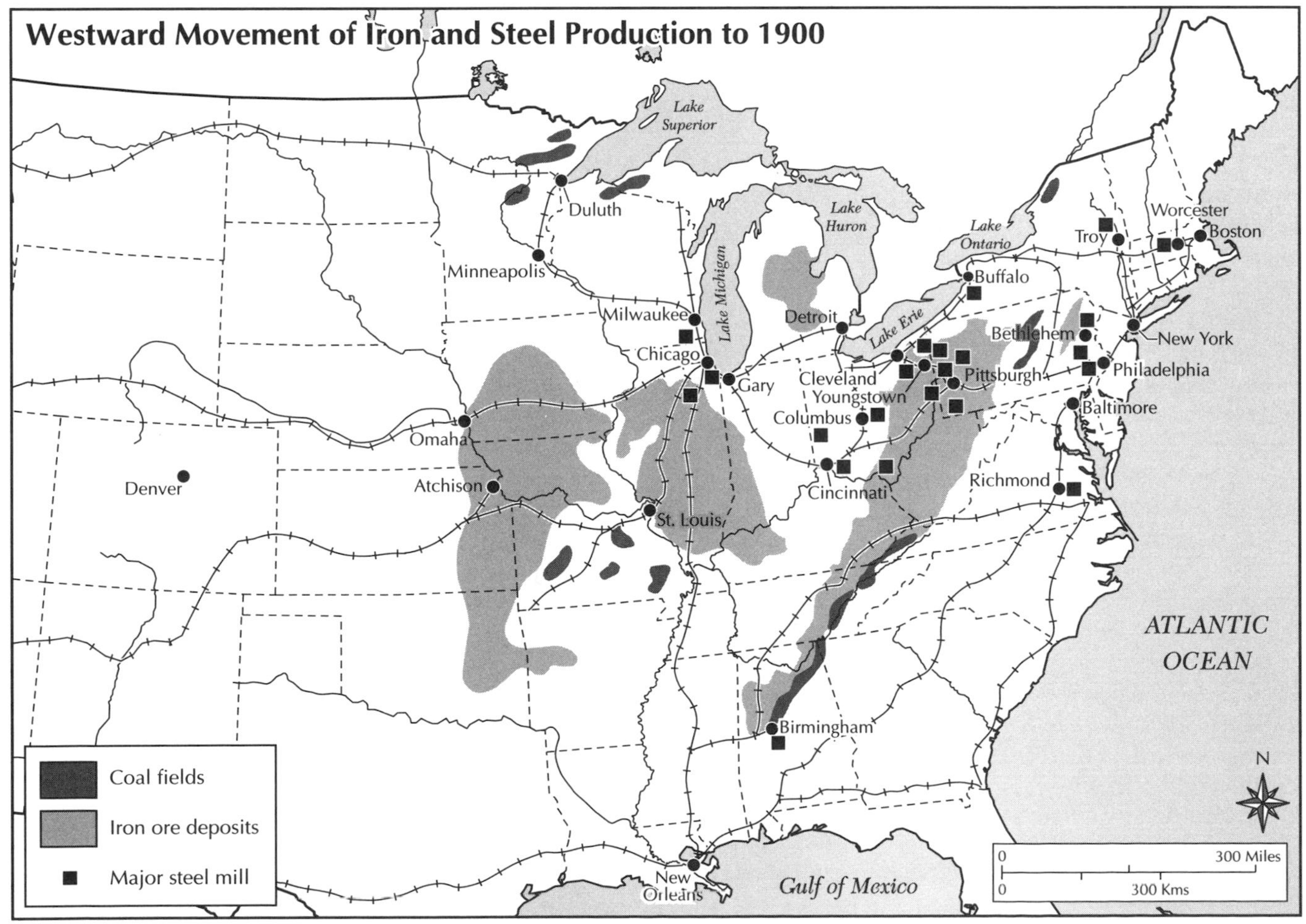

of railroad, and 112 Great Lakes vessels, in addition to vast coal, ore, and limestone deposits.

Further reading: Peter Temin, *Iron and Steel in Nineteenth-Century America: An Economic Inquiry* (Cambridge: Massachusetts Institute of Technology Press, 1964).

Stone, Lucy (1818–1893)

One of the major woman suffrage leaders of the 19th century, Lucy Stone was born on August 13, 1818, on a farm near West Brookfield, Massachusetts. At age 16 she became a teacher, and at 25 she entered Oberlin College. Stone graduated from Oberlin in 1847, becoming the first woman from Massachusetts to earn a bachelor's degree, and became a paid lecturer for the American Anti-Slavery Society. She soon began to talk about WOMEN'S RIGHTS in her antislavery lectures and was rebuked by the Anti-Slavery Society, but a compromise was reached: For a reduced salary, Stone lectured on antislavery on weekends and spoke on women's rights on weekdays at her own expense. Her audiences grew and occasionally numbered as many as 2,000 or 3,000 people. In 1850 Stone helped organize the first national women's rights convention in Worcester, Massachusetts, and she was a primary organizer of several national conventions thereafter.

In 1853 Henry Blackwell, a brother of ELIZABETH BLACKWELL, the first female doctor, began a determined courtship of Stone. She turned him down, but Blackwell persisted, eventually promising to "renounce all the privileges which the law confers on me." They were married on May 1, 1855, and Stone became the first woman to keep her maiden name after her marriage. While Blackwell professed support for her women's rights work, he frequently made it difficult for her to continue her work during the early years of their marriage. And after the birth of her daughter, Alice Stone Blackwell, on September 14, 1857, the organizational work that she had been doing fell to SUSAN B. ANTHONY.

At the conclusion of the Civil War, with her daughter in school, Stone returned full time to suffrage activity. She was involved, along with Anthony and Elizabeth Cady Stanton, in the formation of the American Equal Rights Association (AERA), a coalition dedicated to pushing for both African-American and woman suffrage. Both Stone and Anthony campaigned in Kansas in 1867 for proposals for black and woman suffrage. Both proposals were defeated, and the bitter Kansas campaign caused a rift between Stone and Anthony and Stanton. Midway through that campaign, the REPUBLICAN PARTY withdrew its support for woman suffrage. Stone returned East to raise money for the campaign, while Anthony remained in Kansas and accepted the help of George Francis Train, a Democrat and a blatant racist. Stone was convinced that Train was cynically professing support for woman suffrage in order to split the equal rights movement. She was also furious that her name was used in association with Train's.

Like Anthony and Stanton, Stone was distressed by the inclusion of the word "male" in the Fourteenth Amendment and believed that the equal rights movement should push for an amendment giving the vote to both women and AFRICAN AMERICANS. Unlike Stanton and Anthony, who opposed the Fourteenth and Fifteenth Amendments, she refused to oppose voting rights for African-American men. "I will be thankful in my soul if *any* body can get out of the terrible pit," she said.

In 1869 Anthony and Stanton broke off from the AERA to form the National Woman Suffrage Association (NWSA). Later that same year, Stone formed the American Woman Suffrage Association (AWSA). Stone also started a newspaper, *The Woman's Journal,* which began in 1870 and reported on all aspects of the suffrage movement. It continued to be published until 1931. While the NWSA had a reputation for being more nationally oriented, the AWSA frequently supplied more signatures to petitions for a national suffrage amendment than the NWSA, and both organizations were heavily involved in local suffrage campaigns. The real reason for two organizations was that Stone did not trust Anthony and Stanton, who she feared might discredit the entire movement. Stone, who was more socially conservative, cringed when the NWSA allowed itself to become associated with VICTORIA WOODHULL (and through her to be associated in the public mind with free love). Nor was she happy when Stanton spoke up in favor of relaxed divorce laws. By the 1880s, however, Stone recognized that a merger of the AWSA and NWSA would benefit the movement. The merger took place in 1890. Anthony managed to get Stanton elected president of the merged organization, while Stone became the chair of its executive committee. She died on October 18, 1893.

Further reading: Andrea Moore Kerr, *Lucy Stone: Speaking Out for Equality* (New Brunswick, N.J.: Rutgers University Press, 1992).

— Lynn Hoogenboom

street railways See transportation, urban

strikes See labor: strikes and violence

Strong, Josiah (1847–1916)

The most prominent advocate of the SOCIAL GOSPEL, Josiah Strong was born in Napierville, Illinois, on January

19, 1847, but grew up in Hudson, Ohio. A graduate of Western Reserve College (1869), Strong continued his studies at Lane Theological Seminary, Cincinnati, was ordained a Congregational minister in 1871, and for two years was a home missionary in Cheyenne, Wyoming. He returned to Ohio in 1873 and served as an instructor at Lane, a pastor at Sandusky, secretary of the Ohio Home Mission Society (1881–84), and then for two years as pastor of the Central Congregational Church of Cincinnati. His experience in Cincinnati and especially with the Home Mission Society focused Strong's attention on the challenges to Protestantism by the rapid, unsettling industrialization and urbanization of America.

His response in 1885 was to publish his and the Social Gospel's most important 19th century work, *Our Country: Its Possible Future and Its Present Crisis.* Combining Puritan morality and MANIFEST DESTINY, Strong tried to arouse and inspire Protestants to evangelize and reform America and to utilize its enormous resources to reshape the world for the better. Although Strong is remembered as a racist and imperialist, he wanted the aggressive Anglo-Saxons to spread their superior institutions throughout the world and by so doing promote peace, prosperity, and justice. His ideas were missionary, not military, and he was as opposed to exploiting weak people abroad as he was at home. His contemporaries realized *Our Country* was an attempt to mobilize Protestant America to combat social evils, economic distress, and political corruption and to create an ideal society on earth through reform legislation.

Although Strong was a prolific writer, his main contribution to the Social Gospel was as an organizer. From 1886 to 1898 he was the general secretary of the Evangelical Alliance, calling for ecumenical action on social issues and sponsoring the Interdenominational Congress that met in 1887, 1889, and finally in 1893, at the WORLD'S COLUMBIAN EXPOSITION at Chicago. This last meeting had an immense impact. Strong emphasized a pragmatic religion that linked "fact and faith," tying surveys and statistics to scripture. By 1898 this stance had led to a more daring position than the alliance affirmed, so Strong left the alliance and organized the League for Social Service. Under his leadership until his death in 1916, the league attacked urban and social problems like poverty and drunkenness and tried to improve working conditions with a "safety first" campaign. In 1908 Strong, in keeping with his ecumenical approach, helped form the Federal Council of Churches in Christ in America, the precursor of the National Council of Churches.

Ironically, Strong is remembered for celebrating the "Anglo-Saxon race" and for encouraging IMPERIALISM, but he was motivated by a paternalistic love (not by fear and hatred and a desire to exploit) that wished to achieve social justice at home and abroad and "bring the Kingdom of God on Earth."

Josiah Strong *(New York Historical Society)*

Further reading: Sydney E. Ahlstrom, *A Religious History of the American People* (New Haven, Conn.: Yale University Press, 1972); Martin Marty, *Pilgrims in Their Own Land: Five Hundred Years of Religion in America* (Boston: Little, Brown, 1984).

— W. Frederick Wooden

Sullivan, Louis H. (1856–1924)

With their evident structuralism and ornament derived from nature, Louis H. Sullivan's buildings inspired the phrase "form follows function" and presaged modern architecture. The son of a dancing master, Sullivan was born in Boston, Massachusetts, on September 3, 1856. He received architectural and engineering training at the Massachusetts Institute of Technology and the École des Beaux-Arts in Paris. He then worked briefly in the Philadelphia office of Frank Furness and the Chicago office of William Jenny. In 1881 he entered the office of Dankmar Adler, an established architect with important ties to the Jewish community of Chicago as it rebuilt itself after the fire of 1871. The partnership of Adler and Sullivan was established in 1883 and continued until 1895, marking Sullivan's most productive period as a practicing architect. Although Adler has been credited solely with engineering and managerial skills, historians now acknowledge his innovations in exploiting the structural elements of architecture. On his own after 1895, Sullivan won few major commissions but became more active as a writer and theorist. He died on April 14, 1924, in relative obscurity and poverty. His influence was long felt, however, through his writings and through the "Chicago school," a style promulgated by younger architects such as Frank Lloyd Wright and George Grant Elmslie, both of whom worked in Sullivan's office.

Sullivan's ideas were expressed in a passionate blend of poetry, philosophy, sociology, and architectural criticism. He believed that the historical eclecticism of his era was mindless and that the outward form of modern architecture must derive from inward function. However, he also knew that architecture must be more than mere functionalism; it must also express intellectual, emotional, and spiritual realities. Sullivan's highly distinctive style of ornament derived from his understanding of the rhythms of degeneration and regeneration in living organisms, which provided the model for all architectural development. During his lifetime, Sullivan's ideas were presented mainly to professional audiences. In 1918 his *Kindergarten Chats* first appeared in book form, and in 1924 his *Autobiography of an Idea* was published. Both works remain in print and influential.

Sullivan is probably best remembered for his commercial buildings. His Transportation Building at the WORLD'S COLUMBIAN EXPOSITION of 1893 in Chicago was essentially a polychromatic shed with an enormous ornamented arched entrance, called the "Golden Door." The idiosyncratic building became an aberrant attraction at the fair, which was a bastion of classicist design. In the trading room of the Chicago Stock Exchange (1894), now reconstructed at the Chicago Art Institute, Sullivan's lyrical organic ornament was executed in stenciling, terra-cotta, metal, and stained glass. Sullivan's work in skyscrapers culminated in the Guaranty Building (1896, Buffalo, New York), where the steel skeleton was encased in a thin envelope of brick and structural units were emphasized with terra-cotta ornament. The steel-frame construction of the Schlesinger and Mayer Company Store (now Carson Pirie Scott) in Chicago (1899, 1904) was likewise made evident, and street-level windows were exuberantly framed with Sullivan's ornament in metal. A series of bank buildings in small Midwestern towns closed Sullivan's career, giving him a chance to create functional forms exquisitely ornamented.

See also ART AND ARCHITECTURE.

Further reading: Hugh Morrison, *Louis Sullivan: Prophet of Modern Architecture,* rev. ed. (New York: Norton, 1998); Robert Twombly, *Louis Sullivan: His Life and Work* (New York: Viking, 1986).

— Karen Zukowski

Sumner, William Graham (1840–1910)

William Graham Sumner, America's most influential promoter of SOCIAL DARWINISM, was born on October 30, 1840, in Paterson, New Jersey, and grew up in Hartford, Connecticut. He studied theology at Yale from 1859 to 1863 and abroad between 1863 and 1866. After returning to the United States he was a tutor at Yale from 1866 to 1869. Ordained a Protestant Episcopal priest in 1869, he entered the ministry and served briefly in New York City and as rector from 1870 to 1872 at Morristown, New Jersey. In 1872 Sumner was appointed professor of political and social science at Yale, where he taught until his retirement in 1909. In that year he was elected president of the American Sociological Association, and he died the following year on April 12, 1910.

Sumner's ideas about society emerged from a confluence of Protestant religious beliefs. There were classical laissez-faire economic principles, which advocated a hands-off government policy that would promote a free competitive economy and ensure the greatest prosperity for the largest number, and Charles Darwin's theory of biological evolution. Sumner lived in an era when intellectuals, no longer certain that God created humans in his image, struggled to reconcile their belief in God with the modern evolutionary thinking of geologists and biologists. The evolutionary hypothesis contradicted the biblical account of creation as well as the transcendental notion that God was benevolent and one with nature.

In trying to reconcile traditional Christianity, 19th-century SCIENCE, and the industrial revolution, Sumner achieved great popularity. His efforts to synthesize these elements in a science of society were influenced by the English thinker Herbert Spencer, who applied Darwin's evolutionary theory to society. Possessing the moral fervor of a Puritan preacher, Sumner equated the Protestant ethic of industry, frugality, and temperance with the strengths that enabled the "fittest" individuals not merely to survive but to achieve success. He embraced the ideas that people are unequal, that they have no natural rights, that competition is as much a law of nature as gravity, and that the progress of civilization depends on unrestricted competition.

Accordingly, in Sumner's view, people need total freedom from state intervention in the economy, whether it be tariffs to enrich industrialists, inheritance taxes to level society, safety laws to protect labor, and even anti-monopoly legislation to preserve competition. Since government interference hampered competition and led to the survival of the unfit, Sumner believed that the state should limit itself to defending "the property of men and the honor of women . . . against crime." If people were free from the misguided and hindering effects of the state, competition would yield the best possible results for society. For nearly four decades Sumner lectured and wrote for prestigious journals, advocating his views that competition was glorious, success was the reward of virtue, and that if some were rich and powerful and others were poor and weak, this social reality was the evolutionary, and the only, path toward social progress.

Sumner, however, was progressive in his belief that the state should invest in public EDUCATION. Universal education could not promise students equality, but it could give individuals the chance to show their merit. He served as a member of the Connecticut State Board of Education from 1882 to 1910, where he had an opportunity to carry out his beliefs. But apart from education, Sumner consistently adhered to his Social Darwinian ideas.

Sumner was not the tool of big business, despite its usual appreciation of his laissez-faire ideas. Although he thought "millionaires are a product of natural selection," he also feared they corrupted government with their lobbies. Sumner did not believe that government policies capable of serving private interests should be awarded to the highest bidder. He opposed protective tariffs and overseas imperialistic expansion. Just as he did not oppose corporations, he did not oppose labor unions and believed that their bargaining power would more effectively improve working conditions than government regulations. Sumner argued that he spoke for the "forgotten" middle class that paid taxes to enrich the plutocracy and support the idle. Although few individuals could agree totally with Sumner, conservatives found much, and progressives almost no, support in his Social Darwinism.

Further reading: Richard Hofstadter, *Social Darwinism in American Thought*, rev. ed. (Boston: Beacon Press, 1955).

— Harry Stein

Sunday schools See religion

Supreme Court

During the Gilded Age the Supreme Court, reflecting the growth of large-scale industrial enterprises, became the bastion of property rights, the champion of laissez-faire, and the enemy of state regulation of commerce. Prior to the Civil War the Court interpreted the commerce and contract clauses of the Constitution to allow states considerable regulatory latitude, and in the 1870s it continued that practice. For example, in the slaughterhouse cases (1873), the Court upheld the right of Louisiana to grant a monopoly in order to regulate butchering, and in *Munn v. Illinois* (1877)—one of the Granger cases—the Court approved state regulation of interstate RAILROADS. But by the 1880s economic and political changes had affected the personnel of the Court and changed its attitude.

The dominant Supreme Court jurist during the Gilded Age was neither Chief Justice Morrison R. Waite (1874–88) nor Chief Justice Melville W. Fuller (1888–1910) but rather Associate Justice Stephen J. Field, who served on the Court from 1863 to 1897. Field dissented in the slaughterhouse cases, arguing that the monopoly awarded by the state violated the Fourteenth Amendment by depriving persons of property the due process of law, and he similarly dissented in *Munn* on grounds that state regulation of railroads threatened private property. Field reiterated that argument until, by the late 1880s, it was accepted by the Court. In *Wabash v. Illinois* (1886) the Court adopted Field's view that states could not regulate interstate commerce. The Court, which continued to reflect Field's influence as late as the 1930s, defended private property from the federal government and narrowly defined its regulatory power. Accordingly, the Court in *Pollock v. Farmers' Loan and Trust Co.* (1895) declared the federal income tax, a direct tax, unconstitutional and emasculated the SHERMAN ANTITRUST ACT of 1890 in *United States v. E. C. Knight* (1895) by holding that the sugar trust's monopoly of refining (manufacturing) did not constitute restraint of trade. In 1897 the Court stripped the Interstate Commerce Commission (established in 1887 to regulate railroads as a result of the *Wabash* decision) of its power to regulate rates and to eliminate the long-haul/short-haul abuse.

While Field dominated the Gilded Age Supreme Court, its voice of the future belonged to Associate Justice JOHN MARSHALL HARLAN, who served on the Court from 1877 to 1911 and was its great dissenter. He did not think the court should base its decisions on so-called natural laws like laissez-faire nor should it abuse its power of judicial review. He disagreed with the majority in both the *Pollock* and *Knight* cases. Most notably, while the Court in the Gilded Age became the ardent defender of property rights—ironically, using the civil rights Fourteenth Amendment to do so—it, with the conspicuous exception of Harlan, neglected human rights. He forcefully dissented in the CIVIL RIGHTS CASES (1883), when the majority held that equal rights in public accommodations were not covered by the Fourteenth Amendment, and most notably when the Court, in *PLESSY V. FERGUSON* (1896), agreed that "separate but equal accommodations" did not violate the Fourteenth Amendment. "Our Constitution," Harlan declared, "is color-blind and neither knows nor tolerates classes among citizens."

Further reading: Lauren P. Beth, *John Marshall Harlan: The Last Whig Justice* (Lexington: University of Kentucky Press, 1992); Kermit L. Hall, ed., *The Oxford Companion to the Supreme Court of the United States* (New York: Oxford University Press, 1992); Carl B. Swisher, *Stephen J. Field: Craftsman of the Law* (Washington, D.C.: Brookings Institution, 1930); Tinsley E. Yarbrough, *Judicial Enigma: The First Justice Harlan* (New York: Oxford University Press, 1995).

T

Tammany Hall See corruption, political

Tanner, Benjamin Tucker (1835–1923)

Benjamin Tucker Tanner, an African Methodist Episcopal (AME) bishop, was born in December 1835 in Pittsburgh, Pennsylvania, one of 12 children of Hugh and Isabella Tanner. He celebrated his birthday on December 22 or 23 until about 1860, when he claimed December 25 as his date of birth. Tanner began working at least by age nine, when he delivered copies of Martin Delany's newspaper, *The Mystery.* He left home in his early youth to work as a barber, first in Chicago and then in Cincinnati and other Ohio River ports. Tanner's diary, which he started in 1851, shows an interest in politics, especially in the issues of slavery, and revealed his dismay when he wrote in 1851 that he did not wish to die in the United States. Returning to Pittsburgh, Tanner studied from 1852 to 1857 at Avery College; joined the African Methodist Episcopal (AME) Church in 1856; studied at the Western Theological Seminary from 1857 to 1860; was ordained an AME minister; and in 1860 was chosen to go to California as a missionary. Unable to raise sufficient funds, Tanner was permitted by Bishop Daniel A. Payne to assume the pastorate of the 15th Street Presbyterian Church in Washington, D.C. Subsequent assignments led him to pastor AME Churches in Frederick and Baltimore, Maryland. Tanner was proficient in Latin, Hebrew, and Greek, but he feared that he lacked the spiritual commitment to preach. His diary entry for February 10, 1866, stated, "I pray for a faith that I can believe without a doubt and recommend without an indifferent spirit. Such a faith I have not. O God give it to me lest I die."

Indeed, Tanner is more renowned as an author and editor than as a preacher. His book *An Apology for African Methodism* (1867) led to his appointment as editor of *The Christian Recorder* in 1868. This position provided him an opportunity for 16 years to indulge his passion for scholarship. Tanner became in 1884 the first editor of *The AME Church Review,* a journal that was the culmination of years of anticipation on the part of the church's intellectuals. Tanner used the editor's position of both journals to comment on AME missions, development of clergy, race relations, American and international politics, and other issues of interest to AFRICAN-AMERICAN readers.

Tanner was critical of racial segregation. He stated in 1872 that "we want schools for Americans . . . not for Chinese . . . Negro . . . German . . . Irish nor English Americans but simply Americans." Tanner was equally critical of black nationalists who sought separation or who identified themselves as "Negro." It was his contention that "Negro" was reserved for Africans and not for "Colored" Americans (his preference), who were a racial mixture. He wrote in 1881, "we are not African. Certainly to designate us as Negroes is a fraud. We are Americans [and] the sooner we recognize it the better." His desire for an integrated society led him to declare in 1884 that American geography would lead to a distinctive American race that would combine European, African, and American Indian blood to form a race that would be seven-eighths white, one-eighth African, "with a mottle of yellow."

Tanner was a conservative theologian whose opposition to female preachers conflicted with the more liberal views of HENRY M. TURNER, Bishop John M. Brown, and Theophilus G. Steward. Tanner argued that God, Jesus, and the disciples did not sanction female preachers. He was extremely critical of Steward's theology that embraced the Darwinian theory of evolution as God's plan of creation. Tanner castigated Steward for asserting that the Battle of Armageddon in biblical prophesy would end Anglo-Saxon superiority rather than the world and would result in the rise of true Christianity from Africa and Asia with equality for all races. Tanner contended that Armageddon would lead not to a transfer of power but to the second coming of Christ and the resurrection. Tanner, however, did argue that Africans were major contributors to the origin of Judaism and Christianity. After Tanner was elected to a bishopric in 1888, he wrote little on secular matters and concentrated on advice for ministers and building the church as it sought to open mission fields in Canada, the Caribbean, and Africa. During this period he was at odds with Henry M. Turner, who advocated not only a more aggressive African mission endeavor but emigration to Africa.

Tanner was a prolific writer. In addition to his *Apology* he wrote *The Negro's Origin or Is He Cursed of God?* (1869), *The Color of Solomon—What?* (1895), *The Descent of the Negro* (1898), *The Dispensation in the History of the Church and the Interregnums* (1898), and *The Negro in Holy Writ* (1900). Tanner married Sarah Elizabeth Miller on August 19, 1858. Their union produced nine children, seven of whom survived infancy. Carlton was an AME clergyman and writer, Halle became the first woman licensed to practice medicine in Alabama, and Henry became an internationally famous painter whose art is displayed in the world's museums and art galleries.

Further reading: William Seraile, *Fire in His Heart: Bishop Benjamin Tucker Tanner and the AME Church* (Knoxville: University of Tennessee Press, 1998).

— William Seraile

Tanner, Henry Ossawa See painting

tariff issue

A tariff is a tax on imports, and it has been used by the United States to raise money to pay for the costs of government, to protect domestic goods from foreign competition, and to force foreign nations to change their trade policies. Throughout the history of the United States, the tariff has been a major, often passionate, political issue.

With the triumph of the REPUBLICAN PARTY in 1860, protectionism also triumphed. During and after the Civil War CONGRESS raised rates from roughly 20 percent to a high of 47 percent in 1869. Both major parties, the Republicans explicitly and the Democrats tacitly, accepted protectionism, although not without a measure of dissent within each. The tariff issue became, from time to time, a source of bitter contention between Congress and the president. Occasionally, a president would advocate tariff reform, only to be thwarted in his designs by an uncooperative Congress. It, for example, reluctantly enabled President CHESTER A. ARTHUR to appoint a tariff commission in 1882 that recommended substantial reductions. Congress, however, in 1883 allowed only a 5 percent reduction and retained protectionism. President GROVER CLEVELAND, in December 1887, devoted his entire annual message to the tariff, asking Congress to reduce its rates. The Democratic majority in the House of Representatives approved a tariff reduction bill, but the Republican-controlled Senate rejected the bill. The deadlock made tariff reform a major issue in the ensuing 1888 presidential election. It was close. Cleveland won a plurality of the popular vote, but the Republican candidate BENJAMIN HARRISON, a protectionist, carried the electoral college and with it the presidency.

The Republicans remained focused on the tariff, which they believed won them not only the presidential election but several congressional seats as well. For the first time since 1875, the Republicans controlled the presidency and both Houses of Congress. Under the strong-willed leadership of Speaker THOMAS B. REED of Maine in the House and the protectionist Nelson W. Aldrich of Rhode Island in the Senate, the Republican majority earned the name the "billion dollar Congress" because of the various spending programs it approved. It also passed a new tariff that took the name of one of its sponsors, Representative WILLIAM MCKINLEY of Ohio.

The McKinley Tariff passed in October 1890. Drafted by Aldrich and McKinley, it increased already high rates by another 4 percent and at that time was the highest protective tariff the nation had ever adopted. The McKinley Tariff, however, also included a reciprocity provision designed to encourage foreign trade and discourage foreign retaliation against the high American tariff rates. The president was authorized to remove items from the "free list" if their countries of origin placed unreasonable tariffs on American products. The McKinley Tariff proved to be politically vulnerable. Protectionists had always been careful to stress that American labor benefitted from protection, but attacks on the McKinley Tariff convinced Americans that it was far more friendly to big business than to consumers in general or labor in particular.

Republicans misinterpreted public sentiment on the tariff issue and suffered a major political reversal in the 1890 congressional elections. Their majority in the Senate was reduced to eight seats; in the House, Republicans retained only 88 of 323 seats, with William McKinley among the defeated. The Republican Party also suffered in the presidential election of 1892, which saw Grover Cleveland come back and defeat the incumbent president Harrison. In 1894, President Cleveland again supported a House measure reducing tariff rates, but Senate Republicans, aided by southern Democrats concerned with protecting NEW SOUTH industries in their region, gutted the bill and restored most of the rates. Although Cleveland denounced the restructured tariff bill, he allowed it to become law without his signature as the Wilson-Gorman Tariff. The law also included a small federal income tax provision of 2 percent on all incomes over $4,000, but that was eventually declared unconstitutional by the SUPREME COURT.

The economic depression following the PANIC OF 1893 enabled the Republicans, led by McKinley, to triumph in 1896. Fully committed to raising tariff rates, the Republicans in 1897 passed the Dingley Tariff, expanding reciprocity and raising rates to an average of 57 percent, the highest level in American history.

Further reading: Joanne R. Reitano, *The Tariff Question in the Gilded Age: The Great Debate of 1888* (University Park: Pennsylvania State University Press, 1994); Tom E. Terrill, *The Tariff, Politics, and American Foreign Policy, 1874–1901* (Westport, Conn.: Greenwood Press, 1973).

— Phillip Papas

technology See inventions and technology

telegraph See communications

telephone See communications

temperance See Prohibition Party; Willard, Frances

Tesla, Nikola (1856–1943)

Nikola Tesla, an inventor, was born on July 9, 1856, in Smiljan, Croatia (then part of the Austro-Hungarian Empire), to Serbian parents. His father, an Orthodox clergyman, intended him for the church, but Tesla—uninterested in religion and fascinated by mechanics, physics, and mathematics—ultimately secured parental approval to study engineering (1875–79) at a polytechnic college in Graz, Austria. Tesla also loved literature, especially poetry, and read widely in several languages. To develop these interests, he began studying at Charles University in Prague in 1879, but his father's death cut short his schooling, and Tesla—whose understanding of electricity and its uses was outstanding—was employed by the telegraph office of Hungary, then by the telephone company in Budapest, and in 1882 by the Continental Edison Company in Paris.

While in Budapest, Tesla conceived the basic idea—a rotating electromagnetic field—that made possible an alternating-current (AC) electric motor. Arousing no interest in his idea, Tesla left for America in 1884 with a letter of introduction to THOMAS A. EDISON. Edison was not interested in AC but gave Tesla a job designing better direct-current (DC) motors. Tesla resigned in 1885 following a dispute over his compensation and, with the help of some backers, formed a company to develop arc lamps for street lighting, but when the lamps were in production he was eased out.

Experiencing poverty, Tesla dug ditches for a while, but in 1887 he formed the Tesla Electric Company with the support of executives of the Western Union Telegraph Company and set up a laboratory to explore and perfect his ideas for an AC electric motor. From 1887 to 1891 Tesla patented those and other ideas and in 1888 sold the patents for an AC motor to George Westinghouse. This invention had an enormous effect on the growth of cities, since it provided the motive power for electric street railways, elevated rail lines, and subways.

Tesla's interests went beyond AC motors. He continued working on arc lamps to reduce their annoying hum and found it disappeared if higher frequencies were used, which led to the development of the Tesla coil transformer. In 1893 Tesla's AC polyphase system illuminated the WORLD'S COLUMBIAN EXPOSITION at Chicago. Apart from the AC motor, perhaps Tesla's greatest achievement was the completion in 1896 of the world's first hydroelectric generating plant at Niagara Falls. It was the forerunner of large-scale generating plants and electrical networks. Since AC at a high frequency is the most efficient way to transmit power, Tesla's work on transformers and his development of the "Litz" wire with its many strands were crucial for the development of the electrical industry. Tesla also experimented with wireless radiotelegraphy and in 1898 patented a radio-controlled ship.

Living alone in a New York City hotel room, Tesla was an eccentric who came to prefer the company of pigeons to people. His capacity to visualize mentally what others could not see without a diagram led him to be impatient and offensive with colleagues and left him with few friends. He was independent (he worked as briefly for Westinghouse as he did for Edison), but he was a poor businessman who would not hire a manager and, despite industries built on his genius, spent the last four decades of his life in poverty. Feeling cheated, he became secretive about his ideas, and since his ideas required huge investments, they were not explored. Ignored in America, he was a national hero in Yugoslavia and lived largely off a $7,200 annual gift from its government. He died in his room at the New Yorker Hotel on January 7, 1943.

Further reading: Margaret Cheney, *Tesla: Man Out of Time* (Englewood Cliffs, N.J.: Prentice Hall, 1981); Marc J. Seifer, *Wizard: The Life and Times of Nikola Tesla: Biography of a Genius* (Secaucus, N.J.: Carol Pub., 1996); David Blair Stewart, *Tesla: The Modern Sorcerer* (Berkeley, Calif.: Grog, 1999).

theater

The Gilded Age was a time of transition for the musical theater and drama in the United States. At the beginning of the period, English and Continental influences dominated theater in America; by the turn of the century, the American theater had its own stars, playwrights, and tastes, though a new set of foreign influences was emerging. The period also witnessed important changes in stagecraft and business practices.

Musical entertainments were common during the 19th century, but it was not until *The Black Crook* (1866) that the basic elements of musical theater came together in the United States. The show combined MUSIC, dance, and spectacle to tell a melodramatic story. Moralists denounced the show because the dancers (a French ballet troupe stranded in America) showed too much leg, but *The Black Crook* enjoyed unprecedented success during its original run in New York City. Touring companies and revivals sustained the show until the late 19th century. *The Black Crook* inspired burlesques, spin-offs, and parodies *(The Black Crook Burlesque, The Black Crook Song Book,* and *The White Crook)* and prepared American audiences for such popular musicals as *Evangeline* (1874) and a British import, *Florodora* (1900).

Generally, the musical theater in America hardly differed from its counterparts in England and Europe. Comic operas by French composer Jacques Offenbach were popular during the 1870s and 1880s, while English comic operas by Gilbert and Sullivan dominated the American musical stage after 1879. Operettas, another European import, came into fashion during the 1890s, though an American composer, VICTOR HERBERT, made his mark in the genre with *Prince Ananias* (1894), *The Wizard of the Nile* (1895), and *The Serenade* (1897). Of course, burlesque, minstrelsy, variety, and vaudeville also offered musical entertainment.

Drama, like the musical theater, took its cues from abroad. During these years when there was no "American" drama of consequence, the vitality of theater in America depended largely on the appeal of star actors—Edwin Forrest, JOSEPH JEFFERSON III, John Drew, Minnie Maddern Fiske, Edwin Booth, and such foreign attractions as Sir Henry Irving and Sarah Bernhardt. Shakespeare and melodrama were their stock in trade were the dramatic staples of the period.

During most of the 19th century Shakespeare was not high culture in America but POPULAR ENTERTAINMENT. Shakespeare was performed at a wide range of venues across the country, even in rough-and-tumble mining camps. Some immigrant neighborhoods got their Shakespeare in Yiddish, German, or other foreign language productions. Variety theaters often presented works by Shakespeare on the same bill with magicians, jugglers, acrobats, comedians, and song-and-dance acts. Minstrel and burlesque shows frequently included Shakespeare parodies.

Of course, the appeal of Shakespeare rested largely on the merits of the works themselves, but in America theaters promoted the bard as a moral playwright. This strategy was meant to counter VICTORIANISM and the latent suspicion that theatrical entertainments were somehow immoral. Theater historians with a practical turn of mind note that Shakespeare was in vogue because Shakespeare was in the repertoire of most companies. Touring stars, if they did not have their own traveling companies, could mount a short-term production using the actors, sets, and costumes of local stock companies.

By the 1890s, however, Shakespeare was less popular. The mass audience in America, which had grown increasingly exuberant and aggressive, turned to vaudeville, burlesque, and movies, leaving Shakespeare to more refined theatergoers. Class distinctions became a feature of the American theatrical experience. More discrete and high-minded audiences increasingly favored legitimate drama performed in legitimate theaters, where the price of admission was too high for rowdy workingmen and their families.

Even at such venues, melodrama soon surpassed Shakespeare. Melodrama combined suspense, high emotion, sensationalism, and elaborate plot contrivances in a moralistic framework. In the world of melodrama, virtue always emerged triumphant. Female chastity was usually at the heart of the drama. Women in melodrama generally personified gentleness, selfless love, innocence, and moral virtue, in essence, the Victorian ideal. Naturally, the villain, who embodied worldliness, corruption, and lust (the bane of Victorianism), set out to despoil the heroine, body and soul. Only the hero, the epitome of manly virtue (though typically somewhat dense), could rescue the heroine from "a fate worse than death." Melodramas upheld Victorian notions of gender and domesticity. The home (woman's sphere) was a sanctuary, "a haven in a heartless world." The genre also drew moral distinctions between the city (a dangerous den of vice and temptation) and the country (a peaceful, innocent place of simple, virtuous, hardworking people).

Prior to the 1850s American melodrama was an inferior product. American theaters relied on translations or adaptations of English or European melodramas. But the stage version of Harriet Beecher Stowe's famous novel, *Uncle Tom's Cabin,* changed all that. It caused an immediate sensation in 1856 and remained a homegrown staple of the American theater well into the 20th century. During the 1890s approximately 400 companies toured the country with their versions of the popular melodrama. With *Uncle Tom's Cabin,* American melodrama came of age. The genre enabled American playwrights to dramatize a wide range of social ills, such as drunkenness, urban crime, political corruption, and the exploitation of workers.

A key figure in the maturation of the American theater was Dion Boucicault, a playwright and manager who had enjoyed considerable success in England before

Poster for a popular vaudeville show *(Library of Congress)*

establishing himself in New York City. He specialized in expensively mounted melodramas, though his best-known work was an adaptation of Rip Van Winkle that renowned actor Joseph Jefferson performed for 40 years. After Boucicault, David Belasco, William Gillette, and Augustus Thomas further refined the melodrama by introducing more scenic realism, reducing violence, and minimizing improbable plot twists. Their reforms coincided with the emergence of the "well-made play," a British innovation featuring less improbable plots, well-crafted dialogue, a more restrained acting style, and realistic production values. Playwright Clyde Fitch was the foremost American practitioner of the genre.

The latter years of the 19th century saw other substantial changes in the American theater, some of them originating abroad. Controversial works by Ibsen and Shaw had their first American productions during these years, thus inaugurating modern theater on this side of the Atlantic. American realism found expression in plays by WILLIAM DEAN HOWELLS and Edward (Ned) Harrigan. At the level of stagecraft and production values, the hallmarks of the period were new techniques (improved lighting, versatile stage designs) and greater use of opulence and spectacle. Consolidation was the principal development in the business of theater, culminating in a theatrical trust organized in 1896. The syndicate enabled producer Charles Frohman, booking agents Mark Klaw and Abraham Erlanger, and a few regional partners to dominate commercial theater in the United States into the early 20th century.

See also ENTERTAINMENT, POPULAR.

Further reading: Gerald Bordman, *American Theatre: A Chronicle of Comedy and Drama, 1869–1914* (New York: Oxford University Press, 1994); Lawrence W. Levine, *Highbrow/Lowbrow: The Emergence of Cultural Hierarchy in America* (Cambridge, Mass.: Harvard University Press, 1988); Robert C. Toll, *On With the Show: The First Century of Show Business in America* (New York: Oxford University Press, 1976).

— William Hughes

Theosophy See religion

Thomas, M. Carey (1857–1935)

Martha Carey Thomas, college president, was born on January 2, 1857, in Baltimore into a wealthy, educated, Quaker family. She graduated from Cornell in 1877 and then studied Greek privately at Johns Hopkins but, as a woman, was barred from its seminars. Beginning in 1879 Thomas studied philology for three years at the University of Leipzig, and since no German university would grant the doctor of philosophy to a woman, she transferred to the Swiss University of Zurich and received her Ph.D. summa cum laude in 1882. Academic frustrations coupled with the influence of her mother and her aunt made Thomas a passionate feminist. In part, she pursued the Ph.D. to prove that women could excel in difficult subjects and had the same right to study SCIENCE and culture as men.

With a college for women at Bryn Mawr in the planning stage, Thomas saw an opportunity to further her career and hammer home her conviction that rigorous intellectual pursuits should be open to her sex. Capitalizing on the good fortune that her father and two uncles were trustees of the new college, Thomas—fresh from her triumph at Zurich—audaciously asked to be made its first president. The trustees chose a male but made Thomas its dean and professor of English. In 1894, by the margin of one vote, they named Thomas president, and she served until 1922. As dean and as president, Thomas insisted that the standards at Bryn Mawr be as high as at the leading colleges for men. She required difficult entrance examinations and modeled the curriculum on that of Johns Hopkins, with students taking relevant parallel courses in a prescribed sequence as well as demonstrating to her satisfaction their proficiency in foreign languages. She had no use for either practical courses or for the elective system and retained the traditional faith that the virtue of mental discipline could be achieved by studying languages (preferably dead) and mathematics. As an administrator Thomas was opinionated, vigorous, impetuous, at times devious, and always the autocrat who detested the idea of faculty self-government. Yet, although Bryn Mawr under her idiosyncratic leadership bucked dominant trends in HIGHER EDUCATION toward coeducation and a flexible and practical curriculum, Thomas made it into an outstanding institution.

With roots in Maryland dating back to the 17th century, Thomas had strong aristocratic leanings. Although she worked tirelessly for equal rights and woman suffrage amendments to the Constitution, her egalitarianism ended there. At Bryn Mawr she aimed to train an elite, with the conspicuous exception, inspired by the spirit of noblesse oblige, of a summer school she inaugurated in 1921 to expose working women to social issues and cultural ideas. She believed the white race, especially Nordics, intellectually superior to people of color, favored IMMIGRATION RESTRICTION, hampered the promotion of Jewish instructors, and—stressing heredity over environment—kept statistics on the ancestry of incoming freshmen. An acrimonious depiction of Thomas can be found in Gertrude Stein's novel *Fernhurst.*

Thomas thought women, even if they married, should pursue active careers. She never married but had long-term love affairs with two childhood friends, Mary (Mamie) Gwinn and Mary E. Garrett, the Baltimore & Ohio Railroad heiress. Garrett willed Thomas a fortune, which she utilized for wide travel in a grand style. Just prior to her death on December 2, 1935, Thomas returned to a changed Bryn Mawr College for its 50th anniversary, but her high standards and the inspiration of her pioneering spirit had endured.

Further reading: Helen Lefkowitz Horowitz, *The Power and Passion of M. Carey Thomas* (Urbana: University of Illinois Press, 1994).

— Harry Stein

Tiffany, Louis Comfort (1848–1933)

A designer noted chiefly for his stained glass, Louis Comfort Tiffany was born in New York City on February 18, 1848. He was the son of the founder of Tiffany and Company and had early exposure to fine decorative arts and the methods used to produce them. Instead of entering the family firm, however, Tiffany chose a career as an artist. By the age of 18 he had exhibited at New York City's prestigious National Academy of Design, and he continued to paint in oils and watercolors throughout his life. By 1879 Tiffany had turned to interior design, then a nascent profession. With painter Samuel Colman, textile designer Candace Wheeler, and furniture designer Lockwood de Forest, Tiffany formed Associated Artists, which quickly found success contriving interiors full of intricate patterns and sumptuous color. The firm was dissolved amicably in 1883, and Tiffany formed his own company to decorate interiors, focusing especially on glass architectural fittings such as mosaics, light fixtures, and windows. While conducting innovative experiments in glass, Tiffany oversaw a large corps of craftspeople designing theaters, clubs, and residences. In the early 1890s he began designing blown-glass vessels, which he soon marketed under the name "Favrile Glass." By 1900 he had established Tiffany Studios, which manufactured lamps, ceramics, enamels, and more.

Tiffany was a masterful businessman and promoter. Any of his services or products could be purchased at his Manhattan showroom, and many were also available through his father's company, where he became artistic director in 1902. He organized prominent displays at the WORLD'S COLUMBIAN EXPOSITION of 1893 in Chicago and at subsequent world's fairs; donated his works to museums in America; and sold his products at Siegfried Bing's taste-making shop, L'Art Nouveau, in Paris. He spent much time designing Laurelton Hall, his own home in Cold Spring Harbor, New York, and after 1918 managed the Tiffany Foundation, which offered young artists working retreats. Tiffany Studios declared bankruptcy in 1932, a year before Tiffany died (January 17, 1933, in New York City), and his glass fell out of fashion until the 1960s, when it became highly collectable.

All of Tiffany's work was marked by a sensuous approach to color and light. By introducing variegated colors and textures into individual pieces of glass, Tiffany (along with his rival John La Farge) transformed the art of stained glass. Unlike medieval and baroque craftsmen who painted upon glass, Tiffany's motifs were formed by the play of light through glass that had been mottled, textured, and otherwise colored to produce calculated effects. While he derived motifs from many sources, especially Islamic and Roman glass, nature was his richest source of inspiration. Wisteria, peonies, and dragonflies were favorite motifs for lamp shades, while ecclesiastical windows depicting landscapes, rather than conventional biblical figures, generated controversy. Tiffany was perhaps happiest when he could create a fully integrated interior. He did so for Henry and Louisine Havemeyer, whose New York City house (now demolished) featured a ceiling of Japanese textiles, a fireplace of iridescent tiles, and a suspended staircase of wrought iron. Tiffany's name is now so well known and so identified with richly colored stained glass, the term "Tiffany" is used to describe any stained-glass lampshade.

Further reading: Alastair Duncan, Martin Eidelberg, and Neil Harris, *The Masterworks of Louis Comfort Tiffany* (New York: Harry N. Abrams, 1989); Alastair Duncan, *Louis Comfort Tiffany* (New York: Harry N. Abrams; Washington, D.C.: National Museum of American Art, 1992).

— Karen Zukowski

Tilden, Samuel Jones (1814–1886)

Samuel Jones Tilden, reformer and presidential candidate, was born on February 9, 1814, in New Lebanon, New York, the son of Elam Tilden and Polly Younglove Jones. He attended Yale for one term (1834) and the University of the City of New York (now New York University), where he also studied law. In 1841 he was admitted to the bar and practiced in New York City. A bachelor, Tilden devoted his life to politics and the law. He became a masterful and wealthy railroad attorney and a brilliant political organizer.

Tilden was an active member of the DEMOCRATIC PARTY in New York. As a student, he wrote political articles for New York newspapers in support of Martin Van Buren. In 1843 Tilden was named corporation counsel of New York City, served one term in the New York Assembly (1846), and was identified with Van Buren's antislavery "Barnburner" faction in New York. Tilden was also a delegate to the 1856 Democratic National Convention and the 1860 convention of Douglas Democrats.

During the Civil War Tilden joined other Northern Democrats in supporting a war to restore the Union as it had been and opposed the emancipation of slaves and the growing power of the federal government. During Reconstruction, Tilden favored the policies of President Andrew Johnson. In 1866 he was named chairman of the New York State Democratic Committee, and in 1868 he managed the unsuccessful presidential campaign of Horatio Seymour.

Tilden won a national reputation for attacking the spectacularly corrupt TWEED RING, but he was a tardy political reformer. In the late 1860s William M. Tweed, the "boss" of TAMMANY HALL—New York City's Democratic Party organization—and his associates dominated politics in the city and the state. Tilden, however, did not attack Tweed until after the *New York Times* in 1871 published damning evidence of the Ring's stealings. Tilden's reluctance to attack Tweed stemmed from both his cautious nature and his Democratic partisanship.

In 1874 Tilden's reform reputation gave him the Democratic nomination for governor of New York, and he defeated the incumbent John A. Dix by a plurality of 50,000 votes. As governor, Tilden added to his reform reputation by leading a successful attack against the corrupt "canal ring," which was a bipartisan group of politicians and contractors who made fortunes on the repair and extension of the state's canal system.

Tilden's activities as governor of a pivotal state made him the Democratic presidential nominee in 1876. In the November election he had approximately 250,000 more popular votes than his Republican opponent RUTHERFORD B. HAYES and won 184 electoral votes, which was one short of a majority. Hayes had 163 votes, but 22 electoral votes in Florida, Louisiana, Oregon, and South Carolina were contested. In the ensuing crisis neither Tilden nor Hayes provided much leadership for the contending forces in CONGRESS. Presidential candidates at that time were supposed to be above politics, but the stance especially suited the cautious, passive nature of Tilden and was galling to many of his followers. To resolve the disputed election, Congress created the Electoral Commission of 1877. Ultimately, the commission (which had a Republican majority) declared Hayes the winner by one electoral vote.

Following the disputed election, Tilden remained a significant figure in national politics. However, he suffered various physical ailments that eventually forced him to withdraw from public life. Tilden died on August 4, 1886, and left the bulk of his estate in trust for the establishment of a free library in New York City. His bequest served as the foundation of the New York Public Library.

Further reading: Alexander C. Flick, *Samuel Jones Tilden: A Study in Political Sagacity* (New York: Dodd, Mead, 1939); Jerome Mushkat, *The Reconstruction of the New York Democracy, 1861–1874* (Rutherford, N.J.: Fairleigh Dickinson University Press, 1981); Keith Ian Polakoff, *The Politics of Inertia: The Election of 1876 and the End of Reconstruction* (Baton Rouge: Louisiana State University Press, 1973).

— Phillip Papas

track and field

American interest in track and field began at Princeton University in 1869, when Princeton students participated in track contests called the Caledonian Games. An athletic association at Columbia University also held its first track-and-field meet in 1869. Columbia, Yale, Princeton, and Cornell soon formed track clubs.

In the early 1870s track meets were held at regattas. During the 1873 regatta-sponsored track meet at Hampden Park in Springfield, Massachusetts, James Gordon Bennett, Jr., owner of the *New York Herald,* offered a $500 prize for the winner of a two-mile race. Duncan Bowie of McGill University won the race in 11 minutes, 18.5 seconds. The second regatta-sponsored track meet was held in 1874 at Saratoga, New York. About 30 students from eight colleges participated in the 100-yard dash, one- and three-mile runs, 120-yard hurdles, and seven-mile walk. The 1875 regatta-sponsored track meet at Saratoga included 10 track-and-field field events. Amherst, Cornell, Harvard, Union, Williams, and Yale boasted winners.

Trackmen soon took direct control of their annual meet from the regatta committee. Presidents of the Harvard and Yale Athletic Associations invited 10 colleges in December 1875 to form the Intercollegiate Association of Amateur Athletes of America IC4A). Management was given to a committee of students directly involved in track and field. The first annual IC4A meet was held in 1876 at Saratoga (the day after the regatta) with six running and nine field events. The IC4A prohibited foreigners from competing and awarded prizes to winners. Seventy-one athletes competed in the track and field events. Princeton captured the first IC4A title with four individual champions, including J. M. Mann in the baseball throw and 16-pound shot.

The IC4A remained the dominant college track-and-field event and was moved in 1877 to New York City. From 1880 through 1896, Harvard or Yale won every IC4A meet. American collegians set several track records after Charles Sherrill introduced the sprinter's crouch-start in the late 1880s. Georgetown's Bernie Wefers clocked 9.8 seconds in the 100-yard dash and 22.6 seconds in the 220-yard dash. The Amateur Athletic Union began holding annual track-and-field championships in 1888 and allowed noncollegiate amateurs to compete.

Americans made no concerted effort to send a strong track-and-field team to the first modern Olympic Games at Athens, Greece, in 1896. Princeton professor William Milligan Sloane, head of the American Olympic Committee, recruited four Princeton undergraduates. Eight Boston-area athletes, including seven from either Harvard or the Boston Athletic Association, completed the American team. Americans captured nine of the 12 track-and-field events, finishing second in five more. American victors were Tom Burke in the 100 meters and 400 meters, Tom Curtis in the 110-meter hurdles, Ellery Clark in the high jump and long jump, William Hoyt in the pole vault, Bob Garrett in the shot put and discus, and John Connolly in the triple jump. Americans also finished first in several track-and-field events at the 1900 Olympic Games at Paris, France. American winners were Frank Jarvis in the 100 meters, John Walter Tewksbury in the 200 meters and 400-meter hurdles, Maxey Long in the 400 meters, Alfred Kraenzlein in the 110-meter hurdles and long jump, Irving Baxter in the high jump and pole vault, Meyer Prinstein in the triple jump, Ronald Sheldon in the shot put, and John Flanagan in the hammer throw.

Further reading: Richard Mandell, *The First Modern Olympics* (Berkeley: University of California Press, 1976); Ronald A. Smith, *Sports and Freedom: The Rise of Big-Time College Athletics* (New York: Oxford University Press, 1988).

— David L. Porter

trade, domestic and foreign

The completion in the Gilded Age of a national transportation network—virtually all of it RAILROADS—created a national market for manufacturers and traders to distribute their products. At the same time, the income of Americans was on the rise and ordinary people, farmers and workers, were acquiring more than the bare necessities of life. Consumerism was on the rise, creating mass markets in the United States. The rise of DEPARTMENT STORES, MAIL-ORDER HOUSES, CHAIN STORES, and the growth of ADVERTISING in the late 19th century all led to the increased flow of goods throughout the nation.

With the explosion of economic activity in the Gilded Age, internal trade in the United States multiplied in volume. Railroad freight roughly tripled from 1870 to 1900, when it totaled 141.6 billion ton-miles (a ton-mile is one ton moved one mile). While the MERCHANT MARINE on the whole languished, the tonnage of vessels engaged in coastwise and internal trade jumped from 2,638,000 in 1870 to 4,287,000 in 1900.

Although during the Gilded Age domestic markets absorbed most of the raw materials and finished products Americans produced, foreign trade also increased. In 1870 American exports were valued at $451 million and imports at $462 million, but by 1900 exports were at $1.5 billion and imports at $930 million. The excess of exports over imports throughout most of the Gilded Age was made up—since there has to be an equilibrium in foreign trade—by payments to foreign shipowners and operators, interest paid on European investments in the United States, and a steady inflow of gold that facilitated the resumption of specie payments in 1879 and generally lowered interest rates for Americans.

Most of American foreign commerce was with Europe, much of it with Great Britain. In 1870, 81 percent of American exports were bound for Europe, and Britain received more than half (53 percent) of all exports. In that same year 55 percent of all American imports came from Europe and more than a third (35 percent) originated in Britain. Thirty years later in 1900, American exports to Europe fell slightly to 75 percent (Britain dropped from 53 to 38 percent), while imports from Europe also fell slightly to 52 percent (with Britain falling from 35 to 19 percent). Among the trading partners of the United States in 1900, Germany was second (considerably behind Britain), receiving 13 percent of exports (only a third of what Britain imported from the United States), but as the source of 11 percent of all American imports, it was gaining on Britain.

The principal American export in the late 19th century was baled cotton. In 1870 it was worth $227 million (more than half the value of all exports) and in 1900 $242 million (less than one-fifth of all exports). Increasing exports of wheat and meat from the agricultural sector and of petroleum and machinery from the industrial sector of the economy account for the relative decline of cotton, although it remained the top export. Sugar was the top import in the Gilded Age, with $57 million worth imported in 1870 and $100 million in 1900. The second most important import in 1870 was iron and STEEL manufactures at $40 million, but by 1900 the development of the American steel industry reduced those imports to relative insignificance. After sugar, the most important imports in 1900 were hides and skins, coffee, and then raw silk. The shifts in exports and imports reflects the enormous agricultural and industrial expansion of the United States.

Further reading: Bureau of the Census, *Historical Statistics of the United States* (Washington, D.C.: U.S. Bureau of the Census, 1975).

transportation, urban

Urban public transportation supported the rapid expansion of cities in the late 19th century and made possible the development of residential districts separated from places of work. Converging on a central point, public transportation lines created the "downtown" and the "hundred-percent corner," the point of maximum accessibility where new institutions like DEPARTMENT STORES clustered.

By the 1870s the horse-powered street railway was the prevalent public transportation mode for large and small American cities. Starting in 1832, horsecars had steadily replaced horse-drawn "omnibuses." The smooth rails doubled the load a horse could pull. In flat terrain, horsecars could travel seven miles per hour. Cities granted franchises for tracks on their streets in return for fare limitations (five cents was the norm) and paving or street-sprinkling obligations.

Horses could work for only a few hours, and horsecar companies had to maintain as many as eight to 10 animals for each vehicle they owned. The West End Street Railway of Boston at one time stabled about 8,000 horses. Horses

Electric trolleys competed with automobiles for space on city streets. *(Library of Congress)*

were polluting, generating about 10 pounds of waste per animal per day plus urine. Horses were also subject to disease. An equine epidemic in 1872 killed or disabled 18,000 horses in New York City, crippling public transportation.

Cable cars were the first attempt to overcome the limitations of horsecars. Andrew S. Hallidie, a California manufacturer of wire cable, designed a cable car in 1869 that was drawn by a continuous wire cable beneath the street. By 1873 a Hallidie car scaled Clay Street in San Francisco, and soon Nob Hill was covered with cable lines. The cable, driven by a cable drum in the power house, ran continuously at nine miles per hour. Individual cars used a grip extending downward through a slot to grasp the cable. The "gripman" needed skill to engage and disengage the cable smoothly when stopping or coasting around street corners.

Cable railways had their greatest success in San Francisco, but 30 other cities also operated cable cars. Chicago had the second-largest system, opened in 1882, while other major cable operators included Kansas City, New York City, the Brooklyn Bridge, Cincinnati, Washington, Seattle, and Tacoma. The San Francisco cable cars were designated a National Historic Landmark in 1964. A Washington "grip" car is displayed in the Smithsonian, and a Chicago grip car replica is in the Chicago Museum of Science and Industry.

The biggest urban transportation innovation was the rapid adoption of electric streetcars in the 1890s. After a successful installation in Richmond, Virginia, in 1887, city after city converted their horsecar and cable lines to electricity. The streetcars drew power from a "trolley pole" contacting an overhead wire, and the car itself was soon known as a "trolley." Trolleys were faster than the horsecar, and the expansion of their lines opened new residential areas and recreational opportunities by extending to amusement parks and beaches. The electric trolley would remain the backbone of urban transportation in all but the largest cities until it was replaced by buses and the spread of automobiles starting in the late 1920s. In the largest cities, traffic congestion led to a search for alternatives. The steel-bridge industry made it practical to build continuous elevated viaducts above city streets, separated from pedestrians and vehicles below. New York City initiated the first steam powered "el" trains in 1871. Sioux City, Iowa, opened an elevated steam railway in 1890, and Chicago opened its first elevated line in 1892. The Chicago el lines converged on an elevated loop, which soon replaced the cable car loop as the definition of Chicago's downtown. The West Side elevated line in Chicago was electrified in 1895, and soon electricity replaced steam on other el lines throughout the country.

The other solution was to burrow beneath city streets. London had opened its Metropolitan subway in 1863 using steam locomotives, but the use of coal-burning locomotives underground had obvious limitations. Alfred Beach, the New York publisher of *Scientific American*, advocated pneumatic subways, with differential air pressure moving a car through a closely fitting tunnel. He financed a demonstration line 312 feet long beneath Broadway in 1870. It was not mechanically practical, although further developed. An 1897 subway under Tremont Street in Boston diverted streetcars from the surface for a few congested blocks, but the first true subway, the Interboro Rapid Transit (IRT) in New York City would not open until 1904.

Further reading: Alan Black, *Urban Mass Transportation Planning* (New York: McGraw-Hill, 1995).

— Francis H. Parker

trolley cars

See transportation, urban

trusts

In the Gilded Age companies that monopolized or dominated an industry were called trusts. "Competition is industrial war," a large envelope manufacturer wrote in 1901. "Unrestricted competition, carried to its logical conclusion, means death to some of the combatants and injury for all. Even the victor does not soon recover from the wounds received in combat." An alarming sense that things were dangerously out of control as a result of unrestrained competition was common among business owners throughout the late 19th and early 20th centuries, but never more so than during the years following the PANIC OF 1873.

Before that calamity, businessmen had enjoyed a relatively long period of prosperity that had lasted since the Civil War. This was due mainly to the extension and integration of the RAILROADS. In their rapid growth, they not only absorbed huge supplies of coal, iron, and STEEL, but they also enabled manufacturers in numerous industries to invade markets in distant cities previously closed to them. Combined with a host of technological improvements that greatly lowered the costs of production and made it possible to turn out goods of uniform quality in large amounts, the market expansion stimulated by the railroads opened up vast new opportunities for profit that businessmen rushed headlong to seize. Investment and growth soared in sugar refining, agricultural implements, MEATPACKING, OIL production and refining, as well as in iron and steel and coal. But in their lust to capture new markets many businesses, whether they were in manufacturing or MINING, expanded capacity much too rapidly. This meant that whenever orders for a firm's product declined, it was under enormous pressure to expand sales by cutting prices to meet the new, substantial overhead costs it had taken on. When times were good, as they generally were before the depression of 1873, such price-cutting was not a systemic problem. Moments of falling or stagnant demand, when they appeared, were relatively short and were quickly followed by another burst of growth. But after 1873 conditions changed dramatically. Demand did not rebound but declined sharply, triggering a desperate struggle for survival among producers in every sector of the economy. Cutthroat competition and price wars became the norm as each business tried to hang on as best it could. Marginal firms with older, less efficient facilities and higher fixed costs failed by the thousands. Only those with the lowest costs of production or some other competitive advantage managed to remain afloat even as they reduced prices, laid off workers, and scaled back in anticipation of even more canceled orders.

In this vortex of falling demand, many businesses sought shelter not merely by slashing prices and costs. They saw the solution to the problem of survival as one of taming market forces through strategies aimed at limiting competition. Precedents for this existed well before the depression of 1873. As early as 1817, salt producers along the Kanawha River in the Ohio Valley formed the Kanawha Salt Company to set production quotas and prices for each member firm. Before the Civil War, cotton manufacturers in Rhode Island and Massachusetts sometimes joined together "in unison" to set prices on yarns, and during and after the Civil War, established firms in the anthracite coal industry sought stability in prices and output by entering into agreements with railroads that made it difficult for new entrants to get their coal to market. The depression merely accelerated the search for new and more effective ways to harness what many viewed as suicidal, cutthroat competition.

Railroads serving the anthracite coal fields pioneered one early technique to stanch the bloodletting. Operating on the philosophy that it was better to combine than compete, they entered into a series of "gentlemen's agreements" imposing freight rates, and there were informal, voluntary "understandings" to set quotas or shared percentages of the total coal shipments to market. "Pools" were established to combine both methods of cooperation. Errant members of the pool who exceeded their quota or cut prices below a certain level would suffer fines or, according to the details of each agreement, other punishment to bring them back into line. Such pools soon arose in other battered industries. By the 1880s, observers spoke of a whiskey pool, a cordage pool, a lead pool, a salt pool, as well as multiple railroad and coal pools. But however effective these pools might have been at first in stabilizing prices in various industries, they all eventually unraveled because, as John D. Rockefeller complained, reflecting on the collapse of his own pools in the oil business, they were "ropes of sand." The legal system did not recognize such arrangements. Indeed, they were violations of the common law's prohibition of contracts "in restraint of trade," so when businessmen cheated on their quotas or secretly cut deals on prices, all that their victimized colleagues could do was rail at the unfairness of it all.

But another, far more effective method to stifle competition and stabilize markets would be fashioned by an inventive lawyer, Samuel C. T. Dodd, for his client, John D. Rockefeller and the Standard Oil Company of Ohio. In 1882 Dodd came up with the concept of utilizing an old legal contract, the trust agreement, to get around a barrier in 19th-century commercial law disallowing corporations from owning stock in other companies or to control businesses in jurisdictions outside of the states where they were incorporated. The trust concept would override these legal constraints, and thus it fit in perfectly with John D. Rockefeller's vision and philosophy. Rockefeller, who entered the oil business in 1862 and quickly became the dominant figure in the Standard Oil Company, was appalled by the chaotic, unrestrained competition the oil business exhibited in the 1860s. Even though his own firm did well in that environment, his principal objective from the start was to eliminate what he viewed as wasteful competition. Demanding and getting rebates from railroads on oil shipments (and even getting drawbacks, or kickbacks, on shipments by competitors), Rockefeller and his partners in Standard Oil soon succeeded in driving out independent refining competitors. By 1879 it either owned or had under lease 90 percent of the nation's refining capacity. But the company's management and organization remained cumbersome and ill-suited to Rockefeller's ambitions. When, for example, Standard Oil did business in states outside of Ohio, it was liable for taxes in those jurisdictions. It could have gotten around this by taking out corporate charters in each state, but then it would have had to open its books for inspection, a prospect the secretive Rockefeller was determined to avoid. Equally disturbing, management decisions were often delayed and prolonged because Standard Oil's control of many of the properties it brought into its orbit was not absolute. The holdover owners and managers of those companies still owned stock and had to be consulted.

The Standard Oil Trust Agreement—signed on January 2, 1882, by 41 stockholders holding trust certificates valued at $70 million—resolved many if not all of these issues and more. Under its terms, nine trustees, the functional equivalent of a board of directors, were given absolute control over the management of the properties Standard had in its portfolio. In return for handing over their stock to the trustees, the shareholders in those properties received trust certificates, which were the functional equivalent of common stock but without its voting privileges. This arrangement not only allowed Standard Oil to circumvent the laws of Ohio and many other states barring corporations from holding stock in other corporations, but it enabled the company to transform itself into a highly centralized organization. Just as importantly, under the trust agreement the inner workings of the company were wrapped in secrecy, since, legally, this corporation did not exist, lacking as it did either a legal name or a charter. As a semisecret body having no legal existence, the trust device provided Rockefeller and his fellow trustees with the means to achieve precisely what they had long sought: the ability to employ their assets free from public scrutiny, which allowed them to control from one headquarters the oil refining industry of the nation. And Standard Oil did so on a scale never experienced before. The worth of the various companies that entered into the agreement in 1882 amounted to about $72 million; 10 years later, Standard was conservatively estimated to be worth about $121 million—and growing.

Nevertheless, it was impossible to keep the Standard Oil Trust Agreement entirely secret, and as rumors of its existence were bruited about, numerous stories appeared in newspapers and magazines warning about monopolistic trusts being formed in such disparate industries as lead, school slates, envelopes, linseed oil, cottonseed oil, paving, pitch, salt, cordage, sugar, and countless more. "It is the aim of those who make these combinations," the New York Times intoned, "to kill competition at home, and to exact from consumers a price high enough, . . . [and] as great a tax as they must pay the Government when they buy the same kind of goods from foreign manufacturers." Social reformers and critics like HENRY DEMEREST LLOYD, who had already authored a harsh expose of Standard Oil entitled "The Story of a Great Monopoly" in 1881, were quick to denounce trusts as a new breed of corporate monster that would destroy the competitive system and even the republican form of government itself if not restrained.

Such concerns were justified. The Standard Oil Trust was a monopoly that had absorbed or eliminated virtually all rivals and had successfully imposed its control over both the prices for crude oil it still purchased (Standard Oil would become an oil producer later in its corporate history) and the prices it received for finished petroleum products. Yet, only a few of the many trusts established during these years, like the Sugar Trust, did as well as Standard Oil in eliminating competition and controlling prices—in short, monopolizing its market. Most trusts failed to achieve these goals, and even the Standard Oil Trust—though not its market dominance—turned out to be short-lived.

Even as the SHERMAN ANTITRUST ACT was being enacted in the summer of 1890 in response to the growing public chorus demanding that Washington do something, anything, to rein in the trusts, they were under withering legal assault in state courts. Louisiana brought suit against the Cottonseed Trust in 1887, New York against the Sugar Trust in 1889, and Ohio against the Standard Oil Trust in 1890. In January 1890, a New York court ruled that the Sugar Trust was in violation of the common-law prohibition against restraints of trade, a decision soon affirmed by courts in other states. All trusts brought to book by these rulings appealed, but to no avail. By 1892, when the Ohio Supreme Court upheld the lower court's decision against the Standard Oil Trust and ordered it dissolved, the trust movement came to an end.

However, industrial consolidations and combinations did not cease. They simply continued in a different guise made possible, in 1889, when New Jersey revised its general incorporation laws to allow any corporation situated in the state to hold the securities of subsidiary corporations chartered there. Accordingly, as trusts ran afoul of various state laws, many applied to New Jersey for charters to do business and became "holding companies." The Cottonseed Oil Trust was the first to take advantage of the new law, reconstituting itself in November 1889 as the American Cotton Oil Company. Five months later the Lead Trust became the National Lead and Oil Company of New Jersey, and in January 1891 the Sugar Trust received a New Jersey corporate charter in the name of the American Sugar Refining Company. Standard Oil remained, for complex legal reasons, a "trust in liquidation" after the Ohio Supreme Court's 1892 ruling and remained so for some time, continuing to run its business under an Ohio charter much as before. Finally, in 1899, three years after New Jersey further liberalized its statutes to allow corporations to hold stock in companies chartered elsewhere and only when it was threatened with further court action in Ohio, did Standard Oil reincorporate itself in New Jersey as a holding company, the Standard Oil Company of New Jersey. But except for its new legal form and change of address, the company remained unchanged.

In theory, holding companies had to own more than 50 percent of the voting stock of any subsidiary they acquired. But in practice, operating control could be accomplished with a far smaller slice of outstanding stock, particularly when shares became more widely dispersed. As a financial and organizational tool, therefore, holding companies were perfectly suited to those ambitious businessmen seeking to merge one corporation with another, thereby growing bigger, more powerful, more dominant, more able to control their own destiny without fear of competition.

With the exception of the trusts that reorganized themselves as holding companies, businessmen were slow to take advantage of New Jersey's inviting corporation laws. Consolidations of all sorts virtually ground to a halt during the depression years of 1893–97. But in 1898 and continuing until 1905, an unprecedented wave of mergers, estimated at more than 3,000, swept through the American economy. Startling in its dimensions and scope, this merger wave transformed the structure of American industry as no other combination movement had before. In 1865 most businesses were small. No single company controlled any industry. By 1905, however, about 328 large corporations, most of them the product of mergers after 1898, were estimated to own two-fifths of the $20-billion industrial wealth of the nation. And of those 328 large firms, as many as 156 were dominant enough to have some monopoly control in their particular industry.

Clearly, the oft-expressed desire of businessmen to be free of the debilitating effects of unrestrained competition was one of the major forces propelling this wave of mergers. As J. PIERPONT MORGAN, the investment banker behind many of the largest mergers of this period, put it, "I like a little competition, but I like combination better." But why did so many of the combinations he so obviously wanted and brought to such profitable fruition begin to take shape on the industrial landscape only after 1898? Many compelling reasons have been advanced. For one thing, the SUPREME COURT, in its decision in the *E. C. Knight* case (1895) eviscerated the Sherman Antitrust Act's principal provision, holding "Every contract, combination in the form of trust or otherwise . . . in restraint of trade . . . to be illegal," and by so doing implicitly gave a green light to consolidations under the New Jersey holding-company statutes. Combined with the coincident return to prosperity following the end of the depression of 1893–97, the newly permissive government attitude toward combinations set the stage for an outburst of merger activity. Adding fuel and energy to the process was the maturation of the capital markets under the vigorous leadership of investment bankers like Morgan, who were increasingly employing the stock exchange to float the newly minted securities generated by each merger.

The public's appetite for stocks and bonds was growing substantially during this period, and Morgan and fellow financiers were happy to feed it. Underwriting these mergers proved extremely profitable for them, and the more mergers there were, the greater were the profits to be had. In other words, mergers were a virtual circle of moneymaking, especially for insiders. When, for example, Morgan persuaded ANDREW CARNEGIE and eight of his largest competitors in the steel industry to sell out and created, in 1901, what was the greatest merger of the age, the United States Steel Corporation, everybody involved did fabulously well. Carnegie and his partners came away with $492 million, while Morgan pocketed even more. He sold the shares of the newly formed company for $1.4 billion, which was $700 million in excess of what he paid for all of the firms that became U.S. Steel. Morgan, it is true, pursued mergers because he sincerely believed it was in the public interest to end the economic havoc wrought by unrestrained competition. But he was even more vigorous in his pursuit of money and the countless works of fine art, rare manuscripts, and antiques money allowed him to possess for his personal pleasure and enjoyment. The mergers Morgan engineered clearly enabled him to satisfy both of these passions. Whether they were just as beneficial to the turn-of-the-century American consumer and laboring man, however, is still being debated.

Further reading: Alfred D. Chandler, Jr., *The Visible Hand: The Managerial Resolution in American Business* (Cambridge, Mass.: Harvard University Press, 1977); Neil Fligstein, *The Transformation of Corporate Control* (Cambridge, Mass.: Harvard University Press, 1990); Naomi R. Lamoreaux, *The Great Merger Movements in American Business, 1895–1904* (Cambridge, U.K.: Cambridge University Press, 1985); Ralph Nelson, *Merger Movements in American Industry, 1895–1956* (Princeton, N.J.: Princeton University Press, 1959).

Turner, Frederick Jackson (1861–1932)

Frederick Jackson Turner, born on November 14, 1861, in Portage, Wisconsin, was a distinguished professor of history at the University of Wisconsin and Harvard University. In 1893, three years after the superintendent of the census announced that a frontier line no longer existed, Turner at the annual convention of the American Historical Association discussed the end of the frontier and argued that "the existence of an area of free land, its continuous recession, and the advance of American settlement westward, explain American development" of its democratic institutions and the habits and character of its people.

Turner believed that conquering, occupying, and establishing small communities on the expanding frontier forced Americans to work cooperatively, trust one another to carry out agreements, and reconcile the needs of individualism with democratic government. These human qualities described and explained the greatness of American life. Turner's views were both celebrationist and pessimistic. He was concerned that the passing of the frontier emphasized the depletion of natural resources and also removed the safety valve that enabled the unemployed to seek and find opportunities in the West. With the frontier at an end, how could American democracy and greatness survive if there were no continuing frontier to give renewed birth to American greatness? Turner's vanishing-frontier thesis brought together three major, and for many, troubling forces affecting American society: the end of frontier settlement, the rapid growth of industrial capitalism into an integrated market economy centered in new cities, and the need to extend democratic ideals to new immigrants from eastern and southern Europe coming to America for jobs in the new industrial economy. While Turner believed that the frontier explained much of American development, he also recognized that sectionalism was "fundamental in American history." Indeed, much of his research was on voting patterns and geographical conditions illustrating the persistence of sectionalism, the results of which were summarized in his *Significance of the Sections in American History* (1932), published after his death on March 14, 1932, in Pasadena, California.

Turner's persuasive work on sectionalism has been widely accepted, but the frontier thesis—especially its celebrationist ideas—has provoked critics, many of whom are urban in background. Some have pointed out that there was no safety valve, that the down-and-out in urban America had neither the cash nor the skills to get them out to, or to survive on, the frontier. His rosy picture of the frontier ignored lawlessness and violence, the fate of NATIVE AMERICANS, Asian immigrants, and Chicanos, and the profligate waste of resources. Other critics note that the frontier did not produce unique American forms of government or legal systems. They argue that new states largely imitated the states of the earlier eastern frontier, which in turn had imitated English forms. Turner's critics emphasize that ideas about government, law, voting, and democratic politics were brought to the frontier and did not automatically "germinate" from frontier life. Finally, critics claim that American life was more than its institutions. Turner's thesis could not explain the growth of American SCIENCE, LITERATURE, ART, MUSIC, and other cultural forms. Clearly, Turner's work stimulated research on the frontier and its influence. If it could not explain all American life, it offered for many a compelling argument for American uniqueness.

Further reading: James D. Bennett, *Frederick Jackson Turner* (Boston: Twayne, 1975); Ray A. Billington, *Frederick Jackson Turner: Historian, Scholar, Teacher* (New York: Oxford University Press, 1973).

— Harry Stein

Turner, Henry McNeal (1834–1915)

Henry McNeal Turner, an African Methodist Episcopal (AME) bishop, was born free on February 1, 1834, in Newberry Courthouse, South Carolina. Despite the state prohibition against AFRICAN AMERICANS learning to read, he learned to read and also was tutored in arithmetic, history, law, and theology by lawyers for whom he worked in Abbeville as a janitor. Deeply religious, he was licensed by the Methodist Episcopal Church, South, in 1853 to preach, and in 1858 he joined the AME Church. From 1858 to 1863 he ministered to AME churches in Baltimore and Washington. After organizing a black Civil War regiment, Turner became the war's first black chaplain. He was a gifted orator and successful revivalist and went to Georgia after the end of the war and organized churches.

Turner soon went into politics. The Reconstruction Act of March 2, 1867, called for African Americans to help rewrite the constitutions of those states undergoing Reconstruction. Turner was a delegate to Georgia's constitutional convention. He was elected to the state's legislature in 1868, but white reactionaries in 1869 expelled the two senators and 25 representatives; all were black. Turner, who represented Bibb County, strongly protested his expulsion. He informed the Georgia legislature that he was a duly elected member of their body: "therefore, I shall neither fawn or cringe before any party, nor stoop to beg them for my rights. I am here to demand my rights, and to hurl thunderbolts at the men who would dare to cross the threshold of my manhood." Turner vowed that black men would not fight to defend a nation that would not honor their rights of citizenship and manhood. Thanks to the influence of Senator Charles Sumner, Turner was then appointed postmaster of Macon, but an alleged involvement with a prostitute soon forced his resignation. Congress, however, in 1870 restored the expelled legislators to their seats, and Turner filled out his term but failed to be reelected. Turner then secured a federal civil service appointment in the Savannah customhouse.

At Savannah, Turner also pastored an AME church and remained active in church affairs. He was in 1876 made the manager of the AME Book Concern in Philadelphia, where he was responsible for publishing *The Christian Recorder* and other church publications. During his tenure there he clashed with BENJAMIN TUCKER TANNER, editor of the *Recorder*, over how to settle the Book Concern's debts, how to increase readership, and how to persuade subscribers to pay their arrears.

Turner was elected a bishop in 1880 and served in that capacity until his death in 1915. He was the center of several controversies in the church. There was opposition to his insistence that clergy wear vestments and follow ritual, and fellow bishops questioned his decision in 1885 to ordain Sarah Ann Hughes to the ministry. In 1887 Bishop Jabez Campbell rescinded this act at a North Carolina annual conference of bishops. Turner also shocked many with his declaration that "God is a Negro." He contended that blacks would always feel inferior if they worshiped a European image of God while believing that the devil was black.

With the end of Reconstruction, Turner vigorously advocated African-American emigration to Africa to civilize and Christianize the continent. Turner was a longtime advocate of EMIGRATION TO LIBERIA, and he was criticized for serving since 1876 as a vice president of the American Colonization Society, an organization that had promoted a back-to-Africa program since the 1820s. Turner traveled to Africa several times in the 1890s to oversee the AME Church's mission efforts in Liberia, Sierra Leone, and South Africa. There he founded annual conferences and schools, and upon his return he published exaggerated reports extolling the richness of the land and the possibility of development. Critics castigated him for encouraging people to emigrate to a land of disease, poverty, and high death rates, and among these critics his old adversary Tanner was a major voice. Turner called for a convention in 1893 to meet in Cincinnati to organize emigration to Africa, but he was bitterly disappointed when the delegates rejected migration to Africa as impractical. Turner continued to argue that African Americans would never have the respect of others until black men ruled themselves and that their presence in America would limit them to be nothing more than "menials, scullions, servants, subordinates and underlings." He edited *The Voice of Missions* (1893–1900) and *The Voice of the People* (1901–04) and used both organs to express his personal views on emigration to Africa.

Turner opposed the SPANISH-AMERICAN WAR and suggested that blacks should not fight for a government that could not protect their rights in the South. He was so bitterly opposed to American racism that he vowed never to die in America. His wish was granted when he suffered a severe stroke and died on May 8, 1915, in Windsor, Ontario, Canada. His body was returned to Georgia for burial. Turner is honored throughout the United States with churches named after him. In 1900 the AME Church founded Turner Theological Seminary at Morris Brown College in Atlanta.

See also AFRICAN-AMERICAN CHURCHES, GROWTH OF.

Further reading: Stephen W. Angell, *Bishop Henry McNeal Turner and African American Religion in the South* (Knoxville: University of Tennessee Press, 1992); Edwin, Redkey, *Respect Black: The Writings and Speeches of Henry McNeal Turner* (New York: Arno, 1971).

— William Seraile

Tuskegee Institute See Washington, Booker T.

Twain, Mark (Samuel Langhorne Clemens) (1835–1910)

Perhaps the most influential American literary voice ever, Mark Twain was born Samuel Langhorne Clemens in Florida, Missouri, on November 30, 1835, and grew up in Hannibal, Missouri. His father, a lawyer who speculated unsuccessfully in land, died when Twain was 12, and he was then apprenticed as a printer. As a journeyman printer during 1853 and 1854, he worked his way to St. Louis, New York, Philadelphia, and Keokuk, Iowa. On his way to New Orleans in 1857 he became an apprentice pilot on the Mississippi River and was a full-fledged river pilot when the outbreak of the Civil War shut down the Mississippi.

Mark Twain *(Library of Congress)*

In 1861 Twain joined a volunteer militia affiliated with the Confederacy and discovered that he strongly disliked military life. He was able to quit after two weeks when Missouri did not secede from the union. Feeling deeply conflicted about the war, he moved to Nevada with his brother, Orion, a unionist who had become secretary of the territorial governor of Nevada. In Nevada, Twain became a prospector and later, in 1862, a reporter in Virginia City. It was there that he first used the pseudonym Mark Twain, a river term for two fathoms deep (or safe water). The pseudonym quickly took on a personality of its own, and his adoption of it marked the beginning of his literary career.

In 1864 Twain moved to California, where he found work as a reporter. In 1865 he wrote a short story, "The Celebrated Jumping Frog of Calaveras County." A California newspaper then sent him to the Sandwich Islands (now Hawaii) as a roving reporter. His articles were well received, and in 1866, after his return, he lectured very successfully in the West, beginning a phenomenally successful second career.

Twain's first book, *The Celebrated Jumping Frog of Calaveras County and Other Sketches*, was published in 1867. He gave a triumphant lecture at Cooper Union in New York, then set sail for the Mediterranean and the Holy

Land as a roving reporter for another California paper. The reports he sent back were even more successful than his reports from the Sandwich Islands and formed the basis for *The Innocents Abroad* (1869), which turned him into a national figure. His take on the Old World—and the new type of American tourist that had begun visiting it—was unique, surprising, and funny.

In 1870, after his return to America, he married Olivia Langdon; they made their home in the Northeast, primarily in Hartford, Connecticut. He relied on her, and later on WILLIAM DEAN HOWELLS, to tell him which of his writings were too outrageous to print. Over the next 30 years, his output was impressive. *Roughing It* (1872) recounted, semifictionally, his experiences in the Far West. He followed that up with *THE GILDED AGE* (1873), written with Charles Dudley Warner, an on-target satire on contemporary foibles and corruption that captured the spirit of an era. *The Adventures of Tom Sawyer* (1876), based on memories of his boyhood in Hannibal, demonstrated a sure comic touch. *The Adventures of Huckleberry Finn* (1884), about a runaway boy and an escaped slave on a raft on the Mississippi River, is a certified classic. Its natural use of a wide array of Southern dialects demonstrated just how well Twain understood the spoken word, but that was only a small part of what made the book compelling. Most noteworthy were its comic skewering of human gullibility and venality and its insights into just how twisted conventional morality can get. The passages in which a guilt-racked Huck found himself unable to betray Jim, the runaway slave, even though he was convinced that he would be sent to hell for helping to "steal" the rightful property of someone else, are among the most gripping in literature.

Twain's other books included *A Tramp Abroad* (1880), *The Prince and the Pauper* (1882), *Life on the Mississippi* (1883), *A Connecticut Yankee in King Arthur's Court* (1889), *Tom Sawyer Abroad* (1894), *Tom Sawyer, Detective* (1896), *The Tragedy of Pudd'nhead Wilson and the Comedy, Those Extraordinary Twins* (1894), and *Personal Recollections of Joan of Arc* (1896).

Although his writings often mocked the speculative mania that gripped the nation during the Gilded Age, Twain himself was far from immune, losing a good deal of money on several speculative ventures and spending lavishly on his Hartford home. He continued to write and lecture up until his death on April 21, 1910, with his later writings showing a more bitter cast. At the end of his life, he dictated an autobiography that was published posthumously.

Twain is best remembered for his clear, compelling, and unadorned prose; his remarkable ear for spoken language; his comic flair; and his unique slant on life. "Always do right," he told the young people's society of a Brooklyn Presbyterian Church in 1901. "This will gratify some people and astonish the rest."

Further reading: Justin Kaplan, *Mr. Clemens and Mark Twain* (New York: Simon & Schuster, 1966).

— Lynn Hoogenboom

Tweed Ring

The spectacularly corrupt Tweed Ring was led by William M. Tweed (1823–78), who held a number of municipal posts in New York City in the 1860s, including deputy street commissioner and deputy commissioner of public works. He increased his power through his control of appointments and the awarding of contracts, and by 1868 he was the leader of the Democratic machine, the grand sachem (leader) of TAMMANY HALL, and in complete control of the administration of New York City. Taking advantage of home-rule features in a new city charter secured by bribery from the New York State legislature, Tweed and his close associates—Mayor A. Oakey Hall, Peter B. Sweeny, and Richard B. Connolly—began in 1869 to steal from the city on so spectacular and so organized a scale that the Tweed Ring has overshadowed all other municipal corruptionists in American history. Its most conspicuous, but certainly not the only, source of graft was the construction of the new county courthouse. Not only did contractors purchase building materials from companies in which Tweed had an interest, but they also padded their bills and shared excessive payments with the ring. Since Tweed was on the Board of Audit, these fraudulent bills were not challenged. When construction was finished, the cost of the $12 million courthouse had been multiplied three times.

The Tweed Ring was short-lived. The cartoonist THOMAS NAST began in 1870 to attack Tweed and his cohorts with devastating caricatures in *Harper's Weekly*, and the ring's downfall came in 1871 when disgruntled insiders leaked damning evidence to the *New York Times*. Citizens were aroused. SAMUEL J. TILDEN, the state Democratic leader, belatedly turned on Tweed (enhancing his reform reputation), and Tweed was overthrown, prosecuted, and convicted in 1873 for not properly auditing bills. He was imprisoned, escaped to Spain, but was extradited and returned to jail, where he died.

The effrontery of the Tweed Ring and the sheer volume of its stealings—perhaps as much as the $30 million Tilden alleged—obscures the rapid development of New York during the years Tweed was in power. Extraordinary municipal graft required extensive civic projects, including improved transit facilities, the widening of Broadway, and the development of Central Park. Payoffs and graft were powerful incentives that brought disparate elements, which normally paralyzed action, together to work (and steal) in concert on major undertakings. Indeed, the urban historian Seymour J. Mandelbaum argues that by uniting fragmented neighborhoods and ignoring the frugality prized by

A political cartoon portraying William M. Tweed as a bullying schoolteacher giving New York City comptroller Richard B. Connolly a lesson in arithmetic. The exaggerated bills for the building of a county courthouse are posted on the wall. *(Library of Congress)*

taxpayers and the morals of reformers, Tweed and his accomplices stole the city rich.

Further reading: A. B. Callow, *The Tweed Ring* (New York: Simon & Schuster, 1985); Leo Hershkowitz, *Tweed's New York: Another Look* (Garden City, N.Y.: Anchor Books, 1977); Seymour J. Mandelbaum, *Boss Tweed's New York* (New York: John Wiley & Sons, 1965).

United States v. E. C. Knight Co. (1895) See Sherman Antitrust Act

utopianism

American publishers released more than 150 utopian novels between 1885 and 1900. The outpouring of literary descriptions of the ideal perfect social order betrayed a society uncertain of its future. Part of that uncertainty reflected the fear of cataclysm that accompanies the ending of a century. But the greatest contributor to this doubt was the rift between values and reality caused by industrialization. Labor conflict, the increasing gap between rich and poor, the displacement of farmers, and the growing concentration of economic power—all of which apparently refuted the principles of republicanism—left Americans aghast and seeking answers.

EDWARD BELLAMY's *Looking Backward* (1888) was one of the most widely read utopian solutions for the troubled society. Placed in the year 2000, Bellamy's perfect social order enjoyed an equality of abundance made possible by a nationalized economy. Universal public service guaranteed the production of goods and services. Education, rather than revolution, secured this ideal world, as its unselfish citizens recognized that it made more sense to cooperate and share (rather than compete and amass) surpluses resulting from efficient large-scale production and demanded the abolition of all forms of private property.

The road to utopian bliss was not so peaceful in Ignatius Donnelly's *Caesar's Column,* published in 1890. Donnelly depicted late 20th-century America (the novel is set in 1998) as sated in luxurious splendor. But he has the main character, Gabriel Weltstein, a visitor from Uganda, discover that the grandeur is only a facade disguising a tyranny ruled over by Prince Cabano and the Council of Oligarchy. Their greedy despotism has enslaved the productive classes, reducing them into submissive "automata." The repressive exploitation generates a revolutionary movement, the Brotherhood of Destruction, headed by Caesar Lomellini, a dispossessed farmer. The Brotherhood's victory ignites an orgy of killing and looting. Concerned over the health threat posed by so many exposed cadavers, Caesar orders them placed in a cement column ringed with explosives. But once unleashed, the violence cannot be contained, and Caesar is killed and his head placed on a stake. All, however, is not lost, for Weltstein escapes the bloody chaos and returns to Uganda, where he establishes a harmonious society based upon government ownership of the factors of production.

Utopianism's identification of private property as the source of greed and inequality and the progenitor of evil echoed the views of Christian communes founded before the Civil War. Most of those experiments in utopian communism ultimately succumbed to capitalism. The Oneida Perfectionist Community, renowned for its production of silver flatware, ended its experiment in communal property in 1879 by becoming a joint stock company. The longest-lasting religious commune, the Amana Community, reorganized as a joint stock company in 1932.

Utopianism's rejection of private property also mirrored SOCIALISM. It differed from that doctrine, however, in that it had a clear vision of what might be, but only vague notions on how to achieve utopia. Socialists, whether Lassalleans or Marxists, suggested more concrete strategies for abolishing individual property.

Further reading: Sylvia Bowman, *Edward Bellamy* (Boston: Twayne, 1986); Martin Ridge, *Ignatius Donnelly: The Portrait of a Politician* (Chicago: University of Chicago Press, 1962).

— Harold W. Aurand

V

Vanderbilt, Cornelius See Volume IV

Venezuela boundary dispute (1895)

A serious disagreement arose in 1895 when the United States intervened in the stalled negotiations between Great Britain and Venezuela over the boundary of British Guiana. Britain adhered to the line draw by surveyor Robert Schomburgk in 1840, while Venezuela adhered to a line that enveloped almost all of British Guiana. Intermittent talks went on for years to no avail. When the British, frustrated by Venezuelan intransigence, claimed land beyond the Schomburgk line, where gold had recently been discovered, Venezuela in 1887 suspended diplomatic relations with Great Britain.

In 1894 American concern about the dispute intensified with the publication of a pamphlet, *British Aggressions in Venezuela* or *the Monroe Doctrine on Trial,* whose author, William L. Scruggs, a former American minister to Venezuela, depicted Britain's position as a deliberate violation of the Monroe Doctrine. The essay prompted CONGRESS to unanimously pass a resolution urging arbitration of the matter and convinced President GROVER CLEVELAND of the need to forcefully address the issue. Secretary of State Richard Olney, an impatient, irascible railroad attorney from Boston, sent a letter to London, with Cleveland's approval, claiming in a hyperbolic tone that "the United States is practically sovereign on this continent, and its fiat is law." He also described the insidious nature of the British presence in Latin America and the need to arbitrate the dispute.

The British prime minister, Lord Salisbury, waited four months before responding that the Monroe Doctrine did not apply, since the British presence in Guiana antedated the Republic of Venezuela, and Britain continued to refuse to arbitrate. Outraged by both the delay and the response, Cleveland on December 17, 1895, answered Salisbury by asking Congress for funds for a commission to determine the boundary line and vowed that the United States would use "every means in its power" to uphold that line.

A brief war scare ensued, but tempers cooled after a few days. The British (feeling menaced by Germany and anxious for American friendship) backed off and showed a willingness to arbitrate. Olney also backed off and agreed that territory occupied by either side should not be subject to arbitration for 50 years. Utilizing the good offices of the United States, a treaty of arbitration between Britain and Venezuela was signed on February 2, 1897. On October 3, 1899, the arbitration panel—consisting of two Britons, two Americans, and one Russian—fixed the boundary roughly along the Schomburgk line, although Britain lost control of the mouth of the Orinoco River and 5,000 square miles of territory at the southern end of that line.

Despite the bluster of Cleveland and Olney that could have had disastrous consequences, the Venezuela boundary dispute turned out well for the United States. It forced Britain to recognize American hegemony in the Caribbean, strengthened the Monroe Doctrine, gave impetus to the arbitration of disputes, and ultimately improved Anglo-American relations.

Further reading: Gerald G. Eggert, *Richard Olney: Evolution of a Statesman* (University Park: Pennsylvania State University Press, 1974); Dexter Perkins, *A History of the Monroe Doctrine* (Boston: Little, Brown, 1955); Richard E. Welch, *The Presidencies of Grover Cleveland* (Lawrence: University Press of Kansas, 1988).

— Timothy E. Vislocky

Victorianism

Victorianism is the term used by some social and cultural historians to refer to certain beliefs, assumptions, codes, tastes, behaviors, and social arrangements associated principally, but not exclusively, with the middle class in Britain and the United States during much of the 19th century.

Like any label that purports to cover diverse social and cultural phenomena, *Victorianism* is problematic. Historians do not agree on the exact chronology or content of Victorianism. Some scholars, even allowing for strong transatlantic influences, question whether a label imported from monarchist Britain can accurately describe developments in republican America. Others avoid the term altogether because to moderns it is has long been a pejorative, suggesting narrow-mindedness, hypocrisy, and prudery.

Nevertheless, some of the most subtle and perceptive commentators on 19th-century America have found *Victorianism* to be both valid and useful. That is because, by and large, the American middle class, like its British counterpart, shared well-defined values and tastes during the period. To earn approval, the arts, LITERATURE, and POPULAR ENTERTAINMENT had to be consistent with the social codes of Victorianism. The 1893 Chicago WORLD'S COLUMBIAN EXPOSITION, for instance, celebrated Victorian confidence and faith in progress. In art, Victorianism meant romanticized history, uplift, pathos, and idealizations of middle-class life. In THEATER, Victorians preferred melodrama, in which good conquered evil. In literature, they favored romanticism and gentility. Culture typically upheld such Victorian values as polite behavior, social order (especially patriarchy and Protestantism), duty, and self-restraint.

Victorians, whether in Britain or the United States, considered behavior to be the outward expression of character, hence their emphasis on integrity, good grooming, propriety, and emotional control. Sexual prudence, if not prudery, was an essential part of the code, especially for women, though modern studies have argued that Victorian sexuality differed from that of later eras only in vocabulary, not in passion. Eros, it seems, was as powerful as ever, but it was not admitted into polite discourse or public demeanor.

The behavioral standards of Victorianism were not limited to the middle class. They could be extended to other groups, though expectations varied, depending upon gender, race, class, ethnicity, or RELIGION. Servants, laborers, immigrants, even racial minorities, could earn respect, if not status, by honoring the code. Victorianism also made allowances for (and perpetuated) presumed gender differences by consigning women to a "domestic sphere" and by limiting the "public sphere" almost exclusively to men.

Women were, however, significant agents of Victorianism at both home and church. In their domestic sphere they were arbiters and exemplars of culture, manners, and morals for family and even servants. Also active in church work, women joined with ministers to propagate a "culture of feelings," the sentimental (some would say "feminine") aspect of Victorianism. Beyond hearth and pulpit, schools, armed with their McGuffey readers, were also strongholds of Victorian values.

Of course, not everyone adhered to Victorianism, though it was the standard against which moralists defined deviancy. Even among its adherents, tensions and strains often surfaced. Indeed, women frequently found it difficult to reconcile the contradictory Victorian notions of "true womanhood" (emotional, dependent, gentle, passive) and "ideal motherhood" (practical, self-reliant, strong, protective, nurturing).

As the 19th century drew to a close, Victorianism faced powerful new challenges. Social and political unrest, IMMIGRATION, and economic change jarred the middle class. Gilded Age opportunism undermined Victorian moralism. Popular entertainment offered more amusement and pleasure and less uplift. In art and literature, realism and naturalism challenged gentility and romanticism. On the intellectual front, the theories of Darwin, Marx, and Freud threatened cherished Victorian pieties. Even antimodernists, such as HENRY ADAMS, defected from Victorianism. Although social and cultural reorientation was well advanced by the 1890s, Victorianism did not finally give way to modernism until the second quarter of the 20th century.

See also ART AND ARCHITECTURE; PAINTING.

Further reading: Daniel Walker Howe, ed., *Victorian America* (Philadelphia: University of Pennsylvania Press, 1976); Steve Ickringill and Stephan Mills, eds., *Victorianism in the United States* (Amsterdam: U.V. University Press, 1992); T. J. Jackson Lears, *No Place of Grace: Antimodernism and the Transformation of American Culture, 1880–1920* (New York: Pantheon, 1981); Peter N. Stearns, *Battleground of Desire* (New York: New York University Press, 1999).

— William Hughes

Villard, Henry (1835–1900)

Henry Villard was not only a journalist and a reformer but also a financier and a railroad president. Born in Speyer, Germany, on April 10, 1835, Villard migrated to America in 1853, bouncing from job to job in the Midwest until 1858 when he began a career in journalism as a correspondent for the New York *Staats-Zeitung* and covered the Lincoln-Douglas debates. He switched to the Cincinnati *Commercial* in 1859, reported on the Pikes Peak gold rush in Colorado, and was in Chicago for the 1860 Republican National Convention. He described Civil War battles for the *New York Herald* and later for the *New York Tribune,* and after the war in 1865 he became the Washington correspondent of the *Chicago Tribune* and was its man at the 1867 Paris Exposition.

Like his fellow German immigrant CARL SCHURZ, Villard was a supporter of liberal reforms. Those ties were strengthened in 1866 by his marriage to Helen Frances

"Fanny" Garrison, the daughter of abolitionist William Lloyd Garrison. In 1865 a number of eastern patrician reformers had established the American Social Science Association to analyze problems and to promote the answers—CIVIL SERVICE REFORM, free trade, MONETARY POLICIES—which they already had in hand. Villard became the association's secretary in 1868 and, combining diligence and charm, drummed up support for its program and made useful contacts. By 1870 Villard embarked on a career in finance and was able in 1881 to support the liberal reform agenda by purchasing the *New York Evening Post* and the weekly *THE NATION*, installing Schurz and EDWIN L. GODKIN as coeditors.

After a slow start, Villard succeeded in finance because he took advantage of the depression following the PANIC OF 1873 that plunged many RAILROADS into bankruptcy. In Europe from 1870 to 1873, he used his family connections and returned to the United States as the representative of German investors in the Oregon & California Railroad. With that leverage, Villard helped reorganize it and the Oregon Steamship Company, assumed the presidency of the Oregon Steam and Navigation Company in 1879 and became the dominant force in transportation in the Pacific Northwest. Villard's brilliant accomplishments as a reorganizer earned him the backing of the investment banker J. PIERPONT MORGAN, who supported Villard's acquisition of the Northern Pacific Railroad (NPRR) in 1881. Morgan also backed Villard's optimistic plunge into a massive NPRR construction program that linked the Great Lakes with his Oregon properties. The enormous cost of completing the NPRR just in time to take the brunt of the next economic slump (1883–86) left the NPRR deeply in debt, and Villard was ousted from its presidency in 1884. Morgan, however, did not lose faith in Villard, and he was back on the NPRR board of directors in 1888 and became its chair in 1889. With Morgan's backing, Villard in 1890 gained control of the Edison Lamp Company of Newark, New Jersey, and the Edison Machine Works of Schenectady, New York; he combined them in 1891 as the Edison General Electric Company and named himself president.

Villard's financial career, which took off in the depression of the 1870s, was terminated by the Panic of 1893. His optimistic tendency to overreach again proved to be his undoing, and his two major enterprises had to be reorganized. As a result, in 1893 he was removed from the board of directors of the NPRR and from the presidency of Edison General Electric, which was reconstituted as the General Electric Company. Villard died at Dobbs Ferry, New York, on November 12, 1900.

Further reading: Dietrich G. Buss, *Henry Villard: A Study in Transatlantic Investments and Interest, 1870–1895* (New York: Ohio Press, 1978); James B. Hedges, *Henry Villard and the Railways of the Northwest* (New Haven, Conn.: Yale University Press, 1930).

Virginius affair (1873)

The *Virginius* was a former Confederate blockade runner owned by Cubans that was carrying guns, ammunition, and men to the Cuban insurrectionists, who had been fighting their Spanish masters since 1868. On October 31, 1873, while illegally flying the American flag, it was spotted near CUBA by the Spanish warship *Tornado* (also a former Confederate blockade-runner) and was chased within six miles of Jamaica, where it was captured and towed to Santiago, Cuba.

General Juan Burriel, the governor of Santiago, called an immediate court-martial that convicted the crew of piracy and sentenced all of the passengers and crew to death. On November 4, four of the crew were shot and decapitated, and their heads were placed on pikes. Spaniards on the island celebrated the event with torchlit parades. When the shaky republican government in Madrid learned of the sentencing of the crew, the president Emilio Castelar ordered the executions stayed pending government review, but a break in the telegraph lines prevented Madrid's wishes from reaching Santiago.

Within a few days a total of 53 men (eight of them were American citizens) had been put to death, and the executions were only stopped by the timely arrival of the British warship *Niobe*. Despite the questionable right of the *Virginius* to fly the stars and stripes, Americans were outraged by the insult to the flag and by the sadistic butchery of Burriel and his men. Secretary of State Hamilton Fish instructed the American minister to Spain to demand the return of the ship, its remaining crew and passengers, the payment of an indemnity, and the punishment of Burriel. If these demands were not met, the minister was to break off diplomatic relations and return to the United States.

The Spanish government was in a precarious position in 1873. Having recently overthrown the monarchy, the new Spanish republic still faced a large, powerful bloc of "Carlist" reactionaries and needed to cultivate its popularity. President Emilio Castelar was therefore hesitant to apologize for Burriel's actions because the severe treatment of the *Virginius's* crew was widely supported by Spaniards at home and in Cuba. But after delaying a few days, the Spanish government suggested that negotiations for a settlement be transferred to Washington and pledged to comply with the principles of international law. The Spanish minister Admiral Don Jose Polo was able and conciliatory and, with Fish, worked out an arrangement agreeable to both Madrid and Washington. Basically Spain gave in and released the *Virginius,* including surviving passengers and crew, and paid an indemnity of $80, 000. Spain, however, delayed bringing charges against Burriel. As Spanish procrastination entered its fourth year, the general died.

Further reading: Allan Nevins, *Hamilton Fish: The Inner History of the Grant Administration* (New York: Dodd, Mead & Co., 1937).

— Timothy E. Vislocky

Wabash v. Illinois (1886) See railroads

Ward, Lester Frank (1841–1913)

A founder of modern American sociology, Lester Frank Ward was born on June 18, 1841, in Joliet, Illinois. His father was an itinerant mechanic in the small farming and commercial communities that 20 years earlier had been on the frontier. Following a common-school EDUCATION, Ward worked as a laborer but read widely, studying French, German, and Latin on his own. During the Civil War he served in the Union army, was wounded at Chancellorsville in 1863, and in 1865 secured a position in the Treasury Department at Washington. There he went to evening school and by 1872 he had earned diplomas in law, medicine, and the liberal arts from Columbian College (now George Washington University). During this time he began writing *Dynamic Sociology,* which was published in 1883 and established Ward's scholarly reputation. Ward continued his federal civil service career in the U.S. Geological Survey as chief of the Division of Fossil Plants until 1906. In that year he became the first president of the American Sociological Association, joined the faculty of Brown University, and taught there until his death on April 18, 1913.

Disagreeing with the laissez-faire ideas of WILLIAM GRAHAM SUMNER, Ward believed that the state when guided by SCIENCE could be a powerful means for improving society. He called for "sociocracy," which would give the state a major role in national economic and social planning. The progressive legislation in many states between 1900 and 1920 as well as the New Deal legislation of the 1930s can be traced to his ideas. Ward argued that people through their mental powers could be the subject or creator and not the object of social processes. Acting together, individuals could create citizen communities, identify problems, gather data, and apply cooperative planning to solve social and economic problems. Confronting laissez-faire advocates, Ward pointed to the successful English and French government interventions in transportation and communication systems. He maintained that under an absolute monarchy laissez-faire did make sense, since strict state control severed individuals from one another. In a democracy, however, people could freely associate, unite, plan, and prosper within their own self-created state. Humans had the intellectual capacity to consciously control evolution and to progress. People were not purposeless animals forced to engage in cutthroat competition to survive life's struggles but rather were capable of planning to master nature and the environment. Uncontrolled competition only led to disaster. Modern societies needed planning and "superior systems."

With his stress on intellectual capacity to plan improvements for society, Ward emphasized the role of education, believing it to be the key to progress and the healing of social ills. It only made common sense to educate all children—male and female, rich and poor—to their fullest capacity and that society should bear its costs. As children, the republic's future citizens would learn the need for cooperative planning and scientific methods.

Ward was not a socialist, and while advocating equal opportunity, he did not require equal outcomes. He was an ethical evolutionist who believed that the state should be guided by specialists using scientific planning methods. In his view, education was the nucleus around which individual and social interests could revolve and resolve themselves in harmony.

Further reading: Richard Hofstadter, *Social Darwinism in American Thought,* rev. ed. (Boston: Beacon Press, 1955); Clifford H. Scott, *Lester Frank Ward* (Boston: Twayne, 1976).

— Harry Stein

Washington, Booker T. (1856–1915)

Booker Taliaferro Washington, educator and African-American leader, was born a slave April 5, 1856, on James

Booker T. Washington *(Library of Congress)*

Burroughs's plantation near Hale's Ford, Virginia. His mother was Jane Ferguson, Burroughs's slave cook, but Washington never knew the identity of his white father, who he believed came from a neighboring plantation. After their emancipation in 1865, Washington, his mother, stepfather Washington Ferguson, half brother John, and half sister Amanda moved to Malden, West Virginia. After working hard in a coal mine, Booker became a houseboy for the wife of the mine owner, Viola Ruffner, who tutored the ambitious boy.

Washington was able as well as ambitious. He attended and excelled at Hampton Institute in Virginia from 1872 to 1875. The institute's founder, General Samuel Armstrong, instilled in the impressionable Washington a work ethic and a belief in an educational program for AFRICAN AMERICANS that combined utilitarian skills like agriculture and carpentry with character building. Washington returned to Malden and taught for three years, then studied theology for a few months before deciding that the ministry was not for him. In 1879 he was called back to Hampton Institute by Armstrong to run its night school.

Two years later in 1881 Armstrong strongly recommended Washington to Alabama commissioners of education who were looking for a white principal for an African-American normal school to be established at Tuskegee. They appointed Washington, but he discovered that he had to start a school with only $2,000 and no land or buildings. Working enormously hard and using great tact, Washington secured support from local whites, recruited students, and held Tuskegee's first classes in a shanty. From that rude beginning he built a school that at the time of his death in 1915 boasted a campus of 100 buildings on 2,000 acres, an all-black faculty of almost 200 (including the distinguished botanist GEORGE WASHINGTON CARVER), and 1,500 students. Washington was able to develop Tuskegee Institute into a major industrial education school in large part because he skillfully attracted the financial support of America's leading industrialists and philanthropists, such as ANDREW CARNEGIE, John D. Rockefeller, and GEORGE EASTMAN. Tuskegee, however, was not strictly a vocational school; students also studied composition, history, and mathematics and attended daily chapel services aimed at character building.

Washington married Fanny Norton Smith, a graduate of Hampton Institute, in 1882, but she died two years later from injuries suffered in a fall from a wagon. In 1885 he married Olivia A. Davidson, a graduate of Hampton and the Framingham State Normal School in Massachusetts, who died in 1889. His third wife, whom he married in 1893, was Margaret J. Murray, a Fisk University graduate and a leader of the National Association of Colored Women's Clubs and of the Southern Federation of Colored Women's Clubs.

It was Washington's prominence as an educator that led to his rise as a race leader. The death of Frederick Douglass in February 1895 left a void in national black leadership, and Washington was chosen to speak at the Atlanta Cotton Exposition in late 1895. As he noted in his autobiography, *Up from Slavery* (1901), Washington knew that his words would be carefully monitored for their impact on race relations. His bold call upon whites and blacks to coexist is referred to as the Atlanta compromise. "In all things that are purely social we can be as separate as the fingers, yet one as the hand in all things essential to mutual progress" were the words that cemented his relationship with conservative white America. Washington thought that rather than agitate for civil and political rights, African Americans must first gain the respect of whites by becoming educated, working hard, practicing thrift, acquiring land, and establishing businesses. In 1900 Washington established the National Negro Business League to assist blacks in becoming more economically independent.

Washington's reputation as a successful educator and racial healer earned him the respect and admiration of white Americans, who regarded him as the spokesman of black Americans. Andrew Carnegie extravagantly praised him as "the combined Moses and Joshua of his people." But Washington was also a power broker who instilled both fear and envy in his black critics. President Theodore Roosevelt cleared his appointments of blacks with Washington, and philanthropists counseled with him before giving donations to black institutions of learning. Washington's secret control or influence over newspapers such as the New York *Age* and the Washington *Bee* helped him in his attempts to silence critics. Additionally, his network of spies and informers kept him apprised of what his critics were up to and placed them at a severe disadvantage.

Progressive African Americans and their supporters severely criticized Washington's "accommodationist" approach, his power, and his tactics. In 1903 W. E. B. Du Bois wrote "Of Mr. Booker T. Washington and Others," published in Du Bois's *The Souls of Black Folk*, which helped to galvanize opposition to Washington's leadership. In 1908 a race riot in Springfield, Illinois, also alarmed white progressives who feared the spread of racism in the North. Mary White Ovington and Oswald Garrison Villard, liberal supporters of Du Bois, helped organize the National Association for the Advancement of Colored People (NAACP) because they believed that Washington's accommodationism had resulted in JIM CROW LAWS and disfranchisement and had not resulted in racial harmony or justice.

Despite the accommodationist label, Washington worked for the civil and political rights of African Americans. He secretly provided money to finance suits that challenged discrimination against blacks in voting rights, in jury selection, and in segregated facilities. This facet of his life, however, remained unknown until years after his death. And even though Washington was greatly admired and respected by prominent whites—Harvard bestowed upon him an honorary degree and President Roosevelt in 1901 had him to dinner at the White House—white racists viciously attacked him for seeking social equality. An editorial in the Memphis *Scimitar* proclaimed, "The president of the United States has committed a crime against civilization, and his nigger guest has done his race a wrong which cannot soon be erased." Washington's leadership declined considerably with the election of Woodrow Wilson in 1912, since his Democratic administration ignored African Americans who were staunch Republicans.

Washington, nevertheless, remained a hero among moderates. The *New York Times* noted when he died on November 14, 1915, that "It is doubtful if any American, within the forty years of his active life has rendered to the nation service of greater or more lasting value than his." The *Times* acknowledged that all blacks did not consider Washington to be their leader, but—speaking for most whites—it considered Washington's approach the best for race relations.

Further reading: Louis R. Harlan, *Booker T. Washington*, 2 vols. (Urbana: University of Illinois Press, 1972–83); August Meier, *Negro Thought in America, 1880–1915: Racial Ideologies in the Age of Booker T. Washington* (Ann Arbor: University of Michigan Press, 1963).

— William Seraile

Washington, Treaty of (1871)

The Treaty of Washington arbitrated several contentious issues that had soured relations between Britain, Canada, and the United States in the mid-19th century. First, there was a dispute over the boundary between the United States and Canada on the West Coast. The Oregon Treaty of 1846 had set the boundary at the middle of the channel separating Vancouver Island from the mainland, but since there was no well-defined channel, sovereignty over the mid-channel San Juan Islands was left in question. There was also the fisheries problem, since Americans had been fishing in Canadian coastal waters for many years, much to that dominion's annoyance. A recent irritant to Anglo-American relations was the American failure to prevent the raids in 1866 and 1870 on Canada perpetrated by Irish-American Fenians in the hopes of instigating an Anglo-American war that would free Ireland from British rule.

The foremost issue, however, was the *Alabama* claims. The question of the recompense for damage done to American shipping during the Civil War by British-built cruisers (the *Alabama* and her sister ships) had poisoned Anglo-American relations since that war's conclusion. Britain had repeatedly rebuffed American demands that it express regrets for its actions and make payment to the United States for shipping losses and the costly pursuit of the commerce raiders. Charles Sumner, chair of the Senate Foreign Relations Committee, said the British owed the Americans not only $15 million in direct damages but also an additional $2 billion for prolonging the war two years by its support of the Confederacy. It was obvious that Sumner and like-minded expansionists would accept Canada in lieu of cash.

For years the situation defied settlement, but President Ulysses S. Grant soured on Sumner and gave his moderate Secretary of State Hamilton Fish a free hand. Meanwhile, Britain, fearing that neutrals might build cruisers bent on destroying British commerce in a future conflict, was having second thoughts about its dubious neutrality during the Civil War. On May 8, 1871, Britain, with Canada represented among its negotiators, and the United States signed the Treaty of Washington, which stipulated that the *Alabama* claims would be settled by an international arbitration panel that would meet in Geneva. The British expressed regret for the damage done by British-built warships and agreed to rules defining neutral behavior. Both sides agreed to reciprocal fishing rights in American and Canadian territorial waters, with the price of the Canadian rights, which were of greater value, to be determined by a joint commission. It was also agreed that the emperor of Germany, Wilhelm I, would arbitrate the settlement of the San Juan boundary dispute. The treaty passed the Senate on May 24, 1871, by a vote of 50 to 12.

At the commencement of the arbitration panel in Geneva in December 1871, the United States renewed the Sumner claim for indirect damages, inspired some months of war talk, and jeopardized the treaty until cooler heads prevailed and the Americans retreated. On June 19, 1872, the tribunal's president Count Federico Sclopis of Italy announced that the indirect claims were outside the avowed purview of the panel. Getting down to business, on September 14, 1872, the arbitration panel ordered Great Britain to pay the United States $15.5 million. Later in 1872 the German emperor awarded the San Juan Islands to the United States; in 1873 a commission on the outstanding claims of both the United States and Britain awarded almost $2 million to the latter; and in 1875 the fisheries commission awarded the British $5.5 million. Although Canadians, Britons, and Americans all grumbled, all were winners in the most successful arbitration treaty the world had yet witnessed.

Further reading: Adrian Cook, *The Alabama Claims: American Politics and Anglo-American Relations, 1896–1872* (Ithaca, N.Y.: Cornell University Press, 1975); Allan Nevins, *Hamilton Fish: The Inner History of the Grant Administration* (New York: Dodd, Mead & Co., 1936).

— Timothy E. Vislocky

Weather Bureau, U.S.

From time immemorial the weather has been a universal subject of observation and discussion. As head of the Smithsonian Institution, Joseph Henry made meteorology a major concern. In 1849 he received the first weather observations sent by telegraph in the United States. Henry went on to organize a network of voluntary observers that by 1860 was reporting from 500 stations throughout the nation, but the Civil War seriously handicapped the program. The South was cut off; army observers were withdrawn from the West; and telegraph lines were jammed with war business. After the war, Increase Lapham of Milwaukee, a respected amateur naturalist who had long been a volunteer observer for the Smithsonian, campaigned for a federal storm-warning system and enlisted Wisconsin representative H. E. Paine in the campaign. Paine introduced a bill that won strong support from shippers and other business interests. Colonel Albert J. Myer, chief of the Army Signal Service, persuaded Paine to designate his neglected command as the operating agency, citing its telegraphic network as a major qualification, and CONGRESS adopted Paine's bill on that basis in February 1870.

Joseph Henry cheerfully ceded his volunteer network to Myer, whereupon most of the volunteers dropped out. Myer then turned to civilian meteorologists, notably Lapham and a young astronomer, Cleveland Abbe. Over the next decade the number of stations and the frequency of observations increased substantially under Myer's charge. Forecasts were supplied regularly by telegraph to railroad and weather stations and to the Associated Press. Special warnings of storms and other unusual weather developments were issued to commercial, maritime, and agricultural interests. Myer, now a general, emphasized service over research, to Abbe's private chagrin. Myer, however, showed diplomatic skill in minimizing friction between civilian and military personnel and soothing those who, like Abbe, pined for more research to improve forecasting. As always in meteorology, the inevitable mistaken forecasts brought public complaints, but the overall usefulness of the bureau was generally recognized.

Myer's successor in 1880, General William B. Hazen, proved to be more research-minded, to Abbe's relief. But those who were otherwise-minded resented Hazen, who was also too strict a disciplinarian to suit some. Hazen's tenure was marked by a struggle over the proper degree of Weather Bureau autonomy under the army, and opposition to the cost of the service arose in Congress. Sentiment grew for the transfer of the Weather Bureau to civilian control, and after Hazen's death in 1887, his military successor came around to that idea. The creation of a Department of Agriculture in 1888 offered an administrative home for the bureau, and agricultural interests supported the move. And so it was officially made law as of July 1, 1891.

The bureau's work went on smoothly through the transition to civilian control. The sergeant observers on station were honorably discharged and kept on as civilian employees. Mark Harrington, the new chief, had solid scientific credentials. The bureau was now fully accepted as good for business and industry, but its course was not uniformly smooth. The depression of the 1890s constrained congressional liberality, and the shift from Republican to Democratic political control in 1893 was reflected in bureau appointments. Harrington feuded with the secretary of agriculture and was removed in 1895. But the bureau weathered these setbacks and began the new century with growing effectiveness and public support.

Further reading: Donald R. Whitnah, *A History of the United States Weather Bureau* (Urbana: University of Illinois Press, 1965).

— Robert V. Bruce

Weaver, James B. See currency issue

Wells-Barnett, Ida Bell (1862–1931)

Born into slavery in 1862 in Holly Springs, Mississippi, Ida B. Wells-Barnett became a journalist, lecturer, and social activist who fought for African-American civil rights and WOMEN'S RIGHTS. She became one of the most widely known journalists of the late 19th and early 20th centuries and received more press attention than any AFRICAN AMERICAN except Frederick Douglass.

Encouraged by her father, she attended Rust College (formerly Shaw University, a Freedman's Aid school) during her teen years. At age 16, after yellow fever had killed her parents and baby brother, she took on the care of the five living siblings in the house her father had purchased after the Civil War. She taught primary school and continued to attend Rust between sessions until her dismissal in 1880–81 for what she was later to describe as her "tempestuous, rebellious, hard headed wilfulness." Her determination and fiery spirit were to characterize her life and her tireless work for justice.

Moving to Memphis in 1881, she continued teaching conscientiously but without enthusiasm, despite the social status it afforded. A voracious reader, she was beginning to formulate a political sensibility that was to inform her later work. By the end of 1884 she had won two settlements against railroads for failing to honor first-class tickets. Reported initially only in the African-American press, the case was picked up later by white newspapers as well. Legal battles with railroads continued through 1887, although state courts were less supportive than federal courts of the rights of African Americans. The railroads' smear campaign against Wells was not the only time such a tactic would be employed against her.

The legal cases led Wells into journalism. She contributed articles to the *Freeman,* edited by T. Thomas Fortune, and to church publications, including the *American Baptist,* edited by William J. Simmons, who gave Wells her first contract and adequate compensation. She also wrote letters to white-owned publications. In 1888 Wells bought a one-third interest in the Memphis *Free Speech and Headlight,* managed by the Reverend Taylor Nightingale and J. L. Fleming, and eventually became its editor. By 1889 Wells, whose pen name was Iola, was being called the "Princess of the Press."

In 1892 atrocities in Memphis focused Wells's career on the elimination of LYNCHING. Three African-American men, owners of a grocery store that competed with a white-owned store, had been arrested on trumped-up charges and held in a jail from which they were seized at 3:00 A.M. by a group of men who brutally killed them. Wells's fierce editorials set Memphis in turmoil. The threat of physical violence against Fleming (published in white-owned newspapers) and the destruction of the *Free Speech* office convinced Wells to relocate in New York, where she wrote for Fortune's *New York Age.* Wells was the first to make a connection between the development of successful African-American businesses and the rise of lynching as a form of race terrorism. She countered claims that the rape of white women led to lynching and that lynching was a deterrent, even suggesting that white women entered into consensual sexual relations with black men.

Ida B. Wells-Barnett *(Library of Congress)*

By 1893 Wells had begun a series of antilynching lectures in New York, Philadelphia, and Boston. She then traveled to England, where she was extremely well received. When she returned she started the Women's Era Club (1893), the first civic organization for African-American women. She later founded other women's clubs as well. At the 1893 WORLD'S COLUMBIAN EXPOSITION in Chicago she promoted an antilyching pamphlet she wrote with Frederick Douglass and Ferdinand Barnett of Chicago, who was a prominent African-American attorney and activist. In

1895 she married Barnett; thereafter, she used Wells-Barnett as her surname; edited his paper, the Chicago *Conservator,* and bore four children.

Wells-Barnett joined W. E. B. Du Bois in decrying BOOKER T. WASHINGTON's conservativism and his emphasis on industrial education over higher EDUCATION. In 1910 Barnett founded the Negro Fellowship League to provide lodging, recreation, a reading room, and employment for African-American southern migrants to Chicago. In 1913 she founded the Alpha Suffrage Club, which was the first suffrage organization for African-American women. In the same year, she forced the integration of the American suffrage movement when she refused to march at the back of the National American Woman Suffrage Association's (NAWSA) march in Washington. After the 1918 race riots in East St. Louis, Missouri, Wells-Barnett went there to find legal aid for African-American victims of the mob violence. In 1919 she warned in the *Chicago Tribune* that similar violence could take place in Chicago. Only a few weeks later almost 40 people were killed in a race riot in Chicago.

Wells-Barnett worked with Jane Addams to prevent the city of Chicago from establishing segregated schools. In 1930 she ran as an unsuccessful independent candidate for Illinois state senator. On March 25, 1931 she died of uremia at the age of 69. She maintained a commitment to racial justice throughout her life as a teacher, journalist, and activist. She was one of the foremost civil rights and women's rights leaders in American history.

Further reading: Alfreda M., Duster, ed., *Crusade for Justice: The Autobiography of Ida B. Wells* (Chicago: University of Chicago Press, 1970); Linda O. McMurry, *To Keep the Waters Troubled: The Life of Ida B. Wells* (New York: Oxford University Press, 1998).

— Orlanda Brugnola

Whistler, James Abbott McNeill (1834–1903)

Best known as a painter, James Abbott McNeill Whistler was also a printmaker, an interior designer, and a brilliant publicist. Most of all, he was a tireless promoter for aestheticism.

The son of a railroad engineer, Whistler was born on July 11, 1834, in Lowell, Massachusetts, but raised partly in Russia and England. Whistler entered the United States Military Academy at West Point, where Robert F. Weir, a distinguished painter, taught him art. Whistler went to Paris in 1856, studying in the Academie Gleyre and becoming friends with many in the French avant-garde. Establishing himself by 1863 in the Chelsea section of London, where he lived until 1892, Whistler became associated with the Pre-Raphaelites, a group of painters and writers. Whistler attracted attention for his bohemian lifestyle and his prickly personality. In 1877 John Ruskin, the influential art critic, described an exhibition of Whistler's paintings as "flinging a pot of paint in the public's face," and Whistler sued him for libel. Whistler won the lawsuit but was awarded only a farthing in damages. Simultaneously, the White House, his London residence designed in collaboration with architect E. W. Godwin, generated controversy with municipal officials, who demanded changes to the severe facade. Construction overruns coupled with the legal expenses for the lawsuit resulted in bankruptcy, and Whistler was forced to sell the house. The artist nonetheless continued to devote a great deal of energy to arranging his own houses, studios, and exhibition spaces, devising unorthodox tone-on-tone color schemes for them. In 1888 he married Beatrice Godwin, widow of the architect, and lived happily with her until her death in 1896. Whistler's youthful milieu became the basis for George du Maurier's *Trilby,* a best-selling novel in the 1890s. Whistler died in London on July 17, 1903, after a long period of ill health that curtailed his work. His wit and his thoughts on art remain accessible through his writings, especially *The Gentle Art of Making Enemies* (1890).

Whistler's art revolved around his interest in refined draftsmanship and elegant color harmonies. Carefully calculated balances of color and form, Whistler's works were entitled "arrangements," "symphonies," or "nocturnes" by the artist to mark their affinity with musical compositions. Whistler's best-known painting is also one that clearly illustrates his theories. *Arrangement in Gray and Black: Portrait of the Artist's Mother* (1871, Musée du Louvre, Paris) depicts an elderly Anna Whistler seen in profile; the composition denies narrative and is rather an exercise in tones of grays and blacks. In Frederick R. Leyland's dining room, where blue and white porcelain was displayed against 17th-century Spanish leather, Whistler painted gold peacocks upon a blue ground, upstaging all the other elements. Completed in 1877 and now known as the Peacock Room, it is preserved in the Freer Gallery in Washington, D.C. Whistler was an important figure in the late 19th-century revival of etching. He developed both outline and subtle cross-hatching techniques, drawing equally upon Japanese prints and 17th-century Dutch engravings. All Whistler's art is marked by a simplicity forged from relentless perfectionism.

Further reading: Deanna Marohn Bendix, *Diabolical Designs: Paintings, Interiors, and Exhibitions of James McNeill Whistler* (Washington, D.C.: Smithsonian Institution Press, 1995); Richard Dorment and Margaret F. MacDonald, *James McNeill Whistler* (Washington, D.C.: National Gallery of Art; London: Tate Gallery, 1994).

— Karen Zukowski

Arrangement in Gray and Black: Portrait of the Artist's Mother (1871, Musée du Louvre, Paris), painting by James McNeill Whistler *(Library of Congress)*

White, Stanford (1853–1906)

Stanford White was perhaps the most imaginative design force behind the American Renaissance in the late 19th century. The son of Richard Grant White, music and drama critic, Stanford White was born in New York City on November 9, 1853, and raised among New York's cultured intelligentsia. At age 16, his talents as a draftsman were recognized, and he joined H. H. RICHARDSON, helping to oversee the construction of Trinity Church in Boston. Trips to sketch colonial buildings in New England and medieval buildings in the south of France furthered his training. In 1879 White joined Charles Follen McKim and William R. Mead in their New York City architectural office. With his marriage in 1884 to Elizabeth (Bessie) Smith, White cemented his ties to aristocratic New York. The partnership of McKim, Mead & White endured until White's death, and the firm was responsible for many of the country's most prominent public buildings, including Pennsylvania Station and the Boston Public Library. Among the architects trained in the firm were John M. Carrere, Henry Bacon, and Cass Gilbert.

While McKim, Mead & White is best known for its monumental Beaux Arts buildings, the firm worked in many styles, and White was the most protean and prolific designer of the partnership. Although the three interacted on many projects, some of the firm's work can be largely attributed to White. The shingled facades of the Newport Casino in Newport, Rhode Island (1881), a commercial and entertainment complex surrounding a tennis court, were a creative modernization of colonial forms. The Villard Houses in New York City (1885) were five connected stone palazzi with sumptuous interiors reflecting Florentine models. The Gould Library and other academic buildings for New York University's Bronx, New York, campus (1895–1901) referenced a long tradition of great public rotundas, from the Pantheon to Jefferson's library at the University of Virginia. In many of his buildings, White designed, commissioned, or purchased architectural fittings, furniture, rugs, sculpture, and even silverware. He also produced a staggering variety of independent designs, including sculptural settings, yacht cabins, picture frames, jewelry, trophies, and book covers.

White's life was marked by a boundless appetite for work and play. Tall and rotund, with a large mustache and red hair, his associates thought he radiated energy. He was at the center of New York's cultural elite, and he numbered among his closest friends the sculptor AUGUSTUS SAINT-GAUDENS, the editor Richard Watson Gilder, and the painter Thomas Wilmer Dewing. An insatiable collector, frequently going into debt to buy art, he could often be found in New York's most prestigious private clubs (many of which he designed) or at the THEATER. White's death at the roof theater of Madison Square Garden on June 25, 1906, also made him notorious. He was murdered by Harry Thaw, the husband of Evelyn Nesbit, a former chorus girl, artists' model, and lover of White. Thaw's trials and appeals escalated into an indictment of the private lives of New York's artists and permanently scarred White's reputation. The story has been retold often, notably in the film *Girl in the Red Velvet Swing* (1958) and the novel *Ragtime* (1975) by E. L. Doctorow.

Further reading: David Garrard Lowe, *Stanford White's New York* (New York: Doubleday, 1992); Leland M. Roth, *McKim, Mead & White, Architects* (New York: Harper & Row, 1983); Lawrence Wodehouse, *White of McKim, Mead and White* (New York: Garland, 1988).

— Karen Zukowski

Wilder, Laura Ingalls (1867–1957)

Born Laura Elizabeth Ingalls on February 7, 1867, in Pepin, Wisconsin, the children's book author was the second of four daughters of farmers Charles Philip Ingalls and Caroline Lake Quiner. The future Mrs. Wilder grew up at the edge of the "Big Woods" that she was to make famous. Her pioneer family moved often by covered wagon from the log cabin her father had built in Wisconsin to Missouri, Kansas, back to Wisconsin, to Minnesota, to Iowa, back to Minnesota, and finally in 1879 to their permanent home in De Smet, Dakota Territory (now South Dakota). She studied in traditional one-room schoolhouses as the family moved, leaving school at the age of 15 to become a teacher. She married Almanzo Wilder in 1885 and they had a son, who died in infancy, and a daughter.

After a brief time in an unsettled region in Florida, the young family moved to the Ozarks where, in Mansfield, Missouri, the author spent the rest of her life. From 1911 to 1924 she served as home editor of the Missouri *Ruralist* and contributed occasional articles to local and national periodicals. From 1919 to 1927 she was secretary-treasurer of the Mansfield Farm Loan Association. It was not until her early 60s—when her daughter Rose Wilder Lane, a journalist and novelist, persuaded her to set down her recollections of a childhood on the frontier—that Laura Wilder began work on those autobiographical novels that came to be known as the Little House series. These nine books vividly recall an earlier, simpler life and have taken their place among the most popular children's books in American literature, reportedly selling more than 35 million copies by 1994 and winning numerous prizes.

Beginning with *Little House in the Big Woods* (1932), the Little House books recount the daily events of a warm, close family and their passage from the raw life of the frontier to the beginnings of an established community. Using the names of her real family but told in the third person, the series captures their individual personalities and details of their lives on the frontier. *Little House on the Prairie,* written three years after *Big Woods,* takes the Ingallses to a new home on Indian lands in Kansas, where they lived until the government ordered them to move on. Other books in the saga chronicle the bitter winter of 1880–81 in De Smet, the childhood of her husband Almanzo Wilder, and the Wilders' first years of life together. Neither grimly realistic nor sentimental, the series has become a perennial American classic, presenting a richly textured account of the growth of both the heroine and the society in which she lived during the 1870s and 1880s. In simple, direct prose, it reveals both the hardships and the rewards of American pioneer life and the resourceful and courageous spirit that supported it.

Further reading: Fred Erisman, *Laura Ingalls Wilder* (Boise, Idaho: Boise State University Press, 1994).

— Dennis Wepman

Wild West shows See entertainment, popular

Willard, Frances (1839–1898)

Although primarily a temperance advocate, Frances Elizabeth Caroline Willard embraced a variety of social reforms. Born in Churchville, New York, on September 18, 1839, Willard grew up on a remote but prosperous Wisconsin farm, where she was tutored by her mother. Willard had little formal education prior to attending Milwaukee Female College for a term in 1857 and then (her parents having moved to Evanston, Illinois) the North Western Female College, from which in 1859 she received her Laureate of Science degree. Willard then taught at a variety of schools, most of which were affiliated with the Methodist Church in Illinois, Pennsylvania, and New York. She had in 1861 agreed to marry Charles Henry Fowler, a Chicago Methodist minister, but the engagement was broken after several months, possibly because he wished to dominate an indomitable woman. Willard, who never married, developed close relationships with other women. In 1868, after nursing her father, who eventually died of tuberculosis, Willard and Kate Jackson, whom she had met while teaching (1866–67) at Genesee Wesleyan Seminary in Lima, New York, embarked on a two-year grand tour financed by Jackson's father. They visited Egypt, the Holy Land, Turkey, Russia, and western Europe, and Willard attended lectures and studied languages in Rome, Paris, and Berlin. Returning to Evanston, Willard in 1871 was named president of the new Evanston College for Ladies, which was affiliated with both the Methodist Church and Northwestern University. This ideal situation, however, became intolerable when, by a twist of fate, Charles Fowler became president of Northwestern in 1872, asserted his authority, and harassed Willard in petty ways until she resigned in June 1874.

Willard immediately found a new career. In late 1873 and early 1874 praying groups of women, especially in the Midwest, shut down an estimated 3,000 saloons. Shortly after Willard had resigned, a group of women in Chicago organized a temperance society and asked Willard—a well-known educator—to be their leader. A few months later she became secretary of the state organization, and in November 1874 she was in Cleveland for the organization of the Women's Christian Temperance Union (WCTU) and became its corresponding secretary.

Willard was also a feminist and backed a wide range of social reforms, but the conservative leadership of the WCTU eschewed politics. Using her contacts as secretary and her talents as an orator, Willard fought to secure WCTU backing for woman suffrage and to persuade the leadership to plunge into politics and enable mothers and daughters to shut the "rum-shop beside their homes." By 1879 Willard, aided by her secretary and lifelong close friend Anna A. Gordon, had enough followers to be elected president of the WCTU—a position she retained until her death in 1898—and broaden its reform program. She soon reorganized the WCTU by creating departments (39 by 1889) to promote specific reform. For example, in 1880 the WCTU endorsed woman suffrage and in 1882 it created the Department of the Franchise. Other departments reflecting WCTU concerns included Scientific Temperance Instruction and Peace and Arbitration. The WCTU backed the KINDERGARTEN movement, the eight-hour workday, and prison reform, and addressed problems like prostitution, promoted health and hygiene, and advised young mothers. The WCTU entered politics to press for specific reforms on the state level and also, beginning in 1882, to support the PROHIBITION PARTY.

Frances Willard *(Library of Congress)*

By the 1890s Willard, convinced that poverty was the main cause of intemperance, wished to restructure society. She praised the KNIGHTS OF LABOR in 1886, was influenced by EDWARD BELLAMY's utopian socialist novel *Looking Backward* (1888), began to contribute to the Christian Socialist journal *Dawn* in 1889, and sympathized with the goals of western Populists (see PEOPLE'S PARTY). She consulted with the Populists hoping they would adopt prohibition and woman suffrage and that the various reform elements she favored would unite in 1892 under one banner. To her great disappointment, the Prohibitionists balked and her plans did not materialize. Divisions over FREE SILVER ruined her subsequent attempt in 1895 to unite reformers.

Under Willard's leadership the WCTU had sent temperance missionaries abroad to establish similar organizations, and as a result the World's WCTU organized in 1891 in Boston with Willard as its president. After her failure to unite reformers in 1892, Willard spent most of the remaining six years of her life in England with Isabel Somerset, head of the British Women's Temperance Association, whom she had met in Boston. While in England Willard, not surprisingly, joined the Fabian Society and then preached its version of SOCIALISM at annual conventions of the WCTU, but, surprisingly, Somerset convinced Willard that education would be more effective than prohibition in achieving temperance. Willard's absence and her continuing embrace of social issues caused unease in the WCTU, but she staved off a revolt in 1897. She was, however, in poor health and died in New York City on February 17, 1898. Although the WCTU gradually abandoned the social reforms Willard championed and concentrated on prohibition, under her leadership needed reforms were publicized and some achieved on the state level, and thousands of women were encouraged to demand political equality.

Further reading: Ruth Bordin, *Frances Willard: A Biography* (Chapel Hill: University of North Carolina Press, 1986); Mary Earhart Dillon, *Frances Willard: From Prayers to Politics* (Chicago: University of Chicago Press, 1944).

Wizard of Oz

See currency issue

Women's Christian Temperance Union (WCTU)

See Willard, Frances

women's colleges

HIGHER EDUCATION for women in the late 19th century was strongly influenced by the notion of female intellectual inferiority and the conviction that a woman's place was in the home. Curricula for women mixed watered-down academic subjects with studies that would prepare women for domestic life. Oberlin College, the first coeducational as well as multiracial college, admitted women in 1833 but for a "ladies course" that led to a special degree. The Morrill Land Grant Act of 1862 increased the virtually nonexistent opportunities for women to gain a college education. By 1870 eight state universities, mostly in the West and Midwest, admitted women, and a dozen or so other colleges were coeducational. In 1900 there were approximately 100 coeducational colleges in the country, and most of the women in college were enrolled in these institutions. Prominent women's rights advocates in 1870 promoted coeducation on egalitarian grounds and, in the case of Elizabeth Cady Stanton, in hopes they would lead to "more congenial marriages." Most coeducational colleges, however, were not as rigorous academically as the older established male colleges or the newly established women's colleges. And although coeducation was egalitarian in theory, it was not in practice. Women often got in through the "side door" and were shunted into elementary education or home economics programs.

Women's colleges, on the other hand—addressing the aspirations and needs of women—were founded or matured in the late 19th century. The "Seven Sisters"—including Mount Holyoke (1836, accredited 1888), Vassar (1861), Wellesley (1870), Smith (1871), Radcliffe (1879), Bryn Mawr (1880), and Barnard (1890)—were soon recognized as superior institutions for the education of women. With Vassar leading the way, they proved that women had the intellectual capacity and the physical strength to tackle rigorous academic subjects—including mathematics and the SCIENCES—without suffering either mental or physical breakdowns or sacrificing their femininity. Their curricula included academic subjects similar to those taught at the best male colleges, physical education to keep up their strength, and ART, MUSIC, and some domestic science, although M. CAREY THOMAS of Bryn Mawr—stressing intellect over femininity—offered no home economics and regarded the care of children as a "most utterly unintellectual task." Living in dormitories and eating and studying together forged strong ties of sisterhood.

In 1870 only 1 percent of college-age Americans were in college, but one-fifth of that small number were women. By 1900 4 percent of those aged 18–21 were in college, and roughly one-third were women. Only about half of all who attended college earned a degree, women were more apt to drop out than men, and in 1900 they comprised only one-fifth of those getting degrees. College graduates did, of course, predominate among those women entering the professions, and they were the driving force in the WOMEN'S RIGHTS movement.

Further reading: Roberta Frankfort, *Collegiate Women: Domesticity and Career in Turn of the Century America* (New York: New York University Press, 1977); Mabel Newcomer, *A Century of Higher Education for Women* (New York: Harper & Row Press, 1959).

women's rights

By 1870 the women's rights movement had been underway for more than 20 years but had made little progress beyond defining its objectives. Its adherents demanded the vote, full participation in the political process, and women's equality in marriage, including property rights and custody rights. Unless specifically stated in a marriage contract, a woman who married lost her property and much of her legal identity to her spouse, who, as head of the household, was regarded as her protector. Well into the 20th century, an American family traveling abroad would have one passport issued to the husband, and as late as 1922 a woman born in Brooklyn, New York, who married a Dutch immigrant became a subject of the queen of Holland and had to be naturalized to regain her American citizenship. In addition, feminists wanted equal access to education and to the ministerial, medical, and legal professions. There were a few differences in the demands of women. Some more radical feminists like Elizabeth Cady Stanton favored women's equal rights to divorce, while others like ANTOINETTE BROWN BLACKWELL, who was a minister, were loathe to condone divorce and preferred legal separations.

Although women's rights advocates had few differences over objectives, they split in 1869 over tactics and strategy. They had been in the forefront of the struggle against slavery and rejoiced in the passage of the Thirteenth Amendment to the Constitution freeing slaves. But all were dismayed and many were outraged when Radical Republicans ignored voting rights for women in the Fourteenth Amendment and especially in the Fifteenth Amendment (passed CONGRESS in 1869 and adopted in 1870), which extended voting rights to black men. In 1868, to press for the inclusion of women in the Fifteenth Amendment, Stanton and SUSAN B. ANTHONY published a weekly called *The Revolution* (1868–70). When in 1869 the word *sex* was not included in the Fifteenth Amendment, Stanton, Anthony, and their allies established in New York the National Woman Suffrage Association (NWSA); opposed ratification of the Fifteenth Amendment, stressing that white women were far more qualified to vote than recently emancipated black men; and demanded a constitutional amendment that would enfranchise women. The NWSA leadership was radical in thought and tactics. Stanton, its president, not only advocated free divorce but befriended the notorious VICTORIA WOODHULL and would not abandon her even after she publicly endorsed free love. Failing to get immediate redress in a new amendment, the NWSA adopted the aggressive tactic of attempting to vote, since the Fourteenth Amendment did forbid states from denying anyone their rights as citizens. Anthony in 1872 actually convinced election officials in Rochester, New York, to allow her to register, but she was arrested, tried, found guilty, and fined $100 (which she never paid) when she voted. In 1875 the SUPREME COURT rejected the NWSA's broad interpretation of the Fourteenth Amendment in *Minor v. Happersett,* ruling that while women were citizens, voting was a privilege, not a right, protected by the DUE PROCESS CLAUSE.

More numerous and less radical suffragists led by LUCY STONE and Blackwell, fearful of imperiling the adoption of the Fifteenth Amendment and losing their abolitionist allies, also in 1869 established the Boston-based American Woman Suffrage Association (AWSA). The AWSA was more conservative on matters of divorce and abhorred Woodhull and free love and included men as members and in responsible positions, but both organizations concentrated on acquiring the vote. The AWSA's main strategy—which made sense after *Minor v. Happersett*—was to organize and secure advances on the state and local levels. Ultimately, local and state campaigns began to pay off as women were allowed to participate first in school board elections and, before 1900, were fully enfranchised in four western states. In part, this success resulted from the support of FRANCES WILLARD, a member of the AWSA, and her huge Women's Christian Temperance Union (WCTU), whose 200,000 members demanded the vote so women could protect the home by destroying the liquor traffic.

In 1890 the NWSA and the AWSA joined and formed the National American Woman Suffrage Association (NAWSA) with Stanton as president and Anthony as vice president. The new organization, however—with its largely middle-class, God-fearing membership and its concentration on state campaigns—was more like Stone's AWSA than Stanton's NWSA. In protest, OLYMPIA BROWN founded the Federal Suffrage Association, but it had little influence. The NAWSA avoided any appearance of radicalism. Indeed, when Stanton, after stepping down as president in 1892, helped produce the *Woman's Bible* (1895) in which the scriptures were shorn of their male chauvinism, the NAWSA repudiated the work. By 1900 the NAWSA had begun to taste success, since male voters after campaigns in Colorado (1893) and Idaho (1896) extended the vote to women and joined Wyoming and Utah, which as territories in 1869 and 1870, respectively, had given women the vote without any pressure from suffrage organizations.

Women's rights advocated in the Gilded Age concentrated on the vote but also fought for equality in education, the law, the workplace, and the professions with limited success. Anthony did help secure in 1860 a New York law giving women equal property rights and began a trend among states to give wives sole control of their property and earnings. Similarly, the father's common-law right of custody theoretically remained in force in 1900 in the absence of specific state legislation, which was by no means universal. Marriage laws were not uniform, and in many states adultery remained the sole grounds for a divorce.

Women in the late 19th century did have more opportunities in HIGHER EDUCATION with the increase of coeducational institutions (especially state universities) and of WOMEN'S COLLEGES with rigorous curricula. More teaching positions on the primary and secondary levels and secretarial jobs in business opened up for women, but invariably they received less pay for equal work. And women had to surmount enormous obstacles to secure graduate training in the arts and SCIENCES or to gain admission into divinity, medical, or law schools and enter the professions. ELLEN RICHARDS never rose above the rank of instructor at Massachusetts Institute of Technology (it would not allow her to be a candidate for Ph.D.), although she made distinguished contributions in the field of sanitary chemistry and pioneered the discipline of home economics.

ELIZABETH BLACKWELL, who in 1849 became the first woman doctor in the United States, established in 1868 the Women's Medical College in New York City, which in 1898 merged with Cornell University Medical College and began to admit women. Women aspiring to be physicians could also attend the Female Medical College of Pennsylvania (established in 1850) and the New England Female Medical College (established 1856), but the number of women physicians remained extremely low in the late 19th century. Elizabeth Blackwell's sister-in-law Antoinette Brown Blackwell became the first American woman minister, and Olympia Brown in 1863 was the first to be ordained with full denominational approval, but entering the ministry remained difficult for women in churches whose polity was congregational and impossible in hierarchical denominations.

The legal profession was perhaps the most difficult to enter. When women, after great difficulty, secured an education in the law, they were still refused admission to the bar because of their sex. MYRA BRADWELL sued the state of Illinois when she was refused admission to the bar, and the Supreme Court in *Bradwell v. Illinois* (1873) upheld the state by drawing a distinction between a basic civil right, which could not be denied anyone, and the right to practice a profession. The concurring opinion of Justice Joseph P. Bradley cited the "law of the Creator" that "the paramount destiny and mission of woman are to fulfill the noble and benign offices of wife and mother." In that same year, however, BELVA LOCKWOOD, with the backing of President Ulysses S. Grant, was admitted to the District of Columbia bar. After the Supreme Court in 1876 refused to break tradition and denied her petition to practice before it, she lobbied Congress, and in 1879 it passed a law forcing the Court to reverse itself. Lockwood then became the first woman to be admitted to the Supreme Court bar. Years later, however, when Virginia would not let Lockwood practice in that state because of her sex, the Supreme Court in *In re Lockwood* (1893) reiterated its stand in *Bradwell* and upheld Virginia. By 1900 women in the law had not really come a long way.

Further reading: Joan Hoff, *Law, Gender, and Injustice: A Legal History of U.S. Women* (New York: New York University Press, 1991); Ailene S. Kraditor, *The Ideas of the Woman Suffrage Movement, 1890–1920* (New York: Norton, 1981); Suzanne M. Marilley, *Woman Suffrage and the Origins of Liberal Feminism in the United States, 1820–1920* (Cambridge, Mass.: Harvard University Press, 1996).

Woodhull, Victoria (1838–1927)

Victoria Claflin Woodhull—the first woman to run for the United States PRESIDENCY—was born on September 23, 1838, in Homer, Ohio. Her alcoholic father, always in straitened circumstances, moved the family frequently. At age 15, to escape the instability of her home life, Victoria married Dr. Canning Woodhull, who also turned out to be an alcoholic. After a year or two in Chicago and San Francisco, the couple returned to the Claflin family in Ohio, which by the mid-1850s was being supported by Victoria's younger sister, Tennessee Claflin, who traveled about telling fortunes and selling an elixir she concocted. Victoria joined Tennessee's traveling medicine show as a spiritual healer—a medical clairvoyant—whose touch could heal. The sisters prospered. Victoria had two children and divorced Woodhull in 1865. That same year she married James Harvey Blood who managed her finances, ghosted much of her writings, and involved her in various reform movements.

Audacious and ambitious and accompanied by Blood and assorted Claflins, the sisters came to New York in 1868 expressly to meet CORNELIUS VANDERBILT, the railroad magnate, who was interested in spiritualism. They succeeded, and Vanderbilt, whose wife died in 1868, enjoyed their company and gave them financial advice that enabled Victoria to make a killing on the Gold Exchange in 1869. With those proceeds, Woodhull established Woodhull, Claflin and Company, the first brokerage company to be headed by a woman. Woodhull, an advocate of women's rights, was more interested in politics and reform than in business, and she was influenced by Stephen Pearl Andrews, a radical reformer. In 1869 she attended a woman suffrage convention and in April 1870 announced her candidacy for president of the United States. To promote her campaign she established *Woodhull and Claflin's Weekly*, another first for a woman. Initially, it carried a fair amount of financial news, but it soon became a forum for women's suffrage and radical causes ranging from free love to socialism. The paper lasted six years and claimed as many as 20,000 subscribers.

Her success and audacity catapulted Woodhull into a position of leadership in the WOMEN'S RIGHTS movement. She was prominent at the 1870 suffrage convention and in January 1871 appeared before the House Judiciary Committee arguing for women's suffrage. She became a new symbol of WOMEN'S RIGHTS. SUSAN B. ANTHONY, Elizabeth Cady Stanton, ISABELLA BEECHER HOOKER, and others sought her out, and some like Hooker became lifelong friends. Others, however, were repelled by her spiritualism and her SOCIALISM, her divorce, and her bizarre personal life. (Canning Woodhull had surfaced and joined her extended family.) Woodhull expected RADICAL LABOR to support both woman suffrage and her presidential candidacy, so she took up Karl Marx and financed the first English translation of the *Communist Manifesto.* She and Tennessee joined and led Section 12—the women's section—of the Marxist Workingmen's Association, only to have Section 12 expelled in 1872 because the leadership feared that *Woodhull and Claflin's Weekly,* with its mix of spiritualism and socialism with a dash of free love, made socialism appear ridiculous.

Although by 1872 her support from suffrage advocates and socialists had dwindled, Woodhull persisted in her quest for the presidency. She organized the convention of the Equal Rights Party, which dutifully nominated her. Position papers written by Andrews and a biography by Theodore Tilton had already been published, and she campaigned widely, advocating women's suffrage, labor reforms, spiritualism, and free love. But Woodhull ran out of money and had to curtail her campaigning and even suspend publication of her *Weekly.*

With her campaign a failure, Woodhull defended her own views and exposed hypocritical moralism by publishing in the *Weekly* on November 2, 1872, the details of the adulterous BEECHER-TILTON SCANDAL. Although she and her sister were indicted for sending obscene material through the mails and spent election day in jail, they were acquitted. The scandal revived the *Weekly,* but then it declined and folded in 1876, the same year Woodhull divorced Blood. The following year Woodhull moved to and remained in England, renounced free love and spiritualism, wrote and lectured, achieved respectability, married a banker—John Biddulph Martin—in 1883, and survived him 30 years before she died on June 10, 1927, at Tewkesbury, England. Fascinating and multifaceted, Woodhull was part con artist and part reformer, part adventurer and part humanitarian, part notorious and part respectable.

Further reading: James Brough, *The Vixens: A Biography of Victoria and Tennessee Claflin* (New York: Simon & Schuster, 1980); Barbara Goldsmith, *Other Powers: The Age of Suffrage, Spiritualism and the Scandalous Victoria Woodhull* (New York: Knopf, 1998); Lois Beachy Underhill, *The Woman Who Ran for President: The Many Lives of Victoria Woodhull.* (New York: Penguin Books, 1996).

— W. Frederick Wooden

World's Columbian Exposition (1893)

The Columbian Exposition was scheduled for 1892 to honor the 400th anniversary of Columbus's voyage, but it opened a year late due to construction delays. Chicago civic leaders lobbied so vociferously to host the fair that New York newspapers disparagingly titled Chicago "the windy city." Building on successes like the 1876 PHILADELPHIA CENTENNIAL EXPOSITION and the 1889 Paris Exposition Universelle, the fair was a combination of cultural statement and trade show that epitomized much that was best and worst in American society in the 1890s.

The chosen site was Jackson Park, on the Lake Michigan waterfront south of the Chicago loop. The park had been laid out in 1871 by Olmsted, Vaux & Co. for the Chicago South Park Commission, but the landscape was redesigned by Frederick Law Olmsted for the fair, incorporating a second park and the connecting landscaped "midway" between them. A team of eminent designers, organized by Superintendent of the Works Daniel Burnham, himself a leading Chicago architect, conceived the central court of honor as a Greek or Roman neoclassical city. The vistas of the grand court, with its peristyle and central statue of Columbia, so awed visitors that the neo-

Poster for the World's Columbian Exposition, 1893 *(Library of Congress)*

classical mode became the style of choice for post offices, courthouses, and major public buildings for the next quarter century. The glistening simulated-stone surfaces gave rise to the name "the white city." The vision of order and grandeur, so at odds with the grime and confusion of the working Victorian city, inspired a generation of so-called City Beautiful advocates with plans for urban reconstruction around the country.

Behind the formal facades were the buildings, 200 of them on 633 acres, with the largest of them devoted to the products of America's industrial might. Sixty-two locomotives and complete passenger trains were displayed in the transportation building, whose arched golden portal, designed by LOUIS SULLIVAN, was the largest exception to the general neoclassicism. The manufactures and liberal arts building, with 38 acres of clear space unimpeded by columns under its steel-framed roof, was the largest building in the world and itself a demonstration of American building technology.

Beyond the industrial displays, the visitor encountered the art museum, today rebuilt as the Chicago Museum of Science and Industry, the only remaining structure on the site. Further away, beyond the state exhibits and a "woman's building," came the Midway Plaisance, an amusement area that gives us our term *midway.* The original Ferris wheel, 250 feet high, held 1,400 people at a time in enclosed cabins. The Midway also held foreign displays, arranged in a descending order that reflected the racism prevalent at the time. Half-timbered German and Irish buildings were closest to the White City, with "less civilized" cultures more distant, finally reaching the "primitive," where Eskimos suffered through the summer heat in winter regalia and the Dahomey exhibit denied that its inhabitants were cannibals. "Little Egypt's" belly dance scandalized the nation, and processions from the "primitive cultures," including camels and rickshaws, set out through the white city like emissaries of subject powers sent to the new imperial Rome.

The fair hosted 27 million visitors, the equivalent of almost half the national population. FREDERICK JACKSON TURNER's talk at the fair reflected a Census Bureau report that the American frontier was now officially closed and with it a whole epoch in American history.

Ironically, the "white city," with its vision of order, unity, and imperial domination, took place against a background of social and economic strife. The PANIC OF 1893, marked by business and bank failures, created massive unemployment and led to the PULLMAN STRIKE the following year. Thousands of workers living on the exposition grounds during construction were protected from agitators and labor organizers by barbed wire and guards. AFRICAN AMERICANS were excluded from even the most menial of jobs building and maintaining the fair, and they were provided eating and rest-room facilities only in the Haiti building, provoking Frederick Douglass to call the white city "a whited sepulchre." When the grounds were turned back to the South Park Commission in 1894, the result was a riot of looting, followed the next day by the first of a series of fires that destroyed the white city and its orderly vision of serenity.

Further reading: Robert Muccigrosso, *Celebrating the New World: Chicago's Columbian Exposition of 1893* (Chicago: Ivan R. Dee, 1993); Robert W. Rydell, *All the World's a Fair: Visions of Empire at American International Expositions, 1876–1916* (Chicago: University of Chicago Press, 1984).

— Francis H. Parker

Wounded Knee

See Sioux wars

Y

yellow journalism

Ervin Wardman, editor of the *New York Press,* coined the phrase *yellow journalism* in 1896 to connote the questionable journalistic practices employed by William Randolph Hearst's *New York Journal* and JOSEPH PULITZER's *New York World* in their fight for circulation and readership. Hearst bought the *New York Morning Journal* in 1895, which had been founded in 1882 by Albert Pulitzer (Joseph's younger brother), and he was determined to surpass in popularity Pulitzer's *World,* known for its lively news coverage, low-brow ADVERTISING, and civic mindedness. (The *World* for example had raised $100,000 to complete the base of the STATUE OF LIBERTY.) Hearst began the war with copious illustrations; an emphasis on crime, disasters, and scandals; and abundant feature material that made the *Journal* distinctly sensational and in direct competition with the *World.* Hearst used his considerable wealth to practice "checkbook journalism." He hired away the entire Sunday staff of the *World* and erected huge billboards and plastered blank walls with advertisements of *Journal* features. Circulation bounded upward and soon approached the numbers of the thriving *World.* The *World* responded in kind, and in their newspaper war both Hearst and Pulitzer focused on gossip, scandal, and crime and used questionable reporting techniques to gather as well as create news.

The rivalry came to a head with the papers' Sunday editions; though fairly equal in circulation during the week, Pulitzer's *World* pulled ahead on Sundays with four pages of its eight-page comic section printed in color. The *Journal* began a similar section in 1896, heralding "eight pages of iridescent polychromous effulgence that makes the rainbow look like a lead pipe." The pride of its Sunday comic section and readers' favorite was the strip "The Yellow Kid," drawn by Richard Outcault, whom Hearst had lured away from Pulitzer. Not to be outdone, Pulitzer hired artist George Luks to create a second "Yellow Kid" in the *World,* and the silly boy with the toothless vacant grin and yellow outfit soon symbolized the journalistic depths to which the two newspapers sank in their rivalry.

Further reading: David Nasaw, *Chief: The Life of William Randolph Hearst* (Boston: Houghton Mifflin, 2000); W.A. Swanberg, *Citizen Hearst: A Biography of William Randolph Hearst* (New York: Scribners, 1961); W.A. Swanberg, *Pulitzer* (New York: Scribner's, 1967).

— Ellen Tashie Frisina

Yellowstone National Park See conservation

Yosemite National Park See conservation

Chronology

1870

Hiram Revels becomes the first African American to serve in the U.S. Congress when he is seated as a senator from Mississippi.

The U.S. Weather Bureau is established.

Victoria Woodhull becomes the first woman to run for president of the United States; her magazine *Woodhull & Claflin's Weekly* promotes her radical platform, ranging from woman suffrage to free love to socialism.

The states ratify the Fifteenth Amendment, granting black men the right to vote.

The Standard Oil Company of Ohio is organized by John D. Rockefeller, whose aim is to monopolize the oil refining industry.

New York City runs the first steam-powered elevated train, or "el."

1871

Fire sweeps through Chicago, destroying 18,000 buildings and leaving 90,000 homeless.

U.S. Congress passes the Indian Appropriation Act, with a rider declaring that henceforth Indian tribes or nations would not be regarded as independent nations; in effect, this makes Native Americans wards of the government.

The Ku Klux Klan Enforcement Act of 1871 attempts to curtail the Ku Klux Klan's intimidation of black voters.

The United States and Britain sign the Treaty of Washington of 1871, in which both parties agreed to arbitrate boundary and fishing rights disputes and compensation due to the United States for Britain's dubious neutrality in the U.S. Civil War.

Political leader William "Boss" Tweed is indicted for fraud and corruption in New York City; Thomas Nast's magazine cartoons featuring Tweed help turn public opinion against him.

Showman P. T. Barnum opens a circus called "The Greatest Show on Earth."

American-born artist James Whistler paints his best-known work, a portrait of his mother.

Reacting to Apache raids, vigilantes from Tucson, Arizona, massacre up to 150 Apache men, women, and children at Camp Grant, Arizona, initiating 15 years of intermittent warfare.

1872

The Amnesty Act of 1872 allows a large number of former Confederate supporters to hold civil or military office.

The Yellowstone National Park Act of 1872 establishes the world's first national park in parts of what is now Wyoming, Montana, and Idaho.

The American Public Health Association is founded to improve sanitation in socially disadvantaged neighborhoods.

Horace Greeley, nominated by both the Democratic Party and the Liberal Republican Party, becomes the first candidate to personally campaign for president. Republican incumbent Ulysses S. Grant defeats Greeley, who dies shortly afterward.

1873

U.S. diplomatic relations with Spain are strained when Spanish authorities execute 53 of the passengers and crew of the *Virginius*—supporters of the Cuban Revolution—sailing under the American flag.

The Timber Culture Act of 1873 authorizes any person who keeps 40 acres of timberland in good condition to acquire title to 160 additional acres of timberland.

The Comstock Law of 1873 prohibits the sending of obscene materials through the U.S. mail.

The Panic of 1873 results in an economic depression and widespread unemployment. It is prompted by the collapse of Jay Cooke & Company, a major financial institution.

The Coinage Act of 1873 demonetizes silver and makes gold the sole basis of U.S. currency just as an increased supply of silver becomes available, which, if minted, would have eased payment of debts. Opponents label the law the "Crime of '73."

In *Bradwell v. Illinois,* the U.S. Supreme Court upholds a state's right to deny admission to the bar on the basis of sex.

The "Women's War" breaks out across the United States as thousands of women shut down an estimated 3,000 saloons. Activists form the Women's Christian Temperance Union, led by Frances Willard, to focus attention on the problems associated with drunkenness.

1874

Prospectors discover gold in the Black Hills of South Dakota, sacred hunting territory that was included in the Great Sioux Reservation by the Treaty of Fort Laramie of 1868. The ensuing gold rush touches off a war between the U.S. government and the Sioux.

St. Louis's Eads Bridge opens; it is the first steel bridge in the United States.

Barbed wire is commercially manufactured, permitting fencing of property in treeless regions, especially the West and Southwest.

John Fiske's *Outlines of Cosmic Philosophy* offers a reconciliation of Darwinism and Scripture that many liberal Christians come to embrace.

1875

The Civil Rights Act of 1875 mandates the end of racial discrimination in public accommodations.

Mary Baker Eddy publishes *Science and Health,* the chief text of the Christian Science movement.

The Specie Resumption Act of 1875 authorizes the U.S. Treasury on January 1, 1879, to redeem the paper money issued during the Civil War, known as "greenbacks," with gold coins; this act returns the U.S. to the gold standard.

After successfully advocating for state regulation of railroad freight rates, the Granger movement gathers strength as hundreds of thousands of farmers join its ranks.

In *Minor v. Happersett,* the U.S. Supreme Court rejects the assertion of the National Woman Suffrage Association that the Fourteenth Amendment provides all U.S. citizens, including women, the right to vote.

1876

Physicist Josiah Gibbs publishes his scientific theories, which provide the foundations of the field of physical chemistry.

Johns Hopkins University is established as a center of scholarly research emphasizing its graduate programs. Yale and Harvard had already awarded Ph.Ds but they concentrate on undergraduates.

Inventor Alexander Graham Bell patents the telephone.

Sitting Bull and Crazy Horse lead the Sioux and Cheyenne in major victories against the U.S. Army, first in the Battle of the Rosebud and then at Little Bighorn against General George Armstrong Custer, where Custer's entire force is wiped out.

The United States celebrates its 100th anniversary with the Centennial Exhibition in Philadelphia. On July 4, Susan B. Anthony and her colleagues interrupt official ceremonies to demand women's rights in fulfillment of the ideals of 1776.

Democratic presidential candidate Samuel J. Tilden receives a majority of the votes cast but is defeated by Republican Rutherford B. Hayes in the electoral college following a dispute over the official returns in three southern states.

Thomas Edison establishes his "invention factory" in Menlo Park, New Jersey.

Columbia, Yale, Princeton, and Harvard agree to standardize rules for American football.

1877

Republican governments fall in South Carolina and Louisiana, marking the end of Reconstruction.

During the Nez Perce War, Chief Joseph leads his people more than 1,700 miles through the wilderness toward the Canadian border, eluding the U.S. cavalry. After a final encounter in northern Montana, Joseph surrenders, and the Nez Perce are moved to Indian Territory, but ultimately they are allowed to return to the Pacific Northwest.

Repeated wage cuts spur numerous independent strikes among railroad workers that become known collectively as the Great Strike of 1877.

Thomas Edison invents the phonograph.

1878

A yellow fever epidemic breaks out in Memphis, Tennessee, killing one out of every nine residents.

The Bland-Allison Act of 1878 reinstates the use of limited quantities of silver currency.

The Knights of Labor organizes on a national basis.

1879

The U.S. Geological Survey is established to investigate the nation's mineral resources.

Groups of blacks, led by Benjamin "Pap" Singleton and others, migrate from the South to the West in the "Exodus of '79."

In *Progress and Poverty,* economist Henry George argues that the government should tax property owners for appreciation caused by rising demand, especially in cities; this "Single Tax" would replace all other taxes.

As the result of a bill she drafted, Belva Lockwood becomes the first woman lawyer to argue before the U.S. Supreme Court.

Thomas Edison invents the incandescent light bulb, making electric light practical.

Mary Cassatt exhibits her paintings with the impressionists in Paris.

Second-class postage is created, permitting the shipment of packages of up to four pounds anywhere in the United States for a flat rate of one cent per ounce.

Charles McKim, William Mead, and Stanford White open their New York City architectural office; the firm is to create many of the country's most prominent public buildings in the Beaux Arts style.

1880

Republican James A. Garfield is elected president over Democrat W. S. Hancock.

1881

Humanitarian and former Civil War nurse Clara Barton founds the American Red Cross.

A Century of Dishonor, by Helen Hunt Jackson, is published; the book urges better treatment of Indians.

Booker T. Washington founds the Tuskegee Institute in Alabama.

President James A. Garfield is assassinated; Vice President Chester Arthur becomes president.

Henry Demarest Lloyd's article "The Story of a Great Monopoly" is published in *Atlantic Monthly;* the article establishes Lloyd as the first muckraker.

1882

John L. Sullivan begins a 10-year reign as world heavyweight champion.

Apache warrior Geronimo leads a raid on the San Carlos Reservation in Arizona, freeing several hundred Apache and renewing the Apache War against both U.S. and Mexican authorities.

To better control his oil monopoly, John D. Rockefeller reorganizes Standard Oil using a trust agreement. Other industries soon follow suit.

The U.S. Congress passes the Chinese Exclusion Act prohibiting the immigration of laborers from China.

The *First Modern Suite,* by composer Edward MacDowell, is performed in Zurich, Switzerland. MacDowell is the first American-born composer whose works are performed in Europe.

The *Chicago Tribune* begins its annual accounting of lynchings in the United States, publicizing the practice of terrorism against African Americans and their supporters.

1883

The Council of Bishops convenes in Baltimore and plans a widespread system of Catholic parochial schools.

The Brooklyn Bridge opens.

Buffalo Bill's Wild West show begins touring; it becomes an international entertainment sensation.

U.S. Supreme Court declares the Civil Rights Act of 1875 unconstitutional, opening the way for Jim Crow legislation in the South.

Congress ratifies the Pendleton Act of 1883, ending a long political battle over civil service reform. The act opens some civil offices to competitive entry rather than political patronage; prohibits assessments, the long-standing practice of demanding a percentage of civil servants' salaries for party campaigns; and establishes the U.S. Civil Service Commission to enforce reforms.

1884

Republican James G. Blaine narrowly loses a heated presidential election to Democrat Grover Cleveland.

Samuel Clemens publishes *The Adventures of Huckleberry Finn* under his pen name Mark Twain.

1885

Social Gospel minister Josiah Strong publishes *Our Country: Its Possible Future and Its Present Crisis,* which urges Americans to combat social evils, economic distress, and political corruption at home and to spread "superior" Anglo-Saxon institutions throughout the world.

The decade-long lobbying efforts of the Knights of Labor are rewarded when Congress passes a law prohibiting the importation of contract laborers.

1886

Samuel Gompers founds the American Federation of Labor.

An anarchist rally in Chicago's Haymarket Square turns into a riot when someone throws a bomb at police; the bombing prompts the hasty roundup and conviction of Chicago's known radicals.

Emily Dickinson, a reclusive New Englander, dies; family members discover 1,800 lyric poems in her bedroom.

In *Wabash v. Illinois,* the U.S. Supreme Court strikes down pro-farmer Granger laws, ruling that states cannot regulate interstate commerce.

Harper's magazine first prints the illustrations of Frederic Remington; Remington's art comes to shape Americans' perception of the frontier West.

The Apache Wars conclude when Geronimo surrenders.

In *Santa Clara County v. Southern Pacific Railroad Company,* the U.S. Supreme Court extends the protections of the Fourteenth Amendment to corporations.

Statue of Liberty is dedicated in New York harbor.

1887

U.S. Congress passes the Dawes Severalty Act, which dissolves Native American tribes as legal entities and requires the division of jointly held lands into individual Native American homesteads.

Henry F. Bowers founds the American Protective Association; it becomes the largest of America's many nativist organizations.

Nikola Tesla invents an alternating current (AC) motor and the next year sells his AC patents for generators, transformers, and motors to George Westinghouse. Soon AC electricity becomes the preferred power source for electric streetcars, elevated trains, and subways.

U.S. Congress creates the Interstate Commerce Commission, the first federal regulatory agency.

U.S. Congress passes the Electoral Count Act of 1887, which is designed to prevent disputes over presidential elections such as the one in 1876.

1888

Republican Benjamin Harrison wins a close presidential race over Grover Cleveland.

British diplomat James Bryce publishes *The American Commonwealth,* a perceptive analysis of American political institutions.

George Eastman introduces the Kodak portable box camera and revolutionizes photography.

1889

The *North American Review* publishes Andrew Carnegie's essay "The Gospel of Wealth." The industrialist writes that the duty of the rich man is to be a "trustee for the poor."

Oklahoma, once part of Indian Territory, is opened to white settlement; massive "land rushes" follow.

The former Native American enclaves of North Dakota, South Dakota, and Montana are granted statehood.

Wovoka, a Paiute Indian, sees a vision that gives momentum to the Ghost Dance religion; large numbers of Sioux Indians leave their reservations to join the religious gatherings on the plains.

Jane Addams founds Hull House, an organization whose goal is to improve the lives of the largely immigrant urban poor of Chicago; many similar institutions, known as settlement houses, are established in American cities.

Montgomery Ward & Company is established. Its catalog, containing 24,000 items, brings the department store to rural America.

Elisha Otis invents the electric elevator.

1890

William James publishes *Principles of Psychology,* which helps establish psychology as a field of study in the United States.

U.S. Congress passes the Sherman Antitrust Act in response to growing hostility to industrial monopolies.

The protectionist McKinley Tariff Act imposes the highest import duties in U.S. history to date but also provides for the novel feature of reciprocal trade agreements.

Illustrator Charles Dana Gibson introduces the Gibson Girl.

President Benjamin Harrison signs the Dependents Pension Act, the United States's first social welfare program, which provides pensions for disabled Civil War veterans and their families. The law's passage demonstrates the lobbying power of the Grand Army of the Republic, the largest U.S. veterans' organization.

Ending a long-standing rivalry, the conservative American Woman Suffrage Association merges with the more radical National Woman Suffrage Association to form the National American Woman Suffrage Association.

Jacob Riis publishes *How the Other Half Lives,* which documents the plight of the urban poor through text and photographs.

The superintendent of the census announces that the frontier line no longer exists.

The Sherman Silver Purchase Act increases the minimum amount of silver the federal government is required to buy and mint from $2 million per month to 4.5 million ounces per month at prevailing market prices. The goal of this "soft money" policy is to raise prices by encouraging inflation.

The Association of American Medical Colleges is established to set standards for medical instruction.

At the urging of naturalist John Muir, U.S. Congress creates Yosemite National Park.

The National Farmers' Alliance and Industrial Union meets at Ocala, Florida. Attendees draft a statement that demands abolition of national banks and protective tariffs; free coinage of silver; a graduated income tax; government control of railroads and public utilities; and the direct election of U.S. senators.

U.S. troops massacre more than 200 Sioux at Wounded Knee Creek, South Dakota; Wounded Knee marks the end of the long struggle of Native Americans against white expansion in the West.

1891

The Forest Reserve Act of 1891 authorizes the president to withhold certain public lands from the public domain.

The International Copyright Law of 1891 prohibits the previously common practice of reprinting foreign works without paying for the right to do so. One consequence is a larger market for American authors.

1892

"March King" John Philip Sousa forms the Sousa Band, which performs his marches and other popular American music around the world for nearly 40 years.

Ida B. Wells, editor of the newspaper *Free Speech,* reports on how lynching is used by white businessmen to eliminate black competitors.

Carnegie Steel imports scab workers and Pinkerton detectives to break the Amalgamated Union strike at Homestead Mill; 16 die and 60 are wounded in the failed strike, which suppresses trade unionism in the steel industry for 40 years.

The People's Party (or Populist Party), a reaction by western farmers against eastern business interests, holds its first national convention in Omaha, Nebraska; among its demands are the secret ballot and the unlimited coinage of silver.

State authorities use the militia to break a violent miners strike at Coeur d' Alene, Idaho.

Grover Cleveland is elected president over incumbent Benjamin Harrison. Cleveland is the only U.S. president to serve two nonconsecutive terms. People's Party candidate James B. Weaver also runs, gaining more than 1 million votes.

The General Electric Company is established, underwritten by J. P. Morgan Company.

1893

American businessmen in Hawaii overthrow the government of Queen Liliuokalani and encourage the United States to annex the islands.

The total number of bison on the Great Plains is estimated to be no more than 1,000.

The financial panic of 1893 brings about the most severe economic depression the United States has yet experienced, leaving many Americans destitute and unemployed.

The Sherman Silver Purchase Act is repealed.

1894

Jacob Coxey organizes a march on Washington, D.C., to demand government unemployment relief; capital city police forcibly disperse "Coxey's Army."

U.S. Congress incorporates in the Wilson-Gorman Tariff Act of 1894 the first peacetime income tax; a year later the U.S. Supreme Court rules the tax unconstitutional.

President Grover Cleveland sends federal troops to break the Pullman Strike on the pretext that strikers were illegally obstructing the movement of U.S. mail.

1895

Beginning with South Carolina, seven states use a grandfather clause to disenfranchise African Americans while preserving voting rights for poor and illiterate whites.

William Randolph Hearst's *New York Journal* engages in a circulation war with Joseph Pulitzer's *New York World;* the sensationalist bent of the feuding newspapers, which create as well as gather news, becomes known as "yellow journalism."

In *United States v. E. C. Knight Company,* the U.S. Supreme Court narrowly defines commerce and emasculates the Sherman Antitrust Act of 1890 by declaring that the sugar trust's monopoly of refining (manufacturing) did not restrain trade.

Booker T. Washington delivers his "Atlanta Compromise" speech at the Cotton Exposition in Atlanta. In this controversial speech, Washington accepts segregation in social matters in exchange for economic opportunities for African Americans.

1896

The first publicly screened motion picture is shown in New York City.

George Washington Carver accepts an appointment to Alabama's Tuskegee Institute; his work there helps revive southern agriculture.

The world's first hydroelectric generator, designed by Nikola Tesla, is completed at Niagara Falls.

Plessy v. Ferguson forms the legal basis for segregation by race. Justice John Marshall Harlan dissents from the U.S. Supreme Court's ruling.

Henry Ford builds his first automobile.

William Jennings Bryan delivers his "Cross of Gold" speech, attacking the gold standard at the Democratic National Convention.

A prospector finds gold in Canada's Yukon River Valley, spurring the Klondike gold rush.

Voter participation reaches its all-time high in the presidential race, which Republican William McKinley wins over Democrat William Jennings Bryan.

1897

U.S. Congress passes the Forest Management Act, which designates forest reserves as resources for timber, mining, and grazing.

U.S. Supreme Court prohibits the Interstate Commerce Commission from setting railroad freight rates.

The Dingley Tariff Act raises U.S. protective duties to their highest rate ever.

Alexander Crummell organizes the American Negro Academy to advance the race by developing the "talented tenth" of black Americans.

1898

A piece of private correspondence written by Spain's minister to the United States, the so-called de Lôme letter, attacks U.S. president McKinley. The stolen letter, when published in 1898, is used to feed U.S. desire for war with Spain.

The USS *Maine* explodes in Havana harbor, Cuba. A naval investigation of indeterminate origin concludes that an underwater mine caused the blast, but newspapers blame Spain, increasing American appetite for a war.

U.S. Congress declares war on Spain. In the Pacific Ocean, Admiral George Dewey wins the Philippine Islands for the United States at Manila Bay.

Theodore Roosevelt leads the Rough Riders, a volunteer cavalry regiment, to a victory at San Juan and Kettle Hills in Cuba.

The United States formally annexes Hawaii.

An unprecedented wave of mergers sweeps through the American economy; after seven years and more than 3,000 mergers, two-fifths of the nation's industrial wealth is concentrated in 328 large companies, many of them monopolies.

The Treaty of Paris ends the Spanish-American War; Spain cedes the Philippines and Puerto Rico to the United States; Cuba, nominally independent, in 1901 becomes a U.S. protectorate.

1899

Ragtime composer Scott Joplin publishes "Maple Leaf Rag," which sells more than 1 million copies.

After the United States fails to support Philippine independence, Filipinos wage a guerrilla war against U.S. forces. The Filipino Insurrection fails but stirs sympathy and protest in the United States.

Secretary of State John Hay's Open Door notes instruct U.S. embassies in Germany, Russia, Great Britain, France, Italy, and Japan to seek assurances that those powers will respect the trading rights of other nations within their spheres of influence.

Documents

Susan B. Anthony's Speech on Woman Suffrage, 1871

James Andrews, ed. *American Voices, Significant Speeches in American History, 1640–1945* (New York: Longman, 1989), pp. 300–01

Friends and fellow citizens: I stand before you tonight under indictment for the alleged crime of having voted at the last presidential election, without having a lawful right to vote. It shall be my work this evening to prove to you that in thus voting, I not only committed no crime, but, instead, simply exercised my *citizen's rights,* guaranteed to me and all United States citizens by the National Constitution, beyond the power of any State to deny.

The preamble of the Federal Constitution says:

"We, the people of the United States, in order to form a more perfect union, establish justice, insure *domestic* tranquility, provide for the common defense, promote the general welfare, and secure the blessings of liberty to ourselves and our posterity, do ordain and establish this Constitution for the United States of America."

It was we, the people; not we, the white male citizens; nor yet we, the male citizens; but we, the whole people, who formed the Union. And we formed it, not to give the blessings of liberty, but to secure them; not to the half of ourselves and the half of our posterity, but to the whole people—women as well as men. And it is a downright mockery to talk to women of their enjoyment of the blessings of liberty while they are denied the use of the only means of securing them provided by this democratic-republican government—the ballot.

For any State to make sex a qualification that must ever result in the disfranchisement of one entire half of the people is to pass a bill of attainder, or an *ex post facto* law, and is therefore a violation of the supreme law of the land. By it the blessings of liberty are for ever withheld from women and their female posterity. To them this government has no just powers derived from the consent of the governed. To them this government is not a democracy. It is not a republic. It is an odious aristocracy; a hateful oligarchy of sex; the most hateful aristocracy ever established on the face of the globe; an oligarchy of wealth, where the rich govern the poor. An oligarchy of learning, where the educated govern the ignorant, or even an oligarchy of race, where the Saxon rules the African, might be endured; but this oligarchy of sex, which makes father, brothers, husband, sons, the oligarchs over the mother and sisters, the wife and daughters of every household—which ordains all men sovereigns, all women subjects, carries dissension, discord and rebellion into every home of the nation.

Webster, Worcester and Bouvier all define a citizen to be a person in the United States, entitled to vote and hold office.

The only question left to be settled now is: Are women persons? And I hardly believe any of our opponents will have the hardihood to say they are not. Being persons, then, women are citizens; and no State has a right to make any law, or to enforce any old law, that shall abridge their privileges or immunities. Hence, every discrimination against women in the constitutions and laws of the several States is today null and void, precisely as in every one against Negroes.

Chief Joseph's "I Will Fight No More Forever" Speech, 1877

Courtesy Nez Perce Tribe, Department of Natural Resources, Lapwai, Idaho

I Will Fight No More Forever

Tell General Howard I know his heart. What he told me before, I have in my heart. I am tired of fighting. Our

Chiefs are killed. Looking Glass is dead. Toohoolhoolzote is dead. The old men are all dead. It is the young men who say "yes" or "no." He who led on the young men is dead. It is cold and we have no blankets. The little children are freezing to death. My people, some of them, have run away to the hills and have no blankets, no food; no one knows where they are—perhaps freezing to death. I want to have time to look for my children among the dead. Hear me, my chiefs! I am tired; my heart is sick and sad. From where the sun now stands I will fight no more forever.

A Century of Dishonor (1881)

Helen Hunt Jackson

In Erik Bruun and Jay Crosby, eds. *Our Nation's Archives: The History of the United States in Documents* (New York: Black Dog & Leventhal Publishers, 1999), pp. 425–427

The winter of 1877 and summer of 1878 were terrible seasons for the Cheyennes. Their fall hunt had proved unsuccessful. Indians from other reservations had hunted the ground over before them, and driven the buffalo off; and the Cheyennes made their way home again in straggling parties, destitute and hungry. Their agent reports that the result of this hunt has clearly proved that "in the future the Indian must rely on tilling the ground as the principal means of support; and if this conviction can be firmly established, the greatest obstacle to advancement in agriculture will be overcome. With the buffalo gone, and their pony herds being constantly decimated by the inroads of horse-thieves, they must soon adopt, in all its varieties, the way of the white man."

The ration allowed to these Indians is reported as being "reduced and insufficient," and the small sums they have been able to earn by selling buffalo hides are said to have been "of material assistance" to them in "supplementing" this ration. But in this year there have been sold only $657 worth of skins by the Cheyennes and Arapahoes together. In 1876 they sold $17,600 worth. Here is a falling off enough to cause very great suffering in a little community of five thousand people. But this was only the beginning of their troubles. The summer proved one of unusual heat. Extreme heat, chills and fever, and "a reduced and insufficient ration," all combined, resulted in an amount of sickness heart-rending to read of. "It is no exaggerated estimate," says the agent, "to place the number of sick people on the reservation at two thousand. Many deaths occurred which might have been obviated had there been a proper supply of antimalarial remedies at hand. Hundreds applying for treatment have been refused medicine."

The Northern Cheyennes grew more and more restless and unhappy. "In council and elsewhere they profess an intense desire to be sent North, where they say they will settle down as the others have done," says the report; adding, with an obtuseness which is inexplicable, that "no difference has been made in the treatment of the Indians," but that the "compliance of these Northern Cheyennes has been of an entirely different nature from that of the other Indians," and that it may be "necessary in the future to compel what so far we have been unable to effect by kindness and appeal to their better natures."

If it is "an appeal to men's better natures" to remove them by force from a healthful Northern climate, which they love and thrive in, to a malarial Southern one, where they are struck down by chills and fever—refuse them medicine which can combat chills and fever, and finally starve them—there indeed, might be said to have been most forcible appeals made to the "better natures" of these Northern Cheyennes. What might have been predicted followed.

Early in the autumn, after this terrible summer, a band of some three hundred of these Northern Cheyennes took the desperate step of running off and attempting to make their way back to Dakota. They were pursued, fought desperately, but were finally overpowered, and surrendered. They surrendered, however, only on the condition that they should be taken to Dakota. They were unanimous in declaring that they would rather die than go back to the Indian Territory. This was nothing more, in fact, than saying that they would rather die by bullets than of chills and fever and starvation.

These Indians were taken to Fort Robinson, Nebraska. Here they were confined as prisoners of war, and held subject to the orders of the Department of the Interior. The department was informed of the Indians' determination never to be taken back alive to Indian Territory. The army officers in charge reiterated these statements, and implored the department to permit them to remain at the North; but it was of no avail. Orders came—explicit, repeated, finally stern—insisting on the return of these Indians to their agency. The commanding officer at Fort Robinson has been censured severely for the course he pursued in his effort to carry out those orders. It is difficult to see what else he could have done, except to have resigned his post. He could not take three hundred Indians by sheer brute force and carry them hundreds of miles, especially when they were so desperate that they had broken up the iron stoves in their quarters, and wrought and twisted them into weapons with which to resist. He thought perhaps he could starve them into submission. He stopped the issue of food; he also stopped the issue of fuel to them. It was midwinter; the mercury froze in that month at Fort Robinson. At the end of two days he asked the Indians to let their women and children come out that he might feed them. Not a woman would come out. On the night of the fourth day—or, according to some accounts, the sixth—

these starving, freezing Indians broke prison, overpowered the guards, and fled, carrying their women and children with them. They held the pursuing troops at bay for several days; finally made a last stand in a deep ravine, and were shot down-men, women, and children together. Out of the whole band there were left alive some fifty women and children and seven men, who having been confined in another part of the fort, had not had the good fortune to share in this outbreak and meet their death in the ravine. These, with their wives and children, were sent to Fort Leavenworth to be put in prison; the men to be tried for murders committed in their skirmishes in Kansas on their way to the north. Red Cloud, a Sioux chief, came to Fort Robinson immediately after this massacre and entreated to be allowed to take the Cheyenne widows and orphans into his tribe to be cared for. The Government, therefore, kindly permitted twenty-two Cheyenne widows and thirty-two Cheyenne children—many of them orphans—to be received into the band of the Ogallalla Sioux.

An attempt was made by the Commissioner of Indian Affairs, in his Report for 1879, to show by tables and figures that these Indians were not starving at the time of their flight from Indian Territory. The attempt only redounded to his own disgrace; it being proved, by the testimony given by a former clerk of the Indian Bureau before the Senate committee appointed to investigate the case of the Northern Cheyennes, that the commissioner had been guilty of absolute dishonesty in his estimates, and that the quantity of beef actually issued to the Cheyenne Agency was hundreds of pounds less than he had reported it, and that the Indians were actually, as they had claimed, "starving."

The testimony given before this committee by some of the Cheyenne prisoners themselves is heart-rending. One must have a callous heart who can read it unmoved.

When asked by Senator [John T.] Morgan [of Alabama], "Did you ever really suffer from hunger?" one of the chiefs replied. "We were always hungry; we never had enough. When they that were sick once in awhile felt as though they could eat something, we had nothing to give them."

"Did you not go out on the plains sometimes and hunt buffalo, with the consent of the agent?"

"We went out on a buffalo-hunt, and nearly starved while out; we could not find any buffalo hardly; we could hardly get back with our ponies; we had to kill a good many of our ponies to eat, to save ourselves from starving." "How many children got sick and died?"

"Between the fall of 1877 and 1878 we lost fifty children. A great many of our finest young men died, as well as many women."

"Old Crow," a chief who served faithfully as Indian scout and ally under General [George] Crook for years, said: "I did not feel like doing anything for awhile, because I had no heart. I did not want to be in this country. I was all the time wanting to get back to the better country where I was born, and where my children are buried, and where my mother and sister yet live. So I have laid in my lodge most of the time with nothing to think about but that, and the affair up north at Fort Robinson, and my relatives and friends who were killed there. But now I feel as though, if I had a wagon and a horse or two, and some land, I would try to work. If I had something, so that I could do something, I might not think so much about these other things. As it is now, I feel as though I would just as soon be asleep with the rest."

The wife of one of the chiefs confined at Fort Leavenworth testified before the committee as follows: "The main thing I complained of was that we didn't get enough to eat; my children nearly starved to death; then sickness came, and there was nothing good for them to eat; for a long time the most they had to eat was corn-meal and salt. Three or four children died every day for awhile, and that frightened us."

When asked if there were anything she would like to say to the committee, the poor woman replied: "I wish you would do what you can to get my husband released. I am very poor here, and do not know what is to become of me. If he were released he would come down here, and we would live together quietly, and do no harm to anybody, and make no trouble. But I should never get over my desire to get back north; I should always want to get back where my children were born, and died, and were buried. That country is better than this in every respect. There is plenty of good, cool water there—pure water—while here the water is not good. It is not hot there, nor so sickly. Are you going where my husband is? Can you tell when he is likely to be released?. . .

It is stated also that there was not sufficient clothing to furnish each Indian with a warm suit of clothing, "as promised by the treaty," and that, "by reference to official correspondence, the fact is established that the Cheyennes and Arapahoes are judged as having no legal rights to any lands, having forfeited their treaty reservation by a failure to settle thereon," and their "present reservation not having been, as yet, confirmed by Congress. Inasmuch as the Indians fully understood, and were assured that this reservation was given to them in lieu of their treaty reservation, and have commenced farming in the belief that there was no uncertainty about the matter it is but common justice that definite action be had at an early day, securing to them what is their right."

It would seem that there could be found nowhere in the melancholy record of the experiences of our Indians a more glaring instance of confused multiplication of injustices than this. The Cheyennes were pursued and slain for venturing to leave this very reservation, which, it appears, is not their reservation at all, and they have no legal right to it. Are there any words to fitly characterize such treatment as this from a great, powerful, rich nation, to a handful of helpless people?

Chinese Exclusion Act (1882)

United States Statutes at Large (47th Cong., Sess I, chap. 126), pp. 58–61

May 6, 1882

An Act

To execute certain treaty stipulations relating to Chinese.

Whereas, in the opinion of the Government of the United States the coming of Chinese laborers to this country endangers the good order of certain localities within the territory thereof.

Therefore,

Be it enacted by the Senate and House of Representatives of the United States of America in Congress assembled, That from and after the expiration of ninety days next after the passage of this act, and until the expiration of ten years next after the passage of this act, the coming of Chinese laborers to the United States be, and the same is hereby, suspended; and during such suspension it shall not be lawful for any Chinese laborer to come, or, having so come after the expiration of said ninety days, to remain within the United States.

Sec. 2. That the master of any vessel who shall knowingly bring within the United States on such vessel, and land or permit to be landed, any Chinese laborer, from any foreign port or place, shall be deemed guilty of a misdemeanor, and on conviction thereof shall be punished by a fine of not more than five hundred dollars for each and every such Chinese laborer so brought, and may be also imprisoned for a term not exceeding one year.

Sec. 3. That the two foregoing sections shall not apply to Chinese laborers who were in the United States on the seventeenth day of November, eighteen hundred and eighty, or who shall have come into the same before the expiration of ninety days next after the passage of this act, and who shall produce to such master before going on board such vessel, and shall produce to the collector of the port in the United States at which such vessel shall arrive, the evidence hereinafter in this act required of his being one of the laborers in this section mentioned; nor shall the two foregoing sections apply to the case of any master whose vessel, being bound to a port not within the United States, shall come within the jurisdiction of the United States by reason of being in distress or in stress of weather, or touching at any port of the United States on its voyage to any foreign port or place: *Provided,* That all Chinese laborers brought on such vessel shall depart with the vessel on leaving port.

Sec. 4. That for the purpose of properly identifying Chinese laborers who were in the United States on the seventeenth day of November, eighteen hundred and eighty, or who shall have come into the same before the expiration of ninety days next after the passage of this act, and in order to furnish them with the proper evidence of their right to go from and come to the United States of their free will and accord, as provided by the treaty between the United States and China dated November seventeenth, eighteen hundred and eighty, the collector of customs of the district from which any such Chinese laborer shall depart from the United States shall, in person or by deputy, go on board each vessel having on board any such Chinese laborer and cleared or about to sail from his district for a foreign port, and on such vessel make a list of all such Chinese laborers, which shall be entered in registry-books to be kept for that purpose, in which shall be stated the name, age, occupation, last place of residence, physical marks or peculiarities, and all facts necessary for the identification of each of such Chinese laborers, which books shall be safely kept in the custom-house; and every such Chinese laborer so departing from the United States shall be entitled to, and shall receive, free of any charge or cost upon application therefor, from the collector or his deputy, at the time such list is taken, a certificate, signed by the collector or his deputy and attested by his seal of office, in such form as the Secretary of the Treasury shall prescribe, which certificate shall contain a statement of the name, age, occupation, last place of residence, personal description, and facts of identification of the Chinese laborer to whom the certificate is issued, corresponding with the said list and registry in all particulars. In case any Chinese laborer after having received such certificate shall leave such vessel before her departure he shall deliver his certificate to the master of the vessel, and if such Chinese laborer shall fail to return to such vessel before her departure from port the certificate shall be delivered by the master to the collector of customs for cancellation. The certificate herein provided for shall entitle the Chinese laborer to whom the same is issued to return to and re-enter the United States upon producing and delivering the same to the collector of customs of the district at which such Chinese laborer shall seek to re-enter; and upon delivery of such certificate by such Chinese laborer to the collector of customs at the time of re-entry in the United States, said collector shall cause the same to be filed in the custom-house and duly canceled.

Sec. 5. That any Chinese laborer mentioned in section four of this act being in the United States, and desiring to depart from the United States by land, shall have the right to demand and receive, free of charge or cost, a certificate of identification similar to that provided for in section four of this act to be issued to such Chinese laborers as may desire to leave the United States by water; and it is hereby made the duty of the collector of customs of the district next adjoining the foreign country to which said Chinese laborer desires to go to issue such certificate, free of charge or cost, upon application by such Chinese laborer, and to enter the same upon registry-books to be kept by him for the purpose, as provided for in section four of this act.

Sec. 6. That in order to the faithful execution of articles one and two of the treaty in this act before mentioned, every Chinese person other than a laborer who may be entitled by said treaty and this act to come within the United States, and who shall be about to come to the United States, shall be identified as so entitled by the Chinese Government in each case, such identity to be evidenced by a certificate issued under the authority of said government, which certificate shall be in the English language or (if not in the English language) accompanied by a translation into English, stating such right to come, and which certificate shall state the name, title, or official rank, if any, the age, height, and all physical peculiarities, former and present occupation or profession, and place of residence in China of the person to whom the certificate is issued and that such person is entitled conformably to the treaty in this act mentioned to come within the United States. Such certificate shall be prima-facie evidence of the fact set forth therein, and shall be produced to the collector of customs, or his deputy, of the port in the district in the United States at which the person named therein shall arrive.

Sec. 7. That any person who shall knowingly and falsely alter or substitute any name for the name written in such certificate or forge any such certificate, or knowingly utter any forged or fraudulent certificate, or falsely personate any person named in any such certificate, shall be deemed guilty of a misdemeanor; and upon conviction thereof shall be fined in a sum not exceeding one thousand dollars, and imprisoned in a penitentiary for a term of not more than five years.

Sec. 8. That the master of any vessel arriving in the United States from any foreign port or place shall, at the same time he delivers a manifest of the cargo, and if there be no cargo, then at the time of making a report of the entry of the vessel pursuant to law, in addition to the other matter required to be reported, and before landing, or permitting to land, any Chinese passengers, deliver and report to the collector of customs of the district in which such vessels shall have arrived a separate list of all Chinese passengers taken on board his vessel at any foreign port or place, and all such passengers on board the vessel at that time. Such list shall show the names of such passengers (and if accredited officers of the Chinese Government traveling on the business of that government, or their servants, with a note of such facts), and the names and other particulars, as shown by their respective certificates; and such list shall be sworn to by the master in the manner required by law in relation to the manifest of the cargo. Any willful refusal or neglect of any such master to comply with the provisions of this section shall incur the same penalties and forfeiture as are provided for a refusal or neglect to report and deliver a manifest of the cargo.

Sec. 9. That before any Chinese passengers are landed from any such vessel, the collector, or his deputy, shall proceed to examine such passengers, comparing the certificates with the list and with the passengers; and no passenger shall be allowed to land in the United States from such vessel in violation of law.

Sec. 10. That every vessel whose master shall knowingly violate any of the provisions of this act shall be deemed forfeited to the United States, and shall be liable to seizure and condemnation in any district of the United States into which such vessel may enter or in which she may be found.

Sec. 11. That any person who shall knowingly bring into or cause to be brought into the United States by land, or who shall knowingly aid or abet the same, or aid or abet the landing in the United States from any vessel of any Chinese person not lawfully entitled to enter the United States, shall be deemed guilty of a misdemeanor, and shall, on conviction thereof, be fined in a sum not exceeding one thousand dollars, and imprisoned for a term not exceeding one year.

Sec. 12. That no Chinese person shall be permitted to enter the United States by land without producing to the proper officer of customs the certificate in this act required of Chinese persons seeking to land from a vessel. And any Chinese person found unlawfully within the United States shall be caused to be removed therefrom to the country from whence he came, by direction of the President of the United States, and at the cost of the United States, after being brought before some justice, judge, or commissioner of a court of the United States and found to be one not lawfully entitled to be or remain in the United States.

Sec. 13. That this act shall not apply to diplomatic and other officers of the Chinese Government traveling upon the business of that government, whose credentials shall be taken as equivalent to the certificate in this act mentioned, and shall exempt them and their body and household servants from the provisions of this act as to other Chinese persons.

Sec. 14. That hereafter no State court of the United States shall admit Chinese to citizenship; and all laws in conflict with this act are hereby repealed.

Sec. 15. That the words "Chinese laborers," wherever used in this act, shall be construed to mean both skilled and unskilled laborers and Chinese employed in mining.

Approved, May 6,1882.

The Dawes Severalty Act, 1887

United States Statutes at Large (49th Cong., 2d sess., chap. 119), pp. 388–391

An Act

To provide for the allotment of lands in severalty to Indians on the various reservations, and to extend the protection of the laws of the United States and the Territories over the Indians, and for other purposes.

Be it enacted by the Senate and House of Representatives of the United States of America in Congress assembled, That in all cases where any tribe or band of Indians has been, or shall hereafter be, located upon any reservation created for their use, either by treaty stipulation or by virtue of an act of Congress or executive order setting apart the same for their use, the President of the United States be, and he hereby is, authorized, whenever in his opinion any reservation or any part thereof of such Indians is advantageous for agricultural and grazing purposes, to cause said reservation, or any part thereof, to be surveyed, or resurveyed if necessary, and to allot the lands in said reservation in severalty to any Indian located thereon in quantities as follows:

To each head of a family, one-quarter of a section;

To each single person over eighteen years of age, one-eighth of a section; and

To each orphan child under eighteen years of age, one-eighth of a section; and

To each other single person under eighteen years now living, or who may be born prior to the date of the order of the President directing an allotment of the lands embraced in any reservation, one-sixteenth of a section: *Provided,* That in case there is not sufficient land in any of said reservations to allot lands to each individual of the classes above named in quantities as above provided, the lands embraced in such reservation or reservations shall be allotted to each individual of each of said classes pro rata in accordance with the provisions of this act: *And provided further,* That where the treaty or act of Congress setting apart such reservation provides for the allotment of lands in severalty in quantities in excess of those herein provided, the President, in making allotments upon such reservation, shall allot the lands to each individual Indian belonging thereon in quantity as specified in such treaty or act: *And provided further,* That when the lands allotted are only valuable for grazing purposes, and additional allotment of such grazing lands, in quantities as above provided, shall be made to each individual.

Sec. 2. That all allotments set apart under the provisions of this act shall be selected by the Indians, heads of families selecting for their minor children, and the agents shall select for each orphan child, and in such manner as to embrace the improvements of the Indians making the selection. Where the improvements of two or more Indians have been made on the same legal subdivision of land, unless they shall otherwise agree, a provisional line may be run dividing said lands between them, and the amount to which each is entitled shall be equalized in the assignment of the remainder of the land to which they are entitled under this act: *Provided,* That if any one entitled to an allotment shall fail to make a selection within four years after the President shall direct that allotments may be made on a particular reservation, the Secretary of the Interior may direct the agent of such tribe or band, if such there be, and if there be no agent, then a special agent appointed for that purpose, to make a selection for such Indian, which election shall be allotted as in cases where selections are made by the Indians, and patents shall issue in like manner.

Sec. 3. That the allotments provided for in this act shall be made by special agents appointed by the President for such purpose, and the agents in charge of the respective reservations on which the allotments are directed to be made, under such rules and regulations as the Secretary of the Interior may from time to time prescribe, and shall be certified by such agents to the Commissioner of Indian Affairs, in duplicate, one copy to be retained in the Indian Office and the order to be transmitted to the Secretary of the Interior for his action, and to be deposited in the General Land Office.

Sec. 4. That where any Indian not residing upon a reservation, or for whose tribe no reservation has been provided by treaty, act of Congress, or executive order, shall make settlement upon any surveyed or unsurveyed lands of the United States not otherwise appropriated, he or she shall be entitled, upon application to the local land-office for the district in which the lands are located, to have the same allotted to him or her, and to his or her children, in quantities and manner as provided in this act for Indians residing upon reservations; and when such settlement is made upon unsurveyed lands, the grant to such Indians shall be adjusted upon the survey of the lands so as to conform thereto; and patents shall be issued to them for such lands in the manner and with the restrictions as herein provided. And the fees to which the officers of such local land-office would have been entitled had such lands been entered under the general laws for the disposition of the public lands shall be paid to them, from any moneys in the Treasury of the United States not otherwise appropriated, upon a statement of an account in their behalf for such fees by the Commissioner of the General Land Office, and a certification of such account to the Secretary of the Treasury by the Secretary of the Interior.

Sec. 5. That upon the approval of the allotments provided for in this act by the Secretary of the Interior; he shall cause patents to issue therefor in the name of the allottees, which patents shall be of the legal effect, and declare that the United States does and will hold the land thus allotted, for the period of twenty-five years, in trust for the sole use and benefit of the Indian to whom such allotment shall have been made, or, in case of his decease, of his heirs according to the laws of the State or Territory where such land is located, and that at the expiration of said period the United States will convey the same by patent to said Indian, or his heirs as aforesaid, in fee, discharged of said trust and free of all charge or incumbrance whatsoever: *Provided,* That the President of the United States may in any case in his discretion extend the period. And if any conveyance shall be made of the lands set apart and allotted as herein provided, or any contract made touching the same, before the expiration of the time above mentioned, such conveyance or contract shall be absolutely null and void: *Provided,* That the law of descent and partition in force in the State or Territory where such lands are situate shall apply thereto after patents therefor have been executed and delivered, except as herein otherwise provided; and the laws of the State of Kansas regulating the descent and partition of real estate shall, so far as practicable, apply to all lands in the Indian Territory which may be allotted in severalty under the provisions of this act: *And provided further,* That at any time after lands have been allotted to all the Indians of any tribe as herein provided, or sooner if in the opinion of the President it shall be for the best interests of said tribe, it shall be lawful for the Secretary of the Interior to negotiate with such Indian tribe for the purchase and release by said tribe, in conformity with the treaty or statute under which such reservation is held, of such portions of its reservation not allotted as such tribe shall, from time to time, consent to sell, on such terms and conditions as shall be considered just and equitable between the United States and said tribe of Indians, which purchase shall not be complete until ratified by Congress, and the form and manner of executing such release shall also be prescribed by Congress: *Provided however,* That all lands adapted to agriculture, with or without irrigation so sold or released to the United States by any Indian tribe shall be held by the United States for the sole purpose of securing homes to actual settlers and shall be disposed of by the United States to actual and bona fide settlers only in tracts not exceeding one hundred and sixty acres to any one person, on such terms as Congress shall prescribe, subject to grants which Congress may make in aid of education: *And provided further,* That no patents shall issue therefor except to the person so taking the same as and for a homestead, or his heirs, and after the expiration of five years occupancy thereof as such homestead; and any conveyance of said lands so taken as a homestead, or any contract touching the same, or lien thereon, created prior to the date of such patent, shall be null and void. And the sums agreed to be paid by the United States as purchase money for any portion of any such reservation shall be held in the Treasury of the United States for the sole use of the tribe or tribes of Indians; to whom such reservations belonged; and the same, with interest thereon at three per cent per annum, shall be at all times subject to appropriation by Congress for the education and civilization of such tribe or tribes of Indians or the members thereof. The patents aforesaid shall be recorded in the General Land Office, and afterward delivered, free of charge, to the allottee entitled thereto. And if any religious society or other organization is now occupying any of the public lands to which this act is applicable, for religious or educational work among the Indians, the Secretary of the Interior is hereby authorized to confirm such occupation to such society or organization, in quantity not exceeding one hundred and sixty acres in any one tract, so long as the same shall be so occupied, on such terms as he shall deem just; but nothing herein contained shall change or alter any claim of such society for religious or educational purposes heretofore granted by law. And hereafter in the employment of Indian police, or any other employees in the public service among any of the Indian tribes or bands affected by this act, and where Indians can perform the duties required, those Indians who have availed themselves of the provisions of this act and become citizens of the United States shall be preferred.

Sec. 6. That upon the completion of said allotments and the patenting of the lands to said allottees, each and every member of the respective bands or tribes of Indians to whom allotments have been made shall have the benefit of and be subject to the laws, both civil and criminal, of the State or Territory in which they may reside; and no Territory shall pass or enforce any law denying any such Indian within its jurisdiction the equal protection of the law. And every Indian born within the territorial limits of the United States to whom allotments shall have been made under the provisions of this act, or under any law or treaty, and every Indian born within the territorial limits of the United States who has voluntarily taken up, within said limits, his residence separate and apart from any tribe of Indians therein, and has adopted the habits of civilized life, is hereby declared to be a citizen of the United States, and is entitled to all the rights, privileges, and immunities of such citizens, whether said Indian has been or not, by birth or otherwise, a member of any tribe of Indians within the territorial limits of the United States without in any manner impairing or otherwise affecting the right of any such Indian to tribal or other property.

Sec. 7. That in cases where the use of water for irrigation is necessary to render the lands within any Indian reservation available for agricultural purposes, the Secretary of the Interior be, and he is hereby, authorized to prescribe such rules and regulations as he may deem necessary to secure a just and equal distribution thereof among the Indians residing upon any such reservations; and no other appropriation or grant of water by any riparian proprietor shall be authorized or permitted to the damage of any other riparian proprietor.

Sec. 8. That the provision of this act shall not extend to the territory occupied by the Cherokees, Creeks, Choctaws, Chickasawas, Seminoles, and Osage, Miamies and Peorias, and Sacs and Foxes, in the Indian Territory, nor to any of the reservations of the Seneca Nation of New York Indians in the State of New York, nor to that strip of territory in the State of Nebraska adjoining the Sioux Nation on the south added by executive order.

Sec. 9. That for the purpose of making the surveys and resurveys mentioned in section two of this act, there be, and hereby is, appropriated, out of any moneys in the Treasury not otherwise appropriated, the sum of one hundred thousand dollars, to be repaid proportionately out of the proceeds of the sales of such land as may be acquired from the Indians under the provisions of this act.

Sec. 10. That nothing in this act contained shall be so construed as to affect the right and power of Congress to grant the right of way through any lands granted to an Indian, or a tribe of Indians, for railroads or other highways, or telegraph lines, for the public use, or to condemn such lands to public uses, upon making just compensation.

Sec. 11. That nothing in this act shall be so construed as to prevent the removal of the Southern Ute Indians from their present reservation in Southwestern Colorado to a new reservation by and with the consent of a majority of the adult male members of said tribe.

Approved, February 8, 1887.

Interstate Commerce Act of 1887

United States Statutes at Large (49th Cong., 2d sess., chap. 104), pp. 379–387

An Act

To regulate commerce.

Be it enacted by the Senate and House of Representatives of the United States of America in Congress assembled, That the provisions of this act shall apply to any common carrier or carriers engaged in the transportation of passengers or property wholly by railroad, or partly by railroad and partly by water when both are used, under a common control, management, or arrangement, for a continuous carriage or shipment, from one State or Territory of the United States, or the District of Columbia, to any other State or Territory of the United States, or the District of Columbia, or from any place in the United States to an adjacent foreign country, or from any place in the United States through a foreign country to any other place in the United States, and also to the transportation in like manner of property shipped from any place in the United States to a foreign country and carried from such place to a port of trans-shipment, or shipped from a foreign country to any place in the United States and carried to such place from a port of entry either in the United States or an adjacent foreign country: *Provided, however,* That the provisions of this act shall not apply to the transportation of passengers or property, or to the receiving, delivering, storage, or handling of property, wholly within one State, and not shipped to or from a foreign country from or to any State or Territory as aforesaid.

The term "railroad" as used in this act shall include all bridges and ferries used or operated in connection with any railroad, and also all the road in use by any corporation operating a railroad, whether owned or operated under a contract, agreement, or lease; and the term "transportation" shall include all instrumentalities of shipment or carriage.

All charges made for any service rendered or to be rendered in the transportation of passengers or property as aforesaid, or in connection therewith, or for the receiving, delivering, storage, or handling of such property, shall be reasonable and just; and every unjust and unreasonable charge for such service is prohibited and declared to be unlawful.

Sec. 2. That if any common carrier subject to the provisions of this act shall, directly or indirectly, by any special rate, rebate, drawback, or other device, charge, demand, collect, or receive from any person or persons a greater or less compensation for any service rendered, or to be rendered, in the transportation of passengers or property, subject to the provisions of this act, than it charges, demands, collects, or receives from any other person or persons for doing for him or them a like and contemporaneous service in the transportation of a like kind of traffic under substantially similar circumstances and conditions, such common carrier shall be deemed guilty of unjust discrimination, which is hereby prohibited and declared to be unlawful.

Sec. 3. That it shall be unlawful for any common carrier subject to the provisions of this act to make or give any undue or unreasonable preference or advantage to any particular person, company, firm, corporation, or locality, or any particular description of traffic, in any respect whatsoever, or to subject any particular person, company, firm, corporation, or locality, or any particular description of traffic, to any undue or unreasonable prejudice or disadvantage in any respect whatsoever. Every common carrier subject to the provisions of this act shall according to their respective powers, afford all reasonable, proper, and equal facilities for the interchange of traffic between their respective lines, and for the receiving, forwarding, and delivering of passengers and property to and from their several lines and those connection therewith, and shall not discriminate in their rates and charges between such connecting lines; but this shall not be construed as requiring any such common carrier to give the use of its tracks or terminal facilities to another carrier engaged in like business.

Sec. 4. That it shall be unlawful for any common carrier subject to the provisions of this act to charge or receive any greater compensation in the aggregate for the transportation of passengers or of like kind of property, under substantially similar circumstances and conditions, for a shorter than for a longer distance over the same line, in the same direction, the shorter being included within the longer distance; but this shall not be construed as authorizing any common carrier within the terms of this act to charge and receive as great compensation for a shorter as for a longer distance: *Provided, however,* That upon application to the Commission appointed under the provisions of this act, such common carrier may, in special cases, after investigation by the Commission, be authorized to charge less for longer than for shorter distances for the transportation of passengers or property; and the Commission may from time to time prescribe the extent to which such designated common carrier may be relieved from the operation of this section of this act.

Sec. 5. That it shall be unlawful for any common carrier subject to the provisions of this act to enter into any contract, agreement, or combination with any other common carrier or carriers for the pooling of freights of different and competing railroads, or to divide between them the aggregate or net proceeds of the earnings of such railroads, or any portion thereof; and in any case of an agreement for the pooling of freights as aforesaid, each day of its continuance shall be deemed a separate offense.

Sec. 6. That every common carrier subject to the provisions of this act shall print and keep for public inspection schedules showing the rates and fares and charges for the transportation of passengers and property which any such common carrier has established and which are in force at the time upon its railroad, as defined by the first section of this act. The schedules printed as aforesaid by any such common carrier shall plainly state the places upon its railroad between which property and passengers will be carried, and shall contain the classification of freight in force upon such railroad, and shall also state separately the terminal charges and any rules or regulations which in any wise change, affect, or determine any part or the aggregate of such aforesaid rates and fares and charges. Such schedules shall be plainly printed in large type, of at least the size of ordinary pica, and copies for the use of the public shall be kept in every depot or station upon any such railroad, in such places and in such form that they can be conveniently inspected. . . .

No advance shall be made in the rates, fares, and charges which have been established and published as aforesaid by any common carrier in compliance with the requirements of this section, except after ten days' public notice, which shall plainly state the changes proposed to be made in the schedule then in force, and the time when the increased rates, fares, or charges will go into effect; . . .

And when any such common carrier shall have established and published its rates, fares, and charges in compliance with the provisions of this section, it shall be unlawful for such common carrier to charge, demand, collect, or receive from any person or persons a greater or less compensation for the transportation of passengers or property, or for any services in connection therewith, than is specified in such published schedule of rates, fares, and charges as may at the time be in force.

Every common carrier subject to the provisions of this act shall file with the Commission hereinafter provided for copies of its schedules of rates, fares, and charges which have been established and published in compliance with the requirements of this section, and shall promptly notify said Commission of all changes made in the same. Every such common carrier shall also file with said Commission copies of all contracts, agreements, or arrangements with other common carriers in relation to any traffic affected by the provisions of this act to which it may be a party. . . .

Sec. 9. That any person or persons claiming to be damaged by any common carrier subject to the provisions of this act may either make complaint to the Commission as hereinafter provided for, or may bring suit in his or their own behalf for the recovery of the damages for which such common carrier may be liable under the provisions of this act, in any district or circuit court of the United States of competent jurisdiction; . . .

Sec. 10. That any common carrier subject to the provisions of this act, or, whenever such common carrier is a corporation, any director or officer thereof, or any receiver, trustee, lessee, agent, or person acting for or employed by such corporation, who, alone or with any other corporation, company, person, or party, shall willfully do or cause to be done, or shall willingly suffer or permit to be done, any act, matter, or thing in this act prohibited or declared to be unlawful, or who shall aid or abet therein, or shall willfully omit or fail to do any act, matter, or thing in this act required to be done, or shall cause or willingly suffer or permit any act, matter, or thing so directed or required by this act to be done not to be so done, or shall aid or abet any such omission or failure, or shall be guilty of any infraction of this act, or shall aid or abet therein, shall be deemed guilty of a misdemeanor, and shall, upon conviction thereof in any district court of the United States within the jurisdiction of which such offense was committed, be subject to a fine of not to exceed five thousand dollars for each offense.

Sec. 11. That a Commission is hereby created and established to be known as the Inter-State Commerce Commission, which shall be composed of five Commissioners, who shall be appointed by the President, by and with the advice and consent of the Senate. The Commissioners first appointed under this act shall continue in office for the term of two, three, four, five, and six years, respectively, from the first day of January, anno Domini eighteen hundred and eighty-seven, the term of each to be designated by the President; but their successors shall be appointed for terms of six years, except that any person chosen to fill a vacancy shall be appointed only for the unexpired term of the Commissioner whom he shall succeed. Any Commissioner may be removed by the President for inefficiency, neglect of duty, or malfeasance in office. Not more than three of the Commissioners shall be appointed from the same political party. No person in the employ of or holding any official relation to any common carrier subject to the provisions of this act, or owning stock or bonds thereof, or who is in any manner pecuniarily interested therein, shall enter upon the duties of or hold such office. Said Commissioners shall not engage in any other business, vocation, or employment. No vacancy in the Commission shall impair the right of the remaining Commissioners to exercise all the powers of the Commission.

Sec. 12. That the Commission hereby created shall have authority to inquire into the management of the business of all common carriers subject to the provisions of this act, and shall keep itself informed as to the manner and method in which the same is conducted, and shall have the right to obtain from such common carriers full and complete information necessary to enable the Commission to perform the duties and carry out the objects for which it was created; and for the purposes of this act the Commission shall have power to require the attendance and testimony of witnesses and the production of all books, papers, tariffs, contracts, agreements, and documents relating to any matter under investigation, and to that end may invoke the aid of any court of the United States in requiring the attendance and testimony of witnesses and the production of books, papers, and documents under the provisions of this section. . . .

Sec. 13. That any person, firm, corporation, or association, or any mercantile, agricultural, or manufacturing society, or any body politic or municipal organization complaining of anything done or omitted to be done by any common carrier subject to the provisions of this act in contravention of the provisions thereof, may apply to said Commission by petition, which shall briefly state the facts; whereupon a statement of the charges thus made shall be forwarded by the Commission to such common carrier, who shall be called upon to satisfy the complaint or to answer the same in writing within a reasonable time, to be specified by the Commission. If such common carrier, within the time specified, shall make reparation for the injury alleged to have been done, said carrier shall be relieved of liability to the complainant only for the particular violation of law thus complained of. If such carrier shall not satisfy the complaint within the time specified, or there shall appear to be any reasonable ground for investigating said complaint, it shall be the duty of the Commission to investigate the matters complained of in such manner and by such means as it shall deem proper.

Said Commission shall in like manner investigate any complaint forwarded by the railroad commissioner or railroad commission of any State or Territory, at the request of such commissioner or commission, and may institute any inquiry on its own motion in the same manner and to the same effect as though complaint had been made. . . .

Sec. 16. That whenever any common carrier, as defined in and subject to the provisions of this act, shall violate or refuse or neglect to obey any lawful order or requirement of the Commission in this act named, it shall be the duty of the Commission, and lawful for any company or person interested in such order or requirement, to apply, in a summary way, by petition, to the circuit court of the United States sitting in equity in the judicial district in which the common carrier complained of has its principal office, or in which the violation or disobedience of such order or requirement shall happen, alleging such violation or disobedience, as the case may be; and the said court shall have power to hear and determine the matter, on such short notice to the common carrier complained of as the court shall deem reasonable; . . .

Sec. 20. That the Commission is hereby authorized to require annual reports from all common carriers subject to the provisions of this act, to fix the time and prescribe the manner in which such reports shall be made, and to require from such carriers specific answers to all questions upon which the Commission may need information. Such annual reports shall show in detail the amount of capital stock issued, the amounts paid therefor, and the manner of payment for the same; the dividends paid, the surplus fund, if any, and the number of stockholders; the funded and floating debts and the interest paid thereon; the cost and value of the carrier's property, franchises, and equipment; the number of employees and the salaries paid each class; the amounts expended for improvements each year, how expended, and the character of such improvements; the earnings and receipts from each branch of business and from all sources; the operating and other expenses; the balances of profit and loss; and a complete exhibit of the financial operations of the carrier each year, including an annual balance sheet. Such reports shall also contain such information in relation to rates or regulations concerning fares or freights, or agreements, arrangements, or contracts with other common carriers, as the Commission may require; and the said Commission may, within its discretion, for the purpose of enabling it the better to carry out the purposes of this act, prescribe (if in the opinion of the Commission it is practicable to prescribe such uniformity and methods of keeping accounts) a period of time within which all common carriers subject to the provisions of this act shall have, as near as may be, a uniform system of accounts, and the manner in which such accounts shall be kept. . . .

"Wealth" (1889)
Andrew Carnegie

In John A. Scott, ed. *Living Documents in American History,* Vol. 1 (New York: Washington Square Press, 1964–68), pp. 102–114

The problem of our age is the proper administration of wealth, so that the ties of brotherhood may still bind together the rich and poor in harmonious relationship. The conditions of human life have not only been changed, but revolutionized, within the past few hundred years. In former days there was little difference between the dwelling, dress, food, and environment of the chief and those of his retainers. The Indians are to-day where civilized man then was. When visiting the Sioux, I was led to the wigwam of the chief. It was just like the others in external appearance, and even within the difference was trifling between it and those of the poorest of his braves. The contrast between the palace of the millionaire and the cottage of the laborer with us to-day measures the change which has come with civilization.

This change, however, is not to be deplored, but welcomed as highly beneficial. It is well, nay, essential for the progress of the race, that the houses of some should be homes for all that is highest and best in literature and the arts, and for all the refinements of civilization, rather than that none should be so. Much better this great irregularity than universal squalor. Without wealth there can be no Maecenas. The "good old times" were not good old times. Neither master nor servant was as well situated then as today. A relapse to old conditions would be disastrous to both—not the least so to him who serves—and would sweep away civilization with it. But whether the change be for good or ill, it is upon us, beyond our power to alter, and therefore to be accepted and made the best of. It is a waste of time to criticize the inevitable.

It is easy to see how the change has come. One illustration will serve for almost every phase of the cause. In the manufacture of products we have the whole story. It applies to all combinations of human industry, as stimulated and enlarged by the inventions of this scientific age. Formerly articles were manufactured at the domestic hearth or in small shops which formed part of the household. The master and his apprentices worked side by side, the latter living with the master, and therefore subject to the same conditions. When these apprentices rose to be masters, there was little or no change in their mode of life, and they, in turn, educated in the same routine succeeding apprentices. There was, substantially, social equality, and even political equality, for those engaged in industrial pursuits had then little or no political voice in the State.

But the inevitable result of such a mode of manufacture was crude articles at high prices. To-day the world obtains commodities of excellent quality at prices which even the generation preceding this would have deemed incredible. In the commercial world similar causes have produced similar results, and the race is benefited thereby. The poor enjoy what the rich could not before afford. What were the luxuries have become the necessaries of life. The laborer has now more comforts than the farmer had a few generations ago. The farmer has more luxuries than the landlord had, and is more richly clad and better housed. The landlord has books and pictures rarer, and appointments more artistic, than the King could then obtain.

The price we pay for this salutary change is, no doubt, great. We assemble thousands of operatives in the factory, in the mine, and in the counting-house, of whom the employer can know little or nothing, and to whom the employer is little better than a myth. All intercourse between them is at an end. Rigid Castes are formed, and, as usual, mutual ignorance breeds mutual distrust. Each Caste is without sympathy for the other, and ready to credit anything disparaging in regard to it. Under the law of competition, the employer of thousands is forced into the strictest economies, among which the rates paid to labor figure prominently, and often there is friction between the employer and the employed, between capital and labor, between rich and poor. Human society loses homogeneity.

The price which society pays for the law of competition, like the price it pays for cheap comforts and luxuries, is also great; but the advantages of this law are also greater still, for it is to this law that we owe our wonderful material development, which brings improved conditions in its train. But, whether the law is benign or not, we must say of it, as we say of the change in the conditions of men to which we have referred: It is here, we cannot evade it; no substitutes for it have been found; and while the law may be sometimes hard for the individual, it is best for the race, because it insures the survival of the fittest in every department. We accept and welcome, therefore, as conditions to which we must accommodate ourselves, great inequality of environment, the concentration of business, industrial and commercial, in the hands of a few, and the law of competition between these, as being not only beneficial, but essential for the future progress of the race. Having accepted these, it follows that there must be great scope for the exercise of special ability in the merchant and in the manufacturer who has to conduct affairs upon a great scale. That this talent for organization and management is rare among men is proved by the fact that it invariably secures for its possessor enormous rewards, no matter where or under what laws or conditions. The experienced in affairs always rate the Man whose services can be obtained as a partner as not only the first consideration, but such as to render the question of his capital scarcely worth considering, for such men soon create capital; while, without the special talent required, capital soon takes wings. Such men become interested in forms or corporations using millions; and estimating only simple interest to be made upon the capital invested, it is inevitable that their income must exceed their expenditures, and that they must accumulate wealth. Nor is there any middle ground which such men can occupy, because the great manufacturing or commercial concern which does not earn at least interest upon its capital soon becomes bankrupt. It must either go forward or fall behind: to stand still is impossible. It is a condition essential for its successful operation that it should be thus far profitable, and even that, in addition to interest on capital, it should make profit. It is a law, as certain as any of the others named, that men possessed of this peculiar talent for affairs, under the free play of economic forces, must, of necessity, soon be in receipt of more revenue than can be judiciously expended upon themselves; and this law is as beneficial for the race as the others.

Objections to the foundations upon which society is based are not in order, because the condition of the race is better with these than it has been with any others which have been tried. Of the effect of any new substitutes proposed we cannot be sure. The Socialist or Anarchist who seeks to overturn present conditions is to be regarded as attacking the foundation upon which civilization itself rests, for civilization took its start from the day that the capable, industrious workman said to his incompetent and lazy fellow, "If thou dost not sow, thou shalt not reap," and thus ended primitive Communism by separating the drones from the bees. One who studies this subject will soon be brought face to face with the conclusion that upon the sacredness of property civilization itself depends—the right of the laborer to his hundred dollars in the savings bank, and equally the legal right of the millionaire to his millions. To those who propose to substitute Communism for this intense Individualism the answer, therefore, is: The race has tried that. All progress from that barbarous day to the present time has resulted from its displacement. Not evil, but good, has come to the race from the accumulation of wealth by those who have the ability and energy that produce it.

But even if we admit for a moment that it might be better for the race to discard its present foundation, Individualism, that it is a nobler ideal that man should labor, not for himself alone, but in and for a brotherhood of his fellows, and share with them all in common, realizing Swedenborg's idea of Heaven, where, as he says, the angels derive their happiness, not from laboring for self, but for each other—even admit all this, and a sufficient answer is, This is not evolution, but revolution. It necessitates the changing of human nature itself—a work of aeons, even if it were good to change it, which we cannot know. It is not practicable in our day or in our age. Even if desirable theoretically, it belongs to another and long-succeeding sociological stratum. Our duty is with what is practicable now; with the next step possible in our day and generation. It is criminal to waste our energies in endeavoring to uproot, when all we can profitably or possibly accomplish is to bend the universal tree of humanity a little in the direction most favorable to the production of good fruit under existing circumstances. We might as well urge the destruction of the highest existing type of man because he failed to reach our ideal as to favor the destruction of Individualism, Private Property, the Law of Accumulation of Wealth, and the Law of Competition; for these are the highest results of human experience, the soil in which society so far has produced the best fruit. Unequally or unjustly, perhaps, as these laws sometimes operate, and imperfect as they appear to the Idealist, they are, nevertheless, like the highest type of man, the best and most valuable of all that humanity has yet accomplished.

We start, then, with a condition of affairs under which the best interests of the race are promoted, but which inevitably gives wealth to the few. Thus far, accepting conditions as they exist, the situation can be surveyed and pronounced good. The question then arises—and, if the foregoing be correct, it is the only question with which we have to deal—What is the proper mode of administering wealth after the laws upon which civilization is founded have thrown it into the hands of the few? And it is of this great question that I believe I offer the true solution. It will be understood that *fortunes* are here spoken of, not moderate sums saved by many years of effort, the returns from which are required for the comfortable maintenance and education of families. This is not *wealth,* but only *competence,* which it should be the aim of all to acquire.

There are but three modes in which surplus wealth can be disposed of. It can be left to the families of the decedents; or it can be bequeathed for public purposes; or, finally, it can be administered during their lives by its possessors. Under the first and second modes most of the wealth of the world that has reached the few has hitherto been applied. Let us in turn consider each of these modes. The first is the most injudicious. In monarchical countries, the estates and the greatest portion of the wealth are left to the first son, that the vanity of the parent may be gratified by the thought that his name and title are to descend to succeeding generations unimpaired. The condition of this class in Europe to-day teaches the futility of such hopes or ambitions. The successors have become impoverished through their follies or from the fall in the value of land. Even in Great Britain the strict law of entail has been found inadequate to maintain the status of an hereditary class. Its soil is rapidly passing into the hands of the stranger. Under republican institutions the division of property among the children is much fairer, but the question which forces itself upon thoughtful men in all lands is: Why should men leave great fortunes to their children? If this is done from affection, is it not misguided affection? Observation teaches that, generally speaking, it is not well for the children that they should be so burdened. Neither is it well for the state. Beyond providing for the wife and daughters moderate sources of income, and very moderate allowances indeed, if any, for the sons, men may well hesitate, for it is no longer questionable that great sums bequeathed oftener work more for the injury than for the good of the recipients. Wise men will soon conclude that, for the best interests of the members of their families and of the state, such bequests are an improper use of their means . . .

As to the second mode, that of leaving wealth at death for public uses, it may be said that this is only a means for the disposal of wealth, provided a man is content to wait until he is dead before it becomes of much good in the world. Knowledge of the results of legacies bequeathed is not calculated to inspire the brightest hopes of much posthumous good being accomplished. The cases are not few in which the real object sought by the testator is not attained, nor are they few in which his real wishes are thwarted. In many cases the bequests are so used as to become only monuments of his folly . . .

There remains, then, only one mode of using great fortunes; but in this we have the true antidote for the temporary unequal distribution of wealth, the reconciliation of the rich and the poor—a reign of harmony—another ideal, differing, indeed, from that of the Communist in requiring only the further evolution of existing conditions, not the total overthrow of our civilization. It is founded upon the present most intense individualism, and the race is prepared to put it in practice by degrees whenever it pleases. Under its sway we shall have an ideal state, in which the surplus wealth of the few will become, in the best sense, the property of the many, because administered for the common good; and this wealth, passing through the hands of the few, can be made a much more potent force for the elevation of our race than if it had been distributed in small sums to the people themselves. Even the poorest can be made to see this, and to agree that great sums gathered by some of their fellow-citizens and spent for public purposes, from which the masses reap the principal benefit, are more valuable to them than if scattered among them through the course of many years in trifling amounts.

If we consider what results flow from the Cooper Institute, for instance, to the best portion of the race in New York not possessed of means, and compare these with those which would have arisen for the good of the masses from an equal sum distributed by Mr. Cooper in his lifetime in the form of wages, which is the highest form of distribution, being for work done and not for charity, we can form some estimate of the possibilities for the improvement of the race which lie embedded in the present law of the accumulation of wealth. Much of this sum, if distributed in small quantities among the people, would have been wasted in the indulgence of appetite, some of it in excess; and it may be doubted whether even the part put to the best use, that of adding to the comforts of the home, would have yielded results for the race, as a race, at all comparable to those which are flowing and are to flow from the Cooper Institute from generation to generation. Let the advocate of violent or radical change ponder well this thought.

We might even go so far as to take another instance, that of Mr. Tilden's bequest of five millions of dollars for a free library in the city of New York; but in referring to this one cannot help saying involuntarily, How much better if Mr. Tilden had devoted the last years of his own life to the proper administration of this immense sum; in which case neither legal contest nor any other cause of delay could have interfered with his aims. But let us assume that Mr. Tilden's millions finally become the means of giving to this city a noble public library, where the treasures of the world contained in books will be open to all forever, without money and without price. Considering the good of that part of the race which congregates in and around Manhattan Island, would its permanent benefit have been better promoted had these millions been allowed to circulate in small sums through the hands of the masses? Even the most strenuous advocate of Communism must entertain a doubt upon this subject. Most of those who think will probably entertain no doubt whatever.

Poor and restricted are our opportunities in this life; narrow our horizon; our best work most imperfect; but rich men should be thankful for one inestimable boon. They have it in their power during their lives to busy themselves in organizing benefactions from which the masses of their fellows will derive lasting advantage, and thus dignify their own lives. The highest life is probably to be reached, not by such imitation of the life of Christ as Count Tolstoi gives us, but, while animated by Christ's spirit, by recognizing the changed conditions of this age, and adopting modes of expressing this spirit suitable to the changed conditions under which we live; still laboring for the good of our fellows, which was the essence of his life and teaching, but laboring in a different manner.

This, then, is held to be the duty of the man of Wealth: First, to set an example of modest, unostentatious living, shunning display or extravagance; to provide moderately for the legitimate wants of those dependent upon him; and after doing so to consider all surplus revenues which come to him simply as trust funds, which he is called upon to administer, and strictly bound as a matter of duty to administer in the manner which, in his judgment, is best calculated to produce the most beneficial results for the community—the man of wealth thus becoming the mere agent and trustee for his poorer brethren, bringing to their service his superior wisdom, experience, and ability to administer, doing for them better than they would or could do for themselves . . .

The best uses to which surplus wealth can be put have already been indicated. Those who would administer wisely must, indeed, be wise, for one of the serious obstacles to the improvement of our race is indiscriminate charity. It were better for mankind that the millions of the rich were thrown into the sea than so spent as to encourage the slothful, the drunken, the unworthy. Of every thousand dollars spent in so called charity to-day, it is probable that $950 is unwisely spent; so spent, indeed, as to produce the very evils which it proposes to mitigate or cure. A well-known writer of philosophic books admitted the other day that he had given a quarter of a dollar to a man who approached him as he was coming to visit the house of his friend. He knew nothing of the habits of this beggar, knew not the use that would be made of this money, although he had every reason to suspect that it would be spent improperly. This man professed to be a disciple of Herbert Spencer; yet the quarter-dollar given that night will probably work more injury than all the money which its thoughtless donor will ever be able to give in true charity will do good. He only gratified his own feelings, saved himself from annoyance—and this was probably one of the most selfish and very worst actions of his life, for in all respects he is most worthy.

In bestowing charity, the main consideration should be to help those who will help themselves; to provide part of the means by which those who desire to improve may do so; to give those who desire to rise the aids by which they may rise; to assist, but rarely or never to do all. Neither the individual nor the race is improved by alms-giving. Those worthy of assistance, except in rare cases, seldom require assistance; the really valuable men of the race never do, except in cases of accident or sudden change. Every one has, of course, cases of individuals brought to his own knowledge where temporary assistance can do genuine good, and these he will not overlook. But the amount which can be wisely given by the individual for individuals is necessarily limited by his lack of knowledge of the circumstances connected with each. He is the only true reformer who is as careful and as anxious not to aid the unworthy as he is to aid the worthy, and, perhaps, even more so, for in alms-giving more injury is probably done by rewarding vice than by relieving virtue.

The rich man is thus almost restricted to following the examples of Peter Cooper, Enoch Pratt of Baltimore, Mr. Pratt of Brooklyn, Senator Stanford, and others, who know that the best means of benefiting the community is to place within its reach the ladders upon which the aspiring can rise—parks, and means of recreation, by which men are helped in body and mind; works of art, certain to give pleasure and improve the public taste, and public institutions of various kinds, which will improve the general condition of the people—in this manner returning their surplus wealth to the mass of their fellows in the forms best calculated to do them lasting good.

Thus is the problem of Rich and Poor to be solved. The laws of accumulation will be left free; the laws of distribution free. Individualism will continue, but the millionaire will be but a trustee for the poor; intrusted for a season with a great part of the increased wealth of the community, but administering it for the community far better than it could or would have done for itself. The best minds will thus have reached a stage in the development of the race in which it is clearly seen that there is no mode of disposing of surplus wealth creditable to thoughtful and earnest men into whose hands it flows save by using it year by year for the general good. This day already dawns. But a little while, and although, without incurring the pity of their fellows, men may die sharers in great business enterprises from which their capital cannot be or has not been withdrawn, and is left chiefly at death for public uses; yet the man who dies leaving behind him millions of available wealth, which was his to administer during life, will pass away "unwept, unhonored, and unsung," no matter to what uses he leaves the dross which he cannot take with him. Of such as these the public verdict will then be: "The man who dies thus rich dies disgraced."

Such, in my opinion, is the true Gospel concerning Wealth, obedience to which is destined some day to solve the problem of the Rich and the Poor, and to bring "Peace on earth, among men Good-Will."

How the Other Half Lives (1890)

Jacob A. Riis

In Erik Bruun and Jay Crosby, eds. *Our Nation's Archives: The History of the United States in Documents* (New York: Black Dog & Leventhal Publishers, 1999), pp. 451–458

The street Arab is as much of an institution in New York as Newspaper Row, to which he gravitates naturally, following his Bohemian instinct. Crowded out of the tenements to shift for himself, and quite ready to do it, he meets the host of adventurous runaways from every State in the Union and from across the sea, whom New York attracts with a queer fascination, as it attracts older emigrants from all parts of the world. A census of the population in the Newsboys' Lodging-house on any night will show such an odd mixture of small humanity as could hardly be got together in any other spot. It is a mistake to think that they are helpless little creatures, to be pitied and cried over because they are alone in the world. The unmerciful "guying" the good man would receive, who went to them with such a programme, would soon convince him that that sort of pity was wasted, and would very likely give him the idea that they were a set of hardened little scoundrels, quite beyond the reach of missionary effort.

But that would only be his second mistake. The Street Arab has all the faults and all the virtues of the lawless Life he leads. Vagabond that he is, acknowledging no authority and owing no allegiance to anybody or anything, with his grimy fist raised against society whenever it tries to coerce him, he is as bright and sharp as the weasel, which, among all the predatory beasts, he most resembles. His sturdy independence, love of freedom and absolute self-reliance, together with his rude sense of justice that enables him to govern his little community, not always in accordance with municipal law or city ordinances, but often a good deal closer to the saving line of "doing to others as one would be done by"—these are strong handles by which those who know how can catch the boy and make him useful. Successful bankers, clergymen, and lawyers all over the country, statesmen in some instances of national repute, bear evidence in their lives to the potency of such missionary efforts. There is scarcely a learned profession, or branch of honorable business, that has not in the last twenty years borrowed some of its brightest light from the poverty and gloom of New York's streets.

Anyone, whom business or curiosity has taken through Park Row or across Printing House Square in the midnight hour, when the air is filled with the roar of great presses spinning with printers' ink on endless rolls of white paper the history of the world in twenty-four hours that have just passed away, has seen little groups of these boys hanging about the newspaper offices; in winter, when snow is on the streets, fighting for warm spots around the grated vent-holes that let out the heat and steam from the underground rooms with their noise and clatter, and in summer playing craps and 7-11 on the curb for their hard-earned pennies, with all the absorbing concern of hardened gamblers. This is their beat. Here the agent for the Society for the Prevention of Cruelty to Children finds those he thinks too young for "business," but does not always capture them. Like rabbits in their burrows, the little ragamuffins sleep with at least one eye open, and every sense alert to the approach of danger: of their enemy, the policeman, whose chief business in life is to move them on, and of the agent bent on robbing them of their cherished freedom. At the first warning shot they scatter and are off. To pursue them would be like chasing the fleet-footed mountain goat in his rocky fastnesses.

Sherman Antitrust Act of 1890

United States Statutes at Large (51st Cong., 2d sess., chap. 647), pp. 209–210

An Act

To protect trade and commerce against unlawful restraints and monopolies.

Be it enacted by the Senate and House of Representatives of the United States of America in Congress assembled,

Sec. 1. Every contract, combination in the form of trust or otherwise, or conspiracy, in restraint of trade or commerce among the several States, or with foreign nations, is hereby declared to be illegal. Every person who shall make any such contract or engage in any such combination or conspiracy, shall be deemed guilty of a misdemeanor, and, on conviction thereof, shall be punished by fine not exceeding five thousand dollars, or by imprisonment not exceeding one year, or by both said punishments, in the discretion of the court.

Sec. 2. Every person who shall monopolize, or attempt to monopolize, or combine or conspire with any other person or persons, to monopolize any part of the trade or commerce among the several States, or with foreign nations, shall be deemed guilty of a misdemeanor, and, on conviction thereof, shall be punished by fine not exceeding five thousand dollars, or by imprisonment not exceeding one year, or by both said punishments, in the discretion of the court.

Sec. 3. Every contract, combination in form of trust or otherwise, or conspiracy, in restraint of trade or commerce in any Territory of the United States or of the District of Columbia, or in restraint of trade or commerce between any such Territory and another, or between any such Territory or Territories and any State or States or the District of Columbia, or with foreign nations, or between the District of Columbia and any State or States or foreign nations, is hereby declared illegal. Every person who shall make any such contract or engage in any such combination or conspiracy, shall be deemed guilty of a misdemeanor, and, on conviction thereof, shall be punished by fine not exceeding five thousand dollars, or by imprisonment not exceeding one year, or by both said punishments, in the discretion of the court.

Sec. 4. The several circuit courts of the United States are hereby invested with jurisdiction to prevent and restrain violations of this act; and it shall be the duty of the several district attorneys of the United States, in their respective districts, under the direction of the Attorney-General, to institute proceedings in equity to prevent and restrain such violations. Such proceedings may be by way of petition setting forth the case and praying that such violation shall be enjoined or otherwise prohibited. When the parties complained of shall have been duly notified of such petition the court shall proceed, as soon as may be, to the hearing and determination of the case; and pending such petition and before final decree, the court may at any time make such temporary restraining order or prohibition as shall be deemed just in the premises.

Sec. 5. Whenever it shall appear to the court before which any proceeding under section four of this act may be pending, that the ends of justice require that other parties should be brought before the court, the court may cause them to be summoned, whether they reside in the district in which the court is held or not; and subpoenas to that end may be served in any district by the marshal thereof.

Sec. 6. Any property owned under any contract or by any combination, or pursuant to any conspiracy (and being the subject thereof) mentioned in section one of this act, and being in the course of transportation from one State to another, or to a foreign country, shall be forfeited to the United States, and may be seized and condemned by like proceedings as those provided by law for the forfeiture, seizure, and condemnation of property imported into the United States contrary to law.

Sec. 7. Any person who shall be injured in his business or property by any other person or corporation by reason of anything forbidden or declared to be unlawful by this act, may sue therefor in any circuit court of the United States in the district in which the defendant resides or is found, without respect to the amount in controversy, and shall recover three fold the damages by him sustained, and the costs of suit, including a reasonable attorney's fee.

Sec. 8. That the word "person," or "persons," wherever used in this act shall be deemed to include corporations and associations existing under or authorized by the laws of either the United States, the laws of any of the Territories, the laws of any State, or the laws of any foreign country.

Approved, July 2, 1890.

"The Labor Movement Is a Fixed Fact" (May 1st, 1890)

Samuel Gompers

In Erik Bruun and Jay Crosby, eds. *Our Nation's Archives: The History of the United States in Documents* (New York: Black Dog & Leventhal Publishers, 1999), pp. 458–460

My friends, we have met here today to celebrate the idea that has prompted thousands of workingpeople of Louisville and New Albany to parade the streets of [your city]; that prompts the toilers of Chicago to turn out by their fifty or hundred thousand men; that prompts the vast army of wageworkers in New York to demonstrate their enthusiasm and appreciation of the importance of this idea; that prompts the toilers of England, Ireland, Germany, France, Italy, Spain, and Austria to defy the manifestos of the autocrats of the world and say that on May the first, 1890, the wage-workers of the world will lay down their tools in sympathy with the wage-workers of America, to establish a principle of limitations of hours of labor to eight hours for sleep, eight hours for work, and eight hours for what we will.

It has been charged time and again that were we to have more hours of leisure we would merely devote it to debauchery, to the cultivation of vicious habits-in other words, that we would get drunk. I desire to say this in answer to that charge: As a rule, there are two classes in society who get drunk. One is the class who has no work to do, because it can't get any, and gets drunk on its face. I maintain that that class in our social life that exhibits the greatest degree of sobriety is that class who are able, by a fair number of hours of day's work to earn fair wages-not overworked. The man who works twelve, fourteen, and sixteen hours a day requires some artificial stimulation to restore the life ground out of him in the drudgery of the day. . . .

We ought to be able to discuss this question on a higher ground, and I am pleased to say that the movement in which we are engaged will stimulate us to it. They tell us that the eight-hour movement can not be enforced, for the reason that it must check industrial and commercial progress. I say that the history of this country, in its industrial and commercial relations, shows the reverse. I say that is the plane on which this question ought to be discussed—that is the social question. As long as they make this question an economic one, I am willing to discuss it with them. I would retrace every step I have taken to advance this movement did it mean industrial and commercial stagnation. But it does not mean that. It means greater prosperity; it means a greater degree of progress for the whole people; it means more advancement and intelligence, and a nobler race of people. . . .

They say they can't afford it. Is that true? Let us see for one moment. If a reduction in the hours of labor causes industrial and commercial ruination, it would naturally follow increased hours of labor would increase the prosperity, commercial and industrial. If that were true, England and America ought to be at the tail end, and China at the head of civilization.

Is it not a fact that we find laborers in England and the United States, where the hours are eight, nine and ten hours a day—do we not find that employers and laborers are more successful? Don't we find them selling articles cheaper? We do not need to trust the modern moralist to tell us those things. In all industries where the hours of labor are long, there you will find the least development of the power of invention. Where the hours of labor are long, men are cheap, and where men are cheap there is no necessity for invention. How can you expect a man to work ten or twelve or fourteen hours at his calling and then devote any time to the invention of a machine or discovery of a new principle or force? If he be so fortunate as to be able to read a paper he will fall a sleep before he has read through the second or third line.

Why, when you reduce the hours of labor, say an hour a day, just think what it means. Suppose men who work ten hours a day had the time lessened to nine, or men who work nine hours a day have it reduced to eight hours; what does it mean.It means millions of golden hours and opportunities for thought. Some men might say you will go to sleep. Well, some men might sleep sixteen hours a day; the ordinary man might try that, but he would soon find he could not do it long. He would have to do something. He would probably go to the theater one night, to a concert another night, but could not do that every night. He would probably become interested in some study and the hours that have been taken from manual labor are devoted to mental labor, and the mental labor of one hour will produce for him more wealth than the physical labor of a dozen hours.

I maintain that this is a true proposition—that men under the short-hour system not only have opportunity to improve themselves, but to make a greater degree of prosperity for their employers. Why, my friends, how is it in China, how is it in Spain, how is it in India and Russia, how is it in Italy? Cast your eye throughout the universe and observe the industry that forces nature to yield up its fruits to man's necessities, and you will find that where the hours of labor are the shortest the progress of invention in machinery and the prosperity of the people are the greatest. It is the greatest impediment to progress to hire men cheaply. Wherever men are cheap, there you find the least degree of progress. It has only been under the great influence of our great republic, where our people have exhibited their great senses, that we can move forward, upward and onward, and are watched with interest in our movements of progress and reform. . . .

The man who works the long hours has no necessities except the barest to keep body and soul together, so he can work. He goes to sleep and dreams of work; he rises in the morning to go to work; he takes his frugal lunch to work; he comes home again to throw himself down on a miserable apology for a bed so that he can get that little rest that he may be able to go to work again. He is nothing but a veritable machine. He lives to work instead of working to live.

My friends, the only thing the working people need besides the necessities of life, is time. Time. Time with which our lives begin; time with which our lives close; time to cultivate the better nature within us; time to brighten our homes. Time, which brings us from the lowest condition up to the highest civilization; time, so that we can raise men to a higher plane.

My friends, you will find that it has been ascertained that there is more than a million brothers and sisters—able-bodied men and women—on the streets, and on the highways and byways of our country willing to work but cannot find it. You know that it is the theory of our government that we can work or cease to work at will. It is only a theory. You know that it is only a theory and not a fact. It is true that we can cease to work when we want to, but I deny that we can work when we will, so long as there are a million idle men and women tramping the streets of our cities, searching for work. The theory that we can work or cease to work when we will is a delusion and a snare. It is a lie.

What we want to consider is, first, to make our employment more secure, and, secondly, to make wages more permanent, and, thirdly, to give these poor people a chance to work. The taborer has been regarded as a mere producing machine . . . but the back of labor is the soul of man and honesty of purpose and aspiration. Now you can not, as the political economists and college professors [do], say that labor is a commodity to be bought and sold. I say we are American citizens with the heritage of all the great men who have stood before us; men who have sacrificed all in the cause except honor. Our enemies would like to see this movement thrust into Hades, they would like to see it in a warmer climate, but I say to you that this labor movement has come to stay. Like Banquo's ghost, it will not stay down. I say the labor movement is a fixed fact. It has grown out of the necessities of the people, and, although some may desire to see it fail, still the labor movement will be found to have a strong lodgment in the hearts of the people, and we will go on until success has been achieved.

We want eight hours and nothing less. We have been accused of being selfish, and it has been said that we will want more; that last year we got an advance of ten cents and now we want more. We do want more. You will find that a man generally wants more. Go and ask a tramp what he wants, and if he doesn't want a drink, he wants a good, square meat. You ask a workingman, who is getting two dollars a day, and he will say that he wants ten cents more. Ask a man who gets five dollars a day and he wilt want fifty cents more. The man who receives five thousand dollars a year wants six thousand dollars a year, and the man who owns eight or nine hundred thousand dollars will want a hundred thousand dollars more to make it a million, while the man who has his millions will want everything he can lay his hands on and then raise his voice against the poor devil who wants ten cents more a day. We live in the later part of the nineteenth century. In the age of electricity and steam that has produced wealth a hundred fold, we insist that it has been brought about by the intelligence and energy of the workingmen, and while we find that is now easier to produce it is harder to live. We do want more, and when it becomes more, we shalt stilt want more. And we shall never cease to demand more until we have received the results of our labor.

Populist Party Platform, 1892

Henry Steele Commager and Milton Center, eds. *Documents of American History*, Vol. 1 (Englewood Cliff, N.J.: Prentice Hall, 1988)

Populist Party Platform

Assembled upon the 116th anniversary of the Declaration of Independence, the People's Party of America, in their first national convention, invoking upon their action the blessing of Almighty God, put forth in the name and on behalf of the people of this country, the following preamble and declaration of principles:

Preamble

The conditions which surround us best justify our co-operation; we meet in the midst of a nation brought to the verge of moral, political, and material ruin. Corruption dominates the ballot-box, the Legislatures, the Congress, and touches even the ermine of the bench. The people are demoralized; most of the States have been compelled to isolate the voters at the polling places to prevent universal intimidation and bribery. The newspapers are largely subsidized or muzzled, public opinion silenced, business prostrated, homes covered with mortgages, labor impoverished, and the land concentrating in the hands of capitalists. The urban workmen are denied the right to organize for self-protection, imported pauperized labor beats down their wages, a hireling standing army, unrecognized by our laws, is established to shoot them down, and they are rapidly degenerating into European conditions. The fruits of the toil of millions are boldly stolen to build up colossal fortunes for a few, unprecedented in the history of mankind; and the possessors of these, in turn, despise the Republic and endanger liberty. From the same prolific womb of governmental injustice we breed the two great classes—tramps and millionaires.

The national power to create money is appropriated to enrich bond-holders; a vast public debt payable in legal-tender currency has been funded into gold-bearing bonds, thereby adding millions to the burdens of the people.

Silver, which has been accepted as coin since the dawn of history, has been demonetized to add to the purchasing power of gold by decreasing the value of all forms of property as well as human labor, and the supply of currency is purposely abridged to fatten usurers, bankrupt enterprise, and enslave industry. A vast conspiracy against mankind has been organized on two continents, and it is rapidly taking possession of the world. If not met and overthrown at once it forebodes terrible social convulsions, the destruction of civilization, or the establishment of an absolute despotism.

We have witnessed for more than a quarter of a century the struggles of the two great political parties for power and plunder, while grievous wrongs have been inflicted upon the suffering people. We charge that the controlling influences dominating both these parties have permitted the existing dreadful conditions to develop without serious effort to prevent or restrain them. Neither do they now promise us any substantial reform. They have agreed together to ignore, in the coming campaign, every issue but one. They propose to drown the outcries of a plundered people with the uproar of a sham battle over the tariff, so that capitalists, corporations, national banks, rings, trusts, watered stock, the demonetization of silver and the oppressions of the usurers may all be lost sight of. They propose to sacrifice our homes, lives, and children on the altar of mammon; to destroy the multitude in order to secure corruption funds from the millionaires.

Assembled on the anniversary of the birthday of the nation, and filled with the spirit of the grand general and chief who established our independence, we seek to restore the government of the Republic to the hands of the "plain people," with which class it originated. We assert our purposes to be identical with the purposes of the National Constitution; to form a more perfect union and establish justice, insure domestic tranquillity, provide for the common defence, promote the general welfare, and secure the blessings of liberty for ourselves and our posterity.

We declare that this Republic can only endure as a free government while built upon the love of the people for each other and for the nation; that it cannot be pinned together by bayonets; that the Civil War is over, and that every passion and resentment which grew out of it must die with it, and that we must be in fact, as we are in name, one united brotherhood of free men.

Our country finds itself confronted by conditions for which there is no precedent in the history of the world; our annual agricultural productions amount to billions of dollars in value, which must, within a few weeks or months, be exchanged for billions of dollars' worth of commodities consumed in their production; the existing currency supply is wholly inadequate to make this exchange; the results are falling prices, the formation of combines and rings, the impoverishment of the producing class. We pledge ourselves that if given power we will labor to correct these evils by wise and reasonable legislation, in accordance with the terms of our platform.

We believe that the power of government—in other words, of the people—should be expanded (as in the case of the postal service) as rapidly and as far as the good sense of an intelligent people and the teachings of experience shall justify, to the end that oppression, injustice, and poverty shall eventually cease in the land.

While our sympathies as a party of reform are naturally upon the side of every proposition which will tend to make men intelligent, virtuous, and temperate, we nevertheless regard these questions, important as they are, as secondary to the great issues now pressing for solution, and upon which not only our individual prosperity but the very existence of free institutions depend; and we ask all men to first help us to determine whether we are to have a republic to administer before we differ as to the conditions upon which it is to be administered, believing that the forces of reform this day organized will never cease to move forward until every wrong is righted and equal rights and equal privileges securely established for all the men and women of this country.

Platform

We declare, therefore —

First.— That the union of the labor forces of the United States this day consummated shall be permanent and perpetual; may its spirit enter into all hearts for the salvation of the Republic and the uplifting of mankind.

Second.— Wealth belongs to him who creates it, and every dollar taken from industry without an equivalent is robbery. "If any will not work, neither shall he eat." The interests of rural and civil labor are the same; their enemies are identical.

Third.— We believe that the time has come when the railroad corporations will either own the people or the people must own the railroads; and should the government enter upon the work of owning and managing all railroads, we should favor an amendment to the constitution by which all persons engaged in the government service shall be placed under a civil-service regulation of the most rigid character, so as to prevent the increase of the power of the national administration by the use of such additional government employees.

Finance.— We demand a national currency, safe, sound, and flexible issued by the general government only, a full legal tender for all debts, public and private, and that without the use of banking corporations; a just, equitable, and efficient means of distribution direct to the people, at a tax not to exceed 2 per cent, per annum, to be provided as set forth in the sub-treasury plan of the Farmers' Alliance, or a better system; also by payments in discharge of its obligations for public improvements.

1. We demand free and unlimited coinage of silver and gold at the present legal ratio of 16 to 1.
2. We demand that the amount of circulating medium be speedily increased to not less than $50 per capita.
3. We demand a graduated income tax.
4. We believe that the money of the country should be kept as much as possible in the hands of the people, and hence we demand that all State and national revenues shall be limited to the necessary expenses of the government, economically and honestly administered.
5. We demand that postal savings banks be established by the government for the safe deposit of the earnings of the people and to facilitate exchange.

Transportation.— Transportation being a means of exchange and a public necessity, the government should own and operate the railroads in the interest of the people. The telegraph and telephone, like the post-office system, being a necessity for the transmission of news, should be owned and operated by the government in the interest of the people.

Land.— The land, including all the natural sources of wealth, is the heritage of the people, and should not be monopolized for speculative purposes, and alien ownership of land should be prohibited. All land now held by railroads and other corporations in excess of their actual needs, and all lands now owned by aliens should be reclaimed by the government and held for actual settlers only.

Expression of Sentiments

Your Committee on Platform and Resolutions beg leave unanimously to report the following:

Whereas, Other questions have been presented for our consideration, we hereby submit the following, not as a part of the Platform of the People's Party, but as resolutions expressive of the sentiment of this Convention.

1. Resolved, That we demand a free ballot and a fair count in all elections, and pledge ourselves to secure it to every legal voter without Federal intervention, through the adoption by the States of the unperverted Australian or secret ballot system.
2. Resolved, That the revenue derived from a graduated income tax should be applied to the reduction of the burden of taxation now levied upon the domestic industries of this country.
3. Resolved, That we pledge our support to fair and liberal pensions to ex-Union soldiers and sailors.
4. Resolved, That we condemn the fallacy of protecting American labor under the present system, which opens our ports to the pauper and criminal classes of the world and crowds out our wage-earners; and we denounce the present ineffective laws against

contract labor, and demand the further restriction of undesirable emigration.

5. Resolved, That we cordially sympathize with the efforts of organized workingmen to shorten the hours of labor, and demand a rigid enforcement of the existing eight-hour law on Government work, and ask that a penalty clause be added to the said law.
6. Resolved, That we regard the maintenance of a large standing army of mercenaries, known as the Pinkerton system, as a menace to our liberties, and we demand its abolition; and we condemn the recent invasion of the Territory of Wyoming by the hired assassins of plutocracy, assisted by Federal officers.
7. Resolved, That we commend to the favorable consideration of the people and the reform press the legislative system known as the initiative and referendum.
8. Resolved, That we favor a constitutional provision limiting the office of President and Vice- President to one term, and providing for the election of Senators of the United States by a direct vote of the people.
9. Resolved, That we oppose any subsidy or national aid to any private corporation for any purpose.
10. Resolved, That this convention sympathizes with the Knights of Labor and their righteous contest with the tyrannical combine of clothing manufacturers of Rochester, and declare it to be a duty of all who hate tyranny and oppression to refuse to purchase the goods made by the said manufacturers, or to patronize any merchants who sell such goods.

Booker T. Washington's "Atlanta Compromise" Speech, September 18, 1895

John A. Scott, ed. *Living Documents in American History*, Vol. 1 (New York: Washington Square Press, 1964–68), pp. 609–612

Mr. President and Gentlemen of the Board of Directors and Citizens:

One-third of the population of the South is of the Negro race. No enterprise seeking the material, civil, or moral welfare of this section can disregard this element of our population and reach the highest success. I but convey to you, Mr. President and Directors, the sentiment of the masses of my race when I say that in no way have the value and manhood of the American Negro been more fittingly and generously recognized than by the managers of this magnificent Exposition at every stage of its progress. It is a recognition that will do more to cement the friendship of the two races than any occurrence since the dawn of our freedom.

Not only this, but the opportunity here afforded will awaken among us a new era of industrial progress. Ignorant and inexperienced, it is not strange that in the first years of our new life we began at the top instead of at the bottom; that a seat in Congress or the state legislature was more sought than real estate or industrial skill; that the political convention of stump speaking had more attractions than starting a dairy farm or truck garden.

A ship lost at sea for many days suddenly sighted a friendly vessel. From the mast of the unfortunate vessel was seen a signal, "Water, water; we die of thirst!" The answer from the friendly vessel at once came back, "Cast down your bucket where you are." A second time the signal, "Water, water; send us water!" ran up from the distressed vessel, and was answered, "Cast down your bucket where you are." And a third and fourth signal for water was answered, "Cast down your bucket where you are." The captain of the distressed vessel, at least heeding the injunction, cast down his bucket, and it came up full of fresh, sparkling water from the mouth of the Amazon River. To those of my race who depend on bettering their condition in a foreign land or who underestimate the importance of cultivating friendly relations with the southern white man, who is their next-door neighbour, I would say: "Cast down your bucket where you are"—cast it down in making friends in every manly way of the people of all races by whom we are surrounded.

Cast it down in agriculture, mechanics, in commerce, in domestic service, and in the professions. And in this connection it is well to bear in mind that whatever other sins the South may be called to bear, when it comes to business, pure and simple, it is in the South that the Negro is given a man's chance in the commercial world, and in nothing is this Exposition more eloquent than in emphasizing this chance. Our greatest danger is that in the great leap from slavery to freedom we may overlook the fact that the masses of us are to live by the productions of our hands, and fail to keep in mind that we shall prosper in proportion as we learn to dignify and glorify common labour and put brains and skill into the common occupations of life; shall prosper in proportion as we learn to draw the line between the superficial and the substantial, the ornamental gewgaws of life and the useful. No race can prosper till it learns that there is as much dignity in tilling a field as in writing a poem. It is at the bottom of life we must begin, and not at the top. Nor should we permit our grievances to overshadow our opportunities.

To those of the white race who look to the incoming of those of foreign birth and strange tongue and habits for the prosperity of the South, were I permitted I would repeat what I say to my own race, "Cast down your bucket where you are." Cast it down among the eight millions of Negroes whose habits you know, whose fidelity and love you have tested in days when to have proved treacherous meant the ruin of your firesides. Cast down your bucket among these people who have, without strikes and labor wars, tilled your fields, cleared your forests, builded your railroads and cities, and brought forth treasures from the bowels of the earth, and helped make possible this magnificent representation of the progress of the South. Casting down your bucket among my people, helping and encouraging them as you are doing on these grounds, and to education of head, hand, and heart, you will find that they will buy your surplus land, make blossom the waste places in your fields, and run your factories.

While doing this, you can be sure in the future, as in the past, that you and your families will be surrounded by the most patient, faithful, law-abiding, and unresentful people that the world has seen. As we have proved our loyalty to you in the past, in nursing your children, watching by the sickbed of your mothers and fathers, and often following them with tear-dimmed eyes to their graves, so in the future, in our humble way, we shall stand by you with a devotion that no foreigner can approach, ready to lay down our lives, if need be, in defence of yours, interlacing our industrial, commercial, civil, and religious life with yours in a way that shall make the interests of both races one. In all things that are purely social we can be as separate as the fingers, yet one as the hand in all things essential to mutual progress.

There is no defence or security for any of us except in the highest intelligence and development of all. If anywhere there are efforts tending to curtail the fullest growth of the Negro, let these efforts be turned into stimulating, encouraging, and making him the most useful and intelligent citizen. Effort or means so invested will pay a thousand percent interest. These efforts will be twice blessed—"blessing him that gives and him that takes."

There is no escape through law of man or God from the inevitable:

The laws of changeless justice bind Oppressor with oppressed; And close as sin and suffering joined We march to fate abreast.

Nearly sixteen millions of hands will aid you in pulling the load upward, or they will pull against you the load downward. We shall constitute one-third and more of the ignorance and crime of the South, or one-third of its intelligence and progress; we shall contribute one-third to the business and industrial prosperity of the South, or we shall prove a veritable body of death, stagnating, depressing, retarding every effort to advance the body politic.

Gentlemen of the Exposition, as we present to you our humble effort at an exhibition of our progress, you must not expect overmuch. Starting thirty years ago with ownership here and there in a few quilts and pumpkins and chickens (gathered from miscellaneous sources), remember the path that has led from these to the inventions and production of agricultural implements, buggies, steam-engines, newspapers, books, statuary, carving, paintings, the management of drugstores and banks, has not been trodden without contact with thorns and thistles. While we take pride in what we exhibit as a result of our independent efforts, we do not for a moment forget that our part in this exhibition would fall far short of your expectations but for the constant help that has come to our educational life, not only from the southern States, but especially from northern philanthropists, who have made their gifts a constant stream of blessing and encouragement.

The wisest among my race understand that the agitation of questions of social equality is the extremest folly, and that progress in the enjoyment of all the privileges that will come to us must be the result of severe and constant struggle rather than of artificial forcing. No race that has anything to contribute to the markets of the world is long in any degree ostracized. It is important and right that all privileges of the law be ours, but it is vastly more important that we be prepared for the exercises of these privileges. The opportunity to earn a dollar in a factory just now is worth infinitely more than the opportunity to spend a dollar in an opera-house.

In conclusion, may I repeat that nothing in thirty years has given us more hope and encouragement, and drawn us so near to you of the white race, as this opportunity offered by the Exposition; here bending, as it were, over the altar that represents the results of the struggles of your race and mine, both starting practically empty-handed three decades ago, I pledge that in your effort to work out the great and intricate problem which God has laid at the doors of the South, you shall have at all times the patient, sympathetic help of my race. Only let this be constantly in mind, that, while from representations in these buildings of the product of field, of forest, of mine, of factory, letters, and art, much good will come, yet far above and beyond material benefits will be that higher good, that, let us pray God, will come, in a blotting out of sectional differences and racial animosities and suspicions, and in a determination to administer absolute justice, even in the remotest corner; in a willing obedience among all classes to the mandates of law and a spirit that will tolerate nothing but the highest equity in the enforcement of law. This, then, coupled with our material prosperity, will bring into our beloved South a new heaven and a new earth.

Plessy v. Ferguson (May 18, 1896)
U.S. Supreme Court

163 U.S. 537 (1896). From: *Supreme Court Reporter,* Volume 16, pp. 1138–48. (163 U.S. 537)

Mr. Justice Henry B. Brown for the majority:

This case turns upon the constitutionality of an act of the general assembly of the state of Louisiana, passed in

1890, providing for separate railway carriages for the white and colored races. . . .

The constitutionality of this act is attacked upon the ground that it conflicts both with the thirteenth amendment of the constitution, abolishing slavery, and the fourteenth amendment, which prohibits certain restrictive legislation on the part of the states.

1. That it does not conflict with the thirteenth amendment, which abolished slavery and involuntary servitude, except as a punishment for crime, is too clear for argument. . . .

A statute which implies merely a legal distinction between the white and colored races—a distinction which is founded in the color of the two races, and which must always exist so long as white men are distinguished from the other race by color—has no tendency to destroy the legal equality of the two races, or re-establish a state of involuntary servitude. Indeed, we do not understand that the thirteenth amendment is strenuously relied upon by the plaintiff in error in this connection. . . .

The object of the amendment was undoubtedly to enforce the absolute equality of the two races before the law, but, in the nature of things, it could not have been intended to abolish distinctions based upon color, or to enforce social, as distinguished from political, equality, or a commingling of the two races upon terms unsatisfactory to either. Laws permitting, and even requiring, their separation, in places where they are liable to be brought into contact, do not necessarily imply the inferiority of either race to the other, and have been generally, if not universally, recognized as within the competency of the state legislatures in the exercise of their police power. The most common instance of this is connected with the establishment of separate schools for white and colored children, which have been held to be a valid exercise of the legislative power even by courts of states where the political rights of the colored race have been longest and most earnestly enforced. . . .

It is claimed by the plaintiff in error that, in any mixed community, the reputation of belonging to the dominant race, in this instance the white race, is "property," in the same sense that a right of action or of inheritance is property. Conceding this to be so, for the purposes of this case, we are unable to see how this statute deprives him of, or in any way affects his right to, such property. If he be a white man, and assigned to a colored coach, he may have his action for damages against the company for being deprived of his so-called "property." Upon the other hand, if he be a colored man, and be so assigned, he has been deprived of no property, since he is not lawfully entitled to the reputation of being a white man. . . .

So far, then, as a conflict with the fourteenth amendment is concerned, the case reduces itself to the question whether the statute of Louisiana is a reasonable regulation, and with respect to this there must necessarily be a large discretion on the part of the legislature. In determining the question of reasonableness, it is at liberty to act with reference to the established usages, customs, and traditions of the people, and with a view to the promotion of their comfort, and the preservation of the public peace and good order. Gauged by this standard, we cannot say that a law which authorizes or even requires the separation of the two races in public conveyances is unreasonable, or more obnoxious to the fourteenth amendment than the acts of Congress requiring separate schools for colored children in the District of Columbia, the constitutionality of which does not seem to have been questioned, or the corresponding acts of state legislatures.

We consider the underlying fallacy of the plaintiff's argument to consist in the assumption that the enforced separation of the two races stamps the colored race with a badge of inferiority. If this be so, it is not by reason of anything found in the act, but solely because the colored race chooses to put that construction upon it. The argument necessarily assumes that if, as has been more than once the case, and is not unlikely to be so again, the colored race should become the dominant power in the state legislature, and should enact a law in precisely similar terms, it would thereby relegate the white race to an inferior position. We imagine that the white race, at least, would not acquiesce in this assumption. The argument also assumes that social prejudices may be overcome by legislation, and that equal rights cannot be secured to the negro except by an enforced commingling of the two races. We cannot accept this proposition. If the two races are to meet upon terms of social equality, it must be the result of natural affinities, a mutual appreciation of each other's merits, and a voluntary consent of individuals. As was said by the court of appeals of New York in People v. Gallagher, 93 N. Y. 438, 448: "This end can neither be accomplished nor promoted by laws which conflict with the general sentiment of the community upon whom they are designed to operate. When the government, therefore, has secured to each of its citizens equal rights before the law, and equal opportunities for improvement and progress, it has accomplished the end for which it was organized, and performed all of the functions respecting social advantages with which it is endowed." Legislation is powerless to eradicate racial instincts, or to abolish distinctions based upon physical differences, and the attempt to do so can only result in accentuating the difficulties of the present situation. If the civil and political rights of both races be equal, one cannot be inferior to the other civilly or politically. If one race be inferior to the other socially, the constitution of the United States cannot put them upon the same plane. . . .

Mr. Justice Harlan dissenting.

. . . In respect of civil rights, common to all citizens, the constitution of the United States does not, I think, permit any public authority to know the race of those entitled to be protected in the enjoyment of such rights. Every true man has pride of race, and under appropriate circumstances, when the rights of others, his equals before the law, are not to be affected, it is his privilege to express such pride and to take such action based upon it as to him seems proper. But I deny that any legislative body or judicial tribunal may have regard to the race of citizens when the civil rights of those citizens are involved. Indeed, such legislation as that here in question is inconsistent not only with that equality of rights which pertains to citizenship, national and state, but with the personal liberty enjoyed by every one within the United States.

The thirteenth amendment does not permit the withholding or the deprivation of any right necessarily inhering in freedom. It not only struck down the institution of slavery as previously existing in the United States, but it prevents the imposition of any burdens or disabilities that constitute badges of slavery or servitude. It decreed universal civil freedom in this country. This court has so adjudged. But, that amendment having been found inadequate to the protection of the rights of those who had been in slavery, it was followed by the fourteenth amendment, which added greatly to the dignity and glory of American citizenship, and to the security of personal liberty, by declaring that "all persons born or naturalized in the United States, and subject to the jurisdiction thereof, are citizens of the United States and of the state wherein they reside," and that "no state shall make or enforce any law which shall abridge the privileges or immunities of citizens of the United States; nor shall any state deprive any person of life, liberty or property without due process of law, nor deny to any person within its jurisdiction the equal protection of the laws." These two amendments, if enforced according to their true intent and meaning, will protect all the civil rights that pertain to freedom and citizenship. Finally, and to the end that no citizen should be denied, on account of his race, the privilege of participating in the political control of his country, it was declared by the fifteenth amendment that "the right of citizens of the United States to vote shall not be denied or abridged by the United States or by any state on account of race, color or previous condition of servitude."

These notable additions to the fundamental law were welcomed by the friends of liberty throughout the world. They removed the race line from our governmental systems. They had, as this court has said, a common purpose, namely, to secure "to a race recently emancipated, a race that through many generations have been held in slavery, all the civil rights that the superior race enjoy." They declared, in legal effect, this court has further said, "that the law in the states shall be the same for the black as for the white; that all persons, whether colored or white, shall stand equal before the laws of the states; and in regard to the colored race, for whose protection the amendment was primarily designed, that no discrimination shall be made against them by law because of their color." We also said: "The words of the amendment, it is true, are prohibitory, but they contain a necessary implication of a positive immunity or right, most valuable to the colored race,—the right to exemption from unfriendly legislation against them distinctively as colored; exemption from legal discriminations, implying inferiority in civil society, lessening the security of their enjoyment of the rights which others enjoy; and discriminations which are steps towards reducing them to the condition of a subject race." It was, consequently, adjudged that a state law that excluded citizens of the colored race from juries, because of their race, however well qualified in other respects to discharge the duties of jurymen, was repugnant to the fourteenth amendment. *Strauder v. West Virginia,* 100 U.S. 303, 306, 307; Virginia v. Rives, Id. 313; Ex parte Virginia, Id. 339; *Neal v. Delaware,* 103 U.S. 370, 386; *Bush v. Com.,* 107 U.S. 110, 116, 1 Sup. Ct. 625. At the present term, referring to the previous adjudications, this court declared that "underlying all of those decisions is the principle that the constitution of the United States, in its present form, forbids, so far as civil and political rights are concerned, discrimination by the general government or the states against any citizen because of his race. All citizens are equal before the law." *Gibson v. State,* 162 U.S. 565, 16 Sup. Ct. 904.

The decisions referred to show the scope of the recent amendments of the constitution. They also show that it is not within the power of a state to prohibit colored citizens, because of their race, from participating as jurors in the administration of justice.

It was said in argument that the statute of Louisiana does not discriminate against either race, but prescribes a rule applicable alike to white and colored citizens. But this argument does not meet the difficulty. Every one knows that the statute in question had its origin in the purpose, not so much to exclude white persons from railroad cars occupied by blacks, as to exclude colored people from coaches occupied by or assigned to white persons. Railroad corporations of Louisiana did not make discrimination among whites in the matter of accommodation for travelers. The thing to accomplish was, under the guise of giving equal accommodation for whites and blacks, to compel the latter to keep to themselves while traveling in railroad passenger coaches. No one would be so wanting in candor as to assert the contrary. The fundamental objection, therefore, to the statute, is that it interferes with the personal freedom of citizens. "Personal liberty," it has been well said, "consists in the power of locomotion, of changing situation, or removing one's person to whatsoever places one's own inclination may direct, without imprisonment or restraint, unless by due course of law." 1 Bl. Comm. 134. If a white man and a black man choose to occupy the same public conveyance on a public highway, it is their right to do so; and no government, proceeding alone on grounds of race, can prevent it without infringing the personal liberty of each.

It is one thing for railroad carriers to furnish, or to be required by law to furnish, equal accommodations for all whom they are under a legal duty to carry. It is quite another thing for government to forbid citizens of the white and black races from traveling in the same public conveyance, and to punish officers of railroad companies for permitting persons of the two races to occupy the same passenger coach. If a state can prescribe, as a rule of civil conduct, that whites and blacks shall not travel as passengers in the same railroad coach, why may it not so regulate the use of the streets of its cities and towns as to compel white citizens to keep on one side of a street, and black citizens to keep on the other? Why may it not, upon like grounds, punish whites and blacks who ride together in street cars or in open vehicles on a public road or street? Why may it not require sheriffs to assign whites to one side of a court room, and blacks to the other? And why may it not also prohibit the commingling of the two races in the galleries of legislative halls or in public assemblages convened for the consideration of the political questions of the day? Further, if this statute of Louisiana is consistent with the personal liberty of citizens, why may not the state require the separation in railroad coaches of native and naturalized citizens of the United States, or of Protestants and Roman Catholics?

The answer given at the argument to these questions was that regulations of the kind they suggest would be unreasonable, and could not, therefore, stand before the law. Is it meant that the determination of questions of legislative power depends upon the inquiry whether the statute whose validity is questioned is, in the judgment of the courts, a reasonable one, taking all the circumstances into consideration? A statute may be unreasonable merely because a sound public policy forbade its enactment. But I do not understand that the courts have anything to do with the policy or expediency of legislation. A statute may be valid, and yet, upon grounds of public policy, may well be characterized as unreasonable. Mr. Sedgwick correctly states the rule when he says that, the legislative intention being clearly ascertained, "the courts have no other duty to perform than to execute the legislative will, without any regard to their views as to the wisdom or justice of the particular enactment." Sedg. St. & Const. Law, 324. There is a dangerous tendency in these latter days to enlarge the functions of the courts; by means of judicial interference with the will of the people as expressed by the legislature. Our institutions have the distinguishing characteristic that the three departments of government are co-ordinate and separate. Each must keep within the limits defined by the constitution. And the courts best discharge their duty by executing the will of the lawmaking power, constitutionally expressed, leaving the results of legislation to be dealt with by the people through their representatives. Statutes must always have a reasonable construction. Sometimes they are to be construed strictly, sometimes literally, in order to carry out the legislative will. But, however construed, the intent of the legislature is to be respected if the particular statute in question is valid, although the courts, looking at the public interests, may conceive the statute to be both unreasonable and impolitic. If the power exists to enact a statute, that ends the matter so far as the courts are concerned. The adjudged cases in which statutes have been held to be void, because unreasonable, are those in which the means employed by the legislature were not at all germane to the end to which the legislature was competent.

The white race deems itself to be the dominant race in the country. And so it is, in prestige, in achievements, in education, in wealth, and in power. So, I doubt not, it will continue to be for all time, if it remains true to its great heritage, and holds fast to the principles of constitutional liberty. But in view of the constitution, in the eye of the law, there is in this country no superior, dominant, ruling class of citizens. There is no caste here. Our constitution is color-blind, and neither knows nor tolerates classes among citizens. In respect of civil rights, all citizens are equal before the law. The humblest is the peer of the most powerful. The law regards man as man, and takes no account of his surroundings or of his color when his civil rights as guarantied by the supreme law of the land are involved. It is therefore to be regretted that this high tribunal, the final expositor of the fundamental law of the land, has reached the conclusion that it is competent for a state to regulate the enjoyment by citizens of their civil rights solely upon the basis of race.

In my opinion, the judgment this day rendered will, in time, prove to be quite as pernicious as the decision made by this tribunal in the Dred Scott Case.

It was adjudged in that case that the descendants of Africans who were imported into this country, and sold as slaves, were not included nor intended to be included under the word "citizens" in the constitution, and could not claim any of the rights and privileges which that instrument provided for and secured to citizens of the United States; that, at the time of the adoption of the constitution, they were "considered as a subordinate and inferior class of beings, who had been subjugated by the dominant race, and, whether emancipated or not, yet remained subject to their authority, and had no rights or privileges but such as those who held the power and the government might choose to grant them." 17 How. 393, 404. The recent amendments of the constitution, it was supposed, had eradicated these principles from our institutions. But it seems that we have yet, in some of the states, a dominant race,—a superior class of citizens,—which assumes to regulate the enjoyment of civil rights, common to all citizens, upon the basis of race. The present decision, it may well be apprehended, will not only stimulate aggressions, more or less brutal and irritating, upon the admitted rights of colored citizens, but will encourage the belief that it is possible, by means of state enactments, to defeat the beneficent purposes which the people of the United States had in view when they adopted the recent amendments of the constitution, by one of which the blacks of this country were made citizens of the United States and of the states in which they respectively reside, and whose privileges and immunities, as citizens, the states are forbidden to abridge. Sixty millions of whites are in no danger from the presence here of eight millions of blacks. The destinies of the two races, in this country, are indissolubly linked together, and the interests of both require that the common government of all shall not permit the seeds of race hate to be planted under the sanction of law. What can more certainly arouse race hate, what more certainly create and perpetuate a feeling of distrust between these races, than state enactments which, in fact, proceed on the ground that colored citizens are so inferior and degraded that they cannot be allowed to sit in public coaches occupied by white citizens? That, as all will admit, is the real meaning of such legislation as was enacted in Louisiana.

The sure guaranty of the peace and security of each race is the clear, distinct, unconditional recognition by our governments, national and state, of every right that inheres in civil freedom, and of the equality before the law of all citizens of the United States, without regard to race. State enactments regulating the enjoyment of civil rights upon the basis of race, and cunningly devised to defeat legitimate results of the war, under the pretense of recognizing equality of rights, can have no other result than to render permanent peace impossible, and to keep alive a conflict of races, the continuance of which must do harm to all concerned. This question is not met by the suggestion that social equality cannot exist between the white and black races in this country. That argument, if it can be properly regarded as one, is scarcely worthy of consideration; for social equality no more exists between two races when traveling in a passenger coach or a public highway than when members of the same races sit by each other in a street car or in the jury box, or stand or sit with each other in a political assembly, or when they use in common the streets of a city or town, or when they are in the same room for the purpose of having their names placed on the registry of voters, or when they approach the ballot box in order to exercise the high privilege of voting.

There is a race so different from our own that we do not permit those belonging to it to become citizens of the United States. Persons belonging to it are, with few exceptions, absolutely excluded from our country. I allude to the Chinese race. But, by the statute in question, a Chinaman can ride in the same passenger coach with white citizens of the United States, while citizens of the black race in Louisiana, many of whom, perhaps, risked their lives for the preservation of the Union, who are entitled, by law, to participate in the political control of the state and nation, who are not excluded, by law or by reason of their race, from public stations of any kind, and who have all the legal rights that belong to white citizens, are yet declared to be criminals, liable to imprisonment, if they ride in a public coach occupied by citizens of the white race. It is scarcely just to say that a colored citizen should not object to occupying a public coach assigned to his own race. He does not object, nor, perhaps, would he object to separate coaches for his race if his rights under the law were recognized. But he does object, and he ought never to cease objecting, that citizens of the white and black races can be adjudged criminals because they sit, or claim the right to sit, in the same public coach on a public highway.

The arbitrary separation of citizens, on the basis of race, while they are on a public highway, is a badge of servitude wholly inconsistent with the civil freedom and the equality before the law established by the constitution. It cannot be justified upon any legal grounds.

If evils will result from the commingling of the two races upon public highways established for the benefit of all, they will be infinitely less than those that will surely come from state legislation regulating the enjoyment of civil rights upon the basis of race. We boast of the freedom enjoyed by our people above all other peoples. But it is difficult to reconcile that boast with a state of the law which, practically, puts the brand of servitude and degradation upon a large class of our fellow citizens,—our equals before the law. The thin disguise of "equal" accommodations for passengers in railroad coaches will not mislead any one, nor atone for the wrong this day done.

The result of the whole matter is that while this court has frequently adjudged, and at the present term has recognized the doctrine, that a state cannot, consistently with the constitution of the United States, prevent white and black citizens, having the required qualifications for jury service, from sitting in the same jury box, it is now solemnly held that a state may prohibit white and black citizens from sitting in the same passenger coach on a public highway, or may require that they be separated by a "partition" when in the same passenger coach. May it not now be reasonably expected that astute men of the dominant race, who affect to be disturbed at the possibility that the integrity of the white race may be corrupted, or that its supremacy will be imperiled, by contact on public highways with black people, will endeavor to procure statutes requiring white and black jurors to be separated in the jury box by a "partition," and that, upon retiring from the court room to consult as to their verdict, such partition, if it be a movable one, shall be taken to their consultation room, and set up in such way as to prevent black jurors from coming too close to their brother jurors of the white race. If the "partition" used in the court room happens to be stationary, provision could be made for screens with openings through which jurors of the two races could confer as to their verdict without coming into personal contact with each other. I cannot see but that, according to the principles this day announced, such state legislation, although conceived in hostility to, and enacted for the purpose of humiliating, citizens of the United States of a particular race, would be held to be consistent with the constitution.

I do not deem it necessary to review the decisions of state courts to which reference was made in argument. Some, and the most important, of them, are wholly inapplicable, because rendered prior to the adoption of the last amendments of the constitution, when colored people had very few rights which the dominant race felt obliged to respect. Others were made at a time when public opinion, in many localities, was dominated by the institution of slavery; when it would not have been safe to do justice to the black man; and when, so far as the rights of blacks were concerned, race prejudice was, practically, the supreme law of the land. Those decisions cannot be guides in the era introduced by the recent amendments of the supreme law, which established universal civil freedom, gave citizenship to all born or naturalized in the United States, and residing here, obliterated the race line from our systems of governments, national and state, and placed our free institutions upon the broad and sure foundation of the equality of all men before the law.

I am of opinion that the statute of Louisiana is inconsistent with the personal liberty of citizens, white and black, in that state, and hostile to both the spirit and letter of the constitution of the United States. If laws of like character should be enacted in the several states of the Union, the effect would be in the highest degree mischievous. Slavery, as an institution tolerated by law, would, it is true, have disappeared from our country; but there would remain a power in the states, by sinister legislation, to interfere with the full enjoyment of the blessings of freedom, to regulate civil rights, common to all citizens, upon the basis of race, and to place in a condition of legal inferiority a large body of American citizens, now constituting a part of the political community, called the "People of the United States," for whom, and by whom through representatives, our government is administered. Such a system is inconsistent with the guaranty given by the constitution to each state of a republican form of government, and may be stricken down by congressional action, or by the courts in the discharge of their solemn duty to maintain the supreme law of the land, anything in the constitution or laws of any state to the contrary notwithstanding.

For the reason stated, I am constrained to withhold my assent from the opinion and judgment of the majority.

William Jennings Bryan's "Cross of Gold" Speech, July 9, 1896

The Collections of the Manuscript Division, Library of Congress, Container 49 of the Bryan Papers

Cross of Gold

Mr. Chairman and Gentlemen of the Convention: I would be presumptuous, indeed, to present myself against the distinguished gentlemen to whom you have listened if this was a mere measuring of abilities; but this is not a contest between persons. The humblest citizen in all the land, when clad in the armor of a righteous cause, is stronger than all the hosts of error. I come to speak to you in defense of a cause as holy as the cause of liberty—the cause of humanity.

When this debate is concluded a motion will be made to lay upon the table the resolution offered in commendation of the administration and also the resolution offered in condemnation of the administration. We object to bringing this question down to the level of persons. The individual is but an atom; he is born, he acts, he dies; but principles are eternal; and this has been a contest over a principle.

Principles, not Men

Never before in the history of this country has there been witnessed such a contest as that through which we have just passed. Never before in the history of American politics has a great issue been fought out, as this issue has been, by the voters of a great party. On the fourth of March, 1895, a few democrats, most of them members of congress, issued an address to the democrats of the nation, asserting that the money question was the paramount issue of the hour; declaring that a majority of the democratic party had the right to control the action of the party on this paramount issue; and concluding with the request that the believers in the free coinage of silver in the democratic party should organize, take charge of, and control the policy of the democratic party. Three months later, at Memphis, an organization was perfected, and the silver democrats went forth openly and courageously proclaiming their belief, and declaring that, if successful, they would crystallize into a platform the declaration which they had made. Then began the conflict. With a zeal approaching the zeal which inspired the crusaders who followed Peter the Hermit, our silver democrats went forth from victory unto victory until they are now assembled, not to discuss, not to debate, but to enter up the judgment already rendered by the plain people of this country. In this contest brother has been arrayed against brother, father against son. The warmest ties of love, acquaintance and association have been disregarded; old leaders have been cast aside when they have refused to give expression to the sentiments of those whom they would lead, and new leaders have sprung up to give direction to this cause of truth. Thus has the contest been waged, and we have assembled here under as binding and solemn instructions as were ever imposed upon representatives of the people.

We do not come as individuals. As individuals we might have been glad to compliment the gentleman from New York (Senator Hill), but we know that the people for whom we speak would never be willing to put him in a position where he could thwart the will of the democratic party. I say it was not a question of persons; it was a question of principle, and it is not with gladness, my friends, that we find ourselves brought into conflict with those who are now arrayed on the other side.

The gentleman who preceded me (ex-Governor Russell) spoke of the state of Massachusetts; let me assure him that not one present in all this convention entertains the least hostility to the people of the state of Massachusetts, but we stand here representing people who are the equals before the law of the greatest citizens in the state of Massachusetts. When you (turning to the gold delegates) come before us and tell us that we are about to disturb your business interests, we reply that you have disturbed our business interests by your course.

The Real Business Men

We say to you that you have made the definition of a business man too limited in its application. The man who is employed for wages is as much a business man as his employer; the attorney in a country town is as much a business man as the corporation counsel in a great metropolis; the merchant at the cross-roads store is as much a business man as the merchant of New York; the farmer who goes forth in the morning and toils all day—who begins in the spring and toils all summer—and who by the application of brain and muscle to the natural resources of the country creates wealth, is as much a business man as the man who goes upon the board of trade and bets upon the price of grain; the miners who go down a thousand feet into the earth, or climb two thousand feet upon the cliffs, and bring forth from their hiding places the precious metals to be poured into the channels of trade are as much business men as the few financial magnates who, in a back room, corner the money of the world. We come to speak for this broader class of business men.

Ah, my friends, we say not one word against those who live upon the Atlantic coast, but the hardy pioneers who have braved all the dangers of the wilderness, who have made the desert to blossom as the rose—the pioneers away out there (pointing to the West), who rear their children near to Nature's heart, where they can mingle their voices with the voices of the birds—out there where they have erected school houses for the education of their young, churches where they praise their Creator, and cemeteries where rest the ashes of their dead—these people, we say, are as deserving of the consideration of our party as any people in this country. It is for these that we speak. We do not come as aggressors. Our war is not a war of conquest; we are fighting in the defense of our homes, our families, and posterity. We have petitioned, and our petitions have been scorned; we have entreated, and our entreaties have been disregarded; we have begged, and they have mocked when our calamity came. We beg no longer; we entreat no more; we petition no more. We defy them.

The gentleman from Wisconsin has said that he fears a Robespierre. My friends, in this land of the free you need not fear that a tyrant will spring up from among the people. What we need is an Andrew Jackson to stand, as Jackson stood, against the encroachments of organized wealth.

Must Meet New Conditions

They tell us that this platform was made to catch votes. We reply to them that changing conditions make new issues; that the principles upon which democracy rests are as everlasting as the hills, but that they must be applied to new conditions as they arise. Conditions have arisen, and we are here to meet those conditions. They tell us that the income tax ought not to be brought in here; that it is a new idea. They criticise us for our criticism of the Supreme Court of the United States. My friends, we have not criticised; we have simply called attention to what you already know. If you want criticisms, read the dissenting opinions of the court. There you will find criticisms. They say that we passed an unconstitutional law; we deny it. The income tax law was not unconstitutional when it was passed; it was not unconstitutional when it went before the supreme court for the first time; it did not become unconstitutional until one of the judges changed his mind, and we cannot be expected to know when a judge will change his mind. The income tax is just. It simply intends to put the burdens of government justly upon the backs of the people. I am in favor of an income tax. When I find a man who is not willing to bear his share of the burdens of the government which protects him, I find a man who is unworthy to enjoy the blessings of a government like ours.

Against a National Bank Currency

They say that we are opposing national bank currency; it is true. If you will read what Thomas Benton said, you will find he said that, in searching history, he could find but one parallel to Andrew Jackson; that was Cicero, who destroyed the conspiracy of Cataline and saved Rome. Benton said that Cicero only did for Rome what Jackson did for us when he destroyed the bank conspiracy and saved America. We say in our platform that we believe that the right to coin and issue money is a function of government. We believe it. We believe that it is a part of sovereignty, and can no more with safety be delegated to private individuals than we could afford to delegate to private individuals the power to make penal statutes or levy taxes. Mr. Jefferson, who was once regarded as good democratic authority, seems to have differed in opinion from the gentleman who has addressed us on the part of the minority. Those who are opposed to this proposition tell us that the issue of paper money is a function of the bank, and that the government ought to go out of the banking business. I stand with Jefferson rather than with them, and tell them, as he did, that the issue of money is a function of government, and that the banks ought to go out of the governing business.

They complain about the plank which declares against life tenure in office. They have tried to strain it to mean that which it does not mean. What we oppose by that plank is the life tenure which is being built up in Washington, and which excludes from participation in official benefits the humbler members of society.

The Minority Amendments

Let me call your attention to two or three important things. The gentleman from New York says that he will propose an amendment to the platform providing that the proposed change in our monetary system shall not affect contracts already made. Let me remind you that there is no intention of affecting those contracts which according to present laws are made payable in gold, but if he means to say that we cannot change our monetary system without protecting those who have loaned money before the change was made, I desire to ask him where, in law or morals, he can find justification for not protecting the debtors when the act of 1873 was passed, if he now insists that we must protect the creditors.

He says he will also propose an amendment which will provide for the suspension of free coinage if we fail to maintain the parity within a year. We reply that when we advocate a policy which we believe will be successful, we are not compelled to raise a doubt as to our own sincerity by suggesting what we shall do if we fail. I ask him, if he would apply his logic to us, why he does not apply it to himself. He says he wants this country to try to secure an international agreement. Why does he not tell us what he is going to do if he fails to secure an international agreement? There is more reason for him to do that than there is for us to provide against the failure to maintain the parity. Our opponents have tried for twenty years to secure an international agreement, and those are waiting for it most patiently who do not want it at all.

The Paramount Issue

And now, my friends, let me come to the paramount issue. If they ask us why it is that we say more on the money question than we say upon the tariff question, I reply that, if protection has slain its thousands, the gold standard has slain its tens of thousands. If they ask us why we do not embody in our platform all the things that we believe in, we reply that when we have restored the money of the constitution all other necessary reforms will be possible; but that until this is done there is no other reform that can be accomplished.

Why is it that within three months such a change has come over the country? Three months ago, when it was confidently asserted that those who believe in the gold standard would frame our platform and nominate our candidates, even the advocates of the gold standard did not think that we could elect a president. And they had good reason for their doubt, because there is scarcely a state here to-day asking for the gold standard which is not in the absolute control of the republican party. But note the change. Mr. McKinley was nominated at St. Louis upon a platform which declared for the maintenance of the gold standard until it can be changed into bimetallism by international agreement. Mr. McKinley was the most popular man among the republicans, and three months ago everybody in the republican party prophesied his election. How is it to-day? Why, the man who was once pleased to think that he looked like Napoleon—that man shudders to-day when he remembers that he was nominated on the anniversary of the battle of Waterloo. Not only that, but, as he listens, he can hear with ever-increasing distinctness the sound of the waves as they beat upon the lonely shores of St. Helena.

Why this change? Ah, my friends, is not the reason for the change evident to any one who will look at the matter? No private character, however pure, no personal popularity, however great, can protect from the avenging wrath of an indignant people a man who will declare that he is in favor of fastening the gold standard upon this country or who is willing to surrender the right of self government and place the legislative control of our affairs in the hands of foreign potentates and powers.

Confident of Success

We go forth confident that we shall win. Why? Because upon the paramount issue of this campaign there is not a spot of ground upon which the enemy will dare to challenge battle. If they tell us that the gold standard is a good thing, we shall point to their platform and tell them that their platform pledges the party to get rid of the gold standard and substitute bimetallism. If the gold standard is a good thing, why try to get rid of it? I call your attention to the fact that some of the very people who are in this convention to-day and who tell us that we ought to declare in favor of international bimetallism—thereby declaring that the gold standard is wrong and that the principle of bimetallism is better—these very people four months ago were open and avowed advocates of the gold standard, and were then telling us that we could not legislate two metals together, even with the aid of all the world. If the gold standard is a good thing, we ought to declare in favor of its retention and not in favor of abandoning it; and if the gold standard is a bad thing why should we wait until other nations are willing to help us to let go? Here is the line of battle, and we care not upon which issue they force the fight; we are prepared to meet them on either issue or on both. If they tell us that the gold standard is the standard of civilization, we reply to them that this, the most enlightened of all the nations of the earth, has never declared for a gold standard and that both the great parties this year are declaring against it. If the gold standard is the standard of civilization why, my friends, should we not have it? If they come to meet us on that issue we can present the history of our nation. More than that; we can tell them that they will search the pages of history in vain to find a single instance where the common people of any land have ever declared themselves in favor of the gold standard. They can find where the holders of fixed investments have declared for a gold standard, but not where the masses have.

Carlisle Defines the Issue

Mr. Carlisle said in 1878 that this was a struggle between "the idle holders of idle capital" and "the struggling masses, who produce the wealth and pay the taxes of the country," and, my friends, the question we are to decide is: Upon which side will the Democratic party fight: upon the side of the "idle holders of idle capital" or upon the side of "the struggling masses"? That is the question which the party must answer first, and then it must be answered by each individual hereafter. The sympathies of the Democratic party, as shown by the platform, are on the side of the struggling masses who have ever been the foundation of the Democratic party. There are two ideas of government. There are those who believe that, if you will only legislate to make the well-to-do prosperous, their prosperity will leak through on those below. The Democratic idea, however, has been that if you legislate to make the masses prosperous, their prosperity will find its way up through every class which rests upon them.

You come to us and tell us that the great cities are in favor of the gold standard; we reply that the great cities rest upon our broad and fertile prairies. Burn down your cities and leave our farms, and your cities will spring up again as if by magic; but destroy our farms and the grass will grow in the streets of every city in the country.

A New Declaration of Independence

My friends, we declare that this nation is able to legislate for its own people on every question, without waiting for the aid or consent of any other nation on earth; and upon that issue we expect to carry every state in the Union. I shall not slander the inhabitants of the fair state of Massachusetts nor the inhabitants of the state of New York by saying that, when they are confronted with the proposition, they will declare that this nation is not able to attend to its own business. It is the issue of 1776 over again. Our ancestors when but three millions in number, had the courage to declare their political independence of every other nation; shall we, their descendants, when we have grown to seventy millions, declare that we are less independent than our forefathers? No, my friends, that will never be the verdict of our people. Therefore, we care not upon what lines the battle is fought. If they say bimetallism is good, but that we cannot have it until other nations help us, we reply that, instead of having a gold standard because England has, we will restore bimetallism, and then let England have bimetallism because the United States has it. If they dare to come out in the open field and defend the gold standard as a good thing, we will fight them to the uttermost. Having behind us the producing masses of this nation and the world, supported by the commercial interests, the laboring interests, and the toilers everywhere, we will answer their demand for a gold standard by saying to them: You shall not press down upon the brow of labor this crown of thorns; you shall not crucify mankind upon a cross of gold.

Platform of the American Anti-Imperialist League (1899)

John A. Scott, ed. *Living Documents in American History*, Vol. I (New York: Washington Square Press, 1964–68), pp. 613–614

We hold that the policy known as imperialism is hostile to liberty and tends toward militarism, an evil from which it has been our glory to be free. We regret that it has become necessary in the land of Washington and Lincoln to reaffirm that all men, of whatever race or color, are entitled to life, liberty, and the pursuit of happiness. We maintain that governments derive their just powers from the consent of the governed. We insist that the subjugation of any people is "criminal aggression" and open disloyalty to the distinctive principles of our government.

We earnestly condemn the policy of the present national administration in the Philippines. It seeks to extinguish the spirit of 1776 in those islands. We deplore the sacrifice of our soldiers and sailors, whose bravery deserves admiration even in an unjust war. We denounce the slaughter of the Filipinos as a needless horror. We protest against the extension of American sovereignty by Spanish methods.

We demand the immediate cessation of the war against liberty, begun by Spain and continued by us. We urge that Congress be promptly convened to announce to the Filipinos our purpose to concede to them the independence for which they have so long fought and which of right is theirs.

The United States have always protested against the doctrine of international law which permits the subjugation of the weak by the strong. A self-governing state cannot accept sovereignty over an unwilling people. The United States cannot act upon the ancient heresy that might makes right.

Imperialists assume that with the destruction of self-government in the Philippines by American hands, all opposition here will cease. This is a grievous error. Much as we abhor the war of "criminal aggression" in the Philippines, greatly as we regret that the blood of the Filipinos is on American hands, we more deeply resent the betrayal of American institutions at home. The real firing line is not in the suburbs of Manila. The foe is of our own household. The attempt of 1861 was to divide the country. That of 1899 is to destroy its fundamental principles and noblest ideals.

Whether the ruthless slaughter of the Filipinos shall end next month or next year is but an incident in a contest that must go on until the Declaration of Independence and the Constitution of the United States are rescued from the hands of their betrayers. Those who dispute about standards of value while the foundation of the republic is undermined will be listened to as little as those who would wrangle about the small economies of the household while the house is on fire. The training of a great people for a century, the aspiration for liberty of a vast immigration are forces that will hurl aside those who in the delirium of conquest seek to destroy the character of our institutions.

We deny that the obligation of all citizens to support their government in times of grave national peril applies to the present situation. If an administration may with impunity ignore the issues upon which it was chosen, deliberately create a condition of war anywhere on the face of the globe, debauch the civil service for spoils to promote the adventure, organize a truth-suppressing censorship, and demand of all citizens a suspension of judgment and their unanimous support while it chooses to continue the fighting, representative government itself is imperiled.

We propose to contribute to the defeat of any person or party that stands for the forcible subjugation of any people. We shall oppose for reelection all who in the White House or in Congress betray American liberty in pursuit of un-American ends. We still hope that both of our great political parties will support and defend the Declaration of Independence in the closing campaign of the century.

We hold with Abraham Lincoln, that "no man is good enough to govern another man without that other's consent. When the white man governs himself, that is self-government, but when he governs himself and also governs another man, that is more than self-government—that is despotism." "Our reliance is in the love of liberty which God has planted in us. Our defense is in the spirit which prizes liberty as the heritage of all men in all lands. Those who deny freedom to others deserve it not for themselves, and under a just God, cannot long retain it."

We cordially invite the cooperation of all men and women who remain loyal to the Declaration of Independence and the Constitution of the United States.

Bibliography

Bannister, Robert C. *Social Darwinism: Science and Myth in Anglo-American Social Thought.* Philadelphia: Temple University Press, 1979.

Barry, Kathleen. *Susan B. Anthony: A Biography of a Singular Feminist.* New York: New York University Press, 1988.

Beisner, Robert L. *Twelve against Empire: The Anti-Imperialists, 1898–1900.* New York: McGraw-Hill, 1968.

Blodgett, Geoffrey. *The Gentle Reformers: Massachusetts Reformers in the Cleveland Era.* Cambridge, Mass.: Harvard University Press, 1966.

Bodnar, John E. *The Transplanted: A History of Immigrants in Urban America.* Bloomington: Indiana University Press, 1985.

Bruce, Robert V. *Alexander Graham Bell and the Conquest of Solitude.* Ithaca, N.Y.: Cornell University Press, 1973.

Calhoun, Charles W., ed. *The Gilded Age: Essays on the Origins of Modern America.* Wilmington, Del.: Scholarly Resources, 1996.

Callow, Alexander B., Jr. *The Tweed Ring.* New York: Oxford University Press, 1966.

Campbell, Charles S. *The Transformation of American Foreign Relations, 1865–1900.* New York: Harper & Row, 1976.

Carosso, Vincent P. *The Morgans: Private International Bankers, 1854–1913.* Cambridge, Mass.: Harvard University Press, 1987.

Carter, Paul A. *The Spiritual Crisis of the Gilded Age.* Dekalb: Northern Illinois University Press, 1971.

Chandler, Alfred D., Jr. *The Visible Hand: The Managerial Revolution in American Business.* Cambridge, Mass.: Harvard University Press, 1977.

Chernow, Ron. *Titan: The Life of John D. Rockefeller, Sr.* New York: Random House, 1998

Cochran, Thomas C., and William Miller. *The Age of Enterprise: A Social History of Industrial America.* Rev. ed. New York: Harper & Brothers, 1961.

Cowan, Ruth S. *A Social History of American Technology.* New York: Oxford University Press, 1997.

Cross, Robert D. *The Emergence of Liberal Catholicism in America.* Chicago: Quadrangle, 1968.

Curtis, Susan. *A Consuming Faith: The Social Gospel and Modern American Culture.* Baltimore, Md.: Johns Hopkins University Press, 1991.

Davis, Ronald L. *A History of Music in American Life.* Vol. 2, *The Gilded Years, 1865–1920.* Huntington, N.Y.: Krieger, 1980.

Denning, Michael. *Mechanic Accents: Dime Novels and Working-Class Culture in America.* London: Verso, 1987.

Dinnerstein, Leonard, Roger L. Nichols, and David M. Reimers. *Natives and Strangers: Blacks, Indians, and Immigrants in America.* 2d ed. New York: Oxford University Press, 1990.

Faulkner, Harold U. *Politics, Reform and Expansion, 1890–1900.* New York: Harper & Brothers, 1959.

Fine, Sidney. *Laissez Faire and the General Welfare State: A Study of Conflict in American Thought, 1865–1901.* Ann Arbor: University of Michigan Press, 1956.

Garraty, John A. *The New Commonwealth, 1877–1890.* New York: Harper & Row, 1968.

Ginger, Ray. *The Age of Excess: The United States from 1877 to 1914.* 2d ed. New York: Macmillan, 1975.

Goodwyn, Lawrence. *Democratic Promise: The Populist Moment in America.* New York: Oxford University Press, 1976.

Gould, Lewis L. *The Presidency of William McKinley.* Lawrence: University Press of Kansas, 1980.

Haber, Samuel. *Efficiency and Uplift: Scientific Management in the Progressive Era, 1890–1920.* Chicago: University of Chicago Press, 1964.

Handlin, Oscar. *The Uprooted: The Epic Story of the Great Migrations That Made the American People.* 2d ed. Boston: Little, Brown, 1973.

Haskell, Thomas L. *The Emergence of Professional Social Science: The American Social Science Association and the Nineteenth-Century Crisis of Authority.* Urbana: University of Illinois Press, 1977.

Hays, Samuel P. *The Response to Industrialism, 1877–1920.* Chicago: University of Chicago Press, 1957.

Higham, John. *Strangers in the Land: Patterns of American Nativism, 1860–1925.* 2d ed. New Brunswick, N.J.: Rutgers University Press, 1988.

Hirshson, Stanley P. *Farewell to the Bloody Shirt: Northern Republicans & the Southern Negro, 1877–1893.* Bloomington: Indiana University Press, 1962.

Hofstadter, Richard. *Social Darwinism in American Thought.* Rev. ed. Boston: Beacon Press, 1955.

Hollingsworth, J. Rogers. *The Whirligig of Politics: The Democracy of Cleveland and Bryan.* Chicago: University of Chicago Press, 1963.

Hoogenboom, Ari. *Outlawing the Spoils: A History of the Civil Service Reform Movement, 1865–1883.* Urbana: University of Illinois Press, 1961.

———. *Rutherford B. Hayes: Warrior and President.* Lawrence: University Press of Kansas, 1995.

Hoogenboom, Ari, and Olive Hoogenboom. *A History of the ICC: From Panacea to Palliative.* New York: Norton, 1976.

Jensen, Richard J. *The Winning of the Midwest: Social and Political Conflict, 1888–1896.* Chicago: University of Chicago Press, 1971.

Jones, Howard Mumford. *The Age of Energy: Varieties of American Experience, 1865–1915.* New York: Viking, 1971.

Keller, Morton. *Affairs of State: Public Life in Late Nineteenth-Century America.* Cambridge, Mass.: Harvard University Press, 1977.

Kirkland, Edward C. *Industry Comes of Age: Business, Labor, and Public Policy, 1860–1897.* New York: Holt, Rinehart and Winston, 1961.

Klepner, Paul. *The Cross of Culture: A Social Analysis of Mid-Western Politics, 1850–1890.* 2d ed. New York: Free Press, 1970.

Kousser, J. Morgan. *The Shaping of Southern Politics: Suffrage Restriction and the Establishment of the One-Party South, 1880–1910.* New Haven, Conn.: Yale University Press, 1974.

Kraditor, Ailene S. *The Ideas of the Woman Suffrage Movement, 1890–1920.* New York: Norton, 1981.

Kuklick, Bruce. *The Rise of American Philosophy: Cambridge, Massachusetts, 1860–1930.* New Haven, Conn.: Yale University Press, 1977.

LaFeber, Walter. *The New Empire: An Interpretation of American Expansion, 1860–1898.* Ithaca, N.Y.: Cornell University Press, 1963.

Lamoreaux, Naomi R. *The Great Merger Movement in American Business, 1895–1904.* Cambridge, U.K.: Cambridge University Press, 1985.

McFeely, William S. *Grant: A Biography.* New York: Norton, 1981.

McMath, Robert C., Jr. *American Populism: A Social History, 1877–1898.* New York: Hill & Wang, 1993.

McSeveney, Samuel T. *The Politics of Depression: Political Behavior in the Northeast, 1893–1896.* New York: Oxford University Press, 1972.

Marcus, Robert D. *Grand Old Party: Political Structure in the Gilded Age, 1880–1896.* New York: Oxford University Press, 1971.

Marsden, George M. *Fundamentalism and American Culture: The Shaping of Twentieth-Century Evangelicalism, 1870–1925.* New York: Oxford University Press, 1980.

Martin, Albro. *James J. Hill and the Opening of the Northwest.* New York: Oxford University Press, 1976.

May, Ernest R. *Imperial Democracy: The Emergence of America as a Great Power.* New York: Harper & Row, 1961.

Meier, August. *Negro Thought in America, 1880–1915: Racial Ideologies in the Age of Booker T. Washington.* Ann Arbor: University of Michigan Press, 1963.

Mohl, Raymond A. *The New City: Urban America in the Industrial Age, 1860–1920.* Arlington Heights, Ill.: Harlan Davidson, 1985.

Montgomery, David. *The Fall of the House of Labor: The Workplace, the State, and American Labor Activism, 1865–1925.* New York: Cambridge University Press, 1987.

Morgan, H. Wayne. *From Hayes to McKinley: National Party Politics, 1877–1896.* Syracuse, N.Y.: Syracuse University Press, 1969.

———. *New Muses: Art in American Culture, 1865–1920.* Norman: University of Oklahoma Press, 1978.

———. *William McKinley and His America.* Syracuse, N.Y.: Syracuse University Press, 1963.

Mott, Frank Luther. *A History of American Magazines.* Vol. 4, *1885–1905.* Cambridge, Mass.: Harvard University Press, 1957.

Mrozek, Donald J. *Sport and American Mentality, 1880–1910.* Knoxville: University of Tennessee Press, 1983.

Muccigrosso, Robert. *Celebrating the New World: Chicago's Columbian Exposition of 1893.* Chicago: Ivan R. Dee, 1993.

Mumford, Lewis. *The Brown Decades: A Study of the Arts in America, 1865–1895.* Rev. ed. New York: Dover, 1971.

Norris, James D. *Advertising and the Transformation of American Society, 1865–1920.* New York: Greenwood, 1990.

O'Gorman, James F. *Three American Architects: Richardson, Sullivan, and Wright, 1865–1915.* Chicago: University of Chicago Press, 1991.

Peskin, Allan. *Garfield: A Biography.* Kent, Ohio.: Kent State University Press, 1978.

Porter, Glenn. *The Rise of Big Business, 1869–1920.* Arlington Heights, Ill.: Harlan Davidson, 1992.

Prucha, Francis Paul. *American Indian Policy in Crisis: Christian Reformers and the Indian, 1865–1900.* Norman: University of Oklahoma Press, 1976.

Reeves, Thomas C. *Gentleman Boss: The Life of Chester Alan Arthur.* New York: Knopf, 1975.

Reitano, Joanne. *The Tariff Question in the Gilded Age: The Great Debate of 1888.* University Park: Pennsylvania State University Press, 1994.

Roberts, Jon H. *Darwinism and the Divine in America: Protestant Intellectuals and Organic Evolution, 1859–1900.* Madison: University of Wisconsin Press, 1988.

Rodman, Paul. *The Far West and the Great Plains in Transition, 1859–1900.* New York: Harper & Row, 1988.

Rothman, David J. *Politics and Power: The United States Senate, 1869–1901.* Cambridge, Mass.: Harvard University Press, 1966.

Rydell, Robert W. *All the World's a Fair: Visions of Empire at American International Expositions, 1876–1916.* Chicago: University of Chicago Press, 1984.

Salvatore, Nick. *Eugene V. Debs: Citizen and Socialist.* Urbana: University of Illinois Press, 1982.

Shannon, Fred A. *The Farmer's Last Frontier: Agriculture, 1860–1897.* New York: Holt, Rinehart and Winston, 1945.

Skowronek, Stephen. *Building a New American State: The Expansion of National Administrative Capacities, 1877–1920.* New York: Cambridge University Press, 1982.

Smith, Herbert F. *The Popular American Novel, 1865–1920.* Boston: Twayne, 1980.

Snyder, Robert W. *The Voice of the City: Vaudeville and Popular Culture in New York.* New York: Oxford University Press, 1989.

Socolofsky, Homer E., and Allan B. Spetter. *The Presidency of Benjamin Harrison.* Lawrence: University Press of Kansas, 1987.

Sproat, John G. *"The Best Men": Liberal Reformers in the Gilded Age.* New York: Oxford University Press, 1968.

Summers, Mark Wahlgren. *The Era of Good Stealings.* New York: Oxford University Press, 1993.

Teaford, Jon C. *The Unheralded Triumph: City Government in America,* 1870–1900. Baltimore, Md.: Johns Hopkins University Press, 1984.

Thernstrom, Stephan. *Poverty and Progress: Social Mobility in a Nineteenth-Century City.* Cambridge, Mass.: Harvard University Press, 1964.

Thomas, John L. *Alternative America: Henry George, Edward Bellamy, Henry Demarest Lloyd and the Adversary Tradition.* Cambridge, Mass.: Harvard University Press, 1983.

Thompson, Margaret Susan. *The "Spider Web": Congress and Lobbying in the Age of Grant.* Ithaca, N.Y.: Cornell University Press, 1985.

Trachtenberg, Alan. *The Incorporation of America: Culture and Society in the Gilded Age.* New York: Hill & Wang, 1982.

Unger, Irwin. *The Greenback Era: A Social and Political History of American Finance,* 1865–1879. Princeton, N.J.: Princeton University Press, 1964.

Wall, Joseph Frazier. *Andrew Carnegie.* New York: Oxford University Press, 1970.

Warner, Sam Bass, Jr. *Streetcar Suburbs: The Process of Growth in Boston, 1870–1900.* 2d ed. Cambridge, Mass.: Harvard University Press, 1978.

Welch, Richard E., Jr. *The Presidencies of Grover Cleveland.* Lawrence: University Press of Kansas, 1988.

Wiebe, Robert H. *The Search for Order, 1877–1920.* New York: Hill & Wang, 1967.

Wilkins, Mira. *The Emergence of Multinational Enterprise: American Business Abroad from the Colonial Era to 1914.* Cambridge, Mass.: Harvard University Press, 1970.

Woodward, C. Vann. *Origins of the New South, 1877–1913.* Baton Rouge: Louisiana State University Press, 1951.

———. *The Strange Career of Jim Crow.* 3d ed. New York: Oxford University Press, 1974.

Yellowitz, Irwin. *Industrialism and the American Labor Movement, 1850–1900.* Port Washington, N.Y.: Kennikat, 1977.

Index

Boldface page numbers denote extensive treatment of a topic. *Italic* page numbers refer to illustrations; *c* refers to the Chronology; and *m* indicates a map.

E

F

I

O